CICS/VS Command Level with ANS Cobol Examples

Second Edition

Pacifico A. Lim

VAN NOSTRAND REINHOLD DATA PROCESSING SERIES

VAN NOSTRAND REINHOLD COMPANY
New York

Library of Congress Catalog Card Number: 85-7534
ISBN: 0-442-25814-3

Manufactured in the United States of America

Published by Van Nostrand Reinhold Company Inc.
115 Fifth Avenue
New York, New York 10003

Van Nostrand Reinhold Company Limited
Molly Millars Lane
Wokingham, Berkshire RG11 2PY, England

Van Nostrand Reinhold
480 La Trobe Street
Melbourne, Victoria 3000, Australia

Macmillan of Canada
Division of Canada Publishing Corporation
164 Commander Boulevard
Agincourt, Ontario M1S 3C7, Canada

15 14 13 12 11 10 9 8 7 6 5 4 3 2

Library of Congress Cataloging-in-Publication Data

Lim, Pacifico A.
CICS/VS command level with ANS COBOL examples.

(Van Nostrand Reinhold data processing series)
Includes index.
1. Teleprocessing monitors (Computer programs)
2. CICS/VS (Computer system) 3. COBOL (Computer program language) I. Title. II. Series.
QA76.76.T45L56 1985 001.64'2 85-7534
ISBN 0-442-25814-3

To my brothers,
Alvi, Boy, and Bing
and
my sister, Gloria

Series Introduction

Good examples help make things clear. When discussing capable but extensive software packages, such as IBM's CICS (*C*ustomer *I*nformation *C*ontrol *S*ystem), then good examples can make the difference between confusion and understanding. In this book *CICS/VS Command Level with ANS COBOL Examples,* Mr. Lim provides many practical examples of actual CICS application programs to illustrate important points about CICS usage.

In the first part of the book, Mr. Lim explains CICS features and commands in an organized manner, with attention to cross references and interactions. Mr. Lim shows the importance of local conventions and standard practices, and why some things should be handled in particular ways. Furthermore, the author notes the significance of the systems programmer's supporting role. In the second part of the book, Mr. Lim pulls together and applies the material covered in the first part, and presents six major examples and a number of smaller ones. In discussing and explaining them, Mr. Lim shows screen displays and printed outputs, relating them to what the programmer is trying to accomplish. Mr. Lim closes the book with a chapter on debugging.

In preparing this second edition, Mr. Lim has strengthened the presentation of some topics, and, responding to reader requests, expanded the coverage significantly in three chapters: the introduction to CICS, mapping, and the organization and role of the mainline section. The author has also added additional short examples.

For any reader with a knowledge of COBOL, *CICS/VS Command Level with ANS COBOL Examples* is a readable, useful guide to CICS, illustrated with realistic examples.

Ned Chapin, Ph.D.
Series Editor

THE VAN NOSTRAND REINHOLD DATA PROCESSING SERIES

Edited by Ned Chapin, Ph.D.

IMS Programming Techniques: A Guide to Using DL/1
Dan Kapp and Joseph L. Leben

Reducing COBOL Complexity Through Structured Programming
Carma L. McClure

Composite/Structured Design
Glenford J. Myers

Reliable Software Through Composite Design
Glenford J. Myers

Top-Down Structured Programming Techniques
Clement L. McGowen and John R. Kelly

Operating Systems Principles
Stanley Kurzban, T.S. Heines and A.P. Sayers

Microcomputer Handbook
Charles J. Sippl

Strategic Planning of Management Information Systems
Paul Siegel

Flowcharts
Ned Chapin

Introduction to Artificial Intelligence
Philip C. Jackson, Jr.

Computers and Management for Business
Dougles A. Colbert

Operating Systems Survey
Anthony P. Sayers

Management of Information Technology: Case Studies
Elizabeth B. Adams

Compiler Techniques
Bary W. Pollack

Documentation Manual
J. Van Duyn

Management of ADP Systems
Marvin M. Wofsey

Hospitals: A System Approach
Raymon D. Garrett

Hospital Computer Systems and Procedures, Vol I: Accounting Systems
Hospital Computer Systems and Procedures,
Vol II: Medical Systems
Raymon D. Garrett

Logic Design for Computer Control
K.N. Dodd

Software Engineering Concepts and Techniques
John Buxton, Peter Naur and Brian Randell

Information Management Systems: Data Base Primer
Vivien Prothro

A Programmer's Guide to COBOL
William J. Harrison

A Guide to Structured COBOL with Efficiency Techniques and
Special Algorithms
Pacifico A. Lim

Managing Software Development and Maintenance
Carma L. McClure

Computer-Assisted Data Base Design
George U. Hubbard

Computer Performance Evaluation: Tools and Techniques for Effective Analysis
Michael F. Morris and Paul F. Roth

Evaluating Data Base Management Systems
Judy King

Network Systems
Roshan Lal Sharma, Paulo T. deSousa and Ashok D. Inglé

Logical Data Base Design
Robert M. Curtice and Paul E. Jones, Jr.

Decision Tables in Software Engineering
Richard B. Hurley

CICS/VS Command Level with ANS Cobol Examples, Second Edition
Pacifico A. Lim

Preface to Second Edition

The idea to revise this book came to me while teaching CICS/VS at the New York University School of Continuing Education. Although the students found the book a useful guide for writing Cobol programs that run under CICS/VS, they also occasionally required a more detailed explanation on certain topics presented in it.

To start with, I have confidence that the organization of the book (the chapters and specific topics in each chapter) is very good. This is based on comments from readers and from the fact that the book has been well received by the programming community. It has also been reviewed favorably ("excellent text and reference for COBOL programmers using CICS") in the IBM Systems Journal, Volume 22, Nos. 1/2, 1983, page 165.

I am therefore using the same twenty-four chapters, with basically the same topics in each chapter. However, I have expanded many of the topics to include more details, and sometimes with additional related topics not previously mentioned. It is my belief that this now makes the explanation complete. In addition, I have moved a few topics to a different chapter because they are really best covered in more detail there.

I did not change the program examples. They show how typical CICS/VS programs should be written, and students were satisfied with them. In addition, I also did not change Chapter 24, on debugging.

PACIFICO A. LIM

Preface to First Edition

The development of on-line applications has been with us for quite some time. Management has long realized that there is a need to have certain information available at a moment's notice. Knowing the status of a purchase order, for instance, or the availability of a certain item in inventory helps tremendously in the running of a company.

Such applications often require the use of *c*athode *r*ay *t*ube (CRT) terminals* where the user initiates programs to access on-line files. These terminals may be active concurrently and may access the same files simultaneously. Unfortunately, compilers do not allow the application programmer to control multiple terminals accessing on-line files. If he (or she) were to write an on-line application, he would have the problem of writing routines to control terminals and files. This is like requiring the batch-oriented programmer to write access-method routines for his program.

However, to help users, the hardware manufacturers as well as independent software companies have developed packages to free the application programmer from these problems. Such packages are known as teleprocessing monitors, and one of them is IBM's *C*ustomer *I*nformation *C*ontrol *S*ystem (CICS). It is quite popular, has many useful features, and is written to work with IBM's various virtual-storage (VS) operating systems.

The programmer may think of CICS/VS as an extension of the programming language since he codes the request for on-line services (display data on a terminal, read an on-line file, etc.) right in his program, interspersing them with other statements of the language. He may also think of CICS/VS as an extension of the operating system because it interfaces between the application program and the operating system, using telecommunication and data-access methods available in the latter.

---

*Also known as video display terminals.

CICS/VS first became available in the macro level, where the statements for CICS/VS services were in the form of Assembler macros. In addition, the programmer was required to know some CICS/VS internals. Although a teleprocessing monitor was already a big help, the use of Assembler-type macros was a little bit foreign to high-level application programmers. The introduction of the command-level feature solved this problem. It replaced the macros with commands that were more similar in format to statements that high-level application programmers were used to. In addition, it was no longer necessary to know CICS/VS internals.

CICS/VS is very easy to use, and the experienced programmer can grasp its basic features in a few days. In fact, it is much easier for an experienced programmer to learn CICS/VS than for a novice to learn ANS Cobol. The programmer learning CICS/VS can think of the terminal as the input reader that he reads data from as well as the output printer that he prints data on.

CICS/VS Command Level with ANS Cobol Examples will not present the complete features of CICS/VS. Rather, it will present a coding style based on the author's experience and will cover the most useful and common features that the application programmer will need. Most of the features mentioned will be shown in actual program examples. The reader who is interested in features not mentioned should read the IBM-supplied *CICS/VS Application Programmer's Reference Manual* (Form SC33-0077-1).

This book is written primarily for ANS Cobol application programmers who are interested in or will be involved in writing CICS/VS application programs. They will benefit most from the overall presentation and the program examples. However, non-Cobol application programmers may also benefit from the discussion of CICS/VS techniques. In fact, the commands are basically identical no matter what the language is.

The programs in this book have been tested using an IBM 4341 under DOS/VSE. However, they should execute properly in other operating systems, and IBM hardware that is supported by CICS/VS.

PACIFICO A. LIM

Acknowledgments

The author is indebted to two people at the Van Nostrand Reinhold Publishing Company who helped tremendously in producing this book. Gerry Galbo helped define the target readership, which became the basis for the organization of the book, and he was most patient and encouraging especially when original target dates were missed. Alberta Gordon was most helpful in editing the manuscript, and worked with me from the completion of the manuscript to the final production of the book. She and her staff have done an excellent job.

Contents

CICS/VS Command Level
with
ANS Cobol Examples

1

On-Line Systems

BATCH PROCESSING

The earliest data processing equipment used in business was accounting or tabulating machines. These were slow, primarily mechanical devices which required a deck (or batch) or punched cards as input and either punched cards or printed reports as output. By the nature of these machines, the only processing technique that could be used was to break each application into several relevant steps, where on each step a deck of cards that were in proper sequence were processed one after the other until the end of the deck.

This technique, knows as *batch processing*, was eventually carried over to the early business computer systems. The change from mechanical to electronic components did not immediately result in a change in processing technique. This had to wait until still better hardware was developed and users became more sophisticated and wanted to implement more complex applications.

Characteristics Of Batch Processing

In batch processing, data corresponding to a processing period (e.g., a day, week, or month, etc.) are verified for accuracy through one or more edit runs and are then used to update a master file (usually on magnetic tape) containing records that are sequenced in ascending order according to a key. Once the update is finished, the reports required can then be prepared. Data that belong to the current period, but were not entered, are then entered on the next processing period.

The five most important characteristics of batch processing are:

1. The data needed to update a master file are batched together before the file is updated.
2. It takes some time to prepare the data before final processing.

3. The output usually consists of printed reports (most likely prepared at the computer center).
4. The master file can be used by only one program at any given time. Other programs have to wait for the file to be released.
5. Each step required in the application is scheduled and is started by the computer operator loading the appropriate program.

Figure 1.1 shows a typical batch application.

ON-LINE PROCESSING

Batch processing is still used in applications where only periodic processing is required. Examples are payroll systems and seasonal departmental operating statements. However, it is inadequate where there is a need to get information at a moment's notice.

For instance, an airline reservation system requires the instantaneous access of information on the seat availability of various flights. A Purchase Order system requires the instantaneous access of information on the status of merchandise being ordered.

These required an on-line system whose growth in the commercial sector was helped spurred by three hardware developments. The development of direct access storage devices (of which the magnetic disk is the most popular medium) made it possible to store and access data randomly in fractions of a second, unlike magnetic tapes, whose records have to be read in sequence. Furthermore, faster and faster central processing unit (CPU) speed resulted from better hardware, especially the extensive use of integrated circuits. This fostered the development of multiprogramming, that is, many applications could share CPU time and in effect run simultaneously. While this was not absolutely necessary for on-line applications, it nevertheless helped many commercial installations acquire on-line facilities with minimal additional hardware because they could use the very same CPU they were using for batch applications. Finally, the development of low-cost CRT terminals made feasible the attachment of many such devices to the computer system, allowing many user personnel to run on-line applications simultaneously.

If an installation already has hardware for batch processing, the only additional hardware required to get on-line facilities are terminals and their associated cables and control units. Additional memory,

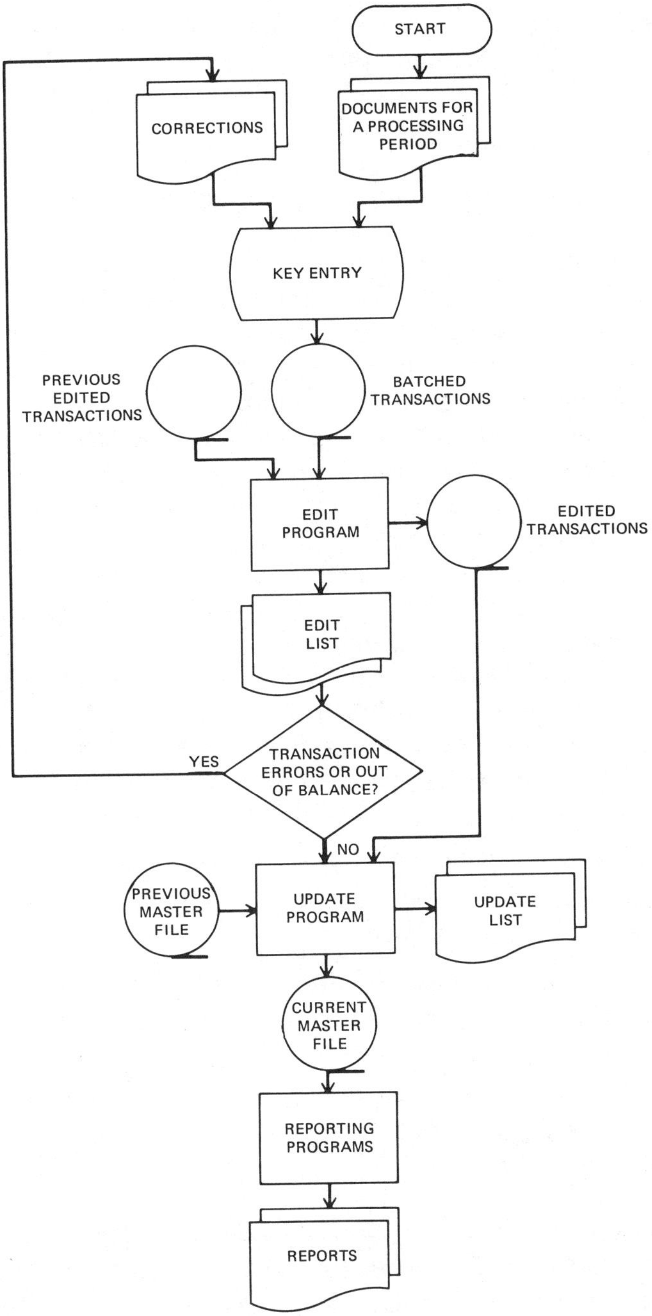

Fig. 1.1. Batch processing. From start to the preparation of the reports takes days or weeks depending on how many edit runs are made to complete the data for a processing period.

disk capacity, and channels may or may not be required depending on need. And as we mentioned before, the same CPU is used.

Characteristics Of On-line Processing

The five most important characteristics of on-line processing are:

1. The data needed to update a master file do not have to be batched and may be used as soon as it is available.
   a. For typical applications, each document being entered is generally independent of another, and there is therefore no need to enter them in batches.
   b. However, if the documents arrive intermittently, and they do not have to be entered immediately, management may decide to batch them anyway to avoid the overhead in starting and terminating applications. This overhead may of course be minimized if the operator keeps the applications "open" or " active" while waiting for a batch to be completed. However, for security reasons, she should not leave the terminal and she can not use it in the meantime for other applications.
   c. If a CICS application is "data entry", that is, a terminal is used to capture data for later use in a batch file update run, documents are generally batched together.
2. Updating is done in a matter of seconds.
3. The output for the user is generally displayed on CRT terminals at the user site.
4. Multiple actions may be done on the file. While some terminals are updating it, others may do inquiry (display information) from it.
5. The user himself usually starts programs for applications right from the terminal any time and without scheduling them with the computer operators.

On-line systems also have the following characteristics: security procedures for files and programs so unauthorized personnel cannot access them through terminals that may be in many locations;

adequate computer response* (generally in terms of seconds); and the capability to generate data (called journals) that is to be used later on as an audit trail of transactions entered or for file recovery. A typical on-line application (File Update) is shown in Figure 1.2.

BENEFITS

Some benefits of on-line processing can be deduced from what we have discussed. The master file is up to date, unlike in batch processing where the master file is only accurate as of the last processing period. Also, data is entered by the user himself, and any question about the data can be easily resolved. In batch processing, documents are translated into machine-readable form generally by data-entry operators who may not be able to resolve questions about the data. Finally, the user may use the computer any time without having to schedule his requirements with computer operators.

The availability of on-line facilities also has several advantages. On-line program development packages can be used, thus increasing programmer productivity. Other packages can give the installation the ability to test programs on-line, which also increases programmer productivity. Still other packages can be used in applications or for computer performance measurements. Lastly, data-entry requirements that are of low volume or have unpredictable schedules can be "off-loaded," freeing the data-entry department to concentrate on large-volume, regularly scheduled input.

TELEPROCESSING MONITORS

The three hardware developments discussed previously were not enough to give commercial installations the ability to develop on-line applications easily. The systems that resulted were more sophisticated and, consequently, more complex than preceding systems. Thus, the new systems required additional functions before the user could run on-line applications. Some of the more important functions are: transmitting data from terminals to computer memory

*Response time is the time it takes for a computer to display the result of a processing step and wait for further operator action after a program is initiated (which is generally done by hitting a key like ENTER).

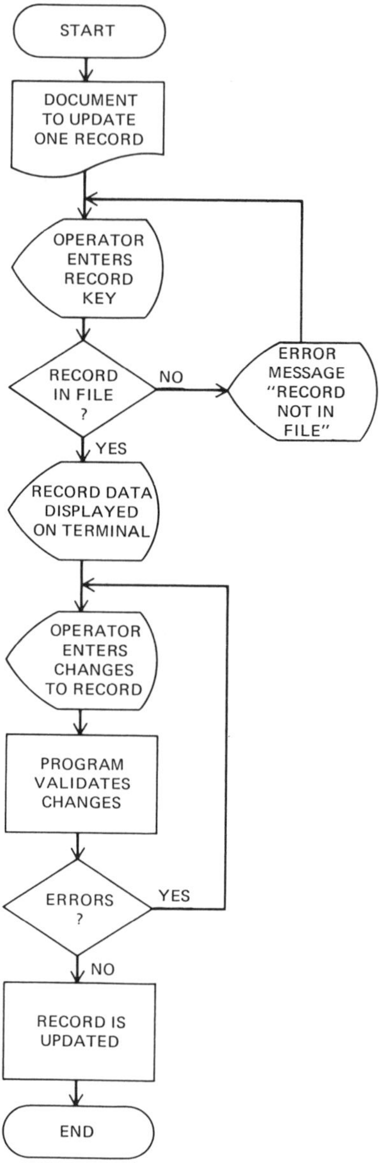

Fig. 1.2. On-line file update. From start to end takes from several seconds to several minutes depending on the amount of changes entered and whether or not the program detects errors during validation.

and vice versa; controlling many concurrently running programs attached to terminals that share the same computer memory and access the same on-line files so that each may be serviced according to some priority: keeping user application programs independent of the physical characteristics of telecommunication devices so that even if the devices are changed, the user does not have to rewrite his programs; and giving the user the ability to develop on-line applications using the very same programming language he is using to write batch applications.

Packages known as teleprocessing monitors solved these problems. They were the last link in the chain of developments that brought on-line capabilities to many commercial installations, freeing the application programmer to concentrate on actual applications. To the programmer, these teleprocessing monitors are extensions of the programming language because requests for on-line services (display data on a terminal, read an on-line file, etc.) are coded right in the application program, which are then provided to the program through the monitor. As a result, on-line programs are in many ways similar to batch programs.

One such teleprocessing monitor is IBM's *C*ustomer *I*nformation *C*ontrol *S*ystem (CICS), which works with IBM's various virtual storage (VS) operating systems. The command-level feature of CICS/VS allows the programmer to code requests for on-line services in statements similar in format to those in the high-level language he is used to.

2

CICS/VS

INTRODUCTION

*C*ustomer *I*nformation *C*ontrol *S*ystem/*V*irtual *S*torage (CICS/VS) is a powerful teleprocessing monitor that provides the support necessary for writing on-line programs and running on-line applications. It aids users in the following ways:

1. Application programmers do not have to learn a new language to write on-line programs. They can use any of four languages they are familiar with, which are ANS Cobol, PL/1, Assembler, or RPG II. Naturally, the coding techniques for programs that run under CICS/VS will be different from those that implement batch applications.
2. They do not have to code routines to implement on-line services (display data on a terminal, read an on-line file, etc.). Instead, with the command-level feature, they code commands in their application programs (PROCEDURE DIVISION for Cobol programs) that invoke CICS-supplied program modules (called control programs) which implement these services. Most commands are short, requiring only 2 to 4 operands, in addition to 2 delimiters (which are always the same).
3. CICS/VS provides a command-language translator (a preprocessor) to convert the commands, which are foreign to these languages, into statements that can then be accepted by the compiler or assembler. Otherwise, there will be error messages when the program is compiled or assembled.
4. It provides a *B*asic *M*apping *S*upport (BMS) facility, which makes it easy for users to enter or display data on terminals in the format he wants.
5. During execution, CICS/VS, which runs in a single partition/region, acts as an "operating system" for the application

programs that run under it and interfaces between the application programs and the operating system. It controls many such programs running concurrently and provides service to these programs.

a. Directly if that service cannot be provided by the operating system itself. An example is when a program requires additional memory.
b. Indirectly, by passing the request to the operating system, if the latter is capable of providing service. An example is when a program requests a record, where the operating system may use an access method like VSAM, etc.

6. CICS/VS provides service to the various programs when requested (usually by commands), switching from one program to another according to a priority that is established by the user himself.

Figure 2.1 shows how CICS/VS interfaces between the application programs and the operating system.

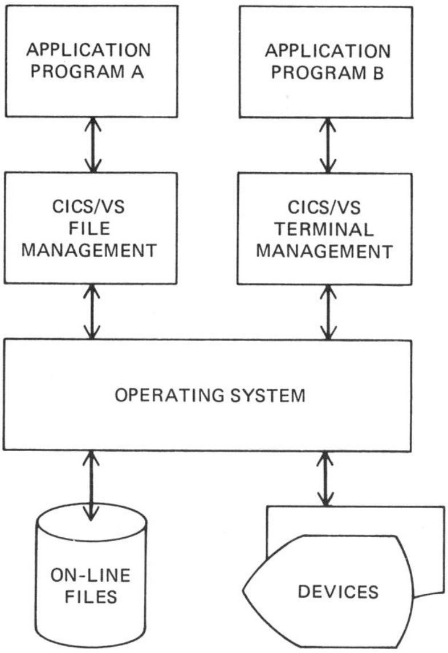

Fig. 2.1. CICS/VS interfaces between application programs and the operating system.

THE CICS/VS PARTITION/REGION

CICS/VS runs in a single partition/region, which has the following general characteristics:

1. It has the highest priority among those assigned to applications. When the CPU is free, the highest-priority task (say an active program at a terminal)* in that partition that is waiting to execute will take control over and above any batch program in other partitions.
2. It consists of the following:
   a. The CICS/VS package. This consists of modules that allow it to function as an "operating system", as well as control programs that execute to implement programmer-written commands.
   b. The dynamic storage area for applications. This is used for the application programs (PROCEDURE DIVISION and WORKING-STORAGE section for Cobol programs) and main storage areas required by the programs (such as for the LINKAGE section).

Initializing CICS/VS

At any time, but usually at the beginning of the day, the console operator initializes CICS/VS. The CICS/VS package and tables are loaded into main storage and the journals are reset to empty. The application programs and mapsets are copied from the program library into virtual storage, except for those defined in the PPT (see "CICS/VS Tables") as resident, which are copied instead into dynamic storage. The users may now use applications.

Terminating CICS/VS

At any time, but usually at the end of the day, the console operator terminates CICS/VS. The journal, as well as production files so designated, are backed up into magnetic tape. The users will no longer be able to use applications until CICS/VS is again initialized.

---

*This definition of a task is sufficient for now. We will define it more accurately in a later section.

CICS/VS APPLICATION PROGRAM

Strictly speaking, there is no such thing as a CICS/VS application program. What the application programmer writes are Cobol, PL/1, Assembler, or RPG II programs that will run under CICS/VS. The object code corresponding to these programs will just make use of the CICS/VS package.

Each application program that runs under CICS/VS does so without interference from other programs. However, since the programs run in a single partition/region, the operating system does not protect one program (or even CICS/VS) from destruction due to say an addressing error such as a wrong index or subscript value in another program. A bug in a program may cause the partition to crash.

Testing Application Programs

To minimize this problem, new application programs should be tested in a partition other than the regular CICS/VS partition. Old application programs being modified may also be tested in like manner, depending on the extend of the modification. This partition may be taken from one of the batch partitions when needed.

CICS/VS Service For Commands

We mentioned before that commands are interspersed with regular statements in the user's application program. For instance, a Cobol program has executed a series of MOVE statements to build up a record image in memory and it is now ready to write out the record.

1. The program will not issue a Cobol WRITE statement because Cobol I/O verbs do not work under CICS/VS.
2. At the point where the Cobol WRITE statement would have been issued, there is instead a command to write out the record.
3. The CICS/VS package recognizes the command and will provide the appropriate service to the program.

CICS/VS TABLES

Some functions of CICS/VS are controlled through tables, which are loaded into the CICS/VS partition/region when it is initialized. Modifications to entries to these tables are therefore effective only on the next CICS/VS initialization, which is usually the next day. The user may however opt to terminate CICS/VS, then immediately reinitialize it in the middle of the day.

Types Of Tables

There are two types of tables:

1. Those of concern to the application programmer:
   a. The *P*rogram *C*ontrol *T*able (PCT). Each application program has an entry in this table, which specifies the transaction identifier, the load module name, and optional parameters such as a priority number, the size of any *T*ransaction *W*ork *A*rea (TWA), etc.
   b. The *P*rocessing *P*rogram *T*able (PPT). Each application program and mapset (see Chapter 4) has an entry in this table, which specifies the load module name, the source language, whether it is an application program or a map, and optional parameters such as whether it is resident or non-resident, etc. Resident modules, which may be specified for heavily-used applications, are loaded into dynamic storage (instead of virtual storage) when CICS/VS is initialized. This puts the overhead in loading them at CICS/VS initialization, not when they are actually required. However, resident modules may be paged out.
   c. The *F*ile *C*ontrol *T*able (FCT). Each new file (new to CICS/VS, not the program) has an entry which specifies the file identifier, what specific services (read, write, update, browse, delete) are allowed on the file, etc.
2. Those of concern only to the systems programmer. One example is the *T*erminal *C*ontrol *T*able (TCT) which has an entry for each terminal and specifies the terminal type, priority number, etc. Another example is the Sign-on Table,

which contains a list of authorized operators, their password, security code, priority, etc.

Maintaining The Tables

Note that in most installations, only the systems programmer, or someone else so designated is allowed to put entries in these tables and then reload them. Most installations do not allow application programmers to do so because erroneous entries may be detrimental to other programs. For tables of the first type (PCT, PPT, and FCT), the application programmer specifies to the systems programmer what he wants or what he is using.

Two Sets Of Tables

Lastly, since application programs are tested in a partition other than the regular CICS/VS partition, there are also two sets of tables. Each set must be complete as far as the terminals, files, application programs, mapsets, etc., that are in production or under test.

TASK

Previously, we loosely defined a task as "an active program at a terminal". We will now define it more accurately by first looking at the concept of jobs and job steps for batch applications. The operating system creates a job step for a program as specified by job control and it includes the housekeeping routines done by the operating system, like loading the program into main storage, and the actual execution of the program itself.

Several such job steps may be stacked together in one job, which is itself created with the // Job card and ends with the /& card. Only one program executes at one time in a partition/region and it will be completed by the end of the job step.

On the other hand, CICS/VS (not the operating system) initiates tasks for programs that run under it. Each task also consists of the housekeeping routines done by CICS/VS, like loading the program into main storage, and the actual execution of the program itself. Several programs may also run (one after the other, not at the same time) in a single task if other programs are "called" into execution.

A batch job, once initiated, will continue under control of the operating system until the latter terminates it. A task, once initiated, will continue under control of CICS/VS until the latter terminates it. However, while a job usually lasts for five, ten, twenty, or thirty minutes or so, a typical task lasts for only fractions of a second.

Initiating And Terminating A Task

A task is most commonly initiated in response to an operator at a terminal hitting a key like ENTER, or any PF or PA key, etc. The task is terminated when the program that first executes, or any other program down the line "called" into execution, issues the command to terminate it. Programs run only within a task and are subordinate to it.

CICS/VS applications are interactive and the operator hits a key like ENTER every time he completes a set of input data to be processed, or PF or PA keys if he wants the program to do something else. Therefore, there are many tasks initiated and terminated to run a single CICS/VS application.

When CICS/VS applications are running, the activity of the task is what counts (not the program), although most activities are triggered by the requirements of the program. For instance, if the program issues a command to "read data" and additional main storage is required for the data, CICS/VS will secure main storage for the task from the dynamic storage area and establish its address so it will ultimately be accessible by the program.

SESSION

A session, which consists of many tasks, constitutes the whole set of activities performed by the operator and the program from the time he starts an application to the time he ends that application.

CONVERSATIONAL MODE OF PROCESSING

A Cobol batch program coded with the "DISPLAY upon console" and "ACCEPT from console" statements may have a "conversation" with the operator through the systems console. Since the program does not leave (i.e., it remains in memory) during this whole "conversation," all the time "patiently" waiting for the operator's answer, this is "true conversation." This mode of processing is known as conversational.

An application program that runs under CICS/VS may also be written in conversational mode, in which case it also remains in memory all the time, "patiently" awaiting the completion of the entry by the operator. This mode of processing is however inherently inefficient and only allows a small number of terminals to run simultaneously and thus, except for certain applications that require it (browse applications, for instance), it is not used.

PSEUDOCONVERSATIONAL MODE OF PROCESSING

In the pseudoconversational mode of processing, a program is purged from the partition/region by terminating the task that corresponds to that program after it has completed whatever function the operator wanted it to do in that particular task (process data entered, display a record from a file, etc.) and is now only awaiting further operator action. The program is really doing nothing and is therefore not needed while the operator is deciding what to do next or is only entering information on the terminal.

Task termination is triggered by a command executed in the program itself and is implemented by a control program called Task Control. If the task is in fact terminated before the next operator action, then the mode of processing is pseudoconversational. It is not a "true conversation" because the program is not there during part of the "conversation".

Efficiency

All resources (main storage, etc.) taken by a terminated task are released back to the system for reuse by other tasks. The more resources are available to all, the more efficient the whole installation becomes (the faster is the overall response time) because a task will wait if a needed resource is not available. And while there is some inefficiency in the additional overhead of terminating tasks and initiating new ones, this inefficiency is far less troublesome than the needless "hogging" of resources, which results from the conversational mode of processing.

For instance, suppose the operator requires 20 seconds to complete the entry of data on the terminal and the CPU requires ¼ second to process them. If the application is written in the pseudoconversational mode of processing, it will be using resources only for ¼ second for every 20¼ seconds it is used (session time). During the 20 seconds of data entry, other tasks may use all resources released by the terminated task.

More Terminals Usable

Applications compete for finite resources (specially main storage). If they are written in the conversational mode of processing, a small number of terminals can easily use up these resources since nobody releases them until the end of the session (which usually takes hours). However, for applications written in the pseudoconversational mode of processing, only a small portion of the terminals being used at any given time are actually using resources and a much larger number of terminals may be used in the installation.

Operator Activity When The Task Is Terminated

Even if the terminal is inactive as far as CICS/VS is concerned because there is no task attached to it, the operator is able to enter data into its buffer (for 3270-type terminals) under control of a map (guide to the format and location of data entered or displayed on a terminal) specified in the program that terminated the task. Naturally, the program specifies what map is to be used before it issues the command that terminates the task.

The operator initiates another task to continue the application by hitting a key like ENTER after the entry is completed or a special key like any PF or PA key if he wants the program to do something else. The operator cannot tell the difference between programs written in the conversational and the pseudoconversational mode of processing.

Data Saved Or Lost At Task Termination

When a task is terminated, the program and all its data in main storage are lost. This means data in working storage, data read from terminals or files (generally placed in the LINKAGE SECTION). etc. On the next task initiation, data from files may however be read again by the program; terminal data (either new data just entered or previously entered data plus corrections for errors) may also be read.

However, for other data that the programmer wants to recall on the next task initiation, CICS/VS provides several options. The most commonly used option is temporary storage on magnetic disk. Before the task is terminated, data to be saved is written out into temporary storage; on the next task initiation, the data is read back by the program into main storage. Thus, while the operator is deciding what to do next or is only entering data at the terminal, the only resource the application is using is some relatively cheap disk space.

FEATURES

The usual characteristics of on-line systems are present in CICS/VS. For instance, it is terminal-oriented, provides security procedures for files and programs, can have fast response time, and provides adequate backup and journal (audit trail) generation procedures. The other features are:

1. *Transaction driven.* A transaction identifier entered by the operator or generated by another program* corresponds to the application program that will first execute in the task.
2. *Multitasking.* CICS/VS controls many tasks running concurrently in a single partition/region through a technique called task switching. In task switching, a task gets control of the CPU until CICS/VS suspends it (generally on a command that causes a wait) and the next highest-priority

*This is by far the most common way of initiating programs. Other methods will be explained later on.

task that is waiting takes control. CICS/VS provides service to the suspended task, and it is then placed in the queue of waiting tasks according to its priority number.

3. *Multithreading.* All terminals requiring the same program will use only one copy of the program (in Cobol, the PROCEDURE DIVISION), thus saving main storage. This feature is possible because multitasking allows each task requiring the same program to use part of the same copy of the program when that task is active.
4. *Quasi-reentrant.* Multithreading requires that application programs be serially reusable. Therefore a task, before it is suspended, must restore any instruction or data it altered, if such instruction or data may be used by another task. The reason is to prevent the other tasks from using a "modified" version. With the command-level feature, ANS Cobol programs are automatically quasi-reentrant since only the PROCEDURE DIVISION is common to all tasks that use the same program. This division is never modified, even by the ALTER* verb which only changes value in the *T*ask *G*roup *T*able (TGT) to control execution, and the TGT is unique for each task.
5. *Priority processing.* Priority ratings can be assigned by the user to each operator, terminal, or transaction identifier (hence program). These ratings are used by CICS/VS to provide the fastest response time to certain operators, terminals, and applications.

CONTROL PROGRAMS

CICS/VS consists of modules that support multitasking, multithreading, priority processing, file security, etc. These are modules that oversee the execution of multiple tasks in a single partition, and application programmers are not really concerned with them. There are, however, other modules that provide services to satisfy commands coded in the application program. These modules are called control programs.

---

*Proponents of structured programming avoid the use of ALTER. It is being deleted from the language in the Cobol-80 standard.

With the command level feature, application programmers do not directly request for specific control programs. CICS/VS will instead provide the necessary control programs in the proper sequence to meet the requirements of a single command.

The control programs that execute in a task are as follows:

When A Task Is Started

1. *Terminal Control.* Upon entry of a transaction identifier, Terminal Control, which monitors terminal operations and uses standard telecommunication access methods available in the operating system, requests Storage Control to create a terminal input/output area, then reads the input into this area. Terminal Control then passes control to Task Control.
2. *Task Control.* Task Control creates a task for the transaction, then checks whether the transaction identifier is valid and present in the Program Control Table (PCT). If the transaction identifier is invalid, an error message is sent to the terminal and the task is terminated. Otherwise, it requests Storage Control to secure a Task Control Area and a Transaction Work Area (if the application requires it). Task Control assigns a priority number to the task, then places it in the queue of waiting tasks. Control then passes to Program Control.
3. *Program Control.* When a program is to execute for the first time in a task, Task Control requests Program Control to take the program from virtual storage and load it into main storage if it is not already in the latter. It also intercepts program abends so that if the program terminates, the whole CICS/VS partition does not terminate.

A Task Executing In Multitasking

1. *Task Control.* Whenever the CICS partition is free, Task Control dispatches the highest-priority task in the wait queue and then transfers control to the corresponding application program. It suspends tasks on commands that cause waits and then places those tasks in the queue according to their priority numbers. It also terminates tasks.

2. *The Application Program.* The application program gets control generally until such time that a command that causes a wait is executed. The task corresponding to the application program is then suspended.
3. *Basic Mapping Support.* The application program requests Basic Mapping Supprt (BMS) to read data from a terminal or to display data on a terminal. BMS uses Terminal Control facilities for data transmission, Program Control to determine the format of the data read or displayed, and Storage Control to secure main storage for the data.
4. *File Control.* The application program requests File Control to retrieve records from files, write records into files, etc. File Control requests Storage Control to secure main storage for records to be read, and uses data-access methods available in the operating system.
5. *Temporary Storage Control.* The application program requests Temporary Storage Control to save information that would normally be lost when a task terminates. It is implemented by CICS/VS as a file with variable records and the programmer can read, write, and rewrite records from it.
6. *Journal Control.* The application program requests Journal Control to write into special-purpose sequential files information that may be used offline as an audit trail or to reconstruct files.
7. *Trace Control.* The program requests Trace Control to provide a trace of the commands as a debugging aid.
8. *Dump Control.* The application program requests Dump Control to write all transaction-related storage areas into a dump file to be printed out later on by a dump utility program. The printout is also used as a debugging aid.
9. *Interval Control.* The application program requests Interval Control to start a task at some future time or at a certain time of day.
10. *Storage Control.* The application program requests Storage Control to acquire main storage for any data required in the program. On input commands, the corresponding control programs automatically request Storage Control to secure

Main Storage for the data that will be read if the area is defined in the LINKAGE section.

Suppose we have a program that reads in data from a terminal and temporary storage, processes the data, then displays it on the same terminal. The flow of control is shown in Figure 2.2.

WAYS TO INITIATE TASKS

We mentioned before that many tasks are initiated and terminated to implement the pseudoconversational mode of processing. There are actually six ways to initiate tasks in CICS/VS:

1. *Transaction identifier entered by the operator.* This is the most common way of starting a session. The task is actually initiated when the operator hits the ENTER key, or any PF or PA key.
2. *Temporary transaction identifier.* The last program that executed at the same terminal, before the task is terminated, specifies the transaction identifier to be used on the next task initiation. This is the method used to continue a session in the pseudoconversational mode of processing. The task is actually initiated when the operator hits the ENTER key, or any PF or PA key.
3. *Interval Control transaction identifier.* The Interval Control command START TRANSID specifies the transaction identifer that will be used for a new task, the time the task will be initiated, and, optionally, a terminal identification if the task is associated with a terminal.
4. *Automatic task initiation.* If the systems programmer specifies a nonzero trigger level for a particular transient data intrapartition destination in the Destination Control Table at systems generation, a task is automatically initiated when the number of entries in the queue (destination) reaches the specified level. Control is passed to an application program that processes the data in the queue.
5. *Permanent transaction identifier.* For terminals that cannot start a task through a transaction identifier because of hardware characteristics, a permanent transaction identifier may be defined for the terminal in the Terminal Control Table. The application program that corresponds to the permanent

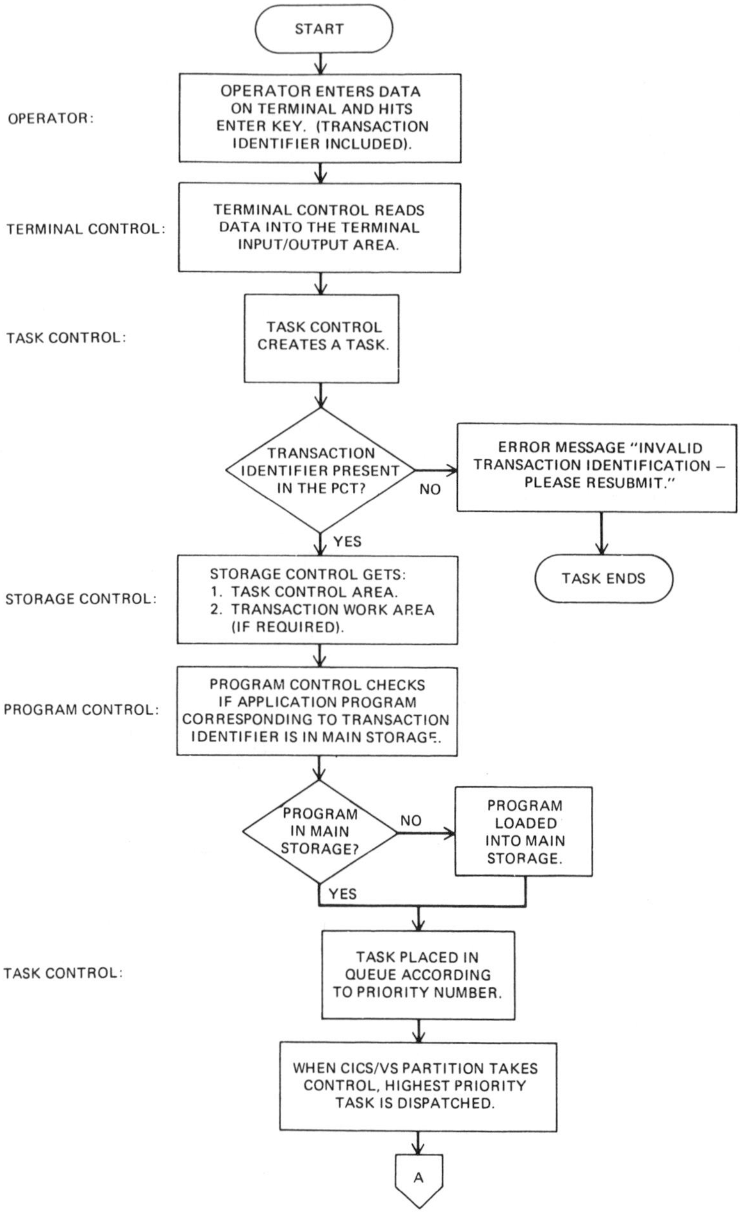

Fig. 2.2. One example of flow of control within a task. Note that the events from the time the task is first dispatched to the time the task is terminated are not done in one contiguous time. The task is suspended and redispatched several times, generally on commands that cause a wait.

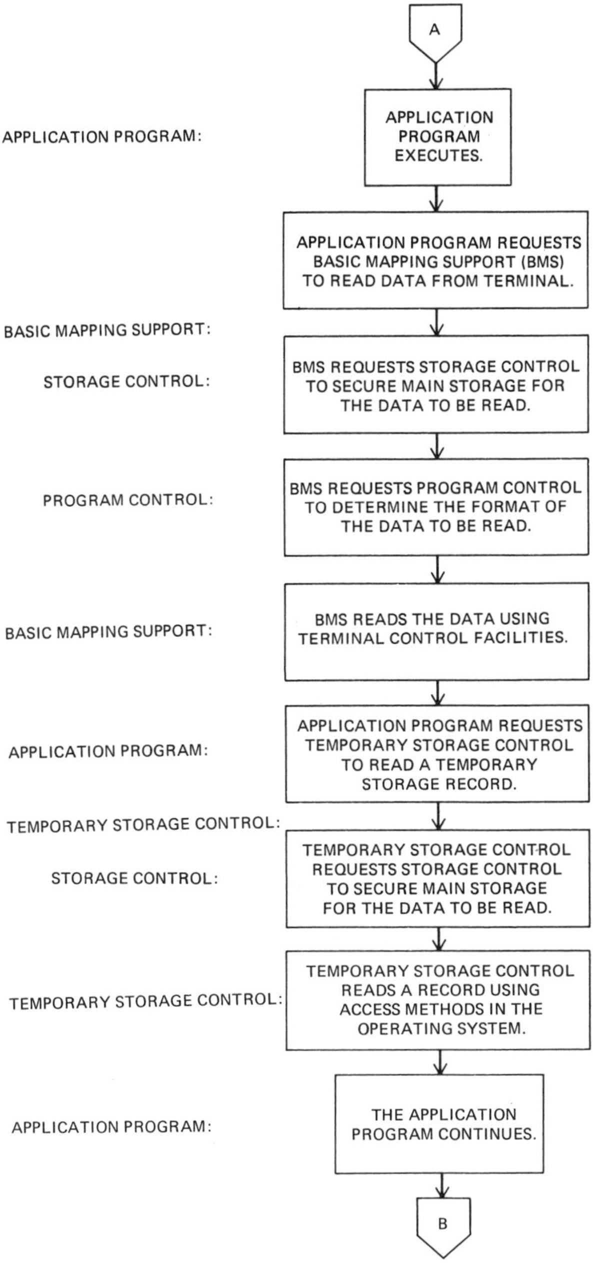

Fig. 2.2. (Continued)

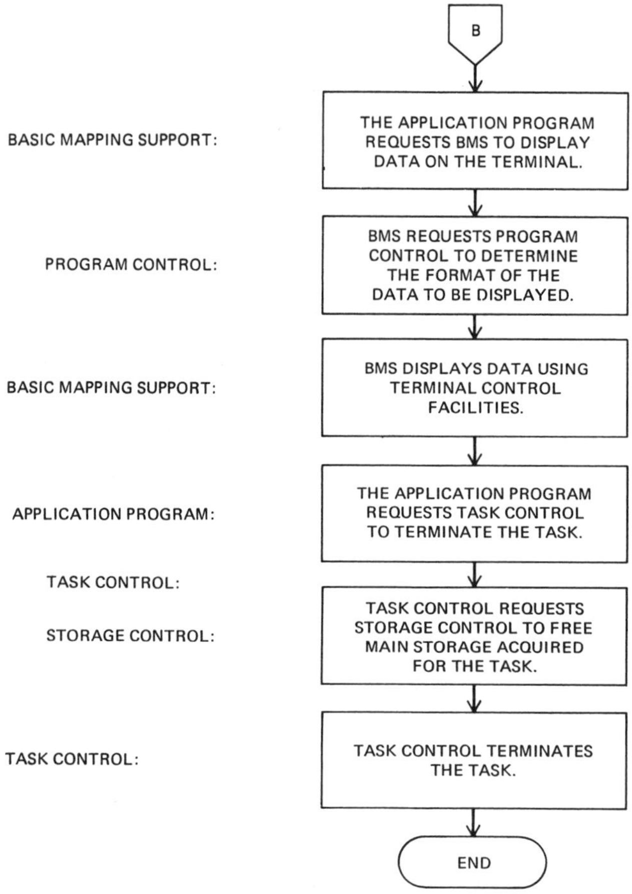
B
BASIC MAPPING SUPPORT:
THE APPLICATION PROGRAM REQUESTS BMS TO DISPLAY DATA ON THE TERMINAL.
PROGRAM CONTROL:
BMS REQUESTS PROGRAM CONTROL TO DETERMINE THE FORMAT OF THE DATA TO BE DISPLAYED.
BASIC MAPPING SUPPORT:
BMS DISPLAYS DATA USING TERMINAL CONTROL FACILITIES.
APPLICATION PROGRAM:
THE APPLICATION PROGRAM REQUESTS TASK CONTROL TO TERMINATE THE TASK.
TASK CONTROL:
STORAGE CONTROL:
TASK CONTROL REQUESTS STORAGE CONTROL TO FREE MAIN STORAGE ACQUIRED FOR THE TASK.
TASK CONTROL:
TASK CONTROL TERMINATES THE TASK.
END

Fig. 2.2. (Continued)

transaction identifier will then select the specific application program that will actually process the transaction.

6. *3270 Attention identifier.* For 3270-type terminals, each of the programmer attention (PA) keys, program function (PF) keys, the selector light pen, the cursor select key, or an operator identification badge can be defined in the PCT to initiate specific programs. Thus by hitting the appropriate PA or PF keys, selecting a detectable field with the selector light pen or

the cursor select key, or using an operator identification badge, the appropriate program is initiated without a transaction identifier.

MAIN STORAGE ALLOCATION FOR COBOL PROGRAMS

Cobol programs used in tasks allocate main storage in the following manner:

1. PROCEDURE DIVISION. All tasks using the same program share one copy.
2. WORKING-STORAGE SECTION. Each task has its own copy.
3. LINKAGE SECTION. Each task has its own copy.
   a. The Transaction Work Area (TWA), Common Work Area (CWA), and Terminal Control Tables User Area (TCTUA), if defined, will have automatic main storage allocation.
   b. Other areas (01-level data blocks) are automatically secured for a task on input commands (RECEIVE MAP to read terminal data, READ DATASET to read a record, etc.) if the locate-mode (SET operand and pointer) option of the command is used.
   c. Otherwise the program has to execute a GETMAIN command.

DEVELOPING NEW APPLICATION PROGRAMS

The steps needed to develop application programs are as follows:

1. The program is passed through a command-language translator (a preprocessor). This creates an output source similar to the original program except that each command is translated into one or more MOVE statements and a CALL statement* to the Execute Interface program, which in turn makes a CALL to the appropriate CICS/VS control programs. The operands in the command are translated into arguments of the CALL statement.

*This is the case for ANS Cobol.

2. The output is then compiled through a regular ANS Cobol compiler and link-edited in the usual way.
3. Each application program must have any entry in the Program Control Table (PCT) and the Processing Program Table (PPT).
4. Each new file (new to CICS/VS, not the program) must have an entry in the File Control Table (FCT).
5. Each old file that has a change in condition (say, a new function like delete is added) must have its entry in the FCT correspondingly changed.

Figure 2.3 shows how application programs are generated.

MODIFYING APPLICATION PROGRAMS

Existing application programs are modified with the same steps in developing new ones, except for the following:

1. There is usually no need to modify entries in the PCT, PPT, or FCT unless an operand changes. One example is when the size of the Transaction Work Area changes, in which case the PCT entry for the program has to be modified.
2. CICS/VS uses the copied versions of application programs (and mapsets) that are in the partition/region, rather than the original ones in the program library. Therefore, any modified application program (or mapset) will not be usable until the next CICS/VS initialization, usually the next day. To make the modified version immediately usable, the programmer should tell the users of that specific application to stop using it for a few minutes while he uses the CICS/VS service:

   CSMT NEW, PGRMID = load module name

   where the load module name is that of the application program or the mapset. He should then get the answer:

   PROGRAM *load module name*
   IS NOW A NEW COPY

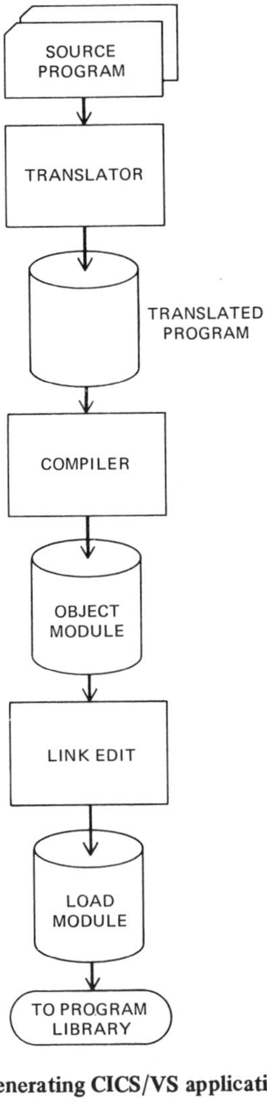

Fig. 2.3. Generating CICS/VS application programs.

The users may now use the new version.

3. If the modification is very trivial (which depends on the experience of the programmer) and thus the modified version does not warrant a separate test, the load module name should be the same as that of the current production version.

4. However, for most modifications, a separate test of the modified version is necessary. In this case, the load module name should be different from that of the current production version. Before the test is conducted, the programmer should use an operating system service (e.g., MAINT) to rename the current production version and then rename the modified version into the current production version. This way, if the modified version fails the test, the current production version can be restored (again with MAINT), and may thus be used until the modified version is declared operational.
5. Modified programs are best tested in a partition separate from the production partition to avoid the possibility of a bug causing problems with the production programs or even causing the CICS/VS partition to crash.
6. If the user needs the production version while a modified version is under test, then both may be used simultaneously, but at different partitions. Special care should be taken that no test data ever goes to a file belonging to the production version.

TRANSLATION OF COMMANDS

We said before that commands are translated into one or more MOVE statements and a CALL statement. For instance, given the command:

```
EXEC CICS
     RECEIVE MAP    ('ORCHM02')
             MAPSET ('ORCHS02')
             SET    (MAP2-POINTER)
END-EXEC.
```

Fig. 2.4. Example of a command.

The translated code is shown in Figure 2.5.

```
*     EXEC CICS
*          RECEIVE MAP     ('ORCHMO2')
*                  MAPSET ('ORCHSO2')
*                  SET     (MAP2-POINTER)
*     END-EXEC.
       MOVE 'ORCHMO2' TO DFHEIV1 MOVE 'ORCHSO2' TO DFHEIV2 MOVE '
-      '            ' TO DFHEIVO CALL 'DFHEI1' USING DFHEIVO
       DFHEIV1 MAP2-POINTER DFHEIV98 DFHEIV2.
```

Fig. 2.5. The command of Fig. 2.4 as translated.

You will observe that the original command has been translated into notes (with asterisks in column 7), and that 3 MOVE and one CALL statements have been generated. Note that the operands of the third MOVE verb are not blanks but unprintable hexadecimal characters.

3

Screen Layout

INTRODUCTION

CICS/VS allows the programmer to specify the format and location of data entered or displayed on a terminal. He can specify the row (line) and column of a field on the terminal screen, whether the keyboard shift of a field being entered is alphabetic or numeric, whether it is of normal, bright, or dark intensity, etc. The screen layout shows this specification on paper and designing it is one of the first steps taken when writing applications. Eventually, it will be translated into an Assembler-format map program which when assembled is used by CICS/VS when the application is run.

This book will deal only with the 3270-type CRT terminal, which is the most popular terminal used with CICS/VS. This terminal has special features like highlighting of fields (some of the displayed information is made to appear much brighter), special keys that allow the programmer to control the program logic, etc.

COMPONENTS OF A LAYOUT

A screen is usually divided into three parts, the title area, the application data area, and the operator message area.

The title area occupies the top one or two lines of the screen and should contain a title that identifies the application to the operator. For example, "PURCHASE ORDER – FILE INQUIRY" for a file inquiry of the Purchase Order master file; or "PURCHASE ORDER – FILE UPDATE" for the update to the purchase order master file. It may also contain a page number, if multiple pages are used.

The application data area is the main body of the screen. It contains relevant information from files, entered by the operator, or generated in the program. Four types of fields are found in this area: field identifiers, the data, STOPPER fields, and SKIP fields.

The field identifiers are constants that identify the data that comes after it or below it in the display. For instance, a field identifier with value "DATE" means that the data following it or below it is a date; a field identifier with value "NAME" means that the data following it or below it is a name. STOPPER and SKIP fields are one-byte fields specified by the programmer to automatically control the cursor as the operator enters data on the screen.

The operator message area, which is the bottom portion of the screen, is where the messages that help the operator are displayed by the program.

DESIGNING THE LAYOUT

The following are pointers in good design:

1. The display is for the benefit of the terminal operator. Thus, the overall considerations are the ease of use and the clarity of information being displayed.
2. The screen layout should correlate with the document being used. As much as possible, the sequence of fields shown on the display should be the same as those of the document. Note that when entering data, the cursor always moves from top to bottom, and from left to right on the same line.
3. A cluttered screen ("PAC MAN") should be avoided as much as possible. This may however become harder to avoid as more data appear on the screen.
4. Align all relevent data being displayed, entered, or modified, preferably in a single column if there is not too much data on the display.
5. Group related data together. You may want to put them in a "box."
6. Be creative in using special characters. For instance, ====> forms an arrow that can point to an important field.
7. Put prompting information on the screen, if such information can help the operator. An example is a set of codes (say, transaction codes) that the operator is not expected to memorize.

8. There must be at least one space between fields. We will learn in the next chapter that the space immediately to the left of the field is the attribute position of the field.
9. If the field identifier is to the left of the data, put a colon and space between the two.
10. Field identifiers for repeating fields are generally placed on top and centered over the fields.
11. Leave enough error message positions on the screen. For most applications, you may use two to six positions, with two positions per line (thus one to three lines for error messages).
12. Improvise when required. For example, if the top lines are being used and therefore cannot accommodate the title, you may put it in a "box" in the middle of the screen.
13. If a field belongs to a repeating line, a good idea is to display error message codes (instead of text) on the same line to the right of the line (assuming there is enough space). This way you can fully edit all the lines and do not have to stop because you have run out of error message positions.
14. Even if you choose to highlight fields in error (thus field identifiers are then defined as bright, data with normal intensity), you may still need error messages to guide the operator.

Design Example #1

1. You are writing a program which is used as a Purchase Order master sign-on (menu) program. All operators are required to sign on to this program to select an application.
2. This program requires a map and the operator enters the following data:

   a. Password — 3 characters, alphabetic.
   b. Employee number — 6 characters, numeric
   c. Code — 1 character, numeric

      code 1 = File Inquiry
      2 = File Add
      3 = File Update
      4 = File Delete

3. The possible error messages are:
   a. INVALID PASSWORD.
   b. INVALID EMPLOYEE NUMBER.
   c. INVALID CODE.
4. Allocate one error message position.
5. Design the layout.

The design is Figure 3.1.

Design Example #2

1. You are writing a program which is used for adding records into a file (File Add). The program requires a map with the following details:
   a. Purchase Order # – 8 digits, numeric
   b. Date of order – format MMDDYY
   c. Total $ amount – 8 digits, numeric; 2 decimal places
   d. from one to four detail lines:
      (1) Item number – 6 digits, numeric
      (2) Number of units – 4 digits, numeric
      (3) Cost of item – 5 digits, numeric; 2 decimal places
      (4) Total $ for line – 8 digits, numeric; 2 decimal places
2. The possible error messages are:
   a. INVALID ORDER NO.
   b. INVALID DATE OF ORDER.
   c. INVALID TOTAL AMOUNT.
3. Allocate three error message positions for the above.
4. The error codes for detail line errors are:
   a. 1 if item number.
   b. 2 if number of units.
   c. 3 if cost of item.
   d. 4 if total $ for line.
5. Design the layout.

The design is Figure 3.2.

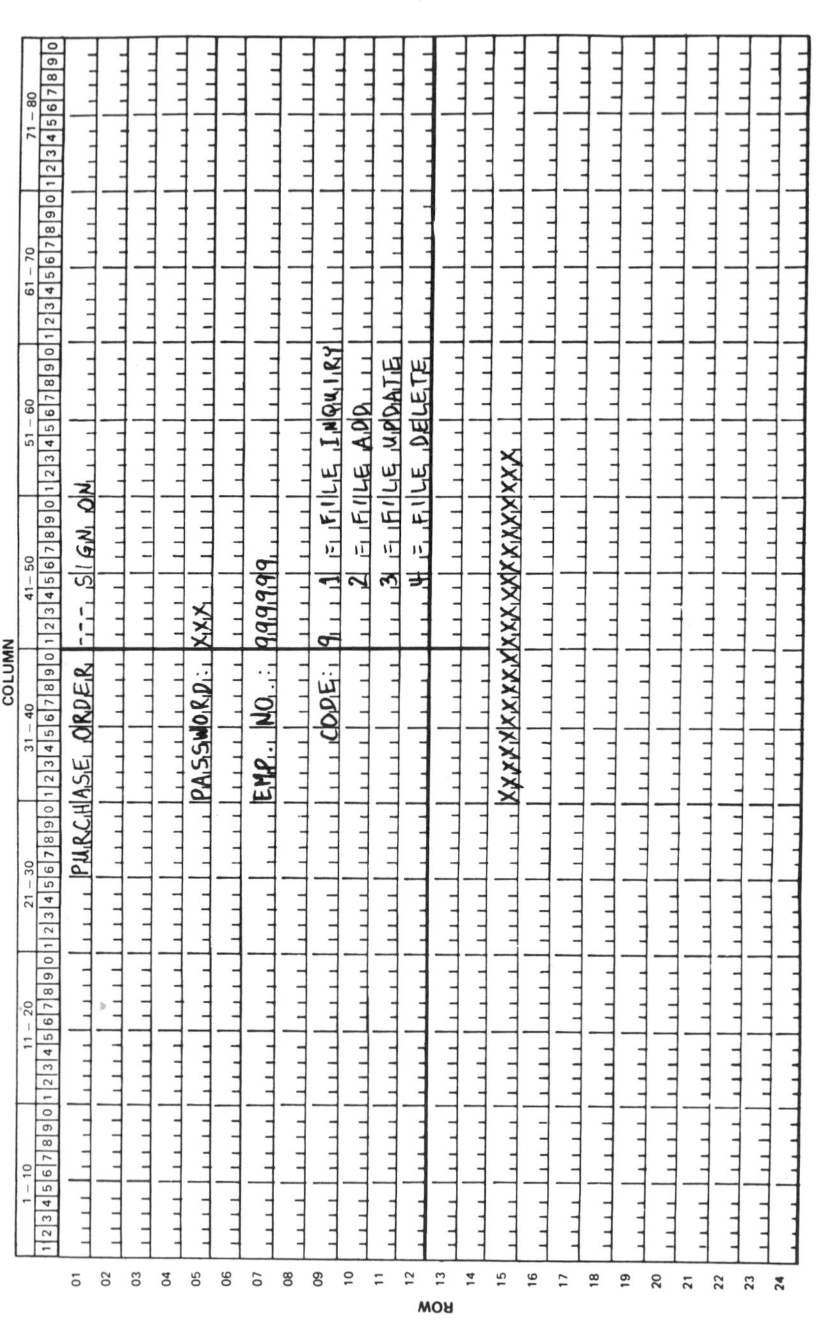

Fig. 3.1. Design Example #1.

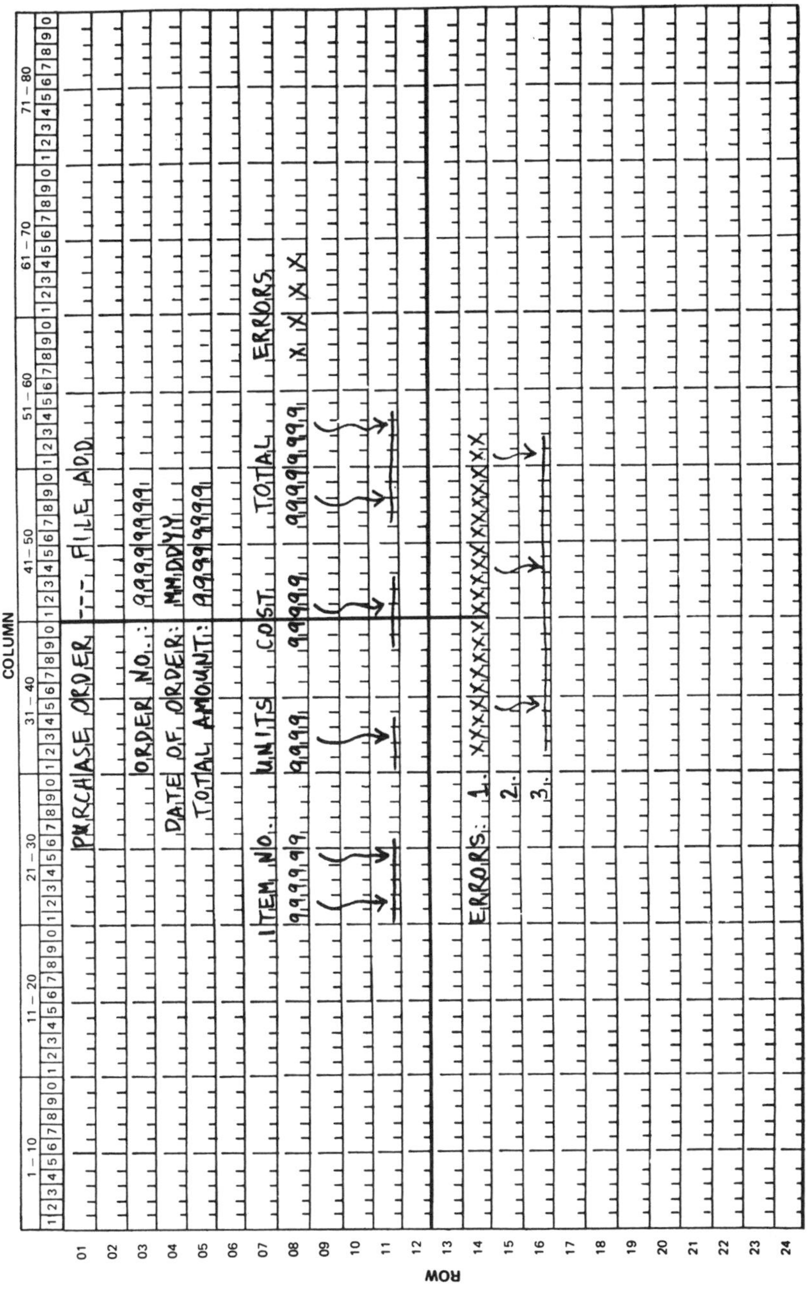

Fig. 3.2. Design Example #2.

FIELD CHARACTERISTICS

Fields on the screen will have different characteristics depending on their use. We will present the usual characteristics of fields as they are generally defined.

Fields In The Title Area

Fields in the title area should have the following characteristics:

1. Bright. They will be much brighter than the surrounding display to stand out.
2. Autoskip. They cannot be modified by the operator because the cursor will automatically skip the fields during normal operation. If he manipulates the cursor positioning keys of the terminal to position the cursor on this field and then attempts to change it, the keyboard will lock.
3. Initial value. They will have an initial value that is the literal constant comprising the title or part of the title. Usually the program does not modify this field, but may do so (for instance, a page number as part of the title).

Field Identifiers

The field identifiers should have the following characteristics:

1. Normal or bright intensity. Some installations prefer to display the field identifiers with normal intensity to contrast them with the fields themselves which will then have bright intensity. Others prefer the reverse. Each installation has its own standard, which should be consistent for all applications.
2. Autoskip. Same as in the Title Area section.
3. Initial value. This is the literal constant comprising the identifier, as in "DATE" or "NAME".

Data Fields

The data fields should have the following characteristics:

1. Bright or normal intensity. The intensity is the reverse of that of the field identifiers so the data stands out. Thus, if the field identifier is of normal intensity, the data is of bright intensity, and vice versa.
2. a. Autoskip. This is defined for data fields that should not be entered or changed by the operator, for instance, data in inquiry, browse applications, or any data that will show on the terminal but should not be touched by the operator.
   b. Unprotected. This is defined for data fields that can be entered or changed by the operator. This will be defined further as either alphabetic or numeric.
3. Initial value. Generally, there will be no initial value since what will show on the terminal is either what was entered by the operator, generated in the program, or came from files. However, in certain fields to be entered by the operator, the programmer may want to define an initial value that may be used as a guide, for instance, MMDDYY in a date field to be entered by the operator so he knows that the format is 2 digits for the month, 2 digits for the day, and 2 digits for the year. The operator will actually type over this initial value when he enters the data.

Operator Messages

The operator messages should have the following characteristics:

1. Bright. Same as in the Data Fields section.
2. Autoskip. Same as in the Data Fields section.
3. Initial value. Generally, there will be no initial value since the messages are generated by the program interactively. However, the programmer may want to display a message whenever a particular screen layout is displayed. For instance, in a data-entry application with multiple screen layouts, the programmer may want to display a prompting message to the operator when one screen comes up, for instance, "ENTER SALES DATA" when the sales data screen comes up.

4

Creating Maps

INTRODUCTION

The screen layouts show on paper the format and location of data entered or displayed on a terminal. However, before they can be used, they are first transformed into maps which are then used by CICS/VS during any data transmission from the terminal to the program and vice versa. There are two types of maps, the physical map and the symbolic description.

GENERATING MAPS

The transformation from screen layouts to maps is shown in Figure 4.1. Note the following:

1. One or more screen layouts are specified in one map program, which is written with Assembler-format macros. The whole map program has a mapset name while each screen layout has a map name.
2. The map program is assembled twice. Once to generate the physical map(s), the other the symbolic description map(s).
3. A physical map is the table equivalent of a screen layout and is stored in the program library. Just like application programs, it is loaded into virtual storage during CICS/VS initialization (except where it is defined in the PPT as resident, in which case it is loaded into dynamic storage instead). During program execution, it is the one actually used by CICS/VS to determine the format and location of data on any command that reads data from or displays data on a terminal.
4. A symbolic description map corresponds to a screen layout and is the set of source statements used by the application program to symbolically refer to data read from or displayed

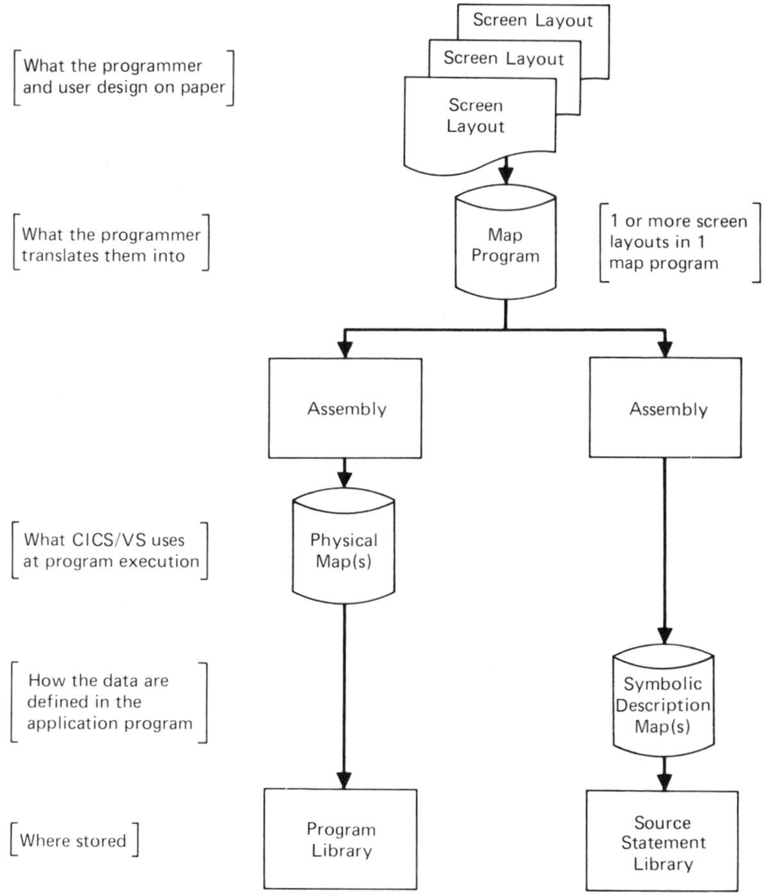

Fig. 4.1. Generating Maps.

on a terminal. In Cobol, it is the set of data-name definitions (data names, PICTURE clauses, USAGE clauses, etc.), grouped under a 01-level entry, that is used in statements in the PROCEDURE DIVISION.

MAP PROGRAM

From Figure 4.1, you will note that in generating maps, the first step is to transform the screen layouts into map programs. Since CICS/VS needs the whole mapset (thus all screen layouts defined in the same map program) in main storage whenever any layout is needed, it is more efficient to combine in one map program only those screen layouts that are used together in one execution of a task in the pseudo-conversational mode of processing. For most applications, there is only one screen layout in a map program.

Options In Creating Map Programs

The map program is written and assembled independent of the application program. There are two options to choose from in creating map programs. First, the programmer may conveniently use an available CICS/VS program where he formats the screen according to what it will look like to the operator. This will then be translated by the program into the map program. Usually, however, there will be some minor modifications to the macros before it can be used.

Second, the programmer may code the program himself. This is not really difficult to do since there are only three macros that will be used. In fact, even if he chooses the first option, he should know how the macros are used since, as we mentioned before, he may have to modify the generated map program before it is used. Also, a minor change to a screen layout does not necessitate the production of a new map program; the programmer may just change a few macros and the modified map program may be used.

Processing Program Table Entry For A Map Program

While an application program has an entry in both the Program Control Table (PCT) and Processing Program Table (PPT), the map program needs an entry only in the latter. The entry identifies this as a map, and specifies the mapset name, which is identical to the load module name specified at assembly. It also includes optional parameters such as whether this mapset is resident in dynamic storage, etc.

Note that just like application programs, map programs modified after CICS/VS initialization will not be usable until the next initialization. The programmer may however make them immediately usable by using the same CICS/VS service "CSMT NEW. . ." mentioned on page 26.

BASIC MAPPING SUPPORT (BMS)

Basic Mapping Support is a CICS/VS control program that gives the application programmer the ability to code map programs without consideration as to what physical device will actually be used as a terminal, to generate the maps independently of the application program, and to read data from or display data on a terminal using simple commands in the PROCEDURE DIVISION. Specifically, BMS has the following functions:

1. It allows the programmer to define operands in the map program without having to know the physical requirements of the actual terminals to be used.
2. It uses Program Control to load the appropriate physical map into main storage when required.
3. On a command to read data from a terminal, it uses Storage Control to secure main storage for the symbolic description map.
4. It uses Terminal Control facilities to transmit data from or to a terminal.
5. On a command to read data from a terminal, it strips formatting information from the transmitted stream so that only relevant data is placed in the main storage corresponding to the symbolic description map. On a command to display data on a terminal, it inserts terminal formatting information into the data being transmitted.
6. It provides the application program with some degree of data independence. The maps are assembled offline and generated before the application program is used. Then, on a change to the screen layout, the application program may not have to be modified; it may or may not even have to be recompiled and relinked.

Device Independence

The capacity to write map programs without having to know the physical requirements of the terminal means that even if the terminal is changed to a different model later on, the map program, in general, does not have to be modified. Exceptions are certain operands in macros that are unique to a specific device or type of device. In either case, the application program does not have to be modified or recompiled and relinked.

Data Independence

BMS gives the programmer some degree of data independence in addition to device independence. If the screen layout is changed, requiring that the physical map be regenerated, the symbolic description map may or may not have to be modified. If the symbolic description map is not modified, then the application program is not modified. If it is modified, then the application program may still not have to be modified, depending on certain factors. The rules for the modifications are as follows:

1. If the screen layout is changed, the map program is correspondingly modified and the physical map is regenerated.
2. Since only fields coded with labels (see page 47) have corresponding entries in the symbolic description map, if the change to the map program adds a new field with a label, deletes a field with a label, rearranges fields, or changes the length or shift (numeric to alphabetic or vice versa) of a field with a label, then and only then will the symbolic description map have to be modified. In many cases it is simpler to just modify the existing symbolic description map rather than regenerate it from the modified map program.
3. If the symbolic description map is modified, then the application program has to be recompiled and relinked to reflect the modifications. Whether it is modified before the compilation depends on the type of modification done to the symbolic description map.
4. If a field with a label is added to the map program, then the programmer will probably add statements in the PROCEDURE DIVISION to process the new field (otherwise why is it added in the first place?).

5. If a field with a label is deleted, then the programmer will have to remove or modify statements that refer to the field since it will no longer be in the symbolic description map.
6. If the length of a field with a label is changed, the programmer may or may not have to modify the program to take account of the change in length. If the application program issues the GETMAIN command for the symbolic description map, then the LENGTH operand of the command will have to be changed.
7. If the shift of a field with a label is changed, then the statements that process that field may have to be changed.

MACROS

BMS macros are coded in the same style as the more common Assembler macros. There are three of them, and the rules for coding are:

1. The label is from one to seven characters long with the first character being alphabetic. This will start in column 1. The programmer may actually code eight characters, but the first seven must be unique.
2. The op code is separated from the label by at least one space. However, we start coding it in column 10 for the sake of readability. It is always six columns long.
3. The operands start in column 17 and are separated by commas. If there is a need for a second line, the last operand must be followed by a comma, and column 72 must have a continuation character (any nonblank character will do but an 'X' or '*' are generally used). The continuation line then starts in column 16 of the next line.
4. The END statement is coded as the last statement to delimit the program. This is coded in columns 10 to 12.

First Macro

The first macro has the following functions:

1. defines a map set which consists of one or more maps;

2. specifies whether the program will generate physical maps or symbolic description maps;
3. specifies whether the maps will be used as input, output, or both;
4. may specify whether the data format is field or block.

The macro is coded in the following manner:

1. Label. This is the name of the map set and will be used in the command in the PROCEDURE DIVISION that reads data (RECEIVE MAP) from or displays data (SEND MAP) on a terminal. This is identical to the load module name when the map program is assembled to get the physical map(s).
2. Op code. This is DFHMSD.
3. Operands.

   a. TYPE = {MAP | DSECT}

   Use MAP to generate the physical map(s), and DSECT to generate the symbolic description map(s). My suggestion is to use MAP as the permanent operand because in a modification of the screen layout, the physical map is always regenerated but the symbolic description map may or may not have to be. To generate the symbolic description map(s) TYPE is temporarily changed to DSECT and later on restored to MAP.

   b. MODE= {IN | *OUT* | INOUT}   *OUT* is the default

   Use IN if the map is used solely to read data from a terminal; OUT if used solely to display data on a terminal; INOUT if used for both. Most maps are defined as INOUT. They can then be used as either input or output in the program.

   c. CTRL=FREEKB
   This operand is normally used so that the keyboard is unlocked after the map is displayed. The operator may then

use the keyboard to enter data on the screen. Alternately, this operand may be omitted if the FREEKB operand is specified in the SEND MAP command.

d. LANG= { *ASM* | COBOL | PL1 } *ASM* is the default

This operand specifies the programming language in whose format the symbolic description map is generated. In this book, we will use Cobol.

e. TIOAPFX=YES

This operand will generate a 12-byte filler prefix for the symbolic description map. When using the command-level feature (as in this book), this operand is always used.

f. DATA= { *FIELD* | BLOCK } *FIELD* is the default

In this book, we omit this operand so it takes on the default. We will then define the fields in the mapset.

g. TERM=terminal type 3270 is the default.

In this book, we omit this operand so it takes on the default.

Second Macro

The second macro has these functions:

1. defines a map within a map set;
2. defines the position of the map on the page (the actual screen);
3. specifies the size of the map;
4. may specify whether the data format is field or block.

The macro is coded in the following manner:

1. Label. This is the name of the map and will be used in the command in the PROCEDURE DIVISION that reads data

(RECEIVE MAP) from or displays data (SEND MAP) on a terminal.

2. Op code. This is DFHMDI.

3. Operands.
   a. SIZE=(lines, columns)
      This defines the size of the map and cannot be greater than the size of the screen being used (the page size).
   b. LINE=n
      On the screen, n specifies the line number where the map starts and can be from 1 to 240; the default is 1 and most maps start at line 1.
   c. COLUMN=n
      The column number is also specified by n and tells where the map starts. It can be from 1 to 240; the default is again 1 and most maps start at column 1.
   d. DATA= { *FIELD* | BLOCK } *FIELD* is the default
      In this book, we omit this operand so it takes on the default. We will then define the fields in the map.

Third Macro

The third macro has the following functions:

1. defines a field within a map;
2. specifies the position of the field;
3. specifies the length of the field;
4. may specify the attributes (characteristics) of the field.
5. may also specify default values, whether the field is part of a group, etc.

The macro is coded in the following manner:

1. Label. Labels are specified for fields that will have entries generated for them when the symbolic description map is generated. Therefore, only fields that will be used in statements in the PROCEDURE DIVISION should really have labels. Coding labels for other fields will just make the symbolic description map larger (consequently requiring a larger main storage allocation) without achieving anything. In fact, data transmission time would be longer. We specify labels for fields entered by the operator (and used in the program), fields used for messages displayed by the program for the operator, fields displayed on the screen from files (as in inquiry applications), etc.

2. Op code. Use DFHMDF.

3. Operands.

   a. $\text{POS=}\left\{\begin{array}{l}\text{line, column}\\ \\ \text{n (0–1919)}\end{array}\right\}$

   This specifies the position of the field's attribute byte, which is one position before the actual start of the field. For example, in Fig. 3.1 the position of the title is given by POS=(01,25), or POS=24. You will notice that the title itself really starts in line 1, column 26. This position is determined relative to the start of the map (line and column operands in the previous macro). Since most maps start in line 1 and column 1, this position is generally with respect to line 1 and column 1 of the actual screen page and is thus easier to interpret.

   Position can be specified with line and column coordinates as in (01,25), or as a number with the first position being 0. Thus POS=(01,25) is identical to POS=24. If we use numbers, the position specification will wrap around to the next line. Therefore, in a screen with a column size of 80, line 1, column 80 is identical to position 79 and line 2, column 1 identical to position 80.

b. LENGTH=n
The maximum length of the field is given by n. It does not include the attribute byte. For instance, the title of Fig. 3.1 has length equal to 31.

c. ATTRB = ($attribute_1$, $attribute_2$, $attribute_3$, . . . $attribute_n$) must be specified for a map defined with mode OUT or INOUT.

1. $attribute_1 = \left\{ \begin{array}{l} \text{ASKIP} \\ \text{PROT} \\ \text{UNPROT} \end{array} \right\}$

   a. ASKIP. The field is autoskip and thus cannot be modified by the operator. It will automatically be skipped by the cursor.
   b. PROT. The field is protected and thus cannot be modified by the operator, but will not be skipped automatically by the cursor. It is used only for STOPPER fields.
   c. UNPROT. The operator may modify the field, and the cursor will at one time fall under this field during normal operation.

   If the whole ATTRB operand is omitted, ASKIP is the default; if the ATTRB operand is specified, but $attribute_1$ is omitted, UNPROT is the default.

2. $attribute_2$ =NUM
   This specifies that the terminal keyboard is in numeric shift and is really only significant for unprotected fields.* If not specified, the keyboard will be in alphabetic shift for an unprotected field. Many CICS/VS programmers do not bother specifying UNPROT if NUM is also specified since in this case UNPROT is the default.

3. $attribute_3 = \left\{ \begin{array}{l} \text{BRT} \\ \textit{NORM} \\ \text{DRK} \end{array} \right\}$ *NORM* is the default

---

*For autoskip or protected fields, the actual value will be what is either specified in the map program (INITIAL = "value") or what is generated in the application program.

a. BRT. This makes the field brighter than normal displays.
b. NORM. The field will appear with normal intensity.
c. DRK. The field will not show on the screen; however, it can still be accessed by the program if the macro has a label. This attribute is useful for information that is used by the program but should not show on the screen; for instance, a password entered.

Note that NORM is the default, regardless whether ATTRB is coded or not.

4. $attribute_4$ = FSET

This attribute requires some knowledge about buffers and modified data tags. It is explained in detail on page 152.

5. $attribute_5$=IC

The insert cursor (IC) attribute specifies the field under which the cursor will be positioned when the physical map is displayed on the screen. This is useful for maps defined with mode IN or INOUT so that the cursor is automatically positioned on the first field that the operator usually enters or modifies. The program may interactively override this during a series of terminal inputs and outputs for a map with mode INOUT so that the cursor will always be under the first field that the operator is supposed to enter or change. This is done through the symbolic cursor positioning technique (page 156).

If the IC operand is missing for a map, then the cursor will be positioned at line 1, column 1 when the map is displayed. The programmer may however specify another line and column through the symbolic cursor positioning technique. If there are multiple IC entries for a map, then the last entry will take effect.

d. INITIAL='literal constant'

This operand specifies the literal value of the field on a command to display the physical map. If the field is defined with a label and the symbolic description map is included in the display, the value in the symbolic description map will override the initial value if the former is not hexadecimal zeroes.

e. PICIN='Cobol PICTURE specification'
For fields defined with labels, this defines the PICTURE specification of the field in the generated symbolic description map if the map is defined with mode IN or INOUT. PICIN is specified only for numeric fields* since the default is alphanumeric (PICTURE X's). Note that PICIN (and PICOUT) are required only if the symbolic description map(s) are generated from the map program.

f. PICOUT='Cobol PICTURE specification'
This is used just like the PICIN operand, but for a map defined with mode OUT or INOUT.

g. GRPNAME=name
GRPNAME identifies this line and succeeding lines defined with the same GRPNAME value as elementary items of the group. There will be only one length field and one attribute byte generated in the symbolic description map for the group. Only the first field in a group must have the ATTRB operands; also, the POS operand for fields after the first in a group must point to where the attribute byte would be if there was one.

h. OCCURS=n
This operand is mutually exclusive with GRPNAME and specifies that this field is repeated a number of times.

The DFHMSD macro is used again as the last macro in the program and the entry is simple:

DFHMSD TYPE=FINAL

MAP PROGRAM EXAMPLE

Let us now show the assembly listing of a complete map program for a screen layout with three labeled data fields. They are a 3-byte

*This includes autoskip fields that are used in statements as numeric.

```
STMT    SOURCE STATEMENT                                    DOS/VSE ASSEMBLER

   1            PRINT NOGEN
   2 MPM010     DFHMSD TYPE=MAP,MODE=INOUT,CTRL=FREEKB,LANG=COBOL,TIOAPFX=YES
  12 MPMA03     DFHMDI SIZE=(24,80)
  40 DUMMY      DFHMDF POS=(01,01),LENGTH=01,ATTRB=(ASKIP,DRK,FSET),          X
                       INITIAL='1'
  51            DFHMDF POS=(01,25),LENGTH=33,ATTRB=(ASKIP,BRT),               X
                       INITIAL='MERCHANDISE PLANS --- FILE DELETE'
  62            DFHMDF POS=(03,31),LENGTH=12,ATTRB=ASKIP,                     X
                       INITIAL='DEPT NUMBER:'
  73 DEPT       DFHMDF POS=(03,44),LENGTH=03,ATTRB=(NUM,BRT,IC)
  83            DFHMDF POS=(03,48),LENGTH=01,ATTRB=PROT
  93            DFHMDF POS=(05,34),LENGTH=09,ATTRB=ASKIP,INITIAL='PASSWORD:'
 104 PASSWD     DFHMDF POS=(05,44),LENGTH=09,ATTRB=(UNPROT,DRK)
 114            DFHMDF POS=(05,54),LENGTH=01
 124 ERROR      DFHMDF POS=(09,20),LENGTH=24,ATTRB=(ASKIP,BRT)
 134            PRINT GEN
 135            DFHMSD TYPE=FINAL
136+***********************************************************************
137+DFHBM601 EQU    90                     MAP SPECIFICATION LENGTH        *
138+DFHBM201 EQU    56                  INPUT WORK AREA LENGTH             *
139+DFHBM301 EQU    142                 OUTPUT WORK AREA LENGTH            *
140+DFHBM401 EQU    204                 CURSOR POSITION                    *
141+DFHBM701 EQU    0                      MAP INDICATOR                   *
142+         DC     2XL1'FF'            END OF MAP                         *
143+DFHBM501 EQU    *                   END OF MAP                         *
144+DFHBM101 EQU    DFHBM501-MPMA03-0      MAP LENGTH             @BA7040 *
145+DFHBM801 EQU    0                   OVERFLOW TRAILER LEN.      @BDAD31 *
146+         DC     4X'FF'              END OF MAPSET              @BDAD32 *
147+***********************************************************************


 149            END
```

Fig. 4.2. Map Program.

department number, a 9-byte password, and 24 bytes for the error message. This is Figure 4.2.

Note the following:

1. PRINT NOGEN at statement 1 is optional but is used so that the expansion of the macros do not print out in the listing.
2. The DUMMY field at statement 40 as the first unlabeled field is explained on page 204. Let it suffice to say that the use of this field is advisable to prevent a certain type of error from abnormally terminating the application.
3. PRINT GEN at statement 134 is required to print certain map statistics, in this case, statements 136 to 147. One piece of statistic is used to check if the length of the corresponding symbolic description map is correct. PRINT GEN would actually not have been needed if PRINT NOGEN was not coded in a previous statement.

4. The END statement at statement 149 is used to indicate the end of the map program.

MAPS IN A MAPSET

When the program reads data from or displays data on a terminal, CICS/VS will require its format as defined in the physical map. However, CICS/VS will always load the whole mapset into main storage, including those physical maps in that mapset which are not needed during that task. This will waste main storage and CPU time.

For most applications, only one map is generally required in a particular task and therefore there is usually only one map in a mapset.

If two or more maps are often used in a single task, then those maps may be conveniently combined in a single mapset. For instance, experienced CICS/VS programmers may combine several maps in overlapping displays in a single task.

To specify several maps in a mapset, the macros are coded as shown in Figure 4.3.

```
map set  name  DFHMSD

     map name  DFHMDI  )
               DFHMDF  |
               DFHMDF  }   First Map
               DFHMDF  )

     map name  DFHMDI  )
               DFHMDF  |
               DFHMDF  }   Second Map
               DFHMDF  |
               DFHMDF  )

     .....             )
     .....             |
     .....             }   Third Map, etc.
     .....             )

               DFHMSD TYPE=FINAL
               END
```

Fig. 4.3. Multiple maps in a mapset.

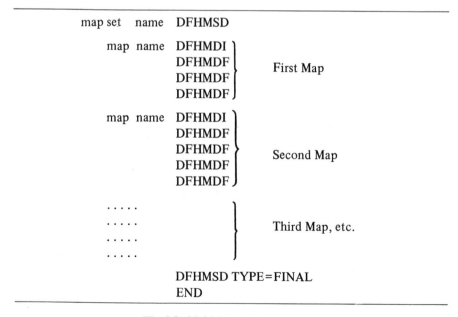

THE PHYSICAL MAPS

When the map program is assembled with the TYPE=MAP operand in the first macro, the physical maps are generated. There is one physical map for every screen layout specified in the map program. However, all physical maps in the mapset are combined in the single generated table that has a load module name that is identical to that of the mapset name.

Whenever there is a command to read terminal data (RECEIVE MAP) or display on a terminal (SEND MAP), CICS/VS has to have the whole mapset in main storage. Naturally, if the mapset is not in main storage when the command is issued, CICS/VS will load it from virtual storage. The command will specify both the map name (hence the physical map) and the mapset name so CICS/VS will know which one to use on that particular command.

THE SYMBOLIC DESCRIPTION MAPS

When the map program is assembled with the TYPE=DSECT (DSECT being dummy section) operand in the first macro, the symbolic description maps are generated. There is one symbolic description map for every screen layout specified in the map program with each one starting with a 01-level entry.

For Cobol programs, the symbolic description map consists of data-name definitions (data names, PICTURE clauses, USAGE clauses, etc.), grouped under a 01-level entry, that are used in statements in the PROCEDURE DIVISION.

Only those entries in the map program where the third macro (thus field) has a label will have entries generated in the symbolic description map. Each labeled entry will actually have three entries generated in the symbolic description map. These are:

1. A two-byte binary (COMP) length field which contains the number of characters the operator entered on the field. I suggest that the data name be identical to that of the field itself but with the "–L" suffix.
2. A one-byte character field which is used if the program changes the attributes (characteristics) of a field interactively

during execution. I suggest that the data name be identical to that of the field itself but with the "–A" suffix.

3. The data field itself.

An example of a symbolic description map is Figure 4.4.

Note that the first entry is a 12-byte filler. This is always the case when using the command-level feature and is generated by the TIOAPFX=YES operand in the first macro.

```
      5         ORIQ01A         12.55.39         08/02/80

00109         ******************************************************************
00110         *                                                                *
00111         *                    DISPLAY MAP DESCRIPTION                      *
00112         *                                                                *
00113         ******************************************************************

00115         01  MAP1-AREA.
00116             05  FILLER                      PIC X(12).
00117             05  MAP1-DUMMY-L                PIC S9999 COMP.
00118             05  MAP1-DUMMY-A                PIC X.
00119             05  MAP1-DUMMY                  PIC X.
00120             05  MAP1-ORDER-NUMBER-L         PIC S9999 COMP.
00121             05  MAP1-ORDER-NUMBER-A         PIC X.
00122             05  MAP1-ORDER-NUMBER           PIC X(10).
00123             05  MAP1-DEPARTMENT-L           PIC S9999 COMP.
00124             05  MAP1-DEPARTMENT-A           PIC X.
00125             05  MAP1-DEPARTMENT             PIC XXX.
00126             05  MAP1-ORDER-DATE-L           PIC S9999 COMP.
00127             05  MAP1-ORDER-DATE-A           PIC X.
00128             05  MAP1-ORDER-DATE.
00129                 10  MAP1-ORDER-DATE-MONTH   PIC XX.
00130                 10  MAP1-ORDER-DATE-DAY     PIC XX.
00131                 10  MAP1-ORDER-DATE-YEAR    PIC XX.
00132             05  MAP1-ORDER-DATE-ENTERED-L   PIC S9999 COMP.
00133             05  MAP1-ORDER-DATE-ENTERED-A   PIC X.
00134             05  MAP1-ORDER-DATE-ENTERED     PIC X(6).
00135             05  MAP1-TOTAL-COST-L           PIC S9999 COMP.
00136             05  MAP1-TOTAL-COST-A           PIC X.
00137             05  MAP1-TOTAL-COST             PIC Z,ZZZ,ZZZ.99.
00138             05  MAP1-TOTAL-PRICE-L          PIC S9999 COMP.
00139             05  MAP1-TOTAL-PRICE-A          PIC X.
00140             05  MAP1-TOTAL-PRICE            PIC Z,ZZZ,ZZZ.99.
00141             05  MAP1-LINE-ITEM              OCCURS 9
00142                                             INDEXED BY MAP1-LINE-I.
00143                 10  MAP1-LINE-NUMBER-L      PIC S9999 COMP.
00144                 10  MAP1-LINE-NUMBER-A      PIC X.
00145                 10  MAP1-LINE-NUMBER        PIC 9.
00146                 10  MAP1-ITEM-NUMBER-L      PIC S9999 COMP.
00147                 10  MAP1-ITEM-NUMBER-A      PIC X.
00148                 10  MAP1-ITEM-NUMBER        PIC 9(8).
00149                 10  MAP1-ITEM-DESCRIPTION-L PIC S9999 COMP.
00150                 10  MAP1-ITEM-DESCRIPTION-A PIC X.
00151                 10  MAP1-ITEM-DESCRIPTION   PIC X(19).
00152                 10  MAP1-ITEM-DATE-L        PIC S9999 COMP.
00153                 10  MAP1-ITEM-DATE-A        PIC X.
00154                 10  MAP1-ITEM-DATE          PIC X(6).
00155                 10  MAP1-UNIT-L             PIC S9999 COMP.
00156                 10  MAP1-UNIT-A             PIC X.
00157                 10  MAP1-UNIT               PIC 9(5).
00158                 10  MAP1-UNIT-COST-L        PIC S9999 COMP.
00159                 10  MAP1-UNIT-COST-A        PIC X.
```

Fig. 4.4. The Symbolic Description Map.

6 ORIQ01A 12.55.39 08/02/80

```
00160          10   MAP1-UNIT-COST        PIC 9(7).
00161          10   MAP1-COST-L           PIC S9999 COMP.
00162          10   MAP1-COST-A           PIC X.
00163          10   MAP1-COST             PIC 9(8).
00164          10   MAP1-UNIT-PRICE-L     PIC S9999 COMP.
00165          10   MAP1-UNIT-PRICE-A     PIC X.
00166          10   MAP1-UNIT-PRICE       PIC 9(7).
00167          10   MAP1-PRICE-L          PIC S9999 COMP.
00168          10   MAP1-PRICE-A          PIC X.
00169          10   MAP1-PRICE            PIC 9(8).
00170       05      MAP1-ERROR-L          PIC S9999 COMP.
00171       05      MAP1-ERROR-A          PIC X.
00172       05      MAP1-ERROR            PIC X(20).
```

Fig. 4.4. (Continued)

Improving The Program-Generated Symbolic Description Map

Actually, the symbolic description maps generated when the map program is assembled (with the TYPE=DSECT operand) are not as streamlined as the one shown in Figure 4.4. Figure 4.5 shows this, and Figure 4.4 in fact is a "corrected version" of it.

Since this is far from the best way to code data names in Cobol, the programmer has to "modify" Figure 4.5 to generate Figure 4.4. Since your installation has CICS/VS, you probably have on-line program development facilities (like On-line LIBRARIAN, etc.) and this is easy to do.

Verifying The Length of The Symbolic Description Map

The DATA DIVISION map in the compilation listing of the application program indicates the length of all data fields, including those of the symbolic description maps. This value can be checked against the corresponding map program assembly listing.

Let us look back at Figure 4.2. There are four labeled fields, which will have entries in the symbolic description map. Each field will be defined with a length equal to the LENGTH specification in the map program, plus two bytes for the length and one byte for the attribute. Thus the length of the symbolic description map should be:

$$\text{length} = 12 \qquad \text{prefix}$$
$$+ (1 + 3) \qquad \text{DUMMY field}$$
$$+ (3 + 3) \qquad \text{DEPT field}$$
$$+ (9 + 3) \qquad \text{PASSWD field}$$
$$+ (24 + 3) \qquad \text{ERROR field}$$

```
01  ORIQM01I.
    02  FILLER PIC X(12).
    02  DUMMYL      COMP  PIC  S9(4).
    02  DUMMYF      PICTURE X.
    02  FILLER REDEFINES DUMMYF.
      03  DUMMYA      PICTURE X.
    02  DUMMYI  PIC X(1).
    02  ORDERL      COMP  PIC  S9(4).
    02  ORDERF      PICTURE X.
    02  FILLER REDEFINES ORDERF.
      03  ORDERA      PICTURE X.
    02  ORDERI  PIC X(10).
    02  DEPTL      COMP  PIC  S9(4).
    02  DEPTF      PICTURE X.
    02  FILLER REDEFINES DEPTF.
      03  DEPTA      PICTURE X.
    02  DEPTI  PIC X(3).
    02  DATEORL      COMP  PIC  S9(4).
    02  DATEORF      PICTURE X.
    02  FILLER REDEFINES DATEORF.
      03  DATEORA      PICTURE X.
    02  DATEORI  PIC X(6).
    02  DATEENTL      COMP  PIC  S9(4).
    02  DATEENTF      PICTURE X.
    02  FILLER REDEFINES DATEENTF.
      03  DATEENTA      PICTURE X.
    02  DATEENTI  PIC X(6).
    02  TOTCOSTL      COMP  PIC  S9(4).
    02  TOTCOSTF      PICTURE X.
    02  FILLER REDEFINES TOTCOSTF.
      03  TOTCOSTA      PICTURE X.
    02  TOTCOSTI  PIC X(12).
    02  TOTPRCEL      COMP  PIC  S9(4).
    02  TOTPRCEF      PICTURE X.
    02  FILLER REDEFINES TOTPRCEF.
      03  TOTPRCEA      PICTURE X.
    02  TOTPRCEI  PIC X(12).
    02  LINE1L      COMP  PIC  S9(4).
    02  LINE1F      PICTURE X.
    02  FILLER REDEFINES LINE1F.
      03  LINE1A      PICTURE X.
    02  LINE1I  PIC X(1).
    02  ITEM1L      COMP  PIC  S9(4).
    02  ITEM1F      PICTURE X.
    02  FILLER REDEFINES ITEM1F.
      03  ITEM1A      PICTURE X.
    02  ITEM1I  PIC 99999999.
    02  DESC1L      COMP  PIC  S9(4).
    02  DESC1F      PICTURE X.
    02  FILLER REDEFINES DESC1F.
      03  DESC1A      PICTURE X.
    02  DESC1I  PIC X(19).
    02  LNDATE1L      COMP  PIC  S9(4).
    02  LNDATE1F      PICTURE X.
    02  FILLER REDEFINES LNDATE1F.
      03  LNDATE1A      PICTURE X.
```

Fig. 4.5. The Symbolic Description Map As Generated From The Map Program. Compare This To Fig. 4.4.

```
02  LNDATE1I  PIC X(6).
02  UNIT1L     COMP  PIC  S9(4).
02  UNIT1F     PICTURE X.
02  FILLER REDEFINES UNIT1F.
  03  UNIT1A     PICTURE X.
02  UNIT1I  PIC 99999.
02  UCOST1L     COMP  PIC  S9(4).
02  UCOST1F     PICTURE X.
02  FILLER REDEFINES UCOST1F.
  03  UCOST1A     PICTURE X.
02  UCOST1I  PIC 9999999.
02  COST1L     COMP  PIC  S9(4).
02  COST1F     PICTURE X.
02  FILLER REDEFINES COST1F.
  03  COST1A     PICTURE X.
02  COST1I  PIC 99999999.
02  UPRICE1L     COMP  PIC  S9(4).
02  UPRICE1F     PICTURE X.
02  FILLER REDEFINES UPRICE1F.
  03  UPRICE1A     PICTURE X.
02  UPRICE1I  PIC 9999999.
02  PRICE1L     COMP  PIC  S9(4).
02  PRICE1F     PICTURE X.
02  FILLER REDEFINES PRICE1F.
  03  PRICE1A     PICTURE X.
02  PRICE1I  PIC 99999999.
02  LINE2L     COMP  PIC  S9(4).
02  LINE2F     PICTURE X.
02  FILLER REDEFINES LINE2F.
  03  LINE2A     PICTURE X.
02  LINE2I  PIC X(1).
02  ITEM2L     COMP  PIC  S9(4).
02  ITEM2F     PICTURE X.
02  FILLER REDEFINES ITEM2F.
  03  ITEM2A     PICTURE X.
02  ITEM2I  PIC 99999999.
02  DESC2L     COMP  PIC  S9(4).
02  DESC2F     PICTURE X.
02  FILLER REDEFINES DESC2F.
  03  DESC2A     PICTURE X.
02  DESC2I  PIC X(19).
02  LNDATE2L     COMP  PIC  S9(4).
02  LNDATE2F     PICTURE X.
02  FILLER REDEFINES LNDATE2F.
  03  LNDATE2A     PICTURE X.
02  LNDATE2I  PIC X(6).
02  UNIT2L     COMP  PIC  S9(4).
02  UNIT2F     PICTURE X.
02  FILLER REDEFINES UNIT2F.
  03  UNIT2A     PICTURE X.
02  UNIT2I  PIC 99999.
02  UCOST2L     COMP  PIC  S9(4).
02  UCOST2F     PICTURE X.
02  FILLER REDEFINES UCOST2F.
  03  UCOST2A     PICTURE X.
02  UCOST2I  PIC 9999999.
```

Fig. 4.5. (Continued)

```
02  COST2L     COMP  PIC  S9(4).
02  COST2F     PICTURE X.
02  FILLER REDEFINES COST2F.
  03  COST2A     PICTURE X.
02  COST2I  PIC 99999999.
02  UPRICE2L     COMP  PIC  S9(4).
02  UPRICE2F     PICTURE X.
02  FILLER REDEFINES UPRICE2F.
  03  UPRICE2A     PICTURE X.
02  UPRICE2I  PIC 9999999.
02  PRICE2L     COMP  PIC  S9(4).
02  PRICE2F     PICTURE X.
02  FILLER REDEFINES PRICE2F.
  03  PRICE2A     PICTURE X.
02  PRICE2I  PIC 99999999.
02  LINE3L     COMP  PIC  S9(4).
02  LINE3F     PICTURE X.
02  FILLER REDEFINES LINE3F.
  03  LINE3A     PICTURE X.
02  LINE3I  PIC X(1).
02  ITEM3L     COMP  PIC  S9(4).
02  ITEM3F     PICTURE X.
02  FILLER REDEFINES ITEM3F.
  03  ITEM3A     PICTURE X.
02  ITEM3I  PIC 99999999.
02  DESC3L     COMP  PIC  S9(4).
02  DESC3F     PICTURE X.
02  FILLER REDEFINES DESC3F.
  03  DESC3A     PICTURE X.
02  DESC3I  PIC X(19).
02  LNDATE3L     COMP  PIC  S9(4).
02  LNDATE3F     PICTURE X.
02  FILLER REDEFINES LNDATE3F.
  03  LNDATE3A     PICTURE X.
02  LNDATE3I  PIC X(6).
02  UNIT3L     COMP  PIC  S9(4).
02  UNIT3F     PICTURE X.
02  FILLER REDEFINES UNIT3F.
  03  UNIT3A     PICTURE X.
02  UNIT3I  PIC 99999.
02  UCOST3L     COMP  PIC  S9(4).
02  UCOST3F     PICTURE X.
02  FILLER REDEFINES UCOST3F.
  03  UCOST3A     PICTURE X.
02  UCOST3I  PIC 9999999.
02  COST3L     COMP  PIC  S9(4).
02  COST3F     PICTURE X.
02  FILLER REDEFINES COST3F.
  03  COST3A     PICTURE X.
02  COST3I  PIC 99999999.
02  UPRICE3L     COMP  PIC  S9(4).
02  UPRICE3F     PICTURE X.
02  FILLER REDEFINES UPRICE3F.
  03  UPRICE3A     PICTURE X.
02  UPRICE3I  PIC 9999999.
02  PRICE3L     COMP  PIC  S9(4).
```

Fig. 4.5. (Continued)

```
02  PRICE3F      PICTURE X.
02  FILLER REDEFINES PRICE3F.
  03  PRICE3A      PICTURE X.
02  PRICE3I  PIC 99999999.
02  LINE4L      COMP  PIC  S9(4).
02  LINE4F      PICTURE X.
02  FILLER REDEFINES LINE4F.
  03  LINE4A      PICTURE X.
02  LINE4I  PIC X(1).
02  ITEM4L      COMP  PIC  S9(4).
02  ITEM4F      PICTURE X.
02  FILLER REDEFINES ITEM4F.
  03  ITEM4A      PICTURE X.
02  ITEM4I  PIC 99999999.
02  DESC4L      COMP  PIC  S9(4).
02  DESC4F      PICTURE X.
02  FILLER REDEFINES DESC4F.
  03  DESC4A      PICTURE X.
02  DESC4I  PIC X(19).
02  LNDATE4L      COMP  PIC  S9(4).
02  LNDATE4F      PICTURE X.
02  FILLER REDEFINES LNDATE4F.
  03  LNDATE4A      PICTURE X.
02  LNDATE4I  PIC X(6).
02  UNIT4L      COMP  PIC  S9(4).
02  UNIT4F      PICTURE X.
02  FILLER REDEFINES UNIT4F.
  03  UNIT4A      PICTURE X.
02  UNIT4I  PIC 99999.
02  UCOST4L      COMP  PIC  S9(4).
02  UCOST4F      PICTURE X.
02  FILLER REDEFINES UCOST4F.
  03  UCOST4A      PICTURE X.
02  UCOST4I  PIC 9999999.
02  COST4L      COMP  PIC  S9(4).
02  COST4F      PICTURE X.
02  FILLER REDEFINES COST4F.
  03  COST4A      PICTURE X.
02  COST4I  PIC 99999999.
02  UPRICE4L      COMP  PIC  S9(4).
02  UPRICE4F      PICTURE X.
02  FILLER REDEFINES UPRICE4F.
  03  UPRICE4A      PICTURE X.
02  UPRICE4I  PIC 9999999.
02  PRICE4L      COMP  PIC  S9(4).
02  PRICE4F      PICTURE X.
02  FILLER REDEFINES PRICE4F.
  03  PRICE4A      PICTURE X.
02  PRICE4I  PIC 99999999.
02  LINE5L      COMP  PIC  S9(4).
02  LINE5F      PICTURE X.
02  FILLER REDEFINES LINE5F.
  03  LINE5A      PICTURE X.
02  LINE5I  PIC X(1).
02  ITEM5L      COMP  PIC  S9(4).
02  ITEM5F      PICTURE X.
```

Fig. 4.5. (Continued)

```
02  FILLER REDEFINES ITEM5F.
  03  ITEM5A     PICTURE X.
02  ITEM5I  PIC 99999999.
02  DESC5L     COMP  PIC  S9(4).
02  DESC5F     PICTURE X.
02  FILLER REDEFINES DESC5F.
  03  DESC5A     PICTURE X.
02  DESC5I  PIC X(19).
02  LNDATE5L     COMP  PIC  S9(4).
02  LNDATE5F     PICTURE X.
02  FILLER REDEFINES LNDATE5F.
  03  LNDATE5A     PICTURE X.
02  LNDATE5I  PIC X(6).
02  UNIT5L     COMP  PIC  S9(4).
02  UNIT5F     PICTURE X.
02  FILLER REDEFINES UNIT5F.
  03  UNIT5A     PICTURE X.
02  UNIT5I  PIC 99999.
02  UCOST5L     COMP  PIC  S9(4).
02  UCOST5F     PICTURE X.
02  FILLER REDEFINES UCOST5F.
  03  UCOST5A     PICTURE X.
02  UCOST5I  PIC 9999999.
02  COST5L     COMP  PIC  S9(4).
02  COST5F     PICTURE X.
02  FILLER REDEFINES COST5F.
  03  COST5A     PICTURE X.
02  COST5I  PIC 99999999.
02  UPRICE5L     COMP  PIC  S9(4).
02  UPRICE5F     PICTURE X.
02  FILLER REDEFINES UPRICE5F.
  03  UPRICE5A     PICTURE X.
02  UPRICE5I  PIC 9999999.
02  PRICE5L     COMP  PIC  S9(4).
02  PRICE5F     PICTURE X.
02  FILLER REDEFINES PRICE5F.
  03  PRICE5A     PICTURE X.
02  PRICE5I  PIC 99999999.
02  LINE6L     COMP  PIC  S9(4).
02  LINE6F     PICTURE X.
02  FILLER REDEFINES LINE6F.
  03  LINE6A     PICTURE X.
02  LINE6I  PIC X(1).
02  ITEM6L     COMP  PIC  S9(4).
02  ITEM6F     PICTURE X.
02  FILLER REDEFINES ITEM6F.
  03  ITEM6A     PICTURE X.
02  ITEM6I  PIC 99999999.
02  DESC6L     COMP  PIC  S9(4).
02  DESC6F     PICTURE X.
02  FILLER REDEFINES DESC6F.
  03  DESC6A     PICTURE X.
02  DESC6I  PIC X(19).
02  LNDATE6L     COMP  PIC  S9(4).
02  LNDATE6F     PICTURE X.
02  FILLER REDEFINES LNDATE6F.
```

Fig. 4.5. (Continued)

```
  03  LNDATE6A     PICTURE X.
02  LNDATE6I  PIC X(6).
02  UNIT6L     COMP  PIC  S9(4).
02  UNIT6F     PICTURE X.
02  FILLER REDEFINES UNIT6F.
  03  UNIT6A     PICTURE X.
02  UNIT6I  PIC 99999.
02  UCOST6L     COMP  PIC  S9(4).
02  UCOST6F     PICTURE X.
02  FILLER REDEFINES UCOST6F.
  03  UCOST6A     PICTURE X.
02  UCOST6I  PIC 9999999.
02  COST6L     COMP  PIC  S9(4).
02  COST6F     PICTURE X.
02  FILLER REDEFINES COST6F.
  03  COST6A     PICTURE X.
02  COST6I  PIC 99999999.
02  UPRICE6L     COMP  PIC  S9(4).
02  UPRICE6F     PICTURE X.
02  FILLER REDEFINES UPRICE6F.
  03  UPRICE6A     PICTURE X.
02  UPRICE6I  PIC 9999999.
02  PRICE6L     COMP  PIC  S9(4).
02  PRICE6F     PICTURE X.
02  FILLER REDEFINES PRICE6F.
  03  PRICE6A     PICTURE X.
02  PRICE6I  PIC 99999999.
02  LINE7L     COMP  PIC  S9(4).
02  LINE7F     PICTURE X.
02  FILLER REDEFINES LINE7F.
  03  LINE7A     PICTURE X.
02  LINE7I  PIC X(1).
02  ITEM7L     COMP  PIC  S9(4).
02  ITEM7F     PICTURE X.
02  FILLER REDEFINES ITEM7F.
  03  ITEM7A     PICTURE X.
02  ITEM7I  PIC 99999999.
02  DESC7L     COMP  PIC  S9(4).
02  DESC7F     PICTURE X.
02  FILLER REDEFINES DESC7F.
  03  DESC7A     PICTURE X.
02  DESC7I  PIC X(19).
02  LNDATE7L     COMP  PIC  S9(4).
02  LNDATE7F     PICTURE X.
02  FILLER REDEFINES LNDATE7F.
  03  LNDATE7A     PICTURE X.
02  LNDATE7I  PIC X(6).
02  UNIT7L     COMP  PIC  S9(4).
02  UNIT7F     PICTURE X.
02  FILLER REDEFINES UNIT7F.
  03  UNIT7A     PICTURE X.
02  UNIT7I  PIC 99999.
02  UCOST7L     COMP  PIC  S9(4).
02  UCOST7F     PICTURE X.
02  FILLER REDEFINES UCOST7F.
  03  UCOST7A     PICTURE X.
```

Fig. 4.5. (Continued)

```
02  UCOST7I  PIC 9999999.
02  COST7L      COMP  PIC  S9(4).
02  COST7F      PICTURE X.
02  FILLER REDEFINES COST7F.
  03  COST7A     PICTURE X.
02  COST7I  PIC 99999999.
02  UPRICE7L     COMP  PIC  S9(4).
02  UPRICE7F     PICTURE X.
02  FILLER REDEFINES UPRICE7F.
  03  UPRICE7A     PICTURE X.
02  UPRICE7I  PIC 9999999.
02  PRICE7L     COMP  PIC  S9(4).
02  PRICE7F     PICTURE X.
02  FILLER REDEFINES PRICE7F.
  03  PRICE7A     PICTURE X.
02  PRICE7I  PIC 99999999.
02  LINE8L      COMP  PIC  S9(4).
02  LINE8F      PICTURE X.
02  FILLER REDEFINES LINE8F.
  03  LINE8A     PICTURE X.
02  LINE8I  PIC X(1).
02  ITEM8L      COMP  PIC  S9(4).
02  ITEM8F      PICTURE X.
02  FILLER REDEFINES ITEM8F.
  03  ITEM8A     PICTURE X.
02  ITEM8I  PIC 99999999.
02  DESC8L      COMP  PIC  S9(4).
02  DESC8F      PICTURE X.
02  FILLER REDEFINES DESC8F.
  03  DESC8A     PICTURE X.
02  DESC8I  PIC X(19).
02  LNDATE8L     COMP  PIC  S9(4).
02  LNDATE8F     PICTURE X.
02  FILLER REDEFINES LNDATE8F.
  03  LNDATE8A     PICTURE X.
02  LNDATE8I  PIC X(6).
02  UNIT8L      COMP  PIC  S9(4).
02  UNIT8F      PICTURE X.
02  FILLER REDEFINES UNIT8F.
  03  UNIT8A     PICTURE X.
02  UNIT8I  PIC 99999.
02  UCOST8L     COMP  PIC  S9(4).
02  UCOST8F     PICTURE X.
02  FILLER REDEFINES UCOST8F.
  03  UCOST8A     PICTURE X.
02  UCOST8I  PIC 9999999.
02  COST8L      COMP  PIC  S9(4).
02  COST8F      PICTURE X.
02  FILLER REDEFINES COST8F.
  03  COST8A     PICTURE X.
02  COST8I  PIC 99999999.
02  UPRICE8L     COMP  PIC  S9(4).
02  UPRICE8F     PICTURE X.
02  FILLER REDEFINES UPRICE8F.
  03  UPRICE8A     PICTURE X.
02  UPRICE8I  PIC 9999999.
```

Fig. 4.5. (Continued)

```
      02  PRICE8L      COMP  PIC   S9(4).
      02  PRICE8F      PICTURE X.
      02  FILLER REDEFINES PRICE8F.
        03  PRICE8A      PICTURE X.
      02  PRICE8I  PIC 99999999.
      02  LINE9L      COMP  PIC   S9(4).
      02  LINE9F      PICTURE X.
      02  FILLER REDEFINES LINE9F.
        03  LINE9A      PICTURE X.
      02  LINE9I  PIC X(1).
      02  ITEM9L      COMP  PIC   S9(4).
      02  ITEM9F      PICTURE X.
      02  FILLER REDEFINES ITEM9F.
        03  ITEM9A      PICTURE X.
      02  ITEM9I  PIC 99999999.
      02  DESC9L      COMP  PIC   S9(4).
      02  DESC9F      PICTURE X.
      02  FILLER REDEFINES DESC9F.
        03  DESC9A      PICTURE X.
      02  DESC9I  PIC X(19).
      02  LNDATE9L      COMP  PIC   S9(4).
      02  LNDATE9F      PICTURE X.
      02  FILLER REDEFINES LNDATE9F.
        03  LNDATE9A      PICTURE X.
      02  LNDATE9I  PIC X(6).
      02  UNIT9L      COMP  PIC   S9(4).
      02  UNIT9F      PICTURE X.
      02  FILLER REDEFINES UNIT9F.
        03  UNIT9A      PICTURE X.
      02  UNIT9I  PIC 99999.
      02  UCOST9L      COMP  PIC   S9(4).
      02  UCOST9F      PICTURE X.
      02  FILLER REDEFINES UCOST9F.
        03  UCOST9A      PICTURE X.
      02  UCOST9I  PIC 9999999.
      02  COST9L      COMP  PIC   S9(4).
      02  COST9F      PICTURE X.
      02  FILLER REDEFINES COST9F.
        03  COST9A      PICTURE X.
      02  COST9I  PIC 99999999.
      02  UPRICE9L      COMP  PIC   S9(4).
      02  UPRICE9F      PICTURE X.
      02  FILLER REDEFINES UPRICE9F.
        03  UPRICE9A      PICTURE X.
      02  UPRICE9I  PIC 9999999.
      02  PRICE9L      COMP  PIC   S9(4).
      02  PRICE9F      PICTURE X.
      02  FILLER REDEFINES PRICE9F.
        03  PRICE9A      PICTURE X.
      02  PRICE9I  PIC 99999999.
      02  ERRORL      COMP  PIC   S9(4).
      02  ERRORF      PICTURE X.
      02  FILLER REDEFINES ERRORF.
        03  ERRORA      PICTURE X.
      02  ERRORI  PIC X(20).
  01  ORIQM01O REDEFINES ORIQM01I.
```

Fig. 4.5. (Continued)

```
02  FILLER PIC X(12).
02  FILLER PICTURE X(3).
02  DUMMYO   PIC X(1).
02  FILLER PICTURE X(3).
02  ORDERO   PIC X(10).
02  FILLER PICTURE X(3).
02  DEPTO   PIC X(3).
02  FILLER PICTURE X(3).
02  DATEORO   PIC X(6).
02  FILLER PICTURE X(3).
02  DATEENTO   PIC X(6).
02  FILLER PICTURE X(3).
02  TOTCOSTO   PIC Z,ZZZ,ZZZ.99.
02  FILLER PICTURE X(3).
02  TOTPRCEO   PIC Z,ZZZ,ZZZ.99.
02  FILLER PICTURE X(3).
02  LINE1O   PIC X(1).
02  FILLER PICTURE X(3).
02  ITEM1O   PIC 99999999.
02  FILLER PICTURE X(3).
02  DESC1O   PIC X(19).
02  FILLER PICTURE X(3).
02  LNDATE1O   PIC X(6).
02  FILLER PICTURE X(3).
02  UNIT1O   PIC 99999.
02  FILLER PICTURE X(3).
02  UCOST1O   PIC 9999999.
02  FILLER PICTURE X(3).
02  COST1O   PIC 99999999.
02  FILLER PICTURE X(3).
02  UPRICE1O   PIC 9999999.
02  FILLER PICTURE X(3).
02  PRICE1O   PIC 99999999.
02  FILLER PICTURE X(3).
02  LINE2O   PIC X(1).
02  FILLER PICTURE X(3).
02  ITEM2O   PIC 99999999.
02  FILLER PICTURE X(3).
02  DESC2O   PIC X(19).
02  FILLER PICTURE X(3).
02  LNDATE2O   PIC X(6).
02  FILLER PICTURE X(3).
02  UNIT2O   PIC 99999.
02  FILLER PICTURE X(3).
02  UCOST2O   PIC 9999999.
02  FILLER PICTURE X(3).
02  COST2O   PIC 99999999.
02  FILLER PICTURE X(3).
02  UPRICE2O   PIC 9999999.
02  FILLER PICTURE X(3).
02  PRICE2O   PIC 99999999.
02  FILLER PICTURE X(3).
02  LINE3O   PIC X(1).
02  FILLER PICTURE X(3).
02  ITEM3O   PIC 99999999.
02  FILLER PICTURE X(3).
```

Fig. 4.5. (Continued)

```
02  DESC30  PIC X(19).
02  FILLER PICTURE X(3).
02  LNDATE30  PIC X(6).
02  FILLER PICTURE X(3).
02  UNIT30  PIC 99999.
02  FILLER PICTURE X(3).
02  UCOST30  PIC 9999999.
02  FILLER PICTURE X(3).
02  COST30  PIC 99999999.
02  FILLER PICTURE X(3).
02  UPRICE30  PIC 9999999.
02  FILLER PICTURE X(3).
02  PRICE30  PIC 99999999.
02  FILLER PICTURE X(3).
02  LINE40  PIC X(1).
02  FILLER PICTURE X(3).
02  ITEM40  PIC 99999999.
02  FILLER PICTURE X(3).
02  DESC40  PIC X(19).
02  FILLER PICTURE X(3).
02  LNDATE40  PIC X(6).
02  FILLER PICTURE X(3).
02  UNIT40  PIC 99999.
02  FILLER PICTURE X(3).
02  UCOST40  PIC 9999999.
02  FILLER PICTURE X(3).
02  COST40  PIC 99999999.
02  FILLER PICTURE X(3).
02  UPRICE40  PIC 9999999.
02  FILLER PICTURE X(3).
02  PRICE40  PIC 99999999.
02  FILLER PICTURE X(3).
02  LINE50  PIC X(1).
02  FILLER PICTURE X(3).
02  ITEM50  PIC 99999999.
02  FILLER PICTURE X(3).
02  DESC50  PIC X(19).
02  FILLER PICTURE X(3).
02  LNDATE50  PIC X(6).
02  FILLER PICTURE X(3).
02  UNIT50  PIC 99999.
02  FILLER PICTURE X(3).
02  UCOST50  PIC 9999999.
02  FILLER PICTURE X(3).
02  COST50  PIC 99999999.
02  FILLER PICTURE X(3).
02  UPRICE50  PIC 9999999.
02  FILLER PICTURE X(3).
02  PRICE50  PIC 99999999.
02  FILLER PICTURE X(3).
02  LINE60  PIC X(1).
02  FILLER PICTURE X(3).
02  ITEM60  PIC 99999999.
02  FILLER PICTURE X(3).
02  DESC60  PIC X(19).
02  FILLER PICTURE X(3).
```

Fig. 4.5. (Continued)

```
02  LNDATE60   PIC X(6).
02  FILLER PICTURE X(3).
02  UNIT60   PIC 99999.
02  FILLER PICTURE X(3).
02  UCOST60   PIC 9999999.
02  FILLER PICTURE X(3).
02  COST60   PIC 99999999.
02  FILLER PICTURE X(3).
02  UPRICE60   PIC 9999999.
02  FILLER PICTURE X(3).
02  PRICE60   PIC 99999999.
02  FILLER PICTURE X(3).
02  LINE70   PIC X(1).
02  FILLER PICTURE X(3).
02  ITEM70   PIC 99999999.
02  FILLER PICTURE X(3).
02  DESC70   PIC X(19).
02  FILLER PICTURE X(3).
02  LNDATE70   PIC X(6).
02  FILLER PICTURE X(3).
02  UNIT70   PIC 99999.
02  FILLER PICTURE X(3).
02  UCOST70   PIC 9999999.
02  FILLER PICTURE X(3).
02  COST70   PIC 99999999.
02  FILLER PICTURE X(3).
02  UPRICE70   PIC 9999999.
02  FILLER PICTURE X(3).
02  PRICE70   PIC 99999999.
02  FILLER PICTURE X(3).
02  LINE80   PIC X(1).
02  FILLER PICTURE X(3).
02  ITEM80   PIC 99999999.
02  FILLER PICTURE X(3).
02  DESC80   PIC X(19).
02  FILLER PICTURE X(3).
02  LNDATE80   PIC X(6).
02  FILLER PICTURE X(3).
02  UNIT80   PIC 99999.
02  FILLER PICTURE X(3).
02  UCOST80   PIC 9999999.
02  FILLER PICTURE X(3).
02  COST80   PIC 99999999.
02  FILLER PICTURE X(3).
02  UPRICE80   PIC 9999999.
02  FILLER PICTURE X(3).
02  PRICE80   PIC 99999999.
02  FILLER PICTURE X(3).
02  LINE90   PIC X(1).
02  FILLER PICTURE X(3).
02  ITEM90   PIC 99999999.
02  FILLER PICTURE X(3).
02  DESC90   PIC X(19).
02  FILLER PICTURE X(3).
02  LNDATE90   PIC X(6).
02  FILLER PICTURE X(3).
```

Fig. 4.5. (Continued)

Thus length = 61 bytes, which should match the length indicated in the DATA DIVISION map. In fact, we did not really have to compute. The "INPUT WORK AREA LENGTH" line (statement 138) always indicates a value (here 56) which is five less than the length of the corresponding symbolic description map.

PICTURE AND USAGE SPECIFICATIONS OF DATA FIELDS*

The following are guidelines on the PICTURE and USAGE specifications of fields in the symbolic description map:

1. All data fields must be defined with USAGE DISPLAY which is the default in Cobol. No field is defined as binary, packed decimal, etc.
2. An alphanumeric field (PIC X's) has, by definition, USAGE DISPLAY.
3. For a numeric field:
   a. If used as output only (for the display, not entry, of data), the field is defined with attribute ASKIP or PROT, not UNPROT. It may then use editing characters like $, –, ., etc. Example –––,–––.99.
   b. If used as input (for the entry of data), the field is defined with attribute NUM (with UNPROT as default).
      1. The PICTURE specification can only have 9's and a V. There are no editing characters.
      2. The PICTURE specification cannot have a sign.
      3. The programmer may however redefine the PICTURE specification because Cobol allows it. But to manipulate the redefined data-name can be tricky.

PROCESSING NEGATIVE NUMBERS

The processing of numeric fields (defined as NUM in the map program) that may contain negative numbers is accomplished with a little trick. The reason is that unlike the "good old days" of punched cards, the operator cannot overpunch with a sign. The solution is as follows:

---

*Here, we mean the fields that contain actual data. Naturally, the length fields are defined as binary.

1. Define the field with PICTURE 9's and the V symbol for the assumed decimal point, if needed. For example:

```
05  MAP1-AMOUNT                    PIC 999V99.
```

2. Redefine it with two entries.
   a. One field with PICTURE 9's and an optional V with length one byte less than the original field. I suggest using a suffix of "NEG" since this field may contain the negative number.
   b. A one-byte field with PICTURE X with suffix "DASH" to contain the negative sign.
   c. Thus, the field is redefined as:

```
05  FILLER REDEFINES MAP1-AMOUNT.
    10  MAP1-AMOUNT-NEG          PIC 99V99.
    10  MAP1-AMOUNT-DASH         PIC X.
```

3. Note that MAP1-AMOUNT-NEG is one byte less than MAP1-AMOUNT and the programmer should allocate enough space to avoid overflow with either positive or negative numbers.

4. To enter a negative number, the operator enters a "–" as the last digit. If the number is positive, the operator enters only digits.

5. If MAP1-AMOUNT-DASH contains a "–", then the program knows that the number is negative.

6. To move an entered number to main storage:
   a. Assume the field in main storage is defined as:

```
05  W005-AMOUNT          PIC S999V99 COMP-3,
```

   Note that the field now contains a sign and is defined as packed decimal.

b. The statements are:

```
IF MAP1-AMOUNT NUMERIC
        MOVE MAP1-AMOUNT TO W005-AMOUNT
ELSE IF       MAP1-AMOUNT-NEG NUMERIC
          AND MAP1-AMOUNT-DASH EQUAL TO '-'
        THEN COMPUTE W005-AMOUNT =MAP1-AMOUNT-NEG * -1
        ELSE "invalid amount" error.
```

7. To display a negative number on the screen, using the previously defined fields:

```
IF W005-AMOUNT LESS THAN ZEROS
        MOVE W005-AMOUNT  TO  MAP1-AMOUNT-NEG
        MOVE '-'          TO  MAP1-AMOUNT-DASH
ELSE    MOVE W005-AMOUNT  TO  MAP1-AMOUNT.
```

FIELD JUSTIFICATION

We said before that each field defined with a label in the map program has three entries in the symbolic description map. These are the length, attribute, and data fields. On any field where the operator enters data, the following are transmitted to the symbolic description map:

1. The length field will contain the number of characters entered.
2. The attributes are not transmitted. The attribute field is useful only if the program changes the attributes of a field during program execution (see page 154).
3. If the field is defined with numeric shift (NUM):
   a. The keyboard is in numeric shift, but may be overridden by the operator by pressing the alphabetic shift key.
   b. Regardless of the above, the data will be transmitted to the symbolic description map with zeros padded on the left.
   c. If the operator enters "167" on a 6-byte field, the length field will contain 3 and the data is transmitted as "000167".

4. If the field is defined with alphabetic shift:
   a. The keyboard is in alphabetic shift, but may be overriden by the operator by pressing the numeric shift key.
   b. Regardless of the above, the data will be transmitted to the symbolic description map with blanks padded on the right.
   c. If the operator enters "BAKER" on a 6-byte field, the length field will contain 5 and the data is transmitted as "BAKERb", where b is a space.

5. Regardless of whether the keyboard is defined as numeric (NUM in the map program) or not, the data will appear on the screen from left to right as the operator enters it. Thus the previous examples will initially appear as "167bbb" and "BAKERb" on the terminal screen while being entered.

6. As we mentioned before, they will of course become "000167" and "BAKERb" in the symbolic description map.

7. Note that if the application validates these data, you will see them on the screen as "000167" and "BAKERb" if errors are detected since you will be displaying the symbolic description map to give the operator the correct error messages. But if a program abend occurs (right after entering them, not on a second or later pass), you will see them in their original entered version as "167bbb" and "BAKERb" since you would not have displayed the symbolic description map.

CODING STOPPER AND SKIP FIELDS

STOPPER and SKIP fields may be needed immediately following unprotected fields (those the operator can enter data on). The reason is to prevent the cursor from stopping and forcing the operator to use special cursor positioning keys to continue, thus wasting her time. The rules are:

1. An unprotected field must be immediately followed (with one space in between, that space being the attribute position of the next field) by an autoskip, protected, or another unprotected field. (Note that if the unprotected field ends in

column 80 of one line, the field following it must have its attribute position in column 1 of the next line). Otherwise, the cursor will stop on the position immediately after the last position of the field after the operator finishes the entry for the field.

2. We do not want this to happen because we want the cursor to go to the next unprotected field once the operator is finished with the current unprotected field. During data entry, the operator is only interested in working with unprotected fields.

3. If the unprotected field is immediately followed by an "actual" field like a field identifier, data field, etc., then that will solve the problem. There is then no need for either a STOPPER or a SKIP field.

4. Otherwise, the programmer will have to code a one-byte autoskip (SKIP) or protected (STOPPER) field immediately after the unprotected field. This will prevent the cursor from stopping at the wrong place.

5. A SKIP field is an unlabeled one-byte autoskip field and is used if the operator consistently enters a fixed number of characters on a field (example, social security number). It is also useful if the field is short (say, three bytes or less) so as to save a keystroke by avoiding the use of the extra key "field skip" that is required if the field is a STOPPER.

6. A STOPPER field is an unlabeled one-byte protected field and is used if the operator consistently enters a variable number of characters on a long field (example, name or address). This will lock the keyboard if the operator attempts to enter more characters than that allocated for the field and is thus a safety measure. STOPPER always requires that the operator hits the "field skip" key once she has finished the entry for the field, regardless on whether she has or has not used up all the character positions allocated for the field. STOPPER is extremely useful for entering names, for instance, since it will tell the operator when a name will not fit in the allocated space so she can do something about it. If a SKIP field is

used instead, the name will be truncated and the rest of the name will "overflow" to the next field.

7. If the operator hits the "field skip" key in the middle of a field, the cursor will immediately go to the next unprotected field, regardless on whether the following field is SKIP or STOPPER (the effect will be the same). For long fields therefore, most of the time there is no difference between SKIP and STOPPER fields.

8. Thus the only advantage of STOPPER over SKIP is if the operator enters more characters than that allocated for a long field where the number of characters entered consistently varies.

9. For a short field, the use of a STOPPER field may be a nuisance since you are forced to hit the "field skip" key all the time. Some installations may prefer to use a SKIP field instead and forgo the extra safety measure to save on keystrokes for such a short field.

Let us see how these principles work by looking at Figure 4.6.

SPACES BETWEEN TWO ADJACENT FIELDS

The following rules apply to the number of spaces allocated between two adjacent fields:

1. If the first field is autoskip or protected, then there is no problem. There is no need for a STOPPER or a SKIP field and the next field can be placed anywhere after the first field.

2. If the first field is unprotected:
   a. If the next "actual" field, like field identifier, data field, etc., follows with one space in between, then there is no problem and there is no need for a SKIP or STOPPER field. Note that the attribute position for the next field is on that space between the two fields.
   b. If the next "actual" field follows with three or more spaces in between, then put a SKIP or STOPPER field

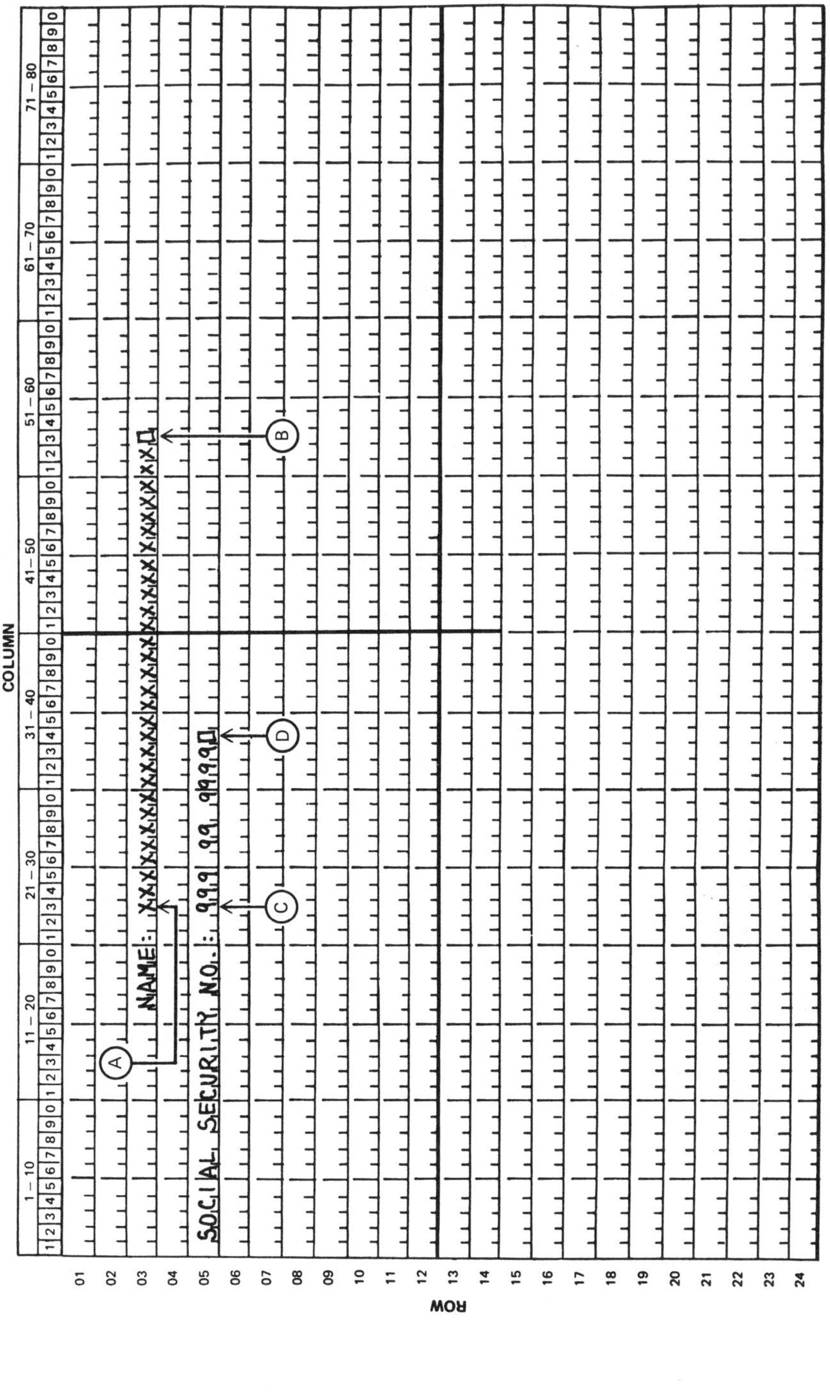

Fig. 4.6. B is a STOPPER field and D is a SKIP field.

between the two, and place it immediately following the unprotected (first) field.

c. If the next "actual" field follows with two spaces in between:
    1. If the second field is also unprotected, there is a problem and the cursor will always stop on the position immediately following the last position of the first field. There is no solution since each field needs two screen positions and one position is already the attribute position of the second field. *Thus, you cannot have two spaces in between two unprotected fields.*
    2. If the second field is autoskip or protected, then the problem is avoided by including the second space as the first character (blank character) of the second field and extending its length by one byte. This will put the attribute byte of the second field on the position immediately following the last position of the first field.

5

Program Components

INTRODUCTION

The Cobol program written to run under CICS/VS is still a Cobol program and thus has many similarities to one written for batch applications. The major differences are:

1. The ENVIRONMENT DIVISION does not have SELECT statements.
2. The DATA DIVISION does not have FD, SD, or RD entries.
3. File records are defined either in the WORKING-STORAGE section or preferably in the LINKAGE section.
4. Most data used are defined in the LINKAGE section, rather than the WORKING-STORAGE section. In typical programs, the former has many more entries than the latter.
5. File Identifiers are specified in the File Control Table (FCT). The commands in the PROCEDURE DIVISION that access file records identify the specific file identifier of the file to be read, written to, etc. Cobol I/O verbs like READ, WRITE, etc., are not used.
6. Files are not opened or closed within the program. Since many tasks access the same file at the same time, the files used in a specific application are opened separately and will be discussed in Chapter 12.
7. The PROCEDURE DIVISION contains the commands that request on-line service (display data on a terminal, etc.).
8. Because of the pseudoconversational mode of processing and other efficiency reasons, the structure of the PROCEDURE DIVISION is somewhat different from one in a program written for a batch application.

```
CBL SUPMAP,STXIT,NOTRUNC,CSYNTAX,SXREF,OPT,VERB,CLIST,BUF=19069
CBL NOOPT,LIB
00001              IDENTIFICATION DIVISION.

00003              PROGRAM-ID. ORADO1A.

00005              ENVIRONMENT DIVISION.

00007      *****************************************************************
00008      *                                                               *
00009      *   1. THIS PROGRAM ADDS NEW ORDERS INTO THE PURCHASE ORDER      *
00010      *      MASTER FILE.                                             *
00011      *                                                               *
00012      *   2. AT LEAST ONE LINE ITEM MUST BE PRESENT FOR EACH ORDER.   *
00013      *                                                               *
00014      *   3. A JOURNAL RECORD IS GENERATED FOR EACH NEW ORDER         *
00015      *      ENTERED.   THE JOURNAL DETAILS ARE                       *
00016      *               A) OPERATOR INITIAL.                            *
00017      *               B) DATE ENTERED.                                *
00018      *               C) ORDER NUMBER.                                *
00019      *               D) DOCUMENT NUMBER.                             *
00020      *               E) TOTAL COST OF ORDER.                         *
00021      *               F) TOTAL PRICE OF ORDER.                        *
00022      *                                                               *
00023      *****************************************************************
```

Fig. 5.1. IDENTIFICATION and ENVIRONMENT DIVISIONS.

THE IDENTIFICATION AND ENVIRONMENT DIVISIONS

These two divisions may actually be coded with three entries. The required lines are:

> IDENTIFICATION DIVISION.
> PROGRAM-ID. program-id.
> ENVIRONMENT DIVISION.

The programmer may wish to add other paragraphs in these two divisions, for instance, SOURCE-COMPUTER, etc. Also, it is a very good idea to put comment cards (asterisks in column 7) after the ENVIRONMENT DIVISION header, explaining what the program does. We should then EJECT before the DATA DIVISION header. An example is given in Figure 5.1.

You will note that SKIP statements are used to improve the presentation of the program.

THE WORKING-STORAGE SECTION

The WORKING-STORAGE section is the first section coded in the DATA DIVISION and is used for the following entries:

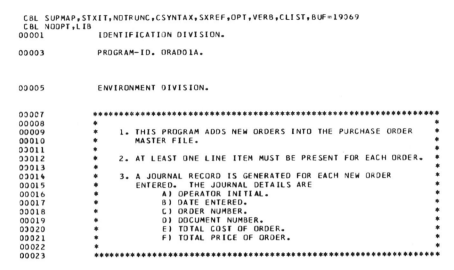

1. If the program sends a communication area to another program, then the field to be sent is defined as the first level-01 entry. For a reason explained on page 111, programs in this book will use this communication area.

2. The next level-01 entry will contain the following level-05 entries:
   a. A 23-byte data area with the label "JOB-NORMAL-END-MESSAGE" and with the value "JOB NORMALLY TERMINATED." This will be displayed on the terminal when the operator decides to terminate the job.
   b. A data area with the label "JOB-ABORTED-MESSAGE," which will be displayed if a job is to be aborted and consists of two level-10 entries:
      1. A 15-byte filler with the value "JOB ABORTED – ;"
      2. A data area with the label "MAJOR-ERROR-MSG" that will contain the message corresponding to the error that caused the job to be aborted. The length will be the maximum error message length.
   c. A data area with the label "OLD-EIB-AREA," which will contain certain information from the Execute Interface Block when the DUMP command is issued on an error that aborts the job. This field will be used for debugging and will be discussed further on page 555. It will contain three level-10 entries:
      1. a 7-byte filler with the value "OLD EIB;"
      2. a 2-byte data area with the label "OLD-EIBFN" and PIC XX;
      3. a 6-byte data area with the label "OLD-EIBRCODE" and PIC X (6).
   d. For areas with fixed values (factors,* "hard coded" tables, etc.).
   e. "Temporary" counters, other storage areas required only within a task and therefore do not have to be saved when the program is purged through task termination in the

*We generally prefer to code constants, including factors, as part of the statement for the sake of efficiency. However, if a factor may change within the lifetime of the program, we should code it as a data name in working storage for easier maintainability.

pseudoconversational mode of processing. These fields may be coded in the Transaction Work Area (TWA) or in working storage.

3. The DFHAID entries and the standard attribute list if required. Each is a level-01 entry and is explained in the next section.

The style used in 2.b. saves main storage since the literal, "JOB ABORTED —," is made common to all messages sent to the terminal to signify an abnormal job termination. To be consistent, the normal termination message in 2.a. is also coded in the WORKING-STORAGE section. The actual error messages appended to "JOB ABORTED —"

```
     2        ORIQ01A        12.55.39        08/02/80

00014        DATA DIVISION.

00016        WORKING-STORAGE SECTION.

00018        01  COMMUNICATION-AREA.
00020            05  COMMAREA-PROCESS-SW     PIC X.

00022        01  AREA1.

00024            05  JOB-NORMAL-END-MESSAGE  PIC X(23) VALUE
00025                'JOB NORMALLY TERMINATED'.

00027            05  JOB-ABORTED-MESSAGE.
00028                10  FILLER              PIC X(15) VALUE 'JOB ABORTED --'.
00029                10  MAJOR-ERROR-MSG     PIC X(16).

00031            05  HEXADECIMAL-ZEROES      PIC 9999 COMP VALUE ZEROES.

00033            05  FILLER REDEFINES HEXADECIMAL-ZEROES.
00034                10  FILLER              PIC X.
00035                10  HEX-ZEROES          PIC X.

00037            05  OLD-EIB-AREA.
00038                10  FILLER              PIC X(7) VALUE 'OLD EIB'.
00039                10  OLD-EIBFN           PIC XX.
00040                10  OLD-EIBRCODE        PIC X(6).
```

Fig. 5.2. Programmer-coded Entries in working storage.

are from the appropriate paragraph in the ABNORMAL-TERMINATION section* that handles the particular error.

My suggestion is that only these data be directly coded in the WORKING-STORAGE section. All other data needed in the program will be stated either as constants in statements or coded in the LINKAGE section.

An example of this part of the WORKING-STORAGE section is shown in Figure 5.2.

The Standard Attention Identifier List

The standard attention identifier list (DFHAID) is used to determine which attention identifier device (specific terminal key, operator badge or light pen) the operator used to initiate a terminal or BMS operation. This list, which resides in a source statement library, should be copied to the WORKING-STORAGE section if the program uses anything other than the ENTER key to control the program logic.

For instance, in a browse application, the program may use the PF1 key to browse forward and the PF2 key to browse backwards. When a task starts, the EIBAID field of the Execute Interface Block contains a value that depends on the attention identifier device used. This value is compared against entries in DFHAID. This is explained in detail on page 123.

The Standard Attribute List

The programmer should also copy a standard attribute list into the program if there is a need to provide for or modify the attributes of a field to be transmitted to a terminal (map defined with mode OUT or INOUT). For instance, a field defined as unprotected, allowing the operator to enter a value on it, may be changed to autoskip so that it can no longer be changed. This may be done in an update application – the operator enters a record number; when it is determined to be valid, the screen comes back with the attribute of the record number changed to autoskip so that the operator can no longer change it when he enters the fields used in the update. The use of this list is shown on page 154.

---

*See page 128.

Figure 5.3 shows this part of the WORKING-STORAGE section. Note that the DFHEIVAR entries are automatically generated by the command-language translator. These are used in the CALL statements generated from the commands.

THE WORKING-STORAGE SECTION AT EXECUTION

Note the following for an executing program:

1. When a new program executes in a task (naturally, we have a new program at the start of a task),* it gets an original (unaltered) copy of the WORKING-STORAGE section. This is important to note since in the pseudoconversational mode of processing, the value of a field in working storage, after the

```
      3          ORDLO1A          13.28.44        08/02/80

   00042            01  DFHAID COPY DFHAID.
   00043 C          01    DFHAID.
   00044 C                02  DFHNULL   PIC  X   VALUE IS ' '.
   00045 C                02  DFHENTER  PIC  X   VALUE IS QUOTE.
   00046 C                02  DFHCLEAR  PIC  X   VALUE IS ' '.
   00047 C                02  DFHPEN    PIC  X   VALUE IS '='.
   00048 C                02  DFHOPID   PIC  X   VALUE IS 'W'.
   00049 C                02  DFHPA1    PIC  X   VALUE IS '%'.
   00050 C                02  DFHPA2    PIC  X   VALUE IS ' '.
   00051 C                02  DFHPA3    PIC  X   VALUE IS ','.
   00052 C                02  DFHPF1    PIC  X   VALUE IS '1'.
   00053 C                02  DFHPF2    PIC  X   VALUE IS '2'.
   00054 C                02  DFHPF3    PIC  X   VALUE IS '3'.
   00055 C                02  DFHPF4    PIC  X   VALUE IS '4'.
   00056 C                02  DFHPF5    PIC  X   VALUE IS '5'.
   00057 C                02  DFHPF6    PIC  X   VALUE IS '6'.
   00058 C                02  DFHPF7    PIC  X   VALUE IS '7'.
   00059 C                02  DFHPF8    PIC  X   VALUE IS '8'.
   00060 C                02  DFHPF9    PIC  X   VALUE IS '9'.
   00061 C                02  DFHPF10   PIC  X   VALUE IS ' '.
   00062 C                02  DFHPF11   PIC  X   VALUE IS '#'.
   00063 C                02  DFHPF12   PIC  X   VALUE IS '@'.
   00064 C                02  DFHPF13   PIC  X   VALUE IS 'A'.
   00065 C                02  DFHPF14   PIC  X   VALUE IS 'B'.
   00066 C                02  DFHPF15   PIC  X   VALUE IS 'C'.
   00067 C                02  DFHPF16   PIC  X   VALUE IS 'D'.
   00068 C                02  DFHPF17   PIC  X   VALUE IS 'E'.
   00069 C                02  DFHPF18   PIC  X   VALUE IS 'F'.
   00070 C                02  DFHPF19   PIC  X   VALUE IS 'G'.
   00071 C                02  DFHPF20   PIC  X   VALUE IS 'H'.
   00072 C                02  DFHPF21   PIC  X   VALUE IS 'I'.
   00073 C                02  DFHPF22   PIC  X   VALUE IS ' '.
   00074 C                02  DFHPF23   PIC  X   VALUE IS '.'.
   00075 C                02  DFHPF24   PIC  X   VALUE IS '□'.
```

Fig. 5.3. Copied or System-generated Entries in working storage.

*We will learn in Chapter 14 that programs can be started or purged anytime within a single task.

```
     4          ORDLO1A           13.28.44          08/02/80

           *     THIS COPY IS A LIST OF ALL VALID 3270 ATTRIBUTE COMBINATIONS
           *     TAKEN FROM 3270 REFERENCE SUMMARY, PAGE 9.

           01    ALL-VALID-ATTRIBUTES.
                 05  ATTR-UNPROT                      PIC X VALUE ' '.
                 05  ATTR-UNPROT-FSET                 PIC X VALUE 'A'.
                 05  ATTR-UNPROT-PEN                  PIC X VALUE 'D'.
                 05  ATTR-UNPROT-PEN-FSET             PIC X VALUE 'E'.
                 05  ATTR-UNPROT-BRT-PEN              PIC X VALUE 'H'.
                 05  ATTR-UNPROT-BRT-PEN-FSET         PIC X VALUE 'I'.
                 05  ATTR-UNPROT-DRK                  PIC X VALUE '¤'.
                 05  ATTR-UNPROT-DRK-FSET             PIC X VALUE '('.
                 05  ATTR-UNPROT-NUM                  PIC X VALUE '&'.
                 05  ATTR-UNPROT-NUM-FSET             PIC X VALUE 'J'.
                 05  ATTR-UNPROT-NUM-PEN              PIC X VALUE 'M'.
                 05  ATTR-UNPROT-NUM-PEN-FSET         PIC X VALUE 'N'.
                 05  ATTR-UNPROT-NUM-BRT-PEN          PIC X VALUE 'Q'.
                 05  ATTR-UNPROT-NUM-BRT-PEN-FSET     PIC X VALUE 'R'.
                 05  ATTR-UNPROT-NUM-DRK              PIC X VALUE '*'.
                 05  ATTR-UNPROT-NUM-DRK-FSET         PIC X VALUE ')'.
                 05  ATTR-PROT                        PIC X VALUE '-'.
                 05  ATTR-PROT-FSET                   PIC X VALUE '/'.
                 05  ATTR-PROT-PEN                    PIC X VALUE 'U'.
                 05  ATTR-PROT-PEN-FSET               PIC X VALUE 'V'.
                 05  ATTR-PROT-BRT-PEN                PIC X VALUE 'Y'.
                 05  ATTR-PROT-BRT-PEN-FSET           PIC X VALUE 'Z'.
                 05  ATTR-PROT-DRK                    PIC X VALUE '%'.
                 05  ATTR-PROT-DRK-FSET               PIC X VALUE ' '.
                 05  ATTR-PROT-ASKIP                  PIC X VALUE '0'.
                 05  ATTR-PROT-ASKIP-FSET             PIC X VALUE '1'.
                 05  ATTR-PROT-ASKIP-PEN              PIC X VALUE '4'.
                 05  ATTR-PROT-ASKIP-PEN-FSET         PIC X VALUE '5'.
                 05  ATTR-PROT-ASKIP-BRT-PEN          PIC X VALUE '8'.
                 05  ATTR-PROT-ASKIP-BRT-PEN-FSET     PIC X VALUE '9'.
                 05  ATTR-PROT-ASKIP-DRK              PIC X VALUE '@'.
                 05  ATTR-PROT-ASKIP-DRK-FSET         PIC X VALUE QUOTE.
```

Fig. 5.3. (Continued)

```
     5          ORDLO1A           13.28.44          08/02/80

           01    DFHEIVAR COPY DFHEIVAR.
  C        01    DFHEIVAR.
  C              02    DFHEIV0  PICTURE X(26).
  C              02    DFHEIV1  PICTURE X(8).
  C              02    DFHEIV2  PICTURE X(8).
  C              02    DFHEIV3  PICTURE X(8).
  C              02    DFHEIV4  PICTURE X(6).
  C              02    DFHEIV5  PICTURE X(4).
  C              02    DFHEIV6  PICTURE X(4).
  C              02    DFHEIV7  PICTURE X(2).
  C              02    DFHEIV8  PICTURE X(2).
  C              02    DFHEIV9  PICTURE X(1).
  C              02    DFHEIV10 PICTURE S9(7) USAGE COMPUTATIONAL-3.
  C              02    DFHEIV11 PICTURE S9(4) USAGE COMPUTATIONAL.
  C              02    DFHEIV12 PICTURE S9(4) USAGE COMPUTATIONAL.
  C              02    DFHEIV13 PICTURE S9(4) USAGE COMPUTATIONAL.
  C              02    DFHEIV14 PICTURE S9(4) USAGE COMPUTATIONAL.
  C              02    DFHEIV15 PICTURE S9(4) USAGE COMPUTATIONAL.
  C              02    DFHEIV16 PICTURE S9(9) USAGE COMPUTATIONAL.
  C              02    DFHEIV17 PICTURE X(4).
  C              02    DFHEIV18 PICTURE X(4).
  C              02    DFHEIV19 PICTURE X(4).
  C              02    DFHEIV97 PICTURE S9(7) USAGE COMPUTATIONAL-3 VALUE ZERO.
  C              02    DFHEIV98 PICTURE S9(4) USAGE COMPUTATIONAL VALUE ZERO.
  C              02    DFHEIV99 PICTURE X(1)  VALUE SPACE.
```

Fig. 5.3. (Continued)

operator starts a task (for instance, by hitting a key like ENTER) is determined by its VALUE clause. It does not retain the value it had when the previous task was terminated because working storage is purged from main storage at task termination. If there is no VALUE clause, the value is unknown.

2. Therefore, you cannot save in working storage data needed for the next task initiation, say in the pseudoconversational mode of processing. However, CICS/VS allows you to save data in several ways, temporary storage on magnetic disk being the most commonly used.

3. As long as a program is active within the task, the whole WORKING-STORAGE section will have memory allocated to it.

4. All tasks using the same program will have their own individual copies of the WORKING-STORAGE section.

THE WORKING-STORAGE SECTION VERSUS THE TRANSACTION WORK AREA

The Transaction Work Area (TWA) is an area that a program may optionally define in the LINKAGE section. It and the WORKING-STORAGE section are often interchangeable and the guidelines on which to use are as follows:

1. For data defined with a VALUE clause, working storage is required. The LINKAGE section cannot have a value clause except for condition names.

2. For "temporary" fields mentioned on page 77, either one may be used.

3. If TWA is used by the program, the size of the TWA must be specified in the PCT entry for the transaction identifier (program). Therefore, if a program modification changes the size of the TWA (for instance, more entries in it), the PCT has to be changed and regenerated. This is not a problem if working storage is used instead.

4. If working storage is used by the program, there is more main storage used since the original copy of working storage is always required in addition to the copies used by the tasks. If there are five tasks using the same program, there will be six copies of working storage but only five copies of the TWA.

5. Since for most applications this additional storage may be small, some installations prefer to use working storage while totally eliminating the TWA. This is primarily a decision made by individual installations.

THE WORKING-STORAGE SECTION VERSUS THE LINKAGE SECTION

The previous discussion only means that for some entries, you decide whether you will use working storage or the Transaction Work Area. There are however other entries that may also be coded either in working storage or as separate blocks (not Transaction Work Area) in the LINKAGE section. The guidelines are:

1. When a program is active (attached to a task), the WORKING-STORAGE section will always have main storage allocation even if many of those entries are not needed in that particular task. This wastes main storage compared to the LINKAGE section where memory will only be allocated when needed (except for such area as the TWA, which will also get main storage at the start of a task).

2. Therefore, except for those entries that we suggest should be coded in working storage, data should be defined in the LINKAGE section.

THE LINKAGE SECTION

In typical programs, most data definitions are in this section. The guidelines for its use are as follows:

1. This section is used for symbolic description maps, file record descriptions, temporary storage areas, etc. – areas which are not needed by the task all the time.

2. It is more efficient to use the LINKAGE section for these areas rather than working storage because this section does not have an automatic main storage allocation (except for some areas like the TWA). The areas defined, except for the exceptions, will be acquired only by CICS/VS when required in the task.
3. These areas are automatically acquired on input commands (read data from a terminal, read an on-line file, etc.) if the programmer uses the more efficient locate-mode option by specifying pointers with the SET operand (I suggest its use) instead of the INTO operand. The programmer may sometimes have to secure the area himself through the GETMAIN command. This is explained in more detail on page 194.
4. For example, if a program uses three screen layouts (thus three maps), the program usually only processes one of these maps at any given task. Therefore, only one of the symbolic description maps should have main storage allocation during a task and this is only done at the point it is required in the task.
5. Compare this to the WORKING-STORAGE section which will always have main storage allocation for the three symbolic description maps all the time the program is active.
6. The Transaction Work Area (TWA), Common Work Area (CWA), and Terminal Control Table User Area (TCTUA), if any, are also coded in this section. However, unlike others, they will be allocated main storage when the task is initiated.
7. This section is also useful for rarely used areas not part of a symbolic description map, file area, etc. The program will issue a GETMAIN command to acquire this area when needed; most of the time there will therefore be no main storage allocation.
8. The VALUE clause is not allowed for the Linkage section.

There is one entry that is automatically generated by the command-language translator. This is the Execute Interface Block, containing information like transaction identifier, terminal identification, results of a command, etc. This block is updated by CICS/VS every time a command is executed, and the information may be used by the application program. A one-byte DFHCOMMAREA field is also generated, if not coded, by the programmer.

SUGGESTED PREFIXES FOR DATA DESCRIPTIONS

For the sake of readability, the following are suggested prefixes for data descriptions:

1. DFH for the DFHCOMMAREA field.
2. MAP1, MAP2, MAP3, etc. for the symbolic description maps.
3. TWA for the transaction work area.
4. TSA for the temporary storage area.

THE PROCEDURE DIVISION

This will be discussed in more detail in Chapter 7. However, the programmer may note the following:

1. The commands that requests on-line services are coded in this division and they are interspersed with regular Cobol statements.
2. Coding techniques, while also stressing readability, must consider efficiency more strongly than in batch programs because response time is very critical. A difference in say 1/4 second in response time is very critical if you consider many terminals contending for CPU time.

GENERAL EFFICIENCY TECHNIQUES

Program efficiency is much more critical in an on-line program than in a batch program. In batch applications, there is not much of a problem if a program runs five or ten minutes longer than it should. But if one task executes even 1/4 second longer than it should because of inefficiency, it will penalize other tasks contending for the same CPU time.

First Goal Is Minimize Paging

There are three major areas of consideration for efficiency. First, since CICS/VS executes in a virtual storage environment, one goal of the programmer is to code his program so as to minimize page faults. Page faults occur when a reference is made to instructions or data that do not currently reside in real storage. When this happens, the page in virtual storage that contains the required instructions or data must be paged into real storage. The more paging occurs, the lower the overall system performance.

Second Goal Is Conserve Main Storage

The second goal is to conserve main storage. Since there is just so much main storage available, the less a task requires main storage (as controlled by the way the program is written), the more tasks (hence terminals) can run at the same time.

Third Goal is Use Language Efficiency Techniques

The third goal is to use efficiency techniques inherent in the programming language used (say, Cobol). However, this book will not deal with this problem because they are best studied in a manual or book that deal solely with the programming language. Instead, we will investigate means to achieve the first two goals. There are three areas to consider, as described in the following sections.

Locality of Reference

The application program should consistently reference, for relatively long periods of time, instructions and data within a relatively small number of pages compared to the total number of pages in the program. This is implemented in the following techniques:

1. The program should execute in a straight line as much as possible, with no branch logic reference beyond a small range of address space (making it short range). However, routines that are executed only rarely, including error-handling routines, should be separated from the main program code. This is explained further on page 101.

2. Subroutines should be placed as near to the caller (PERFORM statement) as possible. This is explained further on page 104.
3. If possible, try to use XCTL instead of LINK to transfer control to another program.
4. Initialize data as close as possible to its first use. This increases the chance that the page the data resides in will still be in main storage when it is first referenced.
5. Define data in the order it is referenced. Refer to elements within arrays in the order they are stored.
6. Avoid GETMAIN commands if possible.
7. For ANS Cobol programs, avoid using the EXAMINE statement or variable move operations because they expand into subroutine executions.

Working Set

The working set is the number and combination of program pages needed during a given period. The application programmer should make this as small as possible by using the following techniques:

1. Programs should be coded in modules (Cobol sections), which are grouped according to their frequency and/or anticipated time of reference. This is explained further on page 101.
2. Do not tie up main storage awaiting a reply from the terminal operator. This can be avoided by using the pseudoconversational mode of processing.
3. Use the locate-mode input/output feature of file control commands rather than move-mode.
4. Specify constants directly rather than as data variables in working storage.
5. Where possible, avoid using LINK commands because they generate requests for main storage.

Validity of Reference

The program should be able to directly determine the correct page where the wanted data resides. This is implemented in the following techniques:

1. Avoid long searches for data.
2. Use data structures that can be addressed directly, such as arrays, rather than structures that must be searched, such as chains.
3. Avoid indirect addressing and any method that simulates indirect addressing.

ANS COBOL TRANSLATOR OPTIONS

The translator options are specified in the CBL card to control options in the command-language translator. For OS/VS, options may also be specified in the EXEC job control statement that invokes the translator. If both methods are used, the last specification for each option takes precedence. The options are:

1. DEBUG/*NODEBUG*. This specifies whether or not the translator is to pass the translator line number to CICS/VS to be displayed by the Execution Diagnostic Facility (EDF).* The default is NODEBUG.
2. FE. The bit pattern corresponding to the first argument of the CALL statement that is generated by the translator is printed in hexadecimal notation. The bit pattern has the encoded message that the Execute Interface program uses to determine which functions (on-line service) are required and which options are specified. With this option, all diagnostic messages are listed regardless of the FLAG option.
3. FLAGI/*FLAGW*/FLAGE. This specifies the diagnostics the translator will list. FLAGI allows all severity levels to print;

*This is the interactive application program debugging feature and will not be explained in the book.

FLAGW allows severity levels W, C, E, and D to print; FLAGE allows severity levels C, E, and D to print. The default is FLAGW.

4. *LIST*/NOLIST (DOS/VS only). LIST will produce a listing of the ANS Cobol input to the translator. The default is LIST.

5. NOSPIE. This prevents the translator from trapping unrecoverable errors; instead, a dump is produced.

6. NUM/*NONUM*. This specifies whether or not the translator is to use the line numbers appearing in columns 1 through 6 of the card, in the diagnostic messages and cross-reference listing. If NUM is not specified, the translator uses its own line numbers. NONUM is the default.

7. OPT/NOOPT. This specifies whether or not the translator is to generate SERVICE RELOAD statements to address the Execute Interface Block and the DFHCOMMAREA. The default is OPT for OS/VS and NOOPT for DOS/VS. The same value for this option must be specified for the translator and the compiler.

8. QUOTE/*APOST*. QUOTE specifies to the translator that double quotation marks (") should be accepted as the character to delineate literals; APOST specifies that the apostrophe character (') be used instead. The default is APOST and the same value for this option must be specified for the translator and the compiler.

9. *SEQ*/NOSEQ. This specifies whether or not the translator is to check for the sequence of source statements. If SEQ is specified and a statement is not in sequence, it is flagged. The default is SEQ.

10. *SOURCE*/NOSOURCE. This specifies whether or not the translator will produce a listing of the source program. The default is SOURCE.

11. *SPACE1*/SPACE2/SPACE3. This specifies the spacing to be used in the output listing: SPACE1 will produce single spacing; SPACE2 double spacing; SPACE3 triple spacing. The default is SPACE1.

12. XREF/*NOXREF.* This specifies whether or not the translator will produce a cross-reference list of all CICS/VS commands in the input. The default is NOXREF.

ANS COBOL LIMITATIONS

ANS Cobol programs written to execute in CICS/VS cannot use the following features:

1. ENVIRONMENT DIVISION and DATA DIVISION entries normally associated with data management;
2. FILE SECTION of the DATA DIVISION;
3. These special features: ACCEPT, DISPLAY, EXHIBIT, REPORT WRITER, SEGMENTATION, SORT, TRACE, and UNSTRING. For OS/VS, any feature that requires an OS/VS GETMAIN;
4. Options that require the use of Operating System services: COUNT, FLOW, STATE, STXIT, or SYMDMP for DOS/VS; COUNT, ENDJOB, FLOW, DYNAM, STATE, SYMDUMP, SYST, or TEST for OS/VS;
5. ANS COBOL statements: READ, WRITE, OPEN, and CLOSE;
6. The optimization feature option of the DOS ANS Cobol V3 compiler;
7. The link-editing of separate ANS Cobol routines.

6

The Linkage Section

INTRODUCTION

We mentioned in the previous chapter why some entries have to be or are best coded in the WORKING-STORAGE section. However, we also mentioned that to conserve main storage, in typical programs there are actually more entries in the LINKAGE section than the WORKING-STORAGE section.

We will now explain the various entries in this section.

THE EXECUTE INTERFACE BLOCK

Actually, the Execute Interface Block is automatically generated by the command-language translator and is placed as the first entry of the LINKAGE section. The programmer may access this block to get information like the terminal identification of the terminal being used, the transaction identifier that initiated the task, the date the task was initiated, the results of the last command executed, etc. For instance, he may use the terminal identification and transaction identifier as the key of a temporary storage record. The date can be used when generating journal records; and the results of the last executed command can be used for debugging.

CICS/VS automatically updates certain fields of this block when the task is initiated and after each command is executed. The Execute Interface Block is shown in Figure 6.1.

The following are the fields of the Execute Interface Block:

1. EIBTIME. This contains the time the task was initiated and is updated when the task is initiated. It may also be updated by the programmer with the ASKTIME command.
2. EIBDATE. This contains the date the task was initiated and is updated when the task is initiated. It may also be updated by the programmer with the ASKTIME command.

```
00139                 LINKAGE SECTION.
00140                 01   DFHEIBLK COPY DFHEIBLK.
00141 C         *        EIBLK EXEC INTERFACE BLOCK
00142 C         01     DFHEIBLK.
00143 C         *          EIBTIME     TIME IN OHHMMSS FORMAT
00144 C                  02 EIBTIME     PICTURE S9(7) USAGE COMPUTATIONAL-3.
00145 C         *          EIBDATE     DATE IN OOYYDDD FORMAT
00146 C                  02 EIBDATE     PICTURE S9(7) USAGE COMPUTATIONAL-3.
00147 C         *          EIBTRNID    TRANSACTION IDENTIFIER
00148 C                  02 EIBTRNID    PICTURE X(4).
00149 C         *          EIBTASKN    TASK NUMBER
00150 C                  02 EIBTASKN    PICTURE S9(7) USAGE COMPUTATIONAL-3.
00151 C         *          EIBTRMID    TERMINAL IDENTIFIER
00152 C                  02 EIBTRMID    PICTURE X(4).
00153 C         *          DFHEIGDI    RESERVED
00154 C                  02 DFHEIGDI    PICTURE S9(4) USAGE COMPUTATIONAL.
00155 C         *          EIBCPOSN    CURSOR POSITION
00156 C                  02 EIBCPOSN    PICTURE S9(4) USAGE COMPUTATIONAL.
00157 C         *          EIBCALEN    COMMAREA LENGTH
00158 C                  02 EIBCALEN    PICTURE S9(4) USAGE COMPUTATIONAL.
00159 C         *          EIBAID      ATTENTION IDENTIFIER
00160 C                  02 EIBAID      PICTURE X(1).
00161 C         *          EIBFN       FUNCTION CODE
00162 C                  02 EIBFN       PICTURE X(2).
00163 C         *          EIBRCODE    RESPONSE CODE
00164 C                  02 EIBRCODE    PICTURE X(6).
00165 C         *          EIBDS       DATASET NAME
00166 C                  02 EIBDS       PICTURE X(8).

       6          ORDLO1A         13.28.44          08/02/80

00167 C         *          EIBREQID    REQUEST IDENTIFIER
00168 C                  02 EIBREQID    PICTURE X(8).
```

Fig. 6.1. The Execute Interface Block.

3. EIBTRNID. This contains the transaction identifier and is
 updated when the task is initiated. The value will remain
 the same within a task even if other programs (which
 have their own transaction identifiers) are "called" into
 execution via the XCTL or LINK command.

4. EIBTASKN. This contains the task number assigned to the
 task by CICS/VS and is the same number that appears in
 trace-table entries generated while the task is in control.

5. EIBTRMID. This field contains the symbolic terminal identifier of the terminal or the logical unit associated with
 the task. It is updated when the task is initiated.

6. EIBPOSN. This contains the cursor address (position) associated with the last terminal control or BMS input operation from a display device such as the 3270.

7. EIBCALEN. This contains the length of the communication area passed to the application program from the previous application program. If no communication area was passed, this field contains zeroes. This field is updated when the program first executes within a task.

8. EIBAID. This contains the attention identifier code associated with the last terminal control or BMS input operation from a display device such as the 3270. This field may be compared against the standard attention identifier list (DFHAID) to check which key the operator used to initiate the terminal control or BMS input operation.

9. EIBFN. This contains a code that identifies the last CICS/VS command issued by the task. This field is updated when the service(s) corresponding to the command has been completed, whether or not an error occured. This field can be used for debugging programs that have been aborted and any time a dump is requested.

10. EIBRCODE. This contains the CICS/VS response code returned after the service(s) corresponding to the command has been completed. Almost all of the information in this field may be used in the HANDLE CONDITION command. This field can also be used in debugging when a program is aborted and any time a dump is requested.

11. EIBDS. This contains the symbolic identifier of the last file used in a File Control command.

12. EIBREQID. This contains the request identifier assigned by CICS/VS to certain Interval Control commands; it is not used if a request identifier is specified in the command.

```
LINKAGE SECTION.
01  DFHCOMMAREA.
    SKIP1
    05  PROCESS-SW                     PIC X.
      88  INITIAL-ENTRY-TIME              VALUE '0'.
      88  ORDER-VALIDATION-TIME           VALUE '1'.
```

Fig. 6.2. The DFHCOMMAREA entry.

DFHCOMMAREA

We mentioned before that the communication area sent by a program is coded in the WORKING-STORAGE section. This communication area, as received by the program invoked (XCTL or LINK command) or the first program that executes on the next task associated with the same terminal (RETURN), is the first programmer-defined entry in the LINKAGE section.

This is the DFHCOMMAREA field and we will use the first byte of the field as a switch to control the pseudoconversational mode of processing. A one-byte DFHCOMMAREA field is actually generated by the command-language translator if not defined by the programmer.

An example of this field is shown in Figure 6.2.

You will note that we are using condition-names for the switch; also, SKIP statements are used to improve the readability of the program.

THE LINKAGE POINTERS

The linkage pointers, known as base locators for linkage (BLL), are the next entries coded by the programmer, and their function is to point to succeeding 01-level entries. Each pointer is a binary fullword and appears in the same sequence as the 01-level entry it points to. Therefore, if the program has two symbolic description maps, an order master file, a Transaction Work Area, and a Temporary Storage area, the LINKAGE section will be as shown in Figure 6.3.

The correspondence between the linkage pointers and the 01-level entries are shown by the arrows. Note also that there is a FILLER fullword in front of the linkage pointers and this is used by CICS/VS to provide addressability to the linkage pointers.

```
         EJECT
     LINKAGE SECTION.
     01  DFHCOMMAREA.
         SKIP1
         05  PROCESS-SW                          PIC X.
           88  INITIAL-ENTRY-TIME                    VALUE '0'.
           88  ORDER-VERIFICATION-TIME               VALUE '1'.
           88  ORDER-VALIDATION-TIME                 VALUE '2'.
         SKIP2
     01  LINKAGE-POINTERS                    COMP.
         SKIP1
         05  FILLER                              PIC S9(8).
   ┌──── 05  MAP1-POINTER                        PIC S9(8).
   │     05  MAP2-POINTER                        PIC S9(8).
   │     05  POM-POINTER                         PIC S9(8).
   │     05  TWA-POINTER                         PIC S9(8).
   │     05  TSA-POINTER ──────────┐             PIC S9(8).
   │     EJECT                     │
   └──>01  MAP1-AREA.              │
         05  .....                 │
         EJECT                     │
     01  MAP2-AREA.                │
         05  .....                 │
         EJECT                     │
     01  ORDER-MASTER-RECORD.      │
         05  .....                 │
         EJECT                     │
     01  TWA-AREA.                 │
         05  .....                 │
         EJECT                     │
     01  TSA-AREA. <───────────────┘
         05  .....
```

Fig. 6.3. Programmer-coded entries in the LINKAGE section.

These pointers are specified in input commands, for instance, to read data from a terminal, a file, Temporary Storage, Transient Storage, etc. For instance, to read in data from a terminal that has the first screen layout, the programmer may code:

```
EXEC CICS
        RECEIVE MAP   ('ORCHM01')
                MAPSET ('ORCHS01')
                SET    (MAP1-POINTER)
END-EXEC.
```

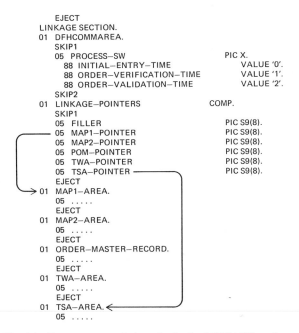

When this command is executed, CICS/VS will, among other things, secure main storage for the area corresponding to MAP1–POINTER (MAP1–AREA in Fig. 6.3) and establish addressability to the area so it can be used in the application program. This method of using pointers to gain access to the corresponding main storage in an input command is known as the locate mode method and will be the one used in this book.

To improve the readability of this section, I would suggest that in addition to the EJECT statement at the beginning of the section, the programmer should code a SKIP2 statement before the linkage pointers and an EJECT statement before each 01-level entry that corresponds to the pointers. See Figure 6.3.

Pointers For Areas Greater Than 4096 Bytes

Actually, this one-to-one correspondence between the linkage pointers and the areas they point to is true only if all of the areas are not greater than 4096 bytes. For an area greater than 4096 bytes, additional pointers have to be specified for each additional 4096 bytes or less. For instance, if the order master record has more than 4096 bytes but not greater than 8192 bytes, the LINKAGE section in Figure 6.3 would have been coded as shown in Figure 6.4.

```
    EJECT
LINKAGE SECTION.
01  DFHCOMMAREA.
    SKIP 1
    05  PROCESS-SW                         PIC X.
      88  INITIAL-ENTRY-TIME                   VALUE '0'.
      88  ORDER-VERIFICATION-TIME              VALUE '1'.
      88  ORDER-VALIDATION-TIME                VALUE '2'.
    SKIP2
01  LINKAGE-POINTERS                    COMP.
    SKIP1
    05  FILLER                             PIC S9(8).
    05  MAP1-POINTER                       PIC S9(8).
    05  MAP2-POINTER                       PIC S9(8).
    05  POM-POINTER1                       PIC S9(8).
    05  POM-POINTER2                       PIC S9(8).
    05  TWA-POINTER                        PIC S9(8).
    05  TSA-POINTER                        PIC S9(8).
    EJECT
01  MAP1-AREA.
    05  .....
    EJECT
01  MAP2-AREA.
    05  .....
    EJECT
01  ORDER-MASTER-RECORD.
    05  .....
    EJECT
01  TWA-AREA.
    05  .....
    EJECT
01  TSA-AREA.
    05  .....
```

Fig. 6.4. Multiple pointers in the LINKAGE section.

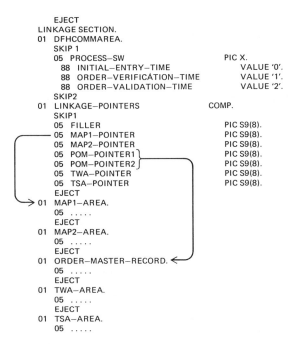

Two linkage pointers now correspond to one area. Also, since the command actually establishes addressability only to the first 4096 bytes of the area, the programmer has to establish addressability to areas beyond 4096 bytes. This is done by adding 4096 to the first extra pointer, 8192 to the next extra pointer, and so on, right after the input command. For Figure 6.4, we establish addressability to the whole ORDER–MASTER–RECORD by:

```
EXEC CICS
     READ DATASET  ('ORMAST')
          RIDFLD   (TWA-ORDER-RECORD-KEY)
          SET      (POM-POINTER1)
END-EXEC.

ADD 4096 POM-POINTER1  GIVING POM-POINTER2.
```

THE SYMBOLIC DESCRIPTION MAPS

Since most CICS/VS programs process terminal data and thus require maps, I suggest that these symbolic description maps be the first entries defined after the linkage pointers.

THE FILE DESCRIPTIONS

The file-record descriptions (including those for journal records) are actually coded just like those in batch processing. These descriptions are best placed in the source statement library so that they may be copied into the program at compilation time.

THE TRANSACTION WORK AREA

If the programmer uses the Transaction Work Area, then it is defined in this section. See Chapter 5 on the merits of the TWA as compared to working storage.

OTHER AREAS

The Temporary Storage Area, Common Work Area, Transient Data Area, and Terminal Control Table User Area are also defined in the

LINKAGE section. The programmer may also define additional areas here, especially if the areas are seldom used in the application program so that main storage will be used for them only when they require it.

VALUES OF ENTRIES IN THE LINKAGE SECTION

The values of entries defined in the LINKAGE section are as follows:

1. *Symbolic description map.* On the RECEIVE MAP command to read terminal data, the length of a field is set to the number of characters entered for a field, else it is zero. The attribute byte contains hexadecimal zeros. The field itself will contain the actual characters entered by the operator, padded with left zeros or right spaces where appropriate. Other fields not touched by the operator will contain hexadecimal zeros, unless the FSET operand is used (see page 152).
2. *Transaction work area.* This contains hexadecimal zeros at the start of a task.
3. *Area acquired through* GETMAIN. This may be set in the command to any value; otherwise the value is unknown.
4. *Other areas.* Values unknown or from files, temporary storage record, etc.

7

The Procedure Division

INTRODUCTION

The most important consideration when coding the PROCEDURE DIVISION for an on-line program is to code it in the most efficient way possible. The response time for such a program is very critical since a loss of even 1/4 second per task is disastrous if we consider many tasks contending for service from the same CPU. This is not the case for batch programs where a loss of five, ten minutes, or even more is generally not a problem.

Thus the structure of the PROCEDURE DIVISION is somewhat different from one written for a batch system. The classical structured programming technique cannot be used "as is" because it promotes too much paging, and thus penalizes efficiency. We will learn in this book how to modify this technique to suit the requirements of CICS/VS.

We mentioned in Chapter 5 some general techniques to promote efficiency. We will now explain these techniques in more detail. Before we do so however, let us mention one efficiency technique that is useful in certain conditions because of multitasking. This is the SUSPEND command and is explained on page 193.

THE PSEUDOCONVERSATIONAL MODE OF PROCESSING

One efficiency technique is the use of the pseudoconversational mode of processing. In it, a program is purged from the partition/region by terminating the task that corresponds to that program, after it has completed whatever function the operator wanted it to do in that particular task (process data entered, display a record from a file, etc.), and is now only awaiting further operator action.

It promotes efficiency because when the program is not needed, expensive resources (especially main storage), are released for reuse by other tasks. Otherwise, some of those tasks may not be able to start to continue after starting for want of resources.

The pseudoconversational mode of processing is accomplished in the following manner.

At The Beginning of The Session

1. The operator enters a transaction identifier that corresponds to the application program he needs.
2. He hits the ENTER key or any PF key.
3. A task is initiated and the transaction identifier is validated by Task Control in the Program Control Table and if valid, Program Control will load the corresponding application program from virtual storage into main storage if it is not yet there.
4. The task is placed in the wait queue. At some point, it will gain control to execute the initial routines (load in a table, get temporary storage if required, etc.).
5. The program displays on the terminal the first map to be used by the operator.
6. The program issues the command to terminate the task. The command will include a temporary transaction identifier, which will be the next one used in the same terminal. Also included is a communication area switch* that will determine the section of the program that will execute the next time.

At this point, the operator indicates the next action to be done by the program, and usually he enters more data on the terminal. He is able to do this, even if there is no task attached to the terminal because it has a buffer. He enters data with the format controlled by the map specified at step 5.

At Other Times During The Session

1. The operator finishes entering data on the terminal.
2. He hits the ENTER key or any PF or PA keys.

*This is my technique. See page 108 for variations.

3. A task is initiated and the transaction identifier sent by the previous task on the same terminal is validated by Task Control in the Program Control Table. If valid, Program Control will load the corresponding program into main storage if it is not yet there. The program to be used is usually the same as the one that sent the transaction identifier. On the ENTER key or any PF key, Terminal Control reads the data into the Terminal Input/Output Area (TIOA).
4. The task is placed in the wait queue. At some point, it will gain control to execute the appropriate section as determined by the value of the communication area switch sent by the previous task on the same terminal.
5. The section issues the command to read the data from the TIOA into the area defined by the symbolic description map.
6. The program processes the data.
7. The program displays the next map to be used by the operator.
8. The program issues the command to terminate the task. This command will likewise include a transaction identifier and a communication area switch.

STRAIGHT LINE CODING

We mentioned that the classical structured programming technique cannot be used "as is" because it promotes too much paging, and thus penalizes efficiency. This is especially true with the heavy use of long-range PERFORM statements.

We can avoid this problem in CICS/VS programs with the second major efficiency technique. We write a program so that there is as much straight-line coding as possible with no branch logic reference beyond a small range of address space. We implement this in two ways: first, by making the overall logic modular; second, by coding each section to make the logic execute in as much of a straight-line as possible.

Overall Program Design

The best way to modularize the overall program logic is to have a MAIN-LINE section control the execution of the whole program.

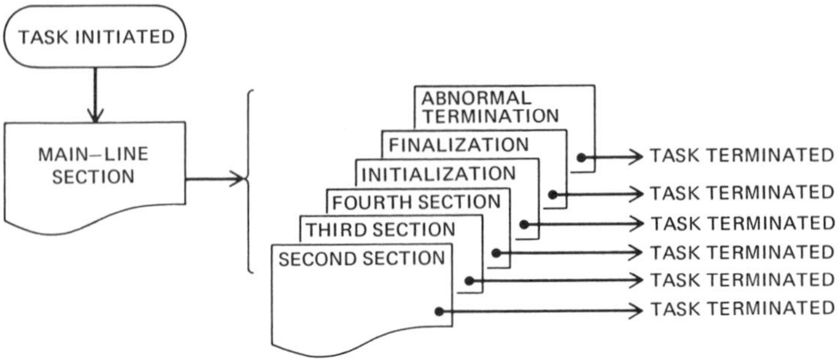

Fig. 7.1. Overall Program Structure.

When a task is initiated by the operator, control goes to this section which in turn selects the subordinate sections (we will learn later on that they are best coded as complete sections) that will actually execute. The last command executed in that section will terminate the task.

The selection of the section required for this current task depends on such factors as which terminal key was used and what happened on the previous task (which previous section was executed). For example, in an inquiry application with multiple pages for each record, if the PF1 key was used, then the program displays the next page of the same record; if the PF2 key was used, then the program displays the previous page of the same record; if the ENTER key was used, then the program reads the next record selected by the operator and displays the first page.

Figure 7.1 shows this structure.

Each of these subordinate sections has the following general characteristics:

1. A section is coded to implement one particular initiation of the task in the pseudoconversational mode of processing. For instance, the section may validate data from a terminal and use it to update a file, or display the record to be updated, etc.

2. Each section is self-contained and will not execute routines in other sections, which minimizes paging. There may be some duplication of code, but this is necessary for optimum response time in a virtual-storage environment.

3. Exceptions are routines to be executed on unrecoverable exceptional conditions* that will force the termination of the session. An example is an I/O error when accessing a file. These routines are coded in the ABNORMAL-TERMINATION section which is the last section of the program.
4. Routines for recoverable exceptional conditions, where the session may continue, should be coded at the end of the section to keep the most commonly used code in as much a straight line as possible.
5. At the end of the section, the command to terminate the task is coded and a communication area switch is set to determine which section is to be used next.
6. The sections controlled by the MAIN-LINE section are arranged according to frequency of use, the most commonly used section coded ahead of the others.
7. The third to the last section is the INITIALIZATION section, which is executed only once in a session and contains the initial routines to be executed when the session is started.
8. The second to the last section is the FINALIZATION section, which is also executed only once in a session and contains housekeeping routines to be executed when the operator decides to terminate the session.
9. The last section is the ABNORMAL-TERMINATION section which contains the routines to be executed on various errors, including unrecoverable exceptional conditions, that will abort the session.

Note that we choose the principle that one section implements one task in the pseudoconversational mode of processing. The choice is "natural" since a section always consists of paragraphs that together do a particular function. However, the use of sections is not mandatory.

---

*Exceptional conditions are "errors" that occur on the execution of commands. See Chapter 8 for more details. It is unrecoverable if it is a "major error" and the session has to be terminated. It is recoverable if it is a "minor error" and the session can continue.

General Design Of A Section

In writing the section, the code can be easily kept in a straight line most of the time. Since the logic of a particular section is generally straightforward, all the programmer has to do is code the statements and CICS/VS commands as they are required. Exceptions occur when there is a need for a logic branch. The following suggestions are offered:

1. Code statements and CICS/VS commands one after the other as they are needed without doing a logic branch unless it is required to implement an iteration logic or unless the code will seldom be executed.
2. To implement an iteration, I suggest the use of PERFORMs. However, the performed paragraph (or paragraphs) should be placed as close as possible to the PERFORM statement. The PERFORM statement itself is followed by a GO TO statement that branches around the paragraph. This way, paging is kept to a minimum. The PERFORM statement should never be used to execute a paragraph that is not executed repeatedly. The code should instead by coded in-line.
3. A set of code that is seldom executed should be placed out of the way, generally at the end of the section.
4. Code corresponding to recoverable exceptional conditions should also be placed out of the way at the end of the section.

To implement an iteration using PERFORMs or to implement a code that is seldom used, we offer the set of codes in Figure 7.2 as an example:

```
section-name  SECTION.
        .......
        .......
        PERFORM ROUTINE-L UNTIL .......
        GO TO AFTER-ROUTINE-L.
ROUTINE-L.
        .......
        .......
AFTER-ROUTINE-L.
        .......
        .......
        IF condition-1 (rare condition)
            PERFORM ROUTINE-S.
        .......
        .......
        Code to terminate task.
ROUTINE-S.
        .......
        .......
```

Fig. 7.2. Straight-line coding.

CICS/VS COMMANDS

CICS/VS commands are coded with two delimiters so the command-language translator can distinguish them from regular ANS Cobol statements. These are the "EXECUTE CICS" or "EXEC CICS" delimiter before the command, and "END-EXEC" after the command.

To make the commands easier to read in the program listing, I suggest the following coding techniques:

1. Separate the delimiters from the other statements in the command.
2. There should be only one operand per line.
3. Align the operands.
4. Always code a SKIP1 or a SKIP2 statement before a command to separate it from the previous statement. Do not

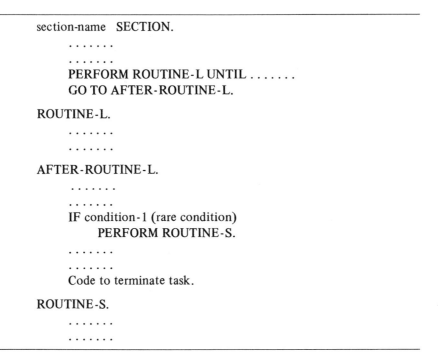

code a SKIP statement after a command because several blank lines are always generated in the compilation listing. Naturally, if a command immediately follows another one, do not code a SKIP statement before the second one.

An example of this is the following:

```
EXEC  CICS
      ADDRESS
               TWA   (TWA-POINTER)
               CWA   (CWA-POINTER)
END-EXEC.
```

However, in this book the delimiters will not be shown, unless the command is used as part of a program code.

INPUT COMMANDS AND THE LINKAGE SECTION

The relationship between the input commands and the LINKAGE section are as follows:

1. Input commands such as RECEIVE MAP (read terminal data), READ DATASET (read file record), READQ TS (read temporary storage record), etc. specify through the SET operand the pointer that corresponds to the appropriate symbolic description map, file record description, etc. This option is the locate-mode method. It is more efficient than using the INTO operand (move-mode) with an area since the area must then be present before the command is executed, in which case the area is either defined in working storage or secured through a GETMAIN command if defined in the LINKAGE section.
2. With the SET operand, CICS/VS will automatically acquire main storage for the area corresponding to the pointer and establish addressability to this area so it can be used in the program.
3. The program can access the area right after the command is executed.

OUTPUT COMMANDS AND THE LINKAGE SECTION

The relationship between the output commands and the LINKAGE section are as follows:

1. Output commands such as SEND MAP (display data on terminal), WRITE DATASET (write file record), WRITEQ TS (write temporary storage record), etc. do not specify the SET operand and a pointer, but the area itself.
2. The area must be present (have main storage allocation) before the command is executed. The area may already be allocated if a RECEIVE MAP, READ DATASET, or READQ TS, etc., command executed within the same task uses the same area. Otherwise, the program has to secure the area with the GETMAIN command if it is defined in the LINKAGE section.

8

The Main-Line Section

INTRODUCTION

We mentioned in the previous chapter that the MAIN-LINE section controls the execution of the whole program. It selects the section to be executed during a single execution of a program in pseudoconversational mode of processing.

SELECTION OF SECTIONS

There are five alternatives in the selection of sections.

Transaction Identifier

Each section may return a different transaction identifier to be used for the next execution of the program. Part of the MAIN-LINE section would then be coded as:

```
if transaction identifier1
    go to section1
else if transaction identifier2
    go to section2
else if transaction identifier3
    go to section3
.....
.....
```

The main problem with this code is that each program is associated with many transaction identifiers, causing the Program Control Table to become large, necessitating a larger space for entries. Also, the search in the PCT to validate the transaction identifier will take longer. However, a transaction identifier other than the one that initiated the current task may be used if another program is to be executed next.

Temporary Storage Switch

In the temporary storage switch method, all sections return the very same transaction identifier, but each sets a different value to the switch that is then used to select the next section to execute. Part of the MAIN-LINE section would then be coded as:

```
read temporary storage.
if switch equal to 1
     go to section1
else if switch equal to 2
     go to section2
else if switch equal to 3
     go to section3
.....
.....
```

The problem here is that not all applications require temporary storage, and we really would not want to use it for a single switch. The use of temporary storage incurs some overhead because we have to read the temporary storage record at the start of every task and re-write it before the end of the task.

Map Switch

In this method, a switch, which is also set to different values by each section, is used as part of a map. The switch is in one of the unused positions of the screen. It is defined as autoskip, so it cannot be modified by the operator, dark, so it cannot be seen, and FSET, so it can be transmitted back to the application program. This field may then be used in place of the DUMMY field, which is defined at the start of the map to prevent MAPFAIL errors. Part of the MAIN-LINE section would then be coded as:

```
read map information.
if switch equal to 1
   go to section1
else if switch equal to 2
   go to section2
else if switch equal to 3
   go to section3
.....
.....
```

The problem with this method is that it can be used only if the application program uses only one map since the map has to be read before the switch is tested and the command that reads the map identifies the specific map required.

Terminal Control Table User Area

The Terminal Control Table User Area may be used to pass data from one task to another if such tasks use the same terminal. Part of the MAIN-LINE section would then be coded as:

```
provide addressability to TCTUA.
if switch equal to 1
    go to section1
else if switch equal to 2
    go to section2
else if switch equal to 3
    go to section3
.....
.....
```

This area is defined in the LINKAGE section and addressability to it established with the ADDRESS command at the beginning of the MAIN-LINE section.

Communication Area Switch

This method does not have the limitations of the first three and is very easy to use. It is the method used in this book. The communication area switch is transmitted by a previous program and can be immediately tested at the start of the MAIN-LINE section of the current program. The EIBCALEN field of the Execute Interface Block will contain the length of the field communicated, and the field itself is the DFHCOMMAREA field in the LINKAGE section. Part of the MAIN-LINE section would then be coded as:

```
if eibcalen not equal to zeroes
    if switch equal to 1
        go to section1
    else if switch equal to 2
        go to section2
    else if switch equal to 3
        go to section3
.....
.....
```

GO TO Statement In Selecting Sections

You will note that in all five alternatives we used GO TO's when selecting the appropriate sections. Although this verb is anathema to many Cobol users, its use here is conceptually more accurate than using PERFORM's, even if the latter works just as well. Control never returns to the MAIN-LINE section once a subordinate section is selected and therefore GO TO's, where no return is expected, are used over PERFORM's, where a return is expected.

COMMUNICATION AREA SWITCH

The use of the communication area switch to control the pseudoconversational mode of processing is based on the following techniques:

1. The area communicated by the current program is defined in the WORKING-STORAGE section as the COMMUNICATION-AREA entry. The switch may or may not be the only item

of this entry. The program will set the value of this switch and then specify it in the command that terminates the task (RETURN).

2. The first program to execute when the task is next initiated on the same terminal will receive this area in the DFHCOMMAREA field. The EIBCALEN field of the Execute Interface Block will specify the length of the field communicated.

EXAMPLE OF MAIN-LINE SECTION CONTROLLING PROGRAM LOGIC

Assume we have an application where the operator starts via a master sign-on (menu) program. This in turn does a XCTL to the actual application program to start the session and send a communication area with a value of 0. Before task termination, the application program does a RETURN to itself to continue the session on the next task initiation and send a communication area with a value of either 1, 2, or 3, depending on which section was executed in that task.

We know that for the application program, EIBCALEN should always be greater than zero since a communication area is always sent to it. However, if the operator accesses this program directly by entering its transaction identifier instead of via the menu program (which can only result from a breakdown in security since in this case the operator should know only the transaction identifier of the menu program, not the applications programs themselves), EIBCALEN is zero and we have a sign-on violation.

The diagram is:

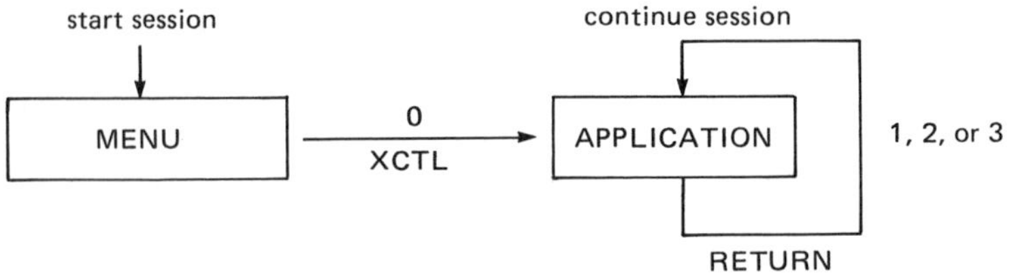

Given the following details:

1. There are three (maps) screens required to enter data for one document.

2. Each map is different and is therefore validated in a separate section.

3. The first section validates the first map, etc.

4. If there are no errors detected, we terminate the task to allow the operator to enter additional data on the next map.

5. If there are errors detected, we terminate the task to allow the operator to enter corrections on the same map.

6. If there are no errors detected on the third map, we write out a record for the document, then display the first map for the next document.

We will use the following table to determine which section should be executed on a particular task.

EIBCALEN	(DFH-PROCESS-SW) (W05-PROCESS-SW)	ACTION
0		Operator bypassed sign-on program. Session aborted. GO TO SIGN-ON-VIOLATION
not 0	VALUE CONDITION-NAME 0 initial-entry 1 first-map-entry 2 second-map-entry 3 third-map-entry	 GO TO INITIALIZATION GO TO FIRST-SECTION GO TO SECOND-SECTION GO TO THIRD-SECTION

To keep this example as simple as possible, we will not deal with the problem of flipping back and forth between screens or using PA keys to abandon a document in the middle of an entry. The MAIN-LINE and subordinate sections would be:

```
MAIN-LINE SECTION.
    IF EIBCALEN NOT EQUAL TO ZEROS
        IF FIRST-MAP-ENTRY
            GO TO FIRST-SECTION
        ELSE IF SECOND-MAP-ENTRY
            GO TO SECOND-SECTION
        ELSE IF THIRD-MAP-ENTRY
            GO TO THIRD-SECTION
        ELSE IF INITIAL-ENTRY
            GO TO INITIALIZATION
        ELSE GO TO PROCESS-SW-ERROR.

    IF EIBCALEN EQUAL TO ZEROS
        GO TO SIGN-ON-VIOLATION.

FIRST-SECTION SECTION.
    .....
    .....
    read the first map.
    validate the data entered on that map.
    .....
    .....
    If there are errors
            redisplay the first map with error messages
            MOVE '1' TO W05-PROCESS-SW
    ELSE display the second map with blank data fields
            MOVE '2' TO W05-PROCESS-SW.
    RETURN w/ trans id and switch (terminate the task).

SECOND-SECTION SECTION.
    .....
    .....
    read the second map.
    validate the data entered on that map.
    .....
    .....
    IF there are errors
            redisplay the second map with error messages
            MOVE '2' TO W05-PROCESS-SW
```

```
    ELSE display the third map with blank data fields
            MOVE '3' TO W05-PROCESS-SW.
    RETURN w/ trans id and switch (terminate the task).

THIRD-SECTION SECTION.
    . . . . .
    . . . . .
    read the third map.
    validate the data entered on that map.
    . . . . .
    . . . . .
    IF there are errors
            redisplay the third map with error messages
            MOVE '3' TO W05-PROCESS-SW
    ELSE write out a record for the document
            display the first map with blank data fields
            MOVE '1' TO W05-PROCESS-SW.
    RETURN w/ trans id and switch (terminate the task).

INITIALIZATION SECTION.
    . . . . .
    . . . . .
    Display the first map with blank data fields.
    MOVE '1' TO W05-PROCESS-SW.
    RETURN w/trans id and switch (terminate the task).

PROCESS-SW-ERROR.
    Display "session aborted -- process switch error"
    RETURN w/ no trans id (terminate the application).

SIGN-ON-VIOLATION.
    Display "session aborted -- sign on violation".
    RETURN w/ no trans id (terminate the application).
```

You will note that for each document, the program executes FIRST-SECTION to process one-third of the document, then SECOND-SECTION to process another one-third and finally THIRD-SECTION to process the last one-third. However, if an error is detected during data validation, the same section is reexecuted. Everything is controlled by W05-PROCESS-SW (DFH-PROCESS-SW when a task is initiated), which is set to the proper value before the end of each task, with the value dependent on whether there was an error detected. It takes a minimum of three tasks to create a record for a single document.

MAIN-LINE SECTION IN A STAND-ALONE PROGRAM

The previous example shows a MAIN-LINE section in a program executed via a XCTL command from the Sign-on (Menu) program. As you note, in our design EIBCALEN will always contain a value. However, for a stand-alone program (one not accessed by another program), EIBCALEN will contain a zero the first time it is executed in a session, when the operator enters its transaction identifier and hits a key like ENTER. In this case, the MAIN-LINE section would be:

```
IF EIBCALEN NOT EQUAL TO ZEROS
  .......
IF EIBCALEN EQUAL TO ZEROS
   GO TO INITIALIZATION.
```

Note that we have conveniently used the fact that when EIBCALEN is equal to zeros, then this is the start of the session. At other times, EIBCALEN will contain a value since each task will transmit one before it is terminated. An actual example of this principle is shown in the sign-on program on page 220 (Figure 17.4), lines 217 to 221.

THE ADDRESS COMMAND

As we mentioned before, CICS/VS automatically acquires main storage on input commands (RECEIVE MAP to "read" terminal data, READ DATASET to read a record from an on-line file, etc.) if the locate-mode option is used (SET with a pointer) and the area corresponding to the pointer is defined in the LINKAGE section.

There are however three storage areas defined in the LINKAGE section that are acquired for the program before it executes in a task.

These are the Transaction Work Area (TWA), the Common Work Area (CWA), and the Terminal Control Table User Area (TCTUA). The program gains access to them through the ADDRESS command, which specifies their pointers. The format is:

```
address
      twa     (twa-pointer)
      cwa     (cwa-pointer)
      tctua   (tctua-pointer)
```

If the program uses any of these storage areas, this command should be coded at the beginning of the MAIN-LINE section. For instance, if a Transaction Work Area is used, part of the MAIN-LINE section would be coded as:

```
EXEC CICS
        ADDRESS TWA (TWA-POINTER)
END-EXEC.

routine to select sections.
```

Note that this command is not needed for the WORKING-STORAGE section.

THE HANDLE AID COMMAND

The HANDLE AID command,* which should be coded at the start of the MAIN-LINE section and any subordinate section, specifies up to twelve attention identifiers and the corresponding routines that the program unconditionally asynchronously executes (a GO TO is effectively done) when certain attention identifiers are used by the operator. The format of the command is:

```
handle aid
        attention identifier1 (routine1)
        attention identifier2 (routine2)
        . . . . . . . .
        . . . . . . . .
```

*The HANDLE AID command is actually a terminal input command but is discussed here instead of Chapter 11 since it is coded in this section.

The attention identifiers that can be used are CLEAR (the Alt/Clear key), ENTER (the ENTER key), PA1 to PA3 (the PA keys), PF1 to PF24 (the PF keys), ANYKEY (any PA, PF, or the CLEAR key), OPERID (the operator identification card reader), and LIGHT-PEN (the light pen attention).

Suggested HANDLE AID Command At The MAIN-LINE Section

I suggest the following attention identifiers specified at the MAIN-LINE section:

1. CLEAR, which is often used as an installation standard to terminate applications (sessions). This requires the simultaneous keying of both the Alternate key and the Clear key, and thus cannot be accidentally used. The corresponding routine should be the FINALIZATION section.

2. PA1 to PA3, which do not allow terminal data to be read into the Terminal Input/Output Area (TIOA) and thus would result in the MAPFAIL exceptional condition on the command to read terminal data (RECEIVE MAP), even if the operator did enter data on the terminal and in spite of the DUMMY field coded in map programs. For programs with data validation (File Add, File Update, etc.), the keys may be conveniently used to bypass the current input if the operator cannot resolve an error that prevents the completion of the input. For other programs, the keys may be used to display the "WRONG KEY USED" message, and then allow the operator to continue with the right key.

A typical MAIN-LINE section for a File Add or File Update application would be:

address command (if any).

```
EXEC CICS
        HANDLE AID
                CLEAR (FINALIZATION)
                PA1   (BYPASS-INPUT)
                PA2   (BYPASS-INPUT)
                PA3   (BYPASS-INPUT)
END–EXEC.
```

routine to select sections.

EXCEPTIONAL CONDITIONS ON COMMANDS

In most cases, we expect the usual result when a command is executed. We expect a record we are looking for to be in the file; we expect to get data to be "read" from a terminal to the program after the operator finishes entering it; we expect main storage to be available when a task needs it.

However, on certain occasions, this does not happen, and an "error" or exceptional condition occurs. Examples are a "record not found" condition when reading a specific record, a "map failure" condition when reading terminal data, a "no storage available" condition when a task requires additional main storage.

The default for most of these commands is for CICS/VS to terminate the task abnormally. This is the case for the "record not found" and "map failure" conditions. A few, like the "no storage available" condition will simply cause the task to be suspended and the command is retried on the next turn of the task in the queue.

The programmer codes HANDLE CONDITION commands if he either wants to process exceptional conditions himself (that is, avoid the system default) or restore that default if it has been overridden.

Types Of Exceptional Conditions

There are two types of exceptional conditions, depending on whether the application can logically continue or not. These are:

1. *Recoverable exceptional conditions.* If the application can continue in spite of the problem, then it is recoverable. An

example is the "record not found" condition on a command to read a record. The program should just display such a message to the operator so she can take whatever action is needed. The programmer should code the specific condition in a HANDLE CONDITION command to unconditionally asynchronously execute a routine (a GO TO is effectively done) when that condition occurs. This will negate the default for that condition, which is the abnormal termination of the task. The routine itself is coded in the same section where the condition occurred, usually at the end of the section. An example is line 00316 on page 256 and lines 00407 to 00410 on pages 257 and 258.

2. *Unrecoverable exceptional conditions.* If the application cannot continue because of the problem, then it is unrecoverable. An example is a "file not open" condition on a command which accesses a file. Since most cases of this type of condition will rarely happen, there is no need to handle them through a specific condition in a HANDLE CONDITION command. We simply allow the ERROR catchall condition coded in a HANDLE CONDITION command at the beginning of the program (MAIN-LINE section) to handle the problem by executing the MAJOR-ERROR paragraph in the ABNORMAL-TERMINATION section that will generate a transaction dump to be used for debugging the problem. An example is line 00315 on page 256 and lines 00536 to 00542 on page 261.

THE HANDLE CONDITION COMMAND

The HANDLE CONDITION command is coded at the MAIN-LINE section and at other sections to specify up to twelve exceptional conditions and their corresponding routines (sections or paragraph names). When a command that executes results in one of the conditions specified, the corresponding routine is unconditionally asynchronously executed (a GO TO is effectively done).

The format of the command is:

```
handle condition
        exceptional condition1 (routine1)
        exceptional condition2 (routine2)
        . . . . . . . . . . . .
        . . . . . . . . . . . .
```

When To Code The Handle Condition Command

The following are general guidelines on when to code this command:

1. CICS/VS maintains a table of all possible exceptional conditions and their corresponding routines. The default for each exceptional condition will hold true at the start of a task. The entries for this table are changed by the execution of HANDLE CONDITION commands where each exceptional condition specified in that command alters the corresponding entry in the table. Naturally, if a particular exceptional condition is specified in more than one HANDLE CONDITION command, the table entry will correspond to the most recently executed HANDLE CONDITION command.

2. On a LINK command, CICS/VS maintains a separate table for the program "called" into execution. That table will itself start off with default values to be optionally changed by HANDLE CONDITION commands. When control returns to the "calling" program, it will continue with the same table values it had when the LINK command was executed.

3. A particular exceptional condition may correspond to different commands. For instance, the NOTOPEN (file not open) exceptional condition may occur when executing the READ DATASET (read an on-line file), REWRITE DATASET (rewrite an old record to an on-line file), etc. command. If these two commands occur in the same task and you want the same routine executed on the NOTOPEN exceptional condition, you only have to specify it once and before the first of the two commands (whichever it is) is executed. Naturally, if these two commands execute in different tasks, then the NOTOPEN exceptional condition must be specified before each command executes.

4. Since CICS/VS uses the table when an exceptional condition occurs, the programmer must make sure that the HANDLE CONDITION command executes ahead of the command that may cause a particular exceptional condition to occur. For instance, if you want to process the NOTOPEN exceptional condition yourself, you must code the program such that within the same task, a HANDLE CONDITION command with the NOTOPEN operand executes before a READ DATASET, REWRITE DATASET, etc. command.

EXECUTION OF ROUTINES WHEN AN EXCEPTIONAL CONDITION OCCURS

When the execution of a command results in an exceptional condition, the routine selected depends on the following:

1. At the beginning of a task, or when a new program is "called" into execution via the LINK command, the system default will take effect.
2. If the table entry for that exceptional condition points to a routine (entry being updated via HANDLE CONDITION commands), then that routine is unconditionally asynchronously executed (a GO TO is effectively done).
3. If the table entry for that exceptional condition does not point to a routine because the most recent HANDLE CONDITION command that specified that condition did not specify a routine, then the default for that exceptional condition will take effect.
4. If the table entry for that exceptional condition does not point to a routine because it was never specified in any HANDLE CONDITION command, then either of two things can happen:
   a. If the default for the exceptional condition is the abnormal termination of the task, and a HANDLE CONDITION command, with the ERROR exceptional condition specified, was executed, then the routine specified for

ERROR is executed. If there was no routine specified for ERROR, then the task is abnormally terminated.

b. Otherwise, the default for that exceptional condition will take effect.

EXCEPTIONAL CONDITION AT THE MAIN-LINE SECTION

I suggest the coding of two exceptional conditions at the MAIN-LINE section. The first is MAPFAIL which occurs when there is no data in the terminal input/output area (TIOA) on the command to read terminal data (RECEIVE MAP). Since most CICS/VS programs deals with terminal data and thus maps, MAPFAIL can occur under certain conditions. The second is ERROR, which is the catch-all condition to avoid the abnormal termination of the task for conditions that are not covered by a corresponding HANDLE CONDITION command.

Since both exceptional conditions are unrecoverable, they should specify routines in the ABNORMAL-TERMINATION section that will terminate the application. A part of the MAIN-LINE section would then be coded as:

```
address command (if any).

handle aid command.

EXEC CICS
          HANDLE CONDITION
                    MAPFAIL  (MAPFAIL-ERROR)
                    ERROR    (MAJOR-ERROR)
END-EXEC.

routine to select sections.
```

USING THE EIBAID FIELDS IN IF STATEMENTS

The HANDLE AID command mentioned before is very useful if the programmer wants specific attention identifiers associated with specific actions. For example, in a File Add application, the program may be written so it will always (therefore unconditionally) abandon the processing of a document if any PA key (PA1, PA2, or PA3) is used by the operator.

However, there are situations where the programmer wants to do a specific action but only under certain conditions. For example, in a File Inquiry application where the data to be displayed cannot fit in one screen, the programmer has to go to a second page for the rest of the data. In this case he wants to display page 2 if the operator hits the PF1 key while on page 1; redisplay page 1 if the operator hits the PF2 key while on page 2.

One way to achieve this is to use an IF condition statement where the condition compares the value of the EIBAID (attention identifier) field of the Execute Interface Block against entries in the DFHAID data block (the standard attention identifier list). A simplified File Inquiry example using 2 maps is:

```
IF EIBCALEN NOT EQUAL TO ZEROS
   IF EIBAID EQUAL TO DFHPF1                (PF1 key used)
      IF DFH-DISPLAY-IS-PAGE1               (current display)
              GO TO DISPLAY-PAGE2
      ELSE GO TO WRONG-KEY-USED
   ELSE IF EIBAID EQUAL TO DFHPF2           (PF2 key used)
              IF DFH-DISPLAY-IS-PAGE2       (current display)
                      GO TO DISPLAY-PAGE1
              ELSE GO TO WRONG-KEY-USED
   ELSE GO TO DISPLAY-NEW-RECORD.
```

Note that if the PF1 key was used, we go to the section that displays the second page only if the current display is page 1; otherwise, we display the "wrong key used" error message. If the PF2 key was used, we go to the section that displays the first page only if the current display is page 2; otherwise, we display the "wrong key used" error message. If the key is other than PF1 or PF2 (except the Clear and PA keys, which should have been defined in previous statements), then we display a new record based on a new record key entered by the operator.

EXAMPLE OF THE MAIN-LINE SECTION

A complete MAIN-LINE section from a File Add application is shown in Figure 8.1.

You see the ADDRESS, HANDLE AID, and HANDLE CONDITION commands. When EIBCALEN is not equal to zero, we either go to the ORDER-VALIDATION section, the INITIALIZATION section, or the PROCESS-SWITCH-ERROR paragraph in the ABNORMAL-TERMINATION section, depending on the value of the communication area switch.

You may have deduced that this program was first executed in a session by the XCTL command from another program. If this were started directly by the operator, then we would go to the SIGN-ON-VIOLATION paragraph of the ABNORMAL-TERMINATION section to abort the session.

```
           EJECT
       PROCEDURE DIVISION.
           SKIP2
      *****************************************************************
      *                                                               *
       MAIN-LINE SECTION.
      *                                                               *
      *****************************************************************
           SKIP2
           EXEC CICS
                ADDRESS TWA (TWA-POINTER)
           END-EXEC.
           EXEC CICS
                HANDLE AID
                       CLEAR (FINALIZATION)
                          PA1 (BYPASS-INPUT)
                          PA2 (BYPASS-INPUT)
                          PA3 (BYPASS-INPUT)
           END-EXEC.
           EXEC CICS
                HANDLE CONDITION
                       MAPFAIL (MAPFAIL-ERROR)
                       ERROR    (MAJOR-ERROR)
           END-EXEC.
           IF EIBCALEN NOT EQUAL TO ZEROES
                IF ORDER-VALIDATION-TIME
                       GO TO ORDER-VALIDATION
                ELSE IF INITIAL-ENTRY-TIME
                       GO TO INITIALIZATION
                ELSE GO TO PROCESS-SWITCH-ERROR.
           SKIP1
           IF EIBCALEN EQUAL TO ZEROES
                GO TO SIGN-ON-VIOLATION.
```

Fig. 8.1. The MAIN-LINE section.

9

The Housekeeping Sections

INTRODUCTION

There are three sections that are coded at the end of the program because they are either executed only once in a session or are only executed on certain errors. They are therefore best kept out of the way of the other sections that are used often.

THE INITIALIZATION SECTION

The routines to be executed when a program is first used in a session are coded in the INITIALIZATION section. This secures, if required, temporary storage for the application, displays the first map required by the operator, then sets the correct values to the communication area switch and terminates the task. To avoid the reexecution of part of this section during the session (thus reducing the possibility of paging), other sections needing to display the first map must do so themselves. An example of this section is shown in Figure 9.1.

The SEND MAP command will display the first map required, the switch is set to '1', and then the RETURN command terminates the task. Note that the TRANSID operand of the RETURN command specifies the transaction identifier as a literal ('ORDL'), unlike other sections which may use EIBTRNID. In many applications, this section executes via a XCTL command from a menu program and EIBTRNID cannot be used because it would contain the wrong value.

THE FINALIZATION SECTION

The routines to be executed when the operator decides to terminate a session are coded in the FINALIZATION section. To standardize the choice of the terminal key that signifies the end of a session, I suggest that applications use the CLEAR key since this actually

```
11          ORDL01A          13.02.04          08/02/80

            ****************************************************************
            *                                                              *
             INITIALIZATION SECTION.
            *                                                              *
            ****************************************************************

            *      EXEC CICS
            *           SEND MAP      ('ORDLM01')
            *                MAPSET  ('ORDLS01')
            *                MAPONLY
            *                ERASE
            *      END-EXEC.
                    MOVE 'ORDLM01' TO DFHEIV1 MOVE 'ORDLS01' TO DFHEIV2 MOVE 'QD
            -      '& D     ESD   -' TO DFHEIV0 CALL 'DFHEI1' USING DFHEIV0
                    DFHEIV1 DFHEIV99 DFHEIV98 DFHEIV2.



                   MOVE '1' TO COMMAREA-PROCESS-SW.

            *      EXEC CICS
            *           RETURN TRANSID  ('ORDL')
            *                  COMMAREA (COMMUNICATION-AREA)
            *                  LENGTH   (1)
            *      END-EXEC.
                    MOVE 'ORDL' TO DFHEIV5 MOVE 1 TO DFHEIV11 MOVE '+H- D  & '
                    TO DFHEIV0 CALL 'DFHEI1' USING DFHEIV0 DFHEIV5
                    COMMUNICATION-AREA DFHEIV11.
```

Fig. 9.1. The INITIALIZATION section.

requires an additional key to be depressed at the same time (the alternate key) and avoids accidental use.

This section displays an unformatted message to the operator, signifying the end of a session, deletes temporary storage taken by the application (unless there is a reason to save it), then terminates the task. An example of this is shown in Figure 9.2.

The SEND command displays the unformatted message "JOB NORMALLY TERMINATED" on top of the screen, the HANDLE CONDITION command specifies the routine to be executed in case the temporary storage queue to be deleted does not exist, the DELETEQ TS command deletes the temporary storage queue, and the RETURN command terminates the task. If the RETURN command does not specify a transaction identifier (as in the case of the other sections) and if the task is at the highest logical level, then a task can no longer be reinitiated by simply using an attention identifier and the operator can no longer continue the session.

```
      ******************************************************************
      *                                                                *
       FINALIZATION SECTION.
      *                                                                *
      ******************************************************************

       PREPARE-TERMINATION-MESSAGE.
           MOVE JOB-NORMAL-END-MESSAGE TO TWA-OPERATOR-MESSAGE.

       JOB-TERMINATED.

      *    EXEC CICS
      *         SEND FROM    (TWA-OPERATOR-MESSAGE)
      *              LENGTH (31)
      *              ERASE
      *    END-EXEC.
            MOVE 31 TO DFHEIV11 MOVE 'DDO D   A       ' TO DFHEIVO CALL '
      -    'DFHEI1' USING DFHEIVO DFHEIV99 DFHEIV98 TWA-OPERATOR-MESSAGE
            DFHEIV11.


      *    EXEC CICS
      *         HANDLE CONDITION
      *              QIDERR (END-OF-JOB)
      *    END-EXEC.
            MOVE 'BD  D%             ' TO DFHEIVO CALL 'DFHEI1' USING
            DFHEIVO GO TO END-OF-JOB DEPENDING ON DFHEIGDI.


           MOVE EIBTRMID  TO   TSA-TERM-ID.
           MOVE EIBTRNID  TO   TSA-TRANS-ID.

      *    EXEC CICS
      *         DELETEQ TS
      *              QUEUE (TSA-QUEUE-ID)
      *    END-EXEC.
            MOVE ' F  D  / ' TO DFHEIVO CALL 'DFHEI1' USING DFHEIVO
            TSA-QUEUE-ID.



       END-OF-JOB.

      *    EXEC CICS
      *         RETURN
      *    END-EXEC.
            MOVE '+H  D  & ' TO DFHEIVO CALL 'DFHEI1' USING DFHEIVO.


```

Fig. 9.2. The FINALIZATION section.

THE ABNORMAL-TERMINATION SECTION

Routines that are to be executed only on unrecoverable exceptional conditions and other "major" errors that will abnormally terminate the session are coded in the ABNORMAL-TERMINATION section. The programmer may code as many routines as he wants in this section. The most common routines are:

1. FILE-NOT-OPEN. This is used for the NOTOPEN exceptional condition for applications using files.

2. MAPFAIL-ERROR. A routine used for the MAPFAIL exceptional condition if no data is sent to the application program from the Terminal Input/Output Area on the RECEIVE MAP command.

3. PROCESS-SWITCH-ERROR. This is employed if the value of the communication area switch that controls pseudoconversational mode of processing is not within the correct range of values.

4. SIGN-ON-VIOLATION. This is used if an application that is supposed to be started only by an XCTL command (as for instance from a sign-on program) is instead directly executed (generally through a transaction identifier).

5. MAJOR-ERROR. This is used for the catchall ERROR exceptional condition for CICS/VS command exceptional condition not covered by a specific HANDLE CONDITION command.

An example of the ABNORMAL-TERMINATION section is shown in Figure 9.3.

Note that I am using an XCTL command to execute a program that displays an installation standard message on a NOTOPEN error. The routines for a MAPFAIL error, a process switch error, and a sign-on violation will display the appropriate message to the operator, then terminate the session.

The routine for the catchall ERROR condition will likewise display a message to the operator, then terminate the session. In addition, I suggest the use of the DUMP command to produce a dump for debugging purposes.

```
13          ORDL01A          13.02.04          08/02/80

      ****************************************************************
      *                                                              *
       ABNORMAL-TERMINATION SECTION.
      *                                                              *
      ****************************************************************

       FILE-NOT-OPEN.

      *    EXEC CICS
      *         XCTL PROGRAM ('TEL2OPEN')
      *    END-EXEC.
            MOVE 'TEL2OPEN' TO DFHEIV3 MOVE '+D  D  B ' TO DFHEIVO CALL
           'DFHEI1' USING DFHEIVO DFHEIV3.

       MAPFAIL-ERROR.
           MOVE 'MAP FAILURE' TO MAJOR-ERROR-MSG.
           GO TO PREPARE-ABORT-MESSAGE.

       PROCESS-SWITCH-ERROR.
           MOVE 'PROCESS ERROR' TO MAJOR-ERROR-MSG.
           GO TO PREPARE-ABORT-MESSAGE.

       SIGN-ON-VIOLATION.
           MOVE 'SIGNON VIOLATION' TO MAJOR-ERROR-MSG.
           GO TO PREPARE-ABORT-MESSAGE.

       MAJOR-ERROR.
           MOVE  EIBFN      TO  OLD-EIBFN.
           MOVE  EIBRCODE   TO  OLD-EIBRCODE.

      *    EXEC CICS
      *         DUMP DUMPCODE ('ERRS')
      *    END-EXEC.
            MOVE 'ERRS' TO DFHEIV5 MOVE '*B  D  = ' TO DFHEIVO CALL 'DFH
      -    'EI1' USING DFHEIVO DFHEIV5.

           MOVE 'MAJOR ERROR' TO MAJOR-ERROR-MSG.
           GO TO PREPARE-ABORT-MESSAGE.

       PREPARE-ABORT-MESSAGE.
           MOVE JOB-ABORTED-MESSAGE TO TWA-OPERATOR-MESSAGE.
           GO TO JOB-TERMINATED.
```

Fig. 9.3. The ABNORMAL-TERMINATION section.

10

Processing Sections

INTRODUCTION

Sections that will be executed one after the other during a session are called processing sections, and they will be coded after the MAIN-LINE section. Their position in the program depends on their frequency of use, the most used sections being coded ahead of the others. Each section is self-contained and will not execute routines beyond that section. This reduces the possibility of paging. There may thus be some redundancy of code among the sections.

An exhaustive discussion on sections is beyond the scope of this book. Rather, this chapter will discuss some typical sections that may be required in various on-line applications.

THE RECORD-KEY-VERIFICATION SECTION

In a File Update or File Inquiry application, the record key entered by the operator must be verified to see if it corresponds to a valid record. If File Control can locate the corresponding record, the data will then be displayed; otherwise, an error message like "RECORD NOT FOUND" is displayed. As a minimum, this section does the following functions:

1. HANDLE CONDITION command for NOTOPEN and NOTFND. NOTOPEN will abnormally terminate the session while NOTFND will display the "RECORD NOT FOUND" message to the operator. In a File Inquiry using an alternate key, DUPKEY must also be specified.
2. RECEIVE MAP command to read the record key entered by the operator.
3. READ DATASET command to read the file.

4. If the record is in the file:
   a. SEND MAP command to display the record information.
   b. Set the communication area switch for the next section (for instance, in an update application, the section that validates the changes to be entered).
   c. RETURN command to terminate the task.
5. If the record is not in the file:
   a. SEND MAP command to display the "RECORD NOT FOUND" message.
   b. Set the communication area switch for the same section to give the operator the option to correct the record key or enter a new one.
   c. RETURN command to terminate the task.

An example of the RECORD-KEY-VERIFICATION section is given in Figure 10.1.

Note that if the record was in the file, we set the communication area switch to '2' (line 366), thus executing the section to validate changes entered by the operator. On the other hand, if the record was not in the file, we set the switch to '1' (line 382) to reexecute the same section and verify the corrected record key or a new record key that would have been entered by the operator.

DATA-VALIDATION SECTION

In a File Update or File Add Application, the DATA-VALIDATION section is the one most used by the operator. Since there is much more data entered in the DATA-VALIDATION section than in the RECORD-KEY-VERIFICATION section, there are also more chances to enter errors in it. There will be instances when the operator will have to correct entered data, in which case this section will be re-executed several times for a single record. For this reason, it is generally coded as the first section after the MAIN-LINE section. As a minimum, this section does the following:

```
10          ORIQ01A          16.10.10          12/27/80

            ****************************************************************
            *                                                              *
             ORDER-VERIFICATION SECTION.                                   *
            *
            ****************************************************************

            *     EXEC CICS
            *          HANDLE CONDITION
            *                 NOTOPEN (FILE-NOT-OPEN)
            *                 NOTFND  (RECORD-NOT-FOUND)
            *     END-EXEC.
                   MOVE '                        ' TO DFHEIV0 CALL 'DFHEI1' USING
                   DFHEIV0 GO TO FILE-NOT-OPEN RECORD-NOT-FOUND DEPENDING ON
                   DFHEIGDI.


            *     EXEC CICS
            *          RECEIVE MAP      ('ORCHM01')
            *                  MAPSET ('ORCHS01')
            *                  SET     (MAP1-POINTER)
            *     END-EXEC.
                   MOVE 'ORCHM01' TO DFHEIV1 MOVE 'ORCHS01' TO DFHEIV2 MOVE '
            -      '               ' TO DFHEIV0 CALL 'DFHEI1' USING DFHEIV0
                   DFHEIV1 MAP1-POINTER DFHEIV98 DFHEIV2.


                  IF MAP1-ORDER-NUMBER NOT NUMERIC
                       GO TO INVALID-ORDER-RTN.

                  MOVE MAP1-ORDER-NUMBER TO TWA-ORDER-RECORD-KEY.

            *     EXEC CICS
            *          READ DATASET ('ORTEST')
            *               SET     (POM-POINTER)
            *               RIDFLD  (TWA-ORDER-RECORD-KEY)
            *     END-EXEC.
                   MOVE 'ORTEST' TO DFHEIV3 MOVE '          ' TO DFHEIV0 CALL 'D
            -      'FHEI1' USING DFHEIV0 DFHEIV3 POM-POINTER DFHEIV98
                   TWA-ORDER-RECORD-KEY.


            *         HERE MOVE RECORD FIELDS INTO THE SYMBOLIC DESC. MAP.


             DISPLAY-ORDER.

            *     EXEC CICS
            *          SEND MAP      ('ORCHM01')
            *               MAPSET ('ORCHS01')
            *               FROM   (MAP1-AREA)
            *               ERASE
```

Fig. 10.1. The RECORD-KEY-VERIFICATION section.

```
    11          ORIQ01A          16.10.10          12/27/80

            *     END-EXEC.
                   MOVE 'ORCHM01' TO DFHEIV1 MOVE 'ORCHS01' TO DFHEIV2 MOVE '
            -     '          S     ' TO DFHEIV0 CALL 'DFHEI1' USING DFHEIV0
                   DFHEIV1 MAP1-AREA DFHEIV98 DFHEIV2.

                  MOVE '2' TO COMMAREA-PROCESS-SW.

             RETURN-AT-RECORD-KEY-VERIFY.

            *     EXEC CICS
            *           RETURN TRANSID  (EIBTRNID)
            *                  COMMAREA (COMMUNICATION-AREA)
            *                  LENGTH   (1)
            *     END-EXEC.
                   MOVE 1 TO DFHEIV11 MOVE '           ' TO DFHEIV0 CALL 'DFHEI1'
                   USING DFHEIV0 EIBTRNID COMMUNICATION-AREA DFHEIV11.

             RECORD-NOT-FOUND.

                  MOVE '1'  TO  COMMAREA-PROCESS-SW.
                  MOVE 'RECORD NOT FOUND' TO MAP1-ERROR.
                  GO TO DISPLAY-INVALID-ORDER-MESSAGE.

             DISPLAY-INVALID-ORDER-MESSAGE.

            *     EXEC CICS
            *          SEND MAP     ('ORCHM01')
            *               MAPSET ('ORCHS01')
            *               FROM    (MAP1-AREA)
            *               ERASE
            *     END-EXEC.
                   MOVE 'ORCHM01' TO DFHEIV1 MOVE 'ORCHS01' TO DFHEIV2 MOVE '
            -     '          S     ' TO DFHEIV0 CALL 'DFHEI1' USING DFHEIV0
                   DFHEIV1 MAP1-AREA DFHEIV98 DFHEIV2.

                  GO TO RETURN-AT-RECORD-KEY-VERIFY.

             INVALID-ORDER-RTN.

                  MOVE  '1'   TO  COMMAREA-PROCESS-SW.
                  MOVE 'INVALID ORDER NUMBER' TO MAP1-ERROR.
                  GO TO DISPLAY-INVALID-ORDER-MESSAGE.
```

Fig. 10.1 (Continued)

File Update Application

1. RECEIVE MAP command to read the data entered by the operator.
2. Edits data.
3. If there are no errors:
   a. HANDLE CONDITION command for NOTOPEN and NOTFND.* NOTOPEN will abnormally terminate the session while NOTFND will display the "RECORD NOT FOUND" message to the operator.
   b. READ DATASET command with UPDATE option to make the record available for update.
   c. Moves the changes to the file record defined in the LINKAGE section.
   d. REWRITE DATASET command to update the record.
   e. SEND MAP command to display the next map required by the operator.
   f. Sets the communication area switch for the next section (the RECORD-KEY-VERIFICATION section).
   g. RETURN command to terminate the task.
4. If there are errors:
   a. SEND MAP command to display the error messages.
   b. Sets the communication area switch to reexecute the DATA-VALIDATION section, to edit the corrections to be entered by the operator.
   c. RETURN command to terminate the task.

An example of this section is shown in Figure 10.2.

---

*The NOTOPEN and NOTFND options are specified because somebody could easily close the file or delete the record between the READ in the RECORD-KEY-VERIFICATION section and the incoming READ.

```
    13          ORCHO1A          16.20.58          12/27/80

           ************************************************************************
           *                                                                      *
            DATA-VALIDATION SECTION.
           *                                                                      *
           ************************************************************************


           *     EXEC CICS
           *          RECEIVE MAP     ('ORCHM02')
           *                  MAPSET ('ORCHS02')
           *                  SET     (MAP2-POINTER)
           *     END-EXEC.
                  MOVE 'ORCHM02' TO DFHEIV1 MOVE 'ORCHS02' TO DFHEIV2 MOVE '
           -     '                ' TO DFHEIV0 CALL 'DFHEI1' USING DFHEIV0
                  DFHEIV1 MAP2-POINTER DFHEIV98 DFHEIV2.


            VALIDATE-ALL-DATA.
                MOVE SPACES TO MAP2-ERRORS (1)
                               MAP2-ERRORS (2)
                               MAP2-ERRORS (3)
                               MAP2-ERRORS (4).
                SET ERROR-I    TO  ZEROES.

                IF MAP2-DOCUMENT NUMERIC
                     NEXT SENTENCE
                ELSE SET ERROR-I UP BY 1
                     MOVE 'INVALID DOCUMENT NUMBER' TO  MAP2-ERRORS (ERROR-I)
                     MOVE -1                        TO  MAP2-DOCUMENT-L.

           *        HERE EDIT THE REST OF THE DATA.


            CHECK-IF-THERE-ARE-ERRORS.

                IF ERROR-I NOT EQUAL TO ZEROES
                     GO TO DISPLAY-ERROR-SCREEN.


            NO-ERRORS-RTN.

                MOVE TSA-ORDER-NUMBER   TO   TWA-ORDER-RECORD-KEY.

           *     EXEC CICS
           *          HANDLE CONDITION
           *                 NOTOPEN (FILE-NOT-OPEN)
           *                 NOTFND  (RECORD-NOT-FOUND)
           *     END-EXEC.
                  MOVE '                    ' TO DFHEIV0 CALL 'DFHEI1' USING
                  DFHEIV0 GO TO FILE-NOT-OPEN RECORD-NOT-FOUND DEPENDING ON
                  DFHEIGDI.
```

Fig. 10.2. The DATA-VALIDATION section For A File Update Application.

```
   14          ORCH01A          16.20.58          12/27/80


       *     EXEC CICS
       *          READ DATASET ('ORTEST')
       *               SET      (POM-POINTER)
       *               RIDFLD   (TWA-ORDER-RECORD-KEY)
       *               UPDATE
       *     END-EXEC.
              MOVE 'ORTEST' TO DFHEIV3 MOVE '         ' TO DFHEIV0 CALL 'D
       -     'FHEI1' USING DFHEIV0 DFHEIV3 POM-POINTER DFHEIV98
              TWA-ORDER-RECORD-KEY.



       *         HERE MOVE CHANGES TO FILE RECORD DEFINITION.


        REWRITE-ORDER-RECORD.
             COMPUTE TWA-POM-LENGTH = 37 + ORDER-LINE-COUNT * 44.

       *     EXEC CICS
       *          REWRITE DATASET ('ORTEST')
       *                  LENGTH  (TWA-POM-LENGTH)
       *                  FROM    (ORDER-MASTER-RECORD)
       *     END-EXEC.
              MOVE 'ORTEST' TO DFHEIV3 MOVE '         ' TO DFHEIV0 CALL 'D
       -     'FHEI1' USING DFHEIV0 DFHEIV3 ORDER-MASTER-RECORD
              TWA-POM-LENGTH.


       *     EXEC CICS
       *          SEND MAP     ('ORCHM01')
       *               MAPSET ('ORCHS01')
       *               MAPONLY
       *               ERASE
       *     END-EXEC.
              MOVE 'ORCHM01' TO DFHEIV1 MOVE 'ORCHS01' TO DFHEIV2 MOVE '
       -     '           ' TO DFHEIV0 CALL 'DFHEI1' USING DFHEIV0
              DFHEIV1 DFHEIV99 DFHEIV98 DFHEIV2.



             MOVE  '1'  TO COMMAREA-PROCESS-SW.


        RETURN-AT-ORDER-VALIDATE.

       *     EXEC CICS
       *          RETURN TRANSID  (EIBTRNID)
       *                 COMMAREA (COMMUNICATION-AREA)
       *                 LENGTH   (1)
       *     END-EXEC.
```

Fig. 10.2. (Continued)

```
    15        ORCH01A          16.20.58         12/27/80

              MOVE 1 TO DFHEIV11 MOVE '          ' TO DFHEIV0 CALL 'DFHEI1'
              USING DFHEIV0 EIBTRNID COMMUNICATION-AREA DFHEIV11.



         DISPLAY-ERROR-SCREEN.

         *    EXEC CICS
         *         SEND MAP        ('ORCHM02')
         *              MAPSET     ('ORCHS02')
         *              FROM       (MAP2-AREA)
         *              DATAONLY
         *              CURSOR
         *    END-EXEC.
               MOVE 'ORCHM02' TO DFHEIV1 MOVE 'ORCHS02' TO DFHEIV2 MOVE -1
              TO DFHEIV11 MOVE '   J          ' TO DFHEIV0 CALL 'DFHEI1'
               USING DFHEIV0 DFHEIV1 MAP2-AREA DFHEIV98 DFHEIV2 DFHEIV99
               DFHEIV99 DFHEIV99 DFHEIV11.



              MOVE  '2'  TO  COMMAREA-PROCESS-SW.

              GO TO RETURN-AT-ORDER-VALIDATE.


         RECORD-NOT-FOUND.

              MOVE 'RECORD NOT FOUND' TO MAP2-ERRORS (1).
              MOVE -1         TO  MAP2-ORDER-NUMBER-L.
              GO TO DISPLAY-ERROR-SCREEN.
```

Fig. 10.2. (Continued)

File Add Application

1. RECEIVE MAP command to read the data entered by the operator.
2. Edits the data.
3. If there are no errors:
   a. GETMAIN command to secure main storage for the new record to be written out.
   b. Moves the data to the file record.
   c. HANDLE CONDITION command for NOTOPEN and DUPREC.* NOTOPEN will abnormally terminate the session while DUPREC will display the "DUPLICATE–NOT ACCEPTED" message to the operator.
   d. WRITE DATASET command to write the new record.
   e. SEND MAP command to display the next map required by the operator.
   f. Sets the communication area switch for the next section (this is generally the same DATA-VALIDATION section).**
   g. RETURN command to terminate the task.
4. If there are errors:
   a. SEND MAP command to display the error messages.
   b. Sets the communication area switch to reexecute the DATA-VALIDATION section to edit the corrections to be entered by the operator.
   c. RETURN command to terminate the task.

An example of this section is shown in Figure 10.3.

---

*The DUPREC exceptional condition is specified to display an error message just in case the record to be created has an existing duplicate.

**In a File Add Application, the record key is generally validated in the same DATA-VALIDATION section. There is generally no need to check in a separate section if the record has a duplicate because this should rarely happen anyway.

```
14            ORAD01A          16.16.28        12/27/80

00422        ************************************************************
00423        *                                                          *
00424         DATA-VALIDATION SECTION.
00425        *                                                          *
00426        ************************************************************

00428        *     EXEC CICS
00429        *          RECEIVE MAP   ('ORADM01')
00430        *                  MAPSET ('ORADS01')
00431        *                  SET    (MAP1-POINTER)
00432        *     END-EXEC.
00433              MOVE 'ORADM01' TO DFHEIV1 MOVE 'ORADS01' TO DFHEIV2 MOVE '
00434        -        '           ' TO DFHEIV0 CALL 'DFHEI1' USING DFHEIV0
00435              DFHEIV1 MAP1-POINTER DFHEIV98 DFHEIV2.
00436
00437
00438         VALIDATE-ALL-DATA.
00439              MOVE SPACES TO MAP1-ERRORS (1)
00440                             MAP1-ERRORS (2)
00441                             MAP1-ERRORS (3)
00442                             MAP1-ERRORS (4).

00444              IF MAP1-ORDER-NUMBER NUMERIC
00445                  MOVE MAP1-ORDER-NUMBER        TO  TSA-ORDER-NUMBER
00446              ELSE SET ERROR-I UP BY 1
00447                  MOVE 'INVALID ORDER NUMBER'   TO  MAP1-ERRORS (ERROR-I)
00448                  MOVE -1                       TO  MAP1-ORDER-NUMBER-L.

00450        *        HERE EDIT THE REST OF THE DATA.

00452         CHECK-IF-THERE-ARE-ERRORS.

00454              IF ERROR-I NOT EQUAL TO ZEROES
00455                  GO TO DISPLAY-ERROR-SCREEN.

00457         NO-ERRORS-RTN.

00459        *     EXEC CICS
00460        *          GETMAIN
00461        *               SET    (POM-POINTER)
00462        *               LENGTH (433)
00463        *     END-EXEC.
00464              MOVE 433 TO DFHEIV11 MOVE '          ' TO DFHEIV0 CALL 'DFHEI
00465        -     '1' USING DFHEIV0 POM-POINTER DFHEIV11.
00466
00467
00468
00469              MOVE TSA-LINE-COUNT      TO  ORDER-LINE-COUNT.
00470              MOVE TSA-POMAST-RECORD   TO  ORDER-MASTER-RECORD.
00471              COMPUTE TWA-POM-LENGTH = 37 + ORDER-LINE-COUNT * 44.
```

Fig. 10.3. The DATA-VALIDATION section For A File Add Application.

```
15          ORAD01A          16.16.28          12/27/80

            MOVE TSA-ORDER-NUMBER    TO   TWA-ORDER-RECORD-KEY.

      *     EXEC CICS
      *          HANDLE CONDITION
      *                 NOTOPEN (FILE-NOT-OPEN)
      *                 DUPREC  (DUPLICATE-RECORD)
      *     END-EXEC.
             MOVE '                        ' TO DFHEIV0 CALL 'DFHEI1' USING
             DFHEIV0 GO TO FILE-NOT-OPEN DUPLICATE-RECORD DEPENDING ON
             DFHEIGDI.


      *     EXEC CICS
      *          WRITE DATASET ('ORTEST')
      *                 LENGTH   (TWA-POM-LENGTH)
      *                 FROM     (ORDER-MASTER-RECORD)
      *                 RIDFLD   (TWA-ORDER-RECORD-KEY)
      *     END-EXEC.
             MOVE 'ORTEST' TO DFHEIV3 MOVE '  0       ' TO DFHEIV0 CALL 'D
      -     'FHEI1' USING DFHEIV0 DFHEIV3 ORDER-MASTER-RECORD
             TWA-POM-LENGTH TWA-ORDER-RECORD-KEY.



       DISPLAY-FRESH-SCREEN.

      *     EXEC CICS
      *          SEND MAP    ('ORADM01')
      *               MAPSET ('ORADS01')
      *               MAPONLY
      *               ERASE
      *     END-EXEC.
             MOVE 'ORADM01' TO DFHEIV1 MOVE 'ORADS01' TO DFHEIV2 MOVE '
      -     '              ' TO DFHEIV0 CALL 'DFHEI1' USING DFHEIV0
             DFHEIV1 DFHEIV99 DFHEIV98 DFHEIV2.



       RETURN-FOR-NEXT-ORDER.

            MOVE '1'  TO COMMAREA-PROCESS-SW.

      *     EXEC CICS
      *          RETURN TRANSID   (EIBTRNID)
      *                 COMMAREA  (COMMUNICATION-AREA)
      *                 LENGTH    (1)
      *     END-EXEC.
             MOVE 1 TO DFHEIV11 MOVE '           ' TO DFHEIV0 CALL 'DFHEI1'
             USING DFHEIV0 EIBTRNID COMMUNICATION-AREA DFHEIV11.



       DISPLAY-ERROR-SCREEN.
```

Fig. 10.3. (Continued)

```
     16        ORAD01A         16.16.28        12/27/80

00526       *      EXEC CICS
00527       *           SEND MAP         ('ORADM01')
00528       *                MAPSET      ('ORADS01')
00529       *                FROM        (MAP1-AREA)
00530       *                DATAONLY
00531       *                CURSOR
00532       *      END-EXEC
00533              MOVE 'ORADM01' TO DFHEIV1 MOVE 'ORADS01' TO DFHEIV2 MOVE -1
00534              TO DFHEIV11 MOVE ' ' J         ' TO DFHEIV0 CALL 'DFHEI1'
00535              USING DFHEIV0 DFHEIV1 MAP1-AREA DFHEIV98 DFHEIV2 DFHEIV99
00536              DFHEIV99 DFHEIV99 DFHEIV11
00537
00538
00539
00540              GO TO RETURN-FOR-NEXT-ORDER.

00542              DUPLICATE-RECORD.

00544              MOVE 'DUPLICATE -- NOT ACCEPTED' TO MAP1-ERRORS (1).
00545              MOVE -1        TO  MAP1-ORDER-NUMBER-L.
00546              GO TO DISPLAY-ERROR-SCREEN.
```

Fig. 10.3. (Continued)

BYPASS-INPUT SECTION

When data is entered for validation, the operator should have the option to discontinue whatever he is working on and start with a new record. This would normally be done only if he could not resolve a validation error message. Otherwise, he would never be able to get out of the DATA-VALIDATION section and continue the session.

I suggest the use of one or all of the programmer attention (PA) keys for this problem by specifying them in a HANDLE AID command. These keys do not allow terminal data to be transmitted to the terminal input/output area (TIOA) and would result in the MAPFAIL exceptional condition if used with the RECEIVE MAP command. This section does the following:

1. GETMAIN command to secure main storage for the map that will contain the message. This is because CICS/VS will get main storage for the symbolic description map only on a RECEIVE MAP command.

2. SEND MAP command to display the "RECORD BYPASSED–CONTINUE" message.

3. Set the communication area switch for the section that processes a new record.

4. RETURN command to terminate the task.

Note that in a File Add application using a single map, the operator may actually be able to just retype over the current entry without doing a "bypass input" function. However, we still have to specify the PA keys anyway. Therefore, I always use the "bypass-input" function for PA keys on all applications with data validation. And it is also good for the operator to see the message "INPUT BYPASSED —— CONTINUE".

An example of this section is shown in Figure 10.4.

```
    17        ORA)01A        16.16.28      12/27/8)

00548    ***********************************************************
00549    *                                                         *
00550    BYPASS-INPUT SECTION.
00551    *                                                         *
00552    ***********************************************************

00554    *    EXEC CICS
00555    *        GETMAIN
00556    *            SET     (MAP1-POINTER)
00557    *            LENGTH  (958)
00558    *            INITIMG (HEX-ZEROES)
00559    *    END-EXEC.
00560         MOVE 958 TO DFHEIV11 MOVE '        ' TO DFHEIV) CALL 'DFHEI
00561    -    '1' USING DFHEIV) MAP1-POINTER DFHEIV11 HEX-ZEROES.
00562
00563
00564
00565
00566         MOVE 'ORDER BYPASSED - CONTINUE' TO MAP1-ERRORS (1).

00568    *    EXEC CICS
00569    *        SEND MAP    ('ORADM01')
00570    *             MAPSET ('ORADS01')
00571    *             FROM   (MAP1-AREA)
00572    *             ERASE
00573    *    END-EXEC.
00574         MOVE 'ORADMC1' TO DFHEIV1 MOVE 'ORADSC1' TO DFHEIV2 MOVE '
00575    -    '     S    ' TO DFHEIV) CALL 'DFHEI1' USING DFHEIV0
00576         DFHEIV1 MAP1-AREA DFHEIV98 DFHEIV2.
00577
00578
00579
00580         MOVE '1' TO COMMAREA-PROCESS-SW.

00582    *    EXEC CICS
00583    *        RETURN TRANSID (EIBTRNID)
00584    *               COMMAREA (COMMUNICATION-AREA)
00585    *               LENGTH  (1)
00586    *    END-EXEC.
00587         MOVE 1 TO DFHEIV11 MOVE '        ' TO DFHEIV) CALL 'DFHEI1'
00588         USING DFHEIV0 EIBTRNID COMMUNICATION-AREA DFHEIV11.
00589
00590
00591
```

Fig. 10.4. The BYPASS-INPUT section.

WRONG-KEY-USED SECTION

In applications where there is no input data to be bypassed, the PA keys may be of no use. However, we still have to specify them in a HANDLE AID command to display an error message if they are used by the operator. This will avoid the same MAPFAIL exceptional condition mentioned in the previous section. This section does the following:

1. GETMAIN command to secure main storage for the map that will contain the message.
2. SEND MAP command to display the "WRONG-KEY-USED" message.
3. Set the communication area switch for the same section to give the operator the chance to use another key (maybe the ENTER key) to continue where he left off without having to reenter any data.
4. RETURN command to terminate the task.

An example of this section is given in Figure 10.5.

```
12          ORIQ01A          16.10.10          12/27/80

***********************************************************************
*                                                                     *
 WRONG-KEY-USED SECTION.
*                                                                     *
***********************************************************************

*      EXEC CICS
*           GETMAIN
*                SET      (MAP1-POINTER)
*                LENGTH   (970)
*                INITIMG  (HEX-ZEROES)
*      END-EXEC.
        MOVE 970 TO DFHEIV11 MOVE '           ' TO DFHEIV0 CALL 'DFHEI
-      '1' USING DFHEIV0 MAP1-POINTER DFHEIV11 HEX-ZEROES.




       MOVE 'WRONG KEY USED' TO MAP1-ERROR.

*      EXEC CICS
*           SEND MAP      ('ORIQM01')
*                MAPSET   ('ORIQS01')
*                FROM     (MAP1-AREA)
*                DATAONLY
*      END-EXEC.
        MOVE 'ORIQM01' TO DFHEIV1 MOVE 'ORIQS01' TO DFHEIV2 MOVE '
-      '            ' TO DFHEIV0 CALL 'DFHEI1' USING DFHEIV0
        DFHEIV1 MAP1-AREA DFHEIV98 DFHEIV2.



       MOVE '1' TO COMMAREA-PROCESS-SW.

*      EXEC CICS
*           RETURN TRANSID   (EIBTRNID)
*                  COMMAREA  (COMMUNICATION-AREA)
*                  LENGTH    (1)
*      END-EXEC.
        MOVE 1 TO DFHEIV11 MOVE '           ' TO DFHEIV0 CALL 'DFHEI1'
        USING DFHEIV0 EIBTRNID COMMUNICATION-AREA DFHEIV11.
```

Fig. 10.5. The WRONG-KEY-USED section.

11

Terminal Input/Output Commands

INTRODUCTION

The most important commands in CICS/VS programs are the Terminal Input/Output commands because most programs read data entered by the operator and display data for the operator. Besides the HANDLE AID command, there are four other commands that are commonly used for terminal operations. To read the terminal data into the program, the RECEIVE MAP command is used; to display data on a terminal, the SEND MAP command is used; to display an unformatted message (a message that is not part of a map) for the operator, the SEND command is used; to save transmission time in a continuous entry application, the ISSUE ERASE UP command is used.

THE 3270 BUFFER

The most popular terminal used in CICS/VS installations is the 3270-type terminal (3278, 3178, etc.). It belongs to the class of editing terminals with a hardware buffer and extensive editing capabilities which allow the operator to enter formatted data into it even if it is not logically connected to the mainframe (i.e., no task attached to it).

There are two ways to enter data into this buffer. One is when the operator enters something on an unprotected field. The other is when the program transmits data to it via the SEND MAP command.

Data in the buffer will remain until it is erased by a command. One common method is the ERASE operand of the SEND MAP command. Note that task termination will not erase the buffer.

Therefore, in applications where data is entered, the operator, in case errors are detected during editing, only corrects those fields that are in error since those fields that are not will be retransmitted along with the corrections when the operator hits a key like ENTER or any PF key, as long as the buffer is not erased.

MODIFIED DATA TAG (MDT)

Of all the fields in the buffer, the application program is only interested in those defined with a label since they are the ones used in statements in the PROCEDURE DIVISION. CICS/VS monitors these fields (those with labels) by attaching a modified data tag (MDT) to each one. It will read into the symbolic description map only those data where the MDT of the field is "ON".

There are 2 ways to set the MDT "ON". One is when the operator enters something on the field. The other is when the program transmits data to it via the SEND MAP command and the field has the FSET attribute. We will discuss the second way later on.

If the buffer is not erased, the status ("ON" or "OFF") of the MDT of fields will also remain as is, unless the FRSET operand is used in the SEND MAP command.

By using the MDT, CICS/VS keeps transmission time to a minimum since only those fields entered by the operator or selectively chosen via the FSET attribute will be read into the symbolic description map. As you already know, fields like field identifiers, operator messages, etc., are not read into the symbolic description map.

TERMINAL INPUT COMMAND

When the operator hits the ENTER or PF keys on the terminal, Terminal Control transmits data with the modified data tag "ON" into the terminal input/output area (TIOA). On a RECEIVE MAP command, CICS/VS secures main storage for the symbolic description map and moves user data from the TIOA into this area. It will also establish the address of the area to the program so it can be accessed.

The RECEIVE MAP command requires BMS modules, which provide the necessary formatting service for the program to interpret input data streams. BMS in turn uses Terminal Control facilities for data transmission.

The format of the command is:

```
RECEIVE  MAP     ('map name')
         MAPSET  ('mapset name')
         SET     (map-pointer)
```

The map name and mapset name are those specified in the map program. The SET operand specifies the linkage pointer that corresponds to the particular symbolic description map. As mentioned before, the use of linkage pointers to gain access to the corresponding main storage constitutes the locate-mode option and will be the one used in this book.

An example of the RECEIVE MAP command is:

```
RECEIVE  MAP     ('ORCHM01')
         MAPSET  ('ORCHS01')
         SET     (MAP1-POINTER)
```

When this command is executed, CICS/VS secures main storage for the symbolic description map corresponding to MAP1-POINTER and moves data from the TIOA into this storage area where the format of the data is defined in the map program that has the mapset name (label) "ORCHS01" and map name (label) "ORCHM01".

Note the following about this command:

1. It is used only if the task is initiated with the ENTER or any PF key. This command will result in the MAPFAIL exceptional condition if the TIOA contains no data, which is always the case if PA keys are used.
2. The use of the DUMMY entry with FSET attribute in the map program avoids MAPFAIL if the ENTER or PF keys are used and the operator does not enter anything on the field (say, she accidentally hits the ENTER key before entering any data) since this 1-byte entry will then be transmitted to the TIOA.
3. CICS/VS will automatically get main storage for the symbolic description map only if the locate-mode (SET operand and pointer) option is used. Otherwise, it has to have main storage before the command is executed.
4. After completion of the command, the program may already access the data in the symbolic description map if there is no exceptional condition.

TERMINAL OUTPUT COMMAND

To display data on a terminal, the SEND MAP command is used. The command uses BMS modules for formatting output data streams, which in turn uses Terminal Control facilities for data transmission. There are three versions of this command: (1) Display initial information (fields defined with the INITIAL operand in the map program) from the physical map; (2) Display data only from the symbolic description map; (3) combine initial information from the physical map with data from the symbolic description map.

Physical Map Only

In many instances, the programmer just wants to display the screen title, the field identifiers, and any user data defined with an initial value. The operator may then start entering data on the terminal. Since only fields defined with the INITIAL operand in the map program are displayed, we are in fact displaying the physical map. The format of the command is:

```
SEND MAP      ('map name')
     MAPSET   ('mapset name')
     MAPONLY
     ERASE
```

The MAPONLY operand specifies that only fields with initial values from the physical map are to be displayed. The ERASE operand specifies that the previous display on the screen will be erased before the new screen is displayed. This is useful if the previous display is a different map because it prevents mixing of displays that can confuse the operator. It also erases the buffer.

An example of this command is:

```
SEND MAP      ('ORCHM01')
     MAPSET   ('ORCHS01')
     MAPONLY
     ERASE
```

This will erase the previous display and then display all fields defined with the INITIAL operand in the map program with the map name (label) "ORCHM01" and the mapset name (label) "ORCHS01".

Symbolic Description Map Only

Once the screen title, field identifiers, etc. have been displayed on the terminal on a MAPONLY option, we do not have to redisplay them on the next screen display as long as we are still using the same map. Current displays are never erased unless specified in the command. We thus save transmission time.

For instance, in an application with data editing, after the program has displayed the title and field identifiers, the operator starts entering data on the terminal. Once he hits the ENTER key or any PF key, the program may validate the data. If there are no errors, the data will presumably be used to update a file. The next map is then displayed. However, if there are any errors, the program has to display error messages along with what the operator entered so that corrections can be entered. We are in fact only displaying data from the symbolic description map. The format of the command is:

```
SEND MAP        ('map name')
     MAPSET     ('mapset name')
     FROM       (map area)
     DATAONLY
```

The DATAONLY operand specifies that only data from map area (the symbolic description map) is to be displayed. We do not use the ERASE operand, so the original display (title, field identifiers) is not erased.

An example of this command is:

```
SEND MAP        ('ORCHM01')
     MAPSET     ('ORCHS01')
     FROM       (MAP1-AREA)
     DATAONLY
```

All fields from MAP1-AREA where the first byte is not hexadecimal zeroes will be displayed on the terminal. Displayed fields will overlay the corresponding fields in the original display, leaving the rest of the original display untouched, unless the ERASE operand is specified.

MAP1-AREA must have main storage allocated to it before this command is given, otherwise the results are unpredictable. However, a RECEIVE MAP command is generally issued earlier in the task, which obtains the necessary storage area. If not, then the programmer has to secure his own main storage area using the GETMAIN command.

Combined Version

In some applications, the displaying of initial values from the map program (hence from the physical map) is not enough when the map displayed is different from the previous display; the programmer may want to add his own display. For example, in an application involving multiple maps, an important field like record key may have been entered on the first map. But when the second map is displayed, this key will also have to appear for the benefit of the operator. Therefore, the first time the second map is displayed, the programmer will have to mix this field, which should be in the symbolic description map, with the title and field identifiers of a map.

The format of the command is:

```
SEND MAP      ('map name')
     MAPSET   ('mapset name')
     FROM     (map area)
     ERASE
```

Note that we are omitting the MAPONLY and DATAONLY operands. If there is no RECEIVE MAP command earlier in the task for this map, the programmer has to use GETMAIN to secure main storage for the symbolic description map before the command is issued. Again, the ERASE option is used to erase the previous display and the buffer.

Any data in the symbolic description map will override the corresponding data in the physical map, unless the former is hexadecimal zeroes; however, attributes from the physical map will be used before corresponding attributes in the symbolic description map, unless it is hexadecimal zeroes.

Note the following about the SEND MAP command:

1. If the symbolic description map is used, then the FROM operand is always required.

2. If the programmer has to use the GETMAIN command to acquire main storage for the symbolic description map, the INITIMG operand should be specified to set it to hexadecimal zeros. This avoids possible extra displays on the terminal screen since only fields in the symbolic description map with the first byte not equal to hexadecimal zeros will be displayed.

THE 12-BYTE PREFIX FOR THE SYMBOLIC DESCRIPTION MAP

Note the following about this prefix:

1. After the RECEIVE MAP command is executed in a task, do not touch the 12-byte prefix of the symbolic description map because it contains information used by BMS. If you destroy this field, the results are unpredictable in the ensuing SEND MAP command for the same map.

2. However, the GETMAIN command (naturally, this command is not needed if the RECEIVE MAP command was executed for the same map) may include this prefix when the symbolic description map is set to hexadecimal zeros.

THE FSET ATTRIBUTE

The reader has already encountered this attribute as used in the DUMMY field in the map program. It is defined for a field if we want a field not entered by the operator on the current map to be transmitted to the symbolic description map on the RECEIVE MAP command if the ENTER or any PF key is used. The FSET attribute sets "ON" the MDT of a field on the SEND MAP command if the field has a value. We will now explain this concept in more detail.

The FSET attribute works in the following manner:

1. The FSET attribute for a field must either be in the map program or is one of the new attributes when the attributes for the field are modified within the program (see later in this chapter).

2. The field must have a label since we want it read into the symbolic description map.

3. The MDT for the field will be set "ON" and its location in the 3270 buffer will contain the value transmitted if either one of the following occurs:
   a. The field in the map program has the "INITIAL=value" operand and the SEND MAP command uses the physical map.
   b. The first byte of the field in the symbolic description map has a value other than hexadecimal zero and the SEND MAP command uses the symbolic description map.
4. Whenever a task is initiated by the ENTER or any PF key, the RECEIVE MAP command will read into the symbolic description map any field from 3 above, along with other fields entered by the operator. These fields will be reread on any RECEIVE MAP command on succeeding tasks initiated by the ENTER or any PF key, until the buffer is deliberately erased or a new map is used.

When Is FSET Required?

The FSET attribute is required in the following cases:

1. It is used in the DUMMY field in the map program.
2. It is required in a File Update application if the value of a field depends on the value of another field in the same map. After the program reads the record to be updated, the fields are displayed so that the operator can make changes by typing over them. The fields that are so related must have the FSET attribute. If not, only the field modified by the operator will be read into the symbolic description map and the other fields will have values of hexadecimal zeros, even if the display shows a value. The modified field will thus always be validated as an error since the other fields will have no data in the symbolic description map. The alternative of having the operator re-enter all related fields if one of them is modified is quite messy and prone to error.
3. It is required in a File Add application if a document (i.e., a record) requires more than one map for entry. In most cases,

as each map is validated to be correct, the data are temporarily held in a temporary storage record which is then moved to the file record area when the whole record is ready to be written out. Also, we always give the operator, during the entry of a single record, the option to flip back and forth between maps so she may correct entries entered in a previous map. Whenever the operator does so, the corresponding fields in temporary storage are moved to the symbolic description map of the map to be recalled and the map is displayed. Those fields that are mandatory in that map must have the FSET attribute. The reason is that in File Add applications, certain fields are mandatory (they have to have valid values) before the record may be written out as valid.

When Is FSET Neutral?

In a File Add application with only one map, it does not matter whether a labeled, unprotected field is defined as FSET or not. The field will only have the MDT "ON" if entered by the operator.

When Is FSET Bad?

In a File Update application, any labeled, unprotected, nonmandatory field (one that is not required to complete the entry) that does not depend for validation on other fields (that is, it is validated by itself) should not have the FSET attribute. We only want this field to go to the symbolic description map for validation if it is actually modified by the operator. If it has the FSET attribute, it will be transmitted unnecessarily, and while the program should work correctly, this reduces efficiency.

MODIFYING ATTRIBUTES

The attributes of fields (whether protected, of bright intensity, etc.) are generally those coming from the physical map as defined in the map program. For maps defined with MODE=INOUT, the programmer has the option to change the attributes from those specified in the map program. One instance occurs in a map that is used for file update: The operator enters the record key and it is verified correct.

When the data from the record is displayed on the same map, the record key is also included for the benefit of the operator. And since we do not want him to be able to modify this field now, the programmer should change the attribute from unprotected to protected.

This is done by moving a value to the attribute byte of the field in the symbolic description map. The specific value is taken from the standard attribute list as in Figure 5.3.

The programmer should understand that there is only one byte to represent the attributes of a field on any modification. The new attributes will completely replace the old ones.

Suppose the record key mentioned is defined as unprotected, numeric, and bright, and we want to modify this to autoskip and bright. We check Fig. 5.3 and verify that the dataname ATTR-PROT-ASKIP-BRT-PEN means autoskip (PROT being included in ASKIP), bright, and pen detectible (this extra attribute will just be ignored). Each field defined with a label (and thus having entries in the symbolic description map) actually has a halfword binary length field, a one-byte attribute field, and the actual field itself. The record key field may be represented in the symbolic description map as:

```
.....
.....
05  MAP1-RECORD-KEY-L         PIC S9999 COMP.
05  MAP1-RECORD-KEY-A         PIC X.
05  MAP1-RECORD-KEY           PIC 9(6).
.....
.....
```

The process of changing the attributes in the program is illustrated in Figure 11.1.

The attributes of MAP1-RECORD-KEY are originally defined in the map program. These are modified by the programmer before the SEND MAP command with the DATAONLY option. As we mentioned before, if the physical map is used, its attributes will be used over any programmer-designated attribute in the symbolic description map. These modified attributes will be the new attributes until they are modified again or until the physical map is redisplayed as either the physical map only version or the combined version of the SEND MAP command.

```
.....
RECEIVE MAP command.
.....
.....
MOVE ATTR-PROT-ASKIP-BRT-PEN TO MAP1-RECORD-KEY-A.
.....
.....
SEND MAP command (DATAONLY option).
.....
.....
RETURN command (task terminates).
```

Fig. 11.1. Modifying Attributes.

After Figure 11.1 is executed, the record key entered by the operator will still show brightly on the screen, but it can not be changed anymore.

SYMBOLIC CURSOR POSITIONING TECHNIQUE

Every time a map is displayed on a screen, the field where the cursor is initially positioned may be controlled in two ways. The choice will always be that field that the operator enters or changes first.

When a new map is being displayed, the programmer generally knows the first field that may be entered or changed by the operator. He specifies this field with the IC operand in the map program.

However, in a map defined with MODE=INOUT, there are two reasons why the programmer has to control the initial position of the cursor every time the same map is redisplayed: (1) The IC operand is effective only when the physical map is included in the display. Thus, on successive displays of the same map (DATAONLY option), the cursor will be positioned at the start of the map (as specified by the LINE and COLUMN operands, else 1, 1 is the default). (2) An INOUT map is generally used interactively. The operator enters a set of data that is validated and redisplayed on the screen in a series of steps.

In a series of terminal inputs and outputs that validate data entered, it is always best to place the cursor on the next display, in case of errors, under the first field validated as an error. This will generally be the first field to be corrected by the operator. For instance, if the operator enters 20 fields and the first error detected was the fourth field entered, then the cursor should be placed under this field on the next display of the map. If the operator enters corrections and on the next display it is now the 15th field that is the first error, then the cursor will be placed under the 15th field.

The cursor can be placed under a specific field by using the symbolic cursor positioning technique. In this method, -1 is moved to the length field of that field in the symbolic description map and then specifying the CURSOR operand in the SEND MAP command.

For instance, assume that this is part of a symbolic description map:

```
01      MAP1-AREA.
        .....
        .....
        05  MAP1-NAME-L          PIC  S9999 COMP.
        05  MAP1-NAME-A          PIC  X.
        05  MAP1-NAME            PIC  X (30).
        .....
        .....
```

A typical use of the cursor positioning technique in an application is shown in Figure 11.2.

```
....
RECEIVE MAP command.
.....
.....
MOVE -1  TO MAP1-NAME-L.
.....
.....
EXEC CICS
         SEND MAP      ('ORCHM01')
              MAPSET   ('ORCHS01')
              FROM     (MAP1-AREA)
              DATAONLY
              CURSOR
END-EXEC.
.....
.....
RETURN command (task terminates).
```

Fig. 11.2. Symbolic Cursor Positioning Technique.

When the SEND MAP command is executed, the CURSOR operand will cause the cursor to be placed under the field whose length field was set to -1. In this case, the field is MAP1-NAME. If we are using the combined version of the SEND MAP command, the symbolic cursor positioning technique will override the insert cursor (IC) specification in the map program.

The technique of cursor positioning may be combined with the technique of modifying attributes. For instance, on page 155 we mentioned a map where we change the attributes of the record key. Presumably, the programmer has specified the IC operand for the record key field in the map program so the cursor will fall under this field when the physical map is first displayed.

However, when the attributes are changed on the next display of the screen so the record key can no longer be modified by the operator, it is necessary to position the cursor on the next unprotected field that follows the record key. Assuming that MAP1-NAME is the next unprotected field, the procedure is given by Figure 11.3.

```
.....
RECEIVE MAP command.
.....
.....
MOVE ATTR-PROT-ASKIP-BRT-PEN TO MAP1-RECORD-KEY-A.
MOVE -1 TO MAP1-NAME-L.
EXEC CICS
        SEND MAP      ('ORCHM01')
             MAPSET   ('ORCHS01')
             FROM     (MAP1-AREA)
             DATAONLY
             CURSOR
END-EXEC.
.....
.....
RETURN command (task terminates).
```

Fig. 11.3. Modifying Attributes and Symbolic Cursor Positioning.

After the procedure in Figure 11.3 is executed, the attributes of the field MAP1-RECORD-KEY are changed and the cursor is positioned under the field MAP1-NAME.

UNFORMATTED MESSAGE

An unformatted message is one that is displayed on a screen but is not part of a map. Thus, the programmer does not have to have a map program to display the message. This is useful for messages sent to the operator when the session is terminated, either normally by the operator, or abnormally, as when a major error occurs on the execution of a command.

The format of the command is:

```
SEND FROM   (message area)
     LENGTH (message length)
     ERASE
```

This command will display, starting at line 1, column 1 of the terminal, as many bytes of message area depending on the message length. ERASE is optional but is usually specified so that the previous display is erased.

For instance, to display the appropriate message when the operator terminates the job, we can code:

```
MOVE JOB-NORMAL-END-MESSAGE TO TWA-OPERATOR-MESSAGE.
EXEC CICS
     SEND FROM   (TWA-OPERATOR-MESSAGE)
          LENGTH (31)
          ERASE
END-EXEC.
```

ISSUE ERASEAUP

In certain applications, the operator may enter data on a terminal that can be used, after validation, to update an on-line file and/or generate journal records. The SEND MAP* command with the ERASE operand is then used on a successful entry to enable the operator to enter the next set of data.

*Usually with the MAPONLY option.

If the next map required is actually the same as the map being displayed, then we would actually be retransmitting fields like the title, the field identifiers, etc., which are already in the current map. The ISSUE ERASEAUP command avoids this retransmission by erasing all user-entered (unprotected) fields on the terminal and setting their modified data tags to "OFF". The operator may then continue entering the next set of data. This command is especially helpful if the terminals are at remote sites where transmission speeds (through modems) are slower than usual.

The format of this command is:

ISSUE ERASEAUP

There is, however, one limitation with the ISSUE ERASEAUP command. Since only unprotected fields are erased and message areas are defined as autoskip, the last set of error messages will remain on the screen, thus confusing the operator. The programmer may go around this problem by defining the message fields as unprotected (instead of the usual autoskip) so that they are erased along with the other unprotected fields on the ISSUE ERASEAUP command. But the problem is that the operator may inadvertently enter data on these fields.

Otherwise, I suggest that we redisplay the physical map instead of using ISSUE ERASEAUP to ensure a prompting message to the operator.

In spite of this, there are four reasons for using the ISSUE ERASEAUP command:

1. A large portion of the display consists of protected fields, with a corresponding large potential for savings.
2. Remote terminals are being used.
3. The application is heavily used.
4. There is an urgent need to save transmission time because the increase in response time is significant to the installation.

12

File Control Commands

INTRODUCTION

CICS/VS supports VSAM (virtual storage access method), ISAM (indexed sequential access method), and DAM (direct access method). This book, however, will show only operations on a VSAM file since it is the one used in the program examples. If the reader is interested in using ISAM or DAM files, he should refer to a regular CICS/VS manual. He will notice that the commands are very similar.

ON-LINE FILES

Application programs work with on-line files and the programmer should know the following about them:

1. If a new file (new to CICS/VS, not the application program) will be used:
   a. The file must have an entry in the File Control Table (FCT). Part of the entry is the type of file, the file identifier, the format of the record(s), the action permitted (add, update, delete, browse, etc.), etc.
   b. The file cluster must be catalogued.
   c. If the file is used for update, it cannot be empty. One solution is to generate a dummy record with low values.
2. If an application program uses an old file:
   a. Check that the action to be done on the file (add, update, delete, browse, etc.) is permitted as defined in the FCT.
   b. If not, modify the FCT and reload it.

File Opening/Closing

These are the details in the opening and closing of a file:

1. Such opening and closing are not done by the application program.
2. A file that is extensively used by many applications (say, a table), is best opened automatically at CICS/VS initialization and closed automatically at CICS/VS termination. The systems programmer will set up the CICS/VS job steps to include these required functions.
3. A file that is used only in an application is generally opened and closed by the lead operator. It is opened before the first use of the application during the day, but after CICS/VS initialization. It is closed after the last use of the application during the day, but before CICS/VS termination. However, if there is a large gap between uses of the application during a day, for reasons of security, the file is generally closed between the gaps of use and just opened when the application is again needed. The systems programmer sets up the facility to open and close the file using transaction identifiers similar in format to those used in starting applications. These however use special macros available under CICS/VS.

ALTERNATE INDEXES

CICS/VS gives the application programmer the facility to have alternate indexes (also known as secondary indexes) for VSAM files so an operator may do a read on or a browse through a file using keys independent of the primary key. For instance, a Purchase Order file may have a primary index based on the order number but may also have an alternate index based on the date of the order. The operator may then have the option of displaying a specific record using either the order number or the date of order or of using any of two browse programs, one using the order number to scan records in order number sequence, and another using the date of order to scan records in date of order sequence.

CICS/VS automatically maintains these indexes on a command that adds, updates, or deletes records.

A browse based on an alternate key is shown in the program example in Chapter 23.

FILE SERVICES

CICS/VS provides the application programmer with the facility to access on-line files using commands in the PROCEDURE DIVISION. Once a file has been opened, he may request a service any time he wants. The commands that provide the services are:

1. READ. Read a record from a file.
2. WRITE. Write a new record into a file.
3. REWRITE. Update an existing record in a file.
4. DELETE (VSAM only). Delete a single record or a group of records from a key-sequenced file.
5. UNLOCK. Release exclusive control over a record or a group of records.
6. STARTBR. Specify the starting point of a browse operation.
7. READNEXT. Read the next record in a file during a browse.
8. READPREV (VSAM only). Read the previous record in a file during a browse.
9. RESETBR. Reset the starting point of a browse.
10. ENDBR. End a browse.

READING INPUT RECORDS

The most common method for getting an input record is to read a specific record. The command for reading a specific record is:

```
read dataset ('file identifier')
     set     (file-pointer)
     ridfld  (data area)
```

The DATASET operand specifies the file identifier of the file in the File Control Table. If the RIDFLD operand specifies an alternate key, then the file identifier corresponds to that of the alternate index. The SET operand specifies the linkage pointer that points to the file record description in the LINKAGE section. The RIDFLD operand specifies the data area that contains the record identification field (key of the record, a relative byte address, or a relative record number).

An example of this command is:

```
MOVE  MAP1-RECORD-KEY TO TWA-RECORD-KEY.
EXEC  CICS
        READ DATASET  ('POMAST')
             SET      (POMAST-POINTER)
             RIDFLD   (TWA-RECORD-KEY)
END-EXEC.
```

When the read command is executed, CICS/VS gets main storage for the file record description pointed to by POMAST-POINTER. Then, using the key equal to that contained in TWA-RECORD-KEY, CICS/VS moves the record from the file 'POMAST' to this storage area. The key value is set to what the operator presumably entered on the terminal (as MAP1-RECORD-KEY).

As another example, it is also possible to read a record using a generic key, that is, only part of the key will be used. The command may be coded as:

```
read dataset    ('file identifier')
     set        (file-pointer)
     ridfld     (data area)
     generic
     keylength  (numeric literal)
     gteq
```

The DATASET operand specifies the file identifier of the file in the File Control Table. The SET operand specifies the linkage pointer that points to the file record description in the LINKAGE section. The RIDFLD operand specifies the data area that contains the record identification field (the generic key). The GENERIC operand specifies that we will be using only part of the key. The KEYLENGTH operand specifies the length of the generic key. And the GTEQ operand is optional and specifies that if the record cannot be found using the key (in this case generic), the next record will be used.

An example of this command is:

```
MOVE MAP1-RECORD-KEY TO TWA-RECORD-KEY.
EXEC CICS
     READ DATASET      ('POMAST')
          SET          (POMAST-POINTER)
          RIDFLD       (TWA-RECORD-KEY)
          GENERIC
          KEYLENGTH    (5)
          GTEQ
END-EXEC.
```

When this command is executed, CICS/VS gets main storage for the file record description pointed to by POMAST-POINTER. Then it moves the first record from the file 'POMAST', whose first 5 bytes of the key are equal to or greater than the first 5 bytes of the value contained in TWA-RECORD-KEY, to this storage area.

The GTEQ opernad is optional and is specified only if the programmer wants to get the first record with a higher key in case the record being requested is not in the file. Otherwise, the NOTFND exceptional condition occurs.

Reading For Update

For a record that will be updated or deleted (VSAM only) after it has been read, the UPDATE option must be specified. That record may then be rewritten or deleted.

CICS/VS will secure exclusive control of the record (ISAM) or of the whole block where the record belongs (DAM), or of the control interval where the record resides (VSAM), so that nobody else (that is, no other task) can access the same record or control interval until the record is rewritten, deleted (VSAM only), the program executes the UNLOCK command, or the task terminates. This makes sure that no one else will modify or delete the same record until the operator either finishes modifying it, deletes it, or no longer needs it.

Exceptional Conditions

Of the many conditions that may occur on a READ command, the programmer should code two, and may code a third, in a HANDLE

CONDITION command: NOTOPEN, NOTFND, and DUPKEY. The NOTOPEN condition should be specified to execute a paragraph in the ABNORMAL-TERMINATION section that displays a message and aborts the session. This condition should in fact always be specified for all commands for file access.

The NOTFND condition should likewise be coded to take care of the condition when a record is not in the file. Generally, this will not abort the session; for instance, in an inquiry or update application, the message that the record is not in the file should be displayed for the operator. He may then correct the record key or enter a new one.

If the READ command is using an alternate key, then the DUPKEY condition should likewise be coded because alternate keys generally have duplicates. Like NOTFND, this should not abort the session.

Other conditions should rarely, if ever, happen. Therefore, the programmer should not bother coding these conditions but instead allow them to be covered by the ERROR condition, which is the catchall condition.

WRITING OUTPUT RECORDS

Adding New Records

We use the WRITE command to add new records to an existing file. The command is:

```
write dataset   ('file identifier')
      from      (file-area)
      ridfld    (data area)
      length    (data value)
```

The DATASET operand specifies the file identifier of the file in the File Control Table. The FROM operand specifies the file record description in the LINKAGE section. The RIDFLD operand specifies the data area that contains the record identification field (key of the record). The LENGTH operand is optional for fixed-length records when the file record description is of the correct size (generally, it is) but it is required for a variable-length record. This may be a numeric literal or a data area.

An example of this command is:

```
COMPUTE TWA-RECORD-LENGTH = 60 + 15 * NUMBER-OF-STORES.
EXEC CICS
       WRITE DATASET  ('POMAST')
             FROM     (POMAST-AREA)
             RIDFLD   (TWA-RECORD-KEY)
             LENGTH   (TWA-RECORD-LENGTH)
END-EXEC.
```

When the WRITE command is executed, CICS/VS will add into the file 'POMAST' a record with the data coming from POMAST-AREA and position it in the file according to the value of TWA-RECORD-KEY. The length of the record added (we assume a variable-length record) is contained in TWA-RECORD-LENGTH as computed before the WRITE command. Naturally, for fixed-length records, the LENGTH operand of the WRITE command and the COMPUTE statement used to compute the record length are not needed.

Securing Storage For The File Record Description

In the READ command, CICS/VS will automatically secure main storage for the file record description. This is not the case for the WRITE command because main storage must already be available for the file record description so that the record can be built up before the (WRITE) command. The programmer will have to use a GETMAIN command to secure an area large enough to contain the largest record to be written out.

The programmer may release the storage area acquired by using the FREEMAIN command when the WRITE command is finished or else let the task release the storage area when it terminates. It is more efficient for the programmer to release storage he has acquired when it is no longer required and the task is not yet about to be terminated.

Exceptional Conditions

Of the many conditions that may occur on a WRITE command, the programmer should code two in a HANDLE CONDITION command: NOTOPEN and DUPREC. The NOTOPEN condition should be specified to execute a paragraph in the ABNORMAL-TERMINATION section to display a message and abort the session. This condition should in fact always be specified for all commands for file access.

The DUPREC condition should likewise be coded to take care of the condition when the key of the record to be added to the file matches that of an existing record. A message should then be displayed for the operator, but the session should not be terminated.

Other conditions should rarely, if ever, happen. Therefore, the programmer should not bother coding these conditions but instead allow them to be covered by the ERROR condition, which is the catchall condition.

UPDATING EXISTING RECORDS

The REWRITE Command

The REWRITE command is used for rewriting (presumably after changes are made) records that were read in the same task, and thus is used to update existing records. The format of the command is:

```
rewrite  dataset   ('file identifier')
         from      (file-area)
         length    (data value)
```

The DATASET operand specifies the file identifier of the file in the File Control Table. The FROM operand specifies the file record description in the LINKAGE section. The LENGTH operand is optional for fixed-length records when the file record description is of the correct size (generally, it is), but is required for a variable-length record. This may be a numeric literal or a data area.

An example of this command is:

```
EXEC CICS
        READ DATASET  ('POMAST')
             SET      (POMAST-POINTER)
             RIDFLD   (TWA-RECORD-KEY)
             UPDATE
END-EXEC.
.....
```

```
.....
COMPUTE TWA-RECORD-LENGTH = 60 + 15 * NUMBER-OF-STORES.
EXEC CICS
        REWRITE DATASET  ('POMAST')
                FROM     (POMAST-AREA)
                LENGTH   (TWA-RECORD-LENGTH)
END-EXEC.
```

When the REWRITE command is executed, CICS/VS will rewrite into the file 'POMAST' the record in POMAST-AREA with the same RIDFLD field used in the previous READ with UPDATE option that secured the record. The LENGTH operand specifies the length (in bytes) of the rewritten record.

Exclusive Control

As we mentioned before, any record to be updated must be initially read with the UPDATE operand. When this is executed, CICS/VS secures the record for the programmer (if it is in the file) and then gets exclusive control of the record (ISAM), the whole block (DAM), or the whole control interval that contains the record (VSAM).

After CICS/VS gets exclusive control for VSAM files, an attempt by another task to use the same control interval before exclusive control is released (by the REWRITE, UNLOCK, or DELETE commands, or when the original task terminates) will cause the second task to go into a wait until exclusive control is released. If the same task does it, an INVREQ condition occurs.

Exceptional Conditions

There is no need to specify error conditions for this command because they will be covered by the corresponding READ for update command.

DELETING EXISTING RECORDS

Only for VSAM files can the programmer delete records in the file. He may choose to delete the record(s) immediately or to delete each record after it is read (he may want to sight verify if this is indeed the record to be deleted).

Immediate Delete

To delete a VSAM record or group of records without reading the record first, the command is:

```
delete dataset    ('file identifier')
       ridfld     (data area)
       keylength  (data value)
       generic
```

The DATASET operand specifies the file identifier of the file in the File Control Table. The RIDFLD operand specifies the data area that contains the record identification field (key of the record, a relative byte address, or a relative record number). The KEYLENGTH operand is mandatory if GENERIC is specified. It specifies the length of the generic key used. The GENERIC operand is optional and specifies that we are deleting a group of records.

An example of this command is:

```
EXEC CICS
     DELETE DATASET     ('POMAST')
            RIDFLD      (TWA-RECORD-KEY)
END-EXEC.
```

This command will delete the specific record whose key is equal to that specified in TWA-RECORD-KEY.

Another example of the command is:

```
EXEC CICS
     DELETE DATASET    ('POMAST')
            RIDFLD     (TWA-RECORD-KEY)
            KEYLENGTH (5)
            GENERIC
END-EXEC.
```

This command will delete the group of records whose first 5 bytes of the key equals the value in TWA-RECORD-KEY.

Delete After Read

The programmer may also delete a specific record after the record has been read for update. The format of the command is similar to that of immediate delete but with the RIDFLD operand omitted since this is the same one specified in the READ for update command. An example is:

```
EXEC  CICS
        READ  DATASET      ('POMAST')
              SET          (POMAST-POINTER)
              RIDFLD       (TWA-RECORD-KEY)
              UPDATE
END-EXEC.
. . . . . . .
. . . . . . .
EXEC  CICS
        DELETE DATASET     ('POMAST')
END-EXEC.
```

Exceptional Conditions

Whether the programmer opts for an immediate delete or does a READ for update first, there should be two conditions specified in a HANDLE CONDITION command, NOTOPEN and NOTFND. The reasons are similar to those mentioned on page 165.

RELEASING EXCLUSIVE CONTROL

For a record read with the UPDATE operand, CICS/VS will secure exclusive control so that the record (along with the whole control interval or the whole block, as the case may be) can not be accessed until it has been updated, deleted (VSAM only), or the task has ended. If, however, the record will not be updated or deleted after all and the task is not about to end, the programmer should release exclusive control so the record can be accessed by other tasks. This is done by using the UNLOCK command, and the format is:

```
unlock dataset ('file identifier')
```

An example of this command is:

```
EXEC CICS
        READ DATASET    ('POMAST')
             SET        (POMAST-POINTER)
             RIDFLD     (TWA-RECORD-KEY)
             UPDATE
END-EXEC.
.......
.......
EXEC CICS
        UNLOCK DATASET   ('POMAST')
END-EXEC.
```

After the unlock command is executed, the record (along with the whole control interval or the whole block, as the case may be) can then be accessed.

Exceptional Conditions

There is no need to specify exceptional conditions for this command because they will be covered by the corresponding READ for UPDATE command.

FILE BROWSE

In many instances where the operator wants to recall previously entered information, he simply enters the record identifier and the program uses this to get the corresponding record in the file and display it. This is known as the inquiry function. However, if the exact record identifier is not known, but can be approximated, then a browse application can be used to pinpoint the record.

In the browse application, the operator enters the approximate record identifier and this is used as the starting point of a search of the file index. By using a single key (the PF1 key is usually used), the operator can continuously scan forward through the file, in ascending sequence, without having to enter another record identifier. With another key (usually the PF2 key is used), he can do it in descending sequence (VSAM file only).

A browse can also be used when there is a need to know which records belong to a particular alternate key value. For instance, in a Purchase Order file with the date of order as an alternate key, there may be a need to see which orders were made on a specific date.

Since CICS/VS maintains pointers to records only within a task, the browse commands require that the task not be terminated for the whole browse session. Thus, this is the only application in CICS/VS where the design has to be pure conversational, not pseudoconversational.

However, this should not degrade the response time for the installation very much for two reasons: First, a browse application should be used rarely and avoided if possible. Secondly, browse applications are often used only for a short time because they are generally written so that only record summaries (but including the exact record identifier) are displayed, allowing many records to be displayed at the same time. Once the required record can be determined from the display, the operator may then terminate the browse and go to a regular inquiry, using the record identifier displayed at the browse to get the complete display of the record.

The application programmer can actually write a browse application using the pseudoconversational mode of processing. He can maintain the pointers to records in between task initiation and termination, but he can not use some of the powerful features available through the CICS/VS browse commands.

The browse function allows an operator to display a series of records singly or as a group. He has the option of starting the browse at any specific record in the file, reading the records in ascending sequence, reading them in descending sequence (VSAM only), restarting the browse at some other record, and terminating the browse.

Browse Starting Point

The STARTBR command specifies the starting point (but does not retrieve the record) of the browse and is usually based on a value entered by the operator. The format of the command is:

```
startbr dataset      ('file identifier')
        ridfld       (data area)
        keylength    (data value)
        generic
        gteq
```

The DATASET operand specifies the file identifier of the file in the File Control Table. If the RIDFLD operand specifies an alternate key, then the file identifier corresponds to that of the alternate index. The RIDFLD operand specifies the data area that contains the record identification field (key of the record, a relative byte address, or a relative record number). The KEYLENGTH operand is mandatory if GENERIC is specified and specifies the length of the generic key used. The GENERIC operand is optional and specifies that we are using a generic key. The GTEQ operand is optional but is generally specified to select the next higher record in case the record specified does not exist (otherwise a NOTFND exceptional condition occurs).

An example of this command is:

```
EXEC CICS
        STARTBR DATASET   ('POMAST')
                RIDFLD    (TWA-RECORD-KEY)
                GTEQ
END-EXEC.
```

When this command is executed, the browse starting point is at the record whose record identification field is equal to the value in TWA-RECORD-KEY or, if there is no such record, the next higher record. If TWA-RECORD-KEY is equal to HIGH-VALUES, then the end of the file is the starting point. A READPREV command will then retrieve the last record in the file.

Exceptional Conditions for STARTBR

The programmer should code the NOTOPEN and NOTFND exceptional conditions in a HANDLE CONDITION command. As we mentioned before, the NOTOPEN condition is always specified for applications that use files; the NOTFND condition is used to display an error message in case the record specified does not exist or, in case

GTEQ is specified, the starting record number is higher than the last record in the file. The NOTFND condition will not occur if RIDFLD specifies a field equal to HIGH-VALUES even if there is no such record.

Browse in Ascending Sequence

The READNEXT command is used to retrieve records in a forward sequence. It is used in the following ways: First, it will retrieve the record specified in the STARTBR or RESETBR command if they were the previous File Control command. Second, it will retrieve the next record in ascending sequence if the previous File Control command is another READNEXT or a READPREV (VSAM only). Third, for VSAM files, it can be used to skip forward to read a record beyond the next higher record in ascending sequence.

The format of the command is:

```
readnext dataset   ('file identifier')
         set       (file-pointer)
         ridfld    (data area)
```

The DATASET operand specifies the file identifier of the file in the File Control Table. If the RIDFLD operand specifies an alternate key, then the file identifier corresponds to that of the alternate index. The SET operand specifies the linkage pointer that points to the file record description in the LINKAGE section. The RIDFLD operand specifies the data area that contains the record identification field (key of the record, a relative byte address, or a relative record number).

An example of this command is:

```
EXEC CICS
        READNEXT DATASET   ('POMAST')
                 SET       (POM-POINTER)
                 RIDFLD    (TWA-RECORD-KEY)
END-EXEC.
```

When this command is executed, a record is retrieved and TWA-RECORD-KEY will be set to the record identification field of the record.

If this command follows a READPREV command and we have not done a skip forward browse or a RESETBR command has not been executed in between, then the same record retrieved by the READPREV command will be retrieved by the READNEXT command. In this case, the programmer should do another READNEXT.

Skip Forward Browse

We mentioned before that the READNEXT command may be used right after a STARTBR or RESETBR command or right after another READNEXT or a READPREV command. A third use is for a skip forward browse, where the operator still retrieves the record in ascending sequence but skips records. In this technique, the operator enters a new record identification field corresponding to the next record to be retrieved, and this will be used on the READNEXT command to retrieve the next record required.

Exceptional Conditions for READNEXT

The programmer should code the NOTFND and ENDFILE exceptional conditions in a HANDLE CONDITION command. NOTFND is used in case the operator opts for the skip forward browse and the record cannot be found.* ENDFILE is used if, during normal browse in ascending sequence, the end of the file is reached. For both conditions, the message "END OF FILE" should be displayed to the operator to guide him in deciding what to do next.

If the browse is being made by using an alternate key, the DUPKEY exceptional condition should likewise be coded in case there are records with duplicate alternate keys; this condition occurs for all records retrieved in a set of duplicates, except the last one.

Browse in Descending Sequence

The READPREV command (VSAM only) retrieves records in descending sequence. The format is:

---

*Since most browses specify the GTEQ operand for STARTBR and RESETBR, this will happen only if the record required is beyond the end of the file.

```
readprev dataset   ('file identifier')
         set       (file-pointer)
         ridfld    (data area)
```

The DATASET operand specifies the file identifier of the file in the File Control Table. If the RIDFLD operand specifies an alternate key, then the file identifier corresponds to that of the alternate index. The SET operand specifies the linkage pointer that points to the file record description in the LINKAGE section. The RIDFLD operand specifies the data area that contains the record identification field (key of the record, a relative byte address, or a relative record number).

An example of this command is:

```
EXEC CICS
     READPREV DATASET   ('POMAST')
              SET       (POM-POINTER)
              RIDFLD    (TWA-RECORD-KEY)
END-EXEC.
```

When this command is executed, the record next in descending sequence is retrieved. TWA-RECORD-KEY will be set to the value of the record retrieved.

If this command follows a READNEXT command, then the very same records are retrieved for both commands. In this case, the programmer should do another READPREV.

Skip Backward Browse

There is no command to do a skip backward browse. If the operator wants to retrieve, in descending sequence, a record beyond the next record, he will have to enter a new record identification field, which will then be used for a RESETBR command, followed by a READNEXT command.

Exceptional Conditions for READPREV

The programmer should code the ENDFILE exceptional condition in a HANDLE CONDITION command. This is used if, during a browse in descending sequence, the end of the file is reached. The message "END OF FILE" should then be displayed to the operator to guide him in deciding what to do next.

If the GTEQ operand is specified in the STARTBR or RESETBR command (generally it is), then the NOTFND exceptional condition need not be coded since this will never happen.

If the browse is being made with the use of an alternate index, the DUPKEY exceptional condition should likewise be coded; in case of records with duplicate alternate keys, this error occurs for all records retrieved except for the last duplicate. Also, in case of duplicates, the records will be retrieved in the order they were added to the file and not in the reverse order.

Reset the Browse Starting Point

The RESETBR command resets the starting point of the browse (but does not retrieve the record) and is usually based on a value entered by the operator. The format is:

```
resetbr dataset     ('file identifier')
        ridfld      (data area)
        keylength   (data value)
        generic
        gteq
```

The DATASET operand specifies the file identifier of the file in the File Control Table. If the RIDFLD operand specifies an alternate key, then the file identifier corresponds to that of the alternate index. The RIDFLD operand specifies the data area that contains the record identification field (key of the record, a relative byte address, or a relative recored record number). The KEYLENGTH operand is mandatory if GENERIC is specified and specifies the length of the generic key used. The GENERIC operand is optional and specifies that we are using a generic key. The GTEQ operand is optional but is generally specified to select the next higher record in case the record specified does not exist (otherwise a NOTFND exceptional condition occurs).

An example of this command is:

```
EXEC CICS
        RESETBR DATASET    ('POMAST')
                RIDFLD     (TWA-RECORD-KEY)
                GTEQ
END-EXEC.
```

When this command is executed, the browse starting point is reset to the value of TWA-RECORD-KEY, or if there is no such record, the next higher record. If TWA-RECORD-KEY is equal to HIGH-VALUES, then the end of the file is the starting point. A READPREV command will then retrieve the last record in the file.

Exceptional Conditions for RESETBR

The same exceptional conditions as for STARTBR should be specified.

Ending the Browse

The ENDBR command is used to end the browse function. The format of the command is:

endbr dataset ('file identifier')

Exceptional Conditions for ENDBR

There are no exceptional conditions specified for this command.

13

Temporary Storage Commands

INTRODUCTION

When a task is terminated, all data corresponding to it is lost. This includes data in working storage, data areas defined in the LINKAGE section, etc. However, on the next task initiation, the program may read back (and thus recover) some of these lost data. Examples are data in a terminal buffer (if the buffer has not been erased), records from files, etc.

Still, there are always some data, not present in a terminal buffer, file record, etc., that are needed by the program on the next task initiation. An example is a counter which contains a value that will be used on the next task. CICS/VS gives the programmer several options to save these type of data and the most common one is the use of temporary storage.

TEMPORARY STORAGE

Temporary storage is a facility that is implemented by CICS/VS as a VSAM file. The program may think of it as an all-purpose VSAM file with variable records (called items). However, it is not a file created for a specific application and therefore the programmer does not have an entry for it in the File Control Table (FCT) nor does he worry about opening or closing it. All he does is define an area for it in the LINKAGE section, with the corresponding pointer, then issue the proper command whenever he wants to write a new record or read, modify, or delete an old record.

Queues

Temporary storage records are maintained in queues with each queue having a unique queue identification code chosen by the programmer.

This code is from one to eight bytes long. There may be multiple records with the same code, in which case a specific record is identified by the ITEM operand of the command. However, in many cases when a program uses temporary storage, it generally uses only one record. This saves overhead compared to one where multiple records are maintained.

The installation should standardize the selection of the queue identification code so no unauthorized task can access or delete records belonging to somebody else.

Auxiliary Storage (Disk) or Main Storage

The programmer may actually choose to use main storage instead of auxiliary storage (magnetic disk) to save records. A good guide is if the combined length of the data is more than 300 bytes long or there is a gap of at least one second from the time it is saved by a task to the time it is required by another task, it is best to save such data in temporary storage on magnetic disk.

Conversely, if the combined length of the data is short and there is practically no gap from the time it is saved to the time it is required by another task, the programmer may use main storage instead to eliminate the overhead in writing and reading temporary storage records.

Except for the operands AUXILIARY (magnetic disk, which is the default) or MAIN (which is mandatory if main storage is used instead), the commands are identical no matter which option the programmer chooses. Even if he chooses main storage, records are still maintained as if they were file records (that is, they may be written out, read, updated, or deleted).

Managing Temporary Storage Records

The following are guidelines in managing temporary storage records:

1. A temporary storage record is saved by writing it or rewriting it before the task is terminated.

2. Whenever a task requires data from a temporary storage record, it must be read within that task.

3. Whenever an old temporary storage record must be saved in its modified version, it must be rewritten within the task (naturally, it is read earlier in the same task).
4. Whenever an old temporary storage queue (consisting of one or more records) is no longer needed, it may be deleted. All records with the same queue identification code are deleted in the same command. There is no command to delete individual records in a queue.

Uses of Temporary Storage

There are two common uses of temporary storage:

1. As a scratch pad in the pseudoconversational mode of processing:
   a. The record is created (written out) in the INITIALIZATION section.
   b. It is deleted at the FINALIZATION section.
   c. To make the queue identification code unique, it is usually a combination of the terminal identifier and the transaction identifier.
   d. It uses auxiliary storage.
2. Suspend data set. In a data collection application, where there is a possibility of the application being suspended so the operator can switch to a higher-priority application, the incomplete data may be written out to temporary storage. After the higher-priority application is finished, the data collection application may then be continued, and all data already written out previously in temporary storage will just be recalled.

There are three commands used for temporary storage. The WRITEQ TS command writes or rewrites one record into a queue, the READQ TS command reads a particular record from a queue, and the DELETEQ TS command deletes the whole queue.

WRITING A NEW RECORD INTO A QUEUE

When a task has completed building up the temporary storage record to be used by another task, it is written out before the task terminates. The format of the command is:

```
writeq ts
       from     (data area)
       queue    (symbolic name)
       length   (data value)
       item     (data area)
       main or auxiliary
```

The FROM operand specifies the main storage area to be written out. The QUEUE operand specifies the queue identification code of the queue. The LENGTH operand specifies the length of the record to be written out. The ITEM operand is optional and sets the half-word binary data area to the value that is set by CICS/VS for the record, depending on the position of the record in the queue. AUXILIARY is the default.

If the queue identification code is defined as:

```
01     TWA-AREA.
       05     .......
       05     .......
       05     TSA-QUEUE-ID.
          10     TSA-TERM-ID          PIC X (4).
          10     TSA-TRANS-ID         PIC X (4).
```

We can code the following:

```
set tsa-queue-id to the proper value.
EXEC CICS
       WRITEQ TS
              FROM    (TSA-AREA)
              QUEUE   (TSA-QUEUE-ID)
              LENGTH (2000)
END-EXEC.
```

When this command is executed, CICS/VS assigns an item number for the record defined in TSA-AREA (if this record starts a new queue, the item number assigned is 1 and subsequent item numbers follow on sequentially), then writes out 2000 bytes of it into the queue identified by TSA-QUEUE-ID.

Note that for every new record written out, the main storage area defined by the FROM operand must be secured through a GETMAIN command so it may be made available to the program. The INITIMG operand is optional for the GETMAIN command and is generally not coded since the fields in the area will be set to the proper value in the program anyway.

READING A RECORD FROM A QUEUE

Whenever a task needs data stored in temporary storage, it must read the particular record where the data resides. The format of the command is:

```
readq  ts
     queue       (symbolic name)
     set         (tsa-pointer)
     length      (data area)
     item        (data value) or next
```

The QUEUE operand specifies the queue identification code of the queue. The SET operand specifies the linkage pointer corresponding to the temporary storage area. The LENGTH operand specifies a halfword binary data area that will be set to the length of the particular record read. The ITEM operand specifies the item number of the record to be read. If ITEM is not specified, NEXT is the default, which means the next sequential record following the last record read (by any task) is read.

An example of the command is:

```
set tsa-queue-id to the proper value.
EXEC CICS
          READQ TS
                    QUEUE       (TSA-QUEUE-ID)
                    SET         (TSA-POINTER)
                    LENGTH      (TSA-LENGTH)
                    ITEM        (1)
END-EXEC.
```

When this command is executed, CICS/VS will secure main storage for the area corresponding to TSA-POINTER and read the first record in the queue identified by TSA-QUEUE-ID into this area. TSA-LENGTH will be set to the length of the record read.

REWRITING A RECORD IN A QUEUE

After a temporary storage record read in a task has been modified within that task, it should be rewritten in the same task so the changes will be reflected when the record is read by another task. The format of the command is:

```
writeq  ts
        from      (data area)
        queue     (symbolic name)
        length    (data area)
        item      (data area)
        rewrite
```

The FROM operand specifies the main storage area to be rewritten. The QUEUE operand specifies the queue identification code of the queue. The LENGTH operand specifies the same data area in the previous READQ TS command that read the particular record. The ITEM operand specifies a halfword binary area that contains the item number of the record to be rewritten. The REWRITE operand specifies that this is a rewrite operation.

An example of this command is:

```
MOVE 1 TO TSA-QUEUE-NO.
EXEC CICS
     WRITEQ TS
            FROM      (TSA-AREA)
            QUEUE     (TSA-QUEUE-ID)
            LENGTH    (TSA-LENGTH)
            ITEM      (TSA-QUEUE-NO)
            REWRITE
END-EXEC.
```

When this command is executed, the first record in the queue defined by TSA-QUEUE-ID is rewritten using the main storage area TSA-AREA and the length TSA-LENGTH. Any task may then access the updated temporary storage record.

DELETING A QUEUE

Any temporary storage queue that is no longer needed may be deleted to free storage areas (main or auxiliary) corresponding to it. The command deletes the whole queue and the format is:

```
deleteq ts
        queue (symbolic name)
```

The QUEUE operand specifies the queue identification code of the queue to be deleted. There is no command to delete individual records in a queue.

An example of the command is:

```
set tsa-queue-id to the proper value.
EXEC CICS
        DELETEQ TS
                QUEUE (TSA-QUEUE-ID)
END-EXEC.
```

TEMPORARY STORAGE COMMAND EXCEPTIONAL CONDITIONS

Scratchpad Facility

Temporary storage queues used as scratchpads, are usually created at the INITIALIZATION section and deleted at the FINALIZATION section. However, in case the FINALIZATION section is never executed, as would occur in a program abend, a CICS/VS abnormal termination, or a hardware error that needs the system to be powered down, we should attempt to delete the queue at the beginning of the INITIALIZATION section. In this case, QIDERR should be specified in a HANDLE CONDITION command just in case the queue was deleted after all to avoid a CICS/VS default that would abort the session on the DELETEQ command.

Generally, this is the only exceptional condition that should be specifically defined in a HANDLE CONDITION command because if the program passed through the normal program test, the other errors should not happen for other commands. If they do, they can always be taken cared of by the catchall ERROR condition.

14

Program Control Commands

INTRODUCTION

Program Control commands allow the programmer to select the flow of control between application programs in CICS/VS. Specifically, they allow the programmer to do five things:

1. RETURN. Return control from one application program to another or to CICS/VS (in which case the task terminates).
2. XCTL. Transfer control from one application program to another with no return to the requesting program.
3. LINK. Effectively "call" another application program, and when the latter is finished, return control to the requesting program.
4. LOAD. Load an application program, table, or mapset into main storage and return control to the requesting program.
5. RELEASE. Delete a previously loaded application program, table, or mapset from main storage.

All programs executed through these commands must be entered in the Processing Program Table (PPT), usually maintained by the systems programmer.

APPLICATION PROGRAM LEVELS

Application programs running under CICS/VS execute at various logical levels. The first program to receive control in a task is at the highest logical level. On a XCTL command, both programs are at the same logical level. On a LINK command, the "called" program is at the next lower logical level. A RETURN command will always return control to the next higher logical level, or if the program is already at the highest logical level, to CICS/VS. In many instances, these commands can also pass data to the next program.

An example of this flow of control is shown in Figure 14.1.

When the task is initiated, application program A executes at the highest logical level. At some point, this issues a XCTL command for application program B, which then executes at the same logical level. This in turn issues a LINK command for application program C, which then executes at the next lower logical level. At some point, application program C in turn issues a XCTL command for application program D, which then executes at the same logical level. Program D in turn issues a LINK command for application program E, which then executes at the next lower logical level (in this example, the lowest logical level).

At some point, application program E issues a RETURN command, which returns control to the next higher logical level at the statement following the LINK command of application program D. At some point in application program D, a RETURN command is issued, which returns control to the next higher logical level at the statement following the LINK command of application program B. When this issues a RETURN command, the task is terminated since this is already at the highest logical level.

Note that only the last application program at each logical level issues the RETURN command.

THE RETURN COMMAND

The RETURN command returns control to another application program at the next higher logical level or to CICS/VS. When the command is issued in a lower logical level application program, the program to which control is returned will have at one point issued the LINK command and will be one logical level higher than the application program issuing the RETURN. Control is returned to the statement following the LINK command. When the application program issuing the command is at the highest logical level, control returns to CICS/VS and the task is terminated. The format of the command is:

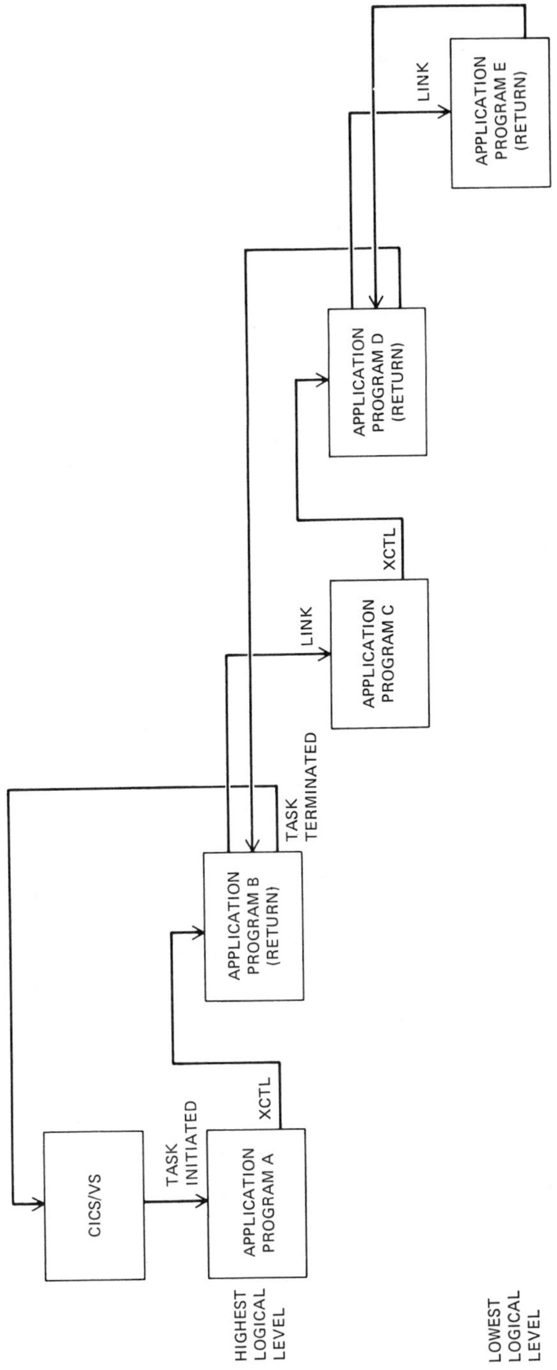

Fig. 14.1. Application Program Logical Levels.

```
return transid      (transaction identifier)
       commarea     (data area)
       length       (data value)
```

The TRANSID operand is used only when the program is at the highest logical level (control is thus being returned to CICS/VS) and the task is associated with a terminal. It specifies the transaction identifier of the next program to execute on that terminal. One common use is in continuing an application in the pseudoconversational mode of processing.

The COMMAREA operand specifies the data area that will be passed on to the next program. The LENGTH operand specifies the length of the data passed. The COMMAREA and LENGTH operands are optional and are used only if we are returning to CICS/VS. Otherwise, the INVREQ exceptional condition will occur.

If the command is issued at a level other than the highest logical level, all conditions set by HANDLE CONDITION commands in the program that issued the LINK command are restored to what they were at the time the LINK command was executed.

Return Command In The Pseudoconversational Mode of Processing

In the pseudoconversational mode of processing, I suggest the following techniques in the use of the transaction buffer:

1. At the INITIALIZATION section, always specify the literal comprising the transaction identifier. This standardizes the specification of the transaction identifier at this section because if a program is initiated by the XCTL command (as in the program examples), we cannot use the EIBTRNID field of the Execute Interface Block.

2. At the other sections, the EIBTRNID is used because we are using the same transaction identifier to implement the pseudoconversational mode of processing.

We mentioned on page 111 that we use the first byte of the communication area as a switch to implement the pseudoconversational mode of processing.

THE XCTL COMMAND

The XCTL command transfers control from one application program to another at the same logical level. The program issuing the command is released and the next program is loaded into main storage if it is not yet there. The format of the command is:

```
xctl program    (name)
     commarea   (data area)
     length     (data value)
```

The PROGRAM operand specifies the phase name of the program that will take over control. The COMMAREA and LENGTH operands are optional and are used to pass data from the requesting program to the new program.

THE LINK COMMAND

The LINK command "calls" another program at the next lower logical level, after which the requesting program regains control when the last program to execute at the lower logical level executes a RETURN command.* The "called" program is loaded into main storage if it is not yet there, but the requesting program is not released. The format of the command is:

```
link program    (name)
     commarea   (data area)
     length     (data value)
```

The operands specify the same things as are in the XCTL command. The "called" program will handle exceptional conditions (HANDLE CONDITION specifications), attention identifiers, and abends independently of the "calling" program.

Note that this command is useful in "calling" a small subprogram. However, since the requesting program is not released, it has a built-in inefficiency. When possible, the XCTL command should be used instead.

---

*The "called" program may itself issue a XCTL command to another program, in which case the latter program will issue the RETURN command.

THE LOAD COMMAND

The load command loads an application program, mapset, or table from the library where they reside into main storage. The format of the command is:

```
load program  (name)
     set      (linkage-pointer)
     length   (data area)
     hold
```

The PROGRAM operand specifies the phase name of the application program, mapset, or the identifier of the table. The SET operand specifies the linkage pointer corresponding to the area where the application program, mapset, or table is loaded. The LENGTH operand is optional and will be set to the length involved. The HOLD operand is also optional and is used if the application program, mapset, or table is to remain in main storage until a RELEASE command is issued. Otherwise, the loaded application program, mapset, or table is released when the task issuing the LOAD command is terminated normally or abnormally.

This command is useful for doing a one-time load of a heavily used application program or mapset into main storage so that the overhead of repeated loading is eliminated. It is also useful in loading a table "as is" into main storage.

THE RELEASE COMMAND

The RELEASE command is used to delete from main storage any application program, mapset, or table previously loaded through a LOAD command. This command is effective regardless of whether the HOLD operand was specified in the corresponding LOAD command or not. The format of the command is:

```
release program (name)
```

15

Miscellaneous Commands

INTRODUCTION

The four most important sets of commands to learn are the Terminal Input/Output commands, the File Control commands, the Temporary Storage commands, and the Program Control commands. The program must be able to read data from and display data on terminals. It should be able to access on-line files easily. It should be able to save data in an environment where the program and main storage are purged many times in a session. The programmer should be able to cause programs to execute in an interactive environment.

However, there are other commands that are useful to the programmer. These commands (with the exception of those used for debugging, which will be discussed in Chapter 24) are presented in this chapter.

THE SUSPEND COMMAND

A task currently in control will remain in control until a command that causes a wait is executed. The task is then suspended and the highest priority task that is ready to execute will take over control. This is the CICS/VS multitasking feature.

However, multitasking can cause a problem because a CPU-intensive task will monopolize the CPU to the exclusion of other tasks. If that task is of low priority, it may cause tasks of higher priority to have slower response times.

To avoid this, the programmer has the option to suspend a program (and thus a task) even before a command that causes a wait is executed, so that the next highest priority task may execute. The suspended task is then placed in the wait queue. The format of the command is:

```
suspend
```

THE GETMAIN COMMAND

The GETMAIN command is used by the programmer to secure main storage for any data block (area consisting of a 01-level entry and subordinate entries) defined in the LINKAGE section if such main storage is required (by another command) and it has not yet been acquired. This command is issued before issuing the other command that will actually use the area. The following are the guidelines in using or not using it:

1. It is not used for the WORKING-STORAGE section, the Transaction Work Area, the Common Work Area, and the Terminal Control Table User Area. These data blocks will always have main storage in a task.

2. It is required/not required for LINKAGE section entries depending on the following:
   a. It is not required before input commands (RECEIVE MAP, READ DATASET, etc.) if the locate-mode option is used since CICS/VS will acquire the area automatically.
   b. It is required before input commands if the move-mode option is used instead.
   c. It is not required before output commands (SEND MAP, WRITE DATASET, etc.) if they use the same main storage area already acquired, say by the corresponding input commands. Otherwise, it is required and if so, the GETMAIN command is issued ahead of the corresponding output command since the area is used when values are moved to it before the output command is issued.

Format Of Getmain

The format of the command is:

```
getmain
      set       (linkage-pointer)
      length    (data value)
      initimg   (data area)
```

The SET operand specifies the linkage pointer that corresponds to the area acquired. The LENGTH operand specifies the length in bytes of the area. The INITIMG operand is optional and specifies a data area whose value the acquired area will be set to.

An example of this command is:

```
EXEC CICS
        GETMAIN
                 SET      (MAP1-POINTER)
                 LENGTH   (900)
                 INITIMG  (HEX-ZEROES)
END-EXEC.
```

When the command is executed, 900 bytes of main storage will be allocated for MAP1-AREA (area that corresponds to MAP1-POINTER), and the area will be set to the value of HEX-ZEROES (generally defined in the WORKING-STORAGE section). HEX-ZEROES will be propagated through the whole area acquired.

Uses of Getmain

Getmain is used for the following:

1. A new map to be displayed (thus there is no corresponding RECEIVE MAP in the task) if the upcoming SEND MAP command includes the symbolic description map. In this case, the INITIMG* operand should be used to initialize the area to hexadecimal zeroes.
2. A record to be added to a file.
3. A new temporary storage record to be created.
4. A journal record to be written out.
5. Any area defined in the LINKAGE section when required in an application program.

---

*The area acquired for a symbolic description map should always be initialized to hexadecimal zeroes since BMS always displays data that is not hexadecimal zeroes. For other areas, INITIMG is optional and is generally not used because the fields will be filled up in the application program anyway.

THE FREEMAIN COMMAND

All main storage areas acquired through the GETMAIN command will not be released until the task terminates. Therefore, on those occasions when the output command that uses the area has already been executed and the task is still not about to be terminated, we may be wasting main storage. If the area is only a few bytes, however, the effort to purge the area may not be worth it; otherwise, the programmer may purge the area through the FREEMAIN command. The format is:

freemain data (data area)

An example of this command is:

```
EXEC CICS
     FREEMAIN DATA  (MAP1-AREA)
END-EXEC.
```

When this command is executed, the main storage corresponding to MAP1-AREA, which was acquired through a previous GETMAIN command, will be released.

WRITING JOURNAL RECORDS

CICS/VS provides special-purpose sequential data sets, called journals, which any task can write to anytime. Journal data sets accept records of varying length from various tasks, and these records generally contain information used either for statistical purposes, for file recovery, or for batch file update.

For instance, a File Add application may also generate a journal record, every time a record is written out, to contain information like operator initials, date, time of day, record number, dollar total of the record, etc. These records may then be used offline to prepare a statistical report as an audit trail.

The format of the command is:

```
journal jfileid   (data value)
        jtypeid   (data value)
        from      (data area)
        length    (data value)
        wait
```

The JFILEID operand specifies the journal data set to be used (02 is the regular journal). The JTYPEID operand specifies a two-byte identifier for the journal record, which is specific for each application or group of applications. The FROM operand specifies the user data* to be included in the record written out. The LENGTH operand specifies the length of the user data. The use of the WAIT operand is optional but is suggested so that the task does not continue until the journal record is completely written out.

The programmer should use the GETMAIN command to secure main storage for the journal record written out.

HANDLE ABEND COMMAND

On a program abend (not CICS/VS exceptional condition), the system default terminates the task with a dump printout used for debugging. However, if the programmer prefers to take care of an abend by executing his own routine in place of the system default, the HANDLE ABEND command can specify a program or label exit. The format of the command is:

```
handle abend
     program    (phase name)
     label      (paragraph/section)
     cancel
     reset
```

All the operands are mutually exclusive. The PROGRAM operand specifies the phase name of the program that will take control. The LABEL operand specifies the section or paragraph name if the same program is used. The CANCEL operand will cancel a previous

*CICS/VS adds a prefix to the journal record.

HANDLE ABEND command at the same logical level of the application program in control. The RESET operand reactivates an exit cancelled by a HANDLE ABEND CANCEL command or by CICS/VS.

Generally, the programmer should opt for the system default instead of issuing this command himself because the dump printout includes the PSW that is used for debugging.

STARTING A TASK

In most applications, a session is initiated when the operator enters a transaction identifier on a terminal. However, if the user wants a session or a task to start at a specified time, the START command is used. The format of this command is:

```
start  transid   (transaction identifier)
       termid    (terminal identification code)
       interval  (hhmmss) / time (hhmmss)
       from      (data area)
```

The TRANSID operand specifies the transaction identifier of the task to be started. The TERMID operand is optional and specifies the terminal identifier if the task is associated with a terminal. The INTERVAL operand specifies the time interval in hours, minutes, and seconds from the time the command is executed to the time the task is started. The TIME operand, which is mutually exclusive with the INTERVAL operand, specifies the exact time in hours, minutes, and seconds the task is started. The FROM operand specifies the location of the data to be passed to the task.

If the INTERVAL operand specifies a zero or the TIME operand a value that is equal to the current time of day (or up to six hours preceding it), the task can be started immediately.

REQUESTING CURRENT TIME OF DAY

When a task is initiated, the EIBDATE and EIBTIME fields of the Execute Interface Block are updated by CICS/VS. The programmer may further update these fields during a task by using the ASKTIME command. The format of the command is:

```
asktime
```

The EIBDATE field is not often critical since the date will probably not have changed from the time the task was initiated. However, the time will have changed and this command may be useful when the programmer needs to use the exact time of day; for instance, when generating journal records.

16

Programming Techniques

INTRODUCTION

In addition to learning CICS/VS features and commands, the programmer needs to learn programming techniques so that he can use these features and commands in the best way possible. There is a need for him to understand security techniques to prevent the unauthorized use of files and applications, techniques for using maps and temporary storage, and techniques for passing data between application programs.

ESTABLISHING SECURITY AND PRIORITY

CICS/VS Sign-On

As an option, the user may require operators to use the CICS/VS sign-on procedure before he or she can use some or all of the applications in the installation. This procedure is used to establish whether the operator is authorized to use a given application and what priority, if any, be given to the tasks that will be initiated during the use of the application. The format of the sign-on entry is:

CSSN NAME=XXXXXXXXXXXXXXXXXXXX, PS=XXXX

The NAME operand is from 1 to 20 characters long. The PS (password) operand is four characters long. These are compared with the sign-on table that is maintained by the systems programmer. This table contains the following information:

1. operator name
2. operator identification

3. operator password
4. operator security codes
5. operator security class
6. operator priority

When the operator enters the name and password and then hits the ENTER key or any PF key, the CICS/VS sign-on program is initiated. The sign-on program loads the sign-on table and verifies whether the name and password match any entry in the table. If not, an error message is displayed.

If an entry is found, the operator identification (usually the operator's initials), security codes, security class, and priority are extracted from the table and moved to the terminal control table (TCT) entry for the terminal that has been signed on. This information remains in the TCT entry until the operator signs off. The message "SIGN ON IS COMPLETE" will be displayed on a successful sign on.

Operator identification (3 characters) is used for statistical purposes. When the operator signs off, a message containing operator identification, number of transactions entered, and number of transaction errors may be sent to transient data on disk, magnetic tape, line printer, or any other CICS/VS supported device. This information may then be used for evaluation or as an audit trail.

Authorization for application use is determined by comparing the operator security codes with the security code of the transaction identifier that corresponds to the required program. The operator may have more than one security code if he is authorized to use applications (hence programs) with different security codes. A security code of 1 generally implies the lowest security while a code of 24 implies the highest security. Thus, many File Inquiry applications (especially for non-sensitive data) will have low security codes while File Update or File Inquiry applications (sensitive data) will have high security codes.

If the transaction identifier is not authorized for the operator, CICS/VS will reject it and send an error message to the operator's terminal and the master terminal, indicating a security violation. Operator identification, terminal identification, and transaction identifier are included in the message. The master terminal operator may then take appropriate action.

The operator security class is used primarily in conjunction with the CICS/VS message routing facility. This facility will not be explained in this book. Let it suffice to say that messages through this facility will be sent to specific operators or specific operator classes only if they have signed on to CICS/VS.

The operator priority is added to the terminal priority and the transaction priority to establish the overall task priority. Each of them can have a value from 0 to 255. The terminal priority is specified in the TCT entry for the terminal. The transaction priority is specified in the PCT entry for the transaction identifier. A task priority number of 255 will have the highest priority while 0 will have the lowest priority. If the task priority as computed is greater than 255, 255 is used.

The use of three factors to establish task priority provides the user with considerable flexibility in selecting which application, operator, or terminal should have the shortest response time.

CICS/VS Sign Off

When the operator is finished, he should sign off so no other operator can use applications using his sign-on data. The format is:

CSSF

The operator should then get the message

"SIGN OFF IS COMPLETE".

Improving Security

While the CICS/VS sign-on procedure is necessary for establishing priority and is used by CICS/VS for statistical purposes and message routing, the security portion may be inadequate to the user. After all, all an operator has to know is the name and password to be able to use an application unauthorized to him.

The user may therefore use procedures in addition to or in place of the CICS/VS sign-on procedures. Some of these are:

1. The operator may be required to enter another password specifically for a particular application, and this password procedure may be as involved as the user wants. In the program examples (Chapter 17 to 23), all operators start a session by entering a password through a master sign-on program.
2. In addition to the password required for a particular application, the user may set up a table of terminal identifications for a given application defined in the application itself and check whether the terminal used (as identified in the EIBTRMID field of the Execute Interface Block) is allowed by the application.
3. An additional password may also be required in the program before an operator is allowed to use a file; optionally, the operator may be required to enter a password to be able to retrieve certain records in a file or even to access certain fields in a record.
4. The passwords or terminal identifications entered for 1, 2, and 3 may be changed dynamically by the operator through a special program. In this case, they should be in direct-access storage devices and not hard coded in the application program. As an option, the password and/or terminal identification file may be maintained in coded form so it cannot be easily deciphered by unauthorized personnel. Each application would then decode the password or terminal identifier through a table before it is evaluated in the application.
5. The sign-on table may be regenerated with new values at certain intervals of time so the password and name may be changed from time to time.

It is really up to the user to determine what level of security is needed for applications. Applications like File Inquiry, especially for non-sensitive data, may be given an easier-to-use security procedure while applications for files that are sensitive must be well protected against unauthorized use. It should be remembered that while there is such a thing as lax security, there is also such a thing as too much security.

FILE OPENING AND CLOSING FOR PROGRAMS UNDER TEST

When we said in Chapter 12 that files are not opened or closed by application programs, we of course meant production programs. However, if the file opening program for a new program under test has not yet been coded, the programmer may open the file himself and thus be able to conduct the test. He uses the CICS/VS file opening service before he conducts the test. The format is:

CSMT DAT, OPE, FILEID=file identifier

The file identifier is the one specified in the File Control Table. The file would then be closed after the testing using the CICS/VS service:

CSMT DAT, CLO, FILEID=file identifier

USING MAPS

1. On a map defined with mode IN or INOUT, it is a good idea to include a one-byte field labeled "DUMMY" with attributes ASKIP, DRK, and FSET and with any initial value. This will guarantee that the field is transmitted to the TIOA when the ENTER or any PF key is used. This will avoid the MAPFAIL error on the RECEIVE MAP command if the operator does not enter anything. The programmer may use any unused position of the screen, usually the first position. See the map programs in Chapters 17 to 23.

2. On any GETMAIN command for the symbolic description map, the INITIMG operand should be specified to initialize the whole area to hexadecimal zeroes. This ensures that only data included in the program will ultimately be displayed on the terminal (on the SEND MAP command) since hexadecimal zeroes will not be transmitted from the symbolic description map to the terminal.

3. When an operator is entering data (File Add or File Update) on a map, it is useful to display an appropriate message when the data entered by the operator has been validated and used to add a new record or update an existing record. A typical message is:

   "RECORD ACCEPTED (or UPDATED)–CONTINUE".

   The operator then knows that everything he has entered has been accepted and he can continue with the next record. This message is best defined as part of the map program (hence physical map) so this will appear on the fresh screen that is displayed every time a record is finished. As a result, only the MAPONLY option need be specified for the fresh screen.

4. When a map that is being used as in (3) is first displayed in a session (at the INITIALIZATION section), it is best to temporarily replace the "RECORD ACCEPTED" message with a message like "ENTER FIRST RECORD" so that the operator will know that the terminal is ready for the first record. We have to use the GETMAIN command to secure main storage for the symbolic description map, then move the message to this area and display it in combination with the physical map.

5. Whenever a currently displayed map is different in format from the previous map displayed, it is wise to always use the ERASE option so that the latter is completely erased and does not confuse the operator. This will also erase the buffer so the terminal is ready for the entry of new data.

6. After the physical map (titles, field identifiers, etc.) is displayed, on succeeding displays of the same map we do not have to include it since it can remain on the screen. We therefore use the DATAONLY option, without the ERASE option.

7. In certain applications, like File Inquiry or File Browse, where new data is continuously displayed, we can use the same technique as in (6). Only data is transmitted for display, saving transmission time. However, if the data displayed is of vari-

able length, a new display will not overlay a previous display if it is shorter than the latter and will mislead the operator reading the data (the extra data coming from the previous display will be mistaken as coming from the current display). If this is so, we are forced to display the physical map with the symbolic description map every time we display the map by omitting MAPONLY and DATAONLY and specifying ERASE. This is shown in the program examples for File Inquiry and File Browse.

8. In many applications, the PF keys can function just like the ENTER key because they can also initiate a task and allow terminal data to be transmitted to the Terminal Input/Output Area. In this case we do not have to specify their use. However, the PA keys always have to be specified (generally in a HANDLE AID command) because they do not allow terminal data to be transmitted to the Terminal Input/Output Area and will result in a MAPFAIL error on the RECEIVE MAP command.

9. In an application where the operator enters data to be validated, the PA keys (or at least one of them, leaving the other two as "wrong keys") may be used to leave the current entry if the operator cannot resolve a data validation error. Otherwise, the error will always appear and he will not be able to continue with the session without terminating it (generally by using the CLEAR key), then restarting it. The program should then issue a GETMAIN for the map to be displayed, then move the message "RECORD BYPASSED–CONTINUE" to the symbolic description map to be included in the next display. This is shown in the program examples in Chapters 19 and 20.

10. In an application where there may not be any need to bypass input data already entered, the PA keys still have to be defined, and in this case they can be used to display the "WRONG KEY USED" message. In a technique similar to that in (9), the program issues a GETMAIN for the map to be displayed, then moves the message to the symbolic description map to be included in the next display. This is shown in the program examples in Chapters 18 and 21.

11. The keyboard shift for a field entered by the operator (whether numeric or alphabetic) depends on whether the data entered is usually numeric or alphabetic. It is convenient for him to have the proper shift automatically provided for so he does not have to use the keyboard shift keys. However, the shift of the field is independent of the PICTURE specification of the field as defined in the symbolic description map. The attribute specification in the map program that provides either numeric (NUM specified) or alphabetic (NUM omitted) shift is different from the PICIN or PICOUT specification that provides the Cobol PICTURE specification. While numeric-shift fields that are used in computation (e.g. amounts) should be defined with PICTURE 9s, and fields with alphabetic shift should always be defined with PICTURE Xs, numeric-shift fields that are not used in computation may also be conveniently defined with PICTURE Xs. For instance, fields like item number or department numbers, which are in numeric shift, may be defined with PICTURE Xs to facilitate editing of these fields.

12. After the RECEIVE MAP command is executed in a task, do not touch the 12-byte prefix of the symbolic description map because it contains information used by BMS. If you destroy this field, the results are unpredictable in the ensuing SEND MAP command for the same map. However, the GETMAIN command (naturally, this command is not needed if the RECEIVE MAP command was executed for the same map) may include this prefix when the symbolic description map is set to hexadecimal zeroes.

DATA VALIDATION TECHNIQUES

1. If the operator needs to enter a lot of data to be validated, the programmer should use several lines at the bottom of the screen for error messages. Since each message will usually be around 30 characters long or less, and each line has 80 characters,*

*The most popular CRT terminals have 80 columns.

there is space for two error messages per line. For most applications, the programmer can use two or three lines, for four or six error messages.

2. The programmer should validate as much data as possible, stopping only when the number of errors detected equals the number of error message positions. This is more efficient than having only one error message position. Otherwise, the operator would be forced to go through the editing steps again for other errors, thus resulting in the multiple reading and displaying of the same map and a delay in the completion of an entry.
3. The programmer should use the symbolic cursor positioning technique. As data is being validated, he should count the number of errors detected. When an error is detected for the first time, the literal -1 should be moved to the length of that field in the symbolic description map so that the cursor will be positioned under that field on the next display and the operator does not have to waste time positioning the cursor to correct the first error entry. This is shown in the DATA-VALIDATION SECTION of the File Add and File Update program examples.
4. The programmer can also use the error count to terminate the editing steps when the number of errors detected equals the number of error message positions. There is no sense in further editing the data once we run out of error message positions because there is no place to put an error message anyway; we would also be wasting processing time. The programmer can effectively use a GO TO to bypass the editing of the rest of the data when this occurs. This is shown in the same program examples as in (3).
5. To display the error messages and the data entered, the programmer simply has to display the symbolic description map without the ERASE operand; thus, the DATAONLY operand is specified. The CURSOR operand is also specified if the technique in (3) is used.
6. At the beginning of the editing steps, the error message positions should be blanked out (move spaces to them). This will

make sure that messages from the previous editing steps, if this is not the first pass through the editing steps for the same set of data, will no longer be displayed. Thus, only error messages for the current editing steps will be displayed. This is more efficient than redisplaying the physical map with the symbolic description map and using the ERASE option.

7. If a field has to be entered (for instance, the record key in a File Add application), the programmer can immediately edit the field for validity. If it has not been entered, the field will contain LOW-VALUES.

8. If the field is optional, then the programmer should first check the length of the field for a value greater than ZERO; if so, data was entered on that field and can be edited.

9. If you highlight a field that is in error (by modifying its attributes to include the BRT attribute when it is validated as an error), then you would have to reset the attributes of all unprotected fields to their original values (that is, as per the map program) before doing the validation steps, by using the same technique for modifying attributes. This makes sure that only errors on the current validation pass will be highlighted in case you still have errors on the second pass or beyond. This is because the use of the DATAONLY operand by itself will retain the attributes as modified.

10. Even if you highlight fields in error, you will still need error messages since highlighting alone may not give a full explanation of the cause of the error.

11. Techniques in temporary "storing" validated fields:
    a. The programmer should define a data group that is a mirror image of the record to be added or updated. Each valid field should be moved to the corresponding field within that group as each one is edited. This simplifies the routine to write or rewrite the record after a successful validation process.
    b. For a File Add application, you may then easily move spaces or zeros for optional fields not entered.

c. For a File Update application, you should initially copy the old record into this data group so that you just replace the corresponding field as you validate each field entered.
d. If only one map is used to enter a document, and the application is File Add, then the record image may be defined in the working storage section or the Transaction Work Area.
e. If more than one map is used to enter a document, then the record image is generally defined in temporary storage. This is required because we want to save data entered on previous maps while we validate data on additional maps. Note that we cannot save data in working storage or the Transaction Work Area since they are purged at task termination.
f. If there are no more errors for the whole document being entered, then the file record image in working storage, the Transaction Work Area, or temporary storage is used to add a new record or update an existing one.

USING TEMPORARY STORAGE

1. Temporary storage is very useful in passing data to another task (may be the same program in pseudoconversational mode). Since we can use direct access storage devices for this instead of main storage, we save a precious resource that otherwise would not be available to other tasks. A good guide is: Any group of data that will remain inactive for more than one second,* especially if it is longer than 300 bytes, should be placed in temporary storage, then read when needed.

2. The programmer may use as many temporary storage records as needed in a single queue and as many queues as he needs for the application. For most applications, however, he will need only one record in a single queue if he uses temporary storage for a scratchpad. It is always more efficient to get a single, long, temporary storage record rather than many smaller ones because of the overhead in reading and rewriting it.

---

*It is inactive from the time it is released by a program (WRITEQ TS) up to the time it is read by the next program (READQ TS).

3. A very useful queue identification code consists of the terminal identification code and the transaction identifier. This way there is no danger that some other terminals or programs will, without permission, use or delete temporary storage queues belonging to somebody else.

4. If the application uses temporary storage for a scratchpad facility, it will no longer need it at the end of the session and should therefore delete it at the FINALIZATION section. At the INITIALIZATION section, this deletion should likewise be attempted since the FINALIZATION section may not have been executed in the previous session. This can happen if there was a program abend, if a hardware error forced the abnormal shutdown of the whole system, or if a CICS/VS error (probably nucleus) forces the termination of the whole CICS/VS partition. This can be seen in the File Add and File Update program examples.

5. At the INITIALIZATION section, after deleting any previous temporary storage queues, we have to do a GETMAIN for the new temporary storage record to be created. Here, the INITIMG operand is generally not coded since all fields will be set to the proper values in the program anyway. After setting the fields to their proper values, we then save the record for the next task by writing it out. The WRITEQ TS command is used.

6. Every time a record in the temporary storage queue is required, it has first to be read in the task. The ITEM operand has to be specified in the READQ TS command so the corresponding record in the queue will be read.

7. Every time a record in the temporary storage queue is updated for the next task, we have to rewrite it. The WRITEQ TS command is used with the ITEM and REWRITE operands.

8. When a temporary storage queue is deleted, all records in that queue are deleted since CICS/VS does not have the facility to delete individual records in a queue.

PASSING DATA BETWEEN PROGRAMS

Temporary Storage

Data may be passed from one application program to another in many ways, depending on the situation. The most common way of passing data from one task to another is through the use of temporary storage records. For example, in the pseudoconversational mode of processing, data may be passed from one execution of the program to the next by using temporary storage queues to implement a scratchpad facility. A good guide is: Data no longer needed by the previous program but which will not be required by the next program until more than one second later, especially if the data is more than 300 bytes long, should be maintained in temporary storage in a direct access storage device.

The Transaction Work Area (TWA)

Another method for passing data between programs employs the Transaction Work Area. However, the two programs involved must execute in the same task since the Transaction Work Area is released when a task terminates. This may be used, for instance, in an XCTL command where two programs have identical TWAs and the second program gets a copy of the first program's TWA and may access it after executing the ADDRESS command with the TWA operand.

The Terminal Control Table User Area

Data may also be passed through the Terminal Control Table User Area. This area is defined as an entry in the LINKAGE section and will have a corresponding linkage pointer. The application programmer establishes addressability to this area in the same ADDRESS command used to establish addressability to the Transaction Work Area and the Common Work Area.

This area can be passed only if the tasks execute at the same terminal. It may therefore be used in the pseudoconversational mode of processing to implement a scratchpad facility, but it does need main storage instead of a direct access storage device, so it may be wasting an important resource. Furthermore, it is limited to 255 bytes.

The Common Work Area

The Common Work Area is part of the Common Systems Area, and all programs in the installation can access it any time to read data from it or to change data in it. However, the user should control the use of this resource because if an error is made by a single application, the results for other applications are unpredictable. It is much easier to pass data through other means, like temporary storage, where applications are not affected by errors in other applications.

The Communication Area

The RETURN, XCTL, and LINK program control commands have the option of passing data to the next program. The data is defined in either the WORKING-STORAGE or LINKAGE section in the first program, but it must be defined in the second program as DFHCOMMAREA, which is the first entry in the LINKAGE section.

On a RETURN command to CICS/VS, the COMMAREA operand specifies the data area and the LENGTH operand the length of the area that is passed to the program that first executes on the next task to be initiated at the same terminal.

On the XCTL or LINK command, the COMMAREA and LENGTH operands pertain to the data area that will be passed to the program specified in the command.

17

Program Examples

INTRODUCTION

We will now present several programs built around a simplified Purchase Order system. The main purpose of the examples is not to show a typical Purchase Order system, but rather to show typical CICS/VS programs. The examples are in fact somewhat simplified and many requirements of a Purchase Order system are not reflected.

The following programs will be presented:

1. Sign-on Program
2. File Inquiry
3. File Add
4. File Update
5. File Delete
6. File Browse (Primary Key)
7. File Browse (Alternate Key)

THE MASTER SIGN-ON PROGRAM

In many applications, the user prefers that all operators start with a master Sign-on program so that the use of the various applications may be properly controlled. This program usually requires each operator to choose one application (add a new record, update an existing record, inquire through the file, etc.) and enter the password for that particular application. The program then validates the password against the particular application and if valid, executes a XCTL command to the particular application. If not, the Sign-on program will be aborted with a message.

The user may choose to have the program send a message to or ring a bell on a master terminal controlled by the user manager stating that there was an invalid sign-on attempt at a particular terminal. The user may also prefer to have all operators use a complicated password procedure to reduce the chance that an unauthorized person might accidentally discover the password. Such passwords (which never show on the terminal screen) may be used in conjunction with the regular CICS/VS sign-on service (CSSN).

In our program examples, the operator will start with the master Sign-on program and continue the session with the particular application selected until he decides to terminate it. A diagram of the procedure is shown in Figure 17.1.

PROGRAM SPECIFICATIONS

The program specifications are as follows:

1. Implement the program using the pseudoconversational mode of processing.
2. Use 'ORAP' as the transaction identifier to initiate the session.
3. The operator selects a particular application and enters the corresponding password for it.
4. If there is more than one application selected, abort the session with the message "JOB ABORTED–MULTIPLE FUNCTION NOT ALLOWED."
5. If there is no application selected, abort the session with the message "JOB ABORTED–NO FUNCTION SELECTED."
6. If the password entered is invalid, abort the session with the message "JOB ABORTED–INVALID PASSWORD."
7. The passwords required for each application are:

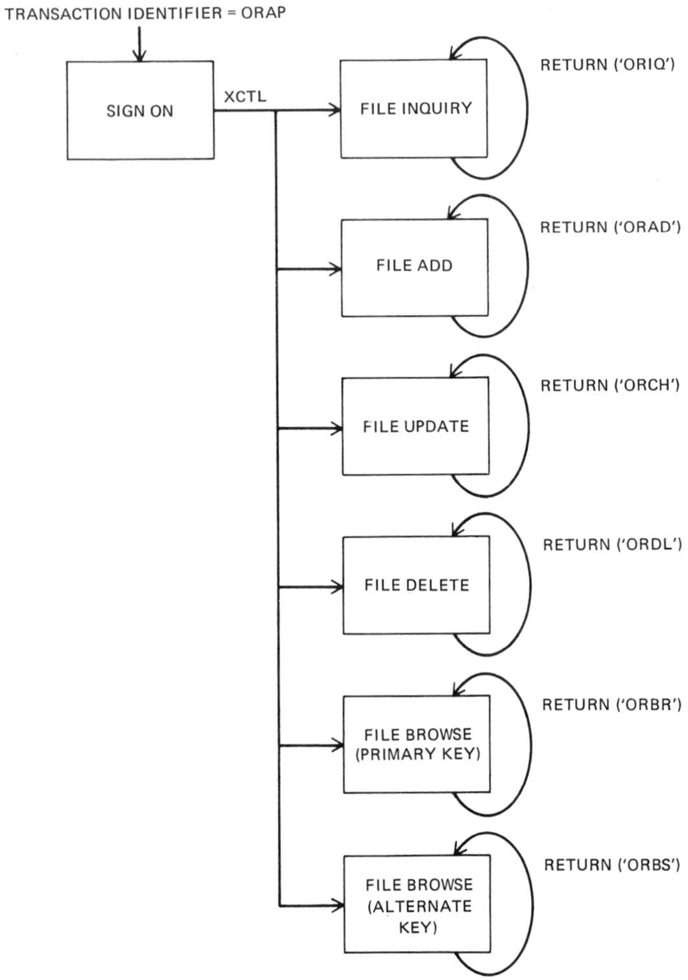

Fig. 17.1. General Procedure Of A Typical Application.

Application	Password
File Inquiry	MMDD* + 1111
File Add	MMDD + 2222
File Update	MMDD + 3333
File Delete	MMDD + 4444
File Browse (Primary key)	MMDD + 5555
File Browse (Alternate key)	MMDD + 6666

*MMDD is the current month and day.

8. The program will transfer control (do a XCTL) to the following programs if the password is valid for the application:

Application	Program
File Inquiry	ORIQ01A
File Add	ORAD01A
File Update	ORCH01A
File Delete	ORDL01A
File Browse (Primary key)	ORBR01A
File Browse (Alternate key)	ORBS01A

9. On any PA key, terminate the session.

SCREEN LAYOUT

The screen layout to be used in the program is shown in Figure 17.2. All 9s are numeric and Xs are alphanumeric fields.

MAP PROGRAM

The map program corresponding to the screen layout is shown in Figure 17.3.

PROGRAM LISTING

The program listing for the sign-on program is shown in Figure 17.4. All program listings in this book will be those of the compiler and

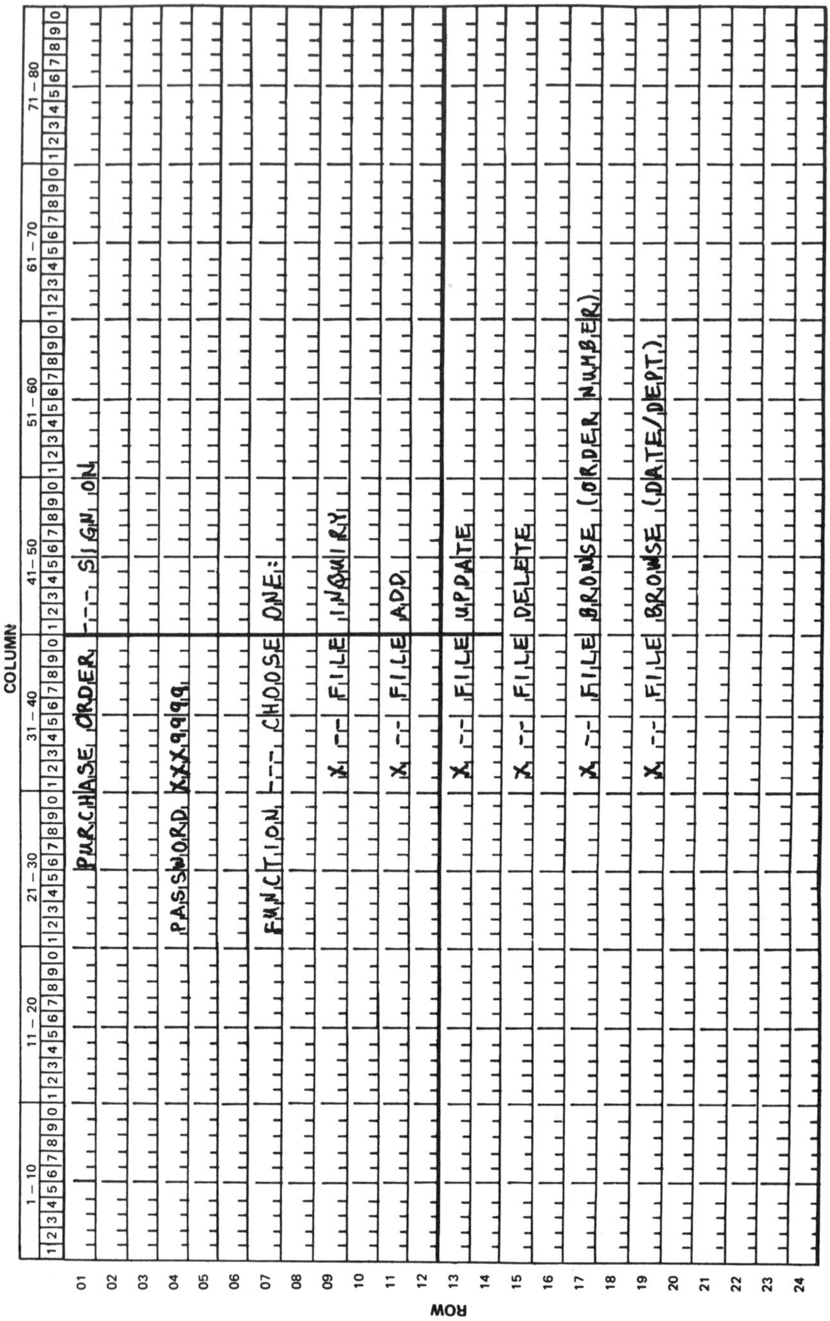

Fig. 17.2. Screen Layout – Sign On Program.

```
STMT    SOURCE STATEMENT                                  DOS/VS ASSEMBLER REL 34.0 13.50

   1             PRINT NOGEN
   2 ORAPSO1     DFHMSD TYPE=MAP,MODE=INOUT,CTRL=FREEKB,LANG=COBOL,           X
                       TIOAPFX=YES
  12 ORAPMO1     DFHMDI SIZE=(24,80)
  40 DUMMY       DFHMDF POS=(01,01),LENGTH=01,ATTRB=(ASKIP,DRK,FSET),         X
                       INITIAL='1'
  52             DFHMDF POS=(01,25),LENGTH=26,ATTRB=(ASKIP,BRT),               X
                       INITIAL='PURCHASE ORDER --- SIGN ON'
  64             DFHMDF POS=(04,21),LENGTH=08,ATTRB=(ASKIP,BRT),               X
                       INITIAL='PASSWORD'
  76 PASSWRD     DFHMDF POS=(04,30),LENGTH=07,ATTRB=(UNPROT,DRK,IC)
  87             DFHMDF POS=(04,38),LENGTH=1
  98             DFHMDF POS=(07,21),LENGTH=24,ATTRB=(ASKIP,BRT),               X
                       INITIAL='FUNCTION --- CHOOSE ONE '
 110 INQUIRY     DFHMDF POS=(09,30),LENGTH=01,ATTRB=(UNPROT,BRT)
 121             DFHMDF POS=(09,32),LENGTH=16,ATTRB=(ASKIP,BRT),               X
                       INITIAL=' -- FILE INQUIRY'
 133 ADD         DFHMDF POS=(11,30),LENGTH=01,ATTRB=(UNPROT,BRT)
 144             DFHMDF POS=(11,32),LENGTH=12,ATTRB=(ASKIP,BRT),               X
                       INITIAL=' -- FILE ADD'
 156 UPDATE      DFHMDF POS=(13,30),LENGTH=01,ATTRB=(UNPROT,BRT)
 167             DFHMDF POS=(13,32),LENGTH=15,ATTRB=(ASKIP,BRT),               X
                       INITIAL=' -- FILE UPDATE'
 179 DELETE      DFHMDF POS=(15,30),LENGTH=01,ATTRB=(UNPROT,BRT)
 190             DFHMDF POS=(15,32),LENGTH=15,ATTRB=(ASKIP,BRT),               X
                       INITIAL=' -- FILE DELETE'
 202 BROWSE      DFHMDF POS=(17,30),LENGTH=01,ATTRB=(UNPROT,BRT)
 213             DFHMDF POS=(17,32),LENGTH=30,ATTRB=(ASKIP,BRT),               X
                       INITIAL=' -- FILE BROWSE (ORDER NUMBER)'
 225 BROWSE2     DFHMDF POS=(19,30),LENGTH=01,ATTRB=(UNPROT,BRT)
 236             DFHMDF POS=(19,32),LENGTH=27,ATTRB=(ASKIP,BRT),               X
                       INITIAL=' -- FILE BROWSE (DATE/DEPT)'
 248             DFHMSD TYPE=FINAL
 262             END
```

Fig. 17.3. Map Program – Sign On Program.

```
      1  IBM DOS VS COBOL

CBL SUPMAP,STXIT,NOTRUNC,CSYNTAX,SXREF,OPT,VERB,CLIST,BUF=19069
CBL NOOPT,LIB
00001              IDENTIFICATION DIVISION.

00003              PROGRAM-ID. ORAP01A.

00005              ENVIRONMENT DIVISION.

00007         ***********************************************************************
00008         *                                                                     *
00009         *    1. THIS IS THE SIGN-ON PROGRAM FOR ALL PURCHASE ORDER             *
00010         *       APPLICATIONS.                                                  *
00011         *                                                                     *
00012         *    2. THE PROGRAM WILL ALLOW THE OPERATOR TO ACCESS THE              *
00013         *       PURCHASE ORDER FILE FOR THE FOLLOWING FUNCTIONS                *
00014         *                                                                     *
00015         *                  (A) INQUIRY (DISPLAY RECORD INFORMATION).           *
00016         *                  (B) ADD NEW RECORDS.                                *
00017         *                  (C) UPDATE EXISTING RECORDS.                        *
00018         *                  (D) DELETE EXISTING RECORDS.                        *
00019         *                  (E) DO A BROWSE VIA RECORD KEY (ORDER NUMBER).      *
00020         *                  (F) DO A BROWSE VIA ALTERNATE KEY,                  *
00021         *                      (DATE OF ORDER WITHIN DEPARTMENT NUMBER).       *
00022         *                                                                     *
00023         *    3. THE FUNCTION SELECTED BY THE OPERATOR IS VALIDATED             *
00024         *       AGAINST THE PASSWORD ENTERED.                                  *
00025         *                                                                     *
00026         ***********************************************************************
```

Fig. 17.4. Sign On Program.

```
2        ORAPO1A          13.23.49        07/26/80

00028         DATA DIVISION.

00030         WORKING-STORAGE SECTION.

00032      01  COMMUNICATION-AREA.

00034          05  COMMAREA-PROCESS-SW          PIC X.

00036          05  COMMAREA-OPERATOR-INITIAL    PIC XXX.

00038      01  AREA1.

00040          05  JOB-NORMAL-END-MESSAGE  PIC X(23) VALUE
00041              'JOB NORMALLY TERMINATED'.

00043          05  JOB-ABORTED-MESSAGE.
00044              10  FILLER                  PIC X(15) VALUE 'JOB ABORTED --'.
00045              10  MAJOR-ERROR-MSG         PIC X(30).

00047          05  OLD-EIB-AREA.
00048              10  FILLER                  PIC X(7) VALUE 'OLD EIB'.
00049              10  OLD-EIBFN               PIC XX.
00050              10  OLD-EIBRCODE            PIC X(6).
```

Fig. 17.4. (Continued)

3 ORAPO1A 13.23.49 07/26/80

```
00052              01  DFHEIVAR COPY DFHEIVAR.
00053 C            01  DFHEIVAR.
00054 C                02   DFHEIV0   PICTURE X(26).
00055 C                02   DFHEIV1   PICTURE X(8).
00056 C                02   DFHEIV2   PICTURE X(8).
00057 C                02   DFHEIV3   PICTURE X(8).
00058 C                02   DFHEIV4   PICTURE X(6).
00059 C                02   DFHEIV5   PICTURE X(4).
00060 C                02   DFHEIV6   PICTURE X(4).
00061 C                02   DFHEIV7   PICTURE X(2).
00062 C                02   DFHEIV8   PICTURE X(2).
00063 C                02   DFHEIV9   PICTURE X(1).
00064 C                02   DFHEIV10  PICTURE S9(7) USAGE COMPUTATIONAL-3.
00065 C                02   DFHEIV11  PICTURE S9(4) USAGE COMPUTATIONAL.
00066 C                02   DFHEIV12  PICTURE S9(4) USAGE COMPUTATIONAL.
00067 C                02   DFHEIV13  PICTURE S9(4) USAGE COMPUTATIONAL.
00068 C                02   DFHEIV14  PICTURE S9(4) USAGE COMPUTATIONAL.
00069 C                02   DFHEIV15  PICTURE S9(4) USAGE COMPUTATIONAL.
00070 C                02   DFHEIV16  PICTURE S9(9) USAGE COMPUTATIONAL.
00071 C                02   DFHEIV17  PICTURE X(4).
00072 C                02   DFHEIV18  PICTURE X(4).
00073 C                02   DFHEIV19  PICTURE X(4).
00074 C                02   DFHEIV97  PICTURE S9(7) USAGE COMPUTATIONAL-3 VALUE ZERO.
00075 C                02   DFHEIV98  PICTURE S9(4) USAGE COMPUTATIONAL VALUE ZERO.
00076 C                02   DFHEIV99  PICTURE X(1)  VALUE SPACE.
00077              LINKAGE SECTION.
00078              01  DFHEIBLK COPY DFHEIBLK.
00079 C            *    EIBLK EXEC INTERFACE BLOCK
00080 C            01  DFHEIBLK.
00081 C            *       EIBTIME        TIME IN 0HHMMSS FORMAT
00082 C                02 EIBTIME        PICTURE S9(7) USAGE COMPUTATIONAL-3.
00083 C            *       EIBDATE        DATE IN 00YYDDD FORMAT
00084 C                02 EIBDATE        PICTURE S9(7) USAGE COMPUTATIONAL-3.
00085 C            *       EIBTRNID       TRANSACTION IDENTIFIER
00086 C                02 EIBTRNID       PICTURE X(4).
00087 C            *       EIBTASKN       TASK NUMBER
00088 C                02 EIBTASKN       PICTURE S9(7) USAGE COMPUTATIONAL-3.
00089 C            *       EIBTRMID       TERMINAL IDENTIFIER
00090 C                02 EIBTRMID       PICTURE X(4).
00091 C            *       DFHEIGDI       RESERVED
00092 C                02 DFHEIGDI       PICTURE S9(4) USAGE COMPUTATIONAL.
00093 C            *       EIBCPOSN       CURSOR POSITION
00094 C                02 EIBCPOSN       PICTURE S9(4) USAGE COMPUTATIONAL.
00095 C            *       EIBCALEN       COMMAREA LENGTH
00096 C                02 EIBCALEN       PICTURE S9(4) USAGE COMPUTATIONAL.
00097 C            *       EIBAID         ATTENTION IDENTIFIER
00098 C                02 EIBAID         PICTURE X(1).
00099 C            *       EIBFN          FUNCTION CODE
00100 C                02 EIBFN          PICTURE X(2).
00101 C            *       EIBRCODE       RESPONSE CODE
00102 C                02 EIBRCODE       PICTURE X(6).
00103 C            *       EIBDS          DATASET NAME
00104 C                02 EIBDS          PICTURE X(8).
```

Fig. 17.4. (Continued)

```
      4          ORAP01A          13.23.49          07/26/80

                *        EIBREQID   REQUEST IDENTIFIER
                           02 EIBREQID   PICTURE X(8).
                 01  DFHCOMMAREA.

                     05  PROCESS-SW                    PIC X.
                       88  PASSWORD-VALIDATION-TIME     VALUE '1'.


                 01  LINKAGE-POINTERS.

                     05  FILLER                        PIC S9(8) COMP.
                     05  MAP1-POINTER                  PIC S9(8) COMP.
                     05  TWA-POINTER                   PIC S9(8) COMP.
```

```
      5          ORAP01A          13.23.49          07/26/80

           ***********************************************************************
           *                                                                     *
           *           SIGN-ON MAP AREA DESCRIPTION                              *
           *                                                                     *
           ***********************************************************************

           01  MAP1-AREA.

               05  FILLER                        PIC X(12).
               05  MAP1-DUMMY-L                  PIC S9999 COMP.
               05  MAP1-DUMMY-A                  PIC X.
               05  MAP1-DUMMY                    PIC X.
               05  MAP1-PASSWORD-L               PIC S9999 COMP.
               05  MAP1-PASSWORD-A               PIC X.
               05  MAP1-PASSWORD.
                 10  MAP1-PASSWORD-ALP           PIC XXX.
                 10  MAP1-PASSWORD-NUM           PIC 9999.
               05  MAP1-INQUIRY-L                PIC S9999 COMP.
               05  MAP1-INQUIRY-A                PIC X.
               05  MAP1-INQUIRY                  PIC X.
               05  MAP1-ADD-L                    PIC S9999 COMP.
               05  MAP1-ADD-A                    PIC X.
               05  MAP1-ADD                      PIC X.
               05  MAP1-UPDATE-L                 PIC S9999 COMP.
               05  MAP1-UPDATE-A                 PIC X.
               05  MAP1-UPDATE                   PIC X.
               05  MAP1-DELETE-L                 PIC S9999 COMP.
               05  MAP1-DELETE-A                 PIC X.
               05  MAP1-DELETE                   PIC X.
               05  MAP1-BROWSE-L                 PIC S9999 COMP.
               05  MAP1-BROWSE-A                 PIC X.
               05  MAP1-BROWSE                   PIC X.
               05  MAP1-BROWSE-ALT-L             PIC S9999 COMP.
               05  MAP1-BROWSE-ALT-A             PIC X.
               05  MAP1-BROWSE-ALT               PIC X.
```

Fig. 17.4. (Continued)

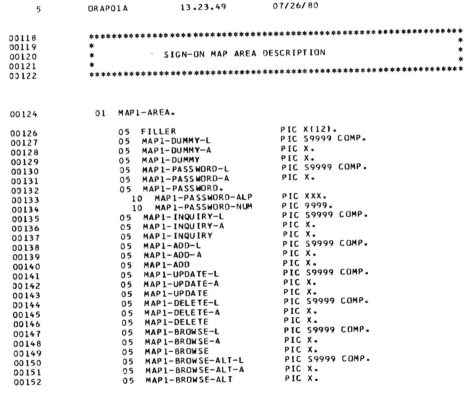

```
       6           ORAPO1A            13.23.49          07/26/80

00154              ****************************************************************
00155              *                                                              *
00156              *                  TRANSACTION WORK AREA                       *
00157              *                                                              *
00158              ****************************************************************

00160              01   TWA-AREA.

00162                   05   TWA-CTR               PIC S9999 COMP.

00164                   05   TWA-OPERATOR-MESSAGE   PIC X(45).

00166                   05   TWA-CURRENT-DATE.
00167                        10   TWA-CURRENT-MM    PIC 99.
00168                        10   FILLER            PIC X.
00169                        10   TWA-CURRENT-DD    PIC 99.
00170                        10   FILLER            PIC XXX.

00172                   05   TWA-PASSWORD-DATE.
00173                        10   TWA-PASSWORD-DATE-MM  PIC 99.
00174                        10   TWA-PASSWORD-DATE-DD  PIC 99.

00176                   05   TWA-DATE REDEFINES TWA-PASSWORD-DATE   PIC 9999.
```

Fig. 17.4. (Continued)

```
7        ORAP01A        13.23.49        07/26/80

          PROCEDURE DIVISION USING DFHEIBLK DFHCOMMAREA.
              CALL 'DFHEI1'.

         *****************************************************************
         *                                                               *
          MAIN-LINE SECTION.
         *                                                               *
         *****************************************************************

         *    EXEC CICS
         *         ADDRESS TWA (TWA-POINTER)
         *    END-EXEC.
               MOVE '                        ' TO DFHEIVO CALL 'DFHEI1' USING
               DFHEIVO TWA-POINTER.

         *    EXEC CICS
         *         HANDLE AID
         *                CLEAR (FINALIZATION)
         *                  PA1 (INITIALIZATION)
         *                  PA2 (INITIALIZATION)
         *                  PA3 (INITIALIZATION)
         *    END-EXEC.
               MOVE '  0                     ' TO DFHEIVO CALL 'DFHEI1' USING
               DFHEIVO GO TO FINALIZATION INITIALIZATION INITIALIZATION
               INITIALIZATION DEPENDING ON DFHEIGDI.




         *    EXEC CICS
         *         HANDLE CONDITION
         *                MAPFAIL (MAPFAIL-ERROR)
         *                ERROR   (MAJOR-ERROR)
         *    END-EXEC.
               MOVE '                        ' TO DFHEIVO CALL 'DFHEI1' USING
               DFHEIVO GO TO MAPFAIL-ERROR MAJOR-ERROR DEPENDING ON
               DFHEIGDI.


              IF EIBCALEN NOT EQUAL TO ZEROES
                   GO TO PASSWORD-VALIDATION.

              IF EIBCALEN EQUAL TO ZEROES
                   GO TO INITIALIZATION.
```

Fig. 17.4. (Continued)

```
     8          ORAP01A          13.23.49          07/26/80

           *****************************************************************
           *                                                               *
            PASSWORD-VALIDATION SECTION.
           *                                                               *
           *****************************************************************

           *    EXEC CICS
           *         RECEIVE MAP     ('ORAPM01')
           *                 MAPSET ('ORAPS01')
           *                 SET     (MAP1-POINTER)
           *    END-EXEC.
                 MOVE 'ORAPM01' TO DFHEIV1 MOVE 'ORAPS01' TO DFHEIV2 MOVE '
           -    '              ' TO DFHEIV0 CALL 'DFHEI1' USING DFHEIV0
                 DFHEIV1 MAP1-POINTER DFHEIV98 DFHEIV2.


                MOVE ZEROES TO TWA-CTR.

                IF MAP1-INQUIRY-L      NOT EQUAL TO ZEROES
                     ADD 1 TO TWA-CTR.

                IF MAP1-ADD-L          NOT EQUAL TO ZEROES
                     ADD 2 TO TWA-CTR.

                IF MAP1-UPDATE-L       NOT EQUAL TO ZEROES
                     ADD 4 TO TWA-CTR.

                IF MAP1-DELETE-L       NOT EQUAL TO ZEROES
                     ADD 8 TO TWA-CTR.

                IF MAP1-BROWSE-L       NOT EQUAL TO ZEROES
                     ADD 16 TO TWA-CTR.

                IF MAP1-BROWSE-ALT-L  NOT EQUAL TO ZEROES
                     ADD 32 TO TWA-CTR.

                IF     TWA-CTR EQUAL TO 1
                    OR TWA-CTR EQUAL TO 2
                    OR TWA-CTR EQUAL TO 4
                    OR TWA-CTR EQUAL TO 8
                    OR TWA-CTR EQUAL TO 16
                    OR TWA-CTR EQUAL TO 32
                THEN NEXT SENTENCE
                ELSE IF TWA-CTR EQUAL TO ZEROES
                          GO TO NO-FUNCTION-ERROR
                     ELSE GO TO MULTIPLE-FUNCTION-ERROR.

                MOVE CURRENT-DATE      TO  TWA-CURRENT-DATE.
                MOVE TWA-CURRENT-MM    TO  TWA-PASSWORD-DATE-MM.
                MOVE TWA-CURRENT-DD    TO  TWA-PASSWORD-DATE-DD.
```

Fig. 17.4. (Continued)

```
    9          ORAP01A          13.23.49          07/26/80

               IF TWA-CTR EQUAL TO 1
                    IF MAP1-PASSWORD-L NOT EQUAL TO ZEROES
                         IF       (MAP1-PASSWORD-ALP EQUAL TO 'PAL'
                                OR MAP1-PASSWORD-ALP EQUAL TO 'ABC')

                            AND MAP1-PASSWORD-NUM NUMERIC
                            AND MAP1-PASSWORD-NUM EQUAL (TWA-DATE + 1111)

                         THEN GO TO INQUIRY-SELECTED
                         ELSE GO TO PASSWORD-ERROR
                    ELSE GO TO PASSWORD-ERROR.

               IF TWA-CTR EQUAL TO 2
                    IF MAP1-PASSWORD-L NOT EQUAL TO ZEROES
                         IF      MAP1-PASSWORD-ALP EQUAL TO 'PAL'
                            AND MAP1-PASSWORD-NUM NUMERIC
                            AND MAP1-PASSWORD-NUM EQUAL (TWA-DATE + 2222)
                         THEN GO TO ADD-SELECTED
                         ELSE GO TO PASSWORD-ERROR
                    ELSE GO TO PASSWORD-ERROR.

               IF TWA-CTR EQUAL TO 4
                    IF MAP1-PASSWORD-L NOT EQUAL TO ZEROES
                         IF      MAP1-PASSWORD-ALP EQUAL TO 'PAL'
                            AND MAP1-PASSWORD-NUM NUMERIC
                            AND MAP1-PASSWORD-NUM EQUAL (TWA-DATE + 3333)
                         THEN GO TO UPDATE-SELECTED
                         ELSE GO TO PASSWORD-ERROR
                    ELSE GO TO PASSWORD-ERROR.

               IF TWA-CTR EQUAL TO 8
                    IF MAP1-PASSWORD-L NOT EQUAL TO ZEROES
                         IF      MAP1-PASSWORD-ALP EQUAL TO 'PAL'
                            AND MAP1-PASSWORD-NUM NUMERIC
                            AND MAP1-PASSWORD-NUM EQUAL (TWA-DATE + 4444)
                         THEN GO TO DELETE-SELECTED
                         ELSE GO TO PASSWORD-ERROR
                    ELSE GO TO PASSWORD-ERROR.

               IF TWA-CTR EQUAL TO 16
                    IF MAP1-PASSWORD-L NOT EQUAL TO ZEROES
                         IF         (MAP1-PASSWORD-ALP EQUAL TO 'PAL'
                                  OR  MAP1-PASSWORD-ALP EQUAL TO 'ABC'
                                  OR  MAP1-PASSWORD-ALP EQUAL TO 'XYZ')

                            AND MAP1-PASSWORD-NUM NUMERIC
                            AND MAP1-PASSWORD-NUM EQUAL (TWA-DATE + 5555)

                         THEN GO TO REGULAR-BROWSE-SELECTED
                         ELSE GO TO PASSWORD-ERROR
                    ELSE GO TO PASSWORD-ERROR.
```

Fig. 17.4. (Continued)

```
   10          ORAP01A          13.23.49          07/26/80

           IF TWA-CTR EQUAL TO 32
               IF MAP1-PASSWORD-L NOT EQUAL TO ZEROES
                   IF         (MAP1-PASSWORD-ALP EQUAL TO 'PAL'
                        OR  MAP1-PASSWORD-ALP EQUAL TO 'ABC'
                        OR  MAP1-PASSWORD-ALP EQUAL TO 'XYZ')

                     AND MAP1-PASSWORD-NUM NUMERIC
                     AND MAP1-PASSWORD-NUM EQUAL (TWA-DATE + 6666)

                   THEN GO TO ALTERNATE-BROWSE-SELECTED
                   ELSE GO TO PASSWORD-ERROR
               ELSE GO TO PASSWORD-ERROR.
```

Fig. 17.4. (Continued)

```
11          ORAP01A          13.23.49          07/26/80

            SUCCESSFUL-SELECTION-ROUTINES.

            INQUIRY-SELECTED.

                MOVE '0'                    TO COMMAREA-PROCESS-SW.
                MOVE MAP1-PASSWORD-ALP TO COMMAREA-OPERATOR-INITIAL.

           *    EXEC CICS
           *         XCTL PROGRAM   ('ORIQ01A')
           *              COMMAREA (COMMUNICATION-AREA)
           *              LENGTH    (4)
           *    END-EXEC.
                 MOVE 'ORIQ01A' TO DFHEIV3 MOVE 4 TO DFHEIV11 MOVE '
           -    '' TO DFHEIV0 CALL 'DFHEI1' USING DFHEIV0 DFHEIV3
                 COMMUNICATION-AREA DFHEIV11.



            ADD-SELECTED.

                MOVE '0'                    TO COMMAREA-PROCESS-SW.
                MOVE MAP1-PASSWORD-ALP TO COMMAREA-OPERATOR-INITIAL.

           *    EXEC CICS
           *         XCTL PROGRAM   ('ORAD01A')
           *              COMMAREA (COMMUNICATION-AREA)
           *              LENGTH    (4)
           *    END-EXEC.
                 MOVE 'ORAD01A' TO DFHEIV3 MOVE 4 TO DFHEIV11 MOVE '
           -    '' TO DFHEIV0 CALL 'DFHEI1' USING DFHEIV0 DFHEIV3
                 COMMUNICATION-AREA DFHEIV11.



            UPDATE-SELECTED.

                MOVE '0'                    TO COMMAREA-PROCESS-SW.
                MOVE MAP1-PASSWORD-ALP TO COMMAREA-OPERATOR-INITIAL.

           *    EXEC CICS
           *         XCTL PROGRAM   ('ORCH01A')
           *              COMMAREA (COMMUNICATION-AREA)
           *              LENGTH    (4)
           *    END-EXEC.
                 MOVE 'ORCH01A' TO DFHEIV3 MOVE 4 TO DFHEIV11 MOVE '
           -    '' TO DFHEIV0 CALL 'DFHEI1' USING DFHEIV0 DFHEIV3
                 COMMUNICATION-AREA DFHEIV11.
```

Fig. 17.4. (Continued)

```
      12           ORAP01A           13.23.49          07/26/80

00389              DELETE-SELECTED.

00391                 MOVE '0'                TO COMMAREA-PROCESS-SW.
00392                 MOVE MAP1-PASSWORD-ALP TO COMMAREA-OPERATOR-INITIAL.

00394        *        EXEC CICS
00395        *            XCTL PROGRAM  ('ORDL01A')
00396        *                COMMAREA (COMMUNICATION-AREA)
00397        *                LENGTH   (4)
00398        *        END-EXEC.
00399                 MOVE 'ORDL01A' TO DFHEIV3 MOVE 4 TO DFHEIV11 MOVE '
00400        -        ' TO DFHEIV0 CALL 'DFHEI1' USING DFHEIV0 DFHEIV3
00401                 COMMUNICATION-AREA DFHEIV11.
00402
00403

00405              REGULAR-BROWSE-SELECTED.

00407                 MOVE '0'                TO COMMAREA-PROCESS-SW.
00408                 MOVE MAP1-PASSWORD-ALP TO COMMAREA-OPERATOR-INITIAL.

00410        *        EXEC CICS
00411        *            XCTL PROGRAM  ('ORBRO1A')
00412        *                COMMAREA (COMMUNICATION-AREA)
00413        *                LENGTH   (4)
00414        *        END-EXEC.
00415                 MOVE 'ORBRO1A' TO DFHEIV3 MOVE 4 TO DFHEIV11 MOVE '
00416        -        ' TO DFHEIV0 CALL 'DFHEI1' USING DFHEIV0 DFHEIV3
00417                 COMMUNICATION-AREA DFHEIV11.
00418
00419

00421              ALTERNATE-BROWSE-SELECTED.

00423                 MOVE '0'                TO COMMAREA-PROCESS-SW.
00424                 MOVE MAP1-PASSWORD-ALP TO COMMAREA-OPERATOR-INITIAL.

00426        *        EXEC CICS
00427        *            XCTL PROGRAM  ('ORBS01A')
00428        *                COMMAREA (COMMUNICATION-AREA)
00429        *                LENGTH   (4)
00430        *        END-EXEC.
00431                 MOVE 'ORBS01A' TO DFHEIV3 MOVE 4 TO DFHEIV11 MOVE '
00432        -        ' TO DFHEIV0 CALL 'DFHEI1' USING DFHEIV0 DFHEIV3
00433                 COMMUNICATION-AREA DFHEIV11.
00434
00435
```

Fig. 17.4. (Continued)

```
  13         ORAP01A          13.23.49          07/26/80

           *****************************************************************
           *                                                               *
            INITIALIZATION SECTION.
           *                                                               *
           *****************************************************************


           *    EXEC CICS
           *         SEND MAP     ('ORAPM01')
           *              MAPSET ('ORAPS01')
           *              MAPONLY
           *              ERASE
           *    END-EXEC.
                 MOVE 'ORAPM01' TO DFHEIV1 MOVE 'ORAPS01' TO DFHEIV2 MOVE '
           -    '              ' TO DFHEIV0 CALL 'DFHEI1' USING DFHEIV0
                 DFHEIV1 DFHEIV99 DFHEIV98 DFHEIV2.



                MOVE '1' TO COMMAREA-PROCESS-SW.

           *    EXEC CICS
           *         RETURN TRANSID  ('ORAP')
           *                COMMAREA (COMMUNICATION-AREA)
           *                LENGTH   (1)
           *    END-EXEC.
                 MOVE 'ORAP' TO DFHEIV5 MOVE 1 TO DFHEIV11 MOVE '          '
                 TO DFHEIV0 CALL 'DFHEI1' USING DFHEIV0 DFHEIV5
                 COMMUNICATION-AREA DFHEIV11.


```

Fig. 17.4. (Continued)

```
    14          ORAP01A         13.23.49        07/26/80

00468       ********************************************************************
00469       *                                                                  *
00470        FINALIZATION SECTION.
00471       *                                                                  *
00472       ********************************************************************

00474        PREPARE-TERMINATION-MESSAGE.
00475            MOVE JOB-NORMAL-END-MESSAGE TO TWA-OPERATOR-MESSAGE.

00477        DISPLAY-OPERATOR-MESSAGE.

00479       *     EXEC CICS
00480       *         SEND FROM   (TWA-OPERATOR-MESSAGE)
00481       *              LENGTH (45)
00482       *              ERASE
00483       *     END-EXEC.
00484             MOVE 45 TO DFHEIV11 MOVE '               ' TO DFHEIVO CALL '
00485       -     'DFHEI1' USING DFHEIVO DFHEIV99 DFHEIV98 TWA-OPERATOR-MESSAGE
00486             DFHEIV11.
00487
00488

00490        END-OF-JOB.

00492       *     EXEC CICS
00493       *          RETURN
00494       *     END-EXEC.
00495             MOVE '          ' TO DFHEIVO CALL 'DFHEI1' USING DFHEIVO.
00496
00497
```

Fig. 17.4. (Continued)

```
15          ORAPO1A          13.23.49          07/26/80

00499       ****************************************************************
00500       *                                                              *
00501       ABNORMAL-TERMINATION SECTION.
00502       *                                                              *
00503       ****************************************************************

00505       PASSWORD-ERROR.
00506           MOVE 'INVALID PASSWORD' TO MAJOR-ERROR-MSG.
00507           GO TO PREPARE-ABORT-MESSAGE.

00509       NO-FUNCTION-ERROR.
00510           MOVE 'NO FUNCTION CHOSEN' TO MAJOR-ERROR-MSG.
00511           GO TO PREPARE-ABORT-MESSAGE.

00513       MULTIPLE-FUNCTION-ERROR.
00514           MOVE 'MULTIPLE FUNCTIONS NOT ALLOWED' TO MAJOR-ERROR-MSG.
00515           GO TO PREPARE-ABORT-MESSAGE.

00517       MAPFAIL-ERROR.
00518           MOVE 'MAP FAILURE' TO MAJOR-ERROR-MSG.
00519           GO TO PREPARE-ABORT-MESSAGE.

00521       MAJOR-ERROR.
00522           MOVE  EIBFN     TO  OLD-EIBFN.
00523           MOVE  EIBRCODE  TO  OLD-EIBRCODE.

00525       *    EXEC CICS
00526       *        DUMP DUMPCODE ('ERRS')
00527       *    END-EXEC.
00528            MOVE 'ERRS' TO DFHEIV5 MOVE '         ' TO DFHEIVO CALL 'DFH
00529       -    'EI1' USING DFHEIVO DFHEIV5.
00530
00531           MOVE 'MAJOR ERROR' TO MAJOR-ERROR-MSG.
00532           GO TO PREPARE-ABORT-MESSAGE.

00534       PREPARE-ABORT-MESSAGE.
00535           MOVE JOB-ABORTED-MESSAGE TO TWA-OPERATOR-MESSAGE.
00536           GO TO DISPLAY-OPERATOR-MESSAGE.
```

Fig. 17.4. (Continued)

not the command-language translator, and thus the commands will already be as translated.

THE MAIN-LINE SECTION

1. Lines 187–191. ADDRESS command for the TWA.
2. Lines 193–202. HANDLE AID command. For this very simple program, the use of the PA keys to restart the session* saves coding extra statements.
3. Lines 207–214. HANDLE CONDITION command.
4. Lines 217–218. If this is not the first execution of the program in the session, the application selected and the corresponding password are validated.
5. Lines 220–221. If this is the first execution of the program in the session, the INITIALIZATION section is executed.

THE INITIALIZATION SECTION

1. Lines 443–451. Display the password map.
2. Line 455. Set the communication area switch to 1.
3. Lines 457–464. Terminate the task.

THE PASSWORD-VALIDATION SECTION

1. Lines 229–236. Read the map containing the password and the application selected.

*The PA keys generally have different functions. See page 206 and the other program examples.

2. Lines 239–257. We use binary integers to detect which application was selected. This is a programming technique.
3. Lines 259–268. If there was more than one application selected, we have a "multiple function" error; if no function was selected, we have a "no function" error.
4. Lines 270–337. Check the password entered against the application selected. If valid, the particular application is selected through a XCTL command; otherwise, there is a password error.
5. Lines 341–433. The paragraphs to select the particular application. Note that a communication area switch with a value of '0' and the password are sent to the program selected.

THE FINALIZATION SECTION

1. Lines 474–486. Display the "JOB NORMALLY TERMINATED" message.
2. Lines 490–495. Terminate the session.

THE ABNORMAL-TERMINATION SECTION

These are the routines used to abnormally terminate the session on errors and CICS/VS command exceptional conditions not covered by a HANDLE CONDITION command.

EXAMPLE

The following are fascimiles of actual photographs taken of a CRT terminal during a session.

Fig. 17.5. The operator keys in the transaction identifier "ORAP," then hits the ENTER key.

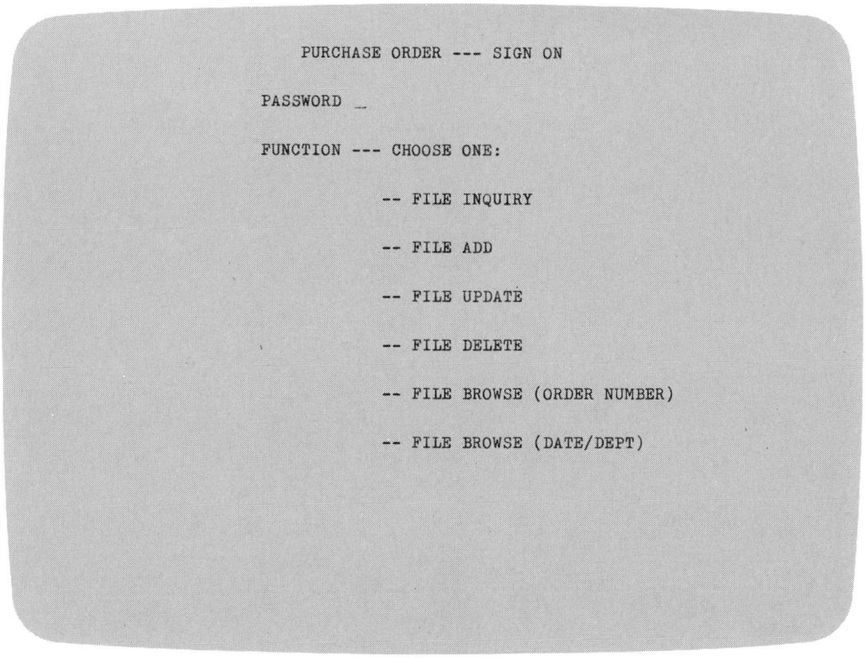

Fig. 17.6. The Sign On program executes and the Sign On map is displayed. The operator may now select the application he wants.

Fig. 17.7. If the operator keys in a transaction identifier not in the Program Control Table, then hits the ENTER key . . . . .

ORAQ DFH2001 INVALID TRANSACTION IDENTIFICATION - PLEASE RESUBMIT

Fig. 17.8. . . . . . Task Control terminates the task and the appropriate message is displayed.

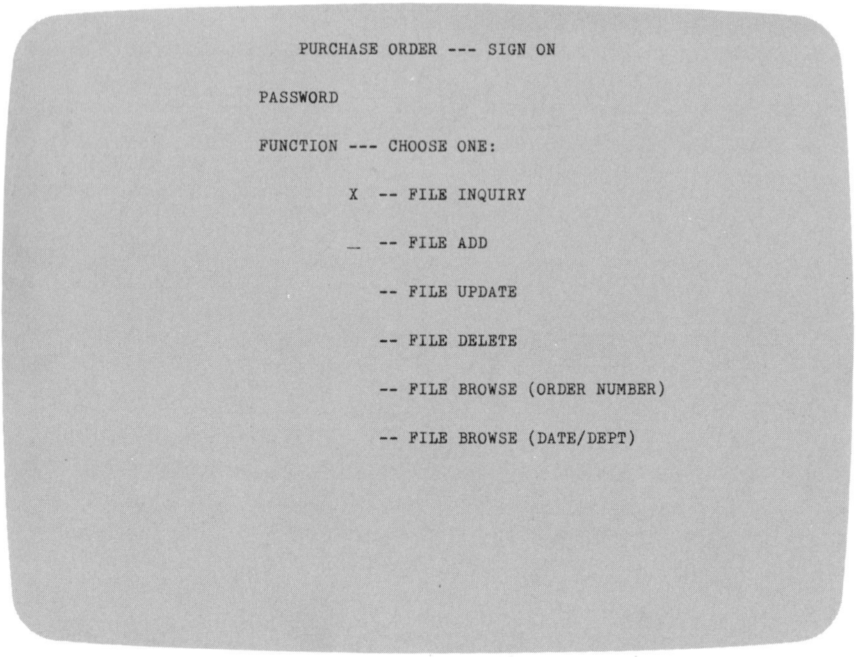

Fig. 17.9. If the operator keys in a password (defined with the DRK attribute) that is invalid for the application selected, then hits the ENTER key, ...

JOB ABORTED -- INVALID PASSWORD

Fig. 17.10. . . . . . The Sign On program is aborted and the appropriate message is displayed.

18

The File Inquiry Program

INTRODUCTION

The File Inquiry program allows the operator to display information from a record selected by using its record key. It executes when selected by the Sign-on program and will continue executing in the session until terminated by the operator. The flow of control to execute this program is shown in Figure 18.1.

PROGRAM SPECIFICATION

The program specifications are as follows:

1. Implement the program using the pseudoconversational mode of processing.
2. Use 'ORIQ' as the transaction identifier. However, the session should not be started by using this identifier, but rather through an XCTL command from the Sign-on program.
3. If the session is started by using the transaction identifier, abort the session with the message "JOB ABORTED–SIGNON VIOLATION."
4. The record to be displayed is based on the order number.
5. If the order number entered is not numeric, display the message "INVALID ORDER NUMBER."
6. If the record is not in the file, display the message "RECORD NOT FOUND."
7. For (5) and (6), allow the operator to correct the order number.

8. If the record is in the file, display it.
9. On any PA key, display the message "WRONG KEY USED"; allow the operator to continue with the session.

SCREEN LAYOUT

The screen layout to be used in the program is shown in Figure 18.2. All 9s are numeric fields and Xs are alphanumeric fields.

MAP PROGRAM

The map program corresponding to the screen layout is Figure 18.3.

PROGRAM LISTING

The program listing for the File Inquiry program is shown in Figure 18.4. The listing is that of the compiler and not the command-language translator, and thus the commands are already as translated.

THE MAIN-LINE SECTION

1. Lines 267–271. ADDRESS command for the TWA.
2. Lines 273–282. HANDLE AID command. The PA keys will result in the "WRONG KEY USED" error.
3. Lines 287–294. HANDLE CONDITION command.
4. Lines 297–302. The selection of sections.

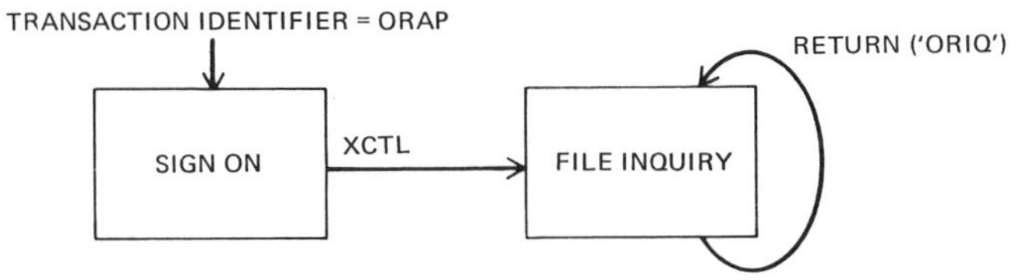

Fig. 18.1. File Inquiry Application.

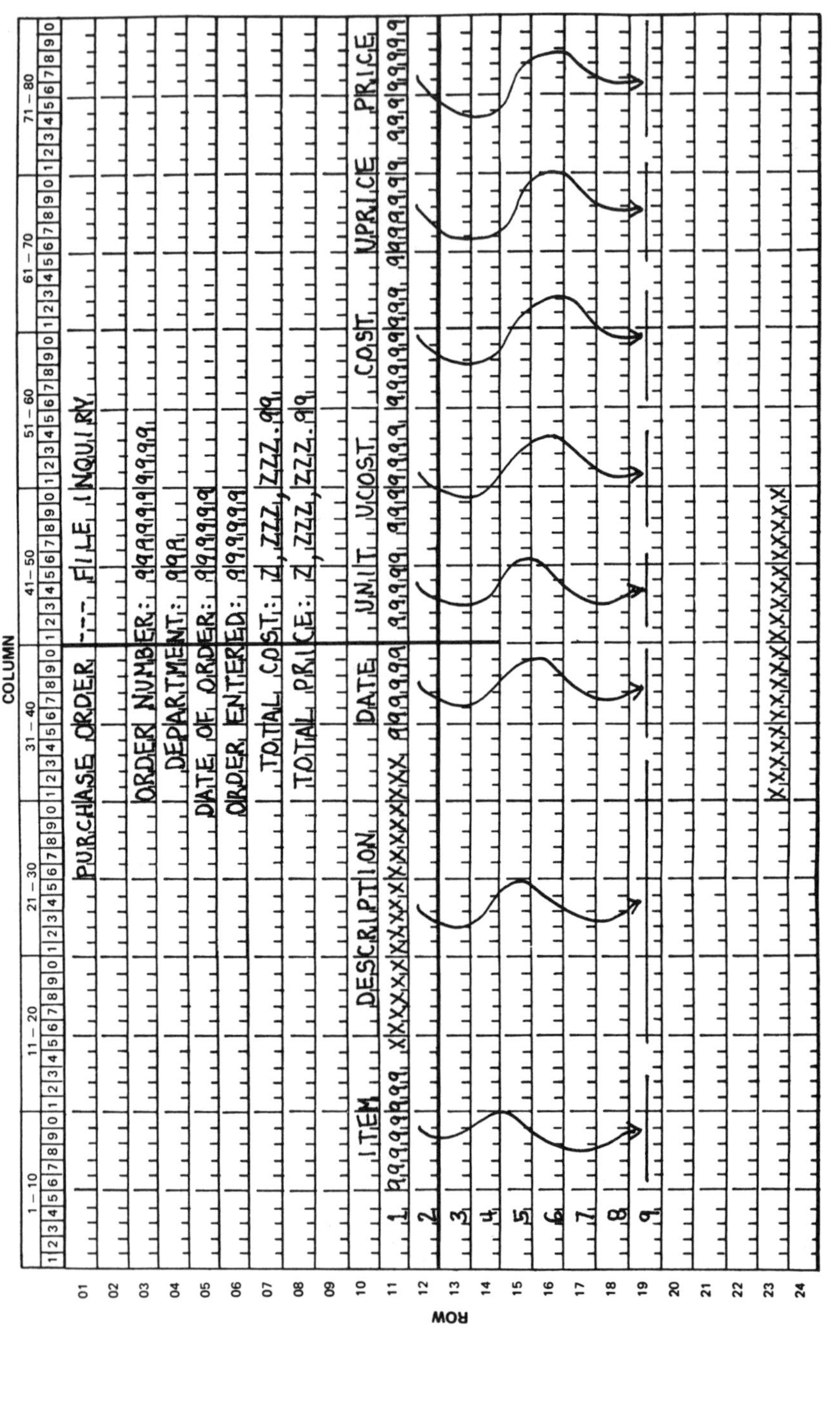

Fig. 18.2. Screen Layout – File Inquiry.

```
STMT    SOURCE STATEMENT                                  DOS/VS ASSEMBLER REL 34.0 14.03

   1             PRINT NOGEN
   2 ORIQS01     DFHMSD TYPE=MAP,MODE=INOUT,CTRL=FREEKB,LANG=COBOL,TIOAPFX=YES
  12 ORIQM01     DFHMDI SIZE=(24,80)
  40 DUMMY       DFHMDF POS=(01,01),LENGTH=01,ATTRB=(ASKIP,DRK,FSET),           X
                       INITIAL='1'
  52             DFHMDF POS=(01,25),LENGTH=31,ATTRB=(ASKIP,BRT),                X
                       INITIAL='PURCHASE ORDER --- FILE INQUIRY'
  64             DFHMDF POS=(03,30),LENGTH=13,ATTRB=ASKIP,                      X
                       INITIAL='ORDER NUMBER '
  76 ORDER       DFHMDF POS=(03,44),LENGTH=10,ATTRB=(NUM,BRT,IC)
  87             DFHMDF POS=(03,55),LENGTH=01,ATTRB=PROT
  98             DFHMDF POS=(04,32),LENGTH=11,ATTRB=ASKIP,INITIAL='DEPARTMENT '
 110 DEPT        DFHMDF POS=(04,44),LENGTH=03,ATTRB=(ASKIP,BRT)
 121             DFHMDF POS=(05,29),LENGTH=14,ATTRB=ASKIP,                      X
                       INITIAL='DATE OF ORDER '
 133 DATEOR      DFHMDF POS=(05,44),LENGTH=06,ATTRB=(ASKIP,BRT)
 144             DFHMDF POS=(06,29),LENGTH=14,ATTRB=ASKIP,                      X
                       INITIAL='ORDER ENTERED '
 156 DATEENT     DFHMDF POS=(06,44),LENGTH=06,ATTRB=(ASKIP,BRT)
 167             DFHMDF POS=(07,32),LENGTH=11,ATTRB=ASKIP,INITIAL='TOTAL COST '
 179 TOTCOST     DFHMDF POS=(07,44),LENGTH=12,ATTRB=(ASKIP,BRT),                X
                       PICOUT='Z,ZZZ,ZZZ.99'
 190             DFHMDF POS=(08,31),LENGTH=12,ATTRB=ASKIP,                      X
                       INITIAL='TOTAL PRICE '
 202 TOTPRCE     DFHMDF POS=(08,44),LENGTH=12,ATTRB=(ASKIP,BRT),                X
                       PICOUT='Z,ZZZ,ZZZ.99'
 213             DFHMDF POS=(10,07),LENGTH=04,ATTRB=ASKIP,INITIAL='ITEM'
 225             DFHMDF POS=(10,17),LENGTH=11,ATTRB=ASKIP,INITIAL='DESCRIPTION'
 237             DFHMDF POS=(10,35),LENGTH=04,ATTRB=ASKIP,INITIAL='DATE'
 249             DFHMDF POS=(10,42),LENGTH=04,ATTRB=ASKIP,INITIAL='UNIT'
 261             DFHMDF POS=(10,48),LENGTH=05,ATTRB=ASKIP,INITIAL='UCOST'
 273             DFHMDF POS=(10,57),LENGTH=04,ATTRB=ASKIP,INITIAL='COST'
 285             DFHMDF POS=(10,65),LENGTH=06,ATTRB=ASKIP,INITIAL='UPRICE'
 297             DFHMDF POS=(10,74),LENGTH=05,ATTRB=ASKIP,INITIAL='PRICE'
 309 LINE1       DFHMDF POS=(11,03),LENGTH=01,ATTRB=ASKIP
 320 ITEM1       DFHMDF POS=(11,05),LENGTH=08,ATTRB=(ASKIP,BRT),                X
                       PICIN='99999999',PICOUT='99999999'
 331 DESC1       DFHMDF POS=(11,14),LENGTH=19,ATTRB=(ASKIP,BRT)
 342 LNDATE1     DFHMDF POS=(11,34),LENGTH=06,ATTRB=(ASKIP,BRT)
 353 UNIT1       DFHMDF POS=(11,41),LENGTH=05,ATTRB=(ASKIP,BRT),                X
                       PICIN='99999',PICOUT='99999'
 364 UCOST1      DFHMDF POS=(11,47),LENGTH=07,ATTRB=(ASKIP,BRT),                X
                       PICIN='9999999',PICOUT='9999999'
 375 COST1       DFHMDF POS=(11,55),LENGTH=08,ATTRB=(ASKIP,BRT),                X
                       PICIN='99999999',PICOUT='99999999'
 386 UPRICE1     DFHMDF POS=(11,64),LENGTH=07,ATTRB=(ASKIP,BRT),                X
                       PICIN='9999999',PICOUT='9999999'
 397 PRICE1      DFHMDF POS=(11,72),LENGTH=08,ATTRB=(ASKIP,BRT),                X
                       PICIN='99999999',PICOUT='99999999'
 408 LINE2       DFHMDF POS=(12,03),LENGTH=01,ATTRB=ASKIP
 419 ITEM2       DFHMDF POS=(12,05),LENGTH=08,ATTRB=(ASKIP,BRT),                X
```

Fig. 18.3. Map Program – File Inquiry.

```
STMT    SOURCE STATEMENT                                    DOS/VS ASSEMBLER REL 34.0 14.03

                          PICIN='99999999',PICOUT='99999999'
 430 DESC2       DFHMDF  POS=(12,14),LENGTH=19,ATTRB=(ASKIP,BRT)
 441 LNDATE2     DFHMDF  POS=(12,34),LENGTH=06,ATTRB=(ASKIP,BRT)
 452 UNIT2       DFHMDF  POS=(12,41),LENGTH=05,ATTRB=(ASKIP,BRT),          X
                          PICIN='99999',PICOUT='99999'
 463 UCOST2      DFHMDF  POS=(12,47),LENGTH=07,ATTRB=(ASKIP,BRT),          X
                          PICIN='9999999',PICOUT='9999999'
 474 COST2       DFHMDF  POS=(12,55),LENGTH=08,ATTRB=(ASKIP,BRT),          X
                          PICIN='99999999',PICOUT='99999999'
 485 UPRICE2     DFHMDF  POS=(12,64),LENGTH=07,ATTRB=(ASKIP,BRT),          X
                          PICIN='9999999',PICOUT='9999999'
 496 PRICE2      DFHMDF  POS=(12,72),LENGTH=08,ATTRB=(ASKIP,BRT),          X
                          PICIN='99999999',PICOUT='99999999'
 507 LINE3       DFHMDF  POS=(13,03),LENGTH=01,ATTRB=ASKIP
 518 ITEM3       DFHMDF  POS=(13,05),LENGTH=08,ATTRB=(ASKIP,BRT),          X
                          PICIN='99999999',PICOUT='99999999'
 529 DESC3       DFHMDF  POS=(13,14),LENGTH=19,ATTRB=(ASKIP,BRT)
 540 LNDATE3     DFHMDF  POS=(13,34),LENGTH=06,ATTRB=(ASKIP,BRT)
 551 UNIT3       DFHMDF  POS=(13,41),LENGTH=05,ATTRB=(ASKIP,BRT),          X
                          PICIN='99999',PICOUT='99999'
 562 UCOST3      DFHMDF  POS=(13,47),LENGTH=07,ATTRB=(ASKIP,BRT),          X
                          PICIN='9999999',PICOUT='9999999'
 573 COST3       DFHMDF  POS=(13,55),LENGTH=08,ATTRB=(ASKIP,BRT),          X
                          PICIN='99999999',PICOUT='99999999'
 584 UPRICE3     DFHMDF  POS=(13,64),LENGTH=07,ATTRB=(ASKIP,BRT),          X
                          PICIN='9999999',PICOUT='9999999'
 595 PRICE3      DFHMDF  POS=(13,72),LENGTH=08,ATTRB=(ASKIP,BRT),          X
                          PICIN='99999999',PICOUT='99999999'
 606 LINE4       DFHMDF  POS=(14,03),LENGTH=01,ATTRB=ASKIP
 617 ITEM4       DFHMDF  POS=(14,05),LENGTH=08,ATTRB=(ASKIP,BRT),          X
                          PICIN='99999999',PICOUT='99999999'
 628 DESC4       DFHMDF  POS=(14,14),LENGTH=19,ATTRB=(ASKIP,BRT)
 639 LNDATE4     DFHMDF  POS=(14,34),LENGTH=06,ATTRB=(ASKIP,BRT)
 650 UNIT4       DFHMDF  POS=(14,41),LENGTH=05,ATTRB=(ASKIP,BRT),          X
                          PICIN='99999',PICOUT='99999'
 661 UCOST4      DFHMDF  POS=(14,47),LENGTH=07,ATTRB=(ASKIP,BRT),          X
                          PICIN='9999999',PICOUT='9999999'
 672 COST4       DFHMDF  POS=(14,55),LENGTH=08,ATTRB=(ASKIP,BRT),          X
                          PICIN='99999999',PICOUT='99999999'
 683 UPRICE4     DFHMDF  POS=(14,64),LENGTH=07,ATTRB=(ASKIP,BRT),          X
                          PICIN='9999999',PICOUT='9999999'
 694 PRICE4      DFHMDF  POS=(14,72),LENGTH=08,ATTRB=(ASKIP,BRT),          X
                          PICIN='99999999',PICOUT='99999999'
 705 LINE5       DFHMDF  POS=(15,03),LENGTH=01,ATTRB=ASKIP
 716 ITEM5       DFHMDF  POS=(15,05),LENGTH=08,ATTRB=(ASKIP,BRT),          X
                          PICIN='99999999',PICOUT='99999999'
 727 DESC5       DFHMDF  POS=(15,14),LENGTH=19,ATTRB=(ASKIP,BRT)
 738 LNDATE5     DFHMDF  POS=(15,34),LENGTH=06,ATTRB=(ASKIP,BRT)
 749 UNIT5       DFHMDF  POS=(15,41),LENGTH=05,ATTRB=(ASKIP,BRT),          X
                          PICIN='99999',PICOUT='99999'
 760 UCOST5      DFHMDF  POS=(15,47),LENGTH=07,ATTRB=(ASKIP,BRT),          X
```

Fig. 18.3. Map Program – File Inquiry.

```
STMT    SOURCE STATEMENT                                   DOS/VS ASSEMBLER REL 34.0 14.03

                              PICIN='9999999',PICOUT='9999999'
 771 COST5     DFHMDF POS=(15,55),LENGTH=08,ATTRB=(ASKIP,BRT),            X
                              PICIN='99999999',PICOUT='99999999'
 782 UPRICE5   DFHMDF POS=(15,64),LENGTH=07,ATTRB=(ASKIP,BRT),            X
                              PICIN='9999999',PICOUT='9999999'
 793 PRICE5    DFHMDF POS=(15,72),LENGTH=08,ATTRB=(ASKIP,BRT),            X
                              PICIN='99999999',PICOUT='99999999'
 804 LINE6     DFHMDF POS=(16,03),LENGTH=01,ATTRB=ASKIP
 815 ITEM6     DFHMDF POS=(16,05),LENGTH=08,ATTRB=(ASKIP,BRT),            X
                              PICIN='99999999',PICOUT='99999999'
 826 DESC6     DFHMDF POS=(16,14),LENGTH=19,ATTRB=(ASKIP,BRT)
 837 LNDATE6   DFHMDF POS=(16,34),LENGTH=06,ATTRB=(ASKIP,BRT)
 848 UNIT6     DFHMDF POS=(16,41),LENGTH=05,ATTRB=(ASKIP,BRT),            X
                              PICIN='99999',PICOUT='99999'
 859 UCOST6    DFHMDF POS=(16,47),LENGTH=07,ATTRB=(ASKIP,BRT),            X
                              PICIN='9999999',PICOUT='9999999'
 870 COST6     DFHMDF POS=(16,55),LENGTH=08,ATTRB=(ASKIP,BRT),            X
                              PICIN='99999999',PICOUT='99999999'
 881 UPRICE6   DFHMDF POS=(16,64),LENGTH=07,ATTRB=(ASKIP,BRT),            X
                              PICIN='9999999',PICOUT='9999999'
 892 PRICE6    DFHMDF POS=(16,72),LENGTH=08,ATTRB=(ASKIP,BRT),            X
                              PICIN='99999999',PICOUT='99999999'
 903 LINE7     DFHMDF POS=(17,03),LENGTH=01,ATTRB=ASKIP
 914 ITEM7     DFHMDF POS=(17,05),LENGTH=08,ATTRB=(ASKIP,BRT),            X
                              PICIN='99999999',PICOUT='99999999'
 925 DESC7     DFHMDF POS=(17,14),LENGTH=19,ATTRB=(ASKIP,BRT)
 936 LNDATE7   DFHMDF POS=(17,34),LENGTH=06,ATTRB=(ASKIP,BRT)
 947 UNIT7     DFHMDF POS=(17,41),LENGTH=05,ATTRB=(ASKIP,BRT),            X
                              PICIN='99999',PICOUT='99999'
 958 UCOST7    DFHMDF POS=(17,47),LENGTH=07,ATTRB=(ASKIP,BRT),            X
                              PICIN='9999999',PICOUT='9999999'
 969 COST7     DFHMDF POS=(17,55),LENGTH=08,ATTRB=(ASKIP,BRT),            X
                              PICIN='99999999',PICOUT='99999999'
 980 UPRICE7   DFHMDF POS=(17,64),LENGTH=07,ATTRB=(ASKIP,BRT),            X
                              PICIN='9999999',PICOUT='9999999'
 991 PRICE7    DFHMDF POS=(17,72),LENGTH=08,ATTRB=(ASKIP,BRT),            X
                              PICIN='99999999',PICOUT='99999999'
1002 LINE8     DFHMDF POS=(18,03),LENGTH=01,ATTRB=ASKIP
1013 ITEM8     DFHMDF POS=(18,05),LENGTH=08,ATTRB=(ASKIP,BRT),            X
                              PICIN='99999999',PICOUT='99999999'
1024 DESC8     DFHMDF POS=(18,14),LENGTH=19,ATTRB=(ASKIP,BRT)
1035 LNDATE8   DFHMDF POS=(18,34),LENGTH=06,ATTRB=(ASKIP,BRT)
1046 UNIT8     DFHMDF POS=(18,41),LENGTH=05,ATTRB=(ASKIP,BRT),            X
                              PICIN='99999',PICOUT='99999'
1057 UCOST8    DFHMDF POS=(18,47),LENGTH=07,ATTRB=(ASKIP,BRT),            X
                              PICIN='9999999',PICOUT='9999999'
1068 COST8     DFHMDF POS=(18,55),LENGTH=08,ATTRB=(ASKIP,BRT),            X
                              PICIN='99999999',PICOUT='99999999'
1079 UPRICE8   DFHMDF POS=(18,64),LENGTH=07,ATTRB=(ASKIP,BRT),            X
                              PICIN='9999999',PICOUT='9999999'
1090 PRICE8    DFHMDF POS=(18,72),LENGTH=08,ATTRB=(ASKIP,BRT),            X
```

Fig. 18.3. Map Program – File Inquiry.

```
STMT    SOURCE STATEMENT                                  DOS/VS ASSEMBLER REL 34.0 14.03

                              PICIN='99999999',PICOUT='99999999'
1101 LINE9      DFHMDF  POS=(19,03),LENGTH=01,ATTRB=ASKIP
1112 ITEM9      DFHMDF  POS=(19,05),LENGTH=08,ATTRB=(ASKIP,BRT),           X
                              PICIN='99999999',PICOUT='99999999'
1123 DESC9      DFHMDF  POS=(19,14),LENGTH=19,ATTRB=(ASKIP,BRT)
1134 LNDATE9    DFHMDF  POS=(19,34),LENGTH=06,ATTRB=(ASKIP,BRT)
1145 UNIT9      DFHMDF  POS=(19,41),LENGTH=05,ATTRB=(ASKIP,BRT),           X
                              PICIN='99999',PICOUT='99999'
1156 UCOST9     DFHMDF  POS=(19,47),LENGTH=07,ATTRB=(ASKIP,BRT),           X
                              PICIN='9999999',PICOUT='9999999'
1167 COST9      DFHMDF  POS=(19,55),LENGTH=08,ATTRB=(ASKIP,BRT),           X
                              PICIN='99999999',PICOUT='99999999'
1178 UPRICE9    DFHMDF  POS=(19,64),LENGTH=07,ATTRB=(ASKIP,BRT),           X
                              PICIN='9999999',PICOUT='9999999'
1189 PRICE9     DFHMDF  POS=(19,72),LENGTH=08,ATTRB=(ASKIP,BRT),           X
                              PICIN='99999999',PICOUT='99999999'
1200 ERROR      DFHMDF  POS=(23,30),LENGTH=20,ATTRB=(ASKIP,BRT)
1211            DFHMSD  TYPE=FINAL
1225            END
```

Fig. 18.3. Map Program – File Inquiry.

```
      1   IBM DOS VS COBOL

 CBL SUPMAP,STXIT,NOTRUNC,CSYNTAX,SXREF,OPT,VERB,CLIST,BUF=19069
 CBL NOOPT,LIB
00001            IDENTIFICATION DIVISION.

00003            PROGRAM-ID. ORIQO1A.


00005            ENVIRONMENT DIVISION.

00007            *****************************************************************
00008            *                                                               *
00009            *    1. THIS PROGRAM DISPLAYS PURCHASE ORDER MASTER RECORDS     *
00010            *       BASED ON THE ORDER NUMBER ENTERED BY THE OPERATOR.      *
00011            *                                                               *
00012            *****************************************************************
```

Fig. 18.4. File Inquiry Program.

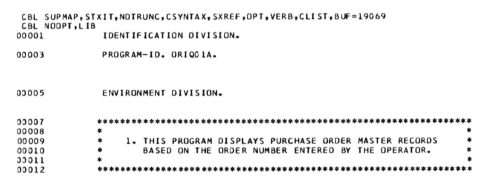

```
2          ORIQ01A          12.55.39          08/02/80

           DATA DIVISION.

           WORKING-STORAGE SECTION.

           01  COMMUNICATION-AREA.

               05  COMMAREA-PROCESS-SW      PIC X.

           01  AREA1.

               05  JOB-NORMAL-END-MESSAGE  PIC X(23) VALUE
                   'JOB NORMALLY TERMINATED'.

               05  JOB-ABORTED-MESSAGE.
                 10  FILLER                 PIC X(15) VALUE 'JOB ABORTED --'.
                 10  MAJOR-ERROR-MSG        PIC X(16).

               05  HEXADECIMAL-ZEROES       PIC 9999 COMP VALUE ZEROES.

               05  FILLER REDEFINES HEXADECIMAL-ZEROES.
                 10  FILLER                 PIC X.
                 10  HEX-ZEROES             PIC X.

               05  OLD-EIB-AREA.
                 10  FILLER                 PIC X(7) VALUE 'OLD EIB'.
                 10  OLD-EIBFN              PIC XX.
                 10  OLD-EIBRCODE           PIC X(6).
```

Fig. 18.4. (Continued)

```
    3        ORIQ01A         12.55.39         08/02/80

                01  DFHEIVAR COPY DFHEIVAR.
    C           01  DFHEIVAR.
    C               02    DFHEIV0   PICTURE X(26).
    C               02    DFHEIV1   PICTURE X(8).
    C               02    DFHEIV2   PICTURE X(8).
    C               02    DFHEIV3   PICTURE X(8).
    C               02    DFHEIV4   PICTURE X(6).
    C               02    DFHEIV5   PICTURE X(4).
    C               02    DFHEIV6   PICTURE X(4).
    C               02    DFHEIV7   PICTURE X(2).
    C               02    DFHEIV8   PICTURE X(2).
    C               02    DFHEIV9   PICTURE X(1).
    C               02    DFHEIV10  PICTURE S9(7)  USAGE COMPUTATIONAL-3.
    C               02    DFHEIV11  PICTURE S9(4)  USAGE COMPUTATIONAL.
    C               02    DFHEIV12  PICTURE S9(4)  USAGE COMPUTATIONAL.
    C               02    DFHEIV13  PICTURE S9(4)  USAGE COMPUTATIONAL.
    C               02    DFHEIV14  PICTURE S9(4)  USAGE COMPUTATIONAL.
    C               02    DFHEIV15  PICTURE S9(4)  USAGE COMPUTATIONAL.
    C               02    DFHEIV16  PICTURE S9(9)  USAGE COMPUTATIONAL.
    C               02    DFHEIV17  PICTURE X(4).
    C               02    DFHEIV18  PICTURE X(4).
    C               02    DFHEIV19  PICTURE X(4).
    C               02    DFHEIV97  PICTURE S9(7)  USAGE COMPUTATIONAL-3 VALUE ZERO.
    C               02    DFHEIV98  PICTURE S9(4)  USAGE COMPUTATIONAL VALUE ZERO.
    C               02    DFHEIV99  PICTURE X(1)   VALUE SPACE.
                LINKAGE SECTION.
                01  DFHEIBLK COPY DFHEIBLK.
    C          *      EIBLK EXEC INTERFACE BLOCK
    C           01    DFHEIBLK.
    C          *         EIBTIME       TIME IN 0HHMMSS FORMAT
    C                 02 EIBTIME       PICTURE S9(7) USAGE COMPUTATIONAL-3.
    C          *         EIBDATE       DATE IN 00YYDDD FORMAT
    C                 02 EIBDATE       PICTURE S9(7) USAGE COMPUTATIONAL-3.
    C          *         EIBTRNID      TRANSACTION IDENTIFIER
    C                 02 EIBTRNID      PICTURE X(4).
    C          *         EIBTASKN      TASK NUMBER
    C                 02 EIBTASKN      PICTURE S9(7) USAGE COMPUTATIONAL-3.
    C          *         EIBTRMID      TERMINAL IDENTIFIER
    C                 02 EIBTRMID      PICTURE X(4).
    C          *         DFHEIGDI      RESERVED
    C                 02 DFHEIGDI      PICTURE S9(4) USAGE COMPUTATIONAL.
    C          *         EIBCPOSN      CURSOR POSITION
    C                 02 EIBCPOSN      PICTURE S9(4) USAGE COMPUTATIONAL.
    C          *         EIBCALEN      COMMAREA LENGTH
    C                 02 EIBCALEN      PICTURE S9(4) USAGE COMPUTATIONAL.
    C          *         EIBAID        ATTENTION IDENTIFIER
    C                 02 EIBAID        PICTURE X(1).
    C          *         EIBFN         FUNCTION CODE
    C                 02 EIBFN         PICTURE X(2).
    C          *         EIBRCODE      RESPONSE CODE
    C                 02 EIBRCODE      PICTURE X(6).
    C          *         EIBDS         DATASET NAME
    C                 02 EIBDS         PICTURE X(8).
```

Fig. 18.4. (Continued)

```
     4          ORIQ01A           12.55.39          08/02/80

                *          EIBREQID   REQUEST IDENTIFIER
                       02 EIBREQID   PICTURE X(8).
                 01  DFHCOMMAREA                       PIC X.

                        88  INITIAL-ENTRY-TIME              VALUE '0'.
                        88  ORDER-DISPLAY-TIME              VALUE '1'.


                 01  LINKAGE-POINTERS.

                     05  FILLER                        PIC S9(8) COMP.
                     05  MAP1-POINTER                  PIC S9(8) COMP.
                     05  POM-POINTER                   PIC S9(8) COMP.
                     05  TWA-POINTER                   PIC S9(8) COMP.
```

Fig. 18.4. (Continued)

```
    5          ORIQ01A          12.55.39          08/02/80

           *****************************************************************
           *                                                               *
           *               DISPLAY MAP DESCRIPTION                         *
           *                                                               *
           *****************************************************************


            01  MAP1-AREA.
                05  FILLER                          PIC X(12).
                05  MAP1-DUMMY-L                    PIC S9999 COMP.
                05  MAP1-DUMMY-A                    PIC X.
                05  MAP1-DUMMY                      PIC X.
                05  MAP1-ORDER-NUMBER-L             PIC S9999 COMP.
                05  MAP1-ORDER-NUMBER-A             PIC X.
                05  MAP1-ORDER-NUMBER               PIC X(10).
                05  MAP1-DEPARTMENT-L               PIC S9999 COMP.
                05  MAP1-DEPARTMENT-A               PIC X.
                05  MAP1-DEPARTMENT                 PIC XXX.
                05  MAP1-ORDER-DATE-L               PIC S9999 COMP.
                05  MAP1-ORDER-DATE-A               PIC X.
                05  MAP1-ORDER-DATE.
                  10  MAP1-ORDER-DATE-MONTH         PIC XX.
                  10  MAP1-ORDER-DATE-DAY           PIC XX.
                  10  MAP1-ORDER-DATE-YEAR          PIC XX.
                05  MAP1-ORDER-DATE-ENTERED-L       PIC S9999 COMP.
                05  MAP1-ORDER-DATE-ENTERED-A       PIC X.
                05  MAP1-ORDER-DATE-ENTERED         PIC X(6).
                05  MAP1-TOTAL-COST-L               PIC S9999 COMP.
                05  MAP1-TOTAL-COST-A               PIC X.
                05  MAP1-TOTAL-COST                 PIC Z,ZZZ,ZZZ.99.
                05  MAP1-TOTAL-PRICE-L              PIC S9999 COMP.
                05  MAP1-TOTAL-PRICE-A              PIC X.
                05  MAP1-TOTAL-PRICE                PIC Z,ZZZ,ZZZ.99.
                05  MAP1-LINE-ITEM              OCCURS 9
                                                INDEXED BY MAP1-LINE-I.
                  10  MAP1-LINE-NUMBER-L            PIC S9999 COMP.
                  10  MAP1-LINE-NUMBER-A            PIC X.
                  10  MAP1-LINE-NUMBER              PIC 9.
                  10  MAP1-ITEM-NUMBER-L            PIC S9999 COMP.
                  10  MAP1-ITEM-NUMBER-A            PIC X.
                  10  MAP1-ITEM-NUMBER              PIC 9(8).
                  10  MAP1-ITEM-DESCRIPTION-L       PIC S9999 COMP.
                  10  MAP1-ITEM-DESCRIPTION-A       PIC X.
                  10  MAP1-ITEM-DESCRIPTION         PIC X(19).
                  10  MAP1-ITEM-DATE-L              PIC S9999 COMP.
                  10  MAP1-ITEM-DATE-A              PIC X.
                  10  MAP1-ITEM-DATE                PIC X(6).
                  10  MAP1-UNIT-L                   PIC S9999 COMP.
                  10  MAP1-UNIT-A                   PIC X.
                  10  MAP1-UNIT                     PIC 9(5).
                  10  MAP1-UNIT-COST-L              PIC S9999 COMP.
                  10  MAP1-UNIT-COST-A              PIC X.
```

Fig. 18.4. (Continued)

```
      6         ORIQ01A          12.55.39          08/02/80

                         10  MAP1-UNIT-COST              PIC 9(7).
                         10  MAP1-COST-L                 PIC S9999 COMP.
                         10  MAP1-COST-A                 PIC X.
                         10  MAP1-COST                   PIC 9(8).
                         10  MAP1-UNIT-PRICE-L           PIC S9999 COMP.
                         10  MAP1-UNIT-PRICE-A           PIC X.
                         10  MAP1-UNIT-PRICE             PIC 9(7).
                         10  MAP1-PRICE-L                PIC S9999 COMP.
                         10  MAP1-PRICE-A                PIC X.
                         10  MAP1-PRICE                  PIC 9(8).
                      05  MAP1-ERROR-L                   PIC S9999 COMP.
                      05  MAP1-ERROR-A                   PIC X.
                      05  MAP1-ERROR                     PIC X(20).
```

Fig. 18.4. (Continued)

```
      7         ORIQ01A          12.55.39          08/02/80

           *****************************************************************
           *                                                               *
           *       PURCHASE ORDER MASTER -- FILE LAYOUT                    *
           *                                                               *
           *****************************************************************

            01  ORDER-MASTER-RECORD.
                05  ORDER-NUMBER                         PIC X(10).
                05  ORDER-ALT-KEY.
                  10  ORDER-DEPARTMENT                   PIC XXX.
                  10  ORDER-DATE.
                    15  ORDER-DATE-YEAR                  PIC XX.
                    15  ORDER-DATE-MONTH                 PIC XX.
                    15  ORDER-DATE-DAY                   PIC XX.
                05  ORDER-DATE-ENTERED.
                  10  ORDER-DATE-ENTERED-MONTH           PIC XX.
                  10  ORDER-DATE-ENTERED-DAY             PIC XX.
                  10  ORDER-DATE-ENTERED-YEAR            PIC XX.
                05  ORDER-TOTAL-COST                     PIC S9(7)V99   COMP-3.
                05  ORDER-TOTAL-PRICE                    PIC S9(7)V99   COMP-3.
                05  ORDER-LINE-COUNT                     PIC S9999      COMP.
                05  ORDER-ALL-LINES.
                  10  ORDER-LINE-ITEM               OCCURS 1 TO 9
                                                    DEPENDING ON ORDER-LINE-COUNT
                                                    INDEXED BY ORDER-LINE-I.
                    15  ORDER-ITEM-NUMBER                PIC X(8).
                    15  ORDER-ITEM-DESCRIPTION           PIC X(19).
                    15  ORDER-ITEM-DATE.
                      20  ORDER-ITEM-DATE-MONTH          PIC XX.
                      20  ORDER-ITEM-DATE-DAY            PIC XX.
                      20  ORDER-ITEM-DATE-YEAR           PIC XX.
                    15  ORDER-UNIT                       PIC S9(5)      COMP-3.
                    15  ORDER-UNIT-COST                  PIC S9(5)V99   COMP-3.
                    15  ORDER-UNIT-PRICE                 PIC S9(5)V99   COMP-3.
```

Fig. 18.4. (Continued)

254 CICS/VS COMMAND LEVEL WITH ANS COBOL EXAMPLES

```
    8          ORIQ01A          12.55.39          08/02/80

00209      ****************************************************************
00210      *                                                              *
00211      *                TRANSACTION WORK AREA                         *
00212      *                                                              *
00213      ****************************************************************

00215          01  TWA-AREA.

00217              05  TWA-LINE-ITEM-MAP.
00218                  10  TWA-LINE-NUMBER-MAP-L          PIC S9999 COMP.
00219                  10  TWA-LINE-NUMBER-MAP-A          PIC X.
00220                  10  TWA-LINE-NUMBER-MAP            PIC 9.
00221                  10  TWA-ITEM-NUMBER-MAP-L          PIC S9999 COMP.
00222                  10  TWA-ITEM-NUMBER-MAP-A          PIC X.
00223                  10  TWA-ITEM-NUMBER-MAP            PIC 9(8).
00224                  10  TWA-ITEM-DESCRIPTION-MAP-L     PIC S9999 COMP.
00225                  10  TWA-ITEM-DESCRIPTION-MAP-A     PIC X.
00226                  10  TWA-ITEM-DESCRIPTION-MAP       PIC X(19).
00227                  10  TWA-ITEM-DATE-MAP-L            PIC S9999 COMP.
00228                  10  TWA-ITEM-DATE-MAP-A            PIC X.
00229                  10  TWA-ITEM-DATE-MAP              PIC X(6).
00230                  10  TWA-UNIT-MAP-L                 PIC S9999 COMP.
00231                  10  TWA-UNIT-MAP-A                 PIC X.
00232                  10  TWA-UNIT-MAP                   PIC 9(5).
00233                  10  TWA-UNIT-COST-MAP-L            PIC S9999 COMP.
00234                  10  TWA-UNIT-COST-MAP-A            PIC X.
00235                  10  TWA-UNIT-COST-MAP              PIC 9(7).
00236                  10  TWA-COST-MAP-L                 PIC S9999 COMP.
00237                  10  TWA-COST-MAP-A                 PIC X.
00238                  10  TWA-COST-MAP                   PIC 9(8).
00239                  10  TWA-UNIT-PRICE-MAP-L           PIC S9999 COMP.
00240                  10  TWA-UNIT-PRICE-MAP-A           PIC X.
00241                  10  TWA-UNIT-PRICE-MAP             PIC 9(7).
00242                  10  TWA-PRICE-MAP-L                PIC S9999 COMP.
00243                  10  TWA-PRICE-MAP-A                PIC X.
00244                  10  TWA-PRICE-MAP                  PIC 9(8).

00246              05  TWA-LINE-ITEM-ORDER.
00247                  10  TWA-ITEM-NUMBER-ORDER          PIC X(8).
00248                  10  TWA-ITEM-DESCRIPTION-ORDER     PIC X(19).
00249                  10  TWA-ITEM-DATE-ORDER            PIC X(6).
00250                  10  TWA-UNIT-ORDER                 PIC S9(5)    COMP-3.
00251                  10  TWA-UNIT-COST-ORDER            PIC S9(5)V99 COMP-3.
00252                  10  TWA-UNIT-PRICE-ORDER           PIC S9(5)V99 COMP-3.

00254              05  TWA-OPERATOR-MESSAGE               PIC X(31).

00256              05  TWA-ORDER-RECORD-KEY               PIC X(10).
```

Fig. 18.4. (Continued)

```
9          ORIQ01A          12.55.39          08/02/80

            PROCEDURE DIVISION USING DFHEIBLK DFHCOMMAREA.
                CALL 'DFHEI1'.

           *****************************************************************
           *                                                               *
            MAIN-LINE SECTION.
           *                                                               *
           *****************************************************************


           *    EXEC CICS
           *         ADDRESS TWA (TWA-POINTER)
           *    END-EXEC.
                 MOVE 'BB  DC             ' TO DFHEIVO CALL 'DFHEI1' USING
                 DFHEIVO TWA-POINTER.

           *    EXEC CICS
           *         HANDLE AID
           *              CLEAR (FINALIZATION)
           *                PA1 (WRONG-KEY-USED)
           *                PA2 (WRONG-KEY-USED)
           *                PA3 (WRONG-KEY-USED)
           *    END-EXEC.
                 MOVE 'BFO DEDFC          ' TO DFHEIVO CALL 'DFHEI1' USING
                 DFHEIVO GO TO FINALIZATION WRONG-KEY-USED WRONG-KEY-USED
                 WRONG-KEY-USED DEPENDING ON DFHEIGDI.




           *    EXEC CICS
           *         HANDLE CONDITION
           *              MAPFAIL (MAPFAIL-ERROR)
           *              ERROR   (MAJOR-ERROR)
           *    END-EXEC.
                 MOVE 'BD  DUA            ' TO DFHEIVO CALL 'DFHEI1' USING
                 DFHEIVO GO TO MAPFAIL-ERROR MAJOR-ERROR DEPENDING ON
                 DFHEIGDI.


                IF EIBCALEN NOT EQUAL TO ZEROES
                     IF ORDER-DISPLAY-TIME
                          GO TO ORDER-DISPLAY
                     ELSE IF INITIAL-ENTRY-TIME
                          GO TO INITIALIZATION
                     ELSE GO TO PROCESS-SWITCH-ERROR.

                IF EIBCALEN EQUAL TO ZEROES
                     GO TO SIGN-ON-VIOLATION.
```

Fig. 18.4. (Continued)

```
  10        ORIQ01A         12.55.39         08/02/80

            ****************************************************************
            *                                                              *
             ORDER-DISPLAY SECTION.
            *                                                              *
            ****************************************************************

            *     EXEC CICS
            *          HANDLE CONDITION
            *               NOTOPEN (FILE-NOT-OPEN)
            *               NOTFND  (RECORD-NOT-FOUND)
            *     END-EXEC.
                   MOVE 'BD  DL(              ' TO DFHEIVO CALL 'DFHEI1' USING
                   DFHEIVO GO TO FILE-NOT-OPEN RECORD-NOT-FOUND DEPENDING ON
                   DFHEIGDI.


            *     EXEC CICS
            *          RECEIVE MAP     ('ORIQM01')
            *                  MAPSET ('ORIQS01')
            *                  SET     (MAP1-POINTER)
            *     END-EXEC.
                   MOVE 'ORIQM01' TO DFHEIV1 MOVE 'ORIQS01' TO DFHEIV2 MOVE 'QB
            -     '& DA    EI    -' TO DFHEIVO CALL 'DFHEI1' USING DFHEIVO
                   DFHEIV1 MAP1-POINTER DFHEIV98 DFHEIV2.


                  IF MAP1-ORDER-NUMBER NOT NUMERIC
                       GO TO INVALID-ORDER-RTN.

                  MOVE MAP1-ORDER-NUMBER TO TWA-ORDER-RECORD-KEY.

            *     EXEC CICS
            *          READ DATASET ('ORTEST')
            *               SET     (POM-POINTER)
            *               RIDFLD  (TWA-ORDER-RECORD-KEY)
            *     END-EXEC.
                   MOVE 'ORTEST' TO DFHEIV3 MOVE 'FB& DA    ' TO DFHEIVO CALL 'D
            -     'FHEI1' USING DFHEIVO DFHEIV3 POM-POINTER DFHEIV98
                   TWA-ORDER-RECORD-KEY.


                  MOVE ORDER-NUMBER          TO   MAP1-ORDER-NUMBER.
                  MOVE ORDER-DEPARTMENT      TO   MAP1-DEPARTMENT.
                  MOVE ORDER-DATE-MONTH      TO   MAP1-ORDER-DATE-MONTH.
                  MOVE ORDER-DATE-DAY        TO   MAP1-ORDER-DATE-DAY.
                  MOVE ORDER-DATE-YEAR       TO   MAP1-ORDER-DATE-YEAR.
                  MOVE ORDER-DATE-ENTERED    TO   MAP1-ORDER-DATE-ENTERED.
                  MOVE ORDER-TOTAL-COST      TO   MAP1-TOTAL-COST.
                  MOVE ORDER-TOTAL-PRICE     TO   MAP1-TOTAL-PRICE.
                  MOVE SPACES                TO   MAP1-ERROR.
                  SET ORDER-LINE-I           TO   1.
                  PERFORM LAYOUT-EACH-LINE
```

Fig. 18.4. (Continued)

```
    11          ORIQ01A          12.55.39          08/02/80

                UNTIL ORDER-LINE-I GREATER THAN ORDER-LINE-COUNT.
            GO TO DISPLAY-ORDER.

        LAYOUT-EACH-LINE.
            SET MAP1-LINE-I                           TO ORDER-LINE-I.
            MOVE ORDER-LINE-ITEM (ORDER-LINE-I) TO TWA-LINE-ITEM-ORDER.
            MOVE MAP1-LINE-ITEM (MAP1-LINE-I)   TO TWA-LINE-ITEM-MAP.
            SET TWA-LINE-NUMBER-MAP               TO ORDER-LINE-I.
            MOVE TWA-ITEM-NUMBER-ORDER     TO  TWA-ITEM-NUMBER-MAP.
            MOVE TWA-ITEM-DESCRIPTION-ORDER TO TWA-ITEM-DESCRIPTION-MAP.
            MOVE TWA-ITEM-DATE-ORDER         TO  TWA-ITEM-DATE-MAP.
            MOVE TWA-UNIT-ORDER              TO  TWA-UNIT-MAP.
            MOVE TWA-UNIT-COST-ORDER         TO  TWA-UNIT-COST-MAP.
            COMPUTE TWA-COST-MAP = TWA-UNIT-ORDER * TWA-UNIT-COST-ORDER.
            MOVE TWA-UNIT-PRICE-ORDER        TO  TWA-UNIT-PRICE-MAP.
            COMPUTE TWA-PRICE-MAP =
                        TWA-UNIT-ORDER * TWA-UNIT-PRICE-ORDER.
            MOVE TWA-LINE-ITEM-MAP    TO  MAP1-LINE-ITEM (MAP1-LINE-I).
            SET ORDER-LINE-I UP BY 1.

        DISPLAY-ORDER.

       *    EXEC CICS
       *         SEND MAP     ('ORIQM01')
       *              MAPSET ('ORIQS01')
       *              FROM   (MAP1-AREA)
       *              ERASE
       *    END-EXEC.
             MOVE 'ORIQM01' TO DFHEIV1 MOVE 'ORIQS01' TO DFHEIV2 MOVE 'QD
       -     '& D    ESD  -' TO DFHEIV0 CALL 'DFHEI1' USING DFHEIV0
             DFHEIV1 MAP1-AREA DFHEIV98 DFHEIV2.



        RETURN-FOR-NEXT-ORDER.

            MOVE '1' TO COMMAREA-PROCESS-SW.

       *    EXEC CICS
       *         RETURN TRANSID  (EIBTRNID)
       *                COMMAREA (COMMUNICATION-AREA)
       *                LENGTH   (1)
       *    END-EXEC.
             MOVE 1 TO DFHEIV11 MOVE '+H- D  & ' TO DFHEIV0 CALL 'DFHEI1'
             USING DFHEIV0 EIBTRNID COMMUNICATION-AREA DFHEIV11.



        RECORD-NOT-FOUND.

            MOVE 'RECORD NOT FOUND' TO MAP1-ERROR.
```

Fig. 18.4. (Continued)

```
    12          ORIQ01A           12.55.39          08/02/80

                     GO TO DISPLAY-INVALID-ORDER-MESSAGE.

                DISPLAY-INVALID-ORDER-MESSAGE.

               *     EXEC CICS
               *          SEND MAP     ('ORIQM01')
               *               MAPSET ('ORIQS01')
               *               FROM    (MAP1-AREA)
               *               ERASE
               *     END-EXEC.
                      MOVE 'ORIQM01' TO DFHEIV1 MOVE 'ORIQS01' TO DFHEIV2 MOVE 'QD
               -     '& D    ESD  -' TO DFHEIV0 CALL 'DFHEI1' USING DFHEIV0
                      DFHEIV1 MAP1-AREA DFHEIV98 DFHEIV2.



                     GO TO RETURN-FOR-NEXT-ORDER.

                INVALID-ORDER-RTN.

                     MOVE 'INVALID ORDER NUMBER' TO MAP1-ERROR.
                     GO TO DISPLAY-INVALID-ORDER-MESSAGE.

    13          ORIQ01A           12.55.39          08/02/80

               ****************************************************************
               *                                                              *
                WRONG-KEY-USED SECTION.
               *                                                              *
               ****************************************************************

               *     EXEC CICS
               *          GETMAIN
               *               SET      (MAP1-POINTER)
               *               LENGTH  (970)
               *               INITIMG (HEX-ZEROES)
               *     END-EXEC.
                      MOVE 970 TO DFHEIV11 MOVE '□8- D  □ ' TO DFHEIV0 CALL 'DFHEI
               -     '1' USING DFHEIV0 MAP1-POINTER DFHEIV11 HEX-ZEROES.




                     MOVE 'WRONG KEY USED' TO MAP1-ERROR.

               *     EXEC CICS
               *          SEND MAP      ('ORIQM01')
               *               MAPSET  ('ORIQS01')
               *               FROM    (MAP1-AREA)
               *               DATAONLY
               *     END-EXEC.
                      MOVE 'ORIQM01' TO DFHEIV1 MOVE 'ORIQS01' TO DFHEIV2 MOVE 'QD
               -     '& D    E-D  -' TO DFHEIV0 CALL 'DFHEI1' USING DFHEIV0
                      DFHEIV1 MAP1-AREA DFHEIV98 DFHEIV2.



                     GO TO RETURN-FOR-NEXT-ORDER.
```

Fig. 18.4. (Continued)

```
14          ORIQ01A          12.55.39          08/02/80

       *****************************************************************
       *                                                               *
        INITIALIZATION SECTION.
       *                                                               *
       *****************************************************************


       *     EXEC CICS
       *          SEND MAP     ('ORIQM01')
       *               MAPSET ('ORIQS01')
       *               MAPONLY
       *               ERASE
       *     END-EXEC.
              MOVE 'ORIQM01' TO DFHEIV1 MOVE 'ORIQS01' TO DFHEIV2 MOVE 'QD
       -     '& D    ESD  -' TO DFHEIV0 CALL 'DFHEI1' USING DFHEIV0
              DFHEIV1 DFHEIV99 DFHEIV98 DFHEIV2.



             MOVE '1' TO COMMAREA-PROCESS-SW.

       *     EXEC CICS
       *          RETURN TRANSID  ('ORIQ')
       *                 COMMAREA (COMMUNICATION-AREA)
       *                 LENGTH   (1)
       *     END-EXEC.
              MOVE 'ORIQ' TO DFHEIV5 MOVE 1 TO DFHEIV11 MOVE '+H- D  & '
              TO DFHEIV0 CALL 'DFHEI1' USING DFHEIV0 DFHEIV5
              COMMUNICATION-AREA DFHEIV11.
```

Fig. 18.4. (Continued)

```
       15          ORIQ01A          12.55.39          08/02/80

00498          *****************************************************************
00499          *                                                               *
00500           FINALIZATION SECTION.
00501          *                                                               *
00502          *****************************************************************

00504           PREPARE-TERMINATION-MESSAGE.

00506               MOVE JOB-NORMAL-END-MESSAGE TO TWA-OPERATOR-MESSAGE.

00508           JOB-TERMINATED.

00510          *     EXEC CICS
00511          *          SEND FROM   (TWA-OPERATOR-MESSAGE)
00512          *               LENGTH (31)
00513          *               ERASE
00514          *     END-EXEC.
00515               MOVE 31 TO DFHEIV11 MOVE 'DDO D   A       ' TO DFHEIVO CALL '
00516          -    'DFHEI1' USING DFHEIVO DFHEIV99 DFHEIV98 TWA-OPERATOR-MESSAGE
00517               DFHEIV11.
00518
00519

00521           END-OF-JOB.

00523          *     EXEC CICS
00524          *          RETURN
00525          *     END-EXEC.
00526               MOVE '+H  D  & ' TO DFHEIVO CALL 'DFHEI1' USING DFHEIVO.
00527
00528
```

Fig. 18.4. (Continued)

```
16         ORIQ01A          12.55.39          08/02/80

           ****************************************************************
           *                                                              *
            ABNORMAL-TERMINATION SECTION.
           *                                                              *
           ****************************************************************

            FILE-NOT-OPEN.

           *     EXEC CICS
           *          XCTL PROGRAM ('TEL2OPEN')
           *     END-EXEC.
                  MOVE 'TEL2OPEN' TO DFHEIV3 MOVE '+D  D  B ' TO DFHEIVO CALL
                 'DFHEI1' USING DFHEIVO DFHEIV3.


            MAPFAIL-ERROR.
                 MOVE 'MAP FAILURE' TO MAJOR-ERROR-MSG.
                 GO TO PREPARE-ABORT-MESSAGE.

            PROCESS-SWITCH-ERROR.
                 MOVE 'PROCESS ERROR' TO MAJOR-ERROR-MSG.
                 GO TO PREPARE-ABORT-MESSAGE.

            SIGN-ON-VIOLATION.
                 MOVE 'SIGNON VIOLATION' TO MAJOR-ERROR-MSG.
                 GO TO PREPARE-ABORT-MESSAGE.

            MAJOR-ERROR.
                 MOVE  EIBFN      TO  OLD-EIBFN.
                 MOVE  EIBRCODE   TO  OLD-EIBRCODE.

           *     EXEC CICS
           *          DUMP DUMPCODE ('ERRS')
           *     END-EXEC.
                  MOVE 'ERRS' TO DFHEIV5 MOVE '*B  D  = ' TO DFHEIVO CALL 'DFH
           -     'EI1' USING DFHEIVO DFHEIV5.

                 MOVE 'MAJOR ERROR' TO MAJOR-ERROR-MSG.
                 GO TO PREPARE-ABORT-MESSAGE.


            PREPARE-ABORT-MESSAGE.
                 MOVE JOB-ABORTED-MESSAGE TO TWA-OPERATOR-MESSAGE.
                 GO TO JOB-TERMINATED.
```

Fig. 18.4. (Continued)

5. Lines 304–305. If the program is executed at the start of the session by an operator-entered transaction identifier instead of through an XCTL command from the Sign-on program, a sign-on violation occurs. This is so if EIBCALEN is equal to zero.

THE INITIALIZATION SECTION

1. Lines 473–481. Display the inquiry map.
2. Line 485. Set the communication area switch to 1.
3. Lines 487–494. Terminate the task.

THE ORDER-DISPLAY SECTION

1. Lines 313–320. HANDLE CONDITION command for the order file.
2. Lines 323–330. Read the map that contains the order number entered by the operator.
3. Lines 333–345. Read the order file using the order number entered.
4. If the record is found:
   a. Lines 348–377. Lay out the fields of the record in the area secured by CICS/VS for the symbolic description map. Note the GO TO of line 360 to keep the code in a "straight line." Lines 363–377 illustrate a Cobol efficiency technique that reduces the use of an index.
   b. Lines 379–389. Display the record. The ERASE option is specified since the data is variable (from 1 to 9 lines). If the data were fixed, this would not be required and DATAONLY would then be specified.
   c. Line 395. Set the communication area switch to 1.
   d. Lines 397–403. Terminate the task.
5. If the record is not found:
   a. Line 409. Lay out the "RECORD NOT FOUND" message in the area secured by CICS/VS for the symbolic description map.

b. Lines 412–422. Display the message. In this case, the ERASE option is mandatory to erase data from the previous display.
c. Line 426. Set the communication area switch to 1 and terminate the task.

THE WRONG-KEY-USED SECTION

1. Lines 439–446. GETMAIN command to secure main storage for the map that will contain the error message. This is because the PA keys do not allow CICS/VS to secure main storage for the symbolic description map through a RECEIVE MAP command.
2. Line 451. Move the "WRONG KEY USED" message into the area secured.
3. Lines 453–461. Display the error message.
4. Line 465. Set the communication area switch to 1 and terminate the task. This GO TO should be of no concern because this section will rarely be executed.

THE FINALIZATION SECTION

1. Lines 504–517. Display the "JOB NORMALLY TERMINATED" message.
2. Lines 521–526. Terminate the session.

THE ABNORMAL-TERMINATION SECTION

These are the routines used to abnormally terminate the session on errors and CICS/VS command exceptional conditions not covered by a HANDLE CONDITION command.

EXAMPLE

The following are facsimiles of actual photographs taken of a CRT terminal during a session.

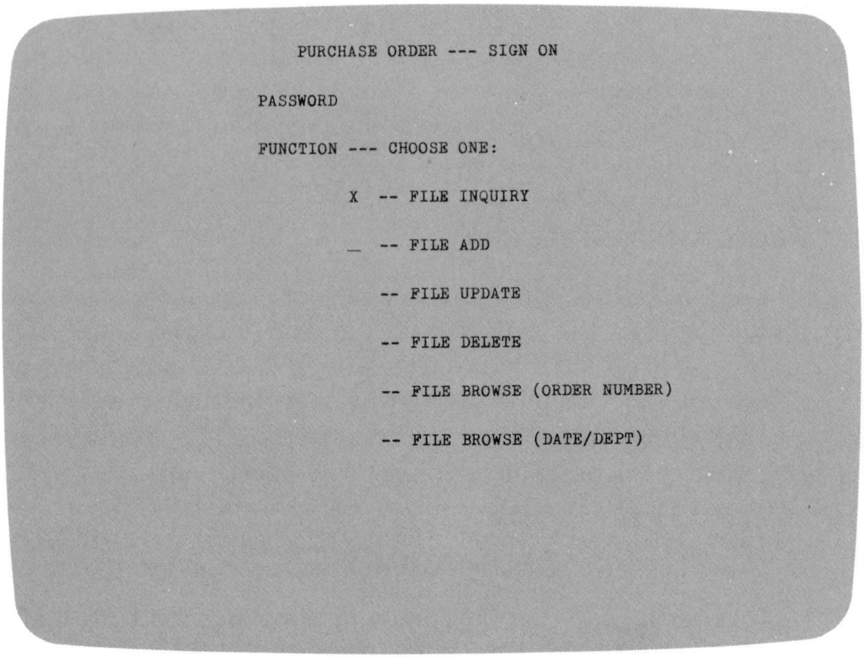

Fig. 18.5. The File Inquiry application is selected by keying in an "X" on the File Inquiry line and the corresponding password, then hitting the ENTER key.

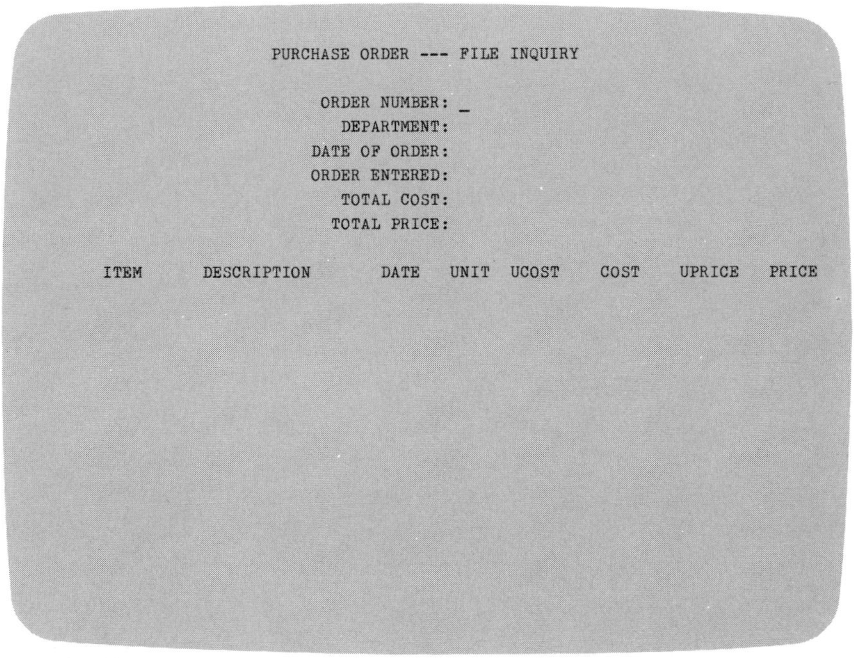

Fig. 18.6. The Sign On program executes which then transfers control to the File Inquiry program. This displays the File Inquiry map.

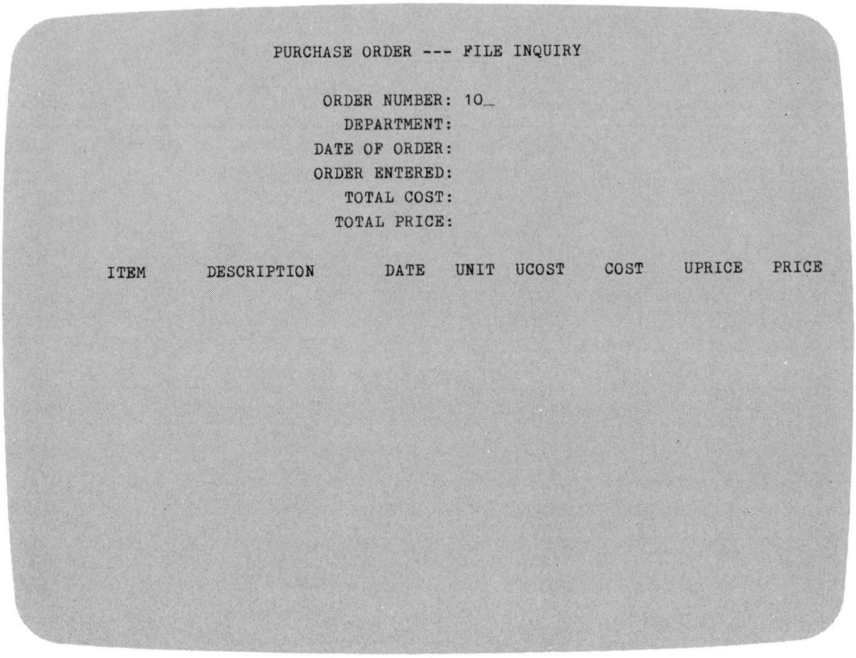

Fig. 18.7. The operator keys in the order number of the record to be displayed, then hits the ENTER key.

```
                    PURCHASE ORDER --- FILE INQUIRY

                         ORDER NUMBER: 0000000010
                           DEPARTMENT: 003
                        DATE OF ORDER: 122480
                        ORDER ENTERED: 122680
                          TOTAL COST:       1,600.00
                         TOTAL PRICE:       3,200.00

    ITEM       DESCRIPTION       DATE   UNIT  UCOST     COST    UPRICE   PRICE
1 00087632 12-INCH CRESCENT     122480 00100 0000600 00060000 0001200 00120000
2 00063271 BENCH VISE           122480 00050 0002000 00100000 0004000 00200000
```

Fig. 18.8. The program displays the record.

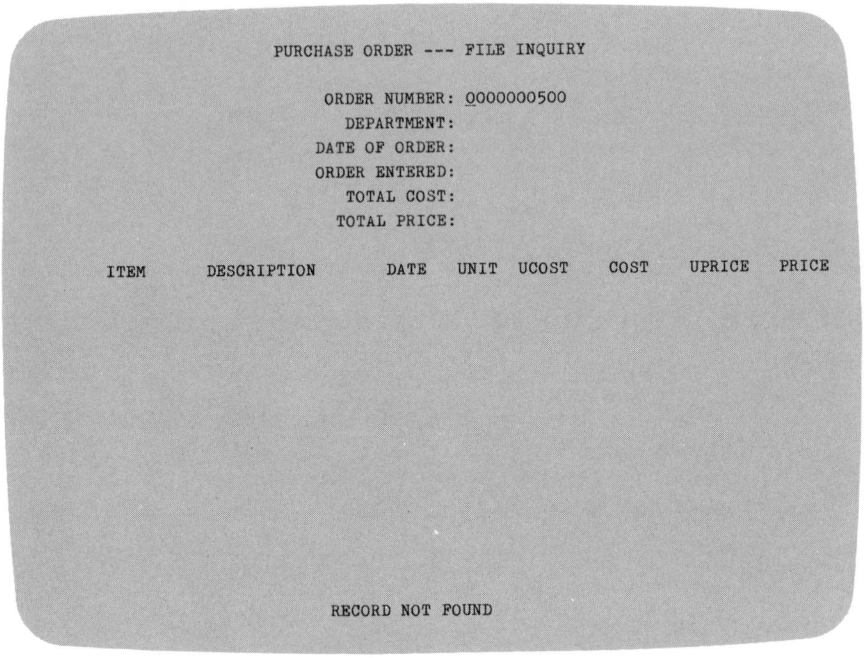

Fig. 18.9. If the record corresponding to the order number entered is not in the file, the "RECORD NOT FOUND" message is displayed.

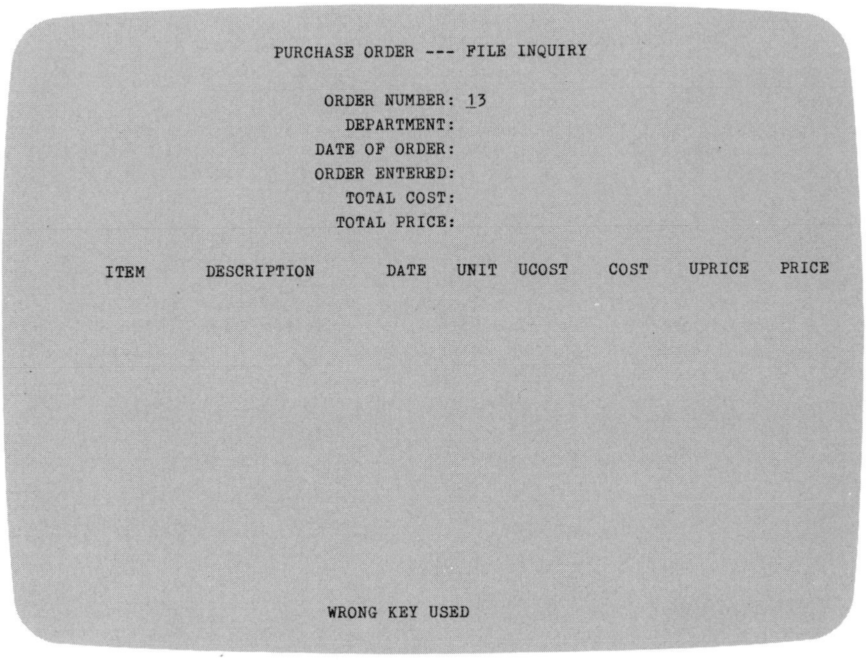

Fig. 18.10. If the operator keys in an order number but then hits one of the PA keys instead of the ENTER key, the "WRONG KEY USED" message is displayed.

```
                         PURCHASE ORDER --- FILE INQUIRY

                              ORDER NUMBER: 0000000013
                                DEPARTMENT: 003
                             DATE OF ORDER: 122680
                             ORDER ENTERED: 122680
                                TOTAL COST:         1,850.00
                               TOTAL PRICE:         3,700.00

     ITEM        DESCRIPTION          DATE   UNIT  UCOST     COST     UPRICE    PRICE
1 00081667 1/2 HP CHAIN SAW        122680 00025 0005000 00125000 0010000 00250000
2 00009152 7 1/4 IN. CIRCL SAW 122680 00040 0001500 00060000 0003000 00120000
```

Fig. 18.11. If the operator then hits the ENTER key, the session continues. The record selected in Fig. 18.10 is now displayed.

19

The File Add Program

INTRODUCTION

This program allows the operator to add new records to the Purchase Order file according to the record key entered. The program executes when selected by the Sign-on program and will continue the session until terminated by the operator. The flow of control to execute this program is shown in Figure 19.1.

PROGRAM SPECIFICATIONS

The program specifications are as follows:

1. Implement the program using the pseudoconversational mode of processing.
2. Use 'ORAD' as the transaction identifier. However, the session should not be started by using this identifier, but rather through an XCTL command from the Sign-on program.
3. If the session is started by using the transaction identifier, abort the session with the message "JOB ABORTED–SIGNON VIOLATION."
4. Edit the data using page 207 as a guide.
5. On any PA key, bypass the input data and display the next fresh screen for the next set of data.

SCREEN LAYOUT

The screen layout to be used in the program is shown in Figure 19.2. All 9s are numeric fields and Xs are alphanumeric fields.

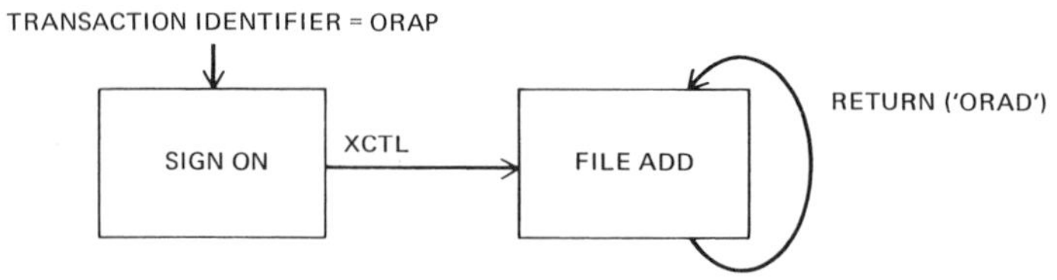

Fig. 19.1. File Add Application.

MAP PROGRAM

The map program corresponding to the screen layout is shown in Figure 19.3.

PROGRAM LISTING

The program listing for the File Add program is shown in Figure 19.4.

MAIN-LINE SECTION

1. Lines 382–386. ADDRESS command for the TWA.
2. Lines 388–397. HANDLE AID command. The PA keys will execute the BYPASS-INPUT section.
3. Lines 402–409. HANDLE CONDITION command.
4. Lines 412–417. The selection of sections.
5. Lines 419–420. If the program is executed at the start of the session by an operator-entered transaction identifier instead of through an XCTL program from the Sign-on program, a sign-on violation occurs. This is so if EIBCALEN is equal to zero.

THE INITIALIZATION SECTION

1. Lines 883–888. HANDLE CONDITION command for the deletion of a specific temporary storage queue.

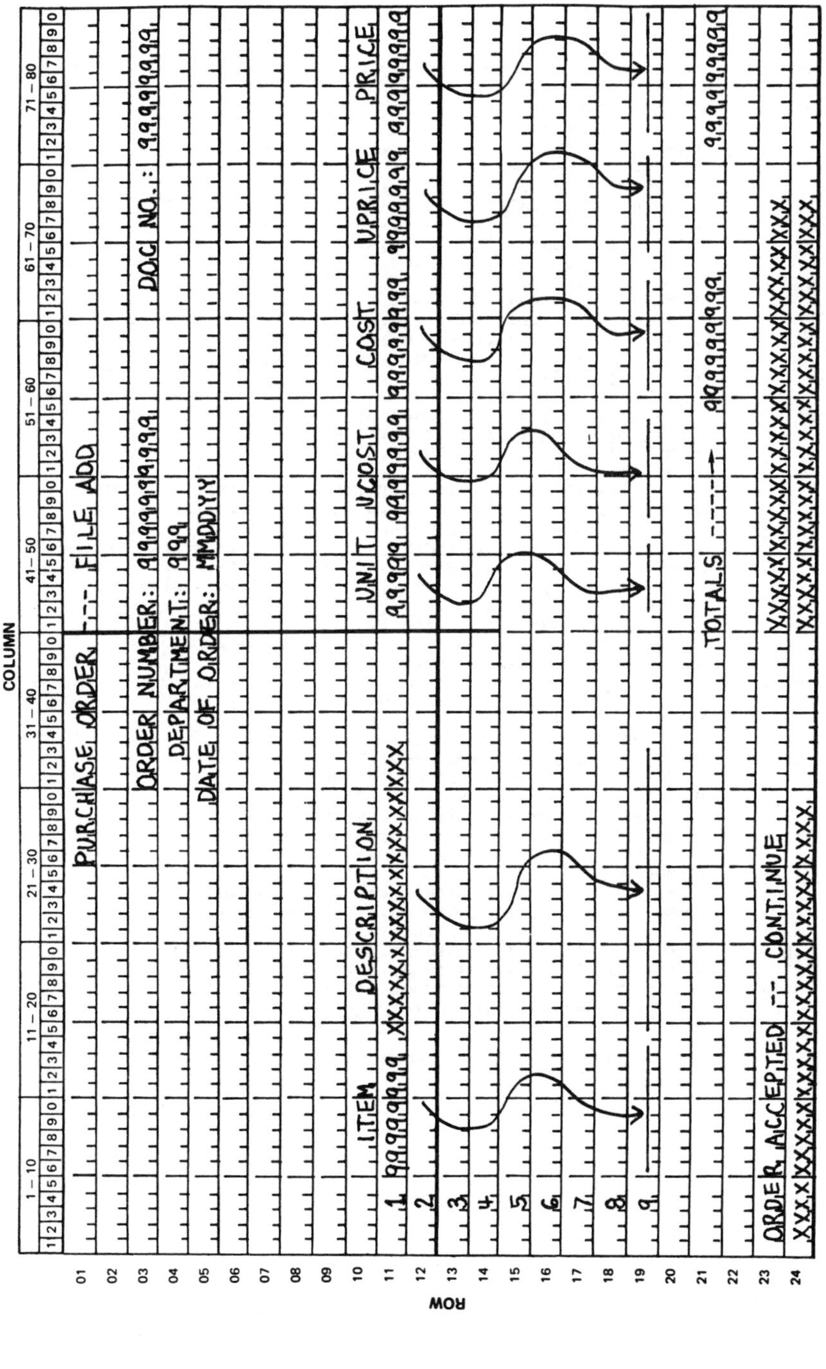

Fig. 19.2. Screen Layout – File Add.

```
STMT    SOURCE STATEMENT                                DOS/VS ASSEMBLER REL 34.0 13.10

   1             PRINT NOGEN
   2 ORADS01     DFHMSD TYPE=MAP,MODE=INOUT,CTRL=FREEKB,LANG=COBOL,TIOAPFX=YES
  12 ORADM01     DFHMDI SIZE=(24,80)
  40 DUMMY       DFHMDF POS=(01,01),LENGTH=01,ATTRB=(ASKIP,DRK,FSET),           X
                       INITIAL='1'
  52             DFHMDF POS=(01,25),LENGTH=27,ATTRB=(ASKIP,BRT),                X
                       INITIAL='PURCHASE ORDER --- FILE ADD'
  64             DFHMDF POS=(03,30),LENGTH=13,ATTRB=ASKIP,                      X
                       INITIAL='ORDER NUMBER '
  76 ORDER       DFHMDF POS=(03,44),LENGTH=10,ATTRB=(NUM,BRT,IC)
  87             DFHMDF POS=(03,55),LENGTH=01,ATTRB=PROT
  98             DFHMDF POS=(03,62),LENGTH=08,ATTRB=ASKIP,INITIAL='DOC NO. '
 110 DOCNO       DFHMDF POS=(03,71),LENGTH=08,ATTRB=(NUM,BRT)
 121             DFHMDF POS=(03,80),LENGTH=01,ATTRB=PROT
 132             DFHMDF POS=(04,32),LENGTH=11,ATTRB=ASKIP,INITIAL='DEPARTMENT '
 144 DEPT        DFHMDF POS=(04,44),LENGTH=03,ATTRB=(NUM,BRT)
 155             DFHMDF POS=(04,48),LENGTH=01,ATTRB=ASKIP
 166             DFHMDF POS=(05,29),LENGTH=14,ATTRB=ASKIP,                      X
                       INITIAL='DATE OF ORDER '
 178 DATEOR      DFHMDF POS=(05,44),LENGTH=06,ATTRB=(NUM,BRT),INITIAL='MMDDYY'
 190             DFHMDF POS=(05,51),LENGTH=01,ATTRB=ASKIP
 201             DFHMDF POS=(10,07),LENGTH=04,ATTRB=ASKIP,INITIAL='ITEM'
 213             DFHMDF POS=(10,17),LENGTH=11,ATTRB=ASKIP,INITIAL='DESCRIPTION'
 225             DFHMDF POS=(10,42),LENGTH=04,ATTRB=ASKIP,INITIAL='UNIT'
 237             DFHMDF POS=(10,48),LENGTH=05,ATTRB=ASKIP,INITIAL='UCOST'
 249             DFHMDF POS=(10,57),LENGTH=04,ATTRB=ASKIP,INITIAL='COST'
 261             DFHMDF POS=(10,65),LENGTH=06,ATTRB=ASKIP,INITIAL='UPRICE'
 273             DFHMDF POS=(10,74),LENGTH=05,ATTRB=ASKIP,INITIAL='PRICE'
 285             DFHMDF POS=(11,03),LENGTH=01,ATTRB=ASKIP,INITIAL='1'
 297 ITEM1       DFHMDF POS=(11,05),LENGTH=08,ATTRB=(NUM,BRT),                  X
                       PICIN='99999999',PICOUT='99999999'
 308 DESC1       DFHMDF POS=(11,14),LENGTH=19,ATTRB=(UNPROT,BRT)
 319             DFHMDF POS=(11,34),LENGTH=01,ATTRB=PROT
 330 UNIT1       DFHMDF POS=(11,41),LENGTH=05,ATTRB=(NUM,BRT),                  X
                       PICIN='99999',PICOUT='99999'
 341 UCOST1      DFHMDF POS=(11,47),LENGTH=07,ATTRB=(NUM,BRT),                  X
                       PICIN='9999999',PICOUT='9999999'
 352 COST1       DFHMDF POS=(11,55),LENGTH=08,ATTRB=(NUM,BRT),                  X
                       PICIN='99999999',PICOUT='99999999'
 363 UPRICE1     DFHMDF POS=(11,64),LENGTH=07,ATTRB=(NUM,BRT),                  X
                       PICIN='9999999',PICOUT='9999999'
 374 PRICE1      DFHMDF POS=(11,72),LENGTH=08,ATTRB=(NUM,BRT),                  X
                       PICIN='99999999',PICOUT='99999999'
 385             DFHMDF POS=(12,01),LENGTH=01,ATTRB=PROT
 396             DFHMDF POS=(12,03),LENGTH=01,ATTRB=ASKIP,INITIAL='2'
 408 ITEM2       DFHMDF POS=(12,05),LENGTH=08,ATTRB=(NUM,BRT),                  X
                       PICIN='99999999',PICOUT='99999999'
 419 DESC2       DFHMDF POS=(12,14),LENGTH=19,ATTRB=(UNPROT,BRT)
 430             DFHMDF POS=(12,34),LENGTH=01,ATTRB=PROT
 441 UNIT2       DFHMDF POS=(12,41),LENGTH=05,ATTRB=(NUM,BRT),                  X
                       PICIN='99999',PICOUT='99999'
```

Fig. 19.3. Map Program – File Add.

```
STMT   SOURCE STATEMENT                                DOS/VS ASSEMBLER REL 34.0 13.10

 452 UCOST2   DFHMDF POS=(12,47),LENGTH=07,ATTRB=(NUM,BRT),                         X
                     PICIN='9999999',PICOUT='9999999'
 463 COST2    DFHMDF POS=(12,55),LENGTH=08,ATTRB=(NUM,BRT),                         X
                     PICIN='99999999',PICOUT='99999999'
 474 UPRICE2  DFHMDF POS=(12,64),LENGTH=07,ATTRB=(NUM,BRT),                         X
                     PICIN='9999999',PICOUT='9999999'
 485 PRICE2   DFHMDF POS=(12,72),LENGTH=08,ATTRB=(NUM,BRT),                         X
                     PICIN='99999999',PICOUT='99999999'
 496          DFHMDF POS=(13,01),LENGTH=01,ATTRB=PROT
 507          DFHMDF POS=(13,03),LENGTH=01,ATTRB=ASKIP,INITIAL='3'
 519 ITEM3    DFHMDF POS=(13,05),LENGTH=08,ATTRB=(NUM,BRT),                         X
                     PICIN='99999999',PICOUT='99999999'
 530 DESC3    DFHMDF POS=(13,14),LENGTH=19,ATTRB=(UNPROT,BRT)
 541          DFHMDF POS=(13,34),LENGTH=01,ATTRB=PROT
 552 UNIT3    DFHMDF POS=(13,41),LENGTH=05,ATTRB=(NUM,BRT),                         X
                     PICIN='99999',PICOUT='99999'
 563 UCOST3   DFHMDF POS=(13,47),LENGTH=07,ATTRB=(NUM,BRT),                         X
                     PICIN='9999999',PICOUT='9999999'
 574 COST3    DFHMDF POS=(13,55),LENGTH=08,ATTRB=(NUM,BRT),                         X
                     PICIN='99999999',PICOUT='99999999'
 585 UPRICE3  DFHMDF POS=(13,64),LENGTH=07,ATTRB=(NUM,BRT),                         X
                     PICIN='9999999',PICOUT='9999999'
 596 PRICE3   DFHMDF POS=(13,72),LENGTH=08,ATTRB=(NUM,BRT),                         X
                     PICIN='99999999',PICOUT='99999999'
 607          DFHMDF POS=(14,01),LENGTH=01,ATTRB=PROT
 618          DFHMDF POS=(14,03),LENGTH=01,ATTRB=ASKIP,INITIAL='4'
 630 ITEM4    DFHMDF POS=(14,05),LENGTH=08,ATTRB=(NUM,BRT),                         X
                     PICIN='99999999',PICOUT='99999999'
 641 DESC4    DFHMDF POS=(14,14),LENGTH=19,ATTRB=(UNPROT,BRT)
 652          DFHMDF POS=(14,34),LENGTH=01,ATTRB=PROT
 663 UNIT4    DFHMDF POS=(14,41),LENGTH=05,ATTRB=(NUM,BRT),                         X
                     PICIN='99999',PICOUT='99999'
 674 UCOST4   DFHMDF POS=(14,47),LENGTH=07,ATTRB=(NUM,BRT),                         X
                     PICIN='9999999',PICOUT='9999999'
 685 COST4    DFHMDF POS=(14,55),LENGTH=08,ATTRB=(NUM,BRT),                         X
                     PICIN='99999999',PICOUT='99999999'
 696 UPRICE4  DFHMDF POS=(14,64),LENGTH=07,ATTRB=(NUM,BRT),                         X
                     PICIN='9999999',PICOUT='9999999'
 707 PRICE4   DFHMDF POS=(14,72),LENGTH=08,ATTRB=(NUM,BRT),                         X
                     PICIN='99999999',PICOUT='99999999'
 718          DFHMDF POS=(15,01),LENGTH=01,ATTRB=PROT
 729          DFHMDF POS=(15,03),LENGTH=01,ATTRB=ASKIP,INITIAL='5'
 741 ITEM5    DFHMDF POS=(15,05),LENGTH=08,ATTRB=(NUM,BRT),                         X
                     PICIN='99999999',PICOUT='99999999'
 752 DESC5    DFHMDF POS=(15,14),LENGTH=19,ATTRB=(UNPROT,BRT)
 763          DFHMDF POS=(15,34),LENGTH=01,ATTRB=PROT
 774 UNIT5    DFHMDF POS=(15,41),LENGTH=05,ATTRB=(NUM,BRT),                         X
                     PICIN='99999',PICOUT='99999'
 785 UCOST5   DFHMDF POS=(15,47),LENGTH=07,ATTRB=(NUM,BRT),                         X
                     PICIN='9999999',PICOUT='9999999'
 796 COST5    DFHMDF POS=(15,55),LENGTH=08,ATTRB=(NUM,BRT),                         X
```

Fig. 19.3. (Continued)

```
STMT    SOURCE STATEMENT                               DOS/VS ASSEMBLER REL 34.0 13.10

                         PICIN='99999999',PICOUT='99999999'
 807 UPRICE5   DFHMDF  POS=(15,64),LENGTH=07,ATTRB=(NUM,BRT),                    X
                         PICIN='9999999',PICOUT='9999999'
 818 PRICE5    DFHMDF  POS=(15,72),LENGTH=08,ATTRB=(NUM,BRT),                    X
                         PICIN='99999999',PICOUT='99999999'
 829           DFHMDF  POS=(16,01),LENGTH=01,ATTRB=PROT
 840           DFHMDF  POS=(16,03),LENGTH=01,ATTRB=ASKIP,INITIAL='6'
 852 ITEM6     DFHMDF  POS=(16,05),LENGTH=08,ATTRB=(NUM,BRT),                    X
                         PICIN='99999999',PICOUT='99999999'
 863 DESC6     DFHMDF  POS=(16,14),LENGTH=19,ATTRB=(UNPROT,BRT)
 874           DFHMDF  POS=(16,34),LENGTH=01,ATTRB=PROT
 885 UNIT6     DFHMDF  POS=(16,41),LENGTH=05,ATTRB=(NUM,BRT),                    X
                         PICIN='99999',PICOUT='99999'
 896 UCOST6    DFHMDF  POS=(16,47),LENGTH=07,ATTRB=(NUM,BRT),                    X
                         PICIN='9999999',PICOUT='9999999'
 907 COST6     DFHMDF  POS=(16,55),LENGTH=08,ATTRB=(NUM,BRT),                    X
                         PICIN='99999999',PICOUT='99999999'
 918 UPRICE6   DFHMDF  POS=(16,64),LENGTH=07,ATTRB=(NUM,BRT),                    X
                         PICIN='9999999',PICOUT='9999999'
 929 PRICE6    DFHMDF  POS=(16,72),LENGTH=08,ATTRB=(NUM,BRT),                    X
                         PICIN='99999999',PICOUT='99999999'
 940           DFHMDF  POS=(17,01),LENGTH=01,ATTRB=PROT
 951           DFHMDF  POS=(17,03),LENGTH=01,ATTRB=ASKIP,INITIAL='7'
 963 ITEM7     DFHMDF  POS=(17,05),LENGTH=08,ATTRB=(NUM,BRT),                    X
                         PICIN='99999999',PICOUT='99999999'
 974 DESC7     DFHMDF  POS=(17,14),LENGTH=19,ATTRB=(UNPROT,BRT)
 985           DFHMDF  POS=(17,34),LENGTH=01,ATTRB=PROT
 996 UNIT7     DFHMDF  POS=(17,41),LENGTH=05,ATTRB=(NUM,BRT),                    X
                         PICIN='99999',PICOUT='99999'
1007 UCOST7    DFHMDF  POS=(17,47),LENGTH=07,ATTRB=(NUM,BRT),                    X
                         PICIN='9999999',PICOUT='9999999'
1018 COST7     DFHMDF  POS=(17,55),LENGTH=08,ATTRB=(NUM,BRT),                    X
                         PICIN='99999999',PICOUT='99999999'
1029 UPRICE7   DFHMDF  POS=(17,64),LENGTH=07,ATTRB=(NUM,BRT),                    X
                         PICIN='9999999',PICOUT='9999999'
1040 PRICE7    DFHMDF  POS=(17,72),LENGTH=08,ATTRB=(NUM,BRT),                    X
                         PICIN='99999999',PICOUT='99999999'
1051           DFHMDF  POS=(18,01),LENGTH=01,ATTRB=PROT
1062           DFHMDF  POS=(18,03),LENGTH=01,ATTRB=ASKIP,INITIAL='8'
1074 ITEM8     DFHMDF  POS=(18,05),LENGTH=08,ATTRB=(NUM,BRT),                    X
                         PICIN='99999999',PICOUT='99999999'
1085 DESC8     DFHMDF  POS=(18,14),LENGTH=19,ATTRB=(UNPROT,BRT)
1096           DFHMDF  POS=(18,34),LENGTH=01,ATTRB=PROT
1107 UNIT8     DFHMDF  POS=(18,41),LENGTH=05,ATTRB=(NUM,BRT),                    X
                         PICIN='99999',PICOUT='99999'
1118 UCOST8    DFHMDF  POS=(18,47),LENGTH=07,ATTRB=(NUM,BRT),                    X
                         PICIN='9999999',PICOUT='9999999'
1129 COST8     DFHMDF  POS=(18,55),LENGTH=08,ATTRB=(NUM,BRT),                    X
                         PICIN='99999999',PICOUT='99999999'
1140 UPRICE8   DFHMDF  POS=(18,64),LENGTH=07,ATTRB=(NUM,BRT),                    X
                         PICIN='9999999',PICOUT='9999999'
```

Fig. 19.3. (Continued)

```
STMT    SOURCE STATEMENT                          DOS/VS ASSEMBLER REL 34.0 13.10

1151 PRICE8   DFHMDF POS=(18,72),LENGTH=08,ATTRB=(NUM,BRT),                    X
                     PICIN='99999999',PICOUT='99999999'
1162          DFHMDF POS=(19,01),LENGTH=01,ATTRB=PROT
1173          DFHMDF POS=(19,03),LENGTH=01,ATTRB=ASKIP,INITIAL='9'
1185 ITEM9    DFHMDF POS=(19,05),LENGTH=08,ATTRB=(NUM,BRT),                    X
                     PICIN='99999999',PICOUT='99999999'
1196 DESC9    DFHMDF POS=(19,14),LENGTH=19,ATTRB=(UNPROT,BRT)
1207          DFHMDF POS=(19,34),LENGTH=01,ATTRB=PROT
1218 UNIT9    DFHMDF POS=(19,41),LENGTH=05,ATTRB=(NUM,BRT),                    X
                     PICIN='99999',PICOUT='99999'
1229 UCOST9   DFHMDF POS=(19,47),LENGTH=07,ATTRB=(NUM,BRT),                    X
                     PICIN='9999999',PICOUT='9999999'
1240 COST9    DFHMDF POS=(19,55),LENGTH=08,ATTRB=(NUM,BRT),                    X
                     PICIN='99999999',PICOUT='99999999'
1251 UPRICE9  DFHMDF POS=(19,64),LENGTH=07,ATTRB=(NUM,BRT),                    X
                     PICIN='9999999',PICOUT='9999999'
1262 PRICE9   DFHMDF POS=(19,72),LENGTH=08,ATTRB=(NUM,BRT),                    X
                     PICIN='99999999',PICOUT='99999999'
1273          DFHMDF POS=(20,01),LENGTH=01,ATTRB=PROT
1284          DFHMDF POS=(21,39),LENGTH=13,ATTRB=ASKIP,                        X
                     INITIAL='TOTALS ----- '
1296 TOTCOST  DFHMDF POS=(21,54),LENGTH=09,ATTRB=(NUM,BRT),                    X
                     PICIN='999999999',PICOUT='999999999'
1307          DFHMDF POS=(21,64),LENGTH=01,ATTRB=PROT
1318 TOTPRCE  DFHMDF POS=(21,71),LENGTH=09,ATTRB=(NUM,BRT),                    X
                     PICIN='999999999',PICOUT='999999999'
1329          DFHMDF POS=(22,01),LENGTH=01,ATTRB=PROT
1340 ERR1     DFHMDF POS=(23,01),LENGTH=28,ATTRB=(ASKIP,BRT),                  X
                     INITIAL='ORDER ACCEPTED -- CONTINUE'
1352 ERR2     DFHMDF POS=(23,40),LENGTH=28,ATTRB=(ASKIP,BRT)
1363 ERR3     DFHMDF POS=(24,01),LENGTH=28,ATTRB=(ASKIP,BRT)
1374 ERR4     DFHMDF POS=(24,40),LENGTH=28,ATTRB=(ASKIP,BRT)
1385          DFHMSD TYPE=FINAL
1399          END
```

Fig. 19.3. (Continued)

```
     1   IBM DOS VS COBOL

 CBL SUPMAP,STXIT,NOTRUNC,CSYNTAX,SXREF,OPT,VERB,CLIST,BUF=19069
 CBL NOOPT,LIB
               IDENTIFICATION DIVISION.

               PROGRAM-ID. ORAD01A.


               ENVIRONMENT DIVISION.

              **********************************************************************
              *                                                                    *
              *    1. THIS PROGRAM ADDS NEW ORDERS INTO THE PURCHASE ORDER         *
              *       MASTER FILE.                                                 *
              *                                                                    *
              *    2. AT LEAST ONE LINE ITEM MUST BE PRESENT FOR EACH ORDER.       *
              *                                                                    *
              *    3. A JOURNAL RECORD IS GENERATED FOR EACH NEW ORDER             *
              *       ENTERED.  THE JOURNAL DETAILS ARE                            *
              *             A) OPERATOR INITIAL.                                   *
              *             B) DATE ENTERED.                                       *
              *             C) ORDER NUMBER.                                       *
              *             D) DOCUMENT NUMBER.                                    *
              *             E) TOTAL COST OF ORDER.                                *
              *             F) TOTAL PRICE OF ORDER.                               *
              *                                                                    *
              **********************************************************************
```

Fig. 19.4. File Add Program.

```
 2        ORADO1A           15.54.49        12/27/80

00025        DATA DIVISION.

00027        WORKING-STORAGE SECTION.

00029        01  COMMUNICATION-AREA.

00031            05  COMMAREA-PROCESS-SW           PIC X.

00033        01  AREA1.

00035            05  VALIDATION-ERROR-MESSAGE.
00036                10  FILLER                   PIC X(5) VALUE 'LINE'.
00037                10  VALIDATION-ERROR-LINE    PIC 9.
00038                10  FILLER                   PIC XXX  VALUE ' - '.
00039                10  VALIDATION-ERROR-MSG     PIC X(19).

00041            05  JOB-NORMAL-END-MESSAGE  PIC X(23) VALUE
00042                'JOB NORMALLY TERMINATED'.

00044            05  JOB-ABORTED-MESSAGE.
00045                10  FILLER                   PIC X(15) VALUE 'JOB ABORTED --'.
00046                10  MAJOR-ERROR-MSG          PIC X(16).

00048            05  HEXADECIMAL-ZEROES           PIC 9999 COMP VALUE ZEROES.

00050            05  FILLER REDEFINES HEXADECIMAL-ZEROES.
00051                10  FILLER                   PIC X.
00052                10  HEX-ZEROES               PIC X.

00054            05  OLD-EIB-AREA.
00055                10  FILLER                   PIC X(7) VALUE 'OLD EIB'.
00056                10  OLD-EIBFN                PIC XX.
00057                10  OLD-EIBRCODE             PIC X(6).
```

Fig. 19.4. (Continued)

```
   3          ORAD01A        15.54.49        12/27/80

00059            01  DFHEIVAR COPY DFHEIVAR.
00060 C          01  DFHEIVAR.
00061 C              02   DFHEIV0   PICTURE X(26).
00062 C              02   DFHEIV1   PICTURE X(8).
00063 C              02   DFHEIV2   PICTURE X(8).
00064 C              02   DFHEIV3   PICTURE X(8).
00065 C              02   DFHEIV4   PICTURE X(6).
00066 C              02   DFHEIV5   PICTURE X(4).
00067 C              02   DFHEIV6   PICTURE X(4).
00068 C              02   DFHEIV7   PICTURE X(2).
00069 C              02   DFHEIV8   PICTURE X(2).
00070 C              02   DFHEIV9   PICTURE X(1).
00071 C              02   DFHEIV10  PICTURE S9(7) USAGE COMPUTATIONAL-3.
00072 C              02   DFHEIV11  PICTURE S9(4) USAGE COMPUTATIONAL.
00073 C              02   DFHEIV12  PICTURE S9(4) USAGE COMPUTATIONAL.
00074 C              02   DFHEIV13  PICTURE S9(4) USAGE COMPUTATIONAL.
00075 C              02   DFHEIV14  PICTURE S9(4) USAGE COMPUTATIONAL.
00076 C              02   DFHEIV15  PICTURE S9(4) USAGE COMPUTATIONAL.
00077 C              02   DFHEIV16  PICTURE S9(9) USAGE COMPUTATIONAL.
00078 C              02   DFHEIV17  PICTURE X(4).
00079 C              02   DFHEIV18  PICTURE X(4).
00080 C              02   DFHEIV19  PICTURE X(4).
00081 C              02   DFHEIV97  PICTURE S9(7) USAGE COMPUTATIONAL-3 VALUE ZERO.
00082 C              02   DFHEIV98  PICTURE S9(4) USAGE COMPUTATIONAL VALUE ZERO.
00083 C              02   DFHEIV99  PICTURE X(1)  VALUE SPACE.
00084        LINKAGE SECTION.
00085            01  DFHEIBLK COPY DFHEIBLK.
00086 C          *    EIBLK EXEC INTERFACE BLOCK
00087 C          01  DFHEIBLK.
00088 C          *        EIBTIME     TIME IN OHHMMSS FORMAT
00089 C              02 EIBTIME       PICTURE S9(7) USAGE COMPUTATIONAL-3.
00090 C          *        EIBDATE     DATE IN OOYYDDD FORMAT
00091 C              02 EIBDATE       PICTURE S9(7) USAGE COMPUTATIONAL-3.
00092 C          *        EIBTRNID    TRANSACTION IDENTIFIER
00093 C              02 EIBTRNID      PICTURE X(4).
00094 C          *        EIBTASKN    TASK NUMBER
00095 C              02 EIBTASKN      PICTURE S9(7) USAGE COMPUTATIONAL-3.
00096 C          *        EIBTRMID    TERMINAL IDENTIFIER
00097 C              02 EIBTRMID      PICTURE X(4).
00098 C          *        DFHEIGDI    RESERVED
00099 C              02 DFHEIGDI      PICTURE S9(4) USAGE COMPUTATIONAL.
00100 C          *        EIBCPOSN    CURSOR POSITION
00101 C              02 EIBCPOSN      PICTURE S9(4) USAGE COMPUTATIONAL.
00102 C          *        EIBCALEN    COMMAREA LENGTH
00103 C              02 EIBCALEN      PICTURE S9(4) USAGE COMPUTATIONAL.
00104 C          *        EIBAID      ATTENTION IDENTIFIER
00105 C              02 EIBAID        PICTURE X(1).
00106 C          *        EIBFN       FUNCTION CODE
00107 C              02 EIBFN         PICTURE X(2).
00108 C          *        EIBRCODE    RESPONSE CODE
00109 C              02 EIBRCODE      PICTURE X(6).
00110 C          *        EIBDS       DATASET NAME
00111 C              02 EIBDS         PICTURE X(8).
```

Fig. 19.4. (Continued)

```
    4        ORADO1A          15.54.49        12/27/80

00112 C    *         EIBREQID     REQUEST IDENTIFIER
00113 C              02 EIBREQID  PICTURE X(8).
00114         01  DFHCOMMAREA.

00116              05  PROCESS-SW              PIC X.
00117                  88  INITIAL-ENTRY-TIME         VALUE '0'.
00118                  88  ORDER-VALIDATION-TIME      VALUE '1'.

00120              05  OPERATOR-INITIAL        PIC XXX.

00122         01  LINKAGE-POINTERS.

00124              05  FILLER              PIC S9(8) COMP.
00125              05  MAP1-POINTER        PIC S9(8) COMP.
00126              05  POM-POINTER         PIC S9(8) COMP.
00127              05  TWA-POINTER         PIC S9(8) COMP.
00128              05  TSA-POINTER         PIC S9(8) COMP.
00129              05  JOURNAL-POINTER     PIC S9(8) COMP.
00130              05  TABLE-POINTER       PIC S9(8) COMP.
```

Fig. 19.4. (Continued)

5 OR AD01A 15.54.49 12/27/80

```
00132          ************************************************************************
00133          *                                                                      *
00134          *               ORDER ENTRY MAP DESCRIPTION                            *
00135          *                                                                      *
00136          ************************************************************************

00138          01  MAP1-AREA.

00140              05  FILLER                        PIC X(12).
00141              05  MAP1-DUMMY-L                  PIC S9999 COMP.
00142              05  MAP1-DUMMY-A                  PIC X.
00143              05  MAP1-DUMMY                    PIC X.
00144              05  MAP1-ORDER-NUMBER-L           PIC S9999 COMP.
00145              05  MAP1-ORDER-NUMBER-A           PIC X.
00146              05  MAP1-ORDER-NUMBER             PIC X(10).
00147              05  MAP1-DOCUMENT-L               PIC S9999 COMP.
00148              05  MAP1-DOCUMENT-A               PIC X.
00149              05  MAP1-DOCUMENT                 PIC X(8).
00150              05  MAP1-DEPARTMENT-L             PIC S9999 COMP.
00151              05  MAP1-DEPARTMENT-A             PIC X.
00152              05  MAP1-DEPARTMENT               PIC XXX.
00153              05  MAP1-ORDER-DATE-L             PIC S9999 COMP.
00154              05  MAP1-ORDER-DATE-A             PIC X.
00155              05  MAP1-ORDER-DATE.
00156                  10  MAP1-ORDER-DATE-MONTH     PIC XX.
00157                  10  MAP1-ORDER-DATE-DAY       PIC XX.
00158                  10  MAP1-ORDER-DATE-YEAR      PIC XX.
00159              05  MAP1-LINE-ITEM                OCCURS 9
00160                                                INDEXED BY MAP1-LINE-I.
00161                  10  MAP1-ITEM-NUMBER-L        PIC S9999 COMP.
00162                  10  MAP1-ITEM-NUMBER-A        PIC X.
00163                  10  MAP1-ITEM-NUMBER          PIC 9(8).
00164                  10  MAP1-ITEM-DESCRIPTION-L   PIC S9999 COMP.
00165                  10  MAP1-ITEM-DESCRIPTION-A   PIC X.
00166                  10  MAP1-ITEM-DESCRIPTION     PIC X(19).
00167                  10  MAP1-UNIT-L               PIC S9999 COMP.
00168                  10  MAP1-UNIT-A               PIC X.
00169                  10  MAP1-UNIT                 PIC 9(5).
00170                  10  MAP1-UNIT-COST-L          PIC S9999 COMP.
00171                  10  MAP1-UNIT-COST-A          PIC X.
00172                  10  MAP1-UNIT-COST            PIC 9(5)V99.
00173                  10  MAP1-COST-L               PIC S9999 COMP.
00174                  10  MAP1-COST-A               PIC X.
00175                  10  MAP1-COST                 PIC 9(6)V99.
00176                  10  MAP1-UNIT-PRICE-L         PIC S9999 COMP.
00177                  10  MAP1-UNIT-PRICE-A         PIC X.
00178                  10  MAP1-UNIT-PRICE           PIC 9(5)V99.
00179                  10  MAP1-PRICE-L              PIC S9999 COMP.
00180                  10  MAP1-PRICE-A              PIC X.
00181                  10  MAP1-PRICE                PIC 9(6)V99.
00182              05  MAP1-TOTAL-COST-L             PIC S9999 COMP.
```

Fig. 19.4. (Continued)

```
      6           ORADO1A          15.54.49          12/27/80

   00183                  05   MAP1-TOTAL-COST-A          PIC X.
   00184                  05   MAP1-TOTAL-COST            PIC 9(7)V99.
   00185                  05   MAP1-TOTAL-PRICE-L         PIC S9999 COMP.
   00186                  05   MAP1-TOTAL-PRICE-A         PIC X.
   00187                  05   MAP1-TOTAL-PRICE           PIC 9(7)V99.
   00188                  05   FILLER                     OCCURS 4
   00189                                                  INDEXED BY ERROR-I.
   00190                      10   MAP1-ERRORS-L          PIC S9999 COMP.
   00191                      10   MAP1-ERRORS-A          PIC X.
   00192                      10   MAP1-ERRORS            PIC X(28).

      7           ORADO1A          15.54.49          12/27/80

   00194    ***********************************************************************
   00195    *                                                                     *
   00196    *          PURCHASE ORDER MASTER -- FILE LAYOUT                       *
   00197    *                                                                     *
   00198    ***********************************************************************

   00200    01   ORDER-MASTER-RECORD.
   00201         05   ORDER-NUMBER                        PIC X(10).
   00202         05   ORDER-ALT-KEY.
   00203              10   ORDER-DEPARTMENT               PIC XXX.
   00204              10   ORDER-DATE.
   00205                   15   ORDER-DATE-YEAR           PIC XX.
   00206                   15   ORDER-DATE-MONTH          PIC XX.
   00207                   15   ORDER-DATE-DAY            PIC XX.
   00208         05   ORDER-DATE-ENTERED.
   00209              10   ORDER-DATE-ENTERED-MONTH       PIC XX.
   00210              10   ORDER-DATE-ENTERED-DAY         PIC XX.
   00211              10   ORDER-DATE-ENTERED-YEAR        PIC XX.
   00212         05   ORDER-TOTAL-COST                    PIC S9(7)V99   COMP-3.
   00213         05   ORDER-TOTAL-PRICE                   PIC S9(7)V99   COMP-3.
   00214         05   ORDER-LINE-COUNT                    PIC S9999      COMP.
   00215         05   ORDER-ALL-LINES.
   00216              10   ORDER-LINE-ITEM                OCCURS 1 TO 9
   00217                                                  DEPENDING ON ORDER-LINE-COUNT
   00218                                                  INDEXED BY ORDER-LINE-I.
   00219                   15   ORDER-ITEM-NUMBER         PIC X(8).
   00220                   15   ORDER-ITEM-DESCRIPTION    PIC X(19).
   00221                   15   ORDER-ITEM-DATE.
   00222                        20   ORDER-ITEM-DATE-MONTH   PIC XX.
   00223                        20   ORDER-ITEM-DATE-DAY     PIC XX.
   00224                        20   ORDER-ITEM-DATE-YEAR    PIC XX.
   00225                   15   ORDER-UNIT                PIC S9(5)      COMP-3.
   00226                   15   ORDER-UNIT-COST           PIC S9(5)V99   COMP-3.
   00227                   15   ORDER-UNIT-PRICE          PIC S9(5)V99   COMP-3.
```

Fig. 19.4. (Continued)

```
         8        ORADO1A          15.54.49        12/27/80

00229            ***************************************************************
00230            *                                                             *
00231            *                  TRANSACTION WORK AREA                      *
00232            *                                                             *
00233            ***************************************************************

00235            01   TWA-AREA.

00237                 05   TWA-LINE-ITEM-MAP.
00238                      10   TWA-ITEM-NUMBER-MAP-L          PIC S9999 COMP.
00239                      10   TWA-ITEM-NUMBER-MAP-A          PIC X.
00240                      10   TWA-ITEM-NUMBER-MAP            PIC X(8).
00241                      10   TWA-ITEM-DESCRIPTION-MAP-L     PIC S9999 COMP.
00242                      10   TWA-ITEM-DESCRIPTION-MAP-A     PIC X.
00243                      10   TWA-ITEM-DESCRIPTION-MAP.
00244                           15   TWA-DESCRIPTION-FIRST-MAP PIC X.
00245                           15   FILLER                   PIC X(18).
00246                      10   TWA-UNIT-MAP-L                 PIC S9999 COMP.
00247                      10   TWA-UNIT-MAP-A                 PIC X.
00248                      10   TWA-UNIT-MAP                   PIC 9(5).
00249                      10   TWA-UNIT-COST-MAP-L            PIC S9999 COMP.
00250                      10   TWA-UNIT-COST-MAP-A            PIC X.
00251                      10   TWA-UNIT-COST-MAP              PIC 9(5)V99.
00252                      10   TWA-COST-MAP-L                 PIC S9999 COMP.
00253                      10   TWA-COST-MAP-A                 PIC X.
00254                      10   TWA-COST-MAP                   PIC 9(6)V99.
00255                      10   TWA-UNIT-PRICE-MAP-L           PIC S9999 COMP.
00256                      10   TWA-UNIT-PRICE-MAP-A           PIC X.
00257                      10   TWA-UNIT-PRICE-MAP             PIC 9(5)V99.
00258                      10   TWA-PRICE-MAP-L                PIC S9999 COMP.
00259                      10   TWA-PRICE-MAP-A                PIC X.
00260                      10   TWA-PRICE-MAP                  PIC 9(6)V99.

00262                 05   TWA-LINE-ITEM-ORDER.
00263                      10   TWA-ITEM-NUMBER-ORDER          PIC X(8).
00264                      10   TWA-ITEM-DESCRIPTION-ORDER     PIC X(19).
00265                      10   TWA-ITEM-DATE-ORDER            PIC X(6).
00266                      10   TWA-UNIT-ORDER                 PIC S9(5)     COMP-3.
00267                      10   TWA-UNIT-COST-ORDER            PIC S9(5)V99  COMP-3.
00268                      10   TWA-UNIT-PRICE-ORDER           PIC S9(5)V99  COMP-3.

00270                 05   TWA-TOTAL-COST                      PIC S9(7)V99  COMP-3.

00272                 05   TWA-TOTAL-PRICE                     PIC S9(7)V99  COMP-3.

00274                 05   TWA-ORDER-RECORD-KEY                PIC X(10).
```

Fig. 19.4. (Continued)

```
9        ORADO1A        15.54.49        12/27/80

               05  TSA-QUEUE-ID.
                 10  TSA-TERM-ID                     PIC XXXX.
                 10  TSA-TRANS-ID                    PIC XXXX.

               05  TWA-BINARY-FIELDS  COMP.
                 10  TWA-LINE-DATA-CNT               PIC S9(8).
                 10  TWA-JOURNAL-ID                  PIC S9(8).
                 10  TWA-POM-LENGTH                  PIC S9(4).
                 10  TSA-LENGTH                      PIC S9(4).
                 10  TSA-QUEUE-NO                    PIC S9(4).
                 10  TWA-JOURNAL-LENGTH              PIC S9(4).

               05  TWA-OPERATOR-MESSAGE              PIC X(31).

               05  TWA-CURRENT-DATE.
                 10  TWA-CURRENT-DATE-MONTH          PIC XX.
                 10  FILLER                          PIC X.
                 10  TWA-CURRENT-DATE-DAY            PIC XX.
                 10  FILLER                          PIC X.
                 10  TWA-CURRENT-DATE-YEAR           PIC XX.

               05  TWA-DEPT-TABLE-KEY.
                 10  TWA-DEPT-TABLE-KEY-CODE         PIC X.
                 10  TWA-DEPT-TABLE-KEY-NUMBER       PIC 9(7) COMP-3.
```

Fig. 19.4. (Continued)

```
   10          ORAD01A           15.54.49          12/27/80

          *****************************************************************
          *                                                               *
          *                TEMPORARY STORAGE AREA                         *
          *                                                               *
          *****************************************************************


           01  TSA-AREA.

               05  TSA-POMAST-RECORD.
                 10  TSA-ORDER-NUMBER                  PIC X(10).
                 10  TSA-DEPARTMENT                    PIC XXX.
                 10  TSA-ORDER-DATE.
                   15  TSA-ORDER-DATE-YEAR             PIC XX.
                   15  TSA-ORDER-DATE-MONTH            PIC XX.
                   15  TSA-ORDER-DATE-DAY              PIC XX.
                 10  TSA-ORDER-ENTERED.
                   15  TSA-ORDER-ENTERED-MONTH         PIC XX.
                   15  TSA-ORDER-ENTERED-DAY           PIC XX.
                   15  TSA-ORDER-ENTERED-YEAR          PIC XX.
                 10  TSA-TOTAL-COST                    PIC S9(7)V99 COMP-3.
                 10  TSA-TOTAL-PRICE                   PIC S9(7)V99 COMP-3.
                 10  TSA-LINE-COUNT                    PIC S9999    COMP.
                 10  TSA-LINE-ITEM                 OCCURS 9
                                                   INDEXED BY TSA-LINE-I.
                   15  TSA-ITEM-NUMBER                 PIC X(8).
                   15  TSA-ITEM-DESCRIPTION            PIC X(19).
                   15  TSA-ITEM-DATE                   PIC X(6).
                   15  TSA-UNIT                        PIC S9(5)    COMP-3.
                   15  TSA-UNIT-COST                   PIC S9(5)V99 COMP-3.
                   15  TSA-UNIT-PRICE                  PIC S9(5)V99 COMP-3.


               05  TSA-OPERATOR-INITIAL                PIC XXX.


               05  TSA-DEPT-CNT                        PIC S9(8)    COMP.


               05  TSA-DEPTS                       OCCURS 300
                                                   DEPENDING ON TSA-DEPT-CNT
                                                   ASCENDING KEY TSA-DEPT-NO
                                                   INDEXED BY DEPT-I.
                 10  TSA-DEPT-NO                       PIC XXX.
```

Fig. 19.4. (Continued)

```
11          ORAD01A          15.54.49          12/27/80

            ****************************************************************
            *                                                              *
            *       JOURNAL RECORD LAYOUT                                  *
            *                                                              *
            ****************************************************************

             01  JOURNAL-RECORD.

                 05  JOURNAL-OPERATOR-INITIAL      PIC XXX.
                 05  JOURNAL-DATE-ENTERED          PIC X(6).
                 05  JOURNAL-ORDER-NUMBER          PIC X(10).
                 05  JOURNAL-DOCUMENT-NUMBER       PIC X(8).
                 05  JOURNAL-TOTAL-COST            PIC S9(7)V99 COMP-3.
                 05  JOURNAL-TOTAL-PRICE           PIC S9(7)V99 COMP-3.
```

```
12          ORAD01A          15.54.49          12/27/80

            ****************************************************************
            *                                                              *
            *           DEPARTMENT TABLE --- RECORD LAYOUT                 *
            *                                                              *
            ****************************************************************

             01  DEPT-TABLE-RECORD.
                 05  DEPT-TABLE-KEY.
                   10  DEPT-TABLE-KEY-CODE         PIC X.
                     88  DEPT-RECORD                   VALUE 'D'.
                   10  DEPT-TABLE-KEY-NUMBER       PIC 9(7) COMP-3.
                 05  DEPT-NO                       PIC XXX.
                 05  FILLER                        PIC X(30).
                 05  DEPT-DIVISION                 PIC XX.
                 05  FILLER                        PIC X(45).
```

Fig. 19.4. (Continued)

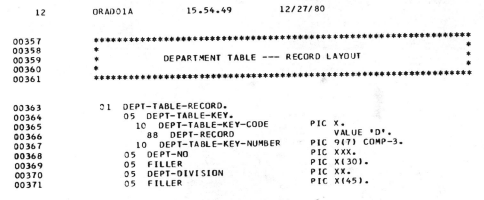

```
   13          ORAD01A          15.54.49          12/27/80

            PROCEDURE DIVISION USING DFHEIBLK DFHCOMMAREA.
                CALL 'DFHEI1'.

           *****************************************************************
           *                                                               *
            MAIN-LINE SECTION.
           *                                                               *
           *****************************************************************


           *    EXEC CICS
           *         ADDRESS TWA (TWA-POINTER)
           *    END-EXEC.
                 MOVE '                     ' TO DFHEIVO CALL 'DFHEI1' USING
                 DFHEIVO TWA-POINTER.

           *    EXEC CICS
           *         HANDLE AID
           *              CLEAR (FINALIZATION)
           *                PA1 (BYPASS-INPUT)
           *                PA2 (BYPASS-INPUT)
           *                PA3 (BYPASS-INPUT)
           *    END-EXEC.
                 MOVE '  0                  ' TO DFHEIVO CALL 'DFHEI1' USING
                 DFHEIVO GO TO FINALIZATION BYPASS-INPUT BYPASS-INPUT
                 BYPASS-INPUT DEPENDING ON DFHEIGDI.




           *    EXEC CICS
           *         HANDLE CONDITION
           *              MAPFAIL (MAPFAIL-ERROR)
           *              ERROR   (MAJOR-ERROR)
           *    END-EXEC.
                 MOVE '                     ' TO DFHEIVO CALL 'DFHEI1' USING
                 DFHEIVO GO TO MAPFAIL-ERROR MAJOR-ERROR DEPENDING ON
                 DFHEIGDI.


                IF EIBCALEN NOT EQUAL TO ZEROES
                     IF ORDER-VALIDATION-TIME
                          GO TO ORDER-VALIDATION
                     ELSE IF INITIAL-ENTRY-TIME
                          GO TO INITIALIZATION
                     ELSE GO TO PROCESS-SWITCH-ERROR.

                IF EIBCALEN EQUAL TO ZEROES
                     GO TO SIGN-ON-VIOLATION.
```

Fig. 19.4. (Continued)

```
14          ORAD01A          15.54.49          12/27/80

           ***************************************************************
           *                                                             *
            ORDER-VALIDATION SECTION.
           *                                                             *
           ***************************************************************

           *    EXEC CICS
           *         RECEIVE MAP    ('ORADM01')
           *                 MAPSET ('ORADS01')
           *                 SET    (MAP1-POINTER)
           *    END-EXEC.
                 MOVE 'ORADM01' TO DFHEIV1 MOVE 'ORADS01' TO DFHEIV2 MOVE '
           -    '             ' TO DFHEIV0 CALL 'DFHEI1' USING DFHEIV0
                 DFHEIV1 MAP1-POINTER DFHEIV98 DFHEIV2.


                MOVE EIBTRMID    TO   TSA-TERM-ID.
                MOVE EIBTRNID    TO   TSA-TRANS-ID.

           *    EXEC CICS
           *         READQ TS
           *              QUEUE  (TSA-QUEUE-ID)
           *              SET    (TSA-POINTER)
           *              LENGTH (TSA-LENGTH)
           *              ITEM   (1)
           *    END-EXEC.
                 MOVE 1 TO DFHEIV11 MOVE '  Y      ' TO DFHEIV0 CALL 'DFHEI1'
                 USING DFHEIV0 TSA-QUEUE-ID TSA-POINTER TSA-LENGTH DFHEIV99
                 DFHEIV11.




                MOVE SPACES TO MAP1-ERRORS (1)
                               MAP1-ERRORS (2)
                               MAP1-ERRORS (3)
                               MAP1-ERRORS (4).
                SET ERROR-I   TO  ZEROES.

            VALIDATE-FIXED-DATA.

                IF MAP1-ORDER-NUMBER NUMERIC
                     MOVE MAP1-ORDER-NUMBER          TO   TSA-ORDER-NUMBER
                ELSE SET ERROR-I UP BY 1
                     MOVE 'INVALID ORDER NUMBER'     TO   MAP1-ERRORS (ERROR-I)
                     MOVE -1                         TO   MAP1-ORDER-NUMBER-L.

                IF MAP1-DOCUMENT NUMERIC
                     NEXT SENTENCE
                ELSE SET ERROR-I UP BY 1
                     MOVE 'INVALID DOCUMENT NUMBER' TO  MAP1-ERRORS (ERROR-I)
```

Fig. 19.4. (Continued)

```
    15         ORA001A          15.54.49        12/27/80

00473                     IF ERROR-I EQUAL TO 1
00474                         MOVE -1                      TO   MAP1-DOCUMENT-L.

00476                SEARCH ALL TSA-DEPTS
00477                     AT END
00478                         GO TO DEPARTMENT-ERROR-RTN
00479                     WHEN MAP1-DEPARTMENT EQUAL   TO   TSA-DEPT-NO (DEPT-I)
00480                         MOVE MAP1-DEPARTMENT     TO   TSA-DEPARTMENT
00481                         GO TO EDIT-ORDER-DATE.

00483                DEPARTMENT-ERROR-RTN.

00485                     SET ERROR-I UP BY 1.
00486                     MOVE 'INVALID DEPARTMENT NUMBER' TO MAP1-ERRORS (ERROR-I).
00487                     IF ERROR-I EQUAL TO 1
00488                         MOVE -1                      TO MAP1-DEPARTMENT-L.

00490                EDIT-ORDER-DATE.

00492                     IF      MAP1-ORDER-DATE-MONTH (GREATER '00' AND LESS '13')
00493                         AND MAP1-ORDER-DATE-DAY    (GREATER '00' AND LESS '32')
00494                         AND MAP1-ORDER-DATE-YEAR   NUMERIC
00495                     THEN MOVE MAP1-ORDER-DATE-MONTH  TO   TSA-ORDER-DATE-MONTH
00496                         MOVE MAP1-ORDER-DATE-DAY    TO   TSA-ORDER-DATE-DAY
00497                         MOVE MAP1-ORDER-DATE-YEAR   TO   TSA-ORDER-DATE-YEAR
00498                     ELSE SET ERROR-I UP BY 1
00499                         MOVE 'INVALID ORDER-DATE'   TO   MAP1-ERRORS (ERROR-I)
00500                         IF ERROR-I EQUAL TO 1
00501                             MOVE -1                 TO   MAP1-ORDER-DATE-L.

00503                VALIDATE-FIXED-DATA-END.

00505                     IF ERROR-I EQUAL TO 4
00506                         GO TO DISPLAY-ERROR-SCREEN.

00508                VALIDATE-VARIABLE-DATA.

00510                     SET MAP1-LINE-I       TO  1.
00511                     MOVE +99              TO  TWA-LINE-DATA-CNT.
00512                     MOVE MAP1-ORDER-DATE  TO  TWA-ITEM-DATE-ORDER.
00513                     MOVE ZEROES           TO  TWA-TOTAL-COST
00514                                               TWA-TOTAL-PRICE.
00515                     PERFORM VALIDATE-EACH-LINE THRU VALIDATE-EACH-LINE-EXIT
00516                         UNTIL TWA-LINE-DATA-CNT EQUAL TO ZEROES
00517                             OR ERROR-I           EQUAL TO 4
00518                             OR MAP1-LINE-I        GREATER THAN 9.
00519                     GO TO VALIDATE-TOTALS.
```

Fig. 19.4. (Continued)

```
16          ORAD01A          15.54.49          12/27/80

        VALIDATE-EACH-LINE.

            MOVE ZEROES                     TO  TWA-LINE-DATA-CNT.
            SET VALIDATION-ERROR-LINE  TO  MAP1-LINE-I.
            MOVE MAP1-LINE-ITEM (MAP1-LINE-I) TO TWA-LINE-ITEM-MAP.

            IF TWA-ITEM-NUMBER-MAP-L NOT EQUAL TO ZEROES
            THEN IF TWA-ITEM-NUMBER-MAP NUMERIC
                    MOVE TWA-ITEM-NUMBER-MAP TO TWA-ITEM-NUMBER-ORDER
                    ADD 1 TO TWA-LINE-DATA-CNT
                ELSE MOVE 'INVALID ITEM NUMBER' TO VALIDATION-ERROR-MSG
                    SET ERROR-I UP BY 1
                    MOVE VALIDATION-ERROR-MESSAGE
                                        TO MAP1-ERRORS (ERROR-I)
                    IF ERROR-I EQUAL TO 1
                        MOVE -1 TO MAP1-ITEM-NUMBER-L (MAP1-LINE-I)
                    ELSE IF ERROR-I EQUAL TO 4
                            GO TO VALIDATE-EACH-LINE-EXIT.

            IF TWA-ITEM-DESCRIPTION-MAP-L EQUAL TO ZEROES
                MOVE SPACES TO TWA-ITEM-DESCRIPTION-ORDER
            ELSE IF TWA-DESCRIPTION-FIRST-MAP EQUAL TO SPACES
                    MOVE 'INVALID DESCRIPTION'
                                        TO VALIDATION-ERROR-MSG
                    SET ERROR-I UP BY 1
                    MOVE VALIDATION-ERROR-MESSAGE
                                        TO MAP1-ERRORS (ERROR-I)
                    IF ERROR-I EQUAL TO 1
                        MOVE -1
                            TO MAP1-ITEM-DESCRIPTION-L (MAP1-LINE-I)
                    ELSE IF ERROR-I EQUAL TO 4
                            GO TO VALIDATE-EACH-LINE-EXIT
                        ELSE NEXT SENTENCE
                ELSE MOVE TWA-ITEM-DESCRIPTION-MAP
                                        TO TWA-ITEM-DESCRIPTION-ORDER
                    ADD 2               TO TWA-LINE-DATA-CNT.

            IF TWA-UNIT-MAP-L NOT EQUAL TO ZEROES
            THEN IF TWA-UNIT-MAP NUMERIC
                    MOVE TWA-UNIT-MAP          TO   TWA-UNIT-ORDER
                    ADD 4 TO TWA-LINE-DATA-CNT
                ELSE MOVE ZEROES               TO   TWA-UNIT-ORDER
                    MOVE 'INVALID UNIT'        TO   VALIDATION-ERROR-MSG
                    SET ERROR-I UP BY 1
                    MOVE VALIDATION-ERROR-MESSAGE
                                               TO   MAP1-ERRORS (ERROR-I)
                    IF ERROR-I EQUAL TO 1
                        MOVE -1            TO   MAP1-UNIT-L (MAP1-LINE-I)
                    ELSE IF ERROR-I EQUAL TO 4
                            GO TO VALIDATE-EACH-LINE-EXIT.

            IF TWA-UNIT-COST-MAP-L NOT EQUAL TO ZEROES
            THEN IF TWA-UNIT-COST-MAP NUMERIC
```

Fig. 19.4. (Continued)

```
     17          ORADO1A              15.54.49         12/27/80

00574                                    MOVE TWA-UNIT-COST-MAP  TO   TWA-UNIT-COST-ORDER
00575                                    ADD 8 TO TWA-LINE-DATA-CNT
00576                           ELSE MOVE ZEROES            TO   TWA-UNIT-COST-ORDER
00577                                MOVE 'INVALID UNIT COST'
00578                                                       TO   VALIDATION-ERROR-MSG
00579                                    SET ERROR-I UP BY 1
00580                                    MOVE VALIDATION-ERROR-MESSAGE
00581                                                       TO   MAP1-ERRORS (ERROR-I)
00582                                    IF ERROR-I EQUAL TO 1
00583                                        MOVE -1   TO   MAP1-UNIT-COST-L (MAP1-LINE-I)
00584                                    ELSE IF ERROR-I EQUAL TO 4
00585                                           GO TO VALIDATE-EACH-LINE-EXIT.

00587                    IF TWA-COST-MAP-L NOT EQUAL TO ZEROES
00588                    THEN IF    TWA-COST-MAP  NUMERIC
00589                          AND TWA-COST-MAP =
00590                                       TWA-UNIT-ORDER * TWA-UNIT-COST-ORDER
00591                          THEN ADD TWA-COST-MAP  TO   TWA-TOTAL-COST
00592                                    ADD 16         TO   TWA-LINE-DATA-CNT
00593                          ELSE MOVE 'INVALID COST'  TO VALIDATION-ERROR-MSG
00594                                    SET ERROR-I UP BY 1
00595                                    MOVE VALIDATION-ERROR-MESSAGE
00596                                                       TO MAP1-ERRORS (ERROR-I)
00597                                    IF ERROR-I EQUAL TO 1
00598                                          MOVE -1 TO MAP1-COST-L (MAP1-LINE-I)
00599                                    ELSE IF ERROR-I EQUAL TO 4
00600                                          GO TO VALIDATE-EACH-LINE-EXIT.

00602                    IF TWA-UNIT-PRICE-MAP-L NOT EQUAL TO ZEROES
00603                    THEN IF TWA-UNIT-PRICE-MAP  NUMERIC
00604                                 MOVE TWA-UNIT-PRICE-MAP  TO   TWA-UNIT-PRICE-ORDER
00605                                 ADD 32 TO TWA-LINE-DATA-CNT
00606                           ELSE MOVE ZEROES            TO   TWA-UNIT-PRICE-ORDER
00607                                MOVE 'INVALID UNIT PRICE'
00608                                                       TO   VALIDATION-ERROR-MSG
00609                                    SET ERROR-I UP BY 1
00610                                    MOVE VALIDATION-ERROR-MESSAGE
00611                                                       TO   MAP1-ERRORS (ERROR-I)
00612                                    IF ERROR-I EQUAL TO 1
00613                                         MOVE -1 TO MAP1-UNIT-PRICE-L (MAP1-LINE-I)
00614                                    ELSE IF ERROR-I EQUAL TO 4
00615                                         GO TO VALIDATE-EACH-LINE-EXIT.

00617                    IF TWA-PRICE-MAP-L NOT EQUAL TO ZEROES
00618                    THEN IF    TWA-PRICE-MAP  NUMERIC
00619                          AND TWA-PRICE-MAP =
00620                                       TWA-UNIT-ORDER * TWA-UNIT-PRICE-ORDER
00621                          THEN ADD TWA-PRICE-MAP  TO   TWA-TOTAL-PRICE
00622                                    ADD 64         TO   TWA-LINE-DATA-CNT
00623                          ELSE MOVE 'INVALID PRICE'  TO VALIDATION-ERROR-MSG
00624                                    SET ERROR-I UP BY 1
00625                                    MOVE VALIDATION-ERROR-MESSAGE
00626                                                       TO   MAP1-ERRORS (ERROR-I)
```

Fig. 19.4. (Continued)

18 OR ADO1A 15.54.49 12/27/80

```
00627                         IF ERROR-I EQUAL TO 1
00628                             MOVE -1 TO MAP1-PRICE-L (MAP1-LINE-I)
00629                         ELSE IF ERROR-I EQUAL TO 4
00630                             GO TO VALIDATE-EACH-LINE-EXIT.

00632               IF TWA-LINE-DATA-CNT EQUAL TO (125 OR 127)
00633                   IF ERROR-I EQUAL TO ZEROES
00634                       SET TSA-LINE-I     TO MAP1-LINE-I
00635                       MOVE TWA-LINE-ITEM-ORDER
00636                                       TO TSA-LINE-ITEM (TSA-LINE-I)
00637                   ELSE NEXT SENTENCE
00638               ELSE IF TWA-LINE-DATA-CNT EQUAL TO ZEROES
00639                       NEXT SENTENCE
00640                   ELSE SET ERROR-I UP BY 1
00641                       MOVE 'INCOMPLETE DATA' TO VALIDATION-ERROR-MSG
00642                       MOVE VALIDATION-ERROR-MESSAGE
00643                                       TO MAP1-ERRORS (ERROR-I)
00644                           IF ERROR-I EQUAL TO 1
00645                               MOVE -1
00646                                       TO MAP1-ITEM-NUMBER-L (MAP1-LINE-I)
00647                           ELSE IF ERROR-I EQUAL TO 4
00648                               GO TO VALIDATE-EACH-LINE-EXIT.

00650               SET MAP1-LINE-I UP BY 1.
00651           VALIDATE-EACH-LINE-EXIT.   EXIT.

00653           VALIDATE-TOTALS.

00655               IF ERROR-I EQUAL TO 4
00656                   GO TO DISPLAY-ERROR-SCREEN.

00658               IF     MAP1-LINE-I EQUAL TO 2
00659                   AND TWA-LINE-DATA-CNT EQUAL TO ZEROES
00660               THEN SET ERROR-I UP BY 1
00661                   MOVE 'NO LINE ITEM ENTERED' TO MAP1-ERRORS (ERROR-I)
00662                   IF ERROR-I EQUAL TO 1
00663                       MOVE -1 TO MAP1-ITEM-NUMBER-L (1)
00664                   ELSE IF ERROR-I EQUAL TO 4
00665                       GO TO VALIDATE-TOTALS-EXIT.

00667               IF     MAP1-TOTAL-COST NUMERIC
00668                   AND MAP1-TOTAL-COST = TWA-TOTAL-COST
00669               THEN MOVE TWA-TOTAL-COST     TO  TSA-TOTAL-COST
00670               ELSE SET ERROR-I UP BY 1
00671                   MOVE 'INCORRECT TOTAL COST' TO  MAP1-ERRORS (ERROR-I)
00672                   IF ERROR-I EQUAL TO 1
00673                       MOVE -1                 TO  MAP1-TOTAL-COST-L
00674                   ELSE IF ERROR-I EQUAL TO 4
00675                       GO TO VALIDATE-TOTALS-EXIT.

00677               IF     MAP1-TOTAL-PRICE NUMERIC
00678                   AND MAP1-TOTAL-PRICE = TWA-TOTAL-PRICE
```

Fig. 19.4. (Continued)

```
19          ORADO1A          15.54.49          12/27/80

           THEN MOVE TWA-TOTAL-PRICE            TO   TSA-TOTAL-PRICE
           ELSE SET ERROR-I UP BY 1
                MOVE 'INCORRECT TOTAL PRICE'  TO   MAP1-ERRORS (ERROR-I)
                IF ERROR-I EQUAL TO 1
                     MOVE -1                  TO   MAP1-TOTAL-PRICE-L
                ELSE IF ERROR-I EQUAL TO 4
                          GO TO VALIDATE-TOTALS-EXIT.
       VALIDATE-TOTALS-EXIT.  EXIT.

       CHECK-IF-THERE-ARE-ERRORS.

           IF ERROR-I NOT EQUAL TO ZEROES
                GO TO DISPLAY-ERROR-SCREEN.

       NO-ERRORS-RTN.

           SET TSA-LINE-COUNT TO MAP1-LINE-I.

           IF TSA-LINE-COUNT GREATER THAN 9
                IF TWA-LINE-DATA-CNT EQUAL TO ZEROES
                     SUBTRACT 2 FROM TSA-LINE-COUNT
                ELSE SUBTRACT 1 FROM TSA-LINE-COUNT
           ELSE SUBTRACT 2 FROM TSA-LINE-COUNT.

      *    EXEC CICS
      *         GETMAIN
      *              SET    (POM-POINTER)
      *              LENGTH (433)
      *    END-EXEC.
            MOVE 433 TO DFHEIV11 MOVE '          ' TO DFHEIVO CALL 'DFHEI
      -    '1' USING DFHEIVO POM-POINTER DFHEIV11.



           MOVE TSA-LINE-COUNT       TO   ORDER-LINE-COUNT.
           MOVE TSA-POMAST-RECORD    TO   ORDER-MASTER-RECORD.
           COMPUTE TWA-POM-LENGTH = 37 + ORDER-LINE-COUNT * 44.
           MOVE TSA-ORDER-NUMBER     TO   TWA-ORDER-RECORD-KEY.

      *    EXEC CICS
      *         HANDLE CONDITION
      *              NOTOPEN (FILE-NOT-OPEN)
      *              DUPREC  (DUPLICATE-RECORD)
      *    END-EXEC.
            MOVE '                  ' TO DFHEIVO CALL 'DFHEI1' USING
            DFHEIVO GO TO FILE-NOT-OPEN DUPLICATE-RECORD DEPENDING ON
            DFHEIGDI.


      *    EXEC CICS
      *         WRITE DATASET ('ORTEST')
```

Fig. 19.4. (Continued)

```
    20          ORADO1A          15.54.49          12/27/80

           *                LENGTH  (TWA-POM-LENGTH)
           *                FROM    (ORDER-MASTER-RECORD)
           *                RIDFLD  (TWA-ORDER-RECORD-KEY)
           *     END-EXEC.
                  MOVE 'ORTEST' TO DFHEIV3 MOVE '   0        ' TO DFHEIV0 CALL 'D
           -     'FHEI1' USING DFHEIV0 DFHEIV3 ORDER-MASTER-RECORD
                  TWA-POM-LENGTH TWA-ORDER-RECORD-KEY.



           *     EXEC CICS
           *          FREEMAIN DATA (ORDER-MASTER-RECORD)
           *     END-EXEC.
                  MOVE '         ' TO DFHEIV0 CALL 'DFHEI1' USING DFHEIV0
                  ORDER-MASTER-RECORD.

           *     EXEC CICS
           *          GETMAIN
           *               SET     (JOURNAL-POINTER)
           *               LENGTH (37)
           *     END-EXEC
                  MOVE 37 TO DFHEIV11 MOVE '         ' TO DFHEIV0 CALL 'DFHEI1
           -     '' USING DFHEIV0 JOURNAL-POINTER DFHEIV11



                 MOVE TSA-OPERATOR-INITIAL   TO  JOURNAL-OPERATOR-INITIAL.
                 MOVE TSA-ORDER-ENTERED      TO  JOURNAL-DATE-ENTERED.
                 MOVE TSA-ORDER-NUMBER       TO  JOURNAL-ORDER-NUMBER.
                 MOVE TSA-TOTAL-COST         TO  JOURNAL-TOTAL-COST.
                 MOVE TSA-TOTAL-PRICE        TO  JOURNAL-TOTAL-PRICE.
                 MOVE MAP1-DOCUMENT          TO  JOURNAL-DOCUMENT-NUMBER.
                 MOVE 37                     TO  TWA-JOURNAL-LENGTH.

           *     EXEC CICS
           *          JOURNAL JFILEID (02)
           *                  JTYPEID ('01')
           *                  FROM     (JOURNAL-RECORD)
           *                  LENGTH   (TWA-JOURNAL-LENGTH)
           *                  REQID    (TWA-JOURNAL-ID)
           *                  WAIT
           *     END-EXEC.
                  MOVE 02 TO DFHEIV11 MOVE '01' TO DFHEIV7 MOVE '   8       ' TO
                  DFHEIV0 CALL 'DFHEI1' USING DFHEIV0 DFHEIV11 TWA-JOURNAL-ID
                 DFHEIV7 JOURNAL-RECORD TWA-JOURNAL-LENGTH.





            DISPLAY-FRESH-SCREEN.

           *     EXEC CICS
```

Fig. 19.4. (Continued)

```
   21          ORAD01A        15.54.49        12/27/80

00783          *              SEND MAP    ('ORADM01')
00784          *                    MAPSET ('ORADS01')
00785          *                    MAPONLY
00786          *                    ERASE
00787          *        END-EXEC.
00788                   MOVE 'ORADM01' TO DFHEIV1 MOVE 'ORADS01' TO DFHEIV2 MOVE '
00789          -        '              ' TO DFHEIVO CALL 'DFHEI1' USING DFHEIVO
00790                   DFHEIV1 DFHEIV99 DFHEIV98 DFHEIV2.
00791
00792
00793
00794          RETURN-FOR-NEXT-ORDER.

00796              MOVE '1'  TO COMMAREA-PROCESS-SW.

00798          *        EXEC CICS
00799          *              RETURN TRANSID  (EIBTRNID)
00800          *                    COMMAREA (COMMUNICATION-AREA)
00801          *                    LENGTH   (1)
00802          *        END-EXEC.
00803                   MOVE 1 TO DFHEIV11 MOVE '        ' TO DFHEIVO CALL 'DFHEI1'
00804                   USING DFHEIVO EIBTRNID COMMUNICATION-AREA DFHEIV11.
00805
00806
00807
00808          DISPLAY-ERROR-SCREEN.

00810          *        EXEC CICS
00811          *              SEND MAP     ('ORADM01')
00812          *                    MAPSET ('ORADS01')
00813          *                    FROM   (MAP1-AREA)
00814          *                    DATAONLY
00815          *                    CURSOR
00816          *        END-EXEC
00817                   MOVE 'ORADM01' TO DFHEIV1 MOVE 'ORADS01' TO DFHEIV2 MOVE -1
00818                   TO DFHEIV11 MOVE '  J           ' TO DFHEIVO CALL 'DFHEI1'
00819                   USING DFHEIVO DFHEIV1 MAP1-AREA DFHEIV98 DFHEIV2 DFHEIV99
00820                   DFHEIV99 DFHEIV99 DFHEIV11
00821
00822
00823
00824              GO TO RETURN-FOR-NEXT-ORDER.

00826          DUPLICATE-RECORD.

00828              MOVE 'DUPLICATE -- NOT ACCEPTED' TO MAP1-ERRORS (1).
00829              MOVE -1      TO  MAP1-ORDER-NUMBER-L.
00830              GO TO DISPLAY-ERROR-SCREEN.
```

Fig. 19.4. (Continued)

```
    22          ORAD01A          15.54.49          12/27/80

                ****************************************************************
                *                                                              *
                 BYPASS-INPUT SECTION.
                *                                                              *
                ****************************************************************


                *     EXEC CICS
                *          GETMAIN
                *               SET      (MAP1-POINTER)
                *               LENGTH   (958)
                *               INITIMG (HEX-ZEROES)
                *     END-EXEC.
                       MOVE 958 TO DFHEIV11 MOVE '          ' TO DFHEIV0 CALL 'DFHEI
                -     '1' USING DFHEIV0 MAP1-POINTER DFHEIV11 HEX-ZEROES.




                      MOVE 'ORDER BYPASSED - CONTINUE' TO MAP1-ERRORS (1).


                *     EXEC CICS
                *          SEND MAP     ('ORADM01')
                *               MAPSET ('ORADS01')
                *               FROM   (MAP1-AREA)
                *               ERASE
                *     END-EXEC.
                       MOVE 'ORADM01' TO DFHEIV1 MOVE 'ORADS01' TO DFHEIV2 MOVE '
                -     '         S    ' TO DFHEIV0 CALL 'DFHEI1' USING DFHEIV0
                       DFHEIV1 MAP1-AREA DFHEIV98 DFHEIV2.



                      MOVE '1' TO COMMAREA-PROCESS-SW.

                *     EXEC CICS
                *          RETURN TRANSID  (EIBTRNID)
                *                 COMMAREA (COMMUNICATION-AREA)
                *                 LENGTH   (1)
                *     END-EXEC.
                       MOVE 1 TO DFHEIV11 MOVE '          ' TO DFHEIV0 CALL 'DFHEI1'
                       USING DFHEIV0 EIBTRNID COMMUNICATION-AREA DFHEIV11.
```

Fig. 19.4. (Continued)

```
23          ORAD01A          15.54.49          12/27/80

            *****************************************************************
            *                                                               *
             INITIALIZATION SECTION.
            *                                                               *
            *****************************************************************


            *    EXEC CICS
            *         HANDLE CONDITION
            *              QIDERR (GET-STORAGE-FOR-TSA)
            *    END-EXEC.
                  MOVE '                  ' TO DFHEIVO CALL 'DFHEI1' USING
                  DFHEIVO GO TO GET-STORAGE-FOR-TSA DEPENDING ON DFHEIGDI.


                 MOVE EIBTRMID    TO  TSA-TERM-ID.
                 MOVE 'ORAD'      TO  TSA-TRANS-ID.

            *    EXEC CICS
            *         DELETEQ TS
            *              QUEUE (TSA-QUEUE-ID)
            *    END-EXEC.
                  MOVE '          ' TO DFHEIVO CALL 'DFHEI1' USING DFHEIVO
                  TSA-QUEUE-ID.


             GET-STORAGE-FOR-TSA.

            *    EXEC CICS
            *         GETMAIN
            *              SET    (TSA-POINTER)
            *              LENGTH (1340)
            *    END-EXEC.
                  MOVE 1340 TO DFHEIV11 MOVE '          ' TO DFHEIVO CALL 'DFHE
            -    'I1' USING DFHEIVO TSA-POINTER DFHEIV11.



             LOAD-DEPARTMENT-TABLE.

                 SET DEPT-I        TO  ZEROES.
                 MOVE 'D'          TO  TWA-DEPT-TABLE-KEY-CODE.
                 MOVE  1           TO  TWA-DEPT-TABLE-KEY-NUMBER.

            *    EXEC CICS
            *         HANDLE CONDITION
            *              ENDFILE (READ-DEPT-TABLE-EXIT)
            *    END-EXEC.
                  MOVE '                  ' TO DFHEIVO CALL 'DFHEI1' USING
                  DFHEIVO GO TO READ-DEPT-TABLE-EXIT DEPENDING ON DFHEIGDI.


            *    EXEC CICS
```

Fig. 19.4. (Continued)

```
24          ORAD01A          15.54.49          12/27/80

       *          STARTBR DATASET ('DSXTABS')
       *                  RIDFLD  (TWA-DEPT-TABLE-KEY)
       *                  GTEQ
       *     END-EXEC.
              MOVE 'DSXTABS' TO DFHEIV3 MOVE '          ' TO DFHEIVO CALL '
       -     'DFHEI1' USING DFHEIVO DFHEIV3 DFHEIV99 DFHEIV98
              TWA-DEPT-TABLE-KEY.


         READ-DEPT-TABLE.

       *     EXEC CICS
       *          READNEXT DATASET ('DSXTABS')
       *                   SET     (TABLE-POINTER)
       *                   RIDFLD  (TWA-DEPT-TABLE-KEY)
       *     END-EXEC.
              MOVE 'DSXTABS' TO DFHEIV3 MOVE '  M      ' TO DFHEIVO CALL '
       -     'DFHEI1' USING DFHEIVO DFHEIV3 TABLE-POINTER DFHEIV98
              TWA-DEPT-TABLE-KEY DFHEIV98 DFHEIV98.


             IF DEPT-RECORD
             THEN IF DEPT-NO EQUAL '999'
                        GO TO READ-DEPT-TABLE-EXIT
                  ELSE IF DEPT-DIVISION LESS THAN '85'
                             SET DEPT-I UP BY 1
                             MOVE DEPT-NO TO TSA-DEPT-NO (DEPT-I).

             GO TO READ-DEPT-TABLE.
         READ-DEPT-TABLE-EXIT.  EXIT.


         CHECK-IF-TABLE-LOADED.

             IF DEPT-I EQUAL TO ZEROES
                  GO TO TABLE-NOT-LOADED-ERROR
             ELSE SET TSA-DEPT-CNT TO DEPT-I.


         INITIALIZE-TSA.

             MOVE CURRENT-DATE                 TO  TWA-CURRENT-DATE.
             MOVE TWA-CURRENT-DATE-MONTH       TO  TSA-ORDER-ENTERED-MONTH.
             MOVE TWA-CURRENT-DATE-DAY         TO  TSA-ORDER-ENTERED-DAY.
             MOVE TWA-CURRENT-DATE-YEAR        TO  TSA-ORDER-ENTERED-YEAR.
             MOVE OPERATOR-INITIAL             TO  TSA-OPERATOR-INITIAL.
             MOVE 1340                         TO  TSA-LENGTH.

       *     EXEC CICS
       *          WRITEQ TS
       *               QUEUE  (TSA-QUEUE-ID)
       *               FROM   (TSA-AREA)
       *               LENGTH (TSA-LENGTH)
```

Fig. 19.4. (Continued)

```
   25          ORADO1A          15.54.49          12/27/80

          *    END-EXEC.
                MOVE '            ' TO DFHEIVO CALL 'DFHEI1' USING DFHEIVO
                TSA-QUEUE-ID TSA-AREA TSA-LENGTH.




          *    EXEC CICS
          *         FREEMAIN DATA (TSA-AREA)
          *    END-EXEC.
                MOVE '            ' TO DFHEIVO CALL 'DFHEI1' USING DFHEIVO
                TSA-AREA.

          *    EXEC CICS
          *         GETMAIN
          *              SET      (MAP1-POINTER)
          *              LENGTH   (958)
          *              INITIMG  (HEX-ZEROES)
          *    END-EXEC.
                MOVE 958 TO DFHEIV11 MOVE '            ' TO DFHEIVO CALL 'DFHEI
          -    '1' USING DFHEIVO MAP1-POINTER DFHEIV11 HEX-ZEROES.




               MOVE 'ENTER FIRST ORDER' TO MAP1-ERRORS (1).

          *    EXEC CICS
          *         SEND MAP     ('ORADM01')
          *              MAPSET ('ORADS01')
          *              FROM   (MAP1-AREA)
          *              ERASE
          *    END-EXEC.
                MOVE 'ORADM01' TO DFHEIV1 MOVE 'ORADS01' TO DFHEIV2 MOVE '
          -    '         S      ' TO DFHEIVO CALL 'DFHEI1' USING DFHEIVO
                DFHEIV1 MAP1-AREA DFHEIV98 DFHEIV2.



               MOVE '1' TO COMMAREA-PROCESS-SW.

          *    EXEC CICS
          *         RETURN TRANSID  ('ORAD')
          *                COMMAREA (COMMUNICATION-AREA)
          *                LENGTH   (1)
          *    END-EXEC.
                MOVE 'ORAD' TO DFHEIV5 MOVE 1 TO DFHEIV11 MOVE '
                TO DFHEIVO CALL 'DFHEI1' USING DFHEIVO DFHEIV5
                COMMUNICATION-AREA DFHEIV11.
```

Fig. 19.4. (Continued)

```
    26          ORAD01A          15.54.49          12/27/80

            *****************************************************************
            *                                                               *
             FINALIZATION SECTION.
            *                                                               *
            *****************************************************************

             PREPARE-TERMINATION-MESSAGE.
                 MOVE JOB-NORMAL-END-MESSAGE TO TWA-OPERATOR-MESSAGE.

             JOB-TERMINATED.

            *    EXEC CICS
            *         SEND FROM   (TWA-OPERATOR-MESSAGE)
            *              LENGTH (31)
            *              ERASE
            *    END-EXEC.
                  MOVE 31 TO DFHEIV11 MOVE '                ' TO DFHEIVO CALL '
            -    'DFHEI1' USING DFHEIVO DFHEIV99 DFHEIV98 TWA-OPERATOR-MESSAGE
                  DFHEIV11.


            *    EXEC CICS
            *         HANDLE CONDITION
            *              QIDERR (END-OF-JOB)
            *    END-EXEC.
                  MOVE '                  ' TO DFHEIVO CALL 'DFHEI1' USING
                  DFHEIVO GO TO END-OF-JOB DEPENDING ON DFHEIGDI.


                 MOVE EIBTRMID  TO  TSA-TERM-ID.
                 MOVE EIBTRNID  TO  TSA-TRANS-ID.

            *    EXEC CICS
            *         DELETEQ TS
            *              QUEUE (TSA-QUEUE-ID)
            *    END-EXEC.
                  MOVE '         ' TO DFHEIVO CALL 'DFHEI1' USING DFHEIVO
                  TSA-QUEUE-ID.



             END-OF-JOB.

            *    EXEC CICS
            *         RETURN
            *    END-EXEC.
                  MOVE '         ' TO DFHEIVO CALL 'DFHEI1' USING DFHEIVO.


```

Fig. 19.4. (Continued)

```
  27          ORAD01A          15.54.49        12/27/80

            *****************************************************************
            *                                                               *
             ABNORMAL-TERMINATION SECTION.
            *                                                               *
            *****************************************************************


             FILE-NOT-OPEN.

            *    EXEC CICS
            *         XCTL PROGRAM ('TEL2OPEN')
            *    END-EXEC.
                  MOVE 'TEL2OPEN' TO DFHEIV3 MOVE '          ' TO DFHEIV0 CALL
                 'DFHEI1' USING DFHEIV0 DFHEIV3.

             MAPFAIL-ERROR.
                 MOVE 'MAP FAILURE' TO MAJOR-ERROR-MSG.
                 GO TO PREPARE-ABORT-MESSAGE.


             PROCESS-SWITCH-ERROR.
                 MOVE 'PROCESS ERROR' TO MAJOR-ERROR-MSG.
                 GO TO PREPARE-ABORT-MESSAGE.


             SIGN-ON-VIOLATION.
                 MOVE 'SIGNON VIOLATION' TO MAJOR-ERROR-MSG.
                 GO TO PREPARE-ABORT-MESSAGE.


             TABLE-NOT-LOADED-ERROR.
                 MOVE 'TABLE NOT LOADED' TO MAJOR-ERROR-MSG.
                 GO TO PREPARE-ABORT-MESSAGE.


             MAJOR-ERROR.
                 MOVE  EIBFN      TO  OLD-EIBFN.
                 MOVE  EIBRCODE   TO  OLD-EIBRCODE.

            *    EXEC CICS
            *         DUMP DUMPCODE ('ERRS')
            *    END-EXEC.
                  MOVE 'ERRS' TO DFHEIV5 MOVE '          ' TO DFHEIV0 CALL 'DFH
            -    'EI1' USING DFHEIV0 DFHEIV5.

                 MOVE 'MAJOR ERROR' TO MAJOR-ERROR-MSG.
                 GO TO PREPARE-ABORT-MESSAGE.


             PREPARE-ABORT-MESSAGE.
                 MOVE JOB-ABORTED-MESSAGE TO TWA-OPERATOR-MESSAGE.
                 GO TO JOB-TERMINATED.
```

Fig. 19.4. (Continued)

2. Lines 891–899. Delete the old temporary storage queue.*
3. Lines 902–910. GETMAIN command to secure main storage for the new temporary storage record to be created.
4. Lines 917–918. The record identification field of a file to be browsed is set to the proper values. We browse this file to load a table of valid department numbers into the temporary storage record to be created.
5. Lines 920–925. HANDLE CONDITION command for the file.
6. Lines 928–958. The table is moved to the temporary storage record.
7. Lines 975–982. WRITEQ TS command to create the new temporary storage record.
8. Lines 987–991. FREEMAIN DATA command to release main storage secured for the temporary storage record by the GETMAIN command in lines 902–910.
9. Lines 993–1000. GETMAIN command to secure main storage for the map to be displayed, which will include a program-generated message.
10. Lines 1007–1015. SEND MAP command to display the map. The "ENTER FIRST ORDER" message is included in the display.
11. Line 1019. Set the communication area switch to 1.
12. Lines 1021–1028. RETURN command to terminate the task.

THE ORDER-VALIDATION SECTION

1. Lines 428–435. READ MAP command to read the data entered by the operator.
2. Lines 441–450. READQ TS command to read the temporary storage record that will be used as a scratchpad.

*This is a precautionary measure. See page 211.

3. Lines 455–686. The editing of the data.

4. If there are no errors:
   a. Lines 703–709. GETMAIN command to secure main storage for the new record to be written out.
   b. Lines 713–715. Move the data to the file record.
   c. Lines 718–725. HANDLE CONDITION command for the order file.
   d. Lines 728–736. WRITE DATASET command to write the new record.
   e. Lines 740–744. FREEMAIN DATA command to release main storage secured for the order record by the GETMAIN command in lines 703–709.
   f. Lines 746–752. GETMAIN command to secure main storage for the journal record to be written out.
   g. Lines 756–762. Move the data into the journal record.
   h. Lines 764–774. JOURNAL command to write out the journal record.
   i. Lines 782–790. SEND MAP command to display the next map required by the operator.
   j. Line 796. Set the communication area switch to 1.
   k. Lines 798–804. RETURN command to terminate the task.

5. If there are errors:
   a. Lines 810–820. SEND MAP command to display the error messages.
   b. Line 824. Set the communication area switch to 1 and RETURN command to terminate the task.

THE BYPASS-INPUT SECTION

1. Lines 838–845. GETMAIN command to secure main storage for the map that will contain the message.

2. Lines 852–860. SEND MAP command to display the "ORDER BYPASSED–CONTINUE" message.

3. Line 864. Set the communication area switch to 1.
4. Lines 866–872. RETURN command to terminate the task.

THE FINALIZATION SECTION

1. Lines 1043–1050. Display the "JOB NORMALLY TERMINATED" message.
2. Lines 1053–1058. HANDLE CONDITION command for the temporary storage queue.
3. Lines 1064–1069. DELETEQ TS command to delete the temporary storage queue used as a scratchpad.
4. Lines 1075–1078. RETURN command to terminate the session.

THE ABNORMAL-TERMINATION SECTION

These are the routines used to abnormally terminate the session on errors and CICS/VS exceptional conditions not covered by a HANDLE CONDITION command.

THE JOURNAL RECORDS

This example of the File Add program generates journal records (see Figure 19.5). We will print these records in hexadecimal format. The system prefix is 72 bytes long and bytes 73 to 109 correspond to statements 350 to 355 of Figure 19.4. The four records correspond to order numbers 10, 11, 12, and 13. The operator initial is PAL and the entry date is December 26, 1980.

EXAMPLE

The following are facsimiles of actual photographs taken of a CRT terminal during a session.

```
* * * * DEVICE  193  SYS020,  3350,  @CICSSQSQ@ CICS JOURNAL TEST                  ,  SAM                          * * * *

BLOCK   1   DATA   109   CHAR                                                  01                      ORADL770PAL122680000000001000000110
                         ZONE  060002008400010001083101000000122912010831040000DF0201000081228DDCCDFFFDCDFFFFFFFFFFFFFFFFFFFFFFFF0
                         NUMR  0D00060005000C200C006F0C000000792F752F006F030000610C0400200C791F6914377071312268000000000100000001100
                               1...5...10...15...20...25...30...35...40...45...50...55...60...65...70...75...80...85...90...95.....

                         CHAR  -
                         ZONE  060000200
                         NUMR  100C0300C
                            101...5...1

BLOCK   2   DATA   109   CHAR                                                  01                      ORADL770PAL122680000000001100000111
                         ZONE  060002008400010002083101000045132912010831040000DF0201000091318DDCCDFFFDCDFFFFFFFFFFFFFFFFFFFFFFFF0
                         NUMR  0D00060005000C200C006F0C0B0197720F752F006F030000610C0400200C729F691437707131226800000000011000001110
                               1...5...10...15...20...25...30...35...40...45...50...55...60...65...70...75...80...85...90...95.....

                         CHAR
                         ZONE  020000500
                         NUMR  060C0020C
                            101...5...1

BLOCK   3   DATA   109   CHAR                                                  01                      ORADL770PAL122680000000001200000112
                         ZONE  06000200840001000308310100 0C43131712010831040000DF0201000001307DDCCDFFFDCDFFFFFFFFFFFFFFFFFFFFFFFF0
                         NUMR  0D00060005000C200C006F0C0B0281730F752F006F030000610C040201C739F691437707131226800000000012000001120
                               1...5...10...15...20...25...30...35...40...45...50...55...60...65...70...75...80...85...90...95.....

                         CHAR
                         ZONE  020000400
                         NUMR  100C0200C
                            101...5...1

BLOCK   4   DATA   109   CHAR                     ¤                            01                      ORADL770PAL122680000000001300000113
                         ZONE  0600020084000100040831010000401319120108310400000F0201000011316DDCCDFFFDCDFFFFFFFFFFFFFFFFFFFFFFFF0
                         NUMR  0D00060005000C200C006F0C0B037B756F752F006F030000610C0400201C755F691437707131226800000000013000001130
                               1...5...10...15...20...25...30...35...40...45...50...55...60...65...70...75...80...85...90...95.....

                         CHAR
                         ZONE  080000700
                         NUMR  150C0300C
                            101...5...1
```

Fig. 19.5. Journal Records In Hexadecimal Format.

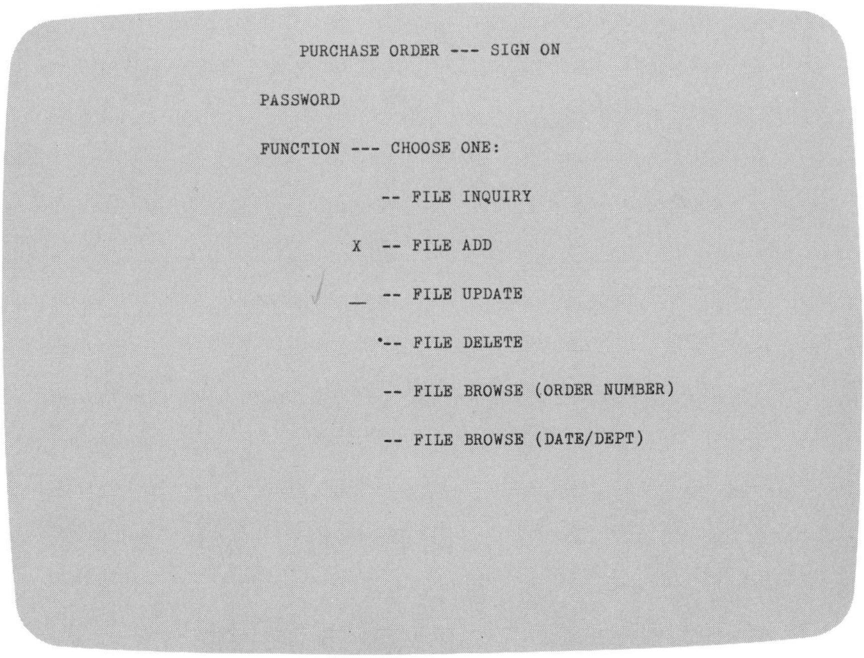

Fig. 19.6. The File Add application is selected by keying in an "X" on the File Add line and the corresponding password, then hitting the ENTER key.

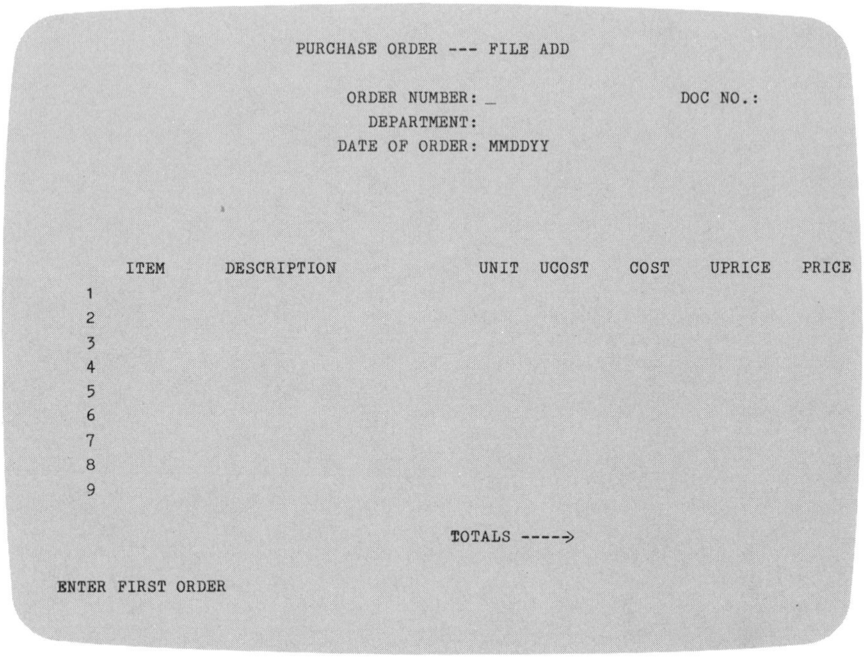

Fig. 19.7. The Sign On program executes which then transfers control to the File Add program. This displays the File Add map.

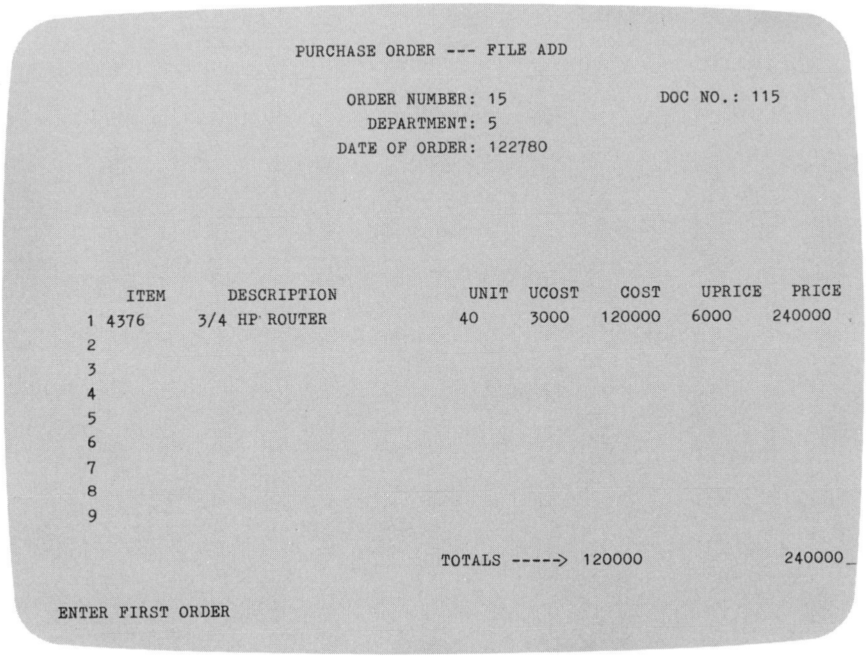

PURCHASE ORDER --- FILE ADD
ORDER NUMBER: 15
DOC NO.: 115
DEPARTMENT: 5
DATE OF ORDER: 122780
ITEM
DESCRIPTION
UNIT
UCOST
COST
UPRICE
PRICE
1 4376 3/4 HP ROUTER 40 3000 120000 6000 240000
2
3
4
5
6
7
8
9
TOTALS -----> 120000 240000_
ENTER FIRST ORDER

Fig. 19.8. The operator keys in the order to be added to the file, then hits the ENTER key.

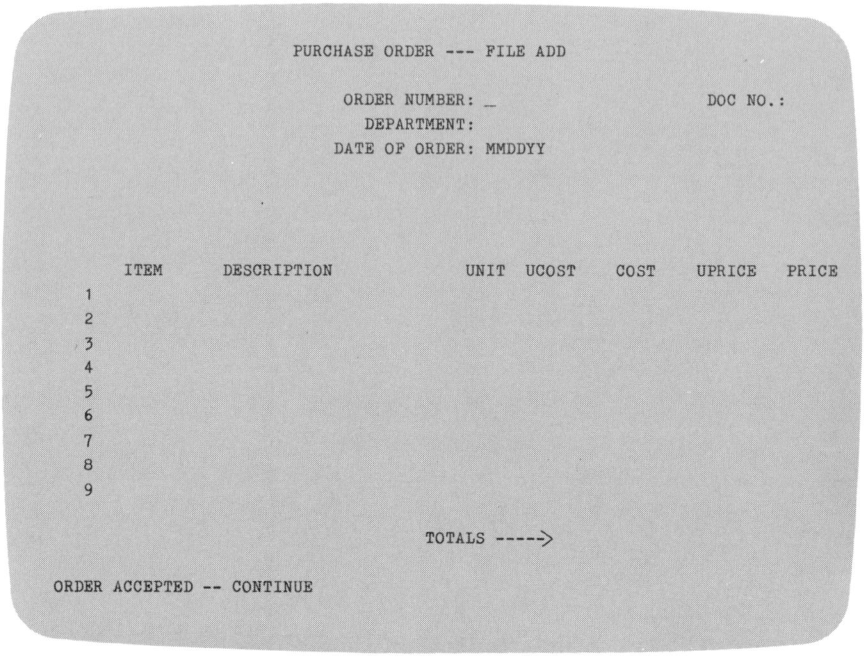

Fig. 19.9. If there are no errors from Fig. 19.8, the order is added to the file. The "ORDER ACCEPTED – CONTINUE" message is then displayed on a fresh map to inform the operator. He may then continue with the next order.

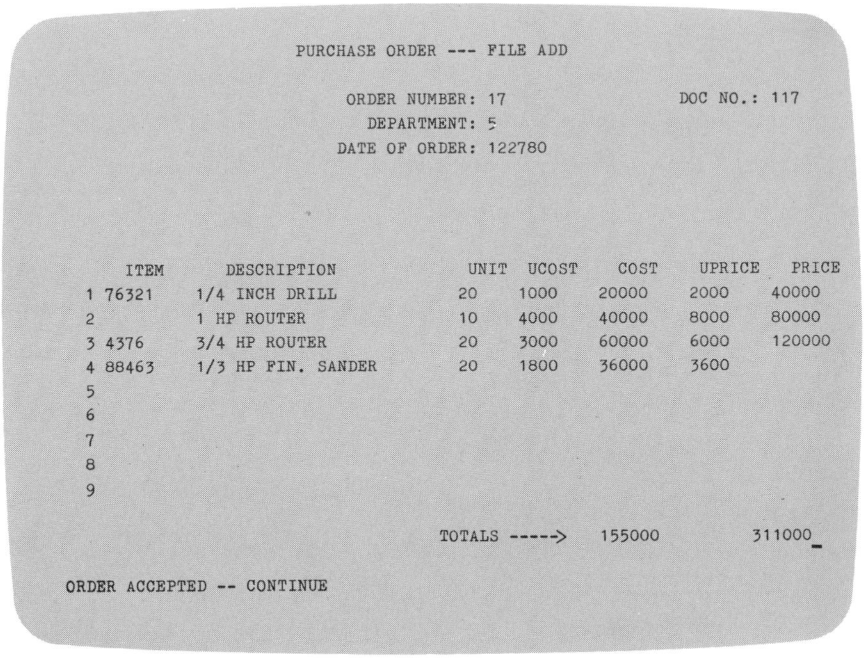

PURCHASE ORDER --- FILE ADD

ORDER NUMBER: 17 DOC NO.: 117
DEPARTMENT: 5
DATE OF ORDER: 122780

	ITEM	DESCRIPTION	UNIT	UCOST	COST	UPRICE	PRICE
1	76321	1/4 INCH DRILL	20	1000	20000	2000	40000
2		1 HP ROUTER	10	4000	40000	8000	80000
3	4376	3/4 HP ROUTER	20	3000	60000	6000	120000
4	88463	1/3 HP FIN. SANDER	20	1800	36000	3600	
5							
6							
7							
8							
9							
			TOTALS ----->		155000		311000_

ORDER ACCEPTED -- CONTINUE

Fig. 19.10. The operator keys in the next order to be added to the file, then hits the ENTER key.

```
                         PURCHASE ORDER --- FILE ADD

                              ORDER NUMBER: 0000000017         DOC NO.: 00000117
                                DEPARTMENT: 005
                             DATE OF ORDER: 122780



      ITEM        DESCRIPTION              UNIT  UCOST     COST     UPRICE    PRICE
  1 00076321 1/4 INCH DRILL               00020 0001000 00020000 0002000 00040000
  2 _         1 HP ROUTER                 00010 0004000 00040000 0008000 00080000
  3 00004376 3/4 HP ROUTER                00020 0003000 00060000 0006000 00120000
  4 00088463 1/3 HP FIN. SANDER           00020 0001800 00036000 0003600
  5
  6
  7
  8
  9

                                        TOTALS -----> 000155000          000311000

LINE 2 - INCOMPLETE DATA                LINE 4 - INCOMPLETE DATA
INCORRECT TOTAL COST                    INCORRECT TOTAL PRICE
```

Fig. 19.11. Four errors are detected. Note that the cursor is under the first error detected.

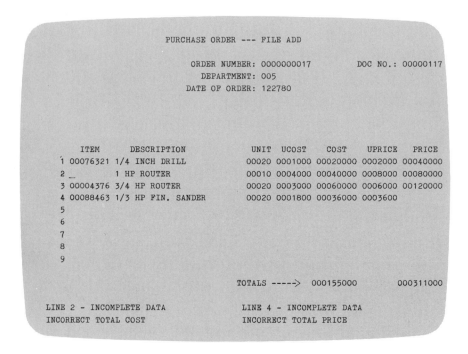

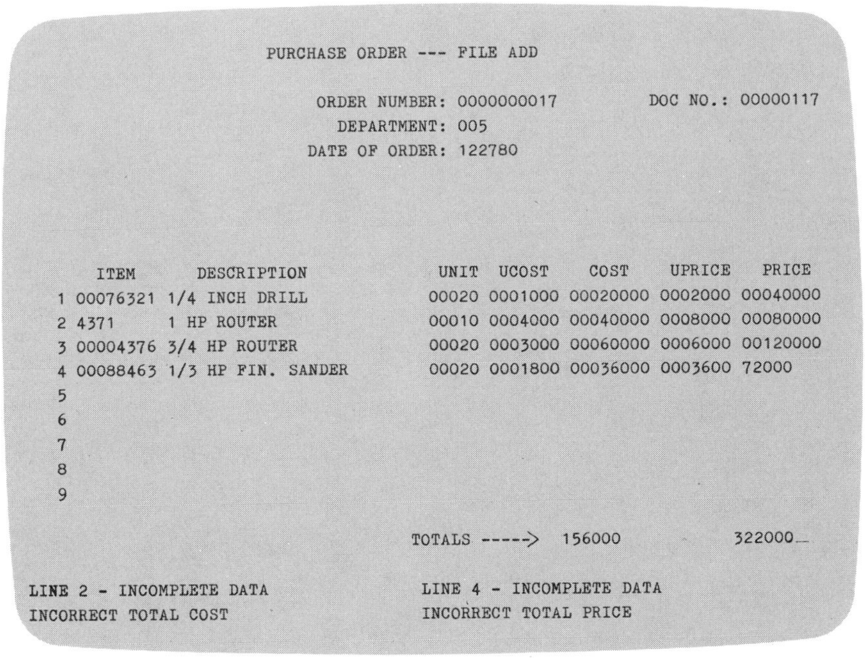

PURCHASE ORDER --- FILE ADD

ORDER NUMBER: 0000000017 DOC NO.: 00000117
DEPARTMENT: 005
DATE OF ORDER: 122780

	ITEM	DESCRIPTION	UNIT	UCOST	COST	UPRICE	PRICE
1	00076321	1/4 INCH DRILL	00020	0001000	00020000	0002000	00040000
2	4371	1 HP ROUTER	00010	0004000	00040000	0008000	00080000
3	00004376	3/4 HP ROUTER	00020	0003000	00060000	0006000	00120000
4	00088463	1/3 HP FIN. SANDER	00020	0001800	00036000	0003600	72000
5							
6							
7							
8							
9							

TOTALS -----> 156000 322000_

LINE 2 - INCOMPLETE DATA
INCORRECT TOTAL COST
LINE 4 - INCOMPLETE DATA
INCORRECT TOTAL PRICE

Fig. 19.12. The operator keys in the corrections, then hits the ENTER key.

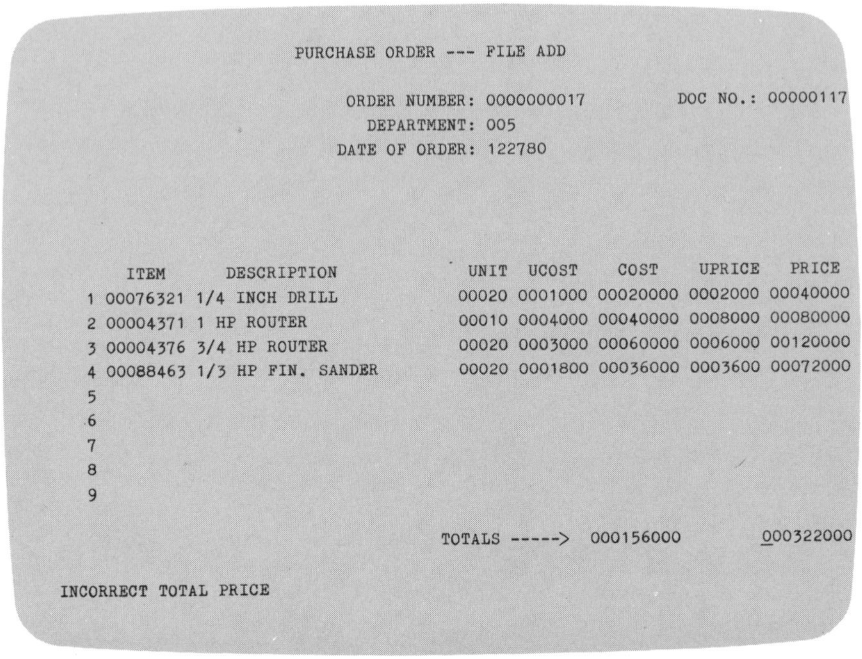

```
                         PURCHASE ORDER --- FILE ADD

                              ORDER NUMBER: 0000000017          DOC NO.: 00000117
                                DEPARTMENT: 005
                             DATE OF ORDER: 122780



     ITEM      DESCRIPTION                  UNIT  UCOST    COST    UPRICE   PRICE
  1 00076321 1/4 INCH DRILL                00020 0001000 00020000 0002000 00040000
  2 00004371 1 HP ROUTER                   00010 0004000 00040000 0008000 00080000
  3 00004376 3/4 HP ROUTER                 00020 0003000 00060000 0006000 00120000
  4 00088463 1/3 HP FIN. SANDER            00020 0001800 00036000 0003600 00072000
  5
  6
  7
  8
  9

                                  TOTALS -----> 000156000         000322000

INCORRECT TOTAL PRICE
```

Fig. 19.13. One error is left. Note again that the cursor is under this field.

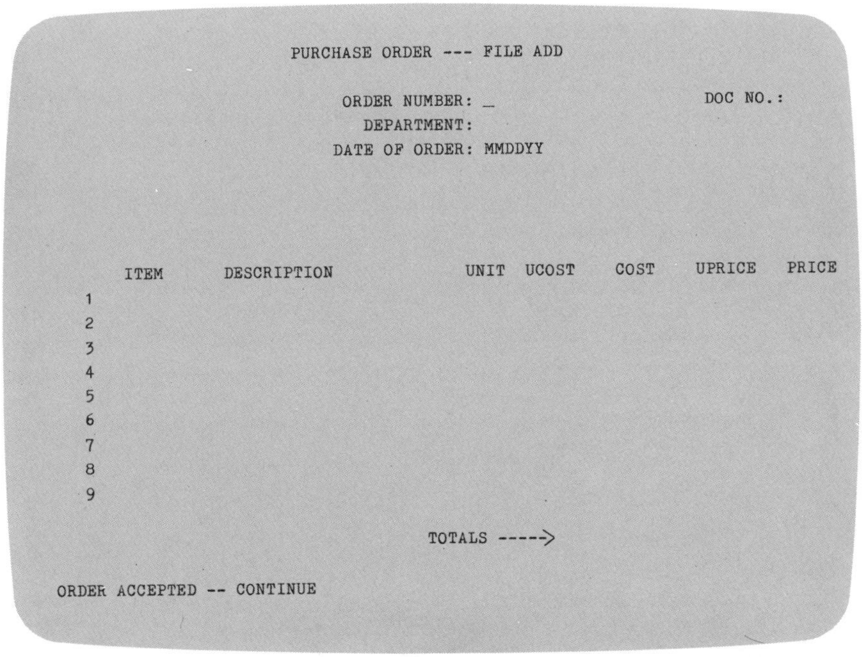

Fig. 19.14. After the operator enters the corrections, the order is added to the file.

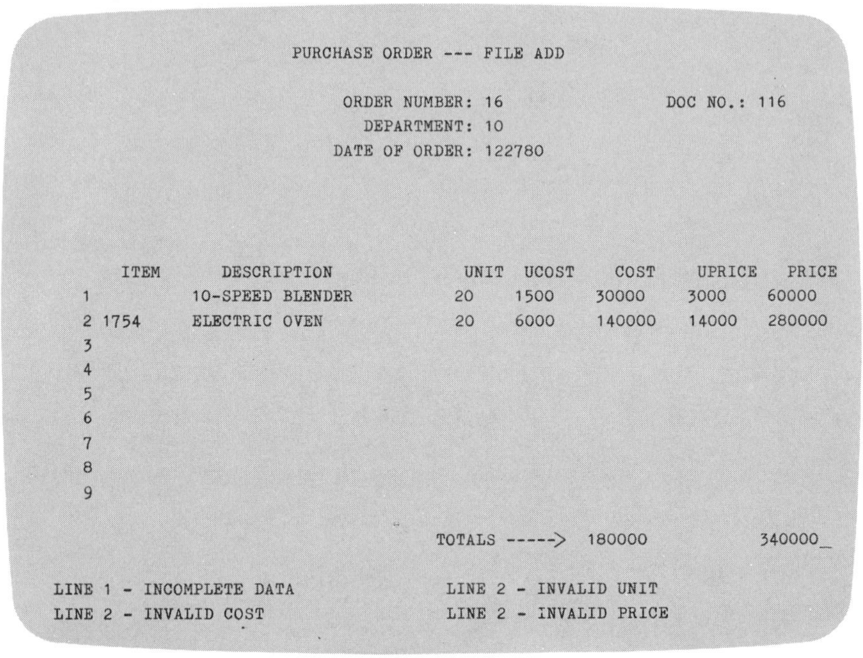

Fig. 19.15. If the operator wishes to discontinue the processing of an order after errors have been detected, he hits any PA key.

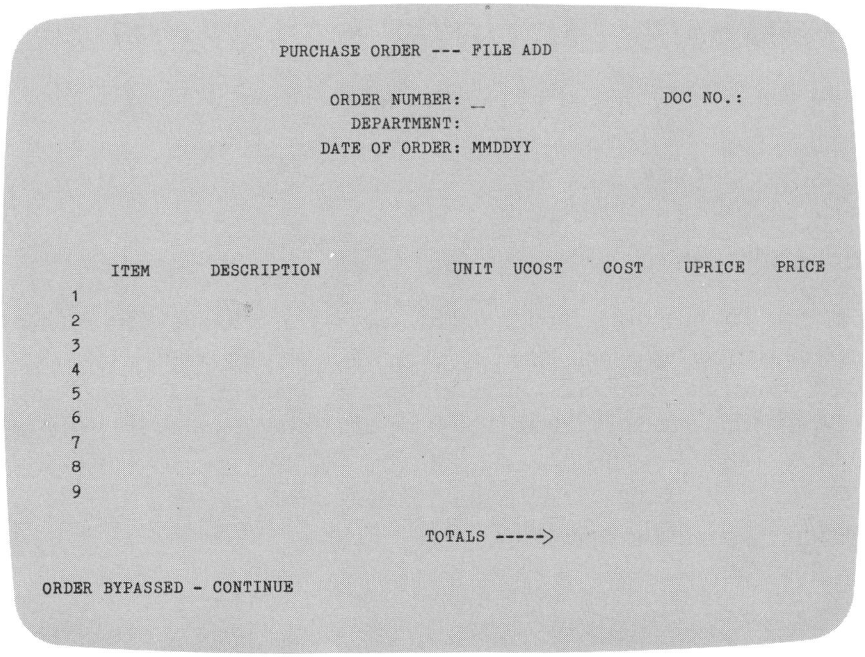

Fig. 19.16. A fresh map is then displayed with the message "ORDER BYPASSED – CONTINUE". The operator may then continue with the next order.

20

The File Update Program

INTRODUCTION

The File Update program allows the operator to change certain fields in an existing order record. The program executes when selected by the Sign-on program and will continue executing in the session until terminated by the operator. The flow of control to execute this program is shown in Figure 20.1.

PROGRAM SPECIFICATIONS

The File Update program specifications are as follows:

1. Implement the program using the pseudoconversational mode of processing.
2. Use 'ORCH' as the transaction identifier. However, the session should not be started by using this identifier, but rather through an XTCL command from the Sign-on program.
3. If the session is started by using the transaction identifier, abort the session with the message "JOB ABORTED–SIGNON VIOLATION."
4. Edit the data using page 207 as a guide.
5. On any PA key, bypass the input data and display the next fresh screen for the next order to be updated.

SCREEN LAYOUTS

These are the screen layouts to be used in the program. Figure 20.2 is for the order number of the order that will be modified, and Figure 20.3 is for the changes themselves. All 9s are numeric fields and Xs are alphanumeric fields.

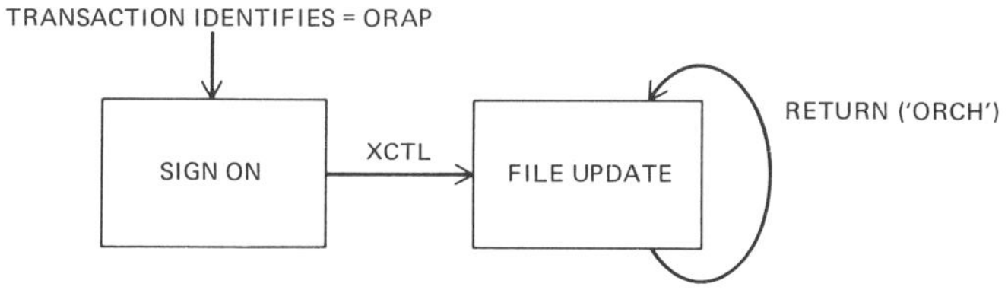

Fig. 20.1. File Update Application.

MAP PROGRAMS

These are the map programs corresponding to the screen layouts. Figure 20.4 corresponds to Figure 20.2 and Figure 20.5 corresponds to Figure 20.3.

PROGRAM LISTING

The program listing for the File Update program is shown in Figure 20.6.

MAIN-LINE SECTION

1. Lines 395–399. ADDRESS command for the TWA.
2. Lines 401–410. HANDLE AID command. The PA keys will execute the BYPASS-INPUT section.
3. Lines 415–422. HANDLE CONDITION command.
4. Lines 425–432. The selection of sections.
5. Lines 434–435. If the program is executed at the start of a session by an operator-entered transaction identifier instead of through an XCTL command from the Sign-on program, a sign-on violation occurs. This is so if EIBCALEN is equal to zero.

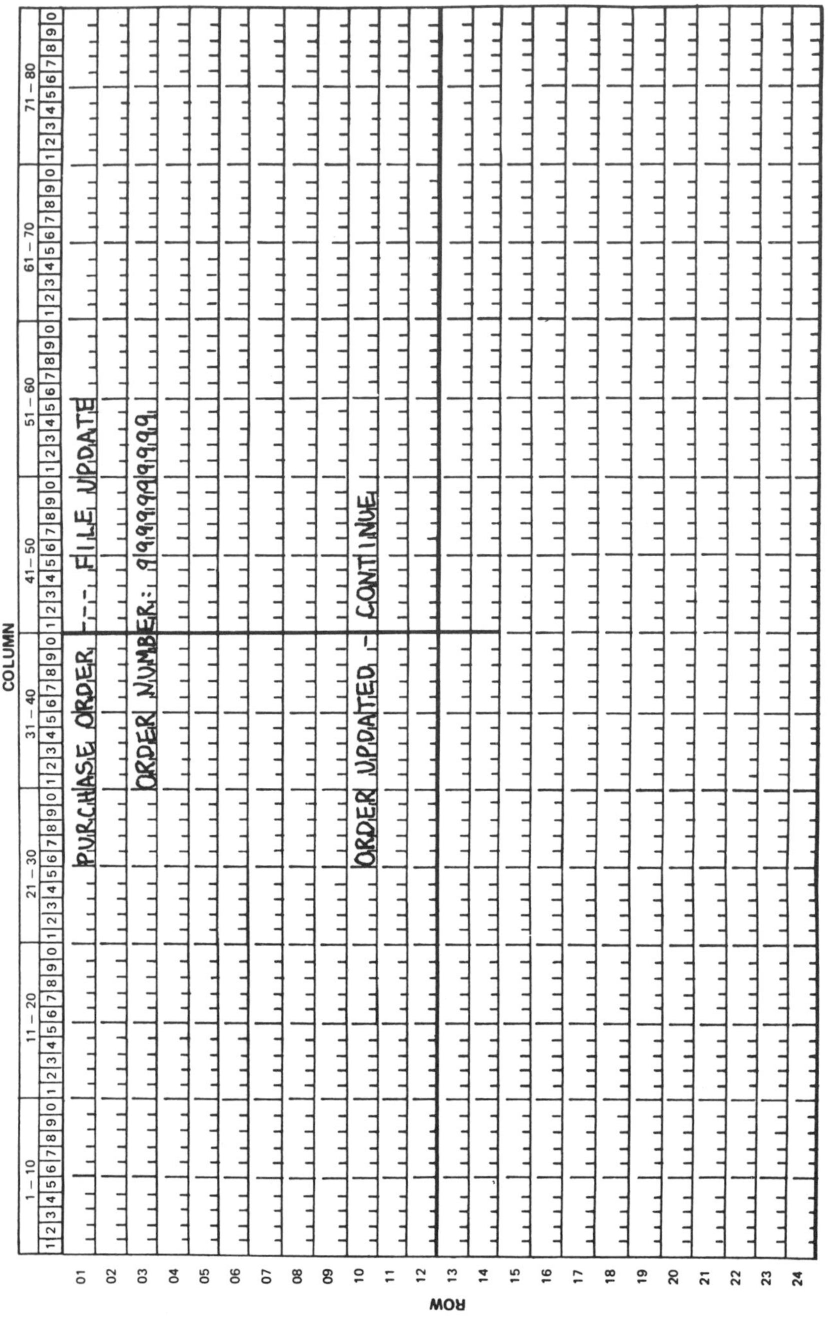

Fig. 20.2. Order Screen Layout – File Update.

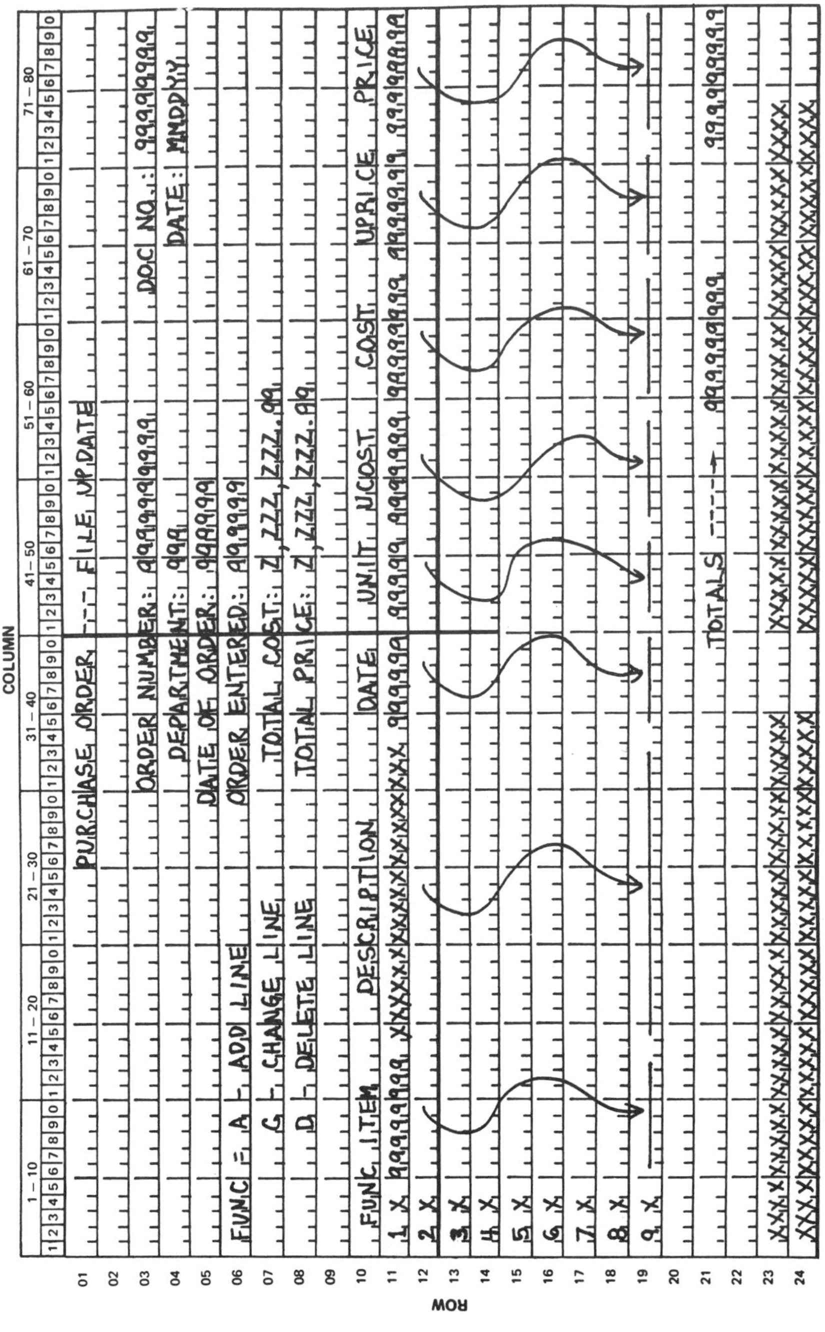

Fig. 20.3. Data Screen Layout – File Update.

```
STMT    SOURCE STATEMENT                              DOS/VS ASSEMBLER REL 34.0 14.10

  1              PRINT NOGEN
  2 ORCHS01      DFHMSD TYPE=MAP,MODE=INOUT,CTRL=FREEKB,LANG=COBOL,TIOAPFX=YES
 12 ORCHM01      DFHMDI SIZE=(24,80)
 40 DUMMY        DFHMDF POS=(01,01),LENGTH=01,ATTRB=(ASKIP,DRK,FSET),          X
                       INITIAL='1'
 52              DFHMDF POS=(01,25),LENGTH=30,ATTRB=(ASKIP,BRT),               X
                       INITIAL='PURCHASE ORDER --- FILE UPDATE'
 64              DFHMDF POS=(03,30),LENGTH=13,ATTRB=ASKIP,                     X
                       INITIAL='ORDER NUMBER '
 76 ORDER        DFHMDF POS=(03,44),LENGTH=10,ATTRB=(NUM,BRT,IC)
 87              DFHMDF POS=(03,55),LENGTH=01,ATTRB=PROT
 98 ERROR        DFHMDF POS=(10,25),LENGTH=25,ATTRB=(ASKIP,BRT),               X
                       INITIAL='ORDER UPDATED - CONTINUE'
110              DFHMSD TYPE=FINAL
124              END
```

Fig. 20.4. Order Screen Map Program – File Update.

```
STMT   SOURCE STATEMENT                          DOS/VS ASSEMBLER REL 34.0 14.50

  1             PRINT NOGEN
  2 ORCHS02     DFHMSD TYPE=MAP,MODE=INOUT,CTRL=FREEKB,LANG=COBOL,TIOAPFX=YES
 12 ORCHM02     DFHMDI  SIZE=(24,80)
 40 DUMMY       DFHMDF  POS=(01,01),LENGTH=01,ATTRB=(ASKIP,DRK,FSET),          X
                      INITIAL='1'
 52             DFHMDF  POS=(01,25),LENGTH=30,ATTRB=(ASKIP,BRT),               X
                      INITIAL='PURCHASE ORDER --- FILE UPDATE'
 64             DFHMDF  POS=(03,30),LENGTH=13,ATTRB=ASKIP,                     X
                      INITIAL='ORDER NUMBER '
 76 ORDER       DFHMDF  POS=(03,44),LENGTH=10,ATTRB=(ASKIP,BRT)
 87             DFHMDF  POS=(03,62),LENGTH=08,ATTRB=ASKIP,INITIAL='DOC NO. '
 99 DOCNO       DFHMDF  POS=(03,71),LENGTH=08,ATTRB=(NUM,BRT,IC)
110             DFHMDF  POS=(03,80),LENGTH=01,ATTRB=PROT
121             DFHMDF  POS=(04,32),LENGTH=11,ATTRB=ASKIP,INITIAL='DEPARTMENT '
133 DEPT        DFHMDF  POS=(04,44),LENGTH=03,ATTRB=(ASKIP,BRT)
144             DFHMDF  POS=(04,65),LENGTH=05,ATTRB=ASKIP,INITIAL='DATE '
156 DATEUPD     DFHMDF  POS=(04,71),LENGTH=06,ATTRB=(NUM,BRT),INITIAL='MMDDYY'
168             DFHMDF  POS=(04,78),LENGTH=01,ATTRB=ASKIP
179             DFHMDF  POS=(05,29),LENGTH=14,ATTRB=ASKIP,                     X
                      INITIAL='DATE OF ORDER '
191 DATEOR      DFHMDF  POS=(05,44),LENGTH=06,ATTRB=(ASKIP,BRT)
202             DFHMDF  POS=(06,01),LENGTH=06,ATTRB=ASKIP,INITIAL='FUNC ='
214             DFHMDF  POS=(06,08),LENGTH=12,ATTRB=ASKIP,                     X
                      INITIAL='A - ADD LINE'
226             DFHMDF  POS=(06,29),LENGTH=14,ATTRB=ASKIP,                     X
                      INITIAL='ORDER ENTERED '
238 DATEENT     DFHMDF  POS=(06,44),LENGTH=06,ATTRB=(ASKIP,BRT)
249             DFHMDF  POS=(07,08),LENGTH=15,ATTRB=ASKIP,                     X
                      INITIAL='C - CHANGE LINE'
261             DFHMDF  POS=(07,32),LENGTH=11,ATTRB=ASKIP,INITIAL='TOTAL COST '
273 TOTCOST     DFHMDF  POS=(07,44),LENGTH=12,ATTRB=(ASKIP,BRT),               X
                      PICOUT='Z,ZZZ,ZZZ.99'
284             DFHMDF  POS=(08,08),LENGTH=15,ATTRB=ASKIP,                     X
                      INITIAL='D - DELETE LINE'
296             DFHMDF  POS=(08,31),LENGTH=12,ATTRB=ASKIP,                     X
                      INITIAL='TOTAL PRICE '
308 TOTPRCE     DFHMDF  POS=(08,44),LENGTH=12,ATTRB=(ASKIP,BRT),               X
                      PICOUT='Z,ZZZ,ZZZ.99'
319             DFHMDF  POS=(10,02),LENGTH=04,ATTRB=ASKIP,INITIAL='FUNC'
331             DFHMDF  POS=(10,07),LENGTH=04,ATTRB=ASKIP,INITIAL='ITEM'
343             DFHMDF  POS=(10,17),LENGTH=11,ATTRB=ASKIP,INITIAL='DESCRIPTION'
355             DFHMDF  POS=(10,35),LENGTH=04,ATTRB=ASKIP,INITIAL='DATE'
367             DFHMDF  POS=(10,42),LENGTH=04,ATTRB=ASKIP,INITIAL='UNIT'
379             DFHMDF  POS=(10,48),LENGTH=05,ATTRB=ASKIP,INITIAL='UCOST'
391             DFHMDF  POS=(10,57),LENGTH=04,ATTRB=ASKIP,INITIAL='COST'
403             DFHMDF  POS=(10,65),LENGTH=06,ATTRB=ASKIP,INITIAL='UPRICE'
415             DFHMDF  POS=(10,74),LENGTH=05,ATTRB=ASKIP,INITIAL='PRICE'
427             DFHMDF  POS=(11,01),LENGTH=01,ATTRB=ASKIP,INITIAL='1'
439 FUNC1       DFHMDF  POS=(11,03),LENGTH=01,ATTRB=(UNPROT,BRT)
450 ITEM1       DFHMDF  POS=(11,05),LENGTH=08,ATTRB=(NUM,BRT),                 X
                      PICIN='99999999',PICOUT='99999999'
```

Fig. 20.5. Data Screen Map Program – File Update.

```
STMT    SOURCE STATEMENT                              DOS/VS ASSEMBLER REL 34.0 14.50

 461 DESC1      DFHMDF POS=(11,14),LENGTH=19,ATTRB=(UNPROT,BRT)
 472 LNDATE1    DFHMDF POS=(11,34),LENGTH=06,ATTRB=(ASKIP,BRT)
 483 UNIT1      DFHMDF POS=(11,41),LENGTH=05,ATTRB=(NUM,BRT),                   X
                      PICIN='99999',PICOUT='99999'
 494 UCOST1     DFHMDF POS=(11,47),LENGTH=07,ATTRB=(NUM,BRT),                   X
                      PICIN='9999999',PICOUT='9999999'
 505 COST1      DFHMDF POS=(11,55),LENGTH=08,ATTRB=(NUM,BRT),                   X
                      PICIN='99999999',PICOUT='99999999'
 516 UPRICE1    DFHMDF POS=(11,64),LENGTH=07,ATTRB=(NUM,BRT),                   X
                      PICIN='9999999',PICOUT='9999999'
 527 PRICE1     DFHMDF POS=(11,72),LENGTH=08,ATTRB=(NUM,BRT),                   X
                      PICIN='99999999',PICOUT='99999999'
 538            DFHMDF POS=(12,01),LENGTH=01,ATTRB=ASKIP,INITIAL='2'
 550 FUNC2      DFHMDF POS=(12,03),LENGTH=01,ATTRB=(UNPROT,BRT)
 561 ITEM2      DFHMDF POS=(12,05),LENGTH=08,ATTRB=(NUM,BRT),                   X
                      PICIN='99999999',PICOUT='99999999'
 572 DESC2      DFHMDF POS=(12,14),LENGTH=19,ATTRB=(UNPROT,BRT)
 583 LNDATE2    DFHMDF POS=(12,34),LENGTH=06,ATTRB=(ASKIP,BRT)
 594 UNIT2      DFHMDF POS=(12,41),LENGTH=05,ATTRB=(NUM,BRT),                   X
                      PICIN='99999',PICOUT='99999'
 605 UCOST2     DFHMDF POS=(12,47),LENGTH=07,ATTRB=(NUM,BRT),                   X
                      PICIN='9999999',PICOUT='9999999'
 616 COST2      DFHMDF POS=(12,55),LENGTH=08,ATTRB=(NUM,BRT),                   X
                      PICIN='99999999',PICOUT='99999999'
 627 UPRICE2    DFHMDF POS=(12,64),LENGTH=07,ATTRB=(NUM,BRT),                   X
                      PICIN='9999999',PICOUT='9999999'
 638 PRICE2     DFHMDF POS=(12,72),LENGTH=08,ATTRB=(NUM,BRT),                   X
                      PICIN='99999999',PICOUT='99999999'
 649            DFHMDF POS=(13,01),LENGTH=01,ATTRB=ASKIP,INITIAL='3'
 661 FUNC3      DFHMDF POS=(13,03),LENGTH=01,ATTRB=(UNPROT,BRT)
 672 ITEM3      DFHMDF POS=(13,05),LENGTH=08,ATTRB=(NUM,BRT),                   X
                      PICIN='99999999',PICOUT='99999999'
 683 DESC3      DFHMDF POS=(13,14),LENGTH=19,ATTRB=(UNPROT,BRT)
 694 LNDATE3    DFHMDF POS=(13,34),LENGTH=06,ATTRB=(ASKIP,BRT)
 705 UNIT3      DFHMDF POS=(13,41),LENGTH=05,ATTRB=(NUM,BRT),                   X
                      PICIN='99999',PICOUT='99999'
 716 UCOST3     DFHMDF POS=(13,47),LENGTH=07,ATTRB=(NUM,BRT),                   X
                      PICIN='9999999',PICOUT='9999999'
 727 COST3      DFHMDF POS=(13,55),LENGTH=08,ATTRB=(NUM,BRT),                   X
                      PICIN='99999999',PICOUT='99999999'
 738 UPRICE3    DFHMDF POS=(13,64),LENGTH=07,ATTRB=(NUM,BRT),                   X
                      PICIN='9999999',PICOUT='9999999'
 749 PRICE3     DFHMDF POS=(13,72),LENGTH=08,ATTRB=(NUM,BRT),                   X
                      PICIN='99999999',PICOUT='99999999'
 760            DFHMDF POS=(14,01),LENGTH=01,ATTRB=ASKIP,INITIAL='4'
 772 FUNC4      DFHMDF POS=(14,03),LENGTH=01,ATTRB=(UNPROT,BRT)
 783 ITEM4      DFHMDF POS=(14,05),LENGTH=08,ATTRB=(NUM,BRT),                   X
                      PICIN='99999999',PICOUT='99999999'
 794 DESC4      DFHMDF POS=(14,14),LENGTH=19,ATTRB=(UNPROT,BRT)
 805 LNDATE4    DFHMDF POS=(14,34),LENGTH=06,ATTRB=(ASKIP,BRT)
 816 UNIT4      DFHMDF POS=(14,41),LENGTH=05,ATTRB=(NUM,BRT),                   X
```

Fig. 20.5. (Continued)

```
STMT   SOURCE STATEMENT                                   DOS/VS ASSEMBLER REL 34.0 14.50

                                 PICIN='99999',PICOUT='99999'
 827 UCOST4      DFHMDF  POS=(14,47),LENGTH=07,ATTRB=(NUM,BRT),                    X
                                 PICIN='9999999',PICOUT='9999999'
 838 COST4       DFHMDF  POS=(14,55),LENGTH=08,ATTRB=(NUM,BRT),                    X
                                 PICIN='99999999',PICOUT='99999999'
 849 UPRICE4     DFHMDF  POS=(14,64),LENGTH=07,ATTRB=(NUM,BRT),                    X
                                 PICIN='9999999',PICOUT='9999999'
 860 PRICE4      DFHMDF  POS=(14,72),LENGTH=08,ATTRB=(NUM,BRT),                    X
                                 PICIN='99999999',PICOUT='99999999'
 871             DFHMDF  POS=(15,01),LENGTH=01,ATTRB=ASKIP,INITIAL='5'
 883 FUNC5       DFHMDF  POS=(15,03),LENGTH=01,ATTRB=(UNPROT,BRT)
 894 ITEM5       DFHMDF  POS=(15,05),LENGTH=08,ATTRB=(NUM,BRT),                    X
                                 PICIN='99999999',PICOUT='99999999'
 905 DESC5       DFHMDF  POS=(15,14),LENGTH=19,ATTRB=(UNPROT,BRT)
 916 LNDATE5     DFHMDF  POS=(15,34),LENGTH=06,ATTRB=(ASKIP,BRT)
 927 UNIT5       DFHMDF  POS=(15,41),LENGTH=05,ATTRB=(NUM,BRT),                    X
                                 PICIN='99999',PICOUT='99999'
 938 UCOST5      DFHMDF  POS=(15,47),LENGTH=07,ATTRB=(NUM,BRT),                    X
                                 PICIN='9999999',PICOUT='9999999'
 949 COST5       DFHMDF  POS=(15,55),LENGTH=08,ATTRB=(NUM,BRT),                    X
                                 PICIN='99999999',PICOUT='99999999'
 960 UPRICE5     DFHMDF  POS=(15,64),LENGTH=07,ATTRB=(NUM,BRT),                    X
                                 PICIN='9999999',PICOUT='9999999'
 971 PRICE5      DFHMDF  POS=(15,72),LENGTH=08,ATTRB=(NUM,BRT),                    X
                                 PICIN='99999999',PICOUT='99999999'
 982             DFHMDF  POS=(16,01),LENGTH=01,ATTRB=ASKIP,INITIAL='6'
 994 FUNC6       DFHMDF  POS=(16,03),LENGTH=01,ATTRB=(UNPROT,BRT)
1005 ITEM6       DFHMDF  POS=(16,05),LENGTH=08,ATTRB=(NUM,BRT),                    X
                                 PICIN='99999999',PICOUT='99999999'
1016 DESC6       DFHMDF  POS=(16,14),LENGTH=19,ATTRB=(UNPROT,BRT)
1027 LNDATE6     DFHMDF  POS=(16,34),LENGTH=06,ATTRB=(ASKIP,BRT)
1038 UNIT6       DFHMDF  POS=(16,41),LENGTH=05,ATTRB=(NUM,BRT),                    X
                                 PICIN='99999',PICOUT='99999'
1049 UCOST6      DFHMDF  POS=(16,47),LENGTH=07,ATTRB=(NUM,BRT),                    X
                                 PICIN='9999999',PICOUT='9999999'
1060 COST6       DFHMDF  POS=(16,55),LENGTH=08,ATTRB=(NUM,BRT),                    X
                                 PICIN='99999999',PICOUT='99999999'
1071 UPRICE6     DFHMDF  POS=(16,64),LENGTH=07,ATTRB=(NUM,BRT),                    X
                                 PICIN='9999999',PICOUT='9999999'
1082 PRICE6      DFHMDF  POS=(16,72),LENGTH=08,ATTRB=(NUM,BRT),                    X
                                 PICIN='99999999',PICOUT='99999999'
1093             DFHMDF  POS=(17,01),LENGTH=01,ATTRB=ASKIP,INITIAL='7'
1105 FUNC7       DFHMDF  POS=(17,03),LENGTH=01,ATTRB=(UNPROT,BRT)
1116 ITEM7       DFHMDF  POS=(17,05),LENGTH=08,ATTRB=(NUM,BRT),                    X
                                 PICIN='99999999',PICOUT='99999999'
1127 DESC7       DFHMDF  POS=(17,14),LENGTH=19,ATTRB=(UNPROT,BRT)
1138 LNDATE7     DFHMDF  POS=(17,34),LENGTH=06,ATTRB=(ASKIP,BRT)
1149 UNIT7       DFHMDF  POS=(17,41),LENGTH=05,ATTRB=(NUM,BRT),                    X
                                 PICIN='99999',PICOUT='99999'
1160 UCOST7      DFHMDF  POS=(17,47),LENGTH=07,ATTRB=(NUM,BRT),                    X
                                 PICIN='9999999',PICOUT='9999999'
```

Fig. 20.5. (Continued)

```
STMT    SOURCE STATEMENT                                DOS/VS ASSEMBLER REL 34.0 14.50

1171 COST7      DFHMDF  POS=(17,55),LENGTH=08,ATTRB=(NUM,BRT),                    X
                        PICIN='99999999',PICOUT='99999999'
1182 UPRICE7    DFHMDF  POS=(17,64),LENGTH=07,ATTRB=(NUM,BRT),                    X
                        PICIN='9999999',PICOUT='9999999'
1193 PRICE7     DFHMDF  POS=(17,72),LENGTH=08,ATTRB=(NUM,BRT),                    X
                        PICIN='99999999',PICOUT='99999999'
1204            DFHMDF  POS=(18,01),LENGTH=01,ATTRB=ASKIP,INITIAL='8'
1216 FUNC8      DFHMDF  POS=(18,03),LENGTH=01,ATTRB=(UNPROT,BRT)
1227 ITEM8      DFHMDF  POS=(18,05),LENGTH=08,ATTRB=(NUM,BRT),                    X
                        PICIN='99999999',PICOUT='99999999'
1238 DESC8      DFHMDF  POS=(18,14),LENGTH=19,ATTRB=(UNPROT,BRT)
1249 LNDATE8    DFHMDF  POS=(18,34),LENGTH=06,ATTRB=(ASKIP,BRT)
1260 UNIT8      DFHMDF  POS=(18,41),LENGTH=05,ATTRB=(NUM,BRT),                    X
                        PICIN='99999',PICOUT='99999'
1271 UCOST8     DFHMDF  POS=(18,47),LENGTH=07,ATTRB=(NUM,BRT),                    X
                        PICIN='9999999',PICOUT='9999999'
1282 COST8      DFHMDF  POS=(18,55),LENGTH=08,ATTRB=(NUM,BRT),                    X
                        PICIN='99999999',PICOUT='99999999'
1293 UPRICE8    DFHMDF  POS=(18,64),LENGTH=07,ATTRB=(NUM,BRT),                    X
                        PICIN='9999999',PICOUT='9999999'
1304 PRICE8     DFHMDF  POS=(18,72),LENGTH=08,ATTRB=(NUM,BRT),                    X
                        PICIN='99999999',PICOUT='99999999'
1315            DFHMDF  POS=(19,01),LENGTH=01,ATTRB=ASKIP,INITIAL='9'
1327 FUNC9      DFHMDF  POS=(19,03),LENGTH=01,ATTRB=(UNPROT,BRT)
1338 ITEM9      DFHMDF  POS=(19,05),LENGTH=08,ATTRB=(NUM,BRT),                    X
                        PICIN='99999999',PICOUT='99999999'
1349 DESC9      DFHMDF  POS=(19,14),LENGTH=19,ATTRB=(UNPROT,BRT)
1360 LNDATE9    DFHMDF  POS=(19,34),LENGTH=06,ATTRB=(ASKIP,BRT)
1371 UNIT9      DFHMDF  POS=(19,41),LENGTH=05,ATTRB=(NUM,BRT),                    X
                        PICIN='99999',PICOUT='99999'
1382 UCOST9     DFHMDF  POS=(19,47),LENGTH=07,ATTRB=(NUM,BRT),                    X
                        PICIN='9999999',PICOUT='9999999'
1393 COST9      DFHMDF  POS=(19,55),LENGTH=08,ATTRB=(NUM,BRT),                    X
                        PICIN='99999999',PICOUT='99999999'
1404 UPRICE9    DFHMDF  POS=(19,64),LENGTH=07,ATTRB=(NUM,BRT),                    X
                        PICIN='9999999',PICOUT='9999999'
1415 PRICE9     DFHMDF  POS=(19,72),LENGTH=08,ATTRB=(NUM,BRT),                    X
                        PICIN='99999999',PICOUT='99999999'
1426            DFHMDF  POS=(20,01),LENGTH=01,ATTRB=PROT
1437            DFHMDF  POS=(21,39),LENGTH=13,ATTRB=ASKIP,                        X
                        INITIAL='TOTALS ----- '
1449 TOTEDCS    DFHMDF  POS=(21,54),LENGTH=09,ATTRB=(NUM,BRT),                    X
                        PICIN='999999999',PICOUT='999999999'
1460            DFHMDF  POS=(21,64),LENGTH=01,ATTRB=PROT
1471 TOTEDPR    DFHMDF  POS=(21,71),LENGTH=09,ATTRB=(NUM,BRT),                    X
                        PICIN='999999999',PICOUT='999999999'
1482            DFHMDF  POS=(22,01),LENGTH=01,ATTRB=PROT
1493 ERR1       DFHMDF  POS=(23,01),LENGTH=34,ATTRB=(ASKIP,BRT)
1504 ERR2       DFHMDF  POS=(23,40),LENGTH=34,ATTRB=(ASKIP,BRT)
1515 ERR3       DFHMDF  POS=(24,01),LENGTH=34,ATTRB=(ASKIP,BRT)
1526 ERR4       DFHMDF  POS=(24,40),LENGTH=34,ATTRB=(ASKIP,BRT)


STMT    SOURCE STATEMENT                                DOS/VS ASSEMBLER REL 34.0 14.50

1537            DFHMSD  TYPE=FINAL
1551            END
```

Fig. 20.5. (Continued)

```
    1   IBM DOS VS COBOL

 CBL SUPMAP,STXIT,NOTRUNC,CSYNTAX,SXREF,OPT,VERB,CLIST,BUF=19069
 CBL NOOPT,LIB
 00001          IDENTIFICATION DIVISION.

 00003          PROGRAM-ID. ORCHO1A.

 00005          ENVIRONMENT DIVISION.

 00007          ****************************************************************
 00008          *                                                              *
 00009          *   1. THIS PROGRAM UPDATES EXISTING ORDERS IN THE PURCHASE     *
 00010          *      ORDER MASTER FILE.                                       *
 00011          *                                                              *
 00012          *   2. THE FIXED DATA AREA WILL REMAIN UNCHANGED.               *
 00013          *                                                              *
 00014          *   3. THE OPERATOR MAY DO THE FOLLOWING.                       *
 00015          *          A) ADD A NEW LINE.                                   *
 00016          *          B) CHANGE AN EXISTING LINE.                          *
 00017          *          C) DELETE AN EXISTING LINE.                          *
 00018          *                                                              *
 00019          ****************************************************************
```

Fig. 20.6. File Update Program.

```
    2          ORCH01A          15.48.02          12/27/80

               DATA DIVISION.

               WORKING-STORAGE SECTION.

               01  COMMUNICATION-AREA.

                   05  COMMAREA-PROCESS-SW              PIC X.

               01  AREA1.

                   05  VALIDATION-ERROR-MESSAGE.
                     10  FILLER                         PIC X(5) VALUE 'LINE'.
                     10  VALIDATION-ERROR-LINE          PIC 9.
                     10  FILLER                         PIC XXX  VALUE ' - '.
                     10  VALIDATION-ERROR-MSG           PIC X(25).

                   05  JOB-NORMAL-END-MESSAGE  PIC X(23) VALUE
                       'JOB NORMALLY TERMINATED'.

                   05  JOB-ABORTED-MESSAGE.
                     10  FILLER                PIC X(15) VALUE 'JOB ABORTED --'.
                     10  MAJOR-ERROR-MSG       PIC X(16).

                   05  HEXADECIMAL-ZEROES      PIC 9999 COMP VALUE ZEROES.

                   05  FILLER REDEFINES HEXADECIMAL-ZEROES.
                     10  FILLER                PIC X.
                     10  HEX-ZEROES            PIC X.

                   05  OLD-EIB-AREA.
                     10  FILLER                PIC X(7) VALUE 'OLD EIB'.
                     10  OLD-EIBFN             PIC XX.
                     10  OLD-EIBRCODE          PIC X(6).
```

Fig. 20.6. (Continued)

```
3          ORCH01A          15.48.02          12/27/80

          01  DFHEIVAR COPY DFHEIVAR.
C         01  DFHEIVAR.
C             02    DFHEIV0   PICTURE X(26).
C             02    DFHEIV1   PICTURE X(8).
C             02    DFHEIV2   PICTURE X(8).
C             02    DFHEIV3   PICTURE X(8).
C             02    DFHEIV4   PICTURE X(6).
C             02    DFHEIV5   PICTURE X(4).
C             02    DFHEIV6   PICTURE X(4).
C             02    DFHEIV7   PICTURE X(2).
C             02    DFHEIV8   PICTURE X(2).
C             02    DFHEIV9   PICTURE X(1).
C             02    DFHEIV10  PICTURE S9(7) USAGE COMPUTATIONAL-3.
C             02    DFHEIV11  PICTURE S9(4) USAGE COMPUTATIONAL.
C             02    DFHEIV12  PICTURE S9(4) USAGE COMPUTATIONAL.
C             02    DFHEIV13  PICTURE S9(4) USAGE COMPUTATIONAL.
C             02    DFHEIV14  PICTURE S9(4) USAGE COMPUTATIONAL.
C             02    DFHEIV15  PICTURE S9(4) USAGE COMPUTATIONAL.
C             02    DFHEIV16  PICTURE S9(9) USAGE COMPUTATIONAL.
C             02    DFHEIV17  PICTURE X(4).
C             02    DFHEIV18  PICTURE X(4).
C             02    DFHEIV19  PICTURE X(4).
C             02    DFHEIV97  PICTURE S9(7) USAGE COMPUTATIONAL-3 VALUE ZERO.
C             02    DFHEIV98  PICTURE S9(4) USAGE COMPUTATIONAL VALUE ZERO.
C             02    DFHEIV99  PICTURE X(1)  VALUE SPACE.
          LINKAGE SECTION.
          01  DFHEIBLK COPY DFHEIBLK.
C         *     EIBLK EXEC INTERFACE BLOCK
C         01    DFHEIBLK.
C         *        EIBTIME       TIME IN 0HHMMSS FORMAT
C               02 EIBTIME       PICTURE S9(7) USAGE COMPUTATIONAL-3.
C         *        EIBDATE       DATE IN 00YYDDD FORMAT
C               02 EIBDATE       PICTURE S9(7) USAGE COMPUTATIONAL-3.
C         *        EIBTRNID      TRANSACTION IDENTIFIER
C               02 EIBTRNID      PICTURE X(4).
C         *        EIBTASKN      TASK NUMBER
C               02 EIBTASKN      PICTURE S9(7) USAGE COMPUTATIONAL-3.
C         *        EIBTRMID      TERMINAL IDENTIFIER
C               02 EIBTRMID      PICTURE X(4).
C         *        DFHEIGDI      RESERVED
C               02 DFHEIGDI      PICTURE S9(4) USAGE COMPUTATIONAL.
C         *        EIBCPOSN      CURSOR POSITION
C               02 EIBCPOSN      PICTURE S9(4) USAGE COMPUTATIONAL.
C         *        EIBCALEN      COMMAREA LENGTH
C               02 EIBCALEN      PICTURE S9(4) USAGE COMPUTATIONAL.
C         *        EIBAID        ATTENTION IDENTIFIER
C               02 EIBAID        PICTURE X(1).
C         *        EIBFN         FUNCTION CODE
C               02 EIBFN         PICTURE X(2).
C         *        EIBRCODE      RESPONSE CODE
C               02 EIBRCODE      PICTURE X(6).
C         *        EIBDS         DATASET NAME
C               02 EIBDS         PICTURE X(8).
```

Fig. 20.6. (Continued)

```
      4          ORCHO1A          15.48.02          12/27/80

  00108 C     *        EIBREQID     REQUEST IDENTIFIER
  00109 C              02 EIBREQID  PICTURE X(8).
  00110        01   DFHCOMMAREA.

  00112             05  PROCESS-SW                  PIC X.
  00113                 88  INITIAL-ENTRY-TIME          VALUE '0'.
  00114                 88  ORDER-VERIFICATION-TIME     VALUE '1'.
  00115                 88  ORDER-VALIDATION-TIME       VALUE '2'.

  00117        01   LINKAGE-POINTERS.

  00119             05  FILLER              PIC S9(8) COMP.
  00120             05  MAP1-POINTER        PIC S9(8) COMP.
  00121             05  MAP2-POINTER        PIC S9(8) COMP.
  00122             05  POM-POINTER         PIC S9(8) COMP.
  00123             05  TWA-POINTER         PIC S9(8) COMP.
  00124             05  TSA-POINTER         PIC S9(8) COMP.
```

Fig. 20.6. (Continued)

```
      5          ORCHO1A          15.48.02          12/27/80

  00126        *****************************************************************
  00127        *                                                               *
  00128        *           ORDER VERIFICATION MAP DESCRIPTION                  *
  00129        *                                                               *
  00130        *****************************************************************

  00132        01  MAP1-AREA.

  00134             05  FILLER                  PIC X(12).
  00135             05  MAP1-DUMMY-L            PIC S9999 COMP.
  00136             05  MAP1-DUMMY-A            PIC X.
  00137             05  MAP1-DUMMY              PIC X.
  00138             05  MAP1-ORDER-NUMBER-L     PIC S9999 COMP.
  00139             05  MAP1-ORDER-NUMBER-A     PIC X.
  00140             05  MAP1-ORDER-NUMBER       PIC X(10).
  00141             05  MAP1-ERROR-L            PIC S9999 COMP.
  00142             05  MAP1-ERROR-A            PIC X.
  00143             05  MAP1-ERROR              PIC X(25).
```

Fig. 20.6. (Continued)

```
6         ORCH01A          15.48.02          12/27/80

          ****************************************************************
          *                                                              *
          *             ORDER VALIDATION MAP DESCRIPTION                 *
          *                                                              *
          ****************************************************************


           01  MAP2-AREA.

               05  FILLER                         PIC X(12).
               05  MAP2-DUMMY-L                   PIC S9999 COMP.
               05  MAP2-DUMMY-A                   PIC X.
               05  MAP2-DUMMY                     PIC X.
               05  MAP2-ORDER-NUMBER-L            PIC S9999 COMP.
               05  MAP2-ORDER-NUMBER-A            PIC X.
               05  MAP2-ORDER-NUMBER              PIC X(10).
               05  MAP2-DOCUMENT-L                PIC S9999 COMP.
               05  MAP2-DOCUMENT-A                PIC X.
               05  MAP2-DOCUMENT                  PIC X(8).
               05  MAP2-DEPARTMENT-L              PIC S9999 COMP.
               05  MAP2-DEPARTMENT-A              PIC X.
               05  MAP2-DEPARTMENT                PIC XXX.
               05  MAP2-CHANGE-DATE-L             PIC S9999 COMP.
               05  MAP2-CHANGE-DATE-A             PIC X.
               05  MAP2-CHANGE-DATE.
                 10  MAP2-CHANGE-DATE-MONTH       PIC XX.
                 10  MAP2-CHANGE-DATE-DAY         PIC XX.
                 10  MAP2-CHANGE-DATE-YEAR        PIC XX.
               05  MAP2-ORDER-DATE-L              PIC S9999 COMP.
               05  MAP2-ORDER-DATE-A              PIC X.
               05  MAP2-ORDER-DATE.
                 10  MAP2-ORDER-DATE-MONTH        PIC XX.
                 10  MAP2-ORDER-DATE-DAY          PIC XX.
                 10  MAP2-ORDER-DATE-YEAR         PIC XX.
               05  MAP2-ORDER-DATE-ENTERED-L      PIC S9999 COMP.
               05  MAP2-ORDER-DATE-ENTERED-A      PIC X.
               05  MAP2-ORDER-DATE-ENTERED        PIC X(6).
               05  MAP2-TOTAL-COST-L              PIC S9999 COMP.
               05  MAP2-TOTAL-COST-A              PIC X.
               05  MAP2-TOTAL-COST                PIC Z,ZZZ,ZZZ.99.
               05  MAP2-TOTAL-PRICE-L             PIC S9999 COMP.
               05  MAP2-TOTAL-PRICE-A             PIC X.
               05  MAP2-TOTAL-PRICE               PIC Z,ZZZ,ZZZ.99.
               05  MAP2-LINE-ITEM             OCCURS 9
                                              INDEXED BY MAP2-LINE-I.
                 10  MAP2-ITEM-FUNCTION-L         PIC S9999 COMP.
                 10  MAP2-ITEM-FUNCTION-A         PIC X.
                 10  MAP2-ITEM-FUNCTION           PIC X.
                 10  MAP2-ITEM-NUMBER-L           PIC S9999 COMP.
                 10  MAP2-ITEM-NUMBER-A           PIC X.
                 10  MAP2-ITEM-NUMBER             PIC 9(8).
                 10  MAP2-ITEM-DESCRIPTION-L      PIC S9999 COMP.
```

Fig. 20.6. (Continued)

```
      7          ORCHO1A          15.48.02          12/27/80

00196                 10   MAP2-ITEM-DESCRIPTION-A    PIC X.
00197                 10   MAP2-ITEM-DESCRIPTION      PIC X(19).
00198                 10   MAP2-ITEM-DATE-L           PIC S9999 COMP.
00199                 10   MAP2-ITEM-DATE-A           PIC X.
00200                 10   MAP2-ITEM-DATE             PIC X(6).
00201                 10   MAP2-UNIT-L                PIC S9999 COMP.
00202                 10   MAP2-UNIT-A                PIC X.
00203                 10   MAP2-UNIT                  PIC 9(5).
00204                 10   MAP2-UNIT-COST-L           PIC S9999 COMP.
00205                 10   MAP2-UNIT-COST-A           PIC X.
00206                 10   MAP2-UNIT-COST             PIC 9(5)V99.
00207                 10   MAP2-COST-L                PIC S9999 COMP.
00208                 10   MAP2-COST-A                PIC X.
00209                 10   MAP2-COST                  PIC 9(6)V99.
00210                 10   MAP2-UNIT-PRICE-L          PIC S9999 COMP.
00211                 10   MAP2-UNIT-PRICE-A          PIC X.
00212                 10   MAP2-UNIT-PRICE            PIC 9(5)V99.
00213                 10   MAP2-PRICE-L               PIC S9999 COMP.
00214                 10   MAP2-PRICE-A               PIC X.
00215                 10   MAP2-PRICE                 PIC 9(6)V99.
00216              05 MAP2-EDIT-TOTAL-COST-L          PIC S9999 COMP.
00217              05 MAP2-EDIT-TOTAL-COST-A          PIC X.
00218              05 MAP2-EDIT-TOTAL-COST            PIC 9(7)V99.
00219              05 MAP2-EDIT-TOTAL-PRICE-L         PIC S9999 COMP.
00220              05 MAP2-EDIT-TOTAL-PRICE-A         PIC X.
00221              05 MAP2-EDIT-TOTAL-PRICE           PIC 9(7)V99.
00222              05 FILLER                     OCCURS 4
00223                                            INDEXED BY ERROR-I.
00224                 10   MAP2-ERRORS-L              PIC S9999 COMP.
00225                 10   MAP2-ERRORS-A              PIC X.
00226                 10   MAP2-ERRORS               PIC X(34).
```

Fig. 20.6. (Continued)

```
     8      ORCHO1A        15.48.02        12/27/80

00228          *************************************************************************
00229          *                                                                       *
00230          *                PURCHASE ORDER MASTER -- FILE LAYOUT                    *
00231          *                                                                       *
00232          *************************************************************************

00234          01   ORDER-MASTER-RECORD.
00235               05   ORDER-NUMBER              PIC X(10).
00236               05   ORDER-ALT-KEY.
00237                 10   ORDER-DEPARTMENT          PIC XXX.
00238                 10   ORDER-DATE.
00239                   15   ORDER-DATE-YEAR          PIC XX.
00240                   15   ORDER-DATE-MONTH         PIC XX.
00241                   15   ORDER-DATE-DAY           PIC XX.
00242               05   ORDER-DATE-ENTERED.
00243                 10   ORDER-DATE-ENTERED-MONTH   PIC XX.
00244                 10   ORDER-DATE-ENTERED-DAY     PIC XX.
00245                 10   ORDER-DATE-ENTERED-YEAR    PIC XX.
00246               05   ORDER-TOTAL-COST             PIC S9(7)V99   COMP-3.
00247               05   ORDER-TOTAL-PRICE            PIC S9(7)V99   COMP-3.
00248               05   ORDER-LINE-COUNT             PIC S9999      COMP.
00249               05   ORDER-ALL-LINES.
00250                 10   ORDER-LINE-ITEM            OCCURS 1 TO 9
00251                                                 DEPENDING ON ORDER-LINE-COUNT
00252                                                 INDEXED BY ORDER-LINE-I.
00253                   15   ORDER-ITEM-NUMBER          PIC X(8).
00254                   15   ORDER-ITEM-DESCRIPTION     PIC X(19).
00255                   15   ORDER-ITEM-DATE.
00256                     20   ORDER-ITEM-DATE-MONTH    PIC XX.
00257                     20   ORDER-ITEM-DATE-DAY      PIC XX.
00258                     2C   ORDER-ITEM-DATE-YEAR     PIC XX.
00259                   15   ORDER-UNIT                 PIC S9(5)      COMP-3.
00260                   15   ORDER-UNIT-COST            PIC S9(5)V99   COMP-3.
00261                   15   ORDER-UNIT-PRICE           PIC S9(5)V99   COMP-3.
```

Fig. 20.6. (Continued)

```
     9        ORCHO1A          15.48.02        12/27/80

00263        ********************************************************************
00264        *                                                                  *
00265        *               TRANSACTION WORK AREA                              *
00266        *                                                                  *
00267        ********************************************************************

00269        01  TWA-AREA.

00271            05  TWA-LINE-ITEM-MAP.
00272                10  TWA-ITEM-FUNCTION-MAP-L         PIC S9999 COMP.
00273                10  TWA-ITEM-FUNCTION-MAP-A         PIC X.
00274                10  TWA-ITEM-FUNCTION-MAP           PIC X.
00275                    88  SCREEN-FUNCTION-IS-ADD          VALUE 'A'.
00276                    88  SCREEN-FUNCTION-IS-CHANGE       VALUE 'C'.
00277                    88  SCREEN-FUNCTION-IS-DELETE       VALUE 'D'.
00278                10  TWA-ITEM-NUMBER-MAP-L          PIC S9999 COMP.
00279                10  TWA-ITEM-NUMBER-MAP-A          PIC X.
00280                10  TWA-ITEM-NUMBER-MAP            PIC X(8).
00281                10  TWA-ITEM-DESCRIPTION-MAP-L     PIC S9999 COMP.
00282                10  TWA-ITEM-DESCRIPTION-MAP-A     PIC X.
00283                10  TWA-ITEM-DESCRIPTION-MAP.
00284                    15  TWA-DESCRIPTION-FIRST-MAP  PIC X.
00285                    15  FILLER                     PIC X(18).
00286                10  TWA-ITEM-DATE-MAP-L            PIC S9999 COMP.
00287                10  TWA-ITEM-DATE-MAP-A            PIC X.
00288                10  TWA-ITEM-DATE-MAP              PIC X(6).
00289                10  TWA-UNIT-MAP-L                 PIC S9999 COMP.
00290                10  TWA-UNIT-MAP-A                 PIC X.
00291                10  TWA-UNIT-MAP                   PIC 9(5).
00292                10  TWA-UNIT-COST-MAP-L            PIC S9999 COMP.
00293                10  TWA-UNIT-COST-MAP-A            PIC X.
00294                10  TWA-UNIT-COST-MAP              PIC 9(5)V99.
00295                10  TWA-COST-MAP-L                 PIC S9999 COMP.
00296                10  TWA-COST-MAP-A                 PIC X.
00297                10  TWA-COST-MAP                   PIC 9(6)V99.
00298                10  TWA-UNIT-PRICE-MAP-L           PIC S9999 COMP.
00299                10  TWA-UNIT-PRICE-MAP-A           PIC X.
00300                10  TWA-UNIT-PRICE-MAP             PIC 9(5)V99.
00301                10  TWA-PRICE-MAP-L                PIC S9999 COMP.
00302                10  TWA-PRICE-MAP-A                PIC X.
00303                10  TWA-PRICE-MAP                  PIC 9(6)V99.

00305            05  TWA-LINE-ITEM-ORDER.
00306                10  TWA-ITEM-NUMBER-ORDER          PIC X(8).
00307                10  TWA-ITEM-DESCRIPTION-ORDER     PIC X(19).
00308                10  TWA-ITEM-DATE-ORDER            PIC X(6).
00309                10  TWA-UNIT-ORDER                 PIC S9(5)       COMP-3.
00310                10  TWA-UNIT-COST-ORDER            PIC S9(5)V99    COMP-3.
00311                10  TWA-UNIT-PRICE-ORDER           PIC S9(5)V99    COMP-3.
```

Fig. 20.6. (Continued)

```
    10            ORCHO1A            15.48.02        12/27/90

00313               05  TWA-TOTAL-COST                          PIC S9(7)V99  COMP-3.

00315               C5  TWA-TOTAL-PRICE                         PIC S9(7)V99  COMP-3.

00317               05  TWA-FUNCTION-COUNTS    COMP.
00318                   10  TWA-FUNCTION-ADD-COUNT              PIC S9(8).
00319                   10  TWA-FUNCTION-CHANGE-COUNT           PIC S9(8).
00320                   10  TWA-FUNCTION-DELETE-COUNT           PIC S9(8).

00322               05  TWA-EDITING-SWITCHES.
00323                   10  TWA-UNIT-SW                         PIC X.
00324                       88  UNIT-WAS-ENTERED                    VALUE 'Y'.
00325                   10  TWA-UNIT-COST-SW                    PIC X.
00326                       88  UNIT-COST-WAS-ENTERED               VALUE 'Y'.
00327                   10  TWA-UNIT-PRICE-SW                   PIC X.
00328                       88  UNIT-PRICE-WAS-ENTERED              VALUE 'Y'.

00330               05  TWA-DELETE-SWITCH                       PIC X.
00331                   88  NO-DELETE-SO-FAR                        VALUE 'N'.

00333               05  TWA-ORDER-RECORD-KEY                    PIC X(10).

00335               05  TSA-QUEUE-ID.
00336                   10  TSA-TERM-ID                         PIC XXXX.
00337                   10  TSA-TRANS-ID                        PIC XXXX.

00339               05  TWA-BINARY-FIELDS   COMP.
00340                   10  TWA-LINE-DATA-CNT                   PIC S9(8).
00341                   10  TWA-POM-LENGTH                      PIC S9(4).
00342                   10  TSA-LENGTH                          PIC S9(4).
00343                   10  TSA-QUEUE-NO                        PIC S9(4).

00345               05  TWA-OPERATOR-MESSAGE                    PIC X(31).

00347               05  TWA-CURRENT-DATE.
00348                   10  TWA-CURRENT-DATE-MONTH              PIC XX.
00349                   10  FILLER                              PIC X.
00350                   10  TWA-CURRENT-DATE-DAY                PIC XX.
00351                   10  FILLER                              PIC X.
00352                   10  TWA-CURRENT-DATE-YEAR               PIC XX.
```

Fig. 20.6. (Continued)

```
   11          ORCH01A           15.48.02          12/27/8

          ***********************************************************************
          *                                                                     *
          *                  TEMPORARY STORAGE AREA                             *
          *                                                                     *
          ***********************************************************************


           01  TSA-AREA.

               05  TSA-ORDER-NUMBER                    PIC X(10).

               05  TSA-ORDER-ALL-LINES.
                 10  TSA-LINE-ITEM                  OCCURS 9
                                                    INDEXED BY TSA-LINE-I.
                   15  TSA-LINE-FUNCTION               PIC X.
                     88  LINE-IS-UNCHANGED                 VALUE SPACE.
                     88  LINE-IS-ADDED                     VALUE 'A'.
                     88  LINE-IS-CHANGED                   VALUE 'C'.
                     88  LINE-IS-DELETED                   VALUE 'D'.
                   15  TSA-ORDER-LINE.
                     20  TSA-ITEM-NUMBER               PIC X(8).
                     20  TSA-ITEM-DESCRIPTION          PIC X(19).
                     20  TSA-ITEM-DATE                 PIC X(6).
                     20  TSA-UNIT                      PIC S9(5)     COMP-3.
                     20  TSA-UNIT-COST                 PIC S9(5)V99  COMP-3.
                     20  TSA-UNIT-PRICE                PIC S9(5)V99  COMP-3.

               05  TSA-POM-NUMBER-OF-LINES             PIC S9(8) COMP.

               05  TSA-SCREEN-NUMBER-OF-LINES          PIC S9(8) COMP.

               05  TSA-CHANGE-DATE                     PIC X(6).
```

Fig. 20.6. (Continued)

```
    12        ORCHO1A          15.48.02        12/27/80

00386         PROCEDURE DIVISION USING DFHEIBLK DFHCOMMAREA.
00387             CALL 'DFHEI1'.

00389         **************************************************************
00390         *                                                            *
00391          MAIN-LINE SECTION.
00392         *                                                            *
00393         **************************************************************

00395         *     EXEC CICS
00396         *         ADDRESS TWA (TWA-POINTER)
00397         *     END-EXEC.
00398               MOVE '                    ' TO DFHEIVO CALL 'DFHEI1' USING
00399               DFHEIVO TWA-POINTER.
00400
00401         *     EXEC CICS
00402         *         HANDLE AID
00403         *             CLEAR (FINALIZATION)
00404         *             PA1 (BYPASS-INPUT)
00405         *             PA2 (BYPASS-INPUT)
00406         *             PA3 (BYPASS-INPUT)
00407         *     END-EXEC.
00408               MOVE ' 0              ' TO DFHEIVO CALL 'DFHEI1' USING
00409               DFHEIVO GO TO FINALIZATION BYPASS-INPUT BYPASS-INPUT
00410               BYPASS-INPUT DEPENDING ON DFHEIGDI.
00411
00412
00413
00414
00415         *     EXEC CICS
00416         *         HANDLE CONDITION
00417         *             MAPFAIL (MAPFAIL-ERROR)
00418         *             ERROR   (MAJOR-ERROR)
00419         *     END-EXEC.
00420               MOVE '                    ' TO DFHEIVO CALL 'DFHEI1' USING
00421               DFHEIVO GO TO MAPFAIL-ERROR MAJOR-ERROR DEPENDING ON
00422               DFHEIGDI.
00423
00424
00425               IF EIBCALEN NOT EQUAL TO ZEROES
00426                   IF ORDER-VALIDATION-TIME
00427                       GO TO ORDER-VALIDATION
00428                   ELSE IF ORDER-VERIFICATION-TIME
00429                       GO TO ORDER-VERIFICATION
00430                   ELSE IF INITIAL-ENTRY-TIME
00431                       GO TO INITIALIZATION
00432                   ELSE GO TO PROCESS-SWITCH-ERROR.

00434               IF EIBCALEN EQUAL TO ZEROES
00435                   GO TO SIGN-ON-VIOLATION.
```

Fig. 20.6. (Continued)

```
    13          ORCH01A        15.48.02        12/27/80

00437       ****************************************************************
00438       *                                                              *
00439        ORDER-VALIDATION SECTION.
00440       *                                                              *
00441       ****************************************************************

00443       *   EXEC CICS
00444       *       RECEIVE MAP     ('ORCHM02')
00445       *               MAPSET  ('ORCHS02')
00446       *               SET     (MAP2-POINTER)
00447       *   END-EXEC.
00448           MOVE 'ORCHM02' TO DFHEIV1 MOVE 'ORCHS02' TO DFHEIV2 MOVE '
00449       -   '              ' TO DFHEIV0 CALL 'DFHEI1' USING DFHEIV0
00450           DFHEIV1 MAP2-POINTER DFHEIV98 DFHEIV2.
00451
00452
00453           MOVE EIBTRMID    TO    TSA-TERM-ID.
00454           MOVE EIBTRNID    TO    TSA-TRANS-ID.

00456       *   EXEC CICS
00457       *       READQ TS
00458       *           QUEUE   (TSA-QUEUE-ID)
00459       *           SET     (TSA-POINTER)
00460       *           LENGTH  (TSA-LENGTH)
00461       *           ITEM    (1)
00462       *   END-EXEC.
00463           MOVE 1 TO DFHEIV11 MOVE '  Y       ' TO DFHEIV0 CALL 'DFHEI1'
00464           USING DFHEIV0 TSA-QUEUE-ID TSA-POINTER TSA-LENGTH DFHEIV99
00465           DFHEIV11.
00466
00467
00468
00469
00470           MOVE SPACES TO MAP2-ERRORS (1)
00471                          MAP2-ERRORS (2)
00472                          MAP2-ERRORS (3)
00473                          MAP2-ERRORS (4).
00474           SET ERROR-I   TO   ZEROES.

00476           IF MAP2-DOCUMENT NUMERIC
00477               NEXT SENTENCE
00478           ELSE SET ERROR-I UP BY 1
00479               MOVE 'INVALID DOCUMENT NUMBER' TO  MAP2-ERRORS (ERROR-I)
00480               MOVE -1                        TO  MAP2-DOCUMENT-L.

00482           IF     MAP2-CHANGE-DATE-MONTH (GREATER '00' AND LESS '13')
00483           AND  MAP2-CHANGE-DATE-DAY    (GREATER '00' AND LESS '32')
00484           AND  MAP2-CHANGE-DATE-YEAR     NUMERIC
00485           THEN MOVE MAP2-CHANGE-DATE   TO  TSA-CHANGE-DATE
00486           ELSE SET ERROR-I UP BY 1
00487               MOVE 'INVALID DATE' TO MAP2-ERRORS (ERROR-I)
```

Fig. 20.6. (Continued)

```
 14          ORCH01A          15.48.02          12/27/80

                      IF ERROR-I EQUAL TO 1
                          MOVE -1 TO MAP2-CHANGE-DATE-L.


               VALIDATE-VARIABLE-DATA.

                   SET MAP2-LINE-I        TO  1.
                   MOVE ZEROES            TO  TWA-LINE-DATA-CNT.
                   MOVE ZEROES            TO  TWA-FUNCTION-ADD-COUNT
                                              TWA-FUNCTION-CHANGE-COUNT
                                              TWA-FUNCTION-DELETE-COUNT.
                   MOVE ZEROES            TO  TWA-TOTAL-COST
                                              TWA-TOTAL-PRICE.
                   PERFORM VALIDATE-EACH-LINE THRU VALIDATE-EACH-LINE-EXIT
                       UNTIL      (TWA-LINE-DATA-CNT EQUAL TO ZEROES
                            AND MAP2-LINE-I GREATER
                                          (TSA-POM-NUMBER-OF-LINES + 1))
                         OR ERROR-I             EQUAL TO 4
                         OR MAP2-LINE-I         GREATER THAN 9.
                   GO TO CHECK-IF-ANY-DATA-ENTERED.


               VALIDATE-EACH-LINE.
                   MOVE SPACES                      TO   TWA-UNIT-SW
                                                         TWA-UNIT-COST-SW
                                                         TWA-UNIT-PRICE-SW.
                   MOVE ZEROES                      TO   TWA-LINE-DATA-CNT.
                   SET VALIDATION-ERROR-LINE  TO   MAP2-LINE-I.
                   MOVE MAP2-LINE-ITEM (MAP2-LINE-I) TO TWA-LINE-ITEM-MAP.
                   SET TSA-LINE-I                   TO   MAP2-LINE-I.
                   MOVE TSA-ORDER-LINE (TSA-LINE-I) TO TWA-LINE-ITEM-ORDER.

                   IF TWA-ITEM-FUNCTION-MAP-L NOT EQUAL TO ZEROES
                       IF SCREEN-FUNCTION-IS-ADD
                           ADD 1 TO TWA-FUNCTION-ADD-COUNT
                           IF MAP2-LINE-I GREATER TSA-POM-NUMBER-OF-LINES
                               NEXT SENTENCE
                           ELSE MOVE 'INVALID ADD FUNCTION'
                                                    TO VALIDATION-ERROR-MSG
                               GO TO ERROR-FUNCTION-RTN
                       ELSE IF SCREEN-FUNCTION-IS-CHANGE
                               ADD 1 TO TWA-FUNCTION-CHANGE-COUNT
                               IF MAP2-LINE-I
                                          NOT GREATER TSA-POM-NUMBER-OF-LINES
                                   NEXT SENTENCE
                               ELSE MOVE 'INVALID CHANGE FUNCTION'
                                                    TO VALIDATION-ERROR-MSG
                                   GO TO ERROR-FUNCTION-RTN
                           ELSE IF SCREEN-FUNCTION-IS-DELETE
                                   ADD 1 TO TWA-FUNCTION-DELETE-COUNT
                                   IF MAP2-LINE-I
                                       NOT GREATER TSA-POM-NUMBER-OF-LINES
                                       NEXT SENTENCE
```

Fig. 20.6. (Continued)

```
15          ORCH01A          15.48.02          12/27/80

                        ELSE MOVE 'INVALID DELETE FUNCTION'
                                        TO VALIDATION-ERROR-MSG
                             GO TO ERROR-FUNCTION-RTN
                   ELSE MOVE 'INVALID FUNCTION CODE'
                                        TO VALIDATION-ERROR-MSG
                        GO TO ERROR-FUNCTION-RTN.

    GO TO VALIDATE-ITEM-NUMBER.


ERROR-FUNCTION-RTN.
    SET ERROR-I UP BY 1.
    MOVE VALIDATION-ERROR-MESSAGE TO MAP2-ERRORS (ERROR-I).
    IF ERROR-I EQUAL TO 1
         MOVE -1 TO MAP2-ITEM-FUNCTION-L (MAP2-LINE-I).
    SET MAP2-LINE-I UP BY 1.
    GO TO VALIDATE-EACH-LINE-EXIT.


VALIDATE-ITEM-NUMBER.

    IF TWA-ITEM-NUMBER-MAP-L NOT EQUAL TO ZEROES
         IF     SCREEN-FUNCTION-IS-ADD
            OR SCREEN-FUNCTION-IS-CHANGE
         THEN IF TWA-ITEM-NUMBER-MAP NUMERIC
                   MOVE TWA-ITEM-NUMBER-MAP
                                  TO TWA-ITEM-NUMBER-ORDER
                   ADD 1 TO TWA-LINE-DATA-CNT
              ELSE MOVE 'INVALID ITEM NUMBER'
                                  TO VALIDATION-ERROR-MSG
                   GO TO ERROR-ITEM-NUMBER-RTN
         ELSE MOVE 'INVALID ITEM NUMBER ENTRY'
                             TO VALIDATION-ERROR-MSG
              GO TO ERROR-ITEM-NUMBER-RTN.

    GO TO VALIDATE-ITEM-DESCRIPTION.


ERROR-ITEM-NUMBER-RTN.
    SET ERROR-I UP BY 1.
    MOVE VALIDATION-ERROR-MESSAGE TO MAP2-ERRORS (ERROR-I).
    IF ERROR-I EQUAL TO 1
         MOVE -1 TO MAP2-ITEM-NUMBER-L (MAP2-LINE-I)
    ELSE IF ERROR-I EQUAL TO 4
              GO TO VALIDATE-EACH-LINE-EXIT.


VALIDATE-ITEM-DESCRIPTION.

    IF TWA-ITEM-DESCRIPTION-MAP-L EQUAL TO ZEROES
         IF SCREEN-FUNCTION-IS-ADD
              MOVE SPACES TO TWA-ITEM-DESCRIPTION-ORDER
         ELSE NEXT SENTENCE
```

Fig. 20.6. (Continued)

16 ORCH01A 15.48.02 12/27/80

```
00588                    ELSE IF    SCREEN-FUNCTION-IS-ADD
00589                         OR SCREEN-FUNCTION-IS-CHANGE
00590                      THEN IF TWA-DESCRIPTION-FIRST-MAP EQUAL TO SPACES
00591                              MOVE 'INVALID DESCRIPTION'
00592                                             TO VALIDATION-ERROR-MSG
00593                              GO TO ERROR-ITEM-DESCRIPTION-RTN
00594                         ELSE MOVE TWA-ITEM-DESCRIPTION-MAP
00595                                             TO TWA-ITEM-DESCRIPTION-ORDER
00596                              ADD 2          TO TWA-LINE-DATA-CNT
00597                      ELSE MOVE 'INVALID ITEM DESC ENTRY'
00598                                     TO VALIDATION-ERROR-MSG
00599                         GO TO ERROR-ITEM-DESCRIPTION-RTN.

00601           GO TO VALIDATE-UNIT.

00603      ERROR-ITEM-DESCRIPTION-RTN.
00604           SET ERROR-I UP BY 1.
00605           MOVE VALIDATION-ERROR-MESSAGE  TO  MAP2-ERRORS (ERROR-I).
00606           IF ERROR-I EQUAL TO 1
00607                MOVE -1 TO MAP2-ITEM-DESCRIPTION-L (MAP2-LINE-I)
00608           ELSE IF ERROR-I EQUAL TO 4
00609                     GO TO VALIDATE-EACH-LINE-EXIT.

00611      VALIDATE-UNIT.

00613           IF TWA-UNIT-MAP-L NOT EQUAL TO ZEROES
00614                    IF    SCREEN-FUNCTION-IS-ADD
00615                     OR SCREEN-FUNCTION-IS-CHANGE
00616                   THEN IF TWA-UNIT-MAP NUMERIC
00617                           MOVE TWA-UNIT-MAP       TO  TWA-UNIT-ORDER
00618                           ADD 4 TO TWA-LINE-DATA-CNT
00619                           MOVE 'Y' TO TWA-UNIT-SW
00620                      ELSE MOVE ZEROES            TO  TWA-UNIT-ORDER
00621                           MOVE 'INVALID UNIT' TO  VALIDATION-ERROR-MSG
00622                           GO TO ERROR-UNIT-RTN
00623                   ELSE MOVE 'INVALID UNIT ENTRY' TO VALIDATION-ERROR-MSG
00624                        GO TO ERROR-UNIT-RTN.

00626           GO TO VALIDATE-UNIT-COST.

00628      ERROR-UNIT-RTN.
00629           SET ERROR-I UP BY 1.
00630           MOVE VALIDATION-ERROR-MESSAGE TO MAP2-ERRORS (ERROR-I).
00631           IF ERROR-I EQUAL TO 1
00632                MOVE -1 TO MAP2-UNIT-L (MAP2-LINE-I)
00633           ELSE IF ERROR-I EQUAL TO 4
00634                     GO TO VALIDATE-EACH-LINE-EXIT.

00636      VALIDATE-UNIT-COST.
```

Fig. 20.6. (Continued)

```
     17              ORCHO1A           15.48.02            12/27/80

00638                  IF TWA-UNIT-COST-MAP-L NOT EQUAL TO ZEROES
00639                     IF     SCREEN-FUNCTION-IS-ADD
00640                     OR SCREEN-FUNCTION-IS-CHANGE
00641                     THEN IF TWA-UNIT-COST-MAP NUMERIC
00642                           MOVE TWA-UNIT-COST-MAP
00643                                        TO TWA-UNIT-COST-ORDER
00644                           ADD 8 TO TWA-LINE-DATA-CNT
00645                           MOVE 'Y' TO TWA-UNIT-COST-SW
00646                     ELSE MOVE 'INVALID UNIT COST'
00647                                        TO   VALIDATION-ERROR-MSG
00648                     GO TO ERROR-UNIT-COST-RTN
00649                     ELSE MOVE 'INVALID UNIT COST ENTRY'
00650                                        TO VALIDATION-ERROR-MSG
00651                     GO TO ERROR-UNIT-COST-RTN.

00653              GO TO VALIDATE-LINE-COST.

00655          ERROR-UNIT-COST-RTN.
00656              SET ERROR-I UP BY 1.
00657              MOVE VALIDATION-ERROR-MESSAGE TO MAP2-ERRORS (ERROR-I).
00658              IF ERROR-I EQUAL TO 1
00659                  MOVE -1 TO MAP2-UNIT-COST-L (MAP2-LINE-I)
00660              ELSE IF ERROR-I EQUAL TO 4
00661                     GO TO VALIDATE-EACH-LINE-EXIT.

00663          VALIDATE-LINE-COST.

00665              IF TWA-COST-MAP-L NOT EQUAL TO ZEROES
00666                 IF     SCREEN-FUNCTION-IS-ADD
00667                 OR SCREEN-FUNCTION-IS-CHANGE
00668                 THEN IF     TWA-COST-MAP    NUMERIC
00669                     AND TWA-COST-MAP =
00670                               TWA-UNIT-ORDER * TWA-UNIT-COST-ORDER
00671                     THEN ADD TWA-COST-MAP   TO   TWA-TOTAL-COST
00672                          ADD 16          TO   TWA-LINE-DATA-CNT
00673                     ELSE MOVE 'INVALID COST'  TO VALIDATION-ERROR-MSG
00674                          GO TO ERROR-LINE-COST-RTN
00675                 ELSE MOVE 'INVALID COST ENTRY'
00676                                        TO VALIDATION-ERROR-MSG
00677                     GO TO ERROR-LINE-COST-RTN
00678              ELSE IF SCREEN-FUNCTION-IS-DELETE
00679                     COMPUTE TWA-TOTAL-COST = TWA-TOTAL-COST
00680                            + TWA-UNIT-ORDER * TWA-UNIT-COST-ORDER
00681              ELSE IF     SCREEN-FUNCTION-IS-CHANGE
00682                     AND    (UNIT-WAS-ENTERED
00683                        OR UNIT-COST-WAS-ENTERED)
00684                     THEN MOVE 'COST NOT ENTERED'
00685                                        TO VALIDATION-ERROR-MSG
00686                     GO TO ERROR-LINE-COST-RTN.
```

Fig. 20.6. (Continued)

18 ORCH01A 15.48.02 12/27/80

```
00688                    GO TO VALIDATE-UNIT-PRICE.

00690          ERROR-LINE-COST-RTN.
00691              SET ERROR-I UP BY 1.
00692              MOVE VALIDATION-ERROR-MESSAGE TO MAP2-ERRORS (ERROR-I).
00693              IF ERROR-I EQUAL TO 1
00694                  MOVE -1 TO MAP2-COST-L (MAP2-LINE-I)
00695              ELSE IF ERROR-I EQUAL TO 4
00696                      GO TO VALIDATE-EACH-LINE-EXIT.

00698          VALIDATE-UNIT-PRICE.

00700              IF TWA-UNIT-PRICE-MAP-L NOT EQUAL TO ZEROES
00701                  IF     SCREEN-FUNCTION-IS-ADD
00702                  OR SCREEN-FUNCTION-IS-CHANGE
00703                  THEN IF TWA-UNIT-PRICE-MAP   NUMERIC
00704                          MOVE TWA-UNIT-PRICE-MAP
00705                                      TO TWA-UNIT-PRICE-ORDER
00706                          ADD 32 TO TWA-LINE-DATA-CNT
00707                          MOVE 'Y' TO TWA-UNIT-PRICE-SW
00708                      ELSE MOVE 'INVALID UNIT PRICE'
00709                                      TO  VALIDATION-ERROR-MSG
00710                          GO TO ERROR-UNIT-PRICE-RTN
00711                  ELSE MOVE 'INVALID UNIT PRICE ENTRY'
00712                                      TO  VALIDATION-ERROR-MSG
00713                      GO TO ERROR-UNIT-PRICE-RTN.

00715              GO TO VALIDATE-LINE-PRICE.

00717          ERROR-UNIT-PRICE-RTN.
00718              SET ERROR-I UP BY 1.
00719              MOVE VALIDATION-ERROR-MESSAGE TO MAP2-ERRORS (ERROR-I).
00720              IF ERROR-I EQUAL TO 1
00721                  MOVE -1 TO MAP2-UNIT-PRICE-L (MAP2-LINE-I)
00722              ELSE IF ERROR-I EQUAL TO 4
00723                      GO TO VALIDATE-EACH-LINE-EXIT.

00725          VALIDATE-LINE-PRICE.

00727              IF TWA-PRICE-MAP-L NOT EQUAL TO ZEROES
00728                  IF     SCREEN-FUNCTION-IS-ADD
00729                  OR SCREEN-FUNCTION-IS-CHANGE
00730                  THEN IF    TWA-PRICE-MAP   NUMERIC
00731                      AND TWA-PRICE-MAP =
00732                                      TWA-UNIT-ORDER * TWA-UNIT-PRICE-ORDER
00733                          THEN ADD TWA-PRICE-MAP   TO   TWA-TOTAL-PRICE
00734                              ADD 64          TO   TWA-LINE-DATA-CNT
00735                          ELSE MOVE 'INVALID PRICE' TO VALIDATION-ERROR-MSG
00736                              GO TO ERROR-LINE-PRICE-RTN
```

Fig. 20.6. (Continued)

```
19          ORCH01A          15.48.02          12/27/80

                  ELSE MOVE 'INVALID PRICE ENTRY' TO VALIDATION-ERROR-MSG
                       GO TO ERROR-LINE-PRICE-RTN
              ELSE IF SCREEN-FUNCTION-IS-DELETE
                       COMPUTE TWA-TOTAL-PRICE = TWA-TOTAL-PRICE
                                + TWA-UNIT-ORDER * TWA-UNIT-PRICE-ORDER
                  ELSE IF      SCREEN-FUNCTION-IS-CHANGE
                            AND    (UNIT-WAS-ENTERED
                                OR UNIT-PRICE-WAS-ENTERED)
                       THEN MOVE 'PRICE NOT ENTERED'
                                                 TO VALIDATION-ERROR-MSG
                           GO TO ERROR-LINE-PRICE-RTN.

              GO TO CHECK-FOR-DATA-COMPLETION.


          ERROR-LINE-PRICE-RTN.
              SET ERROR-I UP BY 1.
              MOVE VALIDATION-ERROR-MESSAGE TO MAP2-ERRORS (ERROR-I).
              IF ERROR-I EQUAL TO 1
                  MOVE -1 TO MAP2-PRICE-L (MAP2-LINE-I)
              ELSE IF ERROR-I EQUAL TO 4
                      GO TO VALIDATE-EACH-LINE-EXIT.


          CHECK-FOR-DATA-COMPLETION.

              IF SCREEN-FUNCTION-IS-ADD
                  IF TWA-LINE-DATA-CNT EQUAL TO (125 OR 127)
                      IF ERROR-I EQUAL TO ZEROES
                          MOVE TSA-CHANGE-DATE
                                        TO TWA-ITEM-DATE-ORDER
                          SET TSA-LINE-I    TO MAP2-LINE-I
                          MOVE TWA-LINE-ITEM-ORDER
                                        TO TSA-ORDER-LINE (TSA-LINE-I)
                          MOVE TWA-ITEM-FUNCTION-MAP
                                        TO TSA-LINE-FUNCTION (TSA-LINE-I)
                      ELSE NEXT SENTENCE
                  ELSE MOVE 'INCOMPLETE ADD' TO VALIDATION-ERROR-MSG
                      GO TO ERROR-INCOMPLETE-DATA-RTN
              ELSE IF SCREEN-FUNCTION-IS-CHANGE
                      IF TWA-LINE-DATA-CNT EQUAL TO ZEROES
                          MOVE 'NO CHANGE DATA' TO VALIDATION-ERROR-MSG
                          GO TO ERROR-INCOMPLETE-DATA-RTN
                      ELSE IF ERROR-I EQUAL TO ZEROES
                              MOVE TSA-CHANGE-DATE
                                                TO TWA-ITEM-DATE-ORDER
                              SET TSA-LINE-I TO MAP2-LINE-I
                              MOVE TWA-LINE-ITEM-ORDER
                                           TO TSA-ORDER-LINE (TSA-LINE-I)
                              MOVE TWA-ITEM-FUNCTION-MAP
                                        TO TSA-LINE-FUNCTION (TSA-LINE-I)
                          ELSE NEXT SENTENCE
                  ELSE IF SCREEN-FUNCTION-IS-DELETE
```

Fig. 20.6. (Continued)

```
    20          ORCH01A          15.48.02          12/27/80

                                MOVE TWA-ITEM-FUNCTION-MAP
                                             TO TSA-LINE-FUNCTION (TSA-LINE-I

                   GO TO VALIDATE-LINE-END.


               ERROR-INCOMPLETE-DATA-RTN.
                   SET ERROR-I UP BY 1.
                   MOVE VALIDATION-ERROR-MESSAGE TO MAP2-ERRORS (ERROR-I).
                   IF ERROR-I EQUAL TO 1
                        MOVE -1 TO MAP2-ITEM-NUMBER-L (MAP2-LINE-I)
                   ELSE IF ERROR-I EQUAL TO 4
                            GO TO VALIDATE-EACH-LINE-EXIT.


               VALIDATE-LINE-END.
                   SET MAP2-LINE-I UP BY 1.
               VALIDATE-EACH-LINE-EXIT.  EXIT.


               CHECK-IF-ANY-DATA-ENTERED.

                   IF ERROR-I EQUAL TO 4
                       GO TO DISPLAY-ERROR-SCREEN.

                   IF  (TWA-FUNCTION-ADD-COUNT
                     + TWA-FUNCTION-CHANGE-COUNT
                     + TWA-FUNCTION-DELETE-COUNT) EQUAL TO ZEROES
                   THEN SET ERROR-I UP BY 1
                        MOVE 'NO UPDATE ENTERED' TO MAP2-ERRORS (ERROR-I)
                        IF ERROR-I EQUAL TO 1
                            MOVE -1 TO MAP2-ITEM-FUNCTION-L (1)
                        ELSE IF ERROR-I EQUAL TO 4
                                GO TO CHECK-IF-ANY-DATA-ENTERED-EXIT
                            ELSE NEXT SENTENCE
                   ELSE IF  (TSA-POM-NUMBER-OF-LINES
                          + TWA-FUNCTION-ADD-COUNT
                          - TWA-FUNCTION-DELETE-COUNT) EQUAL TO ZEROES
                        THEN SET ERROR-I UP BY 1
                            MOVE 'NO LINE ITEM TO BE LEFT'
                                                 TO MAP2-ERRORS (ERROR-I)
                            IF ERROR-I EQUAL TO 1
                                MOVE -1 TO MAP2-ITEM-FUNCTION-L (1)
                            ELSE IF ERROR-I EQUAL TO 4
                                    GO TO CHECK-IF-ANY-DATA-ENTERED-EXIT.

                   IF      MAP2-EDIT-TOTAL-COST NUMERIC
                      AND MAP2-EDIT-TOTAL-COST = TWA-TOTAL-COST
                   THEN NEXT SENTENCE
                   ELSE SET ERROR-I UP BY 1
                        MOVE 'INCORRECT TOTAL COST'  TO  MAP2-ERRORS (ERROR-I)
                        IF ERROR-I EQUAL TO 1
                            MOVE -1                  TO  MAP2-EDIT-TOTAL-COST-L
```

Fig. 20.6. (Continued)

```
    21          ORCH01A          15.48.02          12/27/80

                    ELSE IF ERROR-I EQUAL TO 4
                              GO TO CHECK-IF-ANY-DATA-ENTERED-EXIT.

               IF      MAP2-EDIT-TOTAL-PRICE NUMERIC
                  AND MAP2-EDIT-TOTAL-PRICE = TWA-TOTAL-PRICE
               THEN NEXT SENTENCE
               ELSE SET ERROR-I UP BY 1
                    MOVE 'INCORRECT TOTAL PRICE' TO MAP2-ERRORS (ERROR-I)
                    IF ERROR-I EQUAL TO 1
                         MOVE -1                    TO MAP2-EDIT-TOTAL-PRICE-L
                    ELSE IF ERROR-I EQUAL TO 4
                              GO TO CHECK-IF-ANY-DATA-ENTERED-EXIT.
           CHECK-IF-ANY-DATA-ENTERED-EXIT.  EXIT.


           CHECK-IF-THERE-ARE-ERRORS.

               IF ERROR-I NOT EQUAL TO ZEROES
                    GO TO DISPLAY-ERROR-SCREEN.


           NO-ERRORS-RTN.

               SET TSA-SCREEN-NUMBER-OF-LINES  TO  MAP2-LINE-I.

               IF MAP2-LINE-I GREATER THAN 9
                    IF TWA-ITEM-FUNCTION-MAP-L NOT EQUAL TO ZEROES
                         SUBTRACT 1 FROM TSA-SCREEN-NUMBER-OF-LINES
                    ELSE SUBTRACT 2 FROM TSA-SCREEN-NUMBER-OF-LINES
               ELSE SUBTRACT 2 FROM TSA-SCREEN-NUMBER-OF-LINES.

               MOVE TSA-ORDER-NUMBER  TO  TWA-ORDER-RECORD-KEY.

          *    EXEC CICS
          *         HANDLE CONDITION
          *              NOTOPEN (FILE-NOT-OPEN)
          *              NOTFND  (RECORD-NOT-FOUND)
          *    END-EXEC.
                MOVE '                    ' TO DFHEIVO CALL 'DFHEI1' USING
                DFHEIVO GO TO FILE-NOT-OPEN RECORD-NOT-FOUND DEPENDING ON
                DFHEIGDI.



          *    EXEC CICS
          *         READ DATASET ('ORTEST')
          *              SET     (POM-POINTER)
          *              RIDFLD  (TWA-ORDER-RECORD-KEY)
          *              UPDATE
          *    END-EXEC.
                MOVE 'ORTEST' TO DFHEIV3 MOVE '         ' TO DFHEIVO CALL 'D
          -    'FHEI1' USING DFHEIVO DFHEIV3 POM-POINTER DFHEIV98
```

Fig. 20.6. (Continued)

```
22          ORCH01A          15.48.02          12/27/80

                   TWA-ORDER-RECORD-KEY.



                  MOVE 'N'  TO  TWA-DELETE-SWITCH.
                  SET TSA-LINE-I     TO  1.
                  SET ORDER-LINE-I  TO  1.
                  PERFORM REFORMAT-ORDER-RECORD
                      UNTIL TSA-LINE-I GREATER TSA-SCREEN-NUMBER-OF-LINES.
                  GO TO READJUST-ORDER-TOTALS.

              REFORMAT-ORDER-RECORD.
                  IF LINE-IS-UNCHANGED (TSA-LINE-I)
                      IF NO-DELETE-SO-FAR
                          SET TSA-LINE-I     UP  BY 1
                          SET ORDER-LINE-I  UP  BY 1
                      ELSE MOVE TSA-ORDER-LINE (TSA-LINE-I)
                                      TO ORDER-LINE-ITEM (ORDER-LINE-I)
                          SET TSA-LINE-I     UP  BY 1
                          SET ORDER-LINE-I  UP  BY 1
                  ELSE IF     LINE-IS-ADDED  (TSA-LINE-I)
                          OR LINE-IS-CHANGED (TSA-LINE-I)
                      THEN MOVE TSA-ORDER-LINE (TSA-LINE-I)
                                     TO ORDER-LINE-ITEM (ORDER-LINE-I)
                          SET TSA-LINE-I     UP  BY 1
                          SET ORDER-LINE-I  UP  BY 1
                      ELSE SET TSA-LINE-I UP BY 1
                          MOVE 'Y' TO TWA-DELETE-SWITCH.

              READJUST-ORDER-TOTALS.
                  SET ORDER-LINE-COUNT TO  ORDER-LINE-I.
                  SUBTRACT 1 FROM ORDER-LINE-COUNT.
                  MOVE ZEROES            TO   ORDER-TOTAL-COST
                                              ORDER-TOTAL-PRICE.
                  SET ORDER-LINE-I TO 1.
                  PERFORM READJUST-ORDER-TOTALS2
                      UNTIL ORDER-LINE-I GREATER ORDER-LINE-COUNT.
                  GO TO REWRITE-ORDER-RECORD.

              READJUST-ORDER-TOTALS2.
                  COMPUTE ORDER-TOTAL-COST = ORDER-TOTAL-COST
                          + (ORDER-UNIT (ORDER-LINE-I)
                               * ORDER-UNIT-COST (ORDER-LINE-I)).
                  COMPUTE ORDER-TOTAL-PRICE = ORDER-TOTAL-PRICE
                          + (ORDER-UNIT (ORDER-LINE-I)
                               * ORDER-UNIT-PRICE (ORDER-LINE-I)).
                  SET ORDER-LINE-I UP BY 1.

              REWRITE-ORDER-RECORD.
```

Fig. 20.6. (Continued)

```
    23          ORCH01A          15.48.02        12/27/80

00937               COMPUTE TWA-POM-LENGTH = 37 + ORDER-LINE-COUNT * 44.

00939        *    EXEC CICS
00940        *         REWRITE DATASET ('ORTEST')
00941        *                  LENGTH   (TWA-POM-LENGTH)
00942        *                  FROM     (ORDER-MASTER-RECORD)
00943        *    END-EXEC.
00944             MOVE 'ORTEST' TO DFHEIV3 MOVE '          ' TO DFHEIVO CALL ')
00945        -    'FHEI1' USING DFHEIVO DFHEIV3 ORDER-MASTER-RECORD
00946             TWA-POM-LENGTH.
00947
00948
00949        *    EXEC CICS
00950        *         SEND MAP     ('ORCHM01')
00951        *                  MAPSET ('ORCHS01')
00952        *                  MAPONLY
00953        *                  ERASE
00954        *    END-EXEC.
00955             MOVE 'ORCHM01' TO DFHEIV1 MOVE 'ORCHS01' TO DFHEIV2 MOVE '
00956        -    '          ' TO DFHEIVO CALL 'DFHEI1' USING DFHEIVO
00957             DFHEIV1 DFHEIV99 DFHEIV98 DFHEIV2.
00958
00959
00960
00961             MOVE '1' TO COMMAREA-PROCESS-SW.

00963        RETURN-AT-ORDER-VALIDATE.

00965        *    EXEC CICS
00966        *         RETURN TRANSID (EIBTRNID)
00967        *                  COMMAREA (COMMUNICATION-AREA)
00968        *                  LENGTH   (1)
00969        *    END-EXEC.
00970             MOVE 1 TO DFHEIV11 MOVE '          ' TO DFHEIVO CALL 'DFHEI1'
00971             USING DFHEIVO EIBTRNID COMMUNICATION-AREA DFHEIV11.
00972
00973
00974
00975        DISPLAY-ERROR-SCREEN.

00977        *    EXEC CICS
00978        *         SEND MAP     ('ORCHM02')
00979        *                  MAPSET ('ORCHS02')
00980        *                  FROM   (MAP2-AREA)
00981        *                  DATAONLY
00982        *                  CURSOR
00983        *    END-EXEC.
00984             MOVE 'ORCHM02' TO DFHEIV1 MOVE 'ORCHSC2' TO DFHEIV2 MOVE -1
00985             TO DFHEIV11 MOVE '    J     ' TO DFHEIVO CALL 'DFHEI1'
00986             USING DFHEIVO DFHEIV1 MAP2-AREA DFHEIV98 DFHEIV2 DFHEIV99
00987             DFHEIV99 DFHEIV99 DFHEIV11.
00988
```

Fig. 20.6. (Continued)

```
24          ORCH01A          15.48.02          12/27/80


           MOVE  '2'  TO  COMMAREA-PROCESS-SW.

           GO TO RETURN-AT-ORDER-VALIDATE.


       RECORD-NOT-FOUND.

           MOVE 'RECORD NOT FOUND' TO MAP2-ERRORS (1).
           MOVE -1          TO  MAP2-ORDER-NUMBER-L.
           GO TO DISPLAY-ERROR-SCREEN.
```

Fig. 20.6. (Continued)

```
      25          ORCH01A         15.48.02        12/27/80

01001         *****************************************************************
01002         *
01003           ORDER-VERIFICATION SECTION.                                  *
01004         *
01005         *                                                             **
                                                                            ***

01007         *     EXEC CICS
01008         *         RECEIVE MAP     ('ORCHM01')
01009         *                 MAPSET ('ORCHS01')
01010         *                 SET    (MAP1-POINTER)
01011         *     END-EXEC.
01012               MOVE 'ORCHM01' TO DFHEIV1 MOVE 'ORCHS01' TO DFHEIV2 MOVE '
01013         -     '              ' TO DFHEIVO CALL 'DFHEI1' USING DFHEIVO
01014               DFHEIV1 MAP1-POINTER DFHEIV98 DFHEIV2.
01015
01016
01017               IF MAP1-ORDER-NUMBER NOT NUMERIC
01018                   GO TO INVALID-ORDER-NUMBER.

01020               MOVE MAP1-ORDER-NUMBER TO TWA-ORDER-RECORD-KEY.

01022         *     EXEC CICS
01023         *         HANDLE CONDITION
01024         *             NOTOPEN (FILE-NOT-OPEN)
01025         *             NOTFND  (RECORD-NOT-FOUND-VERIFY)
01026         *     END-EXEC.
01027               MOVE '                      ' TO DFHEIVO CALL 'DFHEI1' USING
01028               DFHEIVO GO TO FILE-NOT-OPEN RECORD-NOT-FOUND-VERIFY
01029               DEPENDING ON DFHEIGDI.
01030
01031
01032         *     EXEC CICS
01033         *         READ DATASET ('ORTEST')
01034         *             SET     (POM-POINTER)
01035         *             RIDFLD  (TWA-ORDER-RECORD-KEY)
01036         *     END-EXEC.
01037               MOVE 'ORTEST' TO DFHEIV3 MOVE '         ' TO DFHEIVO CALL 'D
01038         -     'FHEI1' USING DFHEIVO DFHEIV3 POM-POINTER DFHEIV98
01039               TWA-ORDER-RECORD-KEY.
01040
01041
01042           SECURE-DATA-MAP.

01044         *     EXEC CICS
01045         *         GETMAIN
01046         *             SET     (MAP2-POINTER)
01047         *             LENGTH  (1139)
01048         *             INITIMG (HEX-ZEROES)
01049         *     END-EXEC.
01050               MOVE 1139 TO DFHEIV11 MOVE '        ' TO DFHEIVO CALL 'DFHE
01051         -     'I1' USING DFHEIVO MAP2-POINTER DFHEIV11 HEX-ZEROES.
01052
```

Fig. 20.6. (Continued)

```
 26          ORCHO1A          15.48.02          12/27/80

               MOVE  ORDER-NUMBER            TO   MAP2-ORDER-NUMBER.
               MOVE  ORDER-DEPARTMENT        TO   MAP2-DEPARTMENT.
               MOVE  ORDER-DATE-MONTH        TO   MAP2-ORDER-DATE-MONTH.
               MOVE  ORDER-DATE-DAY          TO   MAP2-ORDER-DATE-DAY.
               MOVE  ORDER-DATE-YEAR         TO   MAP2-ORDER-DATE-YEAR.
               MOVE  ORDER-DATE-ENTERED      TO   MAP2-ORDER-DATE-ENTERED.
               MOVE  ORDER-TOTAL-COST        TO   MAP2-TOTAL-COST.
               MOVE  ORDER-TOTAL-PRICE       TO   MAP2-TOTAL-PRICE.
               SET  ORDER-LINE-I             TO   1.
               PERFORM LAYOUT-EACH-LINE
                   UNTIL ORDER-LINE-I GREATER THAN ORDER-LINE-COUNT.
               GO TO DISPLAY-ORDER.

           LAYOUT-EACH-LINE.
               SET MAP2-LINE-I                              TO ORDER-LINE-I.
               MOVE ORDER-LINE-ITEM (ORDER-LINE-I) TO TWA-LINE-ITEM-ORDER.
               MOVE MAP2-LINE-ITEM (MAP2-LINE-I)     TO TWA-LINE-ITEM-MAP.
               MOVE TWA-ITEM-NUMBER-ORDER      TO   TWA-ITEM-NUMBER-MAP.
               MOVE TWA-ITEM-DESCRIPTION-ORDER TO TWA-ITEM-DESCRIPTION-MAP.
               MOVE TWA-ITEM-DATE-ORDER        TO   TWA-ITEM-DATE-MAP.
               MOVE TWA-UNIT-ORDER             TO   TWA-UNIT-MAP.
               MOVE TWA-UNIT-COST-ORDER        TO   TWA-UNIT-COST-MAP.
               COMPUTE TWA-COST-MAP = TWA-UNIT-ORDER * TWA-UNIT-COST-ORDER.
               MOVE TWA-UNIT-PRICE-ORDER       TO   TWA-UNIT-PRICE-MAP.
               COMPUTE TWA-PRICE-MAP =
                           TWA-UNIT-ORDER * TWA-UNIT-PRICE-ORDER.
               MOVE TWA-LINE-ITEM-MAP     TO   MAP2-LINE-ITEM (MAP2-LINE-I).
               SET ORDER-LINE-I UP BY 1.

           DISPLAY-ORDER.

          *    EXEC CICS
          *         SEND MAP     ('ORCHM02')
          *              MAPSET ('ORCHS02')
          *              FROM    (MAP2-AREA)
          *              ERASE
          *    END-EXEC.
                MOVE 'ORCHM02' TO DFHEIV1 MOVE 'ORCHS02' TO DFHEIV2 MOVE '
          -     '          S      ' TO DFHEIV0 CALL 'DFHEI1' USING DFHEIV0
                DFHEIV1 MAP2-AREA DFHEIV98 DFHEIV2.

          *    EXEC CICS
          *         FREEMAIN DATA (MAP2-AREA)
          *    END-EXEC.
                MOVE '           ' TO DFHEIV0 CALL 'DFHEI1' USING DFHEIV0
                MAP2-AREA.
```

Fig. 20.6. (Continued)

```
     27        ORCH01A           15.48.02          12/27/80

               MOVE EIBTRMID    TO   TSA-TERM-ID.
               MOVE EIBTRNID    TO   TSA-TRANS-ID.

          *    EXEC CICS
          *         READQ TS
          *              QUEUE   (TSA-QUEUE-ID)
          *              SET     (TSA-POINTER)
          *              LENGTH  (TSA-LENGTH)
          *              ITEM    (1)
          *    END-EXEC.
                MOVE 1 TO DFHEIV11 MOVE '  Y       ' TO DFHEIV0 CALL 'DFHEI1'
                USING DFHEIV0 TSA-QUEUE-ID TSA-POINTER TSA-LENGTH DFHEIV99
                DFHEIV11.




               MOVE TWA-ORDER-RECORD-KEY   TO   TSA-ORDER-NUMBER.
               MOVE ORDER-LINE-COUNT       TO   TSA-POM-NUMBER-OF-LINES.
               SET ORDER-LINE-I            TO   1.
               PERFORM MOVE-ORDER-LINES-TO-TSA
                   UNTIL ORDER-LINE-I GREATER THAN ORDER-LINE-COUNT.
               GO TO REWRITE-TSA-AT-VERIFY.

           MOVE-ORDER-LINES-TO-TSA.
               SET TSA-LINE-I           TO   ORDER-LINE-I.
               MOVE ORDER-LINE-ITEM (ORDER-LINE-I)
                                        TO   TSA-ORDER-LINE (TSA-LINE-I).
               MOVE SPACE               TO   TSA-LINE-FUNCTION (TSA-LINE-I).
               SET ORDER-LINE-I UP BY 1.

           REWRITE-TSA-AT-VERIFY.

               MOVE 1    TO   TSA-QUEUE-NO.

          *    EXEC CICS
          *         WRITEQ TS
          *              QUEUE   (TSA-QUEUE-ID)
          *              FROM    (TSA-AREA)
          *              LENGTH  (TSA-LENGTH)
          *              ITEM    (TSA-QUEUE-NO)
          *              REWRITE
          *    END-EXEC.
                MOVE '  Y       ' TO DFHEIV0 CALL 'DFHEI1' USING DFHEIV0
                TSA-QUEUE-ID TSA-AREA TSA-LENGTH DFHEIV99 TSA-QUEUE-NO.
```

Fig. 20.6. (Continued)

```
28        ORCH01A        15.48.02        12/27/80


          MOVE  '2'  TO  COMMAREA-PROCESS-SW.

       RETURN-AT-ORDER-VERIFY.
      *    EXEC CICS
      *         RETURN TRANSID  (EIBTRNID)
      *                COMMAREA (COMMUNICATION-AREA)
      *                LENGTH   (1)
      *    END-EXEC.
            MOVE 1 TO DFHEIV11 MOVE '          ' TO DFHEIV0 CALL 'DFHEI1'
            USING DFHEIV0 EIBTRNID COMMUNICATION-AREA DFHEIV11.




       RECORD-NOT-FOUND-VERIFY.
           MOVE 'RECORD NOT FOUND' TO  MAP1-ERROR.
           GO TO SEND-MAP-VERIFY-ERROR.

       SEND-MAP-VERIFY-ERROR.

      *    EXEC CICS
      *         SEND MAP    ('ORCHM01')
      *              MAPSET ('ORCHS01')
      *              FROM   (MAP1-AREA)
      *              DATAONLY
      *    END-EXEC.
            MOVE 'ORCHM01' TO DFHEIV1 MOVE 'ORCHS01' TO DFHEIV2 MOVE '
      -    '          ' TO DFHEIV0 CALL 'DFHEI1' USING DFHEIV0
            DFHEIV1 MAP1-AREA DFHEIV98 DFHEIV2.



           MOVE  '1'  TO  COMMAREA-PROCESS-SW.
           GO TO RETURN-AT-ORDER-VERIFY.

       INVALID-ORDER-NUMBER.
           MOVE 'INVALID ORDER NUMBER' TO MAP1-ERROR.
           GO TO SEND-MAP-VERIFY-ERROR.
```

Fig. 20.6. (Continued)

```
    29          ORCH01A          15.48.02          12/27/80

           *****************************************************************
           *                                                               *
            BYPASS-INPUT SECTION.
           *                                                               *
           *****************************************************************

           *     EXEC CICS
           *          GETMAIN
           *               SET      (MAP1-POINTER)
           *               LENGTH   (57)
           *               INITIMG  (HEX-ZEROES)
           *     END-EXEC.
                  MOVE 57 TO DFHEIV11 MOVE '          ' TO DFHEIV0 CALL 'DFHEI1
           -     '' USING DFHEIV0 MAP1-POINTER DFHEIV11 HEX-ZEROES.

                 MOVE 'ORDER BYPASSED - CONTINUE' TO MAP1-ERROR.

           *     EXEC CICS
           *          SEND MAP     ('ORCHM01')
           *               MAPSET  ('ORCHS01')
           *               FROM    (MAP1-AREA)
           *               ERASE
           *     END-EXEC.
                  MOVE 'ORCHM01' TO DFHEIV1 MOVE 'ORCHS01' TO DFHEIV2 MOVE '
           -      '         S     ' TO DFHEIV0 CALL 'DFHEI1' USING DFHEIV0
                  DFHEIV1 MAP1-AREA DFHEIV98 DFHEIV2.

                 MOVE '1' TO COMMAREA-PROCESS-SW.

           *     EXEC CICS
           *          RETURN TRANSID   (EIBTRNID)
           *                 COMMAREA  (COMMUNICATION-AREA)
           *                 LENGTH    (1)
           *     END-EXEC.
                  MOVE 1 TO DFHEIV11 MOVE '          ' TO DFHEIV0 CALL 'DFHEI1'
                  USING DFHEIV0 EIBTRNID COMMUNICATION-AREA DFHEIV11.
```

Fig. 20.6. (Continued)

```
   30        ORCHO1A          15.48.02          12/27/80

          ************************************************************************
          *                                                                      *
           INITIALIZATION SECTION.
          *                                                                      *
          ************************************************************************

          *     EXEC CICS
          *          HANDLE CONDITION
          *                QIDERR (GET-STORAGE-FOR-TSA)
          *     END-EXEC.
                 MOVE '                         ' TO DFHEIVO CALL 'DFHEI1' USING
                 DFHEIVO GO TO GET-STORAGE-FOR-TSA DEPENDING ON DFHEIGDI.


                MOVE EIBTRMID    TO   TSA-TERM-ID.
                MOVE 'ORCH'      TO   TSA-TRANS-ID.

          *     EXEC CICS
          *          DELETEQ TS
          *                QUEUE (TSA-QUEUE-ID)
          *     END-EXEC.
                 MOVE '           ' TO DFHEIVO CALL 'DFHEI1' USING DFHEIVO
                 TSA-QUEUE-ID.


           GET-STORAGE-FOR-TSA.

          *     EXEC CICS
          *          GETMAIN
          *                SET    (TSA-POINTER)
          *                LENGTH (429)
          *     END-EXEC.
                 MOVE 429 TO DFHEIV11 MOVE '           ' TO DFHEIVO CALL 'DFHEI
          -     '1' USING DFHEIVO TSA-POINTER DFHEIV11.



                MOVE 429                    TO   TSA-LENGTH.

          *     EXEC CICS
          *          WRITEQ TS
          *                QUEUE   (TSA-QUEUE-ID)
          *                FROM    (TSA-AREA)
          *                LENGTH (TSA-LENGTH)
          *     END-EXEC.
                 MOVE '           ' TO DFHEIVO CALL 'DFHEI1' USING DFHEIVO
                 TSA-QUEUE-ID TSA-AREA TSA-LENGTH.




          *     EXEC CICS
          *          FREEMAIN DATA (TSA-AREA)
```

Fig. 20.6. (Continued)

```
   31        ORCH01A          15.48.02          12/27/80

      *    END-EXEC.
            MOVE '          ' TO DFHEIVO CALL 'DFHEI1' USING DFHEIVO
            TSA-AREA.

      *    EXEC CICS
      *         GETMAIN
      *              SET      (MAP1-POINTER)
      *              LENGTH   (57)
      *              INITIMG  (HEX-ZEROES)
      *    END-EXEC.
            MOVE 57 TO DFHEIV11 MOVE '          ' TO DFHEIVO CALL 'DFHEI1
      -    '' USING DFHEIVO MAP1-POINTER DFHEIV11 HEX-ZEROES.




           MOVE 'ENTER FIRST ORDER' TO MAP1-ERROR.

      *    EXEC CICS
      *         SEND MAP     ('ORCHM01')
      *              MAPSET  ('ORCHS01')
      *              FROM    (MAP1-AREA)
      *              ERASE
      *    END-EXEC.
            MOVE 'ORCHM01' TO DFHEIV1 MOVE 'ORCHS01' TO DFHEIV2 MOVE '
      -    '         S    ' TO DFHEIVO CALL 'DFHEI1' USING DFHEIVO
            DFHEIV1 MAP1-AREA DFHEIV98 DFHEIV2.



           MOVE  '1'  TO COMMAREA-PROCESS-SW.

      *    EXEC CICS
      *         RETURN TRANSID  ('ORCH')
      *                COMMAREA (COMMUNICATION-AREA)
      *                LENGTH   (1)
      *    END-EXEC.
            MOVE 'ORCH' TO DFHEIV5 MOVE 1 TO DFHEIV11 MOVE '
            TO DFHEIVO CALL 'DFHEI1' USING DFHEIVO DFHEIV5
            COMMUNICATION-AREA DFHEIV11.


```

Fig. 20.6. (Continued)

```
32          ORCHO1A          15.48.02          12/27/80

            *****************************************************************
            *                                                               *
             FINALIZATION SECTION.
            *                                                               *
            *****************************************************************

             PREPARE-TERMINATION-MESSAGE.
                 MOVE JOB-NORMAL-END-MESSAGE TO TWA-OPERATOR-MESSAGE.


             JOB-TERMINATED.

            *    EXEC CICS
            *         SEND FROM    (TWA-OPERATOR-MESSAGE)
            *              LENGTH (31)
            *              ERASE
            *    END-EXEC.
                  MOVE 31 TO DFHEIV11 MOVE '                ' TO DFHEIV0 CALL '
            -    'DFHEI1' USING DFHEIV0 DFHEIV99 DFHEIV98 TWA-OPERATOR-MESSAGE
                  DFHEIV11.


            *    EXEC CICS
            *         HANDLE CONDITION
            *              QIDERR (END-OF-JOB)
            *    END-EXEC.
                  MOVE '                  ' TO DFHEIV0 CALL 'DFHEI1' USING
                  DFHEIV0 GO TO END-OF-JOB DEPENDING ON DFHEIGDI.


                 MOVE EIBTRMID   TO   TSA-TERM-ID.
                 MOVE EIBTRNID   TO   TSA-TRANS-ID.

            *    EXEC CICS
            *         DELETEQ TS
            *              QUEUE (TSA-QUEUE-ID)
            *    END-EXEC.
                  MOVE '       ' TO DFHEIV0 CALL 'DFHEI1' USING DFHEIV0
                  TSA-QUEUE-ID.



             END-OF-JOB.

            *    EXEC CICS
            *         RETURN
            *    END-EXEC.
                  MOVE '       ' TO DFHEIV0 CALL 'DFHEI1' USING DFHEIV0.

```

Fig. 20.6. (Continued)

```
    33          ORCH01A           15.48.02          12/27/80

            *****************************************************************
            *                                                               *
             ABNORMAL-TERMINATION SECTION.
            *                                                               *
            *****************************************************************

             FILE-NOT-OPEN.

            *     EXEC CICS
            *          XCTL PROGRAM ('TEL2OPEN')
            *     END-EXEC.
                   MOVE 'TEL2OPEN' TO DFHEIV3 MOVE '            ' TO DFHEIV0 CALL
                  'DFHEI1' USING DFHEIV0 DFHEIV3.

             MAPFAIL-ERROR.
                  MOVE 'MAP FAILURE' TO MAJOR-ERROR-MSG.
                  GO TO PREPARE-ABORT-MESSAGE.


             PROCESS-SWITCH-ERROR.
                  MOVE 'PROCESS ERROR' TO MAJOR-ERROR-MSG.
                  GO TO PREPARE-ABORT-MESSAGE.


             SIGN-ON-VIOLATION.
                  MOVE 'SIGNON VIOLATION' TO MAJOR-ERROR-MSG.
                  GO TO PREPARE-ABORT-MESSAGE.


             MAJOR-ERROR.
                  MOVE   EIBFN      TO   OLD-EIBFN.
                  MOVE   EIBRCODE   TO   OLD-EIBRCODE.

            *     EXEC CICS
            *          DUMP DUMPCODE ('ERRS')
            *     END-EXEC.
                   MOVE 'ERRS' TO DFHEIV5 MOVE '            ' TO DFHEIV0 CALL 'DFH
            -     'EI1' USING DFHEIV0 DFHEIV5.

                  MOVE 'MAJOR ERROR' TO MAJOR-ERROR-MSG.
                  GO TO PREPARE-ABORT-MESSAGE.


             PREPARE-ABORT-MESSAGE.
                  MOVE JOB-ABORTED-MESSAGE TO TWA-OPERATOR-MESSAGE.
                  GO TO JOB-TERMINATED.
```

Fig. 20.6. (Continued)

THE INITIALIZATION SECTION

1. Lines 1246–1251. HANDLE CONDITION command for the temporary storage queue to be deleted.
2. Lines 1257–1262. Delete the old temporary storage queue.*
3. Lines 1267–1273. GETMAIN command to secure main storage for the new temporary storage record to be created.
4. Lines 1279–1286. WRITEQ TS command to write the temporary storage record that will be used as a scratchpad.
5. Lines 1291–1295. FREEMAIN DATA command to release main storage for the temporary storage record secured through the GETMAIN command in lines 1267–1273.
6. Lines 1297–1304. GETMAIN command to secure main storage for the map to be displayed, which will include a program-generated message.
7. Lines 1311–1319. SEND MAP command to display the map. The "ENTER FIRST ORDER" message is included in the display.
8. Line 1323. Set the communication area switch to 1.
9. Lines 1325–1332. RETURN command to terminate the task.

THE ORDER-VERIFICATION SECTION

1. Lines 1007–1014. RECEIVE MAP command to read the order number entered by the operator.
2. Lines 1022–1029. HANDLE CONDITION command for the order file.
3. Lines 1032–1039. READ DATASET command to read the file.

---

*This is a precautionary measure. See page 211.

4. If the record is in the file:
   a. Lines 1044–1051. GETMAIN command for the map that will contain the data from the record just read.
   b. Lines 1056–1083. Move the data from the record into the map to be displayed. Lines 1070–1083 illustrate a Cobol efficiency technique that reduces the use of an index.
   c. Lines 1087–1095. SEND MAP command to display the data from the record.
   d. Lines 1099–1103. FREEMAIN DATA command to release main storage secured for the map in the GETMAIN command in lines 1044–1051.
   e. Lines 1108–1117. READQ TS command to read the temporary storage record to be used as a scratchpad.
   f. Lines 1122–1134. Move the data from the record into the temporary storage record.
   g. Lines 1140–1149. WRITEQ TS command with the REWRITE option to rewrite the temporary storage record.
   h. Line 1156. Set the communication area switch to 2.
   i. Lines 1158–1165. RETURN command to terminate the task.

5. If the record is not in the file:
   a. Lines 1176–1184. SEND MAP command to display the "RECORD NOT FOUND" message.
   b. Line 1188. Set the communication area switch to 1.
   c. Line 1189. RETURN command to terminate the task.

THE ORDER-VALIDATION SECTION

1. Lines 443–450. RECEIVE MAP command to read the data entered by the operator.

2. Lines 456–465. READQ TS command to read the temporary storage record to be used as a scratchpad.

3. Lines 470–850. The editing of the data.

4. If there are no errors:
   a. Lines 869–876. HANDLE CONDITION command for the order file.
   b. Lines 880–888. READ DATASET command with the UPDATE option to make the record available for update.
   c. Lines 892–934. Move the changes to the order record.
   d. Lines 939–946. REWRITE DATASET command to update the record.
   e. Lines 949–957. SEND MAP command to display the next map required by the operator.
   f. Line 961. Set the communication area switch to 1.
   g. Lines 965–971. RETURN command to terminate the task.

5. If there are errors:
   a. Lines 977–987. SEND MAP command to display the error messages.
   b. Line 991. Set the communication area switch to 2.
   c. Line 993. RETURN command to terminate the task.

THE BYPASS-INPUT SECTION

1. Lines 1201–1208. GETMAIN command to secure main storage for the map that will contain the message.
2. Lines 1215–1223. SEND MAP command to display the "ORDER BYPASSED – CONTINUE" message.
3. Line 1227. Set the communication area switch to 1.
4. Lines 1229–1235. RETURN command to terminate the task.

THE FINALIZATION SECTION

1. Lines 1347–1354. Display the "JOB NORMALLY TERMINATED" message.
2. Lines 1357–1362. HANDLE CONDITION command for the temporary storage queue.
3. Lines 1368–1373. DELETEQ TS command to delete the temporary storage queue used as a scratchpad.

4. Lines 1379–1382. RETURN command to terminate the session.

THE ABNORMAL-TERMINATION SECTION

These are the routines used to abnormally terminate the session on errors and CICS/VS exceptional conditions not covered by a HANDLE CONDITION command.

EXAMPLE

The following are facsimiles of actual photographs taken of a CRT terminal during a session.

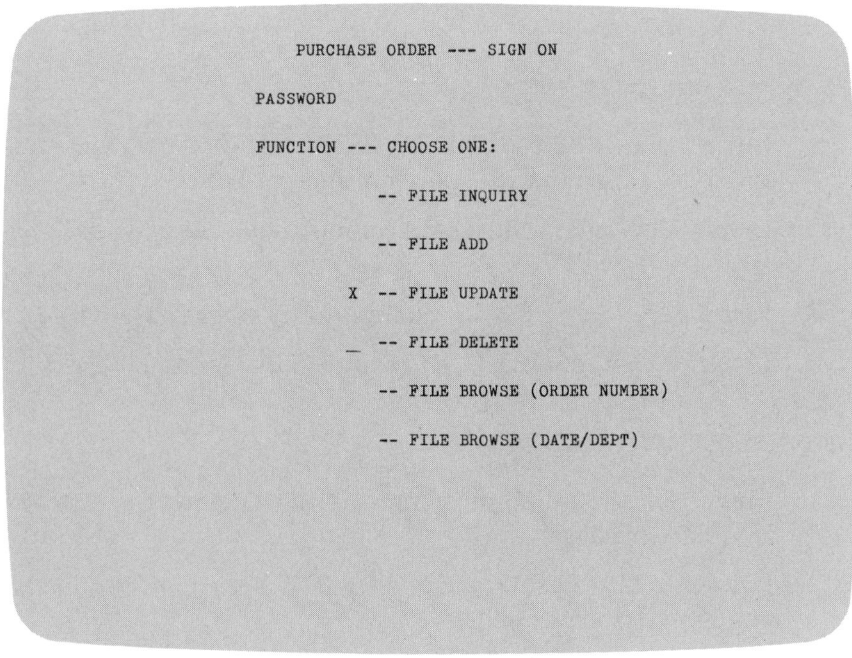

Fig. 20.7. The File Update application is selected by keying in an "X" on the File Update line and the corresponding password, then hitting the ENTER key.

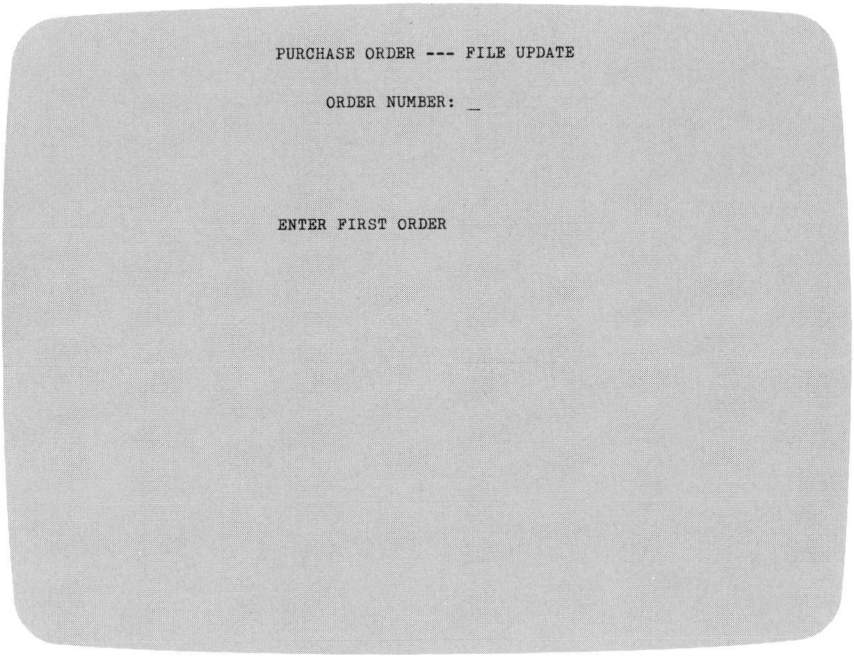

Fig. 20.8. The Sign On program executes which then transfers control to the File Update program. This displays the order number map.

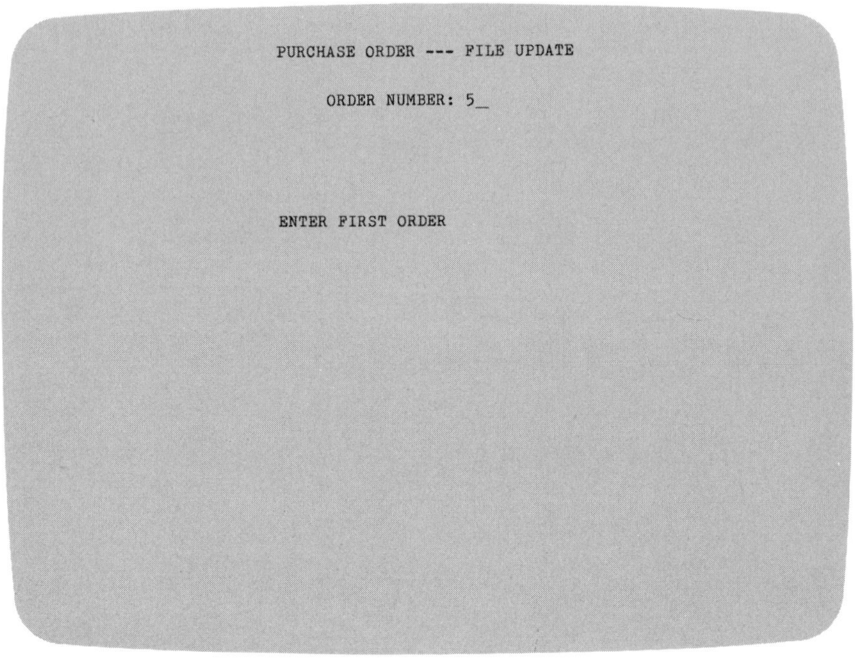

Fig. 20.9. The operator keys in the order number of the record to be updated, then hits the ENTER key.

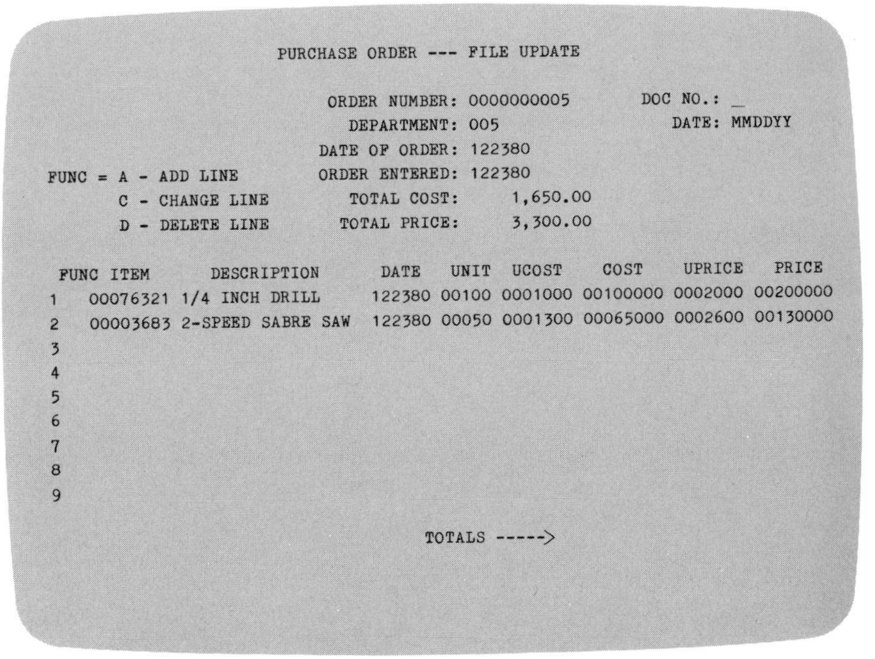
PURCHASE ORDER --- FILE UPDATE
ORDER NUMBER: 0000000005
DOC NO.: _
DEPARTMENT: 005
DATE: MMDDYY
DATE OF ORDER: 122380
FUNC = A - ADD LINE
ORDER ENTERED: 122380
C - CHANGE LINE
TOTAL COST: 1,650.00
D - DELETE LINE
TOTAL PRICE: 3,300.00
FUNC ITEM DESCRIPTION DATE UNIT UCOST COST UPRICE PRICE
1 00076321 1/4 INCH DRILL 122380 00100 0001000 00100000 0002000 00200000
2 00003683 2-SPEED SABRE SAW 122380 00050 0001300 00065000 0002600 00130000
3
4
5
6
7
8
9
TOTALS ----->

Fig. 20.10. The program displays the record.

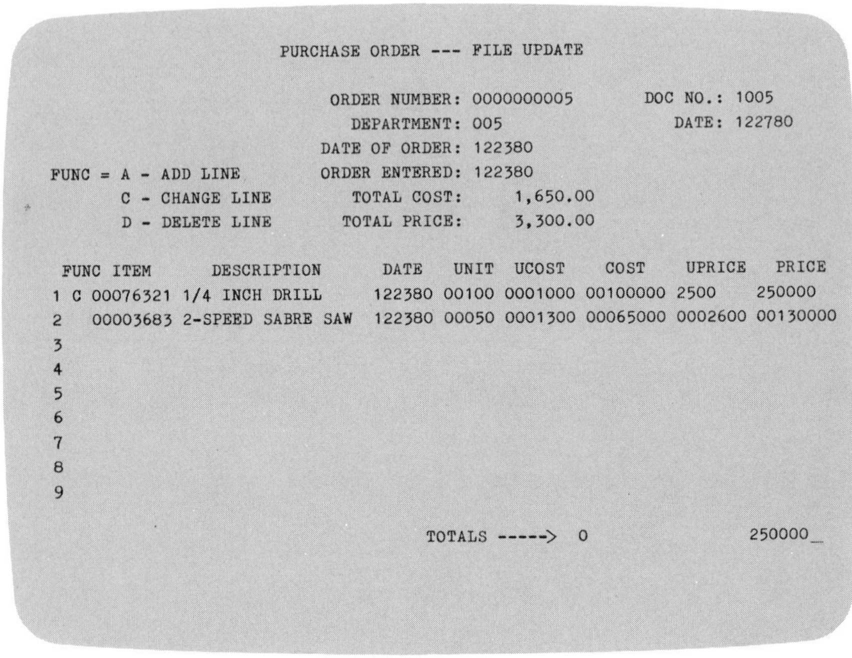

```
                         PURCHASE ORDER --- FILE UPDATE

                            ORDER NUMBER: 0000000005         DOC NO.: 1005
                              DEPARTMENT: 005                  DATE: 122780
                           DATE OF ORDER: 122380
FUNC = A - ADD LINE       ORDER ENTERED: 122380
       C - CHANGE LINE       TOTAL COST:        1,650.00
       D - DELETE LINE      TOTAL PRICE:        3,300.00

 FUNC ITEM       DESCRIPTION        DATE   UNIT  UCOST     COST     UPRICE    PRICE
1 C 00076321 1/4 INCH DRILL       122380 00100 0001000 00100000 2500      250000
2   00003683 2-SPEED SABRE SAW    122380 00050 0001300 00065000 0002600 00130000
3
4
5
6
7
8
9
                                   TOTALS ----->  0                      250000_
```

Fig. 20.11. The operator keys in the changes to the record, then hits the ENTER key.

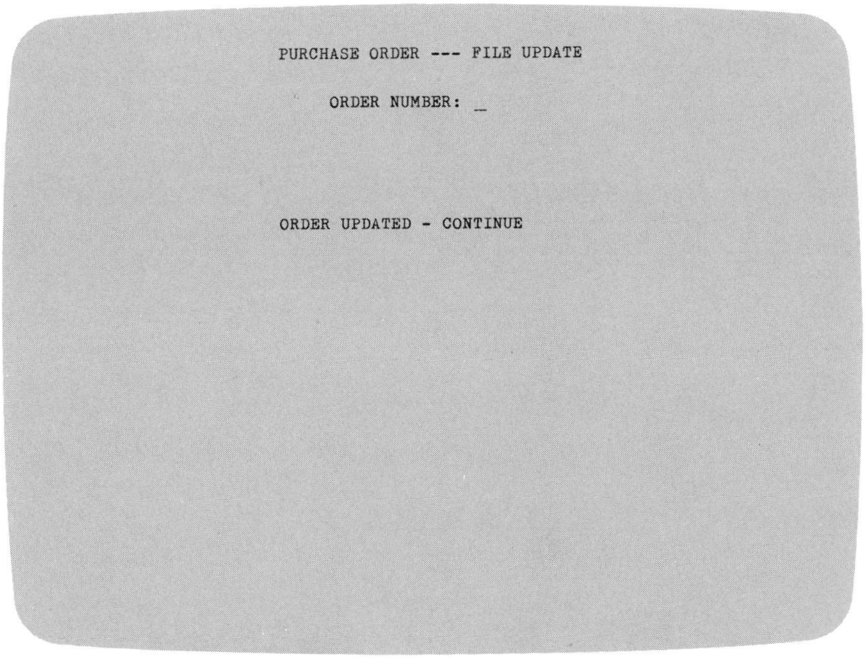

Fig. 20.12. If there are no errors from Fig. 20.11, the order is updated. The "ORDER UPDATED – CONTINUE" message is then displayed to inform the operator. He may then continue with the next order.

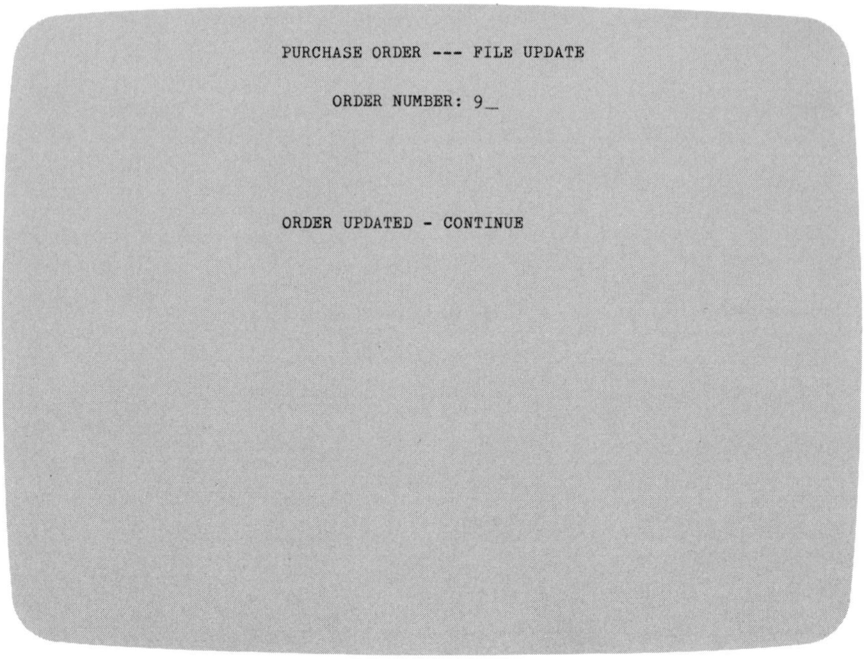

Fig. 20.13. The operator keys in the order number of the next order to be updated, then hits the ENTER key.

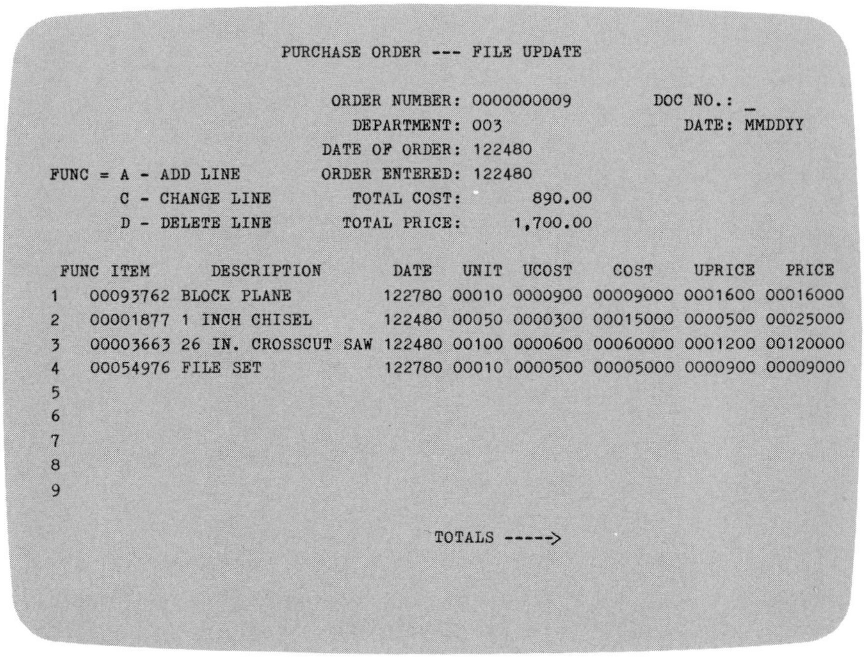
PURCHASE ORDER --- FILE UPDATE
ORDER NUMBER: 0000000009
DOC NO.: _
DEPARTMENT: 003
DATE: MMDDYY
DATE OF ORDER: 122480
FUNC = A - ADD LINE
ORDER ENTERED: 122480
C - CHANGE LINE
TOTAL COST: 890.00
D - DELETE LINE
TOTAL PRICE: 1,700.00
FUNC ITEM DESCRIPTION DATE UNIT UCOST COST UPRICE PRICE
1 00093762 BLOCK PLANE 122780 00010 0000900 00009000 0001600 00016000
2 00001877 1 INCH CHISEL 122480 00050 0000300 00015000 0000500 00025000
3 00003663 26 IN. CROSSCUT SAW 122480 00100 0000600 00060000 0001200 00120000
4 00054976 FILE SET 122780 00010 0000500 00005000 0000900 00009000
5
6
7
8
9
TOTALS ----->

Fig. 20.14. The program displays the record.

```
                         PURCHASE ORDER --- FILE UPDATE

                              ORDER NUMBER: 0000000009          DOC NO.: 1009
                                DEPARTMENT: 003                    DATE: 122780
                             DATE OF ORDER: 122480
FUNC = A - ADD LINE         ORDER ENTERED: 122480
       C - CHANGE LINE         TOTAL COST:         890.00
       D - DELETE LINE        TOTAL PRICE:       1,700.00

 FUNC ITEM        DESCRIPTION          DATE   UNIT  UCOST     COST     UPRICE    PRICE
1    00093762 BLOCK PLANE            122780 00010 0000900 00009000 0001600 00016000
2 C  00001877 1 INCH CHISEL          122480 00050 350     00015000 0000500 00025000
3 D  00003663 26 IN. CROSSCUT SAW    122480 00100 0000600 00060000 0001200 00120000
4    00054976 FILE SET               122780 00010 0000500 00005000 0000900 00009000
5 A           10 INCH HACKSAW               10    400     4000     800     8000_
6
7
8
9

                                          TOTALS ---->
```

Fig. 20.15. The operator keys in the changes to the record, then hits the ENTER key.

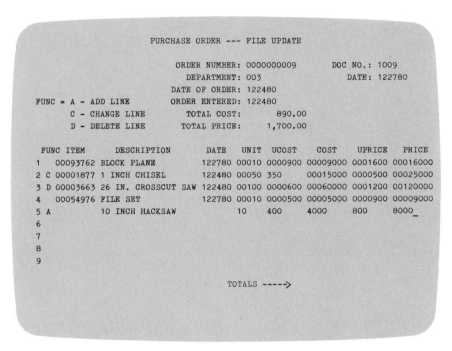

```
                           PURCHASE ORDER --- FILE UPDATE

                              ORDER NUMBER: 0000000009          DOC NO.: 00001009
                                DEPARTMENT: 003                     DATE: 122780
                             DATE OF ORDER: 122480
FUNC = A - ADD LINE          ORDER ENTERED: 122480
       C - CHANGE LINE          TOTAL COST:           890.00
       D - DELETE LINE         TOTAL PRICE:         1,700.00

FUNC ITEM        DESCRIPTION         DATE   UNIT   UCOST    COST     UPRICE   PRICE
1    00093762 BLOCK PLANE            122780 00010 0000900 00009000 0001600 00016000
2 C  00001877 1 INCH CHISEL          122480 00050 0000350 00015000 0000500 00025000
3 D  00003663 26 IN. CROSSCUT SAW    122480 00100 0000600 00060000 0001200 00120000
4    00054976 FILE SET               122780 00010 0000500 00005000 0000900 00009000
5 A           10 INCH HACKSAW               00010 0000400 00004000 0000800 00008000
6
7
8
9

                                        TOTALS ----->

LINE 2 - COST NOT ENTERED                  LINE 5 - INCOMPLETE ADD
INCORRECT TOTAL COST                       INCORRECT TOTAL PRICE
```

Fig. 20.16. Four errors are detected. Note that the cursor is under the first error detected.

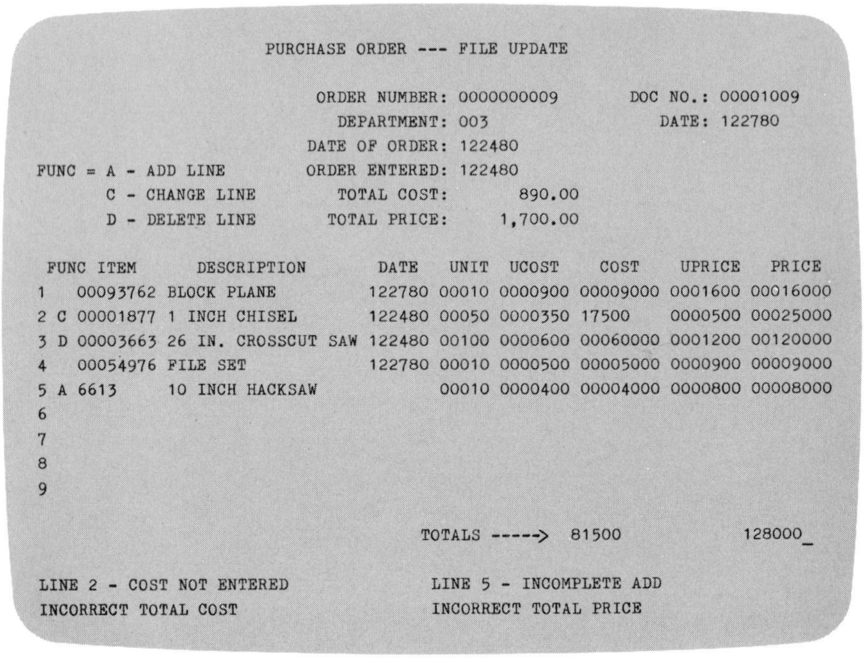

```
                         PURCHASE ORDER --- FILE UPDATE

                              ORDER NUMBER: 0000000009         DOC NO.: 00001009
                                DEPARTMENT: 003                   DATE: 122780
                             DATE OF ORDER: 122480
FUNC = A - ADD LINE         ORDER ENTERED: 122480
       C - CHANGE LINE         TOTAL COST:          890.00
       D - DELETE LINE        TOTAL PRICE:        1,700.00

 FUNC ITEM       DESCRIPTION         DATE   UNIT  UCOST    COST     UPRICE   PRICE
1    00093762 BLOCK PLANE          122780 00010 0000900 00009000 0001600 00016000
2 C 00001877 1 INCH CHISEL         122480 00050 0000350 17500    0000500 00025000
3 D 00003663 26 IN. CROSSCUT SAW  122480 00100 0000600 00060000 0001200 00120000
4    00054976 FILE SET             122780 00010 0000500 00005000 0000900 00009000
5 A 6613      10 INCH HACKSAW             00010 0000400 00004000 0000800 00008000
6
7
8
9

                                TOTALS ----> 81500                  128000_

LINE 2 - COST NOT ENTERED             LINE 5 - INCOMPLETE ADD
INCORRECT TOTAL COST                  INCORRECT TOTAL PRICE
```

Fig. 20.17. The operator keys in the corrections, then hits the ENTER key.

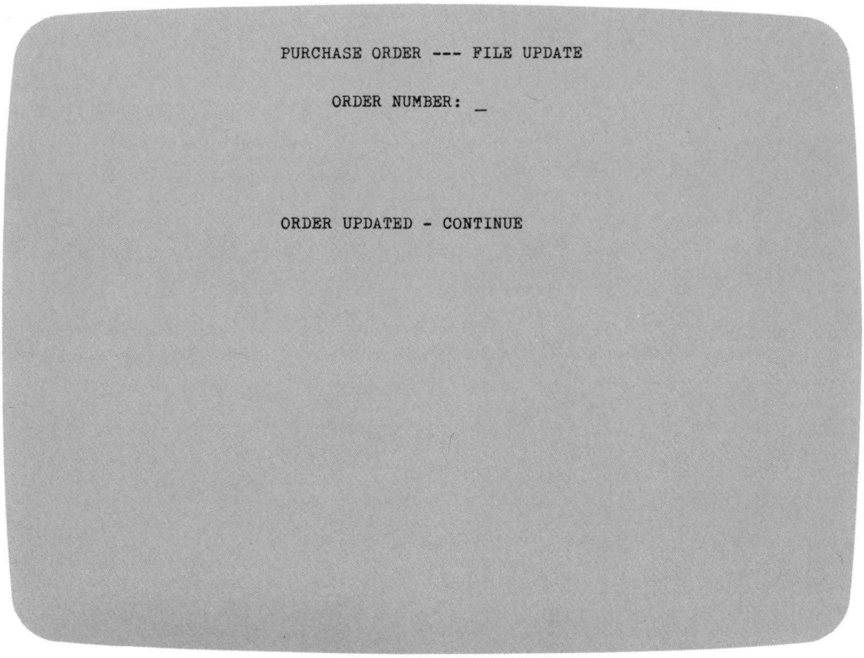

Fig. 20.18. If there are no more errors, the order is updated.

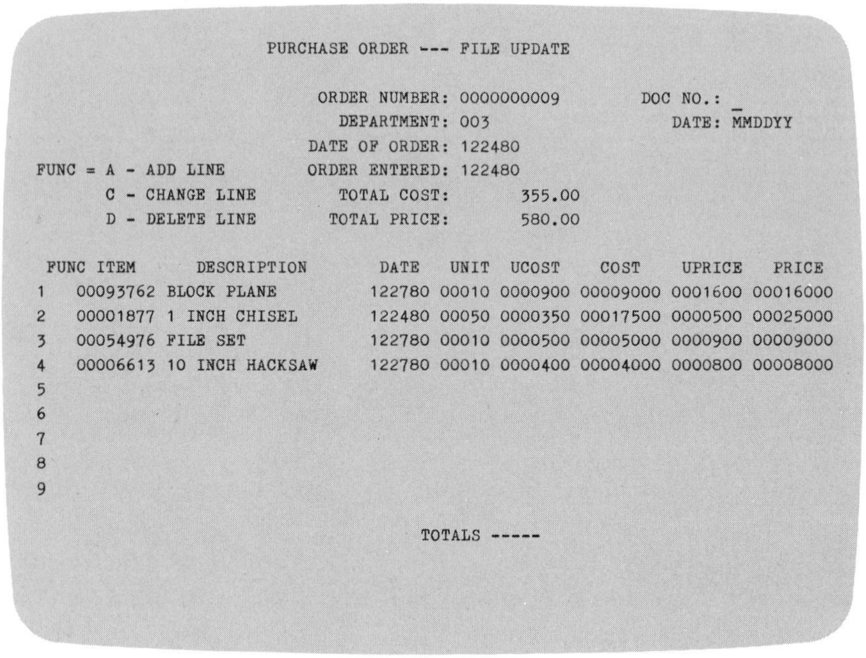

PURCHASE ORDER --- FILE UPDATE
ORDER NUMBER: 0000000009
DOC NO.: _
DEPARTMENT: 003
DATE: MMDDYY
DATE OF ORDER: 122480
FUNC = A - ADD LINE
ORDER ENTERED: 122480
C - CHANGE LINE
TOTAL COST: 355.00
D - DELETE LINE
TOTAL PRICE: 580.00
FUNC ITEM DESCRIPTION DATE UNIT UCOST COST UPRICE PRICE
1 00093762 BLOCK PLANE 122780 00010 0000900 00009000 0001600 00016000
2 00001877 1 INCH CHISEL 122480 00050 0000350 00017500 0000500 00025000
3 00054976 FILE SET 122780 00010 0000500 00005000 0000900 00009000
4 00006613 10 INCH HACKSAW 122780 00010 0000400 00004000 0000800 00008000
5
6
7
8
9
TOTALS -----

Fig. 20.19. The just-updated order is redisplayed. Note that the changes in Fig. 20.15 are reflected.

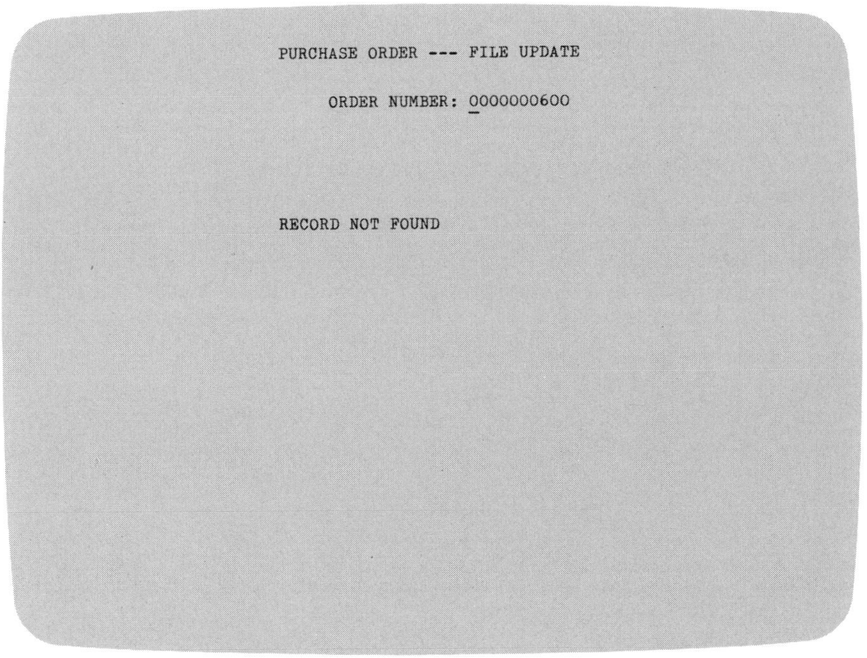

Fig. 20.20. If the record corresponding to the order number entered is not in the file, the "RECORD NOT FOUND" message is displayed.

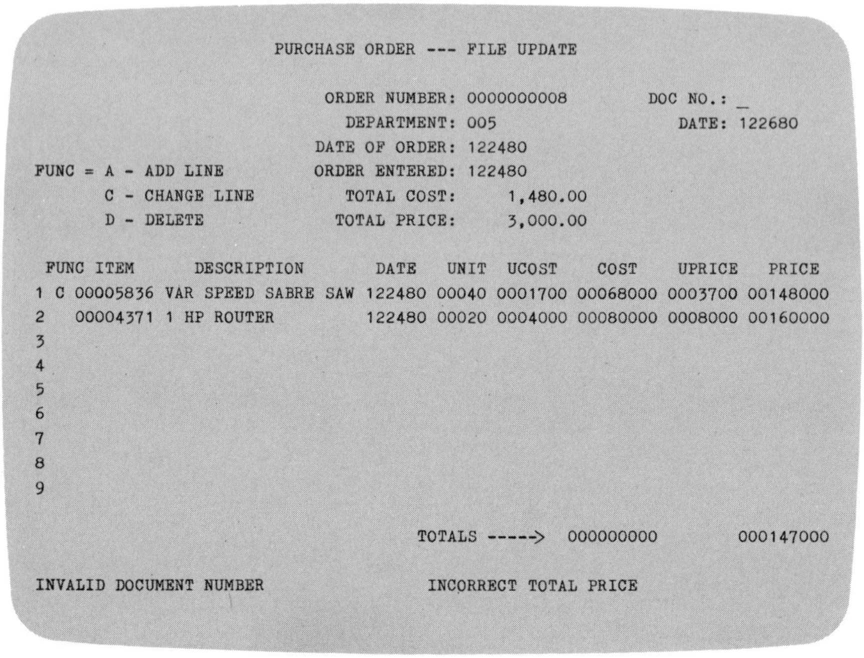

Fig. 20.21. If the operator wishes to discontinue the processing of an order after it has been displayed, he hits any PA key.

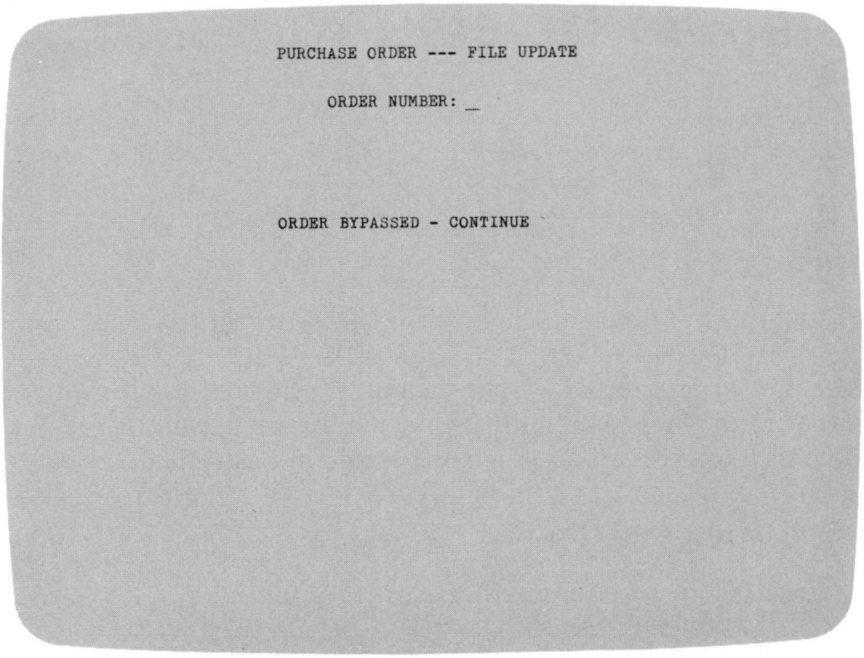

Fig. 20.22. A fresh order map is then displayed, along with the message "ORDER BYPASSED – CONTINUE". The operator may then continue with the next order.

21

The File Delete Program

INTRODUCTION

The File Delete program allows the operator to delete records from the order file according to the record key entered. The program executes when selected by the Sign-on program and will continue executing in the session until terminated by the operator. The flow of control to execute this program is shown in Figure 21.1.

PROGRAM SPECIFICATION

The File Delete program specifications are as follows:

1. Implement the program using the pseudoconversational mode of processing.
2. Use 'ORDL' as the transaction identifier. However, the session should not be started by using this identifier, but rather through an XCTL command from the Sign-on program.
3. If the session is started by using the transaction identifier, abort the session with the message "JOB ABORTED – SIGN-ON VIOLATION."
4. The record to be deleted is based on the order number.
5. If the order number entered is not numeric, display the message "INVALID ORDER NUMBER."
6. If the record is not in the file, display the message "RECORD NOT FOUND."
7. For (5) and (6), allow the operator to correct the order number.
8. If the record is in the file, delete it.
9. On any PA key, display the message "WRONG KEY USED"; allow the operator to continue with the session.

SCREEN LAYOUT

The screen layout to be used in the program is shown in Figure 21.2. All 9s are numeric fields and Xs are alphanumeric fields.

MAP PROGRAM

The map program corresponding to the screen layout is shown in Figure 21.3.

PROGRAM LISTING

The program listing for the File Delete program is given in Figure 21.4. The listing is that of the compiler and not the command-language translator, and thus the commands are already as translated.

THE MAIN-LINE SECTION

1. Lines 148–152. ADDRESS command for the TWA.
2. Lines 154–163. HANDLE AID command. The PA keys will result in the "WRONG KEY USED" error.
3. Lines 168–175. HANDLE CONDITION command.
4. Lines 178–183. The selection of sections.
5. Lines 185–186. If the program is executed at the start of the session by an operator-entered transaction identifier instead of through an XCTL command from the Sign-on program, a sign-on violation occurs. This is so if EIBCALEN is equal to zero.

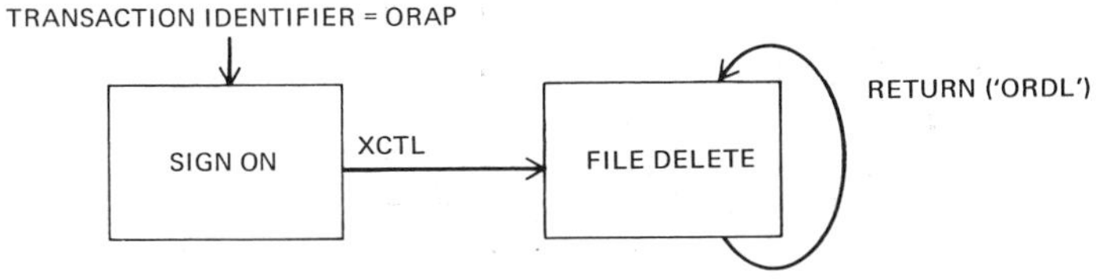

Fig. 21.1. File Delete Application.

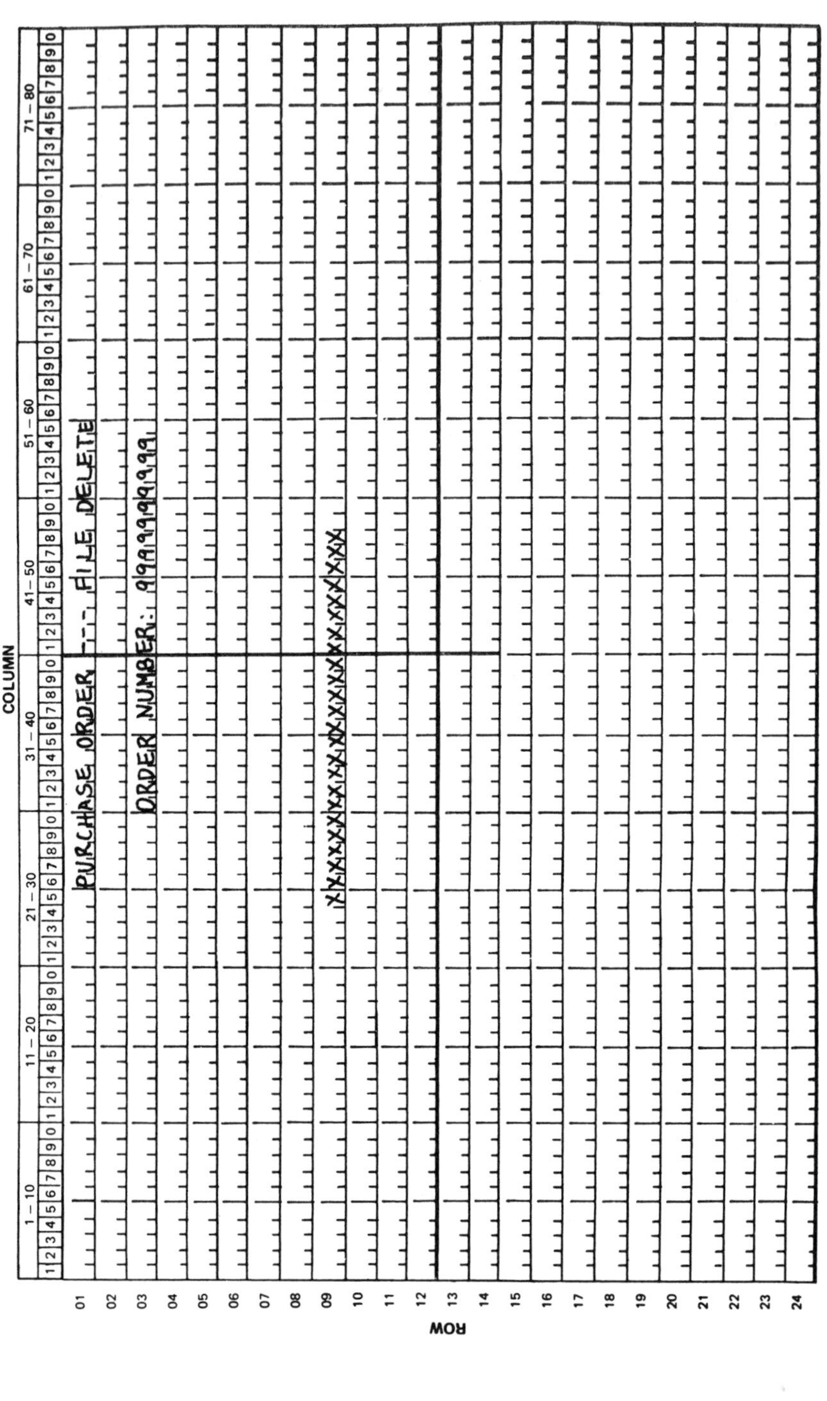

Fig. 21.2. Screen Layout – File Delete.

```
STMT    SOURCE STATEMENT                        DOS/VS ASSEMBLER REL 34.0 14.14

    1              PRINT NOGEN
    2 ORDLSO1      DFHMSD TYPE=MAP,MODE=INOUT,CTRL=FREEKB,LANG=COBOL,TIOAPFX=YES
   12 ORDLMO1      DFHMDI SIZE=(24,80)
   40 DUMMY        DFHMDF POS=(01,01),LENGTH=01,ATTRB=(ASKIP,DRK,FSET),        X
                          INITIAL='1'
   52              DFHMDF POS=(01,25),LENGTH=30,ATTRB=(ASKIP,BRT),             X
                          INITIAL='PURCHASE ORDER --- FILE DELETE'
   64              DFHMDF POS=(03,30),LENGTH=13,ATTRB=ASKIP,                   X
                          INITIAL='ORDER NUMBER '
   76 ORDER        DFHMDF POS=(03,44),LENGTH=10,ATTRB=(NUM,BRT,IC)
   87              DFHMDF POS=(03,55),LENGTH=01,ATTRB=PROT
   98 ERROR        DFHMDF POS=(09,24),LENGTH=24,ATTRB=(ASKIP,BRT)
  109              DFHMSD TYPE=FINAL
  123              END
```

Fig. 21.3. Map Program – File Delete.

```
    1  IBM DOS VS COBOL

CBL SUPMAP,STXIT,NOTRUNC,CSYNTAX,SXREF,OPT,VERB,CLIST,BUF=19069
CBL NOOPT,LIB
00001           IDENTIFICATION DIVISION.

00003           PROGRAM-ID. ORDL01A.

00005           ENVIRONMENT DIVISION.

00007           ***********************************************************
00008           *                                                         *
00009           *    1. THIS PROGRAM DELETES RECORDS FROM THE PURCHASE ORDER *
00010           *       MASTER FILE.                                      *
00011           *                                                         *
00012           ***********************************************************
```

Fig. 21.4. File Delete Program.

```
    2          ORDL01A          13.02.04         08/02/80

               DATA DIVISION.


               WORKING-STORAGE SECTION.


               01  COMMUNICATION-AREA.
                   05  COMMAREA-PROCESS-SW      PIC X.


               01  AREA1.


                   05  JOB-NORMAL-END-MESSAGE  PIC X(23) VALUE
                       'JOB NORMALLY TERMINATED'.

                   05  JOB-ABORTED-MESSAGE.
                     10  FILLER                PIC X(15) VALUE 'JOB ABORTED --'.
                     10  MAJOR-ERROR-MSG       PIC X(16).

                   05  HEXADECIMAL-ZEROES      PIC 9999 COMP VALUE ZEROES.

                   05  FILLER REDEFINES HEXADECIMAL-ZEROES.
                     10  FILLER                PIC X.
                     10  HEX-ZEROES            PIC X.

                   05  OLD-EIB-AREA.
                     10  FILLER                PIC X(7) VALUE 'OLD EIB'.
                     10  OLD-EIBFN             PIC XX.
                     10  OLD-EIBRCODE          PIC X(6).
```

Fig. 21.4. (Continued)

```
00042                 01  DFHEIVAR COPY DFHEIVAR.
00043 C               01  DFHEIVAR.
00044 C                   02   DFHEIVO  PICTURE X(26).
00045 C                   02   DFHEIV1  PICTURE X(8).
00046 C                   02   DFHEIV2  PICTURE X(8).
00047 C                   02   DFHEIV3  PICTURE X(8).
00048 C                   02   DFHEIV4  PICTURE X(6).
00049 C                   02   DFHEIV5  PICTURE X(4).
00050 C                   02   DFHEIV6  PICTURE X(4).
00051 C                   02   DFHEIV7  PICTURE X(2).
00052 C                   02   DFHEIV8  PICTURE X(2).
00053 C                   02   DFHEIV9  PICTURE X(1).
00054 C                   02   DFHEIV10 PICTURE S9(7) USAGE COMPUTATIONAL-3.
00055 C                   02   DFHEIV11 PICTURE S9(4) USAGE COMPUTATIONAL.
00056 C                   02   DFHEIV12 PICTURE S9(4) USAGE COMPUTATIONAL.
00057 C                   02   DFHEIV13 PICTURE S9(4) USAGE COMPUTATIONAL.
00058 C                   02   DFHEIV14 PICTURE S9(4) USAGE COMPUTATIONAL.
00059 C                   02   DFHEIV15 PICTURE S9(4) USAGE COMPUTATIONAL.
00060 C                   02   DFHEIV16 PICTURE S9(9) USAGE COMPUTATIONAL.
00061 C                   02   DFHEIV17 PICTURE X(4).
00062 C                   02   DFHEIV18 PICTURE X(4).
00063 C                   02   DFHEIV19 PICTURE X(4).
00064 C                   02   DFHEIV97 PICTURE S9(7) USAGE COMPUTATIONAL-3 VALUE ZERO.
00065 C                   02   DFHEIV98 PICTURE S9(4) USAGE COMPUTATIONAL VALUE ZERO.
00066 C                   02   DFHEIV99 PICTURE X(1)  VALUE SPACE.
00067             LINKAGE SECTION.
00068             01  DFHEIBLK COPY DFHEIBLK.
00069 C           *    EIBLK EXEC INTERFACE BLOCK
00070 C           01  DFHEIBLK.
00071 C           *      EIBTIME     TIME IN OHHMMSS FORMAT
00072 C                  02 EIBTIME     PICTURE S9(7) USAGE COMPUTATIONAL-3.
00073 C           *      EIBDATE     DATE IN OOYYDDD FORMAT
00074 C                  02 EIBDATE     PICTURE S9(7) USAGE COMPUTATIONAL-3.
00075 C           *      EIBTRNID    TRANSACTION IDENTIFIER
00076 C                  02 EIBTRNID    PICTURE X(4).
00077 C           *      EIBTASKN    TASK NUMBER
00078 C                  02 EIBTASKN    PICTURE S9(7) USAGE COMPUTATIONAL-3.
00079 C           *      EIBTRMID    TERMINAL IDENTIFIER
00080 C                  02 EIBTRMID    PICTURE X(4).
00081 C           . *    DFHEIGDI    RESERVED
00082 C                  02 DFHEIGDI    PICTURE S9(4) USAGE COMPUTATIONAL.
00083 C           *      EIBCPOSN    CURSOR POSITION
00084 C                  02 EIBCPOSN    PICTURE S9(4) USAGE COMPUTATIONAL.
00085 C           *      EIBCALEN    COMMAREA LENGTH
00086 C                  02 EIBCALEN    PICTURE S9(4) USAGE COMPUTATIONAL.
00087 C           *      EIBAID      ATTENTION IDENTIFIER
00088 C                  02 EIBAID      PICTURE X(1).
00089 C           *      EIBFN       FUNCTION CODE
00090 C                  02 EIBFN       PICTURE X(2).
00091 C           *      EIBRCODE    RESPONSE CODE
00092 C                  02 EIBRCODE    PICTURE X(6).
00093 C           *      EIBDS       DATASET NAME
00094 C                  02 EIBDS       PICTURE X(8).
```

Fig. 21.4. (Continued)

```
     4          ORDL01A            13.02.04          08/02/80

                *          EIBREQID    REQUEST IDENTIFIER
                       02 EIBREQID    PICTURE X(8).
                 01  DFHCOMMAREA.

                     05  PROCESS-SW                 PIC X.
                         88  INITIAL-ENTRY-TIME            VALUE '0'.
                         88  DELETE-TIME                   VALUE '1'.


                 01  LINKAGE-POINTERS.

                     05  FILLER                     PIC S9(8) COMP.
                     05  MAP1-POINTER               PIC S9(8) COMP.
                     05  TWA-POINTER                PIC S9(8) COMP.


     5          ORDL01A            13.02.04          08/02/80

                ****************************************************************
                *                                                              *
                *              DELETE MAP DESCRIPTION                          *
                *                                                              *
                ****************************************************************

                 01  MAP1-AREA.
                     05  FILLER                     PIC X(12).
                     05  MAP1-DUMMY-L               PIC S9999 COMP.
                     05  MAP1-DUMMY-A               PIC X.
                     05  MAP1-DUMMY                 PIC X.
                     05  MAP1-ORDER-NUMBER-L        PIC S9999 COMP.
                     05  MAP1-ORDER-NUMBER-A        PIC X.
                     05  MAP1-ORDER-NUMBER          PIC X(10).
                     05  MAP1-ERROR-L               PIC S9999 COMP.
                     05  MAP1-ERROR-A               PIC X.
                     05  MAP1-ERROR                 PIC X(24).


     6          ORDL01A            13.02.04          08/02/80

                ****************************************************************
                *                                                              *
                *              TRANSACTION WORK AREA                           *
                *                                                              *
                ****************************************************************


                 01  TWA-AREA.


                     05  TWA-OPERATOR-MESSAGE    PIC X(31).


                     05  TWA-ORDER-RECORD-KEY    PIC X(10).
```

Fig. 21.4. (Continued)

```
     7         ORDLO1A         13.02.04        08/02/80

00139            PROCEDURE DIVISION USING DFHEIBLK DFHCOMMAREA.
00140                CALL 'DFHEI1'.

00142            ****************************************************************
00143            *                                                              *
00144            MAIN-LINE SECTION.
00145            *                                                              *
00146            ****************************************************************

00148            *    EXEC CICS
00149            *        ADDRESS TWA (TWA-POINTER)
00150            *    END-EXEC.
00151                MOVE 'BB   DC             ' TO DFHEIVO CALL 'DFHEI1' USING
00152                DFHEIVO TWA-POINTER.
00153
00154            *    EXEC CICS
00155            *        HANDLE AID
00156            *            CLEAR (FINALIZATION)
00157            *            PA1 (WRONG-KEY-USED)
00158            *            PA2 (WRONG-KEY-USED)
00159            *            PA3 (WRONG-KEY-USED)
00160            *    END-EXEC.
00161                MOVE 'BFO DEDFC           ' TO DFHEIVO CALL 'DFHEI1' USING
00162                DFHEIVO GO TO FINALIZATION WRONG-KEY-USED WRONG-KEY-USED
00163                WRONG-KEY-USED DEPENDING ON DFHEIGDI.
00164
00165
00166
00167
00168            *    EXEC CICS
00169            *        HANDLE CONDITION
00170            *            MAPFAIL (MAPFAIL-ERROR)
00171            *            ERROR   (MAJOR-ERROR)
00172            *    END-EXEC.
00173                MOVE 'BD   DUA            ' TO DFHEIVO CALL 'DFHEI1' USING
00174                DFHEIVO GO TO MAPFAIL-ERROR MAJOR-ERROR DEPENDING ON
00175                DFHEIGDI.
00176
00177
00178                IF EIBCALEN NOT EQUAL TO ZEROES
00179                    IF DELETE-TIME
00180                        GO TO DELETE-THE-RECORD
00181                    ELSE IF INITIAL-ENTRY-TIME
00182                        GO TO INITIALIZATION
00183                    ELSE GO TO PROCESS-SWITCH-ERROR.

00185                IF EIBCALEN EQUAL TO ZEROES
00186                    GO TO SIGN-ON-VIOLATION.
```

Fig. 21.4. (Continued)

```
    8          ORDL01A          13.02.04          08/02/80

           *****************************************************************
           *                                                               *
            DELETE-THE-RECORD SECTION.
           *                                                               *
           *****************************************************************

           *     EXEC CICS
           *          HANDLE CONDITION
           *               NOTOPEN (FILE-NOT-OPEN)
           *               NOTFND  (RECORD-NOT-FOUND)
           *     END-EXEC.
                  MOVE 'BD  DL(              ' TO DFHEIVO CALL 'DFHEI1' USING
                  DFHEIVO GO TO FILE-NOT-OPEN RECORD-NOT-FOUND DEPENDING ON
                  DFHEIGDI.


           *     EXEC CICS
           *          RECEIVE MAP     ('ORDLM01')
           *                  MAPSET ('ORDLS01')
           *                  SET     (MAP1-POINTER)
           *     END-EXEC.
                  MOVE 'ORDLM01' TO DFHEIV1 MOVE 'ORDLS01' TO DFHEIV2 MOVE 'QB
           -     '& DA    EI    -' TO DFHEIVO CALL 'DFHEI1' USING DFHEIVO
                  DFHEIV1 MAP1-POINTER DFHEIV98 DFHEIV2.


                 IF MAP1-ORDER-NUMBER NOT NUMERIC
                      GO TO INVALID-ORDER-RTN.

                 MOVE MAP1-ORDER-NUMBER TO TWA-ORDER-RECORD-KEY.

           *     EXEC CICS
           *          DELETE DATASET ('ORTEST')
           *                 RIDFLD  (TWA-ORDER-RECORD-KEY)
           *     END-EXEC.
                  MOVE 'ORTEST' TO DFHEIV3 MOVE 'FH& D   A ' TO DFHEIVO CALL 'D
           -     'FHEI1' USING DFHEIVO DFHEIV3 DFHEIV99 DFHEIV98
                  TWA-ORDER-RECORD-KEY.

                 MOVE 'ORDER DELETED - CONTINUE' TO MAP1-ERROR.

           *     EXEC CICS
           *          SEND MAP     ('ORDLM01')
           *               MAPSET ('ORDLS01')
           *               FROM    (MAP1-AREA)
           *               DATAONLY
           *     END-EXEC.
                  MOVE 'ORDLM01' TO DFHEIV1 MOVE 'ORDLS01' TO DFHEIV2 MOVE 'QD
           -     '& D     E-D   -' TO DFHEIVO CALL 'DFHEI1' USING DFHEIVO
                  DFHEIV1 MAP1-AREA DFHEIV98 DFHEIV2.
```

Fig. 21.4. (Continued)

```
   9        ORDL01A          13.02.04        08/02/80

00240
00241          RETURN-FOR-NEXT-ORDER.

00243              MOVE '1' TO COMMAREA-PROCESS-SW.

00245      *     EXEC CICS
00246      *         RETURN TRANSID  (EIBTRNID)
00247      *                 COMMAREA (COMMUNICATION-AREA)
00248      *                 LENGTH    (1)
00249      *     END-EXEC.
00250            MOVE 1 TO DFHEIV11 MOVE '+H- D  & ' TO DFHEIVO CALL 'DFHEI1'
00251            USING DFHEIVO EIBTRNID COMMUNICATION-AREA DFHEIV11.
00252
00253
00254

00256          RECORD-NOT-FOUND.
00257              MOVE 'RECORD NOT FOUND' TO MAP1-ERROR.
00258              GO TO DISPLAY-INVALID-ORDER-MESSAGE.

00260          DISPLAY-INVALID-ORDER-MESSAGE.

00262      *     EXEC CICS
00263      *         SEND MAP   ('ORDLM01')
00264      *              MAPSET ('ORDLS01')
00265      *              FROM   (MAP1-AREA)
00266      *              DATAONLY
00267      *     END-EXEC.
00268            MOVE 'ORDLM01' TO DFHEIV1 MOVE 'ORDLS01' TO DFHEIV2 MOVE 'QD
00269      -     '& D    E-D -' TO DFHEIVO CALL 'DFHEI1' USING DFHEIVO
00270            DFHEIV1 MAP1-AREA DFHEIV98 DFHEIV2.
00271
00272
00273
00274              GO TO RETURN-FOR-NEXT-ORDER.

00276          INVALID-ORDER-RTN.

00278              MOVE 'INVALID ORDER NUMBER' TO MAP1-ERROR.
00279              GO TO DISPLAY-INVALID-ORDER-MESSAGE.
```

Fig. 21.4. (Continued)

```
10          ORDL01A          13.02.04          08/02/80

            ****************************************************************
            *                                                              *
             WRONG-KEY-USED SECTION.
            *                                                              *
            ****************************************************************

            *     EXEC CICS
            *          GETMAIN
            *               SET      (MAP1-POINTER)
            *               LENGTH   (56)
            *               INITIMG (HEX-ZEROES)
            *     END-EXEC.
                   MOVE 56 TO DFHEIV11 MOVE '□B- D   □ ' TO DFHEIV0 CALL 'DFHEI1
            -      '' USING DFHEIV0 MAP1-POINTER DFHEIV11 HEX-ZEROES.




                  MOVE 'WRONG KEY USED' TO MAP1-ERROR.

            *     EXEC CICS
            *          SEND MAP     ('ORDLM01')
            *               MAPSET ('ORDLS01')
            *               FROM    (MAP1-AREA)
            *               DATAONLY
            *     END-EXEC.
                   MOVE 'ORDLM01' TO DFHEIV1 MOVE 'ORDLS01' TO DFHEIV2 MOVE 'QD
            -      '& D     E-D  -' TO DFHEIV0 CALL 'DFHEI1' USING DFHEIV0
                   DFHEIV1 MAP1-AREA DFHEIV98 DFHEIV2.



                  GO TO RETURN-FOR-NEXT-ORDER.
```

Fig. 21.4. (Continued)

11 ORDLO1A 13.02.04 08/02/80

```
00315          *******************************************************************
00316          *                                                                 *
00317           INITIALIZATION SECTION.
00318          *                                                                 *
00319          *******************************************************************

00321          *    EXEC CICS
00322          *        SEND MAP    ('ORDLMO1')
00323          *             MAPSET ('ORDLSO1')
00324          *             MAPONLY
00325          *             ERASE
00326          *    END-EXEC.
00327                MOVE 'ORDLMO1' TO DFHEIV1 MOVE 'ORDLSO1' TO DFHEIV2 MOVE 'QD
00328          -     '& D    ESO  -' TO DFHEIVO CALL 'DFHEI1' USING DFHEIVO
00329                DFHEIV1 DFHEIV99 DFHEIV98 DFHEIV2.
00330
00331
00332
00333                MOVE '1' TO COMMAREA-PROCESS-SW.

00335          *    EXEC CICS
00336          *        RETURN TRANSID  ('ORDL')
00337          *               COMMAREA (COMMUNICATION-AREA)
00338          *               LENGTH   (1)
00339          *    END-EXEC.
00340                MOVE 'ORDL' TO DFHEIV5 MOVE 1 TO DFHEIV11 MOVE '+H- D  & '
00341                TO DFHEIVO CALL 'DFHEI1' USING DFHEIVO DFHEIV5
00342                COMMUNICATION-AREA DFHEIV11.
00343
00344
```

Fig. 21.4. (Continued)

```
   12          ORDLO1A        13.02.04        08/02/80

00346       ******************************************************************
00347       *                                                                *
00348        FINALIZATION SECTION.
00349       *                                                                *
00350       ******************************************************************

00352        PREPARE-TERMINATION-MESSAGE.
00353            MOVE JOB-NORMAL-END-MESSAGE TO TWA-OPERATOR-MESSAGE.

00355        JOB-TERMINATED.
00356       *    EXEC CICS
00357       *         SEND FROM   (TWA-OPERATOR-MESSAGE)
00358       *              LENGTH (31)
00359       *              ERASE
00360       *    END-EXEC.
00361            MOVE 31 TO DFHEIV11 MOVE 'DDO D    A       ' TO DFHEIVO CALL '
00362       -    'DFHEI1' USING DFHEIVO DFHEIV99 DFHEIV98 TWA-OPERATOR-MESSAGE
00363            DFHEIV11.
00364
00365

00367        END-OF-JOB.
00368       *    EXEC CICS
00369       *         RETURN
00370       *    END-EXEC.
00371            MOVE '+H  D  & ' TO DFHEIVO CALL 'DFHEI1' USING DFHEIVO.
00372
00373
```

Fig. 21.4. (Continued)

```
13        ORDL01A        13.02.04        08/02/80

00375     ***********************************************************************
00376     *                                                                     *
00377      ABNORMAL-TERMINATION SECTION.
00378     *                                                                     *
00379     ***********************************************************************

00381      FILE-NOT-OPEN.

00383     *    EXEC CICS
00384     *         XCTL PROGRAM ('TEL2OPEN')
00385     *    END-EXEC.
00386           MOVE 'TEL2OPEN' TO DFHEIV3 MOVE '+D  D  B ' TO DFHEIV0 CALL
00387          'DFHEI1' USING DFHEIV0 DFHEIV3.
00388
00389      MAPFAIL-ERROR.
00390          MOVE 'MAP FAILURE' TO MAJOR-ERROR-MSG.
00391          GO TO PREPARE-ABORT-MESSAGE.

00393      PROCESS-SWITCH-ERROR.
00394          MOVE 'PROCESS ERROR' TO MAJOR-ERROR-MSG.
00395          GO TO PREPARE-ABORT-MESSAGE.

00397      SIGN-ON-VIOLATION.
00398          MOVE 'SIGNON VIOLATION' TO MAJOR-ERROR-MSG.
00399          GO TO PREPARE-ABORT-MESSAGE.

00401      MAJOR-ERROR.
00402          MOVE  EIBFN     TO  OLD-EIBFN.
00403          MOVE  EIBRCODE  TO  OLD-EIBRCODE.

00405     *    EXEC CICS
00406     *         DUMP DUMPCODE ('ERRS')
00407     *    END-EXEC.
00408           MOVE 'ERRS' TO DFHEIV5 MOVE '*B  D  = ' TO DFHEIV0 CALL 'DFH
00409     -    'EI1' USING DFHEIV0 DFHEIV5.
00410
00411          MOVE 'MAJOR ERROR' TO MAJOR-ERROR-MSG.
00412          GO TO PREPARE-ABORT-MESSAGE.

00414      PREPARE-ABORT-MESSAGE.
00415          MOVE JOB-ABORTED-MESSAGE TO TWA-OPERATOR-MESSAGE.
00416          GO TO JOB-TERMINATED.
```

Fig. 21.4. (Continued)

THE INITIALIZATION SECTION

1. Lines 321–329. Display the delete map.
2. Line 333. Set the communication area switch to 1.
3. Lines 335–342. Terminate the task.

THE DELETE-THE-RECORD SECTION

1. Lines 194–201. HANDLE CONDITION command for the order file.
2. Lines 204–211. Read the map that contains the order number entered by the operator.
3. Lines 214–225. Delete the record using the order number entered.
4. If the record is found:
   a. Line 227. Lay out the "ORDER DELETED – CONTINUE" message in the area secured by CICS/VS for the symbolic description map.
   b. Lines 229–237. Display the message.
   c. Line 243. Set the communication area switch to 1.
   d. Lines 245–251. Terminate the task.
5. If the record is not found:
   a. Line 257. Lay out the "RECORD NOT FOUND" message in the area secured by CICS/VS for the symbolic description map.
   b. Lines 260–270. Display the message.
   c. Line 243. Set the communication area switch to 1.
   d. Lines 245–251. Terminate the task.

THE WRONG-KEY-USED SECTION

1. Lines 287–294. GETMAIN command to secure main storage for the map that will contain the error message. This is because the PA keys do not allow CICS/VS to secure main storage for the symbolic description map through a RECEIVE MAP command.
2. Line 299. Move the "WRONG KEY USED" message into the area secured.
3. Lines 301–309. Display the error message.
4. Line 313. Set the communication area switch to 1 and terminate the task. This GO TO should be of no concern because this section will rarely be executed.

THE FINALIZATION SECTION

1. Lines 352–363. Display the "JOB NORMALLY TERMINATED" message.
2. Lines 367–371. Terminate the session.

THE ABNORMAL-TERMINATION SECTION

These are the routines used to abnormally terminate the session on errors and CICS/VS command exceptional conditions not covered by a HANDLE CONDITION command.

EXAMPLE

The following are facsimiles of actual photographs taken of a CRT terminal during a session.

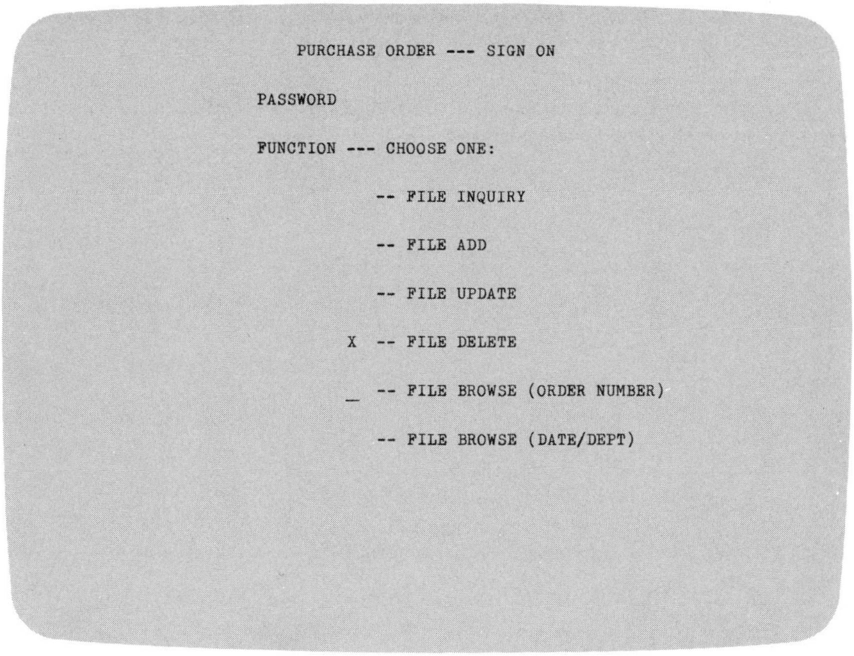

Fig. 21.5. The File Delete application is selected by keying in an "X" on the File Delete line and the corresponding password, then hitting the ENTER key.

Fig. 21.6. The Sign On program executes which then transfers control to the File Delete program. This displays the File Delete map.

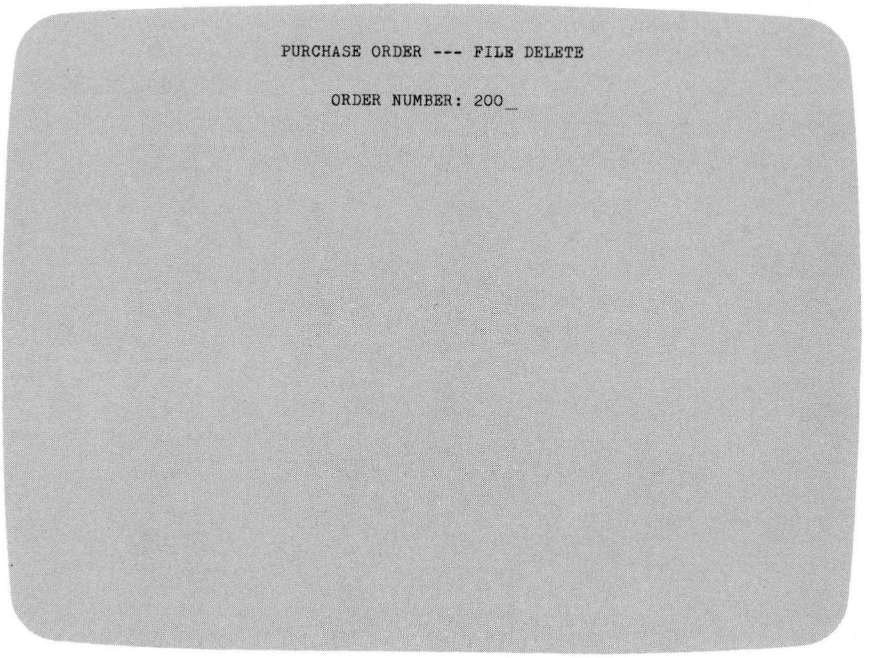

Fig. 21.7. The operator keys in the order number of the record to be deleted, then hits the ENTER key.

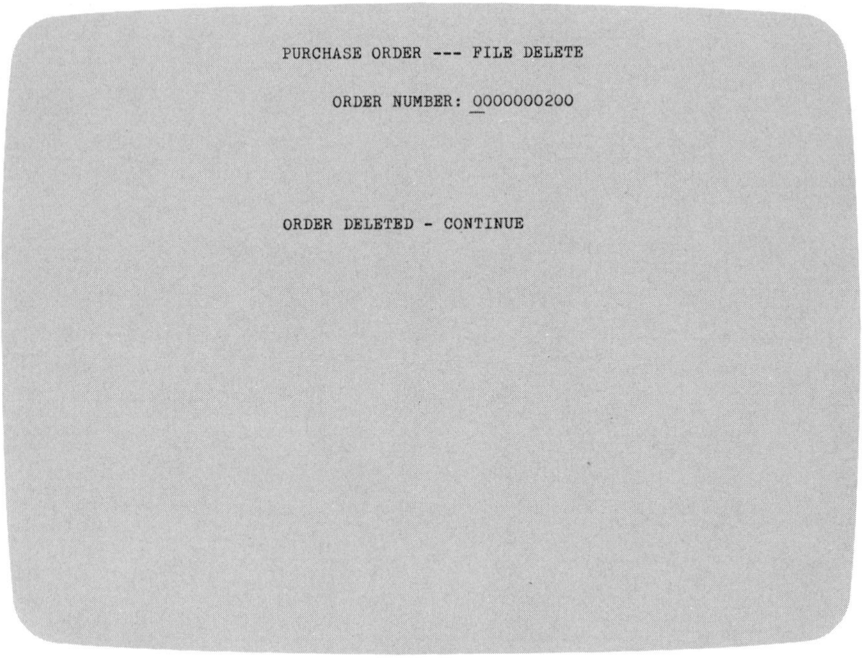

Fig. 21.8. The program deletes the record. The "ORDER DELETED – CONTINUE" message is then displayed to inform the operator. He may then continue with the next order.

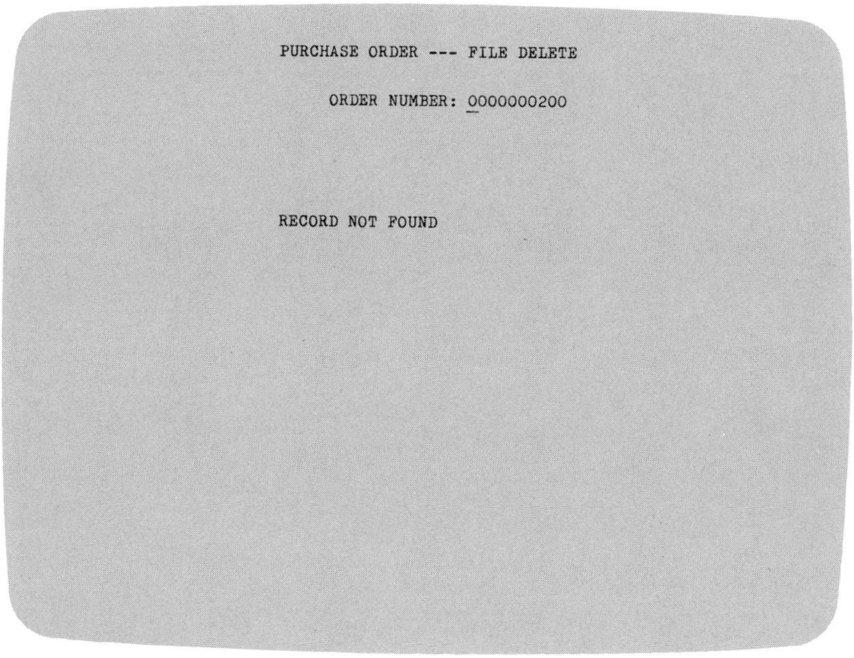

Fig. 21.9. If the record to be deleted is not in the file (as for example the previously deleted record), the "RECORD NOT FOUND" message is displayed.

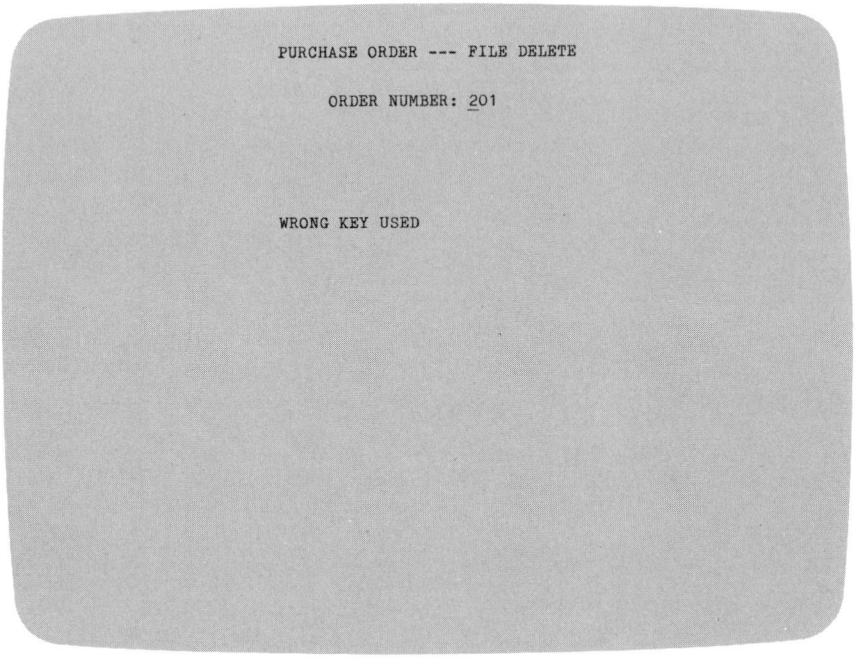

Fig. 21.10. If the operator keys in an order number but hits one of the PA keys instead of the ENTER key, the "WRONG KEY USED" message is displayed.

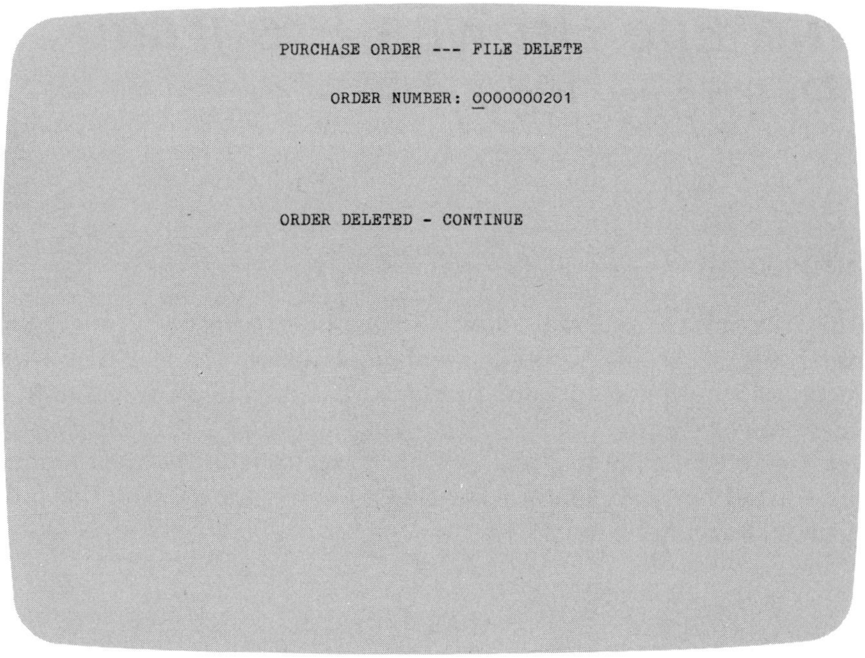

Fig. 21.11. If the operator then hits the ENTER key, the session continues. The record selected in Fig. 21.10 is now deleted.

22

The File Browse Program (Primary Key)

INTRODUCTION

This File Browse program allows the operator to browse through the order file according to order number sequence. He may also skip records in both the forward and backward directions by entering a new browse starting point. The program executes when selected by the Sign-on program and will continue executing in the session until terminated by the operator. The flow of control to execute this program is shown in Figure 22.1.

PROGRAM SPECIFICATION

The File Browse program (primary key) specifications are as follows:

1. Implement the program using the conversational mode of processing.
2. Use 'ORBR' as the transaction identifier. However, the session should be started not by this identifier, but rather through an XCTL command from the Sign-on program.
3. If the session is started by using the transaction identifier, abort the session with the message "JOB ABORTED – SIGNON VIOLATION."
4. The browse starting point is the order number entered by the operator; if the record is not in the file, the record next in ascending sequence is used; if the order number is higher than the last record in the file, the last record is used.

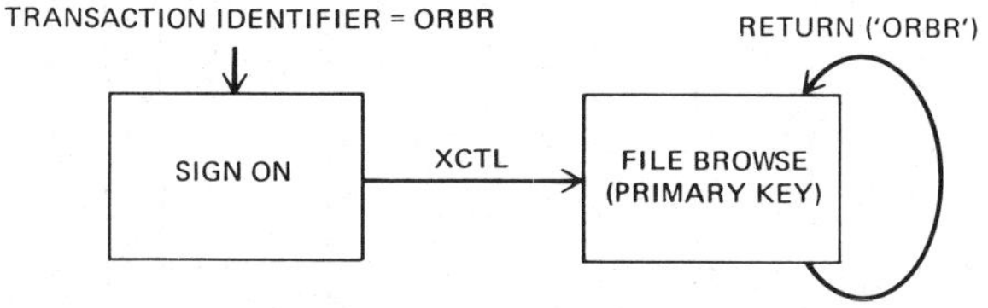

Fig. 22.1. File Browse Application (Primary Key).

5. On the PF1 key, display the record next in ascending sequence.
6. On the PF2 key, display the record next in descending sequence.
7. The operator may restart the browse at some other point by entering a new order number.
8. On any PA key, display the message "WRONG KEY USED"; allow the operator to continue on with the session.
9. In this example, display only one record per page.

SCREEN LAYOUT

The screen layout to be used in the program is shown in Figure 22.2. All 9s are numeric fields and Xs are alphanumeric fields.

MAP PROGRAM

The map program corresponding to the screen layout is shown in Figure 22.3.

PROGRAM LISTING

The program listing for the File Browse program (primary key) is shown in Figure 22.4. The listing is that of the compiler and not the command-language translator, and thus the commands are already as translated.

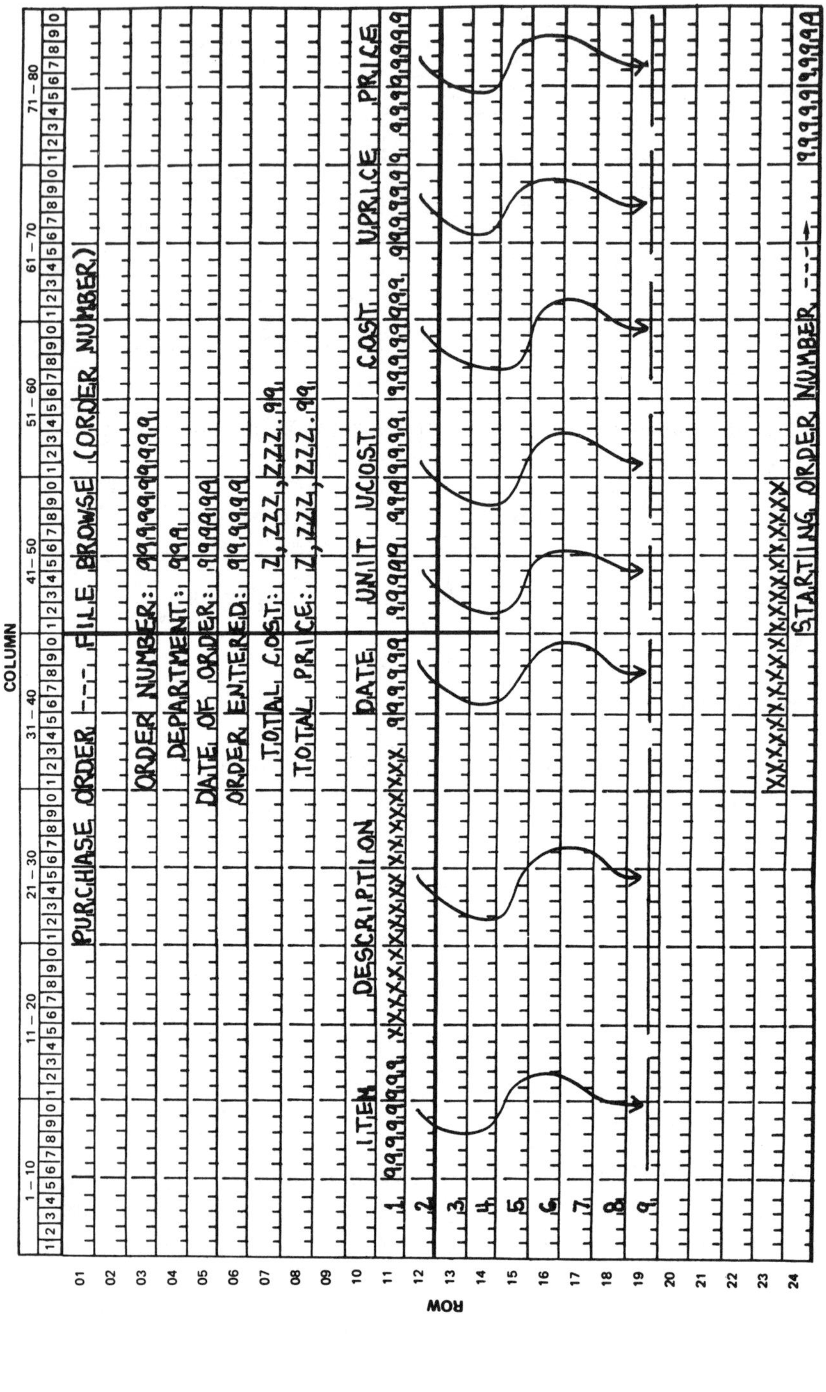

Fig. 22.2. Screen Layout – File Browse (Primary Key).

```
STMT    SOURCE STATEMENT                                        DOS/VS ASSEMBLER REL 34.0 14.07

   1              PRINT NOGEN
   2 ORBRS01      DFHMSD TYPE=MAP,MODE=INOUT,CTRL=FREEKB,LANG=COBOL,TIOAPFX=YES
  12 ORBRM01      DFHMDI SIZE=(24,80)
  40 DUMMY        DFHMDF POS=(01,01),LENGTH=01,ATTRB=(ASKIP,DRK,FSET),           X
                        INITIAL='1'
  52              DFHMDF POS=(01,20),LENGTH=45,ATTRB=(ASKIP,BRT),                X
                        INITIAL='PURCHASE ORDER --- FILE BROWSE (ORDER NUMBER)'
  64              DFHMDF POS=(03,30),LENGTH=13,ATTRB=ASKIP,                      X
                        INITIAL='ORDER NUMBER '
  76 ORDER        DFHMDF POS=(03,44),LENGTH=10,ATTRB=(ASKIP,BRT)
  87              DFHMDF POS=(04,32),LENGTH=11,ATTRB=ASKIP,INITIAL='DEPARTMENT '
  99 DEPT         DFHMDF POS=(04,44),LENGTH=03,ATTRB=(ASKIP,BRT)
 110              DFHMDF POS=(05,29),LENGTH=14,ATTRB=ASKIP,                      X
                        INITIAL='DATE OF ORDER '
 122 DATEOR       DFHMDF POS=(05,44),LENGTH=06,ATTRB=(ASKIP,BRT)
 133              DFHMDF POS=(06,29),LENGTH=14,ATTRB=ASKIP,                      X
                        INITIAL='ORDER ENTERED '
 145 DATEENT      DFHMDF POS=(06,44),LENGTH=06,ATTRB=(ASKIP,BRT)
 156              DFHMDF POS=(07,32),LENGTH=11,ATTRB=ASKIP,INITIAL='TOTAL COST '
 168 TOTCOST      DFHMDF POS=(07,44),LENGTH=12,ATTRB=(ASKIP,BRT),                X
                        PICOUT='Z,ZZZ,ZZZ.99'
 179              DFHMDF POS=(08,31),LENGTH=12,ATTRB=ASKIP,                      X
                        INITIAL='TOTAL PRICE '
 191 TOTPRCE      DFHMDF POS=(08,44),LENGTH=12,ATTRB=(ASKIP,BRT),                X
                        PICOUT='Z,ZZZ,ZZZ.99'
 202              DFHMDF POS=(10,07),LENGTH=04,ATTRB=ASKIP,INITIAL='ITEM'
 214              DFHMDF POS=(10,17),LENGTH=11,ATTRB=ASKIP,INITIAL='DESCRIPTION'
 226              DFHMDF POS=(10,35),LENGTH=04,ATTRB=ASKIP,INITIAL='DATE'
 238              DFHMDF POS=(10,42),LENGTH=04,ATTRB=ASKIP,INITIAL='UNIT'
 250              DFHMDF POS=(10,48),LENGTH=05,ATTRB=ASKIP,INITIAL='UCOST'
 262              DFHMDF POS=(10,57),LENGTH=04,ATTRB=ASKIP,INITIAL='COST'
 274              DFHMDF POS=(10,65),LENGTH=06,ATTRB=ASKIP,INITIAL='UPRICE'
 286              DFHMDF POS=(10,74),LENGTH=05,ATTRB=ASKIP,INITIAL='PRICE'
 298 LINE1        DFHMDF POS=(11,03),LENGTH=01,ATTRB=ASKIP
 309 ITEM1        DFHMDF POS=(11,05),LENGTH=08,ATTRB=(ASKIP,BRT),                X
                        PICIN='99999999',PICOUT='99999999'
 320 DESC1        DFHMDF POS=(11,14),LENGTH=19,ATTRB=(ASKIP,BRT)
 331 LNDATE1      DFHMDF POS=(11,34),LENGTH=06,ATTRB=(ASKIP,BRT)
 342 UNIT1        DFHMDF POS=(11,41),LENGTH=05,ATTRB=(ASKIP,BRT),                X
                        PICIN='99999',PICOUT='99999'
 353 UCOST1       DFHMDF POS=(11,47),LENGTH=07,ATTRB=(ASKIP,BRT),                X
                        PICIN='9999999',PICOUT='9999999'
 364 COST1        DFHMDF POS=(11,55),LENGTH=08,ATTRB=(ASKIP,BRT),                X
                        PICIN='99999999',PICOUT='99999999'
 375 UPRICE1      DFHMDF POS=(11,64),LENGTH=07,ATTRB=(ASKIP,BRT),                X
                        PICIN='9999999',PICOUT='9999999'
 386 PRICE1       DFHMDF POS=(11,72),LENGTH=08,ATTRB=(ASKIP,BRT),                X
                        PICIN='99999999',PICOUT='99999999'
 397 LINE2        DFHMDF POS=(12,03),LENGTH=01,ATTRB=ASKIP
 408 ITEM2        DFHMDF POS=(12,05),LENGTH=08,ATTRB=(ASKIP,BRT),                X
                        PICIN='99999999',PICOUT='99999999'
```

Fig. 22.3. Map Program – File Browse (Primary Key).

```
STMT    SOURCE STATEMENT                                  DOS/VS ASSEMBLER REL 34.0 14.07

 419 DESC2      DFHMDF POS=(12,14),LENGTH=19,ATTRB=(ASKIP,BRT)
 430 LNDATE2    DFHMDF POS=(12,34),LENGTH=06,ATTRB=(ASKIP,BRT)
 441 UNIT2      DFHMDF POS=(12,41),LENGTH=05,ATTRB=(ASKIP,BRT),              X
                       PICIN='99999',PICOUT='99999'
 452 UCOST2     DFHMDF POS=(12,47),LENGTH=07,ATTRB=(ASKIP,BRT),              X
                       PICIN='9999999',PICOUT='9999999'
 463 COST2      DFHMDF POS=(12,55),LENGTH=08,ATTRB=(ASKIP,BRT),              X
                       PICIN='99999999',PICOUT='99999999'
 474 UPRICE2    DFHMDF POS=(12,64),LENGTH=07,ATTRB=(ASKIP,BRT),              X
                       PICIN='9999999',PICOUT='9999999'
 485 PRICE2     DFHMDF POS=(12,72),LENGTH=08,ATTRB=(ASKIP,BRT),              X
                       PICIN='99999999',PICOUT='99999999'
 496 LINE3      DFHMDF POS=(13,03),LENGTH=01,ATTRB=ASKIP
 507 ITEM3      DFHMDF POS=(13,05),LENGTH=08,ATTRB=(ASKIP,BRT),              X
                       PICIN='99999999',PICOUT='99999999'
 518 DESC3      DFHMDF POS=(13,14),LENGTH=19,ATTRB=(ASKIP,BRT)
 529 LNDATE3    DFHMDF POS=(13,34),LENGTH=06,ATTRB=(ASKIP,BRT)
 540 UNIT3      DFHMDF POS=(13,41),LENGTH=05,ATTRB=(ASKIP,BRT),              X
                       PICIN='99999',PICOUT='99999'
 551 UCOST3     DFHMDF POS=(13,47),LENGTH=07,ATTRB=(ASKIP,BRT),              X
                       PICIN='9999999',PICOUT='9999999'
 562 COST3      DFHMDF POS=(13,55),LENGTH=08,ATTRB=(ASKIP,BRT),              X
                       PICIN='99999999',PICOUT='99999999'
 573 UPRICE3    DFHMDF POS=(13,64),LENGTH=07,ATTRB=(ASKIP,BRT),              X
                       PICIN='9999999',PICOUT='9999999'
 584 PRICE3     DFHMDF POS=(13,72),LENGTH=08,ATTRB=(ASKIP,BRT),              X
                       PICIN='99999999',PICOUT='99999999'
 595 LINE4      DFHMDF POS=(14,03),LENGTH=01,ATTRB=ASKIP
 606 ITEM4      DFHMDF POS=(14,05),LENGTH=08,ATTRB=(ASKIP,BRT),              X
                       PICIN='99999999',PICOUT='99999999'
 617 DESC4      DFHMDF POS=(14,14),LENGTH=19,ATTRB=(ASKIP,BRT)
 628 LNDATE4    DFHMDF POS=(14,34),LENGTH=06,ATTRB=(ASKIP,BRT)
 639 UNIT4      DFHMDF POS=(14,41),LENGTH=05,ATTRB=(ASKIP,BRT),              X
                       PICIN='99999',PICOUT='99999'
 650 UCOST4     DFHMDF POS=(14,47),LENGTH=07,ATTRB=(ASKIP,BRT),              X
                       PICIN='9999999',PICOUT='9999999'
 661 COST4      DFHMDF POS=(14,55),LENGTH=08,ATTRB=(ASKIP,BRT),              X
                       PICIN='99999999',PICOUT='99999999'
 672 UPRICE4    DFHMDF POS=(14,64),LENGTH=07,ATTRB=(ASKIP,BRT),              X
                       PICIN='9999999',PICOUT='9999999'
 683 PRICE4     DFHMDF POS=(14,72),LENGTH=08,ATTRB=(ASKIP,BRT),              X
                       PICIN='99999999',PICOUT='99999999'
 694 LINE5      DFHMDF POS=(15,03),LENGTH=01,ATTRB=ASKIP
 705 ITEM5      DFHMDF POS=(15,05),LENGTH=08,ATTRB=(ASKIP,BRT),              X
                       PICIN='99999999',PICOUT='99999999'
 716 DESC5      DFHMDF POS=(15,14),LENGTH=19,ATTRB=(ASKIP,BRT)
 727 LNDATE5    DFHMDF POS=(15,34),LENGTH=06,ATTRB=(ASKIP,BRT)
 738 UNIT5      DFHMDF POS=(15,41),LENGTH=05,ATTRB=(ASKIP,BRT),              X
                       PICIN='99999',PICOUT='99999'
 749 UCOST5     DFHMDF POS=(15,47),LENGTH=07,ATTRB=(ASKIP,BRT),              X
                       PICIN='9999999',PICOUT='9999999'
```

Fig. 22.3. (Continued)

```
STMT   SOURCE STATEMENT                                       DOS/VS ASSEMBLER REL 34.0 14.07

 760 COST5     DFHMDF POS=(15,55),LENGTH=08,ATTRB=(ASKIP,BRT),                X
                      PICIN='99999999',PICOUT='99999999'
 771 UPRICE5   DFHMDF POS=(15,64),LENGTH=07,ATTRB=(ASKIP,BRT),                X
                      PICIN='9999999',PICOUT='9999999'
 782 PRICE5    DFHMDF POS=(15,72),LENGTH=08,ATTRB=(ASKIP,BRT),                X
                      PICIN='99999999',PICOUT='99999999'
 793 LINE6     DFHMDF POS=(16,03),LENGTH=01,ATTRB=ASKIP
 804 ITEM6     DFHMDF POS=(16,05),LENGTH=08,ATTRB=(ASKIP,BRT),                X
                      PICIN='99999999',PICOUT='99999999'
 815 DESC6     DFHMDF POS=(16,14),LENGTH=19,ATTRB=(ASKIP,BRT)
 826 LNDATE6   DFHMDF POS=(16,34),LENGTH=06,ATTRB=(ASKIP,BRT)
 837 UNIT6     DFHMDF POS=(16,41),LENGTH=05,ATTRB=(ASKIP,BRT),                X
                      PICIN='99999',PICOUT='99999'
 848 UCOST6    DFHMDF POS=(16,47),LENGTH=07,ATTRB=(ASKIP,BRT),                X
                      PICIN='9999999',PICOUT='9999999'
 859 COST6     DFHMDF POS=(16,55),LENGTH=08,ATTRB=(ASKIP,BRT),                X
                      PICIN='99999999',PICOUT='99999999'
 870 UPRICE6   DFHMDF POS=(16,64),LENGTH=07,ATTRB=(ASKIP,BRT),                X
                      PICIN='9999999',PICOUT='9999999'
 881 PRICE6    DFHMDF POS=(16,72),LENGTH=08,ATTRB=(ASKIP,BRT),                X
                      PICIN='99999999',PICOUT='99999999'
 892 LINE7     DFHMDF POS=(17,03),LENGTH=01,ATTRB=ASKIP
 903 ITEM7     DFHMDF POS=(17,05),LENGTH=08,ATTRB=(ASKIP,BRT),                X
                      PICIN='99999999',PICOUT='99999999'
 914 DESC7     DFHMDF POS=(17,14),LENGTH=19,ATTRB=(ASKIP,BRT)
 925 LNDATE7   DFHMDF POS=(17,34),LENGTH=06,ATTRB=(ASKIP,BRT)
 936 UNIT7     DFHMDF POS=(17,41),LENGTH=05,ATTRB=(ASKIP,BRT),                X
                      PICIN='99999',PICOUT='99999'
 947 UCOST7    DFHMDF POS=(17,47),LENGTH=07,ATTRB=(ASKIP,BRT),                X
                      PICIN='9999999',PICOUT='9999999'
 958 COST7     DFHMDF POS=(17,55),LENGTH=08,ATTRB=(ASKIP,BRT),                X
                      PICIN='99999999',PICOUT='99999999'
 969 UPRICE7   DFHMDF POS=(17,64),LENGTH=07,ATTRB=(ASKIP,BRT),                X
                      PICIN='9999999',PICOUT='9999999'
 980 PRICE7    DFHMDF POS=(17,72),LENGTH=08,ATTRB=(ASKIP,BRT),                X
                      PICIN='99999999',PICOUT='99999999'
 991 LINE8     DFHMDF POS=(18,03),LENGTH=01,ATTRB=ASKIP
1002 ITEM8     DFHMDF POS=(18,05),LENGTH=08,ATTRB=(ASKIP,BRT),                X
                      PICIN='99999999',PICOUT='99999999'
1013 DESC8     DFHMDF POS=(18,14),LENGTH=19,ATTRB=(ASKIP,BRT)
1024 LNDATE8   DFHMDF POS=(18,34),LENGTH=06,ATTRB=(ASKIP,BRT)
1035 UNIT8     DFHMDF POS=(18,41),LENGTH=05,ATTRB=(ASKIP,BRT),                X
                      PICIN='99999',PICOUT='99999'
1046 UCOST8    DFHMDF POS=(18,47),LENGTH=07,ATTRB=(ASKIP,BRT),                X
                      PICIN='9999999',PICOUT='9999999'
1057 COST8     DFHMDF POS=(18,55),LENGTH=08,ATTRB=(ASKIP,BRT),                X
                      PICIN='99999999',PICOUT='99999999'
1068 UPRICE8   DFHMDF POS=(18,64),LENGTH=07,ATTRB=(ASKIP,BRT),                X
                      PICIN='9999999',PICOUT='9999999'
1079 PRICE8    DFHMDF POS=(18,72),LENGTH=08,ATTRB=(ASKIP,BRT),                X
                      PICIN='99999999',PICOUT='99999999'
```

Fig. 22.3. (Continued)

```
STMT    SOURCE STATEMENT                               DOS/VS ASSEMBLER REL 34.0 14.07 ·

1090 LINE9      DFHMDF  POS=(19,03),LENGTH=01,ATTRB=ASKIP
1101 ITEM9      DFHMDF  POS=(19,05),LENGTH=08,ATTRB=(ASKIP,BRT),                    X
                        PICIN='99999999',PICOUT='99999999'
1112 DESC9      DFHMDF  POS=(19,14),LENGTH=19,ATTRB=(ASKIP,BRT)
1123 LNDATE9    DFHMDF  POS=(19,34),LENGTH=06,ATTRB=(ASKIP,BRT)
1134 UNIT9      DFHMDF  POS=(19,41),LENGTH=05,ATTRB=(ASKIP,BRT),                    X
                        PICIN='99999',PICOUT='99999'
1145 UCOST9     DFHMDF  POS=(19,47),LENGTH=07,ATTRB=(ASKIP,BRT),                    X
                        PICIN='9999999',PICOUT='9999999'
1156 COST9      DFHMDF  POS=(19,55),LENGTH=08,ATTRB=(ASKIP,BRT),                    X
                        PICIN='99999999',PICOUT='99999999'
1167 UPRICE9    DFHMDF  POS=(19,64),LENGTH=07,ATTRB=(ASKIP,BRT),                    X
                        PICIN='9999999',PICOUT='9999999'
1178 PRICE9     DFHMDF  POS=(19,72),LENGTH=08,ATTRB=(ASKIP,BRT),                    X
                        PICIN='99999999',PICOUT='99999999'
1189 ERROR      DFHMDF  POS=(23,30),LENGTH=20,ATTRB=(ASKIP,BRT)
1200            DFHMDF  POS=(24,40),LENGTH=27,ATTRB=ASKIP,                          X
                        INITIAL='STARTING ORDER NUMBER ---- '
1212 STARTOR    DFHMDF  POS=(24,70),LENGTH=10,ATTRB=(NUM,BRT,FSET,IC)
1223            DFHMSD TYPE=FINAL
1237            END
```

Fig. 22.3. (Continued)

```
      1   IBM DOS VS COBOL

 CBL SUPMAP,STXIT,NOTRUNC,CSYNTAX,SXREF,OPT,VERB,CLIST,BUF=19069
 CBL NOOPT,LIB
00001              IDENTIFICATION DIVISION.

00003              PROGRAM-ID. ORBRO1A.


00005              ENVIRONMENT DIVISION.

00007              ****************************************************************
00008              *                                                              *
00009              *    1. THIS PROGRAM ALLOWS A BROWSE (BY ORDER NUMBER) ON THE  *
00010              *       PURCHASE ORDER MASTER FILE.                            *
00011              *                                                              *
00012              *    2. THE OPERATOR MAY START AT THE BEGINNING OF THE FILE    *
00013              *       BY ENTERING ALL ZEROES ON THE STARTING ORDER NUMBER    *
00014              *       FIELD.                                                 *
00015              *                                                              *
00016              *    3. SHE MAY ALSO START AT THE END OF THE FILE (FOR A       *
00017              *       BROWSE BACKWARDS) BY ENTERING ALL NINES.               *
00018              *                                                              *
00019              *    4. BROWSE FORWARD -    PF1 OR ENTER KEY.                  *
00020              *                                                              *
00021              *    5. BROWSE BACKWARDS - PF2 KEY.                            *
00022              *                                                              *
00023              ****************************************************************
```

Fig. 22.4. File Browse Program (Primary Key).

```
     2          ORBRO1A           12.59.17          08/02/80

                DATA DIVISION.

                WORKING-STORAGE SECTION.

                01  COMMUNICATION-AREA.

                    05  COMMAREA-PROCESS-SW      PIC X.


                01  AREA1.

                    05  JOB-NORMAL-END-MESSAGE   PIC X(23) VALUE
                        'JOB NORMALLY TERMINATED'.

                    05  JOB-ABORTED-MESSAGE.
                      10  FILLER                 PIC X(15) VALUE 'JOB ABORTED --'.
                      10  MAJOR-ERROR-MSG        PIC X(16).

                    05  HEXADECIMAL-ZEROES       PIC 9999 COMP VALUE ZEROES.

                    05  FILLER REDEFINES HEXADECIMAL-ZEROES.
                      10  FILLER                 PIC X.
                      10  HEX-ZEROES             PIC X.

                    05  OLD-EIB-AREA.
                      10  FILLER                 PIC X(7) VALUE 'OLD EIB'.
                      10  OLD-EIBFN              PIC XX.
                      10  OLD-EIBRCODE           PIC X(6).


                01  DFHAID COPY DFHAID.
                01      DFHAID.
                  02    DFHNULL    PIC   X    VALUE IS ' '.
                  02    DFHENTER   PIC   X    VALUE IS QUOTE.
                  02    DFHCLEAR   PIC   X    VALUE IS ' '.
                  02    DFHPEN     PIC   X    VALUE IS '='.
                  02    DFHOPID    PIC   X    VALUE IS 'W'.
                  02    DFHPA1     PIC   X    VALUE IS '%'.
                  02    DFHPA2     PIC   X    VALUE IS ' '.
                  02    DFHPA3     PIC   X    VALUE IS ','.
                  02    DFHPF1     PIC   X    VALUE IS '1'.
                  02    DFHPF2     PIC   X    VALUE IS '2'.
                  02    DFHPF3     PIC   X    VALUE IS '3'.
                  02    DFHPF4     PIC   X    VALUE IS '4'.
```

Fig. 22.4. (Continued)

```
        3            ORBR01A           12.59.17          08/02/80

                  02   DFHPF5      PIC   X   VALUE IS '5'.
                  02   DFHPF6      PIC   X   VALUE IS '6'.
                  02   DFHPF7      PIC   X   VALUE IS '7'.
                  02   DFHPF8      PIC   X   VALUE IS '8'.
                  02   DFHPF9      PIC   X   VALUE IS '9'.
                  02   DFHPF10     PIC   X   VALUE IS ' '.
                  02   DFHPF11     PIC   X   VALUE IS '#'.
                  02   DFHPF12     PIC   X   VALUE IS '@'.
                  02   DFHPF13     PIC   X   VALUE IS 'A'.
                  02   DFHPF14     PIC   X   VALUE IS 'B'.
                  02   DFHPF15     PIC   X   VALUE IS 'C'.
                  02   DFHPF16     PIC   X   VALUE IS 'D'.
                  02   DFHPF17     PIC   X   VALUE IS 'E'.
                  02   DFHPF18     PIC   X   VALUE IS 'F'.
                  02   DFHPF19     PIC   X   VALUE IS 'G'.
                  02   DFHPF20     PIC   X   VALUE IS 'H'.
                  02   DFHPF21     PIC   X   VALUE IS 'I'.
                  02   DFHPF22     PIC   X   VALUE IS ' '.
                  02   DFHPF23     PIC   X   VALUE IS '.'.
                  02   DFHPF24     PIC   X   VALUE IS '□'.
```

Fig. 22.4. (Continued)

4 ORBRO1A 12.59.17 08/02/80

```
00088              01  DFHEIVAR COPY DFHEIVAR.
00089 C            01  DFHEIVAR.
00090 C                02    DFHEIV0  PICTURE X(26).
00091 C                02    DFHEIV1  PICTURE X(8).
00092 C                02    DFHEIV2  PICTURE X(8).
00093 C                02    DFHEIV3  PICTURE X(8).
00094 C                02    DFHEIV4  PICTURE X(6).
00095 C                02    DFHEIV5  PICTURE X(4).
00096 C                02    DFHEIV6  PICTURE X(4).
00097 C                02    DFHEIV7  PICTURE X(2).
00098 C                02    DFHEIV8  PICTURE X(2).
00099 C                02    DFHEIV9  PICTURE X(1).
00100 C                02    DFHEIV10 PICTURE S9(7) USAGE COMPUTATIONAL-3.
00101 C                02    DFHEIV11 PICTURE S9(4) USAGE COMPUTATIONAL.
00102 C                02    DFHEIV12 PICTURE S9(4) USAGE COMPUTATIONAL.
00103 C                02    DFHEIV13 PICTURE S9(4) USAGE COMPUTATIONAL.
00104 C                02    DFHEIV14 PICTURE S9(4) USAGE COMPUTATIONAL.
00105 C                02    DFHEIV15 PICTURE S9(4) USAGE COMPUTATIONAL.
00106 C                02    DFHEIV16 PICTURE S9(9) USAGE COMPUTATIONAL.
00107 C                02    DFHEIV17 PICTURE X(4).
00108 C                02    DFHEIV18 PICTURE X(4).
00109 C                02    DFHEIV19 PICTURE X(4).
00110 C                02    DFHEIV97 PICTURE S9(7) USAGE COMPUTATIONAL-3 VALUE ZERO.
00111 C                02    DFHEIV98 PICTURE S9(4) USAGE COMPUTATIONAL VALUE ZERO.
00112 C                02    DFHEIV99 PICTURE X(1)  VALUE SPACE.
00113              LINKAGE SECTION.

00115              01  DFHEIBLK COPY DFHEIBLK.
00116 C            *       EIBLK EXEC INTERFACE BLOCK
00117 C            01    DFHEIBLK.
00118 C            *       EIBTIME     TIME IN 0HHMMSS FORMAT
00119 C                02 EIBTIME     PICTURE S9(7) USAGE COMPUTATIONAL-3.
00120 C            *       EIBDATE     DATE IN 00YYDDD FORMAT
00121 C                02 EIBDATE     PICTURE S9(7) USAGE COMPUTATIONAL-3.
00122 C            *       EIBTRNID    TRANSACTION IDENTIFIER
00123 C                02 EIBTRNID    PICTURE X(4).
00124 C            *       EIBTASKN    TASK NUMBER
00125 C                02 EIBTASKN    PICTURE S9(7) USAGE COMPUTATIONAL-3.
00126 C            *       EIBTRMID    TERMINAL IDENTIFIER
00127 C                02 EIBTRMID    PICTURE X(4).
00128 C            *       DFHEIGDI    RESERVED
00129 C                02 DFHEIGDI    PICTURE S9(4) USAGE COMPUTATIONAL.
00130 C            *       EIBCPOSN    CURSOR POSITION
00131 C                02 EIBCPOSN    PICTURE S9(4) USAGE COMPUTATIONAL.
00132 C            *       EIBCALEN    COMMAREA LENGTH
00133 C                02 EIBCALEN    PICTURE S9(4) USAGE COMPUTATIONAL.
00134 C            *       EIBAID      ATTENTION IDENTIFIER
00135 C                02 EIBAID      PICTURE X(1).
00136 C            *       EIBFN       FUNCTION CODE
00137 C                02 EIBFN       PICTURE X(2).
00138 C            *       EIBRCODE    RESPONSE CODE
00139 C                02 EIBRCODE    PICTURE X(6).
```

Fig. 22.4. (Continued)

```
     5          ORBRO1A          12.59.17        08/02/80

00140 C         *          EIBDS        DATASET NAME
00141 C                 02 EIBDS        PICTURE X(8).
00142 C         *          EIBREQID     REQUEST IDENTIFIER
00143 C                 02 EIBREQID     PICTURE X(8).
00144             01  DFHCOMMAREA                     PIC X.

00146                 88  INITIAL-ENTRY-TIME              VALUE '0'.
00147                 88  BROWSE-START-TIME               VALUE '1'.



00149             01  LINKAGE-POINTERS.

00151                 05  FILLER                      PIC S9(8) COMP.
00152                 05  MAP1-POINTER                PIC S9(8) COMP.
00153                 05  POM-POINTER                 PIC S9(8) COMP.
00154                 05  TWA-POINTER                 PIC S9(8) COMP.
```

Fig. 22.4. (Continued)

```
    6           ORBR01A          12.59.17          08/02/80

            ************************************************************************
            *                                                                      *
            *              DISPLAY MAP DESCRIPTION                                 *
            *                                                                      *
            ************************************************************************


             01  MAP1-AREA.
                 05  FILLER                           PIC X(12).
                 05  MAP1-DUMMY-L                     PIC S9999 COMP.
                 05  MAP1-DUMMY-A                     PIC X.
                 05  MAP1-DUMMY                       PIC X.
                 05  MAP1-ORDER-NUMBER-L              PIC S9999 COMP.
                 05  MAP1-ORDER-NUMBER-A              PIC X.
                 05  MAP1-ORDER-NUMBER                PIC X(10).
                 05  MAP1-DEPARTMENT-L                PIC S9999 COMP.
                 05  MAP1-DEPARTMENT-A                PIC X.
                 05  MAP1-DEPARTMENT                  PIC XXX.
                 05  MAP1-ORDER-DATE-L                PIC S9999 COMP.
                 05  MAP1-ORDER-DATE-A                PIC X.
                 05  MAP1-ORDER-DATE.
                   10  MAP1-ORDER-DATE-MONTH          PIC XX.
                   10  MAP1-ORDER-DATE-DAY            PIC XX.
                   10  MAP1-ORDER-DATE-YEAR           PIC XX.
                 05  MAP1-ORDER-DATE-ENTERED-L        PIC S9999 COMP.
                 05  MAP1-ORDER-DATE-ENTERED-A        PIC X.
                 05  MAP1-ORDER-DATE-ENTERED          PIC X(6).
                 05  MAP1-TOTAL-COST-L                PIC S9999 COMP.
                 05  MAP1-TOTAL-COST-A                PIC X.
                 05  MAP1-TOTAL-COST                  PIC Z,ZZZ,ZZZ.99.
                 05  MAP1-TOTAL-PRICE-L               PIC S9999 COMP.
                 05  MAP1-TOTAL-PRICE-A               PIC X.
                 05  MAP1-TOTAL-PRICE                 PIC Z,ZZZ,ZZZ.99.
                 05  MAP1-LINE-ITEM               OCCURS 9
                                                  INDEXED BY MAP1-LINE-I.
                   10  MAP1-LINE-NUMBER-L             PIC S9999 COMP.
                   10  MAP1-LINE-NUMBER-A             PIC X.
                   10  MAP1-LINE-NUMBER               PIC 9.
                   10  MAP1-ITEM-NUMBER-L             PIC S9999 COMP.
                   10  MAP1-ITEM-NUMBER-A             PIC X.
                   10  MAP1-ITEM-NUMBER               PIC X(8).
                   10  MAP1-ITEM-DESCRIPTION-L        PIC S9999 COMP.
                   10  MAP1-ITEM-DESCRIPTION-A        PIC X.
                   10  MAP1-ITEM-DESCRIPTION          PIC X(19).
                   10  MAP1-ITEM-DATE-L               PIC S9999 COMP.
                   10  MAP1-ITEM-DATE-A               PIC X.
                   10  MAP1-ITEM-DATE                 PIC X(6).
                   10  MAP1-UNIT-L                    PIC S9999 COMP.
                   10  MAP1-UNIT-A                    PIC X.
                   10  MAP1-UNIT                      PIC 9(5).
                   10  MAP1-UNIT-COST-L               PIC S9999 COMP.
                   10  MAP1-UNIT-COST-A               PIC X.
```

Fig. 22.4. (Continued)

```
     7        ORBR01A        12.59.17        08/02/80

                        10  MAP1-UNIT-COST          PIC 9(7).
                        10  MAP1-COST-L             PIC S9999 COMP.
                        10  MAP1-COST-A             PIC X.
                        10  MAP1-COST               PIC 9(8).
                        10  MAP1-UNIT-PRICE-L       PIC S9999 COMP.
                        10  MAP1-UNIT-PRICE-A       PIC X.
                        10  MAP1-UNIT-PRICE         PIC 9(7).
                        10  MAP1-PRICE-L            PIC S9999 COMP.
                        10  MAP1-PRICE-A            PIC X.
                        10  MAP1-PRICE              PIC 9(8).
                    05  MAP1-ERROR-L                PIC S9999 COMP.
                    05  MAP1-ERROR-A                PIC X.
                    05  MAP1-ERROR                  PIC X(20).
                    05  MAP1-START-ORDER-L          PIC S9999 COMP.
                    05  MAP1-START-ORDER-A          PIC X.
                    05  MAP1-START-ORDER            PIC X(10).
```

```
     8        ORBR01A        12.59.17        08/02/80

      ****************************************************************
      *                                                              *
      *         PURCHASE ORDER MASTER -- FILE LAYOUT                 *
      *                                                              *
      ****************************************************************

       01  ORDER-MASTER-RECORD.
           05  ORDER-NUMBER                        PIC X(10).
           05  ORDER-ALT-KEY.
             10  ORDER-DEPARTMENT                  PIC XXX.
             10  ORDER-DATE.
               15  ORDER-DATE-YEAR                 PIC XX.
               15  ORDER-DATE-MONTH                PIC XX.
               15  ORDER-DATE-DAY                  PIC XX.
           05  ORDER-DATE-ENTERED.
             10  ORDER-DATE-ENTERED-MONTH          PIC XX.
             10  ORDER-DATE-ENTERED-DAY            PIC XX.
             10  ORDER-DATE-ENTERED-YEAR           PIC XX.
           05  ORDER-TOTAL-COST                    PIC S9(7)V99   COMP-3.
           05  ORDER-TOTAL-PRICE                   PIC S9(7)V99   COMP-3.
           05  ORDER-LINE-COUNT                    PIC S9999      COMP.
           05  ORDER-ALL-LINES.
             10  ORDER-LINE-ITEM               OCCURS 1 TO 9
                                               DEPENDING ON ORDER-LINE-COUNT
                                               INDEXED BY ORDER-LINE-I.
               15  ORDER-ITEM-NUMBER               PIC X(8).
               15  ORDER-ITEM-DESCRIPTION          PIC X(19).
               15  ORDER-ITEM-DATE.
                 20  ORDER-ITEM-DATE-MONTH         PIC XX.
                 20  ORDER-ITEM-DATE-DAY           PIC XX.
                 20  ORDER-ITEM-DATE-YEAR          PIC XX.
               15  ORDER-UNIT                      PIC S9(5)      COMP-3.
               15  ORDER-UNIT-COST                 PIC S9(5)V99   COMP-3.
               15  ORDER-UNIT-PRICE                PIC S9(5)V99   COMP-3.
```

Fig. 22.4. (Continued)

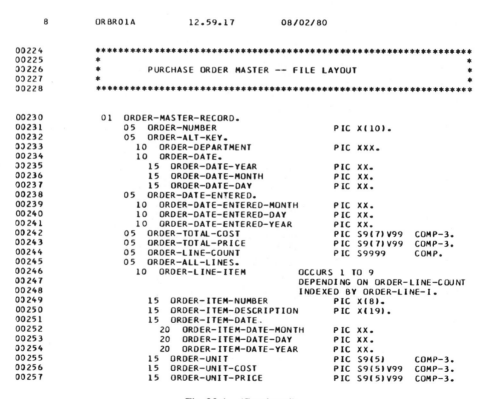

```
9          ORBR01A          12.59.17          08/02/80

           *****************************************************************
           *                                                               *
           *                 TRANSACTION WORK AREA                         *
           *                                                               *
           *****************************************************************

            01  TWA-AREA.

                05  TWA-LINE-ITEM-MAP.
                  10  TWA-LINE-NUMBER-MAP-L            PIC S9999 COMP.
                  10  TWA-LINE-NUMBER-MAP-A            PIC X.
                  10  TWA-LINE-NUMBER-MAP              PIC 9.
                  10  TWA-ITEM-NUMBER-MAP-L            PIC S9999 COMP.
                  10  TWA-ITEM-NUMBER-MAP-A            PIC X.
                  10  TWA-ITEM-NUMBER-MAP              PIC X(8).
                  10  TWA-ITEM-DESCRIPTION-MAP-L       PIC S9999 COMP.
                  10  TWA-ITEM-DESCRIPTION-MAP-A       PIC X.
                  10  TWA-ITEM-DESCRIPTION-MAP         PIC X(19).
                  10  TWA-ITEM-DATE-MAP-L              PIC S9999 COMP.
                  10  TWA-ITEM-DATE-MAP-A              PIC X.
                  10  TWA-ITEM-DATE-MAP                PIC X(6).
                  10  TWA-UNIT-MAP-L                   PIC S9999 COMP.
                  10  TWA-UNIT-MAP-A                   PIC X.
                  10  TWA-UNIT-MAP                     PIC 9(5).
                  10  TWA-UNIT-COST-MAP-L              PIC S9999 COMP.
                  10  TWA-UNIT-COST-MAP-A              PIC X.
                  10  TWA-UNIT-COST-MAP                PIC 9(7).
                  10  TWA-COST-MAP-L                   PIC S9999 COMP.
                  10  TWA-COST-MAP-A                   PIC X.
                  10  TWA-COST-MAP                     PIC 9(8).
                  10  TWA-UNIT-PRICE-MAP-L             PIC S9999 COMP.
                  10  TWA-UNIT-PRICE-MAP-A             PIC X.
                  10  TWA-UNIT-PRICE-MAP               PIC 9(7).
                  10  TWA-PRICE-MAP-L                  PIC S9999 COMP.
                  10  TWA-PRICE-MAP-A                  PIC X.
                  10  TWA-PRICE-MAP                    PIC 9(8).

                05  TWA-LINE-ITEM-ORDER.
                  10  TWA-ITEM-NUMBER-ORDER            PIC X(8).
                  10  TWA-ITEM-DESCRIPTION-ORDER       PIC X(19).
                  10  TWA-ITEM-DATE-ORDER              PIC X(6).
                  10  TWA-UNIT-ORDER                   PIC S9(5)    COMP-3.
                  10  TWA-UNIT-COST-ORDER              PIC S9(5)V99 COMP-3.
                  10  TWA-UNIT-PRICE-ORDER             PIC S9(5)V99 COMP-3.

                05  TWA-OPERATOR-MESSAGE               PIC X(31).
```

Fig. 22.4. (Continued)

```
   10        ORBR01A         12.59.17        08/02/80

                05  TWA-ORDER-RECORD-KEY              PIC X(10).

                05  PREV-ACTION                       PIC X.
                    88  PREV-ACTION-FORWARD                VALUE '1'.
                    88  PREV-ACTION-BACKWARDS              VALUE '2'.
                    88  PREV-ACTION-FORWARD-EOF            VALUE '3'.
                    88  PREV-ACTION-BACKWARDS-EOF          VALUE '4'.
                    88  PREV-ACTION-FORWARD-NOTFOUND       VALUE '5'.
                    88  PREV-ACTION-IMMATERIAL             VALUE '9'.

   11        ORBR01A         12.59.17        08/02/80

            PROCEDURE DIVISION USING DFHEIBLK DFHCOMMAREA.
                CALL 'DFHEI1'.

           ******************************************************************
           *                                                                *
            MAIN-LINE SECTION.
           *                                                                *
           ******************************************************************

           *    EXEC CICS
           *         ADDRESS TWA (TWA-POINTER)
           *    END-EXEC.
                 MOVE 'BB  DC            ' TO DFHEIVO CALL 'DFHEI1' USING
                 DFHEIVO TWA-POINTER.

           *    EXEC CICS
           *         HANDLE AID
           *              CLEAR (FINALIZATION)
           *                PA1 (WRONG-KEY-USED)
           *                PA2 (WRONG-KEY-USED)
           *                PA3 (WRONG-KEY-USED)
           *    END-EXEC.
                 MOVE 'BFO DEDFC          ' TO DFHEIVO CALL 'DFHEI1' USING
                 DFHEIVO GO TO FINALIZATION WRONG-KEY-USED WRONG-KEY-USED
                 WRONG-KEY-USED DEPENDING ON DFHEIGDI.




           *    EXEC CICS
           *         HANDLE CONDITION
           *              MAPFAIL (MAPFAIL-ERROR)
           *              NOTOPEN (FILE-NOT-OPEN)
           *              ERROR   (MAJOR-ERROR)
           *    END-EXEC.
                 MOVE 'BD- DULA           ' TO DFHEIVO CALL 'DFHEI1' USING
                 DFHEIVO GO TO MAPFAIL-ERROR FILE-NOT-OPEN MAJOR-ERROR
                 DEPENDING ON DFHEIGDI.



                IF EIBCALEN NOT EQUAL TO ZEROES
                     IF BROWSE-START-TIME
                          GO TO BROWSE-START
                     ELSE IF INITIAL-ENTRY-TIME
                          GO TO INITIALIZATION
                     ELSE GO TO PROCESS-SWITCH-ERROR.

                IF EIBCALEN EQUAL TO ZEROES
                     GO TO SIGN-ON-VIOLATION.
```

Fig. 22.4. (Continued)

```
    12        ORBRO1A        12.59.17        08/02/80

00367        ***************************************************************
00368        *                                                             *
00369         BROWSE-CONTINUE SECTION.
00370        *                                                             *
00371        ***************************************************************

00373        *    EXEC CICS
00374        *        RECEIVE MAP    ('ORBRMO1')
00375        *                MAPSET ('ORBRSO1')
00376        *                SET    (MAP1-POINTER)
00377        *    END-EXEC.
00378             MOVE 'ORBRMO1' TO DFHEIV1 MOVE 'ORBRSO1' TO DFHEIV2 MOVE 'Q8
00379        -    '& DA   EI  -' TO DFHEIVO CALL 'DFHEI1' USING DFHEIVO
00380             DFHEIV1 MAP1-POINTER DFHEIV98 DFHEIV2.
00381
00382
00383             IF MAP1-START-ORDER NOT NUMERIC
00384                 GO TO INVALID-ORDER.

00386             IF MAP1-START-ORDER EQUAL TO TWA-ORDER-RECORD-KEY
00387                 IF    EIBAID EQUAL TO DFHPF1
00388                     OR EIBAID EQUAL TO DFHENTER
00389                 THEN GO TO BROWSE-FORWARD
00390                 ELSE IF EIBAID EQUAL TO DFHPF2
00391                         IF PREV-ACTION-FORWARD-NOTFOUND
00392                             MOVE HIGH-VALUES TO TWA-ORDER-RECORD-KEY

00394        *                    EXEC CICS
00395        *                        RESETBR
00396        *                            DATASET ('ORTEST')
00397        *                            RIDFLD  (TWA-ORDER-RECORD-KEY)
00398        *                            GTEQ
00399        *                    END-EXEC
00400                             MOVE 'ORTEST' TO DFHEIV3 MOVE 'FMO D -U
00401        -    '' TO DFHEIVO CALL 'DFHEI1' USING DFHEIVO DFHEIV3 DFHEIV99
00402             DFHEIV98 TWA-ORDER-RECORD-KEY
00403
00404
00405
00406                             GO TO BROWSE-BACKWARD
00407                         ELSE GO TO BROWSE-BACKWARD
00408                     ELSE GO TO WRONG-KEY-USED
00409             ELSE MOVE '9' TO PREV-ACTION
00410                 IF MAP1-START-ORDER GREATER THAN TWA-ORDER-RECORD-KEY
00411                     MOVE MAP1-START-ORDER TO TWA-ORDER-RECORD-KEY
00412                     GO TO BROWSE-FORWARD
00413                 ELSE MOVE MAP1-START-ORDER TO TWA-ORDER-RECORD-KEY
00414        *            EXEC CICS
00415        *                RESETBR
00416        *                    DATASET ('ORTEST')
00417        *                    RIDFLD  (TWA-ORDER-RECORD-KEY)
00418        *                    GTEQ
00419        *            END-EXEC

    13        ORBRO1A        12.59.17        08/02/80

00420                     MOVE 'ORTEST' TO DFHEIV3 MOVE 'FMO D -U ' TO
00421             DFHEIVO CALL 'DFHEI1' USING DFHEIVO DFHEIV3 DFHEIV99
00422             DFHEIV98 TWA-ORDER-RECORD-KEY
00423
00424
00425
00426                     GO TO BROWSE-FORWARD.
```

Fig. 22.4. (Continued)

```
   14          ORBR01A          12.59.17         08/02/80

           *****************************************************************
           *                                                               *
            BROWSE-FORWARD SECTION.
           *                                                               *
           *****************************************************************

           *    EXEC CICS
           *         HANDLE CONDITION
           *              ENDFILE (END-OF-FILE-FORWARD)
           *              NOTFND  (RECORD-NOT-FOUND-FORWARD)
           *    END-EXEC.
                 MOVE 'BD  DM(             ' TO DFHEIVO CALL 'DFHEI1' USING
                 DFHEIVO GO TO END-OF-FILE-FORWARD RECORD-NOT-FOUND-FORWARD
                 DEPENDING ON DFHEIGDI.


            READ-NEXT-RECORD.

           *    EXEC CICS
           *         READNEXT DATASET ('ORTEST')
           *                  SET     (POM-POINTER)
           *                  RIDFLD  (TWA-ORDER-RECORD-KEY)
           *    END-EXEC.
                 MOVE 'ORTEST' TO DFHEIV3 MOVE 'F+M DA 0 ' TO DFHEIVO CALL 'D
           -    'FHEI1' USING DFHEIVO DFHEIV3 POM-POINTER DFHEIV98
                 TWA-ORDER-RECORD-KEY DFHEIV98 DFHEIV98.


                IF PREV-ACTION-BACKWARDS
                     MOVE '1' TO PREV-ACTION
                     GO TO READ-NEXT-RECORD.


            LAYOUT-ORDER-SCREEN.
                MOVE TWA-ORDER-RECORD-KEY  TO  MAP1-START-ORDER.
                MOVE ORDER-NUMBER          TO  MAP1-ORDER-NUMBER.
                MOVE ORDER-DEPARTMENT      TO  MAP1-DEPARTMENT.
                MOVE ORDER-DATE-MONTH      TO  MAP1-ORDER-DATE-MONTH.
                MOVE ORDER-DATE-DAY        TO  MAP1-ORDER-DATE-DAY.
                MOVE ORDER-DATE-YEAR       TO  MAP1-ORDER-DATE-YEAR.
                MOVE ORDER-DATE-ENTERED    TO  MAP1-ORDER-DATE-ENTERED.
                MOVE ORDER-TOTAL-COST      TO  MAP1-TOTAL-COST.
                MOVE ORDER-TOTAL-PRICE     TO  MAP1-TOTAL-PRICE.
                MOVE SPACES                TO  MAP1-ERROR.
                SET ORDER-LINE-I           TO  1.
                PERFORM LAYOUT-EACH-LINE
                    UNTIL ORDER-LINE-I GREATER THAN ORDER-LINE-COUNT.
                GO TO DISPLAY-ORDER.


            LAYOUT-EACH-LINE.
                SET MAP1-LINE-I                      TO ORDER-LINE-I.
```

Fig. 22.4. (Continued)

```
15          ORBR01A          12.59.17          08/02/80

                 MOVE ORDER-LINE-ITEM (ORDER-LINE-I) TO TWA-LINE-ITEM-ORDER.
                 MOVE MAP1-LINE-ITEM (MAP1-LINE-I)    TO TWA-LINE-ITEM-MAP.
                 SET TWA-LINE-NUMBER-MAP              TO ORDER-LINE-I.
                 MOVE TWA-ITEM-NUMBER-ORDER     TO  TWA-ITEM-NUMBER-MAP.
                 MOVE TWA-ITEM-DESCRIPTION-ORDER TO TWA-ITEM-DESCRIPTION-MAP.
                 MOVE TWA-ITEM-DATE-ORDER       TO  TWA-ITEM-DATE-MAP.
                 MOVE TWA-UNIT-ORDER            TO  TWA-UNIT-MAP.
                 MOVE TWA-UNIT-COST-ORDER       TO  TWA-UNIT-COST-MAP.
                 COMPUTE TWA-COST-MAP = TWA-UNIT-ORDER * TWA-UNIT-COST-ORDER.
                 MOVE TWA-UNIT-PRICE-ORDER      TO  TWA-UNIT-PRICE-MAP.
                 COMPUTE TWA-PRICE-MAP =
                              TWA-UNIT-ORDER * TWA-UNIT-PRICE-ORDER.
                 MOVE TWA-LINE-ITEM-MAP    TO  MAP1-LINE-ITEM (MAP1-LINE-I).
                 SET ORDER-LINE-I UP BY 1.

             DISPLAY-ORDER.

            *    EXEC CICS
            *         SEND MAP     ('ORBRM01')
            *              MAPSET ('ORBRS01')
            *              FROM    (MAP1-AREA)
            *              ERASE
            *    END-EXEC.
                  MOVE 'ORBRM01' TO DFHEIV1 MOVE 'ORBRS01' TO DFHEIV2 MOVE 'QD
            -    '& D    ESD  -' TO DFHEIV0 CALL 'DFHEI1' USING DFHEIV0
                  DFHEIV1 MAP1-AREA DFHEIV98 DFHEIV2.



             AFTER-DISPLAY.
                 MOVE '1' TO PREV-ACTION.
                 GO TO BROWSE-CONTINUE.

             END-OF-FILE-FORWARD.
                 MOVE TWA-ORDER-RECORD-KEY  TO  MAP1-START-ORDER.
                 MOVE   '3'                 TO  PREV-ACTION.
                 GO TO END-OF-FILE-FORWARD-MESSAGE.

             END-OF-FILE-FORWARD-MESSAGE.
                 MOVE 'END OF FILE' TO MAP1-ERROR.

            *    EXEC CICS
            *         SEND MAP     ('ORBRM01')
            *              MAPSET ('ORBRS01')
            *              FROM    (MAP1-AREA)
            *              ERASE
            *    END-EXEC.
                  MOVE 'ORBRM01' TO DFHEIV1 MOVE 'ORBRS01' TO DFHEIV2 MOVE 'QD
            -    '& D    ESD  -' TO DFHEIV0 CALL 'DFHEI1' USING DFHEIV0
                  DFHEIV1 MAP1-AREA DFHEIV98 DFHEIV2.
```

Fig. 22.4. (Continued)

```
        16          ORBROlA          12.59.17        08/02/80

00528
00529
00530
00531               GO TO BROWSE-CONTINUE.

00533           RECORD-NOT-FOUND-FORWARD.
00534               MOVE TWA-ORDER-RECORD-KEY   TO  MAP1-START-ORDER.
00535               MOVE    '5'                  TO  PREV-ACTION.
00536               GO TO END-OF-FILE-FORWARD-MESSAGE.

        17          ORBROlA          12.59.17        08/02/80

00538           ***************************************************************
00539           *                                                             *
00540            BROWSE-BACKWARD SECTION.
00541           *                                                             *
00542           ***************************************************************

00544           *   EXEC CICS
00545           *       HANDLE CONDITION
00546           *           ENDFILE (END-OF-FILE-BACKWARDS)
00547           *   END-EXEC.
00548               MOVE 'BD  DM              ' TO DFHEIVO CALL 'DFHEI1' USING
00549               DFHEIVO GO TO END-OF-FILE-BACKWARDS DEPENDING ON DFHEIGDI.
00550
00551
00552           READ-PREVIOUS-RECORD.
00553           *   EXEC CICS
00554           *       READPREV DATASET ('ORTEST')
00555           *                SET     (POM-POINTER)
00556           *                RIDFLD  (TWA-ORDER-RECORD-KEY)
00557           *   END-EXEC.
00558               MOVE 'ORTEST' TO DFHEIV3 MOVE 'F&M DA 4 ' TO DFHEIVO CALL 'D
00559           -   'FHEI1' USING DFHEIVO DFHEIV3 POM-POINTER DFHEIV98
00560               TWA-ORDER-RECORD-KEY DFHEIV98 DFHEIV98.
00561
00562
00563               IF PREV-ACTION-FORWARD
00564                   MOVE '2' TO PREV-ACTION
00565                   GO TO READ-PREVIOUS-RECORD.

00567               PERFORM LAYOUT-ORDER-SCREEN THRU DISPLAY-ORDER.
00568               MOVE '2' TO PREV-ACTION.
00569               GO TO BROWSE-CONTINUE.

00571           END-OF-FILE-BACKWARDS.
00572               MOVE TWA-ORDER-RECORD-KEY   TO  MAP1-START-ORDER.
00573               MOVE    'END OF FILE'       TO  MAP1-ERROR.
00574               MOVE    '4'                 TO  PREV-ACTION.

00576           *   EXEC CICS
00577           *       SEND MAP   ('ORBRMO1')
00578           *           MAPSET ('ORBRSO1')
00579           *           FROM   (MAP1-AREA)
00580           *           ERASE
00581           *   END-EXEC.
00582               MOVE 'ORBRMO1' TO DFHEIV1 MOVE 'ORBRSO1' TO DFHEIV2 MOVE 'QO
00583           -   '& D   ESD -' TO DFHEIVO CALL 'DFHEI1' USING DFHEIVO
00584               DFHEIV1 MAP1-AREA DFHEIV98 DFHEIV2.
00585
00586
00587
00588               GO TO BROWSE-CONTINUE.
```

Fig. 22.4. (Continued)

```
18          ORBRO1A          12.59.17          08/02/80

             INVALID-ORDER.
                 MOVE 'INVALID ORDER NUMBER' TO MAP1-ERROR.

            *    EXEC CICS
            *         SEND MAP     ('ORBRMO1')
            *              MAPSET ('ORBRSO1')
            *              FROM    (MAP1-AREA)
            *              ERASE
            *    END-EXEC.
                  MOVE 'ORBRMO1' TO DFHEIV1 MOVE 'ORBRSO1' TO DFHEIV2 MOVE 'QD
            -    '& D    ESD  -' TO DFHEIVO CALL 'DFHEI1' USING DFHEIVO
                  DFHEIV1 MAP1-AREA DFHEIV98 DFHEIV2.



                 GO TO BROWSE-CONTINUE.


19          ORBRO1A          12.59.17          08/02/80

            ****************************************************************
            *                                                              *
             WRONG-KEY-USED SECTION.
            *                                                              *
            ****************************************************************

            *    EXEC CICS
            *         GETMAIN
            *              SET      (MAP1-POINTER)
            *              LENGTH   (983)
            *              INITIMG (HEX-ZEROES)
            *    END-EXEC.
                  MOVE 983 TO DFHEIV11 MOVE '¤B- D  ¤ ' TO DFHEIVO CALL 'DFHEI
            -    '1' USING DFHEIVO MAP1-POINTER DFHEIV11 HEX-ZEROES.




                 MOVE 'WRONG KEY USED' TO MAP1-ERROR.

            *    EXEC CICS
            *         SEND MAP     ('ORBRMO1')
            *              MAPSET ('ORBRSO1')
            *              FROM    (MAP1-AREA)
            *              DATAONLY
            *    END-EXEC.
                  MOVE 'ORBRMO1' TO DFHEIV1 MOVE 'ORBRSO1' TO DFHEIV2 MOVE 'QD
            -    '& D    E-D  -' TO DFHEIVO CALL 'DFHEI1' USING DFHEIVO
                  DFHEIV1 MAP1-AREA DFHEIV98 DFHEIV2.



            *    EXEC CICS
            *         FREEMAIN DATA (MAP1-AREA)
            *    END-EXEC.
                  MOVE '¤D  D    ' TO DFHEIVO CALL 'DFHEI1' USING DFHEIVO
                  MAP1-AREA.

                 GO TO BROWSE-CONTINUE.
```

Fig. 22.4. (Continued)

```
   20         ORBR01A          12.59.17         08/02/80

              ***************************************************************
              *                                                             *
               BROWSE-START SECTION.
              *                                                             *
              ***************************************************************


              *    EXEC CICS
              *         RECEIVE MAP     ('ORBRM01')
              *                 MAPSET ('ORBRS01')
              *                 SET     (MAP1-POINTER)
              *    END-EXEC.
                    MOVE 'ORBRM01' TO DFHEIV1 MOVE 'ORBRS01' TO DFHEIV2 MOVE 'QB
              -    '& DA   EI   -' TO DFHEIV0 CALL 'DFHEI1' USING DFHEIV0
                    DFHEIV1 MAP1-POINTER DFHEIV98 DFHEIV2.


               BROWSE-STARTING-RECORD.

                   IF MAP1-START-ORDER NOT NUMERIC
                        GO TO INVALID-ORDER-NUMBER-START.

                   MOVE MAP1-START-ORDER  TO  TWA-ORDER-RECORD-KEY.

              *    EXEC CICS
              *         HANDLE CONDITION
              *              NOTFND (RECORD-NOT-FOUND-STARTBROWSE)
              *    END-EXEC.
                    MOVE 'BD  D(              ' TO DFHEIV0 CALL 'DFHEI1' USING
                    DFHEIV0 GO TO RECORD-NOT-FOUND-STARTBROWSE DEPENDING ON
                    DFHEIGDI.

               BROWSE-COMMAND.

              *    EXEC CICS
              *         STARTBR DATASET ('ORTEST')
              *                 RIDFLD  (TWA-ORDER-RECORD-KEY)
              *                 GTEQ
              *    END-EXEC.
                    MOVE 'ORTEST' TO DFHEIV3 MOVE 'F¤0 D -- ' TO DFHEIV0 CALL 'D
              -    'FHEI1' USING DFHEIV0 DFHEIV3 DFHEIV99 DFHEIV98
                    TWA-ORDER-RECORD-KEY.


                   IF TWA-ORDER-RECORD-KEY NUMERIC
                        GO TO BROWSE-FORWARD
                   ELSE GO TO BROWSE-BACKWARD.


               RECORD-NOT-FOUND-STARTBROWSE.
                   MOVE HIGH-VALUES TO TWA-ORDER-RECORD-KEY.
                   GO TO BROWSE-COMMAND.
```

Fig. 22.4. (Continued)

```
    21        ORBR01A          12.59.17        08/02/80

               INVALID-ORDER-NUMBER-START.
                   MOVE 'INVALID ORDER NUMBER' TO MAP1-ERROR.

              *    EXEC CICS
              *         SEND MAP    ('ORBRM01')
              *              MAPSET ('ORBRS01')
              *              FROM   (MAP1-AREA)
              *              DATAONLY
              *    END-EXEC.
                    MOVE 'ORBRM01' TO DFHEIV1 MOVE 'ORBRS01' TO DFHEIV2 MOVE 'QD
              -    '& D    E-D  -' TO DFHEIV0 CALL 'DFHEI1' USING DFHEIV0
                    DFHEIV1 MAP1-AREA DFHEIV98 DFHEIV2.



                   MOVE  '1'  TO COMMAREA-PROCESS-SW.

              *    EXEC CICS
              *         RETURN TRANSID  (EIBTRNID)
              *                COMMAREA (COMMUNICATION-AREA)
              *                LENGTH   (1)
              *    END-EXEC.
                    MOVE 1 TO DFHEIV11 MOVE '+H- D  & ' TO DFHEIV0 CALL 'DFHEI1'
                    USING DFHEIV0 EIBTRNID COMMUNICATION-AREA DFHEIV11.



    22        ORBR01A          12.59.17        08/02/80

              *****************************************************************
              *                                                               *
               INITIALIZATION SECTION.
              *                                                               *
              *****************************************************************


              *    EXEC CICS
              *         SEND MAP    ('ORBRM01')
              *              MAPSET ('ORBRS01')
              *              MAPONLY
              *              ERASE
              *    END-EXEC.
                    MOVE 'ORBRM01' TO DFHEIV1 MOVE 'ORBRS01' TO DFHEIV2 MOVE 'QD
              -    '& D    ESD  -' TO DFHEIV0 CALL 'DFHEI1' USING DFHEIV0
                    DFHEIV1 DFHEIV99 DFHEIV98 DFHEIV2.



                   MOVE  '1'  TO  COMMAREA-PROCESS-SW.

              *    EXEC CICS
              *         RETURN TRANSID  ('ORBR')
              *                COMMAREA (COMMUNICATION-AREA)
              *                LENGTH   (1)
              *    END-EXEC.
                    MOVE 'ORBR' TO DFHEIV5 MOVE 1 TO DFHEIV11 MOVE '+H- D  & '
                    TO DFHEIV0 CALL 'DFHEI1' USING DFHEIV0 DFHEIV5
                    COMMUNICATION-AREA DFHEIV11.
```

Fig. 22.4. (Continued)

```
    23          ORBR01A          12.59.17          08/02/80

           ***********************************************************************
           *                                                                     *
            FINALIZATION SECTION.
           *                                                                     *
           ***********************************************************************


            PREPARE-TERMINATION-MESSAGE.
                MOVE JOB-NORMAL-END-MESSAGE TO TWA-OPERATOR-MESSAGE.

            JOB-TERMINATED.
           *    EXEC CICS
           *          SEND FROM   (TWA-OPERATOR-MESSAGE)
           *               LENGTH (31)
           *               ERASE
           *    END-EXEC.
                 MOVE 31 TO DFHEIV11 MOVE 'DDO D    A       ' TO DFHEIV0 CALL '
           -    'DFHEI1' USING DFHEIV0 DFHEIV99 DFHEIV98 TWA-OPERATOR-MESSAGE
                 DFHEIV11.



            END-OF-JOB.
           *    EXEC CICS
           *         RETURN
           *    END-EXEC.
                 MOVE '+H  D  & ' TO DFHEIV0 CALL 'DFHEI1' USING DFHEIV0.

```

Fig. 22.4. (Continued)

```
    24          ORBRO1A          12.59.17          08/02/80

00787          ***********************************************************************
00788          *                                                                     *
00789          ABNORMAL-TERMINATION SECTION.
00790          *                                                                     *
00791          ***********************************************************************

00793          FILE-NOT-OPEN.

00795     *       EXEC CICS
00796     *          XCTL PROGRAM ('TEL2OPEN')
00797     *       END-EXEC.
00798             MOVE 'TEL2OPEN' TO DFHEIV3 MOVE '+0   D   B ' TO DFHEIVO CALL
00799             'DFHEI1' USING DFHEIVO DFHEIV3.
00800

00802          MAPFAIL-ERROR.
00803             MOVE 'MAP FAILURE' TO MAJOR-ERROR-MSG.
00804             GO TO PREPARE-ABORT-MESSAGE.

00806          PROCESS-SWITCH-ERROR.
00807             MOVE 'PROCESS ERROR' TO MAJOR-ERROR-MSG.
00808             GO TO PREPARE-ABORT-MESSAGE.

00810          SIGN-ON-VIOLATION.
00811             MOVE 'SIGNON VIOLATION' TO MAJOR-ERROR-MSG.
00812             GO TO PREPARE-ABORT-MESSAGE.

00814          MAJOR-ERROR.
00815             MOVE   EIBFN     TO  OLD-EIBFN.
00816             MOVE   EIBRCODE  TO  OLD-EIBRCODE.

00818     *       EXEC CICS
00819     *          DUMP DUMPCODE ('ERRS')
00820     *       END-EXEC.
00821             MOVE 'ERRS' TO DFHEIV5 MOVE '*B   D   = ' TO DFHEIVO CALL 'DFH
00822     -       'EI1' USING DFHEIVO DFHEIV5.
00823
00824             MOVE 'MAJOR ERROR' TO MAJOR-ERROR-MSG.
00825             GO TO PREPARE-ABORT-MESSAGE.

00827          PREPARE-ABORT-MESSAGE.
00828             MOVE JOB-ABORTED-MESSAGE TO TWA-OPERATOR-MESSAGE.
00829             GO TO JOB-TERMINATED.
```

Fig. 22.4. (Continued)

THE MAIN-LINE SECTION

1. Lines 325–329. ADDRESS command for the TWA.
2. Lines 331–340. HANDLE AID command. The PA keys will result in the "WRONG KEY USED" error.
3. Lines 345–353. HANDLE CONDITION command. The NOTOPEN condition for the order file is specified here rather than in other sections because the program is in conversational mode and this specification will not change during the session.
4. Lines 357–362. The selection of sections.
5. Lines 364–365. If the program is executed at the start of the session by an operator-entered transaction identifier instead of through an XCTL command from the Sign-on program, a sign-on violation occurs. This is so if EIBCALEN is equal to zero.

THE INITIALIZATION SECTION

1. Lines 733–741. Display the browse map.
2. Line 745. Set the communication area switch to 1.
3. Lines 747–754. Terminate the task. This section is implemented in the pseudoconversational mode so the task is terminated while the operator enters the browse starting point.

THE BROWSE-START SECTION

1. Lines 654–661. Read the map that contains the order number that is the starting point of the browse.
2. Lines 671–677. HANDLE CONDITION command for the order file.
3. Lines 679–688. STARTBR command to establish the starting point of the browse.

4. Lines 691–693. Line 691 will be executed if a record was found based on the order number and is always executed because of the GTEQ operand of STARTBR unless the order number entered is greater than the last order number in the file. We then go into a forward browse to display this record. Line 693 will be executed if a record was not found, in which case lines 696–697 would have been executed to mark the end of the file. We therefore go into a backward browse to display the last record in the file.

5. Line 696. If the record is not found, we set the key to HIGH-VALUES to mark the end of the file as the starting point of the browse (in this case, we have to browse backwards).

6. If the order number (as entered by the operator) is not numeric:
   a. Line 700. Lay out the message "INVALID ORDER NUMBER" in the area secured by CICS/VS for the symbolic description map.
   b. Lines 702–710. Display the error message.
   c. Line 714. Set the communication area switch to 1.
   d. Lines 716–722. Terminate the task.

THE BROWSE-FORWARD SECTION

1. Lines 434–441. HANDLE CONDITION command for the order file. The ENDFILE option is for the routine if the end of the file is reached in a normal forward browse. The NOTFND option is for the routine if we do not find a record during skip-browse forward.

2. Lines 444–453. Read the next record in ascending sequence.

3. Lines 456–458. If the previous File read was a READPREV command, then we bypass this record; otherwise we would be displaying the same record as in the previous display.

4. Lines 460–491. Move the record data into the symbolic description map. Lines 477–491 illustrate a Cobol efficiency technique that reduces the use of an index.

5. Lines 493–503. Display the record. The ERASE option is specified since the data is variable (from 1 to 9 lines). If the data were fixed, this would not be required and DATAONLY would then be specified.
6. Lines 508–509. The forward browse is finished; wait for the next action from the operator.
7. Lines 512–531. If the end of the file is reached during normal forward browse, we display the "END OF FILE" message.
8. Lines 534–536. If the record is not found in a skip-forward browse, we likewise display the "END OF FILE" message.

THE BROWSE-BACKWARD SECTION

1. Lines 544–549. HANDLE CONDITION command for the order file. The ENDFILE option is for the routine if the end of the file is reached in a normal backward browse. The NOTFND option is not specified because it will never happen in a READPREV command if the GTEQ operand is specified in the browse.
2. Lines 552–560. Read the next record in descending sequence.
3. Lines 563–565. If the previous File read was a READNEXT command, then we bypass this record; otherwise we would be displaying the same record as in the previous display.
4. Line 567. Display the record.
5. Lines 568–569. The backward browse is finished; wait for the next action from the operator.
6. Lines 571–588. If the end of the file is reached during normal backward browse, we display the "END OF FILE" message.
7. Lines 593–601. If any new browse starting point entered is not numeric, we display the "INVALID ORDER NUMBER" message.

THE BROWSE-CONTINUE SECTION

1. Lines 373–380. Read the map containing the record key.

2. If a new order number was not entered:
   a. Lines 387–389. If the PF1 or ENTER key was used, do a forward browse.
   b. If the PF2 key was used:
      1. Lines 391–406. If the previous action was a skip-forward browse and the record was not found (this can happen if the last order number entered by the operator was higher than the last record in the file), the browse is reset to the end of the file and the last record is displayed.
      2. Line 407. Otherwise, do a backward browse.
   c. Line 408. Otherwise, the wrong key was used.

3. If a new order number was entered:
   a. Lines 410–412. If the new order number is greater than the previously displayed order, then do a skip-forward browse.
   b. Lines 413–426. Otherwise, the browse starting point is reset using the new order number, and do a forward browse.

THE WRONG-KEY-USED SECTION

1. Lines 614–621. GETMAIN command to secure main storage for the map that will contain the error message. This is because the PA keys do not allow CICS/VS to secure main storage for the symbolic description map through a RECEIVE MAP command.

2. Line 626. Move the "WRONG KEY USED" message into the area secured.

3. Lines 628–636. Display the error message.

4. Lines 640–644. FREEMAIN command to free main storage secured in the previous GETMAIN command. We have to do this to save main storage because, since we are using the conversational mode of processing, the area will not otherwise be freed through task termination.

5. Line 646. The operator may continue the browse.

THE FINALIZATION SECTION

1. Lines 768–775. Display the "JOB NORMALLY TERMINATED" message.
2. Lines 780–783. Terminate the session.

THE ABNORMAL-TERMINATION SECTION

These are the routines used to abnormally terminate the session on errors and CICS/VS command exceptional conditions not covered by a HANDLE CONDITION command.

EXAMPLE

The following are facsimiles of actual photographs taken of a CRT terminal during a session.

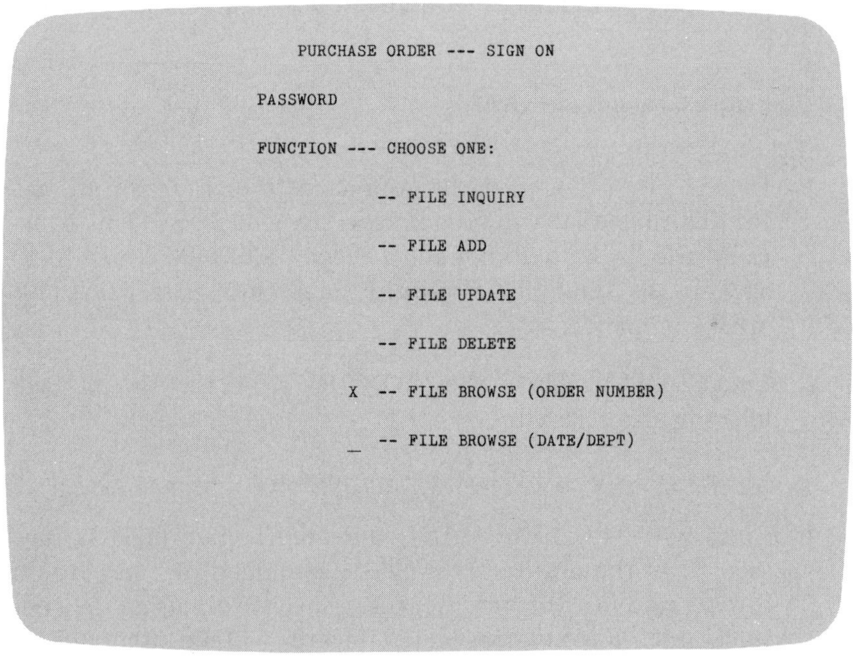

Fig. 22.5. The File Browse (by order number) application is selected by keying in an "X" on the File Browse line and the corresponding password, then hitting the ENTER key.

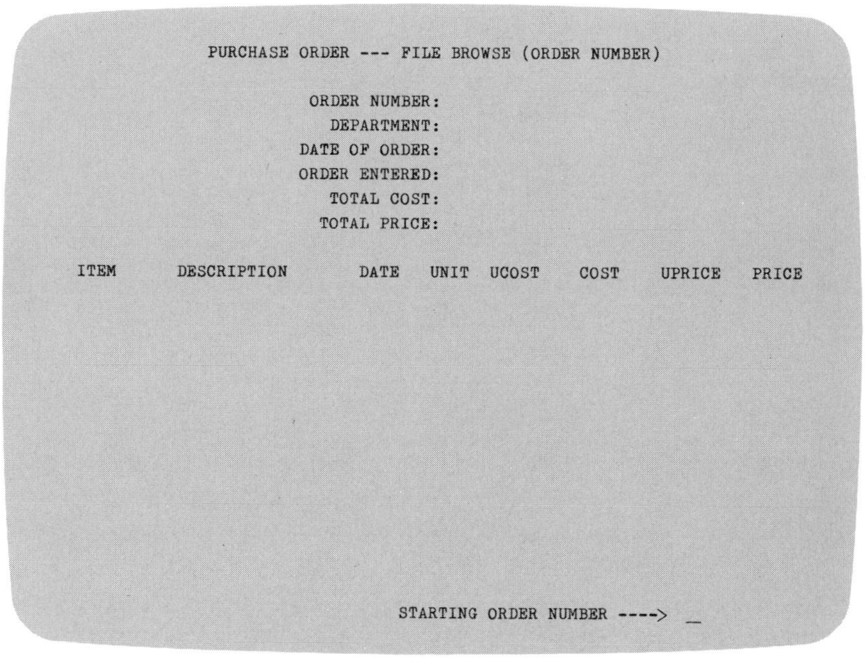

Fig. 22.6. The Sign On program executes which then transfers control to the File Browse program. This displays the File Browse map.

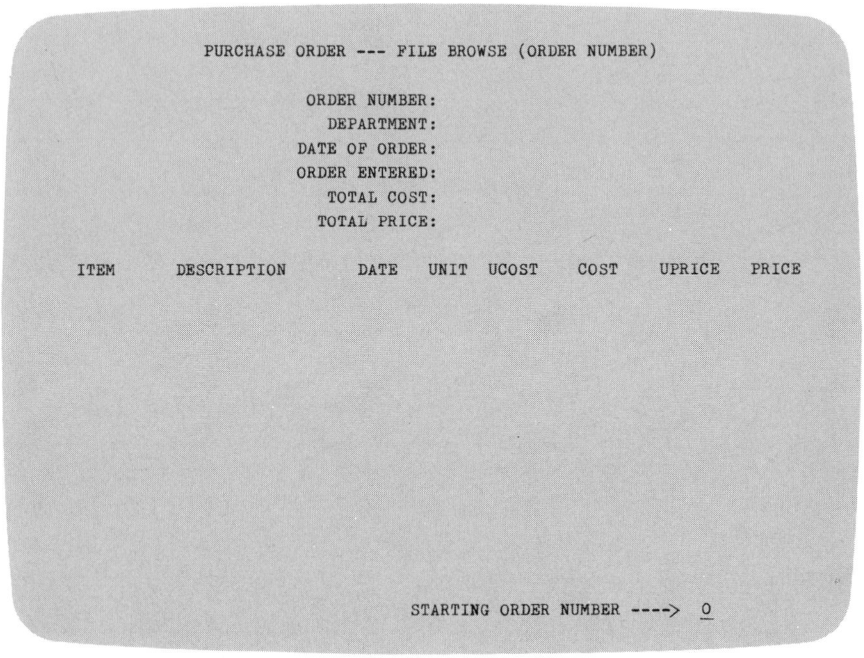

Fig. 22.7. The operator keys in the browse starting point, then hits the ENTER key.

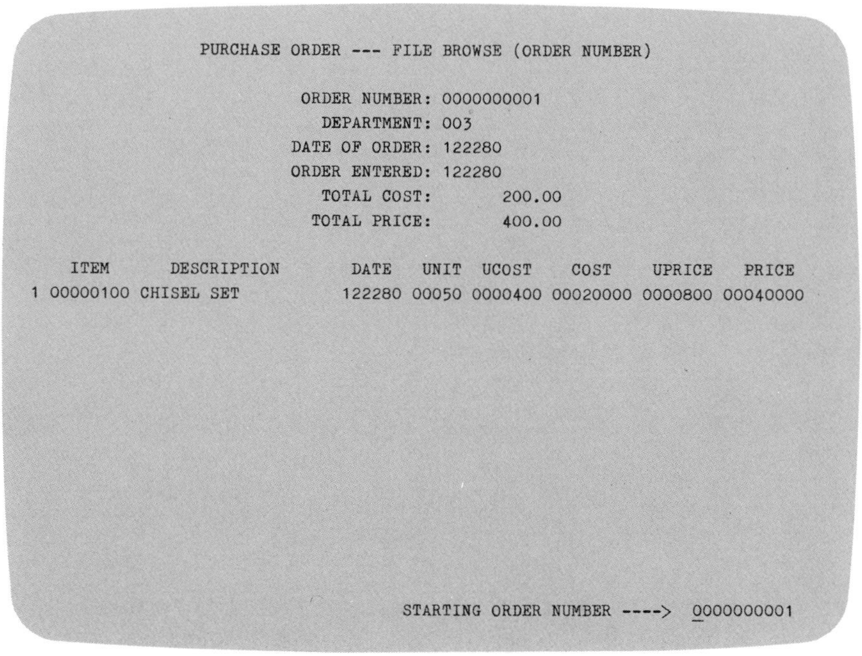

Fig. 22.8. The program displays the record whose order number is equal to the starting point. Since the record does not exist, the next higher one is used.

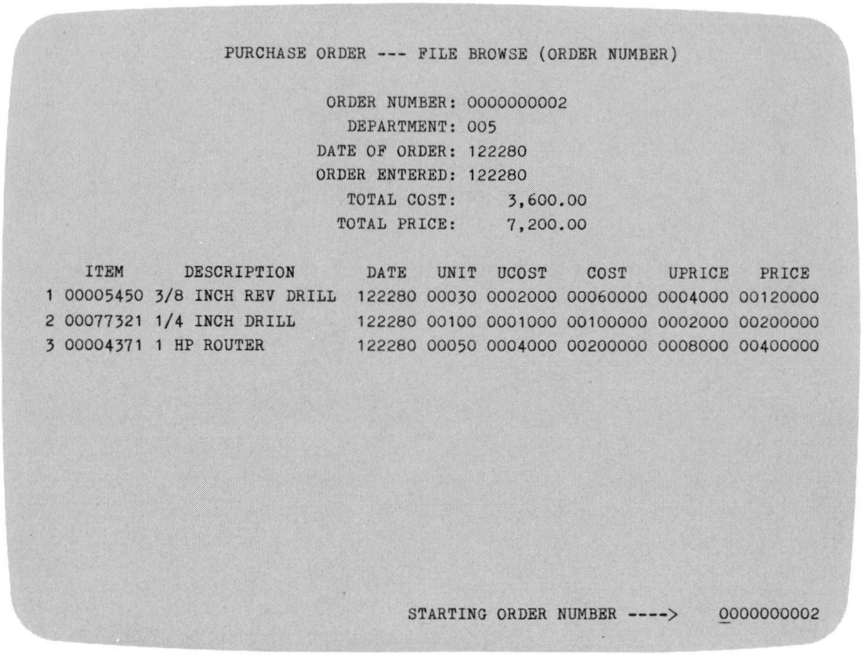

```
                PURCHASE ORDER --- FILE BROWSE (ORDER NUMBER)

                           ORDER NUMBER: 0000000002
                             DEPARTMENT: 005
                          DATE OF ORDER: 122280
                          ORDER ENTERED: 122280
                             TOTAL COST:      3,600.00
                            TOTAL PRICE:      7,200.00

     ITEM       DESCRIPTION          DATE   UNIT  UCOST     COST     UPRICE   PRICE
1 00005450 3/8 INCH REV DRILL      122280 00030 0002000 00060000 0004000 00120000
2 00077321 1/4 INCH DRILL          122280 00100 0001000 00100000 0002000 00200000
3 00004371 1 HP ROUTER             122280 00050 0004000 00200000 0008000 00400000

                                    STARTING ORDER NUMBER ---->     0000000002
```

Fig. 22.9. The operator hits the PF1 key, which results in the display of the record next in ascending sequence.

```
                 PURCHASE ORDER --- FILE BROWSE (ORDER NUMBER)

                           ORDER NUMBER: 0000000002
                             DEPARTMENT: 005
                          DATE OF ORDER: 122280
                          ORDER ENTERED: 122280
                             TOTAL COST:        3,600.00
                            TOTAL PRICE:        7,200.00

     ITEM        DESCRIPTION        DATE   UNIT  UCOST     COST    UPRICE    PRICE
1 00005450 3/8 INCH REV DRILL 122280 00030 0002000 00060000 0004000 00120000
2 00076321 1/4 INCH DRILL     122280 00100 0001000 00100000 0002000 00200000
3 00004371 1 HP ROUTER        122280 00050 0004000 00200000 0008000 00400000











                                  STARTING ORDER NUMBER ---->    16_
```

Fig. 22.10. The operator keys in another browse starting point, then hits the ENTER key.

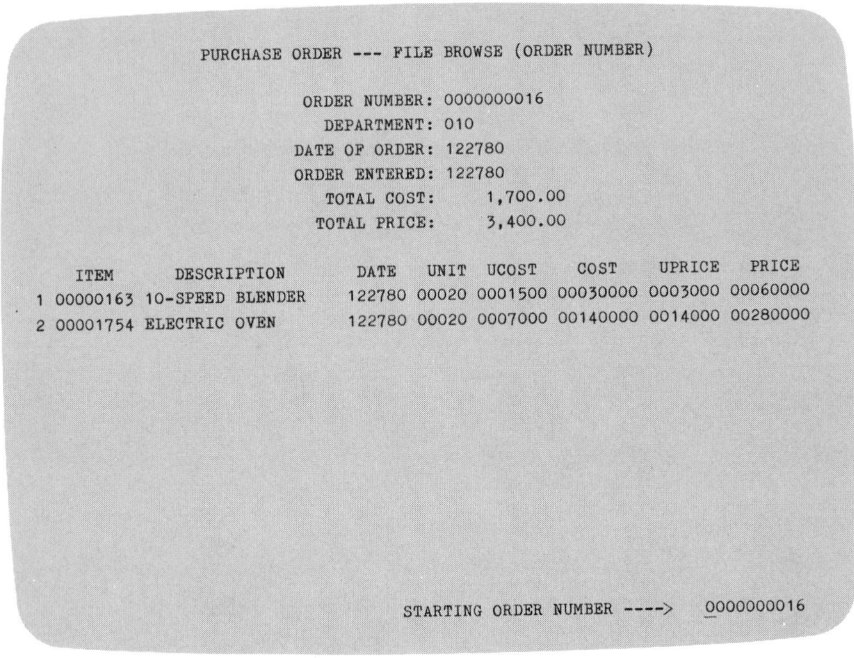

PURCHASE ORDER --- FILE BROWSE (ORDER NUMBER)
ORDER NUMBER: 0000000016
DEPARTMENT: 010
DATE OF ORDER: 122780
ORDER ENTERED: 122780
TOTAL COST: 1,700.00
TOTAL PRICE: 3,400.00
ITEM DESCRIPTION DATE UNIT UCOST COST UPRICE PRICE
1 00000163 10-SPEED BLENDER 122780 00020 0001500 00030000 0003000 00060000
2 00001754 ELECTRIC OVEN 122780 00020 0007000 00140000 0014000 00280000
STARTING ORDER NUMBER ----> 0000000016

Fig. 22.11. The program displays the record whose order number is equal to the new starting point. The skip-forward function is executed to do this.

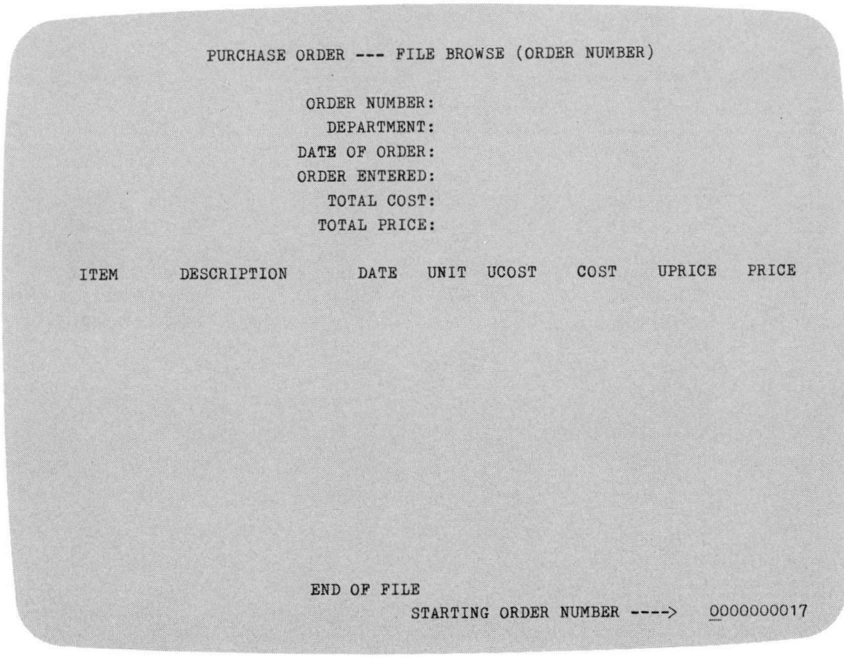

Fig. 22.12. After repeated PF1's, the end of the file is reached. Order number 17 was the last order displayed.

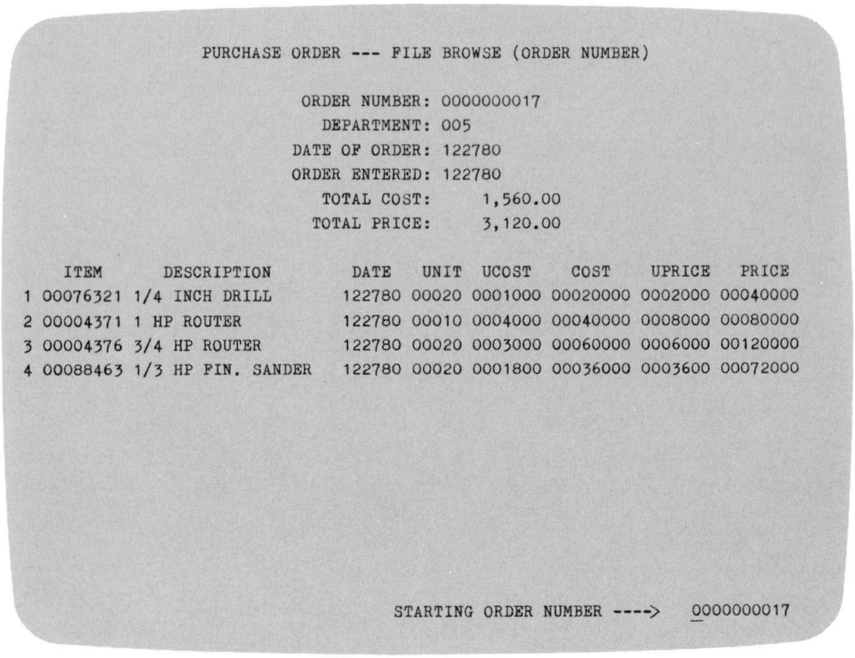

Fig. 22.13. The operator hits the PF2 key, which results in the display of the record next in descending sequence.

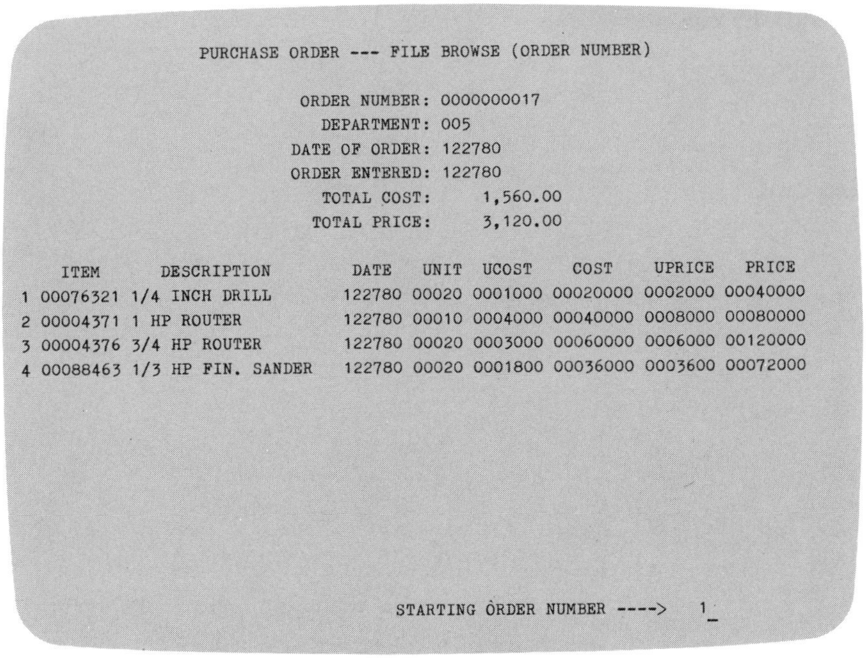

PURCHASE ORDER --- FILE BROWSE (ORDER NUMBER)

ORDER NUMBER: 0000000017
DEPARTMENT: 005
DATE OF ORDER: 122780
ORDER ENTERED: 122780
TOTAL COST: 1,560.00
TOTAL PRICE: 3,120.00

	ITEM	DESCRIPTION	DATE	UNIT	UCOST	COST	UPRICE	PRICE
1	00076321	1/4 INCH DRILL	122780	00020	0001000	00020000	0002000	00040000
2	00004371	1 HP ROUTER	122780	00010	0004000	00040000	0008000	00080000
3	00004376	3/4 HP ROUTER	122780	00020	0003000	00060000	0006000	00120000
4	00088463	1/3 HP FIN. SANDER	122780	00020	0001800	00036000	0003600	00072000

STARTING ORDER NUMBER ----> 1_

Fig. 22.14. The operator keys in another browse starting point, then hits the ENTER key.

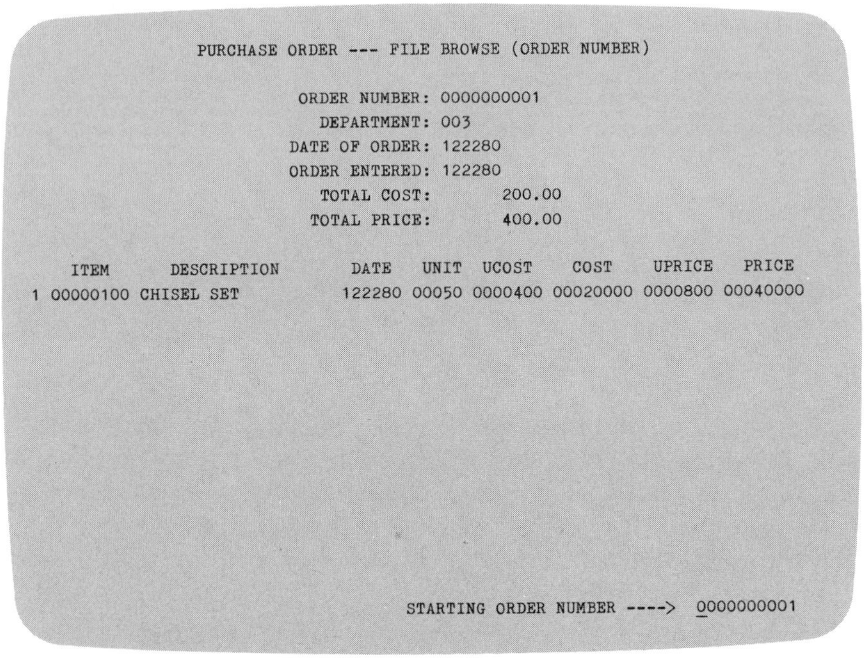

```
                 PURCHASE ORDER --- FILE BROWSE (ORDER NUMBER)

                        ORDER NUMBER: 0000000001
                          DEPARTMENT: 003
                       DATE OF ORDER: 122280
                      ORDER ENTERED: 122280
                          TOTAL COST:          200.00
                         TOTAL PRICE:          400.00

    ITEM       DESCRIPTION         DATE   UNIT  UCOST    COST      UPRICE  PRICE
1 00000100 CHISEL SET            122280 00050 0000400 00020000 0000800 00040000



                                STARTING ORDER NUMBER ----> 0000000001
```

Fig. 22.15. The program displays the record whose order number is equal to the new starting point. The skip-backward function is executed to do this.

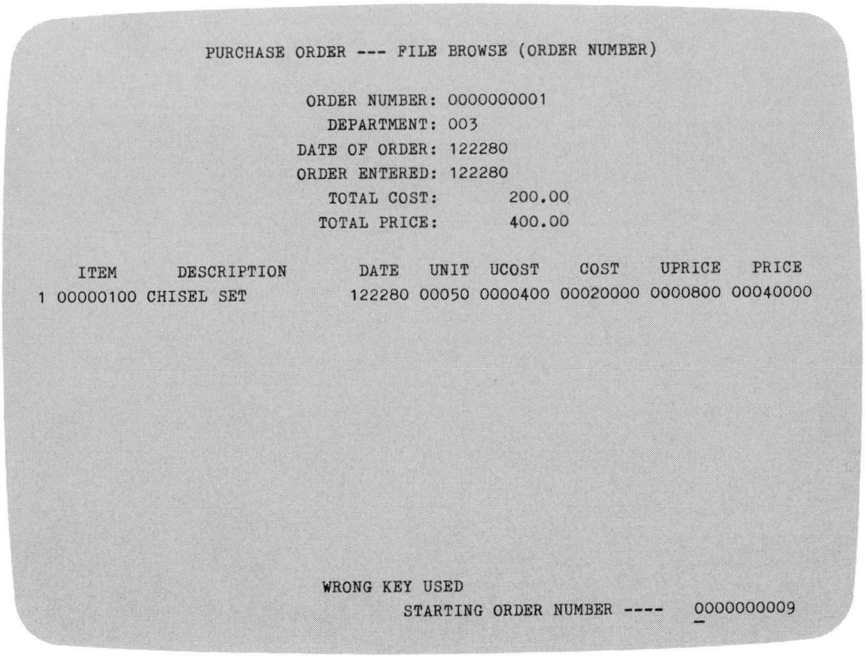

Fig. 22.16. If the operator keys in another browse starting point but then hits one of the PA keys instead of the ENTER key, the "WRONG KEY USED" message is displayed.

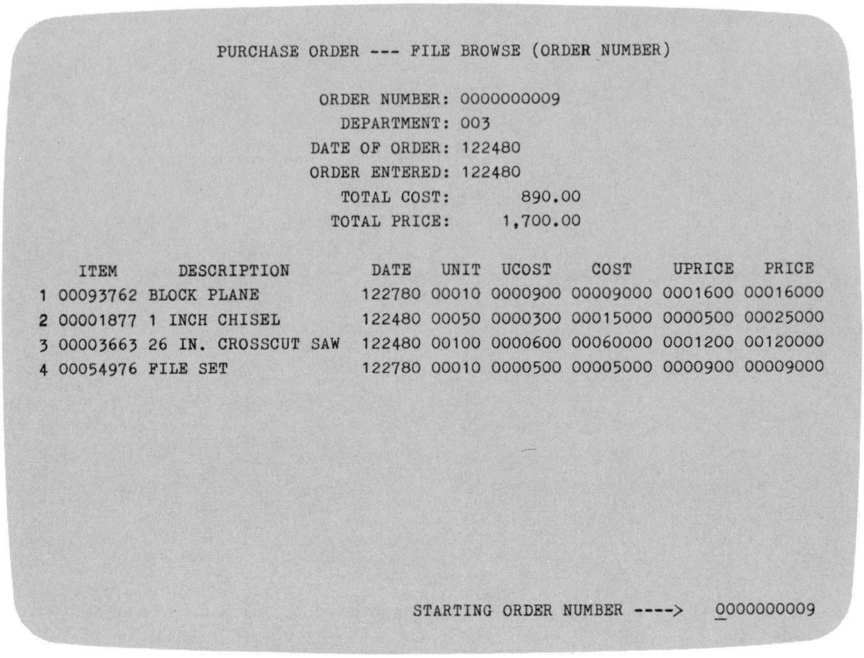

```
                    PURCHASE ORDER --- FILE BROWSE (ORDER NUMBER)

                              ORDER NUMBER: 0000000009
                                DEPARTMENT: 003
                             DATE OF ORDER: 122480
                             ORDER ENTERED: 122480
                                TOTAL COST:       890.00
                               TOTAL PRICE:     1,700.00

     ITEM       DESCRIPTION          DATE   UNIT  UCOST     COST     UPRICE   PRICE
1 00093762 BLOCK PLANE              122780 00010 0000900 00009000 0001600 00016000
2 00001877 1 INCH CHISEL            122480 00050 0000300 00015000 0000500 00025000
3 00003663 26 IN. CROSSCUT SAW      122480 00100 0000600 00060000 0001200 00120000
4 00054976 FILE SET                 122780 00010 0000500 00005000 0000900 00009000

                                        STARTING ORDER NUMBER ---->   0000000009
```

Fig. 22.17. If the operator then hits the ENTER key, the session continues. The record selected in Fig. 22.16 is now displayed.

23

The File Browse Program (Alternate Key)

INTRODUCTION

This File Browse program allows the operator to browse through the order file according to order date within department number sequence (alternate key). He may also skip records in both the forward and backward directions by entering a new browse starting point. The program executes when selected by the Sign-on program and will continue executing in the session until terminated by the operator. The flow of control to execute this program is shown in Figure 23.1.

PROGRAM SPECIFICATION

The File Browse program (alternate key) specifications are as follows:

1. Implement the program using the conversational mode of processing.
2. Use 'ORBS' as the transaction identifier. However, the session should not be started by using this identifier, but rather through an XCTL command from the Sign-on program.
3. If the session is started by using the transaction identifier, abort the session with the message "JOB ABORTED – SIGNON VIOLATION."
4. The browse starting point is based on the order date within the department number entered by the operator. If the record is not in the file, the record next in ascending sequence is used. If the starting point is higher than the last record in the file, the last record is used.
5. On the PF1 key, display the record next in ascending sequence.

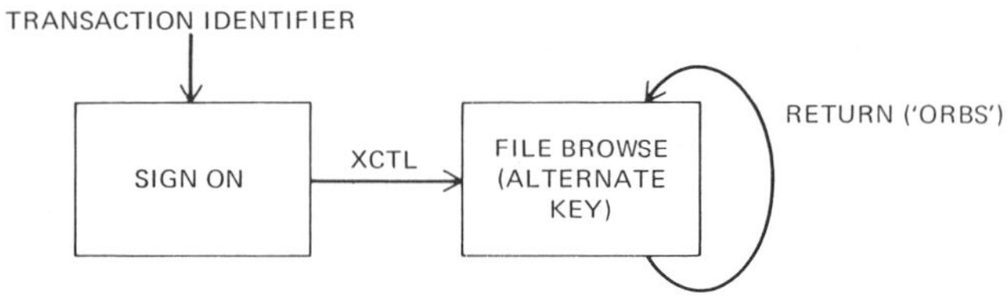

Fig. 23.1. File Browse Application (Alternate Key).

6. On the PF2 key, display the record next in descending sequence.
7. The operator may restart the browse at some other point by entering a new starting point.
8. On any PA key, display the message "WRONG KEY USED"; allow the operator to continue on with the session.
9. In this example, display only one record per page.

SCREEN LAYOUT

The screen layout to be used in the program is shown in Figure 23.2. All 9s are numeric fields and Xs are alphanumeric fields.

MAP PROGRAM

The map program corresponding to the screen layout is shown in Figure 23.3.

PROGRAM LISTING

The program listing for the File Browse program (date of order within department number) is shown in Figure 23.4. The listing is that of the compiler and not the command-language translator, and thus the commands are already as translated.

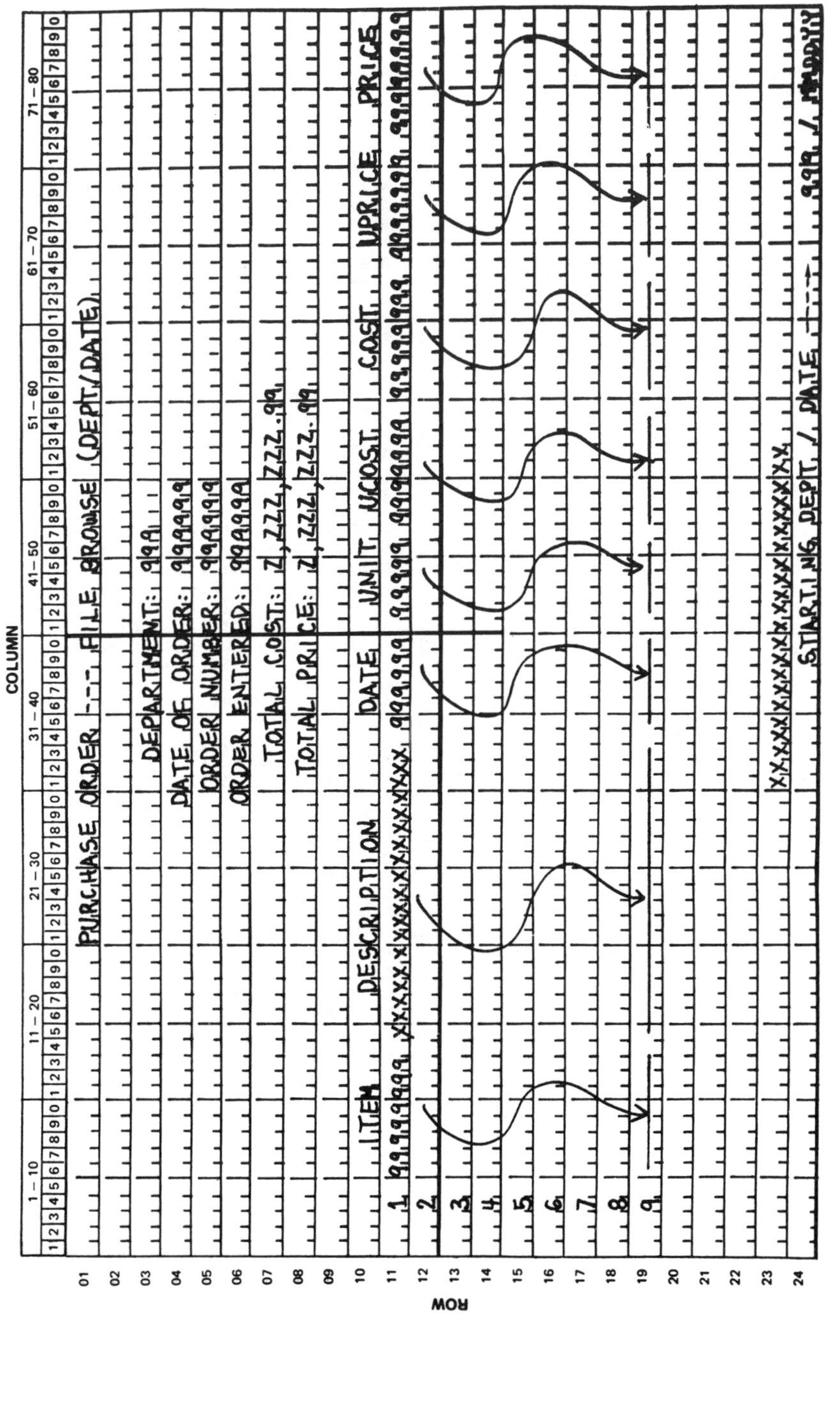

Fig. 23.2. Screen Layout – File Browse (Alternate Key).

```
STMT    SOURCE STATEMENT                              DOS/VS ASSEMBLER REL 34.0 13.13

   1             PRINT NOGEN
   2 ORBSS01     DFHMSD TYPE=MAP,MODE=INOUT,CTRL=FREEKB,LANG=COBOL,TIOAPFX=YES
  12 ORBSM01     DFHMDI SIZE=(24,80)
  40 DUMMY       DFHMDF POS=(01,01),LENGTH=01,ATTRB=(ASKIP,DRK,FSET),            X
                       INITIAL='1'
  52             DFHMDF POS=(01,20),LENGTH=42,ATTRB=(ASKIP,BRT),                 X
                       INITIAL='PURCHASE ORDER --- FILE BROWSE (DEPT/DATE)'
  64             DFHMDF POS=(03,32),LENGTH=11,ATTRB=ASKIP,INITIAL='DEPARTMENT '
  76 DEPT        DFHMDF POS=(03,44),LENGTH=03,ATTRB=(ASKIP,BRT)
  87             DFHMDF POS=(04,29),LENGTH=14,ATTRB=ASKIP,                       X
                       INITIAL='DATE OF ORDER '
  99 DATEOR      DFHMDF POS=(04,44),LENGTH=06,ATTRB=(ASKIP,BRT)
 110             DFHMDF POS=(05,30),LENGTH=13,ATTRB=ASKIP,                       X
                       INITIAL='ORDER NUMBER '
 122 ORDER       DFHMDF POS=(05,44),LENGTH=10,ATTRB=(ASKIP,BRT)
 133             DFHMDF POS=(06,29),LENGTH=14,ATTRB=ASKIP,                       X
                       INITIAL='ORDER ENTERED '
 145 DATEENT     DFHMDF POS=(06,44),LENGTH=06,ATTRB=(ASKIP,BRT)
 156             DFHMDF POS=(07,32),LENGTH=11,ATTRB=ASKIP,INITIAL='TOTAL COST '
 168 TOTCOST     DFHMDF POS=(07,44),LENGTH=12,ATTRB=(ASKIP,BRT),                 X
                       PICOUT='Z,ZZZ,ZZZ.99'
 179             DFHMDF POS=(08,31),LENGTH=12,ATTRB=ASKIP,                       X
                       INITIAL='TOTAL PRICE '
 191 TOTPRCE     DFHMDF POS=(08,44),LENGTH=12,ATTRB=(ASKIP,BRT),                 X
                       PICOUT='Z,ZZZ,ZZZ.99'
 202             DFHMDF POS=(10,07),LENGTH=04,ATTRB=ASKIP,INITIAL='ITEM'
 214             DFHMDF POS=(10,17),LENGTH=11,ATTRB=ASKIP,INITIAL='DESCRIPTION'
 226             DFHMDF POS=(10,35),LENGTH=04,ATTRB=ASKIP,INITIAL='DATE'
 238             DFHMDF POS=(10,42),LENGTH=04,ATTRB=ASKIP,INITIAL='UNIT'
 250             DFHMDF POS=(10,48),LENGTH=05,ATTRB=ASKIP,INITIAL='UCOST'
 262             DFHMDF POS=(10,57),LENGTH=04,ATTRB=ASKIP,INITIAL='COST'
 274             DFHMDF POS=(10,65),LENGTH=06,ATTRB=ASKIP,INITIAL='UPRICE'
 286             DFHMDF POS=(10,74),LENGTH=05,ATTRB=ASKIP,INITIAL='PRICE'
 298 LINE1       DFHMDF POS=(11,03),LENGTH=01,ATTRB=ASKIP
 309 ITEM1       DFHMDF POS=(11,05),LENGTH=08,ATTRB=(ASKIP,BRT),                 X
                       PICIN='99999999',PICOUT='99999999'
 320 DESC1       DFHMDF POS=(11,14),LENGTH=19,ATTRB=(ASKIP,BRT)
 331 LNDATE1     DFHMDF POS=(11,34),LENGTH=06,ATTRB=(ASKIP,BRT)
 342 UNIT1       DFHMDF POS=(11,41),LENGTH=05,ATTRB=(ASKIP,BRT),                 X
                       PICIN='99999',PICOUT='99999'
 353 UCOST1      DFHMDF POS=(11,47),LENGTH=07,ATTRB=(ASKIP,BRT),                 X
                       PICIN='9999999',PICOUT='9999999'
 364 COST1       DFHMDF POS=(11,55),LENGTH=08,ATTRB=(ASKIP,BRT),                 X
                       PICIN='99999999',PICOUT='99999999'
 375 UPRICE1     DFHMDF POS=(11,64),LENGTH=07,ATTRB=(ASKIP,BRT),                 X
                       PICIN='9999999',PICOUT='9999999'
 386 PRICE1      DFHMDF POS=(11,72),LENGTH=08,ATTRB=(ASKIP,BRT),                 X
                       PICIN='99999999',PICOUT='99999999'
 397 LINE2       DFHMDF POS=(12,03),LENGTH=01,ATTRB=ASKIP
 408 ITEM2       DFHMDF POS=(12,05),LENGTH=08,ATTRB=(ASKIP,BRT),                 X
                       PICIN='99999999',PICOUT='99999999'
```

Fig. 23.3. Map Program – File Browse (Alternate Key).

```
STMT    SOURCE STATEMENT                              DOS/VS ASSEMBLER REL 34.0 13.13

  419 DESC2       DFHMDF  POS=(12,14),LENGTH=19,ATTRB=(ASKIP,BRT)
  430 LNDATE2     DFHMDF  POS=(12,34),LENGTH=06,ATTRB=(ASKIP,BRT)
  441 UNIT2       DFHMDF  POS=(12,41),LENGTH=05,ATTRB=(ASKIP,BRT),                  X
                          PICIN='99999',PICOUT='99999'
  452 UCOST2      DFHMDF  POS=(12,47),LENGTH=07,ATTRB=(ASKIP,BRT),                  X
                          PICIN='9999999',PICOUT='9999999'
  463 COST2       DFHMDF  POS=(12,55),LENGTH=08,ATTRB=(ASKIP,BRT),                  X
                          PICIN='99999999',PICOUT='99999999'
  474 UPRICE2     DFHMDF  POS=(12,64),LENGTH=07,ATTRB=(ASKIP,BRT),                  X
                          PICIN='9999999',PICOUT='9999999'
  485 PRICE2      DFHMDF  POS=(12,72),LENGTH=08,ATTRB=(ASKIP,BRT),                  X
                          PICIN='99999999',PICOUT='99999999'
  496 LINE3       DFHMDF  POS=(13,03),LENGTH=01,ATTRB=ASKIP
  507 ITEM3       DFHMDF  POS=(13,05),LENGTH=08,ATTRB=(ASKIP,BRT),                  X
                          PICIN='99999999',PICOUT='99999999'
  518 DESC3       DFHMDF  POS=(13,14),LENGTH=19,ATTRB=(ASKIP,BRT)
  529 LNDATE3     DFHMDF  POS=(13,34),LENGTH=06,ATTRB=(ASKIP,BRT)
  540 UNIT3       DFHMDF  POS=(13,41),LENGTH=05,ATTRB=(ASKIP,BRT),                  X
                          PICIN='99999',PICOUT='99999'
  551 UCOST3      DFHMDF  POS=(13,47),LENGTH=07,ATTRB=(ASKIP,BRT),                  X
                          PICIN='9999999',PICOUT='9999999'
  562 COST3       DFHMDF  POS=(13,55),LENGTH=08,ATTRB=(ASKIP,BRT),                  X
                          PICIN='99999999',PICOUT='99999999'
  573 UPRICE3     DFHMDF  POS=(13,64),LENGTH=07,ATTRB=(ASKIP,BRT),                  X
                          PICIN='9999999',PICOUT='9999999'
  584 PRICE3      DFHMDF  POS=(13,72),LENGTH=08,ATTRB=(ASKIP,BRT),                  X
                          PICIN='99999999',PICOUT='99999999'
  595 LINE4       DFHMDF  POS=(14,03),LENGTH=01,ATTRB=ASKIP
  606 ITEM4       DFHMDF  POS=(14,05),LENGTH=08,ATTRB=(ASKIP,BRT),                  X
                          PICIN='99999999',PICOUT='99999999'
  617 DESC4       DFHMDF  POS=(14,14),LENGTH=19,ATTRB=(ASKIP,BRT)
  628 LNDATE4     DFHMDF  POS=(14,34),LENGTH=06,ATTRB=(ASKIP,BRT)
  639 UNIT4       DFHMDF  POS=(14,41),LENGTH=05,ATTRB=(ASKIP,BRT),                  X
                          PICIN='99999',PICOUT='99999'
  650 UCOST4      DFHMDF  POS=(14,47),LENGTH=07,ATTRB=(ASKIP,BRT),                  X
                          PICIN='9999999',PICOUT='9999999'
  661 COST4       DFHMDF  POS=(14,55),LENGTH=08,ATTRB=(ASKIP,BRT),                  X
                          PICIN='99999999',PICOUT='99999999'
  672 UPRICE4     DFHMDF  POS=(14,64),LENGTH=07,ATTRB=(ASKIP,BRT),                  X
                          PICIN='9999999',PICOUT='9999999'
  683 PRICE4      DFHMDF  POS=(14,72),LENGTH=08,ATTRB=(ASKIP,BRT),                  X
                          PICIN='99999999',PICOUT='99999999'
  694 LINE5       DFHMDF  POS=(15,03),LENGTH=01,ATTRB=ASKIP
  705 ITEM5       DFHMDF  POS=(15,05),LENGTH=08,ATTRB=(ASKIP,BRT),                  X
                          PICIN='99999999',PICOUT='99999999'
  716 DESC5       DFHMDF  POS=(15,14),LENGTH=19,ATTRB=(ASKIP,BRT)
  727 LNDATE5     DFHMDF  POS=(15,34),LENGTH=06,ATTRB=(ASKIP,BRT)
  738 UNIT5       DFHMDF  POS=(15,41),LENGTH=05,ATTRB=(ASKIP,BRT),                  X
                          PICIN='99999',PICOUT='99999'
  749 UCOST5      DFHMDF  POS=(15,47),LENGTH=07,ATTRB=(ASKIP,BRT),                  X
                          PICIN='9999999',PICOUT='9999999'
```

Fig. 23.3. (Continued)

```
STMT    SOURCE STATEMENT                                   DOS/VS ASSEMBLER REL 34.0 13.13

 760 COST5      DFHMDF POS=(15,55),LENGTH=08,ATTRB=(ASKIP,BRT),                    X
                       PICIN='99999999',PICOUT='99999999'
 771 UPRICE5    DFHMDF POS=(15,64),LENGTH=07,ATTRB=(ASKIP,BRT),                    X
                       PICIN='9999999',PICOUT='9999999'
 782 PRICE5     DFHMDF POS=(15,72),LENGTH=08,ATTRB=(ASKIP,BRT),                    X
                       PICIN='99999999',PICOUT='99999999'
 793 LINE6      DFHMDF POS=(16,03),LENGTH=01,ATTRB=ASKIP
 804 ITEM6      DFHMDF POS=(16,05),LENGTH=08,ATTRB=(ASKIP,BRT),                    X
                       PICIN='99999999',PICOUT='99999999'
 815 DESC6      DFHMDF POS=(16,14),LENGTH=19,ATTRB=(ASKIP,BRT)
 826 LNDATE6    DFHMDF POS=(16,34),LENGTH=06,ATTRB=(ASKIP,BRT)
 837 UNIT6      DFHMDF POS=(16,41),LENGTH=05,ATTRB=(ASKIP,BRT),                    X
                       PICIN='99999',PICOUT='99999'
 848 UCOST6     DFHMDF POS=(16,47),LENGTH=07,ATTRB=(ASKIP,BRT),                    X
                       PICIN='9999999',PICOUT='9999999'
 859 COST6      DFHMDF POS=(16,55),LENGTH=08,ATTRB=(ASKIP,BRT),                    X
                       PICIN='99999999',PICOUT='99999999'
 870 UPRICE6    DFHMDF POS=(16,64),LENGTH=07,ATTRB=(ASKIP,BRT),                    X
                       PICIN='9999999',PICOUT='9999999'
 881 PRICE6     DFHMDF POS=(16,72),LENGTH=08,ATTRB=(ASKIP,BRT),                    X
                       PICIN='99999999',PICOUT='99999999'
 892 LINE7      DFHMDF POS=(17,03),LENGTH=01,ATTRB=ASKIP
 903 ITEM7      DFHMDF POS=(17,05),LENGTH=08,ATTRB=(ASKIP,BRT),                    X
                       PICIN='99999999',PICOUT='99999999'
 914 DESC7      DFHMDF POS=(17,14),LENGTH=19,ATTRB=(ASKIP,BRT)
 925 LNDATE7    DFHMDF POS=(17,34),LENGTH=06,ATTRB=(ASKIP,BRT)
 936 UNIT7      DFHMDF POS=(17,41),LENGTH=05,ATTRB=(ASKIP,BRT),                    X
                       PICIN='99999',PICOUT='99999'
 947 UCOST7     DFHMDF POS=(17,47),LENGTH=07,ATTRB=(ASKIP,BRT),                    X
                       PICIN='9999999',PICOUT='9999999'
 958 COST7      DFHMDF POS=(17,55),LENGTH=08,ATTRB=(ASKIP,BRT),                    X
                       PICIN='99999999',PICOUT='99999999'
 969 UPRICE7    DFHMDF POS=(17,64),LENGTH=07,ATTRB=(ASKIP,BRT),                    X
                       PICIN='9999999',PICOUT='9999999'
 980 PRICE7     DFHMDF POS=(17,72),LENGTH=08,ATTRB=(ASKIP,BRT),                    X
                       PICIN='99999999',PICOUT='99999999'
 991 LINE8      DFHMDF POS=(18,03),LENGTH=01,ATTRB=ASKIP
1002 ITEM8      DFHMDF POS=(18,05),LENGTH=08,ATTRB=(ASKIP,BRT),                    X
                       PICIN='99999999',PICOUT='99999999'
1013 DESC8      DFHMDF POS=(18,14),LENGTH=19,ATTRB=(ASKIP,BRT)
1024 LNDATE8    DFHMDF POS=(18,34),LENGTH=06,ATTRB=(ASKIP,BRT)
1035 UNIT8      DFHMDF POS=(18,41),LENGTH=05,ATTRB=(ASKIP,BRT),                    X
                       PICIN='99999',PICOUT='99999'
1046 UCOST8     DFHMDF POS=(18,47),LENGTH=07,ATTRB=(ASKIP,BRT),                    X
                       PICIN='9999999',PICOUT='9999999'
1057 COST8      DFHMDF POS=(18,55),LENGTH=08,ATTRB=(ASKIP,BRT),                    X
                       PICIN='99999999',PICOUT='99999999'
1068 UPRICE8    DFHMDF POS=(18,64),LENGTH=07,ATTRB=(ASKIP,BRT),                    X
                       PICIN='9999999',PICOUT='9999999'
1079 PRICE8     DFHMDF POS=(18,72),LENGTH=08,ATTRB=(ASKIP,BRT),                    X
                       PICIN='99999999',PICOUT='99999999'
```

Fig. 23.3. (Continued)

```
STMT    SOURCE STATEMENT                         DOS/VS ASSEMBLER REL 34.0 13.13

1090 LINE9      DFHMDF POS=(19,03),LENGTH=01,ATTRB=ASKIP
1101 ITEM9      DFHMDF POS=(19,05),LENGTH=08,ATTRB=(ASKIP,BRT),         X
                PICIN='99999999',PICOUT='99999999'
1112 DESC9      DFHMDF POS=(19,14),LENGTH=19,ATTRB=(ASKIP,BRT)
1123 LNDATE9    DFHMDF POS=(19,34),LENGTH=06,ATTRB=(ASKIP,BRT)
1134 UNIT9      DFHMDF POS=(19,41),LENGTH=05,ATTRB=(ASKIP,BRT),         X
                PICIN='99999',PICOUT='99999'
1145 UCOST9     DFHMDF POS=(19,47),LENGTH=07,ATTRB=(ASKIP,BRT),         X
                PICIN='9999999',PICOUT='9999999'
1156 COST9      DFHMDF POS=(19,55),LENGTH=08,ATTRB=(ASKIP,BRT),         X
                PICIN='99999999',PICOUT='99999999'
1167 UPRICE9    DFHMDF POS=(19,64),LENGTH=07,ATTRB=(ASKIP,BRT),         X
                PICIN='9999999',PICOUT='9999999'
1178 PRICE9     DFHMDF POS=(19,72),LENGTH=08,ATTRB=(ASKIP,BRT),         X
                PICIN='99999999',PICOUT='99999999'
1189 ERROR      DFHMDF POS=(23,30),LENGTH=22,ATTRB=(ASKIP,BRT)
1200            DFHMDF POS=(24,38),LENGTH=26,ATTRB=ASKIP,              X
                INITIAL='STARTING DEPT / DATE ---- '
1212 STRDEPT    DFHMDF POS=(24,68),LENGTH=03,ATTRB=(NUM,BRT,FSET,IC),   X
                INITIAL='999'
1224            DFHMDF POS=(24,72),LENGTH=01,ATTRB=ASKIP,INITIAL='/'
1236 STRDATE    DFHMDF POS=(24,74),LENGTH=06,ATTRB=(NUM,BRT,FSET),      X
                INITIAL='MMDDYY'
1248            DFHMSD TYPE=FINAL
1262            END
```

Fig. 23.3. (Continued)

```
1   IBM DOS VS COBOL

CBL SUPMAP,STXIT,NOTRUNC,CSYNTAX,SXREF,OPT,VERB,CLIST,BUF=19069
CBL NOOPT,LIB
00001           IDENTIFICATION DIVISION.

00003           PROGRAM-ID. ORBSC1A.

00005           ENVIRONMENT DIVISION.

00007           **********************************************************
00008           *                                                        *
00009           *   1. THIS PROGRAM ALLOWS A BROWSE (BY ORDER DATE WITHIN *
00010           *      DEPARTMENT NUMBER) ON THE PURCHASE ORDER MASTER FILE.*
00011           *                                                        *
00012           *   2. THE OPERATOR MAY START AT THE EARLIEST ORDER DATE OF*
00013           *      THE LOWEST DEPARTMENT NUMBER BY ENTERING ALL ZEROES*
00014           *      ON THE DEPT/DATE STARTING FIELD.                   *
00015           *                                                        *
00016           *   3. SHE MAY ALSO START AT THE LATEST DATE OF THE HIGHEST*
00017           *      DEPARTMENT NUMBER (FOR A BROWSE BACKWARDS) BY ENTERING*
00018           *      ALL NINES.                                         *
00019           *                                                        *
00020           *   4. BROWSE FORWARD -   PF1 OR ENTER KEY.               *
00021           *                                                        *
00022           *   5. BROWSE BACKWARDS - PF2 KEY.                        *
00023           *                                                        *
00024           **********************************************************
```

Fig. 23.4. File Browse Program (Alternate Key).

```
      2          ORBS01A         15.59.55         12/27/80

                 DATA DIVISION.

                 WORKING-STORAGE SECTION.

                 01  COMMUNICATION-AREA.

                     05  COMMAREA-PROCESS-SW       PIC X.

                 01  AREA1.

                     05  JOB-NORMAL-END-MESSAGE  PIC X(23) VALUE
                         'JOB NORMALLY TERMINATED'.

                     05  JOB-ABORTED-MESSAGE.
                       10  FILLER                  PIC X(15) VALUE 'JOB ABORTED --'.
                       10  MAJOR-ERROR-MSG         PIC X(16).

                     05  HEXADECIMAL-ZEROES        PIC 9999 COMP VALUE ZEROES.

                     05  FILLER REDEFINES HEXADECIMAL-ZEROES.
                       10  FILLER                  PIC X.
                       10  HEX-ZEROES              PIC X.

                     05  OLD-EIB-AREA.
                       10  FILLER                  PIC X(7) VALUE 'OLD EIB'.
                       10  OLD-EIBFN               PIC XX.
                       10  OLD-EIBRCODE            PIC X(6).

                     05  DUPLICATE-MESSAGE.
                       10  FILLER                  PIC X(12) VALUE 'DUPLICATE - '.
                       10  DUPLICATE-COUNT         PIC 999.
                       10  DUPLICATE-LAST          PIC X(7).

                 01  DFHAID COPY DFHAID.
                 01    DFHAID.
                   02  DFHNULL    PIC   X   VALUE IS ' '.
                   02  DFHENTER   PIC   X   VALUE IS QUOTE.
                   02  DFHCLEAR   PIC   X   VALUE IS ' '.
                   02  DFHPEN     PIC   X   VALUE IS '='.
                   02  DFHOPID    PIC   X   VALUE IS 'W'.
                   02  DFHPA1     PIC   X   VALUE IS '%'.
```

Fig. 23.4. (Continued)

```
     3          ORBSO1A          15.59.55          12/27/80

00067 C              02   DFHPA2      PIC   X   VALUE IS ' '.
00068 C              02   DFHPA3      PIC   X   VALUE IS ','.
00069 C              02   DFHPF1      PIC   X   VALUE IS '1'.
00070 C              02   DFHPF2      PIC   X   VALUE IS '2'.
00071 C              02   DFHPF3      PIC   X   VALUE IS '3'.
00072 C              02   DFHPF4      PIC   X   VALUE IS '4'.
00073 C              02   DFHPF5      PIC   X   VALUE IS '5'.
00074 C              02   DFHPF6      PIC   X   VALUE IS '6'.
00075 C              02   DFHPF7      PIC   X   VALUE IS '7'.
00076 C              02   DFHPF8      PIC   X   VALUE IS '8'.
00077 C              02   DFHPF9      PIC   X   VALUE IS '9'.
00078 C              02   DFHPF10     PIC   X   VALUE IS ' '.
00079 C              02   DFHPF11     PIC   X   VALUE IS '#'.
00080 C              02   DFHPF12     PIC   X   VALUE IS '@'.
00081 C              02   DFHPF13     PIC   X   VALUE IS 'A'.
00082 C              02   DFHPF14     PIC   X   VALUE IS 'B'.
00083 C              02   DFHPF15     PIC   X   VALUE IS 'C'.
00084 C              02   DFHPF16     PIC   X   VALUE IS 'D'.
00085 C              02   DFHPF17     PIC   X   VALUE IS 'E'.
00086 C              02   DFHPF18     PIC   X   VALUE IS 'F'.
00087 C              02   DFHPF19     PIC   X   VALUE IS 'G'.
00088 C              02   DFHPF20     PIC   X   VALUE IS 'H'.
00089 C              02   DFHPF21     PIC   X   VALUE IS 'I'.
00090 C              02   DFHPF22     PIC   X   VALUE IS ' '.
00091 C              02   DFHPF23     PIC   X   VALUE IS '.'.
00092 C              02   DFHPF24     PIC   X   VALUE IS '¤'.
```

Fig. 23.4. (Continued)

4 ORBSO1A 15.59.55 12/27/80

```
00094            01  DFHEIVAR COPY DFHEIVAR.
00095 C          01  DFHEIVAR.
00096 C              02    DFHEIV0   PICTURE X(26).
00097 C              02    DFHEIV1   PICTURE X(8).
00098 C              02    DFHEIV2   PICTURE X(8).
00099 C              02    DFHEIV3   PICTURE X(8).
00100 C              02    DFHEIV4   PICTURE X(6).
00101 C              02    DFHEIV5   PICTURE X(4).
00102 C              02    DFHEIV6   PICTURE X(4).
00103 C              02    DFHEIV7   PICTURE X(2).
00104 C              02    DFHEIV8   PICTURE X(2).
00105 C              02    DFHEIV9   PICTURE X(1).
00106 C              02    DFHEIV10  PICTURE S9(7) USAGE COMPUTATIONAL-3.
00107 C              02    DFHEIV11  PICTURE S9(4) USAGE COMPUTATIONAL.
00108 C              02    DFHEIV12  PICTURE S9(4) USAGE COMPUTATIONAL.
00109 C              02    DFHEIV13  PICTURE S9(4) USAGE COMPUTATIONAL.
00110 C              02    DFHEIV14  PICTURE S9(4) USAGE COMPUTATIONAL.
00111 C              02    DFHEIV15  PICTURE S9(4) USAGE COMPUTATIONAL.
00112 C              02    DFHEIV16  PICTURE S9(9) USAGE COMPUTATIONAL.
00113 C              02    DFHEIV17  PICTURE X(4).
00114 C              02    DFHEIV18  PICTURE X(4).
00115 C              02    DFHEIV19  PICTURE X(4).
00116 C              02    DFHEIV97  PICTURE S9(7) USAGE COMPUTATIONAL-3 VALUE ZERO.
00117 C              02    DFHEIV98  PICTURE S9(4) USAGE COMPUTATIONAL VALUE ZERO.
00118 C              02    DFHEIV99  PICTURE X(1)  VALUE SPACE.
00119            LINKAGE SECTION.

00121            01  DFHEIBLK COPY DFHEIBLK.
00122 C          *     EIBLK EXEC INTERFACE BLOCK
00123 C          01  DFHEIBLK.
00124 C          *       EIBTIME     TIME IN OHHMMSS FORMAT
00125 C              02 EIBTIME      PICTURE S9(7) USAGE COMPUTATIONAL-3.
00126 C          *       EIBDATE     DATE IN OOYYDDD FORMAT
00127 C              02 EIBDATE      PICTURE S9(7) USAGE COMPUTATIONAL-3.
00128 C          *       EIBTRNID    TRANSACTION IDENTIFIER
00129 C              02 EIBTRNID     PICTURE X(4).
00130 C          *       EIBTASKN    TASK NUMBER
00131 C              02 EIBTASKN     PICTURE S9(7) USAGE COMPUTATIONAL-3.
00132 C          *       EIBTRMID    TERMINAL IDENTIFIER
00133 C              02 EIBTRMID     PICTURE X(4).
00134 C          *       DFHEIGDI    RESERVED
00135 C              02 DFHEIGDI     PICTURE S9(4) USAGE COMPUTATIONAL.
00136 C          *       EIBCPOSN    CURSOR POSITION
00137 C              02 EIBCPOSN     PICTURE S9(4) USAGE COMPUTATIONAL.
00138 C          *       EIBCALEN    COMMAREA LENGTH
00139 C              02 EIBCALEN     PICTURE S9(4) USAGE COMPUTATIONAL.
00140 C          *       EIBAID      ATTENTION IDENTIFIER
00141 C              02 EIBAID       PICTURE X(1).
00142 C          *       EIBFN       FUNCTION CODE
00143 C              02 EIBFN        PICTURE X(2).
00144 C          *       EIBRCODE    RESPONSE CODE
00145 C              02 EIBRCODE     PICTURE X(6).
```

Fig. 23.4. (Continued)

```
5          ORBSO1A          15.59.55          12/27/80

           *         EIBDS       DATASET NAME
                  02 EIBDS       PICTURE X(8).
           *         EIBREQID    REQUEST IDENTIFIER
                  02 EIBREQID    PICTURE X(8).
             01  DFHCOMMAREA                       PIC X.

                 88  INITIAL-ENTRY-TIME                VALUE '0'.
                 88  BROWSE-START-TIME                 VALUE '1'.



             01  LINKAGE-POINTERS.

                 05  FILLER                        PIC S9(8) COMP.
                 05  MAP1-POINTER                  PIC S9(8) COMP.
                 05  POM-POINTER                   PIC S9(8) COMP.
                 05  TWA-POINTER                   PIC S9(8) COMP.
```

Fig. 23.4. (Continued)

```
6          ORBS01A          15.59.55          12/27/80

       ******************************************************************
       *                                                                *
       *                 DISPLAY MAP DESCRIPTION                        *
       *                                                                *
       ******************************************************************


        01  MAP1-AREA.
            05  FILLER                          PIC X(12).
            05  MAP1-DUMMY-L                    PIC S9999 COMP.
            05  MAP1-DUMMY-A                    PIC X.
            05  MAP1-DUMMY                      PIC X.
            05  MAP1-DEPARTMENT-L               PIC S9999 COMP.
            05  MAP1-DEPARTMENT-A               PIC X.
            05  MAP1-DEPARTMENT                 PIC XXX.
            05  MAP1-ORDER-DATE-L               PIC S9999 COMP.
            05  MAP1-ORDER-DATE-A               PIC X.
            05  MAP1-ORDER-DATE.
              10  MAP1-ORDER-DATE-MONTH         PIC XX.
              10  MAP1-ORDER-DATE-DAY           PIC XX.
              10  MAP1-ORDER-DATE-YEAR          PIC XX.
            05  MAP1-ORDER-NUMBER-L             PIC S9999 COMP.
            05  MAP1-ORDER-NUMBER-A             PIC X.
            05  MAP1-ORDER-NUMBER               PIC X(10).
            05  MAP1-ORDER-DATE-ENTERED-L       PIC S9999 COMP.
            05  MAP1-ORDER-DATE-ENTERED-A       PIC X.
            05  MAP1-ORDER-DATE-ENTERED         PIC X(6).
            05  MAP1-TOTAL-COST-L               PIC S9999 COMP.
            05  MAP1-TOTAL-COST-A               PIC X.
            05  MAP1-TOTAL-COST                 PIC Z,ZZZ,ZZZ.99.
            05  MAP1-TOTAL-PRICE-L              PIC S9999 COMP.
            05  MAP1-TOTAL-PRICE-A              PIC X.
            05  MAP1-TOTAL-PRICE                PIC Z,ZZZ,ZZZ.99.
            05  MAP1-LINE-ITEM              OCCURS 9
                                            INDEXED BY MAP1-LINE-I.
              10  MAP1-LINE-NUMBER-L            PIC S9999 COMP.
              10  MAP1-LINE-NUMBER-A            PIC X.
              10  MAP1-LINE-NUMBER              PIC 9.
              10  MAP1-ITEM-NUMBER-L            PIC S9999 COMP.
              10  MAP1-ITEM-NUMBER-A            PIC X.
              10  MAP1-ITEM-NUMBER              PIC X(8).
              10  MAP1-ITEM-DESCRIPTION-L       PIC S9999 COMP.
              10  MAP1-ITEM-DESCRIPTION-A       PIC X.
              10  MAP1-ITEM-DESCRIPTION         PIC X(19).
              10  MAP1-ITEM-DATE-L              PIC S9999 COMP.
              10  MAP1-ITEM-DATE-A              PIC X.
              10  MAP1-ITEM-DATE                PIC X(6).
              10  MAP1-UNIT-L                   PIC S9999 COMP.
              10  MAP1-UNIT-A                   PIC X.
              10  MAP1-UNIT                     PIC 9(5).
              10  MAP1-UNIT-COST-L              PIC S9999 COMP.
              10  MAP1-UNIT-COST-A              PIC X.
```

Fig. 23.4. (Continued)

```
7          ORBS01A          15.59.55          12/27/80

               10  MAP1-UNIT-COST              PIC 9(5)V99.
               10  MAP1-COST-L                 PIC S9999 COMP.
               10  MAP1-COST-A                 PIC X.
               10  MAP1-COST                   PIC 9(6)V99.
               10  MAP1-UNIT-PRICE-L           PIC S9999 COMP.
               10  MAP1-UNIT-PRICE-A           PIC X.
               10  MAP1-UNIT-PRICE             PIC 9(5)V99.
               10  MAP1-PRICE-L                PIC S9999 COMP.
               10  MAP1-PRICE-A                PIC X.
               10  MAP1-PRICE                  PIC 9(6)V99.
             05  MAP1-ERROR-L                  PIC S9999 COMP.
             05  MAP1-ERROR-A                  PIC X.
             05  MAP1-ERROR                    PIC X(22).
             05  MAP1-START-DEPARTMENT-L       PIC S9999 COMP.
             05  MAP1-START-DEPARTMENT-A       PIC X.
             05  MAP1-START-DEPARTMENT         PIC XXX.
             05  MAP1-START-DATE-L             PIC S9999 COMP.
             05  MAP1-START-DATE-A             PIC X.
             05  MAP1-START-DATE.
               10  MAP1-START-DATE-MONTH       PIC XX.
               10  MAP1-START-DATE-DAY         PIC XX.
               10  MAP1-START-DATE-YEAR        PIC XX.

8          ORBS01A          15.59.55          12/27/80

      *****************************************************************
      *                                                               *
      *       PURCHASE ORDER MASTER -- FILE LAYOUT                    *
      *                                                               *
      *****************************************************************

       01  ORDER-MASTER-RECORD.
           05  ORDER-NUMBER                        PIC X(10).
           05  ORDER-ALT-KEY.
             10  ORDER-DEPARTMENT                  PIC XXX.
             10  ORDER-DATE.
               15  ORDER-DATE-YEAR                 PIC XX.
               15  ORDER-DATE-MONTH                PIC XX.
               15  ORDER-DATE-DAY                  PIC XX.
           05  ORDER-DATE-ENTERED.
             10  ORDER-DATE-ENTERED-MONTH          PIC XX.
             10  ORDER-DATE-ENTERED-DAY            PIC XX.
             10  ORDER-DATE-ENTERED-YEAR           PIC XX.
           05  ORDER-TOTAL-COST                    PIC S9(7)V99  COMP-3.
           05  ORDER-TOTAL-PRICE                   PIC S9(7)V99  COMP-3.
           05  ORDER-LINE-COUNT                    PIC S9999     COMP.
           05  ORDER-ALL-LINES.
             10  ORDER-LINE-ITEM               OCCURS 1 TO 9
                                               DEPENDING ON ORDER-LINE-COUNT
                                               INDEXED BY ORDER-LINE-I.
               15  ORDER-ITEM-NUMBER               PIC X(8).
               15  ORDER-ITEM-DESCRIPTION          PIC X(19).
               15  ORDER-ITEM-DATE.
                 20  ORDER-ITEM-DATE-MONTH         PIC XX.
                 20  ORDER-ITEM-DATE-DAY           PIC XX.
                 20  ORDER-ITEM-DATE-YEAR          PIC XX.
               15  ORDER-UNIT                      PIC S9(5)     COMP-3.
               15  ORDER-UNIT-COST                 PIC S9(5)V99  COMP-3.
               15  ORDER-UNIT-PRICE                PIC S9(5)V99  COMP-3.
```

Fig. 23.4. (Continued)

```
    9         ORBS01A        15.59.55        12/27/80

00271         ****************************************************************
00272         *                                                              *
00273         *              TRANSACTION WORK AREA                           *
00274         *                                                              *
00275         ****************************************************************

00277         01  TWA-AREA.

00279             05  TWA-LINE-ITEM-MAP.
00280                 10  TWA-LINE-NUMBER-MAP-L        PIC S9999 COMP.
00281                 10  TWA-LINE-NUMBER-MAP-A        PIC X.
00282                 10  TWA-LINE-NUMBER-MAP          PIC 9.
00283                 10  TWA-ITEM-NUMBER-MAP-L        PIC S9999 COMP.
00284                 10  TWA-ITEM-NUMBER-MAP-A        PIC X.
00285                 10  TWA-ITEM-NUMBER-MAP          PIC X(8).
00286                 10  TWA-ITEM-DESCRIPTION-MAP-L   PIC S9999 COMP.
00287                 10  TWA-ITEM-DESCRIPTION-MAP-A   PIC X.
00288                 10  TWA-ITEM-DESCRIPTION-MAP     PIC X(19).
00289                 10  TWA-ITEM-DATE-MAP-L          PIC S9999 COMP.
00290                 10  TWA-ITEM-DATE-MAP-A          PIC X.
00291                 10  TWA-ITEM-DATE-MAP            PIC X(6).
00292                 10  TWA-UNIT-MAP-L               PIC S9999 COMP.
00293                 10  TWA-UNIT-MAP-A               PIC X.
00294                 10  TWA-UNIT-MAP                 PIC 9(5).
00295                 10  TWA-UNIT-COST-MAP-L          PIC S9999 COMP.
00296                 10  TWA-UNIT-COST-MAP-A          PIC X.
00297                 10  TWA-UNIT-COST-MAP            PIC 9(5)V99.
00298                 10  TWA-COST-MAP-L               PIC S9999 COMP.
00299                 10  TWA-COST-MAP-A               PIC X.
00300                 10  TWA-COST-MAP                 PIC 9(6)V99.
00301                 10  TWA-UNIT-PRICE-MAP-L         PIC S9999 COMP.
00302                 10  TWA-UNIT-PRICE-MAP-A         PIC X.
00303                 10  TWA-UNIT-PRICE-MAP           PIC 9(5)V99.
00304                 10  TWA-PRICE-MAP-L              PIC S9999 COMP.
00305                 10  TWA-PRICE-MAP-A              PIC X.
00306                 10  TWA-PRICE-MAP                PIC 9(6)V99.

00308             05  TWA-LINE-ITEM-ORDER.
00309                 10  TWA-ITEM-NUMBER-ORDER        PIC X(8).
00310                 10  TWA-ITEM-DESCRIPTION-ORDER   PIC X(19).
00311                 10  TWA-ITEM-DATE-ORDER          PIC X(6).
00312                 10  TWA-UNIT-ORDER               PIC S9(5)    COMP-3.
00313                 10  TWA-UNIT-COST-ORDER          PIC S9(5)V99 COMP-3.
00314                 10  TWA-UNIT-PRICE-ORDER         PIC S9(5)V99 COMP-3.

00316             05  TWA-OPERATOR-MESSAGE             PIC X(31).
```

Fig. 23.4. (Continued)

```
   10          ORBSO1A          15.59.55          12/27/80

00318                 05   TWA-ALTERNATE-KEY.
00319                      10   TWA-ALTERNATE-KEY-DEPT          PIC XXX.
00320                      10   TWA-ALTERNATE-KEY-DATE.
00321                           15   TWA-ALTERNATE-KEY-DATE-YEAR      PIC XX.
00322                           15   TWA-ALTERNATE-KEY-DATE-MONTH     PIC XX.
00323                           15   TWA-ALTERNATE-KEY-DATE-DAY       PIC XX.

00325                 05   TWA-PREV-ALTERNATE-KEY          PIC X(9).

00327                 05   TWA-START-ALTERNATE-KEY.
00328                      10   TWA-START-DEPARTMENT          PIC XXX.
00329                      10   TWA-START-DATE.
00330                           15   TWA-START-DATE-YEAR      PIC XX.
00331                           15   TWA-START-DATE-MONTH     PIC XX.
00332                           15   TWA-START-DATE-DAY       PIC XX.

00334                 05   TWA-DUPLICATE-COUNT          PIC S999 COMP-3.

00336                 05   PREV-ACTION          PIC X.
00337                      88   PREV-ACTION-FORWARD              VALUE '1'.
00338                      88   PREV-ACTION-BACKWARDS            VALUE '2'.
00339                      88   PREV-ACTION-FORWARD-EOF          VALUE '3'.
00340                      88   PREV-ACTION-BACKWARDS-EOF        VALUE '4'.
00341                      88   PREV-ACTION-FORWARD-NOTFOUND     VALUE '5'.
00342                      88   PREV-ACTION-IMMATERIAL           VALUE '9'.
```

Fig. 23.4. (Continued)

```
   11          ORBS01A          15.59.55          12/27/80

           PROCEDURE DIVISION USING DFHEIBLK DFHCOMMAREA.
               CALL 'DFHEI1'.

          ***************************************************************
          *                                                             *
           MAIN-LINE SECTION.
          *                                                             *
          ***************************************************************

          *    EXEC CICS
          *         ADDRESS TWA (TWA-POINTER)
          *    END-EXEC.
                MOVE '                 ' TO DFHEIVO CALL 'DFHEI1' USING
                DFHEIVO TWA-POINTER.

          *    EXEC CICS
          *         HANDLE AID
          *              CLEAR (FINALIZATION)
          *                PA1 (WRONG-KEY-USED)
          *                PA2 (WRONG-KEY-USED)
          *                PA3 (WRONG-KEY-USED)
          *    END-EXEC.
                MOVE '  0              ' TO DFHEIVO CALL 'DFHEI1' USING
                DFHEIVO GO TO FINALIZATION WRONG-KEY-USED WRONG-KEY-USED
                WRONG-KEY-USED DEPENDING ON DFHEIGDI.




          *    EXEC CICS
          *         HANDLE CONDITION
          *              MAPFAIL (MAPFAIL-ERROR)
          *              NOTOPEN (FILE-NOT-OPEN)
          *              ERROR   (MAJOR-ERROR)
          *    END-EXEC.
                MOVE '                 ' TO DFHEIVO CALL 'DFHEI1' USING
                DFHEIVO GO TO MAPFAIL-ERROR FILE-NOT-OPEN MAJOR-ERROR
                DEPENDING ON DFHEIGDI.



               IF EIBCALEN NOT EQUAL TO ZEROES
                    IF BROWSE-START-TIME
                         GO TO BROWSE-START
                    ELSE IF INITIAL-ENTRY-TIME
                         GO TO INITIALIZATION
                    ELSE GO TO PROCESS-SWITCH-ERROR.

               IF EIBCALEN EQUAL TO ZEROES
                    GO TO SIGN-ON-VIOLATION.
```

Fig. 23.4. (Continued)

```
   12        ORBS01A         15.59.55        12/27/80

          ***************************************************************
          *                                                             *
           BROWSE-CONTINUE SECTION.
          *                                                             *
          ***************************************************************

          *    EXEC CICS
          *         RECEIVE MAP      ('ORBSM01')
          *                 MAPSET   ('ORBSS01')
          *                 SET      (MAP1-POINTER)
          *    END-EXEC.
                MOVE 'ORBSM01' TO DFHEIV1 MOVE 'ORBSS01' TO DFHEIV2 MOVE '
          -    '                ' TO DFHEIV0 CALL 'DFHEI1' USING DFHEIV0
                DFHEIV1 MAP1-POINTER DFHEIV98 DFHEIV2.


               IF     MAP1-START-DEPARTMENT NOT NUMERIC
                  OR MAP1-START-DATE        NOT NUMERIC
               THEN GO TO INVALID-START-KEY.

               MOVE MAP1-START-DEPARTMENT  TO  TWA-START-DEPARTMENT.
               MOVE MAP1-START-DATE-MONTH  TO  TWA-START-DATE-MONTH.
               MOVE MAP1-START-DATE-DAY    TO  TWA-START-DATE-DAY.
               MOVE MAP1-START-DATE-YEAR   TO  TWA-START-DATE-YEAR.

               IF TWA-START-ALTERNATE-KEY = TWA-ALTERNATE-KEY
                    IF     EIBAID EQUAL TO DFHPF1
                        OR EIBAID EQUAL TO DFHENTER
                    THEN GO TO BROWSE-FORWARD
                    ELSE IF EIBAID EQUAL TO DFHPF2
                              IF PREV-ACTION-FORWARD-NOTFOUND
                                   MOVE ZEROES TO TWA-DUPLICATE-COUNT
                                   MOVE SPACES TO TWA-PREV-ALTERNATE-KEY
                                   MOVE HIGH-VALUES TO TWA-ALTERNATE-KEY

          *                        EXEC CICS
          *                             RESETBR
          *                                  DATASET ('ORTAIX')
          *                                  RIDFLD  (TWA-ALTERNATE-KEY)
          *                                  GTEQ
          *                        END-EXEC
                                    MOVE 'ORTAIX' TO DFHEIV3 MOVE '
          -    '' TO DFHEIV0 CALL 'DFHEI1' USING DFHEIV0 DFHEIV3 DFHEIV99
                DFHEIV98 TWA-ALTERNATE-KEY



                                   GO TO BROWSE-BACKWARD
                              ELSE GO TO BROWSE-BACKWARD
                         ELSE GO TO WRONG-KEY-USED
               ELSE MOVE ZEROES                TO  TWA-DUPLICATE-COUNT
                    MOVE SPACES                TO  TWA-PREV-ALTERNATE-KEY
                    MOVE '9'                   TO  PREV-ACTION
```

Fig. 23.4. (Continued)

13 ORBSO1A 15.59.55 12/27/80

```
00448                            IF TWA-START-ALTERNATE-KEY GREATER TWA-ALTERNATE-KEY
00449                                MOVE TWA-START-ALTERNATE-KEY TO TWA-ALTERNATE-KEY
00450                                GO TO BROWSE-FORWARD
00451                            ELSE MOVE TWA-START-ALTERNATE-KEY TO TWA-ALTERNATE-KEY

00453         *                  EXEC CICS
00454         *                      RESETBR
00455         *                          DATASET ('ORTAIX')
00456         *                          RIDFLD  (TWA-ALTERNATE-KEY)
00457         *                          GTEQ
00458         *                  END-EXEC
00459                            MOVE 'ORTAIX' TO DFHEIV3 MOVE '        ' TO
00460          DFHEIVO CALL 'DFHEI1' USING DFHEIVO DFHEIV3 DFHEIV99
00461          DFHEIV98 TWA-ALTERNATE-KEY
00462
00463
00464
00465                            GO TO BROWSE-FORWARD.
```

Fig. 23.4. (Continued)

```
14          ORBS01A          15.59.55          12/27/80

           *****************************************************************
           *                                                               *
            BROWSE-FORWARD SECTION.
           *                                                               *
           *****************************************************************

           *    EXEC CICS
           *         HANDLE CONDITION
           *              ENDFILE (END-OF-FILE-FORWARD)
           *              NOTFND  (RECORD-NOT-FOUND-FORWARD)
           *              DUPKEY  (DUPLICATE-KEY-FORWARD)
           *    END-EXEC.
                 MOVE '                    ' TO DFHEIVO CALL 'DFHEI1' USING
                 DFHEIVO GO TO END-OF-FILE-FORWARD RECORD-NOT-FOUND-FORWARD
                 DUPLICATE-KEY-FORWARD DEPENDING ON DFHEIGDI.



            READ-NEXT-RECORD.

           *    EXEC CICS
           *         READNEXT DATASET ('ORTAIX')
           *                  SET     (POM-POINTER)
           *                  RIDFLD  (TWA-ALTERNATE-KEY)
           *    END-EXEC.
                 MOVE 'ORTAIX' TO DFHEIV3 MOVE '  M      ' TO DFHEIVO CALL 'D
           -    'FHEI1' USING DFHEIVO DFHEIV3 POM-POINTER DFHEIV98
                 TWA-ALTERNATE-KEY DFHEIV98 DFHEIV98.


                IF PREV-ACTION-BACKWARDS
                     MOVE '1' TO PREV-ACTION
                     GO TO READ-NEXT-RECORD.

                IF TWA-ALTERNATE-KEY EQUAL TWA-PREV-ALTERNATE-KEY
                     ADD 1                      TO   TWA-DUPLICATE-COUNT
                     MOVE TWA-DUPLICATE-COUNT   TO   DUPLICATE-COUNT
                     MOVE ZEROES                TO   TWA-DUPLICATE-COUNT
                     MOVE ' / LAST'             TO   DUPLICATE-LAST
                     MOVE DUPLICATE-MESSAGE     TO   MAP1-ERROR
                ELSE MOVE TWA-ALTERNATE-KEY     TO   TWA-PREV-ALTERNATE-KEY
                     MOVE SPACES                TO   MAP1-ERROR.


            LAYOUT-ORDER-SCREEN.
                MOVE TWA-ALTERNATE-KEY-DEPT          TO   MAP1-START-DEPARTMENT.
                MOVE TWA-ALTERNATE-KEY-DATE-MONTH    TO   MAP1-START-DATE-MONTH.
                MOVE TWA-ALTERNATE-KEY-DATE-DAY      TO   MAP1-START-DATE-DAY.
                MOVE TWA-ALTERNATE-KEY-DATE-YEAR     TO   MAP1-START-DATE-YEAR.
                MOVE ORDER-NUMBER                    TO   MAP1-ORDER-NUMBER.
                MOVE ORDER-DEPARTMENT                TO   MAP1-DEPARTMENT.
                MOVE ORDER-DATE-MONTH                TO   MAP1-ORDER-DATE-MONTH.
```

Fig. 23.4. (Continued)

```
   15            ORBS01A           15.59.55            12/27/80

00518                   MOVE  ORDER-DATE-DAY                  TO   MAP1-ORDER-DATE-DAY.
00519                   MOVE  ORDER-DATE-YEAR                 TO   MAP1-ORDER-DATE-YEAR.
00520                   MOVE  ORDER-DATE-ENTERED           TO   MAP1-ORDER-DATE-ENTERED.
00521                   MOVE  ORDER-TOTAL-COST               TO   MAP1-TOTAL-COST.
00522                   MOVE  ORDER-TOTAL-PRICE              TO   MAP1-TOTAL-PRICE.
00523                   SET  ORDER-LINE-I                          TO   1.
00524                   PERFORM LAYOUT-EACH-LINE
00525                        UNTIL ORDER-LINE-I GREATER THAN ORDER-LINE-COUNT.
00526                   GO TO DISPLAY-ORDER.

00528              LAYOUT-EACH-LINE.
00529                   SET MAP1-LINE-I                             TO ORDER-LINE-I.
00530                   MOVE ORDER-LINE-ITEM (ORDER-LINE-I) TO TWA-LINE-ITEM-ORDER.
00531                   MOVE MAP1-LINE-ITEM (MAP1-LINE-I)   TO TWA-LINE-ITEM-MAP.
00532                   SET TWA-LINE-NUMBER-MAP                 TO ORDER-LINE-I.
00533                   MOVE TWA-ITEM-NUMBER-ORDER          TO  TWA-ITEM-NUMBER-MAP.
00534                   MOVE TWA-ITEM-DESCRIPTION-ORDER TO TWA-ITEM-DESCRIPTION-MAP.
00535                   MOVE TWA-ITEM-DATE-ORDER            TO  TWA-ITEM-DATE-MAP.
00536                   MOVE TWA-UNIT-ORDER                    TO  TWA-UNIT-MAP.
00537                   MOVE TWA-UNIT-COST-ORDER            TO  TWA-UNIT-COST-MAP.
00538                   COMPUTE TWA-COST-MAP = TWA-UNIT-ORDER * TWA-UNIT-COST-ORDER.
00539                   MOVE TWA-UNIT-PRICE-ORDER          TO  TWA-UNIT-PRICE-MAP.
00540                   COMPUTE TWA-PRICE-MAP =
00541                               TWA-UNIT-ORDER * TWA-UNIT-PRICE-ORDER.
00542                   MOVE TWA-LINE-ITEM-MAP       TO  MAP1-LINE-ITEM (MAP1-LINE-I).
00543                   SET ORDER-LINE-I UP BY 1.

00545              DISPLAY-ORDER.

00547              *     EXEC CICS
00548              *          SEND MAP     ('ORBSM01')
00549              *               MAPSET ('ORBSS01')
00550              *               FROM   (MAP1-AREA)
00551              *               ERASE
00552              *     END-EXEC.
00553                   MOVE 'ORBSM01' TO DFHEIV1 MOVE 'ORBSS01' TO DFHEIV2 MOVE '
00554              -    '          S    ' TO DFHEIV0 CALL 'DFHEI1' USING DFHEIV0
00555                   DFHEIV1 MAP1-AREA DFHEIV98 DFHEIV2.
00556
00557
00558
00559              AFTER-DISPLAY.
00560                   MOVE '1' TO PREV-ACTION.
00561                   GO TO BROWSE-CONTINUE.

00563              DUPLICATE-KEY-FORWARD.
00564                   ADD 1                                    TO   TWA-DUPLICATE-COUNT.
00565                   MOVE TWA-DUPLICATE-COUNT          TO   DUPLICATE-COUNT.
00566                   MOVE SPACES                           TO   DUPLICATE-LAST.
00567                   MOVE DUPLICATE-MESSAGE            TO   MAP1-ERROR.
```

Fig. 23.4. (Continued)

```
16          ORBS01A          15.59.55          12/27/80

                IF TWA-DUPLICATE-COUNT EQUAL  TO  1
                     MOVE TWA-ALTERNATE-KEY   TO  TWA-PREV-ALTERNATE-KEY.
                GO TO LAYOUT-ORDER-SCREEN.

            END-OF-FILE-FORWARD.
                MOVE TWA-ALTERNATE-KEY-DEPT        TO  MAP1-START-DEPARTMENT.
                MOVE TWA-ALTERNATE-KEY-DATE-MONTH TO  MAP1-START-DATE-MONTH.
                MOVE TWA-ALTERNATE-KEY-DATE-DAY   TO  MAP1-START-DATE-DAY.
                MOVE TWA-ALTERNATE-KEY-DATE-YEAR  TO  MAP1-START-DATE-YEAR.
                MOVE SPACES                     TO  TWA-PREV-ALTERNATE-KEY.
                MOVE   '3'                        TO  PREV-ACTION.
                GO TO END-OF-FILE-FORWARD-MESSAGE.

            END-OF-FILE-FORWARD-MESSAGE.
                MOVE 'END OF FILE' TO MAP1-ERROR.

           *    EXEC CICS
           *         SEND MAP     ('ORBSM01')
           *              MAPSET ('ORBSS01')
           *              FROM    (MAP1-AREA)
           *              ERASE
           *    END-EXEC.
                 MOVE 'ORBSM01' TO DFHEIV1 MOVE 'ORBSS01' TO DFHEIV2 MOVE '
           -    '          S     ' TO DFHEIV0 CALL 'DFHEI1' USING DFHEIV0
                 DFHEIV1 MAP1-AREA DFHEIV98 DFHEIV2.



                GO TO BROWSE-CONTINUE.

            RECORD-NOT-FOUND-FORWARD.
                MOVE TWA-ALTERNATE-KEY-DEPT        TO  MAP1-START-DEPARTMENT.
                MOVE TWA-ALTERNATE-KEY-DATE-MONTH TO  MAP1-START-DATE-MONTH.
                MOVE TWA-ALTERNATE-KEY-DATE-DAY   TO  MAP1-START-DATE-DAY.
                MOVE TWA-ALTERNATE-KEY-DATE-YEAR  TO  MAP1-START-DATE-YEAR.
                MOVE SPACES                     TO  TWA-PREV-ALTERNATE-KEY.
                MOVE   '5'                        TO  PREV-ACTION.
                GO TO END-OF-FILE-FORWARD-MESSAGE.
```

Fig. 23.4. (Continued)

```
17          ORBS01A          15.59.55          12/27/80

            ****************************************************************
            *                                                              *
             BROWSE-BACKWARD SECTION.
            *                                                              *
            ****************************************************************


            *    EXEC CICS
            *         HANDLE CONDITION
            *              ENDFILE (END-OF-FILE-BACKWARDS)
            *              DUPKEY  (DUPLICATE-KEY-BACKWARDS)
            *    END-EXEC.
                  MOVE '                        ' TO DFHEIVO CALL 'DFHEI1' USING
                  DFHEIVO GO TO END-OF-FILE-BACKWARDS DUPLICATE-KEY-BACKWARDS
                 DEPENDING ON DFHEIGDI.


             READ-PREVIOUS-RECORD.
            *    EXEC CICS
            *         READPREV DATASET ('ORTAIX')
            *                  SET     (POM-POINTER)
            *                  RIDFLD  (TWA-ALTERNATE-KEY)
            *    END-EXEC.
                  MOVE 'ORTAIX' TO DFHEIV3 MOVE '  M      ' TO DFHEIVO CALL 'D
            -    'FHEI1' USING DFHEIVO DFHEIV3 POM-POINTER DFHEIV98
                  TWA-ALTERNATE-KEY DFHEIV98 DFHEIV98.


                 IF PREV-ACTION-FORWARD
                      MOVE '2' TO PREV-ACTION
                      GO TO READ-PREVIOUS-RECORD.

                 IF TWA-ALTERNATE-KEY  EQUAL     TO  TWA-PREV-ALTERNATE-KEY
                      ADD 1                      TO  TWA-DUPLICATE-COUNT
                      MOVE TWA-DUPLICATE-COUNT   TO  DUPLICATE-COUNT
                      MOVE ZEROES                TO  TWA-DUPLICATE-COUNT
                      MOVE ' / LAST'             TO  DUPLICATE-LAST
                      MOVE DUPLICATE-MESSAGE     TO  MAP1-ERROR
                 ELSE MOVE TWA-ALTERNATE-KEY     TO  TWA-PREV-ALTERNATE-KEY
                      MOVE SPACES                TO  MAP1-ERROR.


             LAYOUT-ORDER-SCREEN-BACKWARDS.
                 PERFORM LAYOUT-ORDER-SCREEN THRU DISPLAY-ORDER.
                 MOVE '2' TO PREV-ACTION.
                 GO TO BROWSE-CONTINUE.


             DUPLICATE-KEY-BACKWARDS.
                 ADD 1                          TO  TWA-DUPLICATE-COUNT.
                 MOVE TWA-DUPLICATE-COUNT       TO  DUPLICATE-COUNT.
                 MOVE SPACES                    TO  DUPLICATE-LAST.
                 MOVE DUPLICATE-MESSAGE         TO  MAP1-ERROR.
```

Fig. 23.4. (Continued)

```
18          ORBS01A          15.59.55          12/27/80

               IF TWA-DUPLICATE-COUNT EQUAL  TO  1
                    MOVE TWA-ALTERNATE-KEY   TO  TWA-PREV-ALTERNATE-KEY.
               GO TO LAYOUT-ORDER-SCREEN-BACKWARDS.

           END-OF-FILE-BACKWARDS.
               MOVE TWA-ALTERNATE-KEY-DEPT           TO  MAP1-START-DEPARTMENT.
               MOVE TWA-ALTERNATE-KEY-DATE-MONTH TO  MAP1-START-DATE-MONTH.
               MOVE TWA-ALTERNATE-KEY-DATE-DAY     TO  MAP1-START-DATE-DAY.
               MOVE TWA-ALTERNATE-KEY-DATE-YEAR   TO  MAP1-START-DATE-YEAR.
               MOVE SPACES                        TO  TWA-PREV-ALTERNATE-KEY.
               MOVE   '4'                         TO  PREV-ACTION.
               MOVE 'END OF FILE' TO MAP1-ERROR.

      *        EXEC CICS
      *             SEND MAP     ('ORBSM01')
      *                  MAPSET ('ORBSS01')
      *                  FROM    (MAP1-AREA)
      *                  ERASE
      *        END-EXEC.
                MOVE 'ORBSM01' TO DFHEIV1 MOVE 'ORBSS01' TO DFHEIV2 MOVE '
      -        '         S     ' TO DFHEIV0 CALL 'DFHEI1' USING DFHEIV0
                DFHEIV1 MAP1-AREA DFHEIV98 DFHEIV2.



               GO TO BROWSE-CONTINUE.

           INVALID-START-KEY.
               MOVE 'INVALID ALTERNATE KEY' TO MAP1-ERROR.

      *        EXEC CICS
      *             SEND MAP     ('ORBSM01')
      *                  MAPSET ('ORBSS01')
      *                  FROM    (MAP1-AREA)
      *                  ERASE
      *        END-EXEC.
                MOVE 'ORBSM01' TO DFHEIV1 MOVE 'ORBSS01' TO DFHEIV2 MOVE '
      -        '         S     ' TO DFHEIV0 CALL 'DFHEI1' USING DFHEIV0
                DFHEIV1 MAP1-AREA DFHEIV98 DFHEIV2.



               GO TO BROWSE-CONTINUE.
```

Fig. 23.4. (Continued)

```
    19          ORBS01A           15.59.55          12/27/80

           *****************************************************************
           *                                                               *
            WRONG-KEY-USED SECTION.
           *                                                               *
           *****************************************************************

           *     EXEC CICS
           *          GETMAIN
           *               SET      (MAP1-POINTER)
           *               LENGTH   (987)
           *               INITIMG  (HEX-ZEROES)
           *     END-EXEC.
                  MOVE 987 TO DFHEIV11 MOVE '          ' TO DFHEIVO CALL 'DFHEI
           -     '1' USING DFHEIVO MAP1-POINTER DFHEIV11 HEX-ZEROES.




                 MOVE 'WRONG KEY USED' TO MAP1-ERROR.

           *     EXEC CICS
           *          SEND MAP     ('ORBSM01')
           *               MAPSET ('ORBSS01')
           *               FROM    (MAP1-AREA)
           *               DATAONLY
           *     END-EXEC.
                  MOVE 'ORBSM01' TO DFHEIV1 MOVE 'ORBSS01' TO DFHEIV2 MOVE '
           -     '            ' TO DFHEIVO CALL 'DFHEI1' USING DFHEIVO
                  DFHEIV1 MAP1-AREA DFHEIV98 DFHEIV2.



           *     EXEC CICS
           *          FREEMAIN DATA (MAP1-AREA)
           *     END-EXEC.
                  MOVE '          ' TO DFHEIVO CALL 'DFHEI1' USING DFHEIVO
                  MAP1-AREA.

                 GO TO BROWSE-CONTINUE.
```

Fig. 23.4. (Continued)

```
20          ORBS01A          15.59.55          12/27/80

      ***********************************************************************
      *                                                                     *
       BROWSE-START SECTION.
      *                                                                     *
      ***********************************************************************


      *    EXEC CICS
      *         RECEIVE MAP     ('ORBSM01')
      *                 MAPSET  ('ORBSS01')
      *                 SET     (MAP1-POINTER)
      *    END-EXEC.
            MOVE 'ORBSM01' TO DFHEIV1 MOVE 'ORBSS01' TO DFHEIV2 MOVE '
      -    '             ' TO DFHEIV0 CALL 'DFHEI1' USING DFHEIV0
            DFHEIV1 MAP1-POINTER DFHEIV98 DFHEIV2.


       BROWSE-STARTING-RECORD.

           IF     MAP1-START-DEPARTMENT   NOT   NUMERIC
              OR MAP1-START-DATE          NOT   NUMERIC
           THEN GO TO INVALID-ALTERNATE-KEY-START.

           MOVE MAP1-START-DEPARTMENT        TO   TWA-START-DEPARTMENT.
           MOVE MAP1-START-DATE-MONTH        TO   TWA-START-DATE-MONTH.
           MOVE MAP1-START-DATE-DAY          TO   TWA-START-DATE-DAY.
           MOVE MAP1-START-DATE-YEAR         TO   TWA-START-DATE-YEAR.
           MOVE TWA-START-ALTERNATE-KEY      TO   TWA-ALTERNATE-KEY.

      *    EXEC CICS
      *         HANDLE CONDITION
      *              NOTFND (RECORD-NOT-FOUND-STARTBROWSE)
      *    END-EXEC.
            MOVE '                          ' TO DFHEIV0 CALL 'DFHEI1' USING
            DFHEIV0 GO TO RECORD-NOT-FOUND-STARTBROWSE DEPENDING ON
            DFHEIGDI.

       BROWSE-COMMAND.

      *    EXEC CICS
      *         STARTBR DATASET ('ORTAIX')
      *                 RIDFLD  (TWA-ALTERNATE-KEY)
      *                 GTEQ
      *    END-EXEC.
            MOVE 'ORTAIX' TO DFHEIV3 MOVE '          ' TO DFHEIV0 CALL 'D
      -    'FHEI1' USING DFHEIV0 DFHEIV3 DFHEIV99 DFHEIV98
            TWA-ALTERNATE-KEY.


           MOVE ZEROES TO TWA-DUPLICATE-COUNT.

           IF TWA-ALTERNATE-KEY NUMERIC
                GO TO BROWSE-FORWARD
```

Fig. 23.4. (Continued)

```
  21          ORBS01A          15.59.55          12/27/80

                 ELSE GO TO BROWSE-BACKWARD.


            RECORD-NOT-FOUND-STARTBROWSE.
                 MOVE HIGH-VALUES TO TWA-ALTERNATE-KEY.
                 GO TO BROWSE-COMMAND.


            INVALID-ALTERNATE-KEY-START.
                 MOVE 'INVALID ALTERNATE KEY' TO MAP1-ERROR.

           *     EXEC CICS
           *          SEND MAP      ('ORBSM01')
           *               MAPSET ('ORBSS01')
           *               FROM     (MAP1-AREA)
           *               DATAONLY
           *     END-EXEC.
                  MOVE 'ORBSM01' TO DFHEIV1 MOVE 'ORBSS01' TO DFHEIV2 MOVE '
           -     '               ' TO DFHEIVO CALL 'DFHEI1' USING DFHEIVO
                  DFHEIV1 MAP1-AREA DFHEIV98 DFHEIV2.



                 MOVE  '1'  TO COMMAREA-PROCESS-SW.

           *     EXEC CICS
           *          RETURN TRANSID  (EIBTRNID)
           *                 COMMAREA (COMMUNICATION-AREA)
           *                 LENGTH    (1)
           *     END-EXEC.
                  MOVE 1 TO DFHEIV11 MOVE '           ' TO DFHEIVO CALL 'DFHEI1'
                  USING DFHEIVO EIBTRNID COMMUNICATION-AREA DFHEIV11.



```

Fig. 23.4. (Continued)

```
22          ORBS01A          15.59.55          12/27/80

      ******************************************************************
      *                                                                *
       INITIALIZATION SECTION.
      *                                                                *
      ******************************************************************


      *     EXEC CICS
      *          SEND MAP      ('ORBSM01')
      *               MAPSET ('ORBSS01')
      *               MAPONLY
      *               ERASE
      *     END-EXEC.
             MOVE 'ORBSM01' TO DFHEIV1 MOVE 'ORBSS01' TO DFHEIV2 MOVE '
      -     '              ' TO DFHEIV0 CALL 'DFHEI1' USING DFHEIV0
             DFHEIV1 DFHEIV99 DFHEIV98 DFHEIV2.



            MOVE   '1'   TO   COMMAREA-PROCESS-SW.

      *     EXEC CICS
      *          RETURN TRANSID   ('ORBS')
      *                 COMMAREA (COMMUNICATION-AREA)
      *                 LENGTH    (1)
      *     END-EXEC.
             MOVE 'ORBS' TO DFHEIV5 MOVE 1 TO DFHEIV11 MOVE '
             TO DFHEIV0 CALL 'DFHEI1' USING DFHEIV0 DFHEIV5
             COMMUNICATION-AREA DFHEIV11.
```

Fig. 23.4. (Continued)

```
   23          ORBS01A           15.59.55         12/27/80

           *****************************************************************
           *                                                               *
            FINALIZATION SECTION.
           *                                                               *
           *****************************************************************


            PREPARE-TERMINATION-MESSAGE.
                MOVE JOB-NORMAL-END-MESSAGE TO TWA-OPERATOR-MESSAGE.

            JOB-TERMINATED.
           *    EXEC CICS
           *         SEND FROM   (TWA-OPERATOR-MESSAGE)
           *              LENGTH (31)
           *              ERASE
           *    END-EXEC.
                 MOVE 31 TO DFHEIV11 MOVE '                  ' TO DFHEIVO CALL '
           -    'DFHEI1' USING DFHEIVO DFHEIV99 DFHEIV98 TWA-OPERATOR-MESSAGE
                 DFHEIV11.



            END-OF-JOB.
           *    EXEC CICS
           *         RETURN
           *    END-EXEC.
                 MOVE '          ' TO DFHEIVO CALL 'DFHEI1' USING DFHEIVO.


```

Fig. 23.4. (Continued)

```
    24          ORBS01A          15.59.55          12/27/80

            *****************************************************************
            *                                                               *
             ABNORMAL-TERMINATION SECTION.
            *                                                               *
            *****************************************************************

             FILE-NOT-OPEN.

            *    EXEC CICS
            *         XCTL PROGRAM ('TEL2OPEN')
            *    END-EXEC.
                  MOVE 'TEL2OPEN' TO DFHEIV3 MOVE '          ' TO DFHEIVO CALL
                 'DFHEI1' USING DFHEIVO DFHEIV3.


             MAPFAIL-ERROR.
                 MOVE 'MAP FAILURE' TO MAJOR-ERROR-MSG.
                 GO TO PREPARE-ABORT-MESSAGE.


             PROCESS-SWITCH-ERROR.
                 MOVE 'PROCESS ERROR' TO MAJOR-ERROR-MSG.
                 GO TO PREPARE-ABORT-MESSAGE.


             SIGN-ON-VIOLATION.
                 MOVE 'SIGNON VIOLATION' TO MAJOR-ERROR-MSG.
                 GO TO PREPARE-ABORT-MESSAGE.


             MAJOR-ERROR.
                 MOVE  EIBFN      TO  OLD-EIBFN.
                 MOVE  EIBRCODE   TO  OLD-EIBRCODE.

            *    EXEC CICS
            *         DUMP DUMPCODE ('ERRS')
            *    END-EXEC.
                  MOVE 'ERRS' TO DFHEIV5 MOVE '          ' TO DFHEIVO CALL 'DFH
            -    'EI1' USING DFHEIVO DFHEIV5.

                 MOVE 'MAJOR ERROR' TO MAJOR-ERROR-MSG.
                 GO TO PREPARE-ABORT-MESSAGE.


             PREPARE-ABORT-MESSAGE.
                 MOVE JOB-ABORTED-MESSAGE TO TWA-OPERATOR-MESSAGE.
                 GO TO JOB-TERMINATED.
```

Fig. 23.4. (Continued)

THE MAIN-LINE SECTION

1. Lines 353–357. ADDRESS command for the TWA.
2. Lines 359–368. HANDLE AID command. The PA keys will result in the "WRONG KEY USED" error.
3. Lines 373–381. HANDLE CONDITION command. The NOT-OPEN condition for the order file is specified here rather than in other sections because the program is in the conversational mode and this specification will not change during the session.
4. Lines 385–390. The selection of sections.
5. Lines 392–393. If the program is executed at the start of the session by an operator-entered transaction identifier instead of through an XCTL command from the Sign-on program, a sign-on violation occurs. This is so if EIBCALEN is equal to zero.

THE INITIALIZATION SECTION

1. Lines 834–842. SEND MAP command to display the browse map.
2. Line 846. Set the communication area switch to 1.
3. Lines 848–855. RETURN command to terminate the task. This section is implemented in the pseudoconversational mode so the task is terminated while the operator enters the browse starting point.

THE BROWSE-START SECTION

1. Lines 748–755. RECEIVE MAP command to read the map that contains the department number and date of order that is the starting point of the browse.
2. Lines 770–776. HANDLE CONDITION command for the order file.
3. Lines 780–787. STARTBR command to establish the starting point of the browse.
4. Lines 792–794. Line 792 will be executed if a record was found, which was based on the starting point, and is always

executed because of the GTEQ operand of STARTBR unless the starting point is greater than the last record in the file. We then go into a forward browse to display this record. Line 794 will be executed if a record was not found, in which case lines 797–798 would have been executed to mark the end of the file. We therefore go into a backward browse to display the last record in the file.

5. Line 797. If the record is not found, we set the key to HIGH-VALUES to mark the end of the file as the starting point of the browse (in this case, we have to browse backwards).
6. If the department number and date of order (as entered by the operator) are not numeric:
   a. Lines 803–811. Display the error message "INVALID ALTERNATE KEY."
   b. Line 815. Set the communication area switch to 1.
   c. Lines 817–823. RETURN command to terminate the task.

THE BROWSE-FORWARD SECTION

1. Lines 473–481. HANDLE CONDITION command for the order file. The ENDFILE option is for the routine if the end of the file is reached in a normal forward browse. The NOTFND option is for the routine if we do not find a record during skip-forward browse. The DUPKEY option is for the routine if the alternate key is a duplicate.
2. Lines 487–494. Read the next record in ascending sequence.
3. Lines 497–499. If the previous File read was a READPREV command, then we bypass this record; otherwise we would be displaying the same record as in the previous display.
4. Lines 501–506. If this is the last in a group of duplicate records.
5. Lines 507–508. This record has no duplicate.
6. Lines 511–543. Move the record data into the symbolic description map.
7. Lines 547–555. Display the record. The ERASE option is specified since the data is variable (from 1 to 9 lines). If the data were fixed, this would not be required and DATAONLY would then be specified.

8. Lines 560–561. The forward browse is finished; wait for the next action from the operator.
9. Lines 564–570. If this record has duplicates but is not the last in the group.
10. Lines 584–592. If the end of the file is reached during normal forward browse, we display the "END OF FILE" message.
11. Lines 599–605. If the record is not found in a skip-forward browse, we likewise display the "END OF FILE" message.

THE BROWSE-BACKWARD SECTION

1. Lines 613-620. HANDLE CONDITION command for the order file. The ENDFILE option is for the routine if the end of the file is reached in a normal backward browse. The DUPKEY option is for the routine in case of duplicate alternate keys. The NOTFND option is not specified because it will never happen in a READPREV command if the GTEQ operand is specified in the browse.
2. Lines 624–631. Read the next record in descending sequence.
3. Lines 634–636. If the previous File read was a READNEXT command, then we bypass this record; otherwise, we would be displaying the same record as in the previous display.
4. Line 648. Display the record.
5. Lines 649–650. The backward browse is finished; wait for the next action from the operator.
6. Lines 670–678. If the end of the file is reached during normal backward browse, we display the "END OF FILE" message.
7. Lines 687–695. If any new browse starting point entered is invalid in format, we display the "INVALID ALTERNATE KEY" message.

THE BROWSE-CONTINUE SECTION

1. Lines 401–408. Read the map containing the alternate key.

2. If a new starting point was not entered:
   a. Lines 421–423. If the PF1 or ENTER key was used, do a forward browse.
   b. If the PF2 key was used:
      1. Lines 425–442. If the previous action was a skip-forward browse and the record was not found (this can happen if the starting point entered by the operator was higher than the last record in the file), the browse is reset to the end of the file and the last record is displayed.
      2. Line 443. Otherwise, do a backward browse.
   c. Line 444. Otherwise, the wrong key was used.

3. If a new starting point was entered:
   a. Lines 448–450. If the new starting point is greater than the previously displayed order, do a skip-forward browse.
   b. Lines 451–465. Otherwise, the browse starting point is reset and do a forward browse.

THE WRONG-KEY-USED SECTION

1. Lines 708–715. GETMAIN command to secure main storage for the map that will contain the error message. This is because the PA keys do not allow CICS/VS to secure main storage for the symbolic description map through the RECEIVE MAP command.

2. Line 720. Move the "WRONG KEY USED" message into the area secured.

3. Lines 722–730. Display the error message.

4. Lines 734–738. FREEMAIN command to free main storage secured in the previous GETMAIN command. We have to do this to save main storage because, since we are using the conversational mode of processing, the area will not otherwise be freed by task termination.

5. Line 740. The operator may continue the browse.

THE FINALIZATION SECTION

1. Lines 869–876. Display the "JOB NORMALLY TERMINATED" message.
2. Lines 881–884. Terminate the session.

THE ABNORMAL-TERMINATION SECTION

These are the routines to abnormally terminate the session on errors and CICS/VS command exceptional conditions not covered by a HANDLE CONDITION command.

EXAMPLE

The following are facsimiles of actual photographs taken of a CRT terminal during a session.

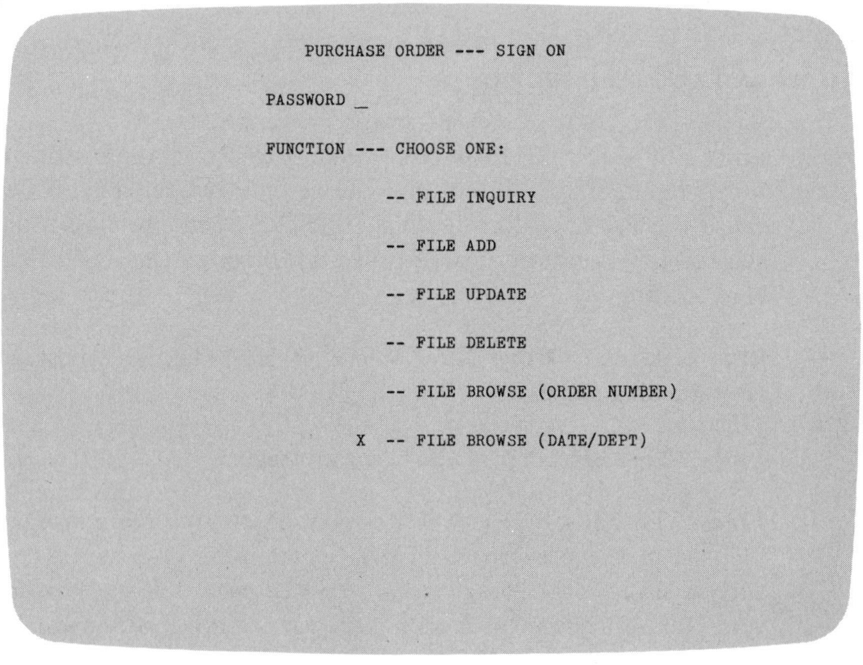

Fig. 23.5. The File Browse (by date/department number) application is selected by keying in an "X" on the File Browse line and the corresponding password, then hitting the ENTER key.

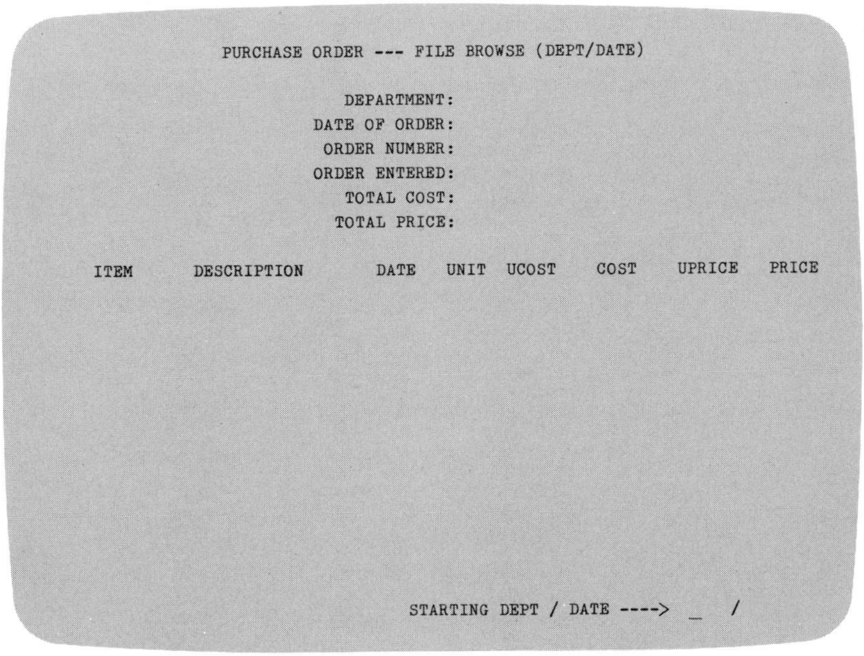

Fig. 23.6. The Sign On program executes which then transfers control to the File Browse program. This displays the File Browse map.

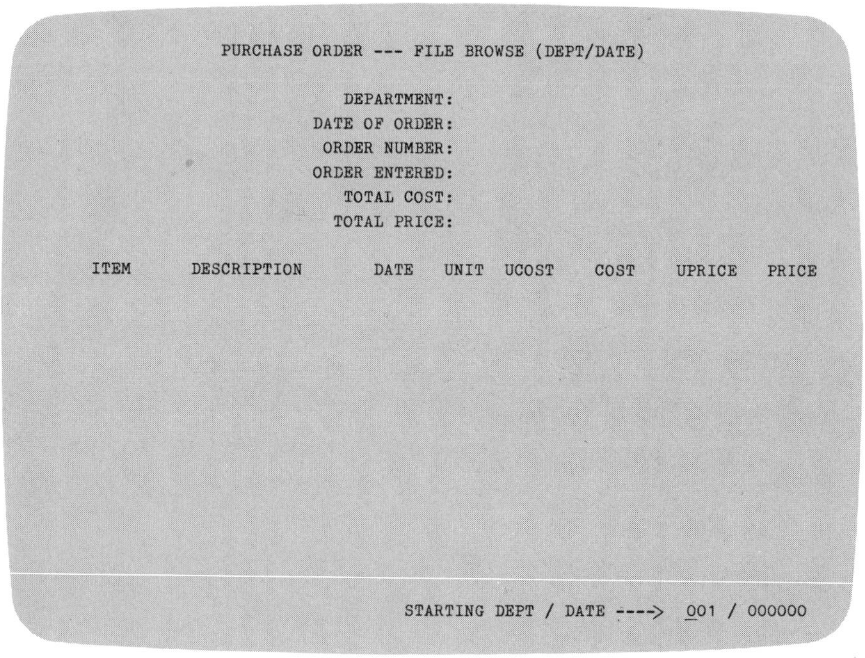

Fig. 23.7. The operator keys in the browse starting point, then hits the ENTER key.

```
                PURCHASE ORDER --- FILE BROWSE (DEPT/DATE)

                         DEPARTMENT: 003
                      DATE OF ORDER: 122280
                       ORDER NUMBER: 0000000001
                      ORDER ENTERED: 122280
                         TOTAL COST:        200.00
                        TOTAL PRICE:        400.00

   ITEM       DESCRIPTION          DATE   UNIT  UCOST    COST     UPRICE   PRICE
 1 00000100 CHISEL SET            122280 00050 0000400 00020000 0000800 00040000




                                  STARTING DEPT / DATE ----> 003 / 122280
```

Fig. 23.8. The program displays the record whose date and department number are equal to the starting point. Since the record does not exist, the next higher one is used.

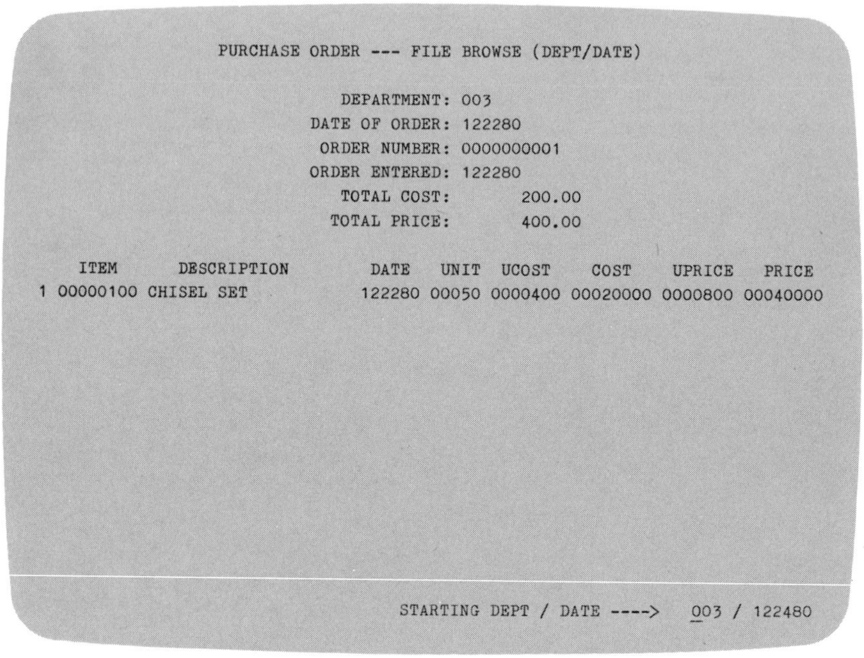

Fig. 23.9. The operator keys in another browse starting point, then hits the ENTER key.

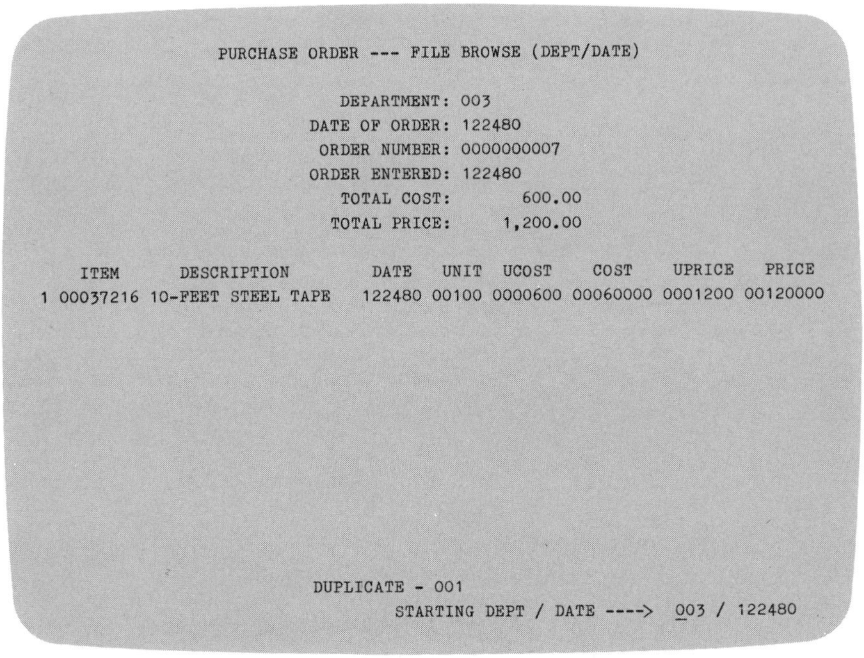

Fig. 23.10. The program displays the record whose date and department number are equal to the new starting point. This is the first record in a set of duplicates. The skip-forward function is executed to do this.

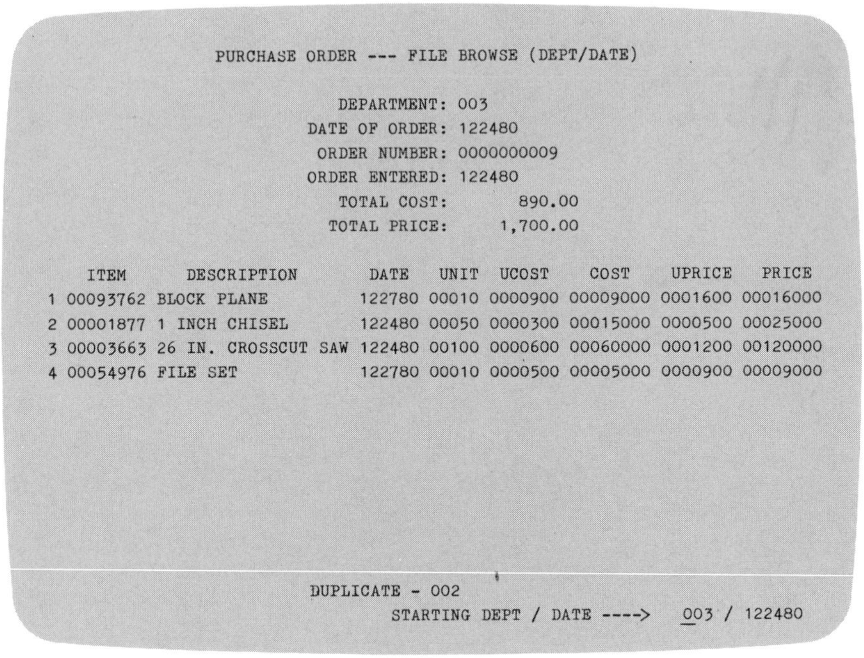
PURCHASE ORDER --- FILE BROWSE (DEPT/DATE)

DEPARTMENT: 003
DATE OF ORDER: 122480
ORDER NUMBER: 0000000009
ORDER ENTERED: 122480
TOTAL COST: 890.00
TOTAL PRICE: 1,700.00

ITEM		DESCRIPTION	DATE	UNIT	UCOST	COST	UPRICE	PRICE
1	00093762	BLOCK PLANE	122780	00010	0000900	00009000	0001600	00016000
2	00001877	1 INCH CHISEL	122480	00050	0000300	00015000	0000500	00025000
3	00003663	26 IN. CROSSCUT SAW	122480	00100	0000600	00060000	0001200	00120000
4	00054976	FILE SET	122780	00010	0000500	00005000	0000900	00009000

DUPLICATE - 002
STARTING DEPT / DATE ----> 003 / 122480

Fig. 23.11. The operator hits the PF1 key, which results in the display of the record next in ascending sequence. This is the second record in a set of duplicates.

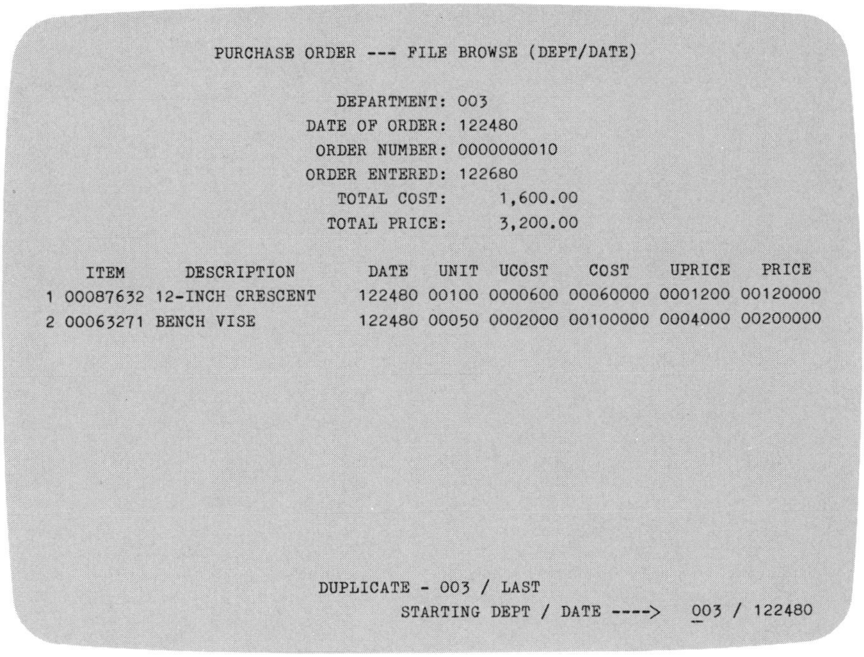

```
                PURCHASE ORDER --- FILE BROWSE (DEPT/DATE)

                            DEPARTMENT: 003
                         DATE OF ORDER: 122480
                          ORDER NUMBER: 0000000010
                         ORDER ENTERED: 122680
                            TOTAL COST:        1,600.00
                           TOTAL PRICE:        3,200.00

     ITEM        DESCRIPTION          DATE   UNIT  UCOST     COST     UPRICE    PRICE
1 00087632 12-INCH CRESCENT         122480 00100 0000600 00060000 0001200 00120000
2 00063271 BENCH VISE               122480 00050 0002000 00100000 0004000 00200000

                       DUPLICATE - 003 / LAST
                               STARTING DEPT / DATE ---->   003 / 122480
```

Fig. 23.12. The operator hits the PF1 key, which results in the display of the record next in ascending sequence. This is the third (and last) record in a set of duplicates.

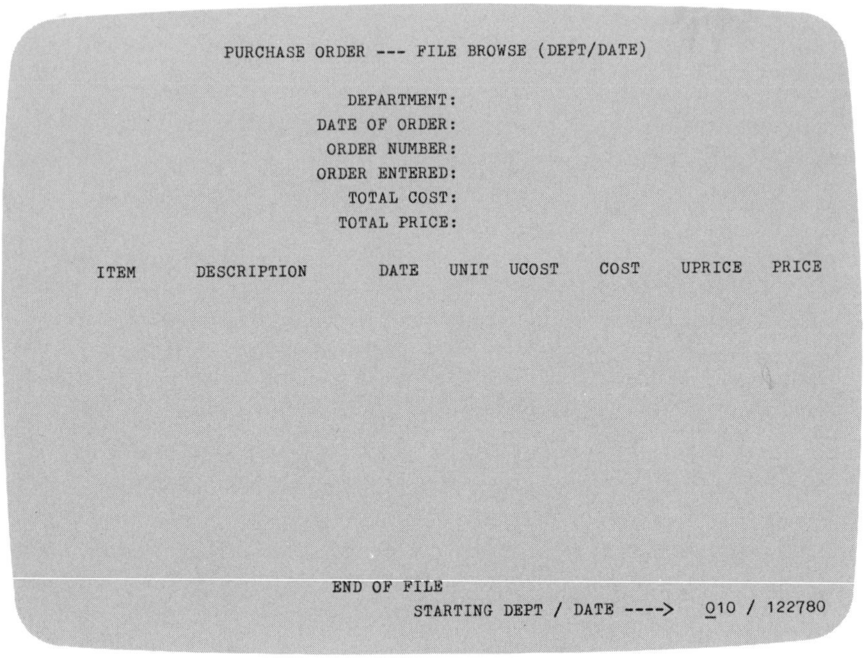

Fig. 23.13. After repeated PF1's, the end of the file is reached. The record with department number of 010 and date of 122780 was the last record displayed.

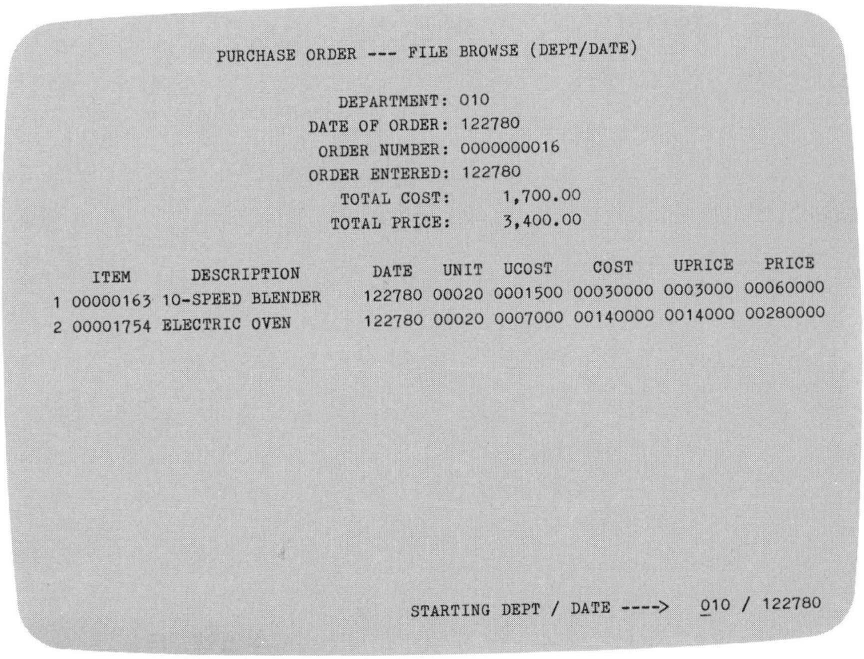

PURCHASE ORDER --- FILE BROWSE (DEPT/DATE)
DEPARTMENT: 010
DATE OF ORDER: 122780
ORDER NUMBER: 0000000016
ORDER ENTERED: 122780
TOTAL COST: 1,700.00
TOTAL PRICE: 3,400.00
ITEM DESCRIPTION DATE UNIT UCOST COST UPRICE PRICE
1 00000163 10-SPEED BLENDER 122780 00020 0001500 00030000 0003000 00060000
2 00001754 ELECTRIC OVEN 122780 00020 0007000 00140000 0014000 00280000
STARTING DEPT / DATE ----> 010 / 122780

Fig. 23.14. The operator hits the PF2 key, which results in the display of the record next in descending sequence.

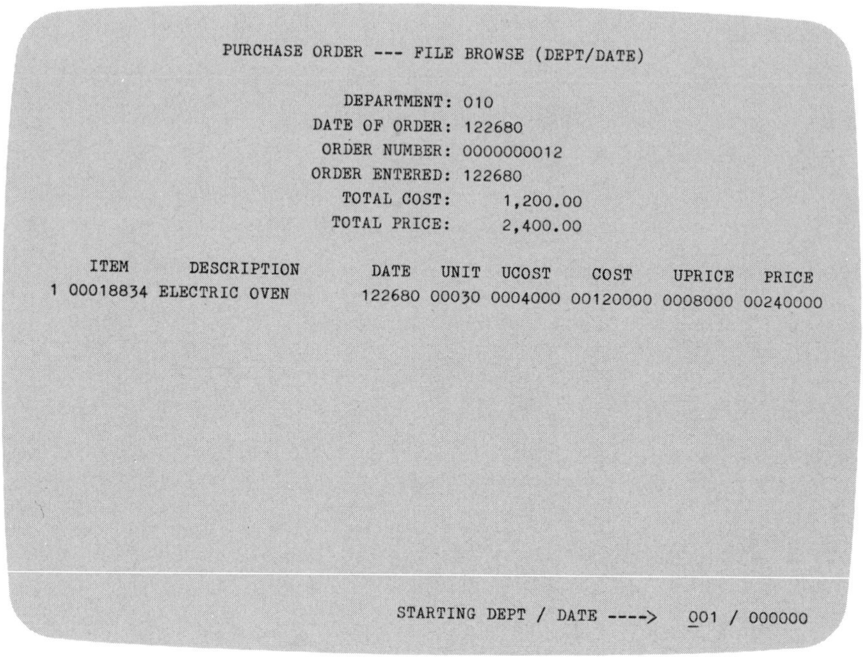

PURCHASE ORDER --- FILE BROWSE (DEPT/DATE)
DEPARTMENT: 010
DATE OF ORDER: 122680
ORDER NUMBER: 0000000012
ORDER ENTERED: 122680
TOTAL COST: 1,200.00
TOTAL PRICE: 2,400.00
ITEM DESCRIPTION DATE UNIT UCOST COST UPRICE PRICE
1 00018834 ELECTRIC OVEN 122680 00030 0004000 00120000 0008000 00240000
STARTING DEPT / DATE ----> 001 / 000000

Fig. 23.15. The operator keys in another browse starting point, then hits the ENTER key.

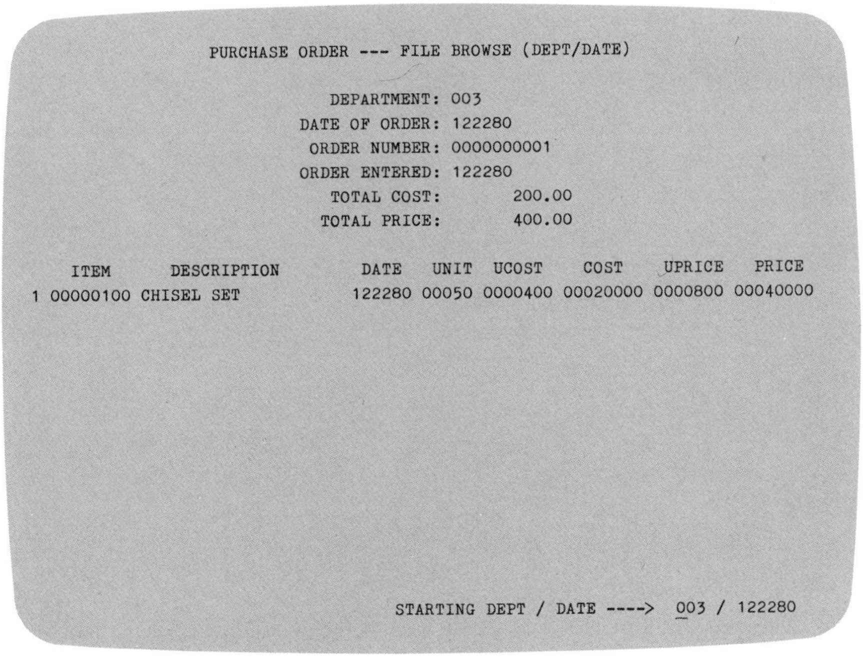

Fig. 23.16. The program displays the record whose date and department number are equal to the new starting point. Since the record does not exist, the next higher one is used.

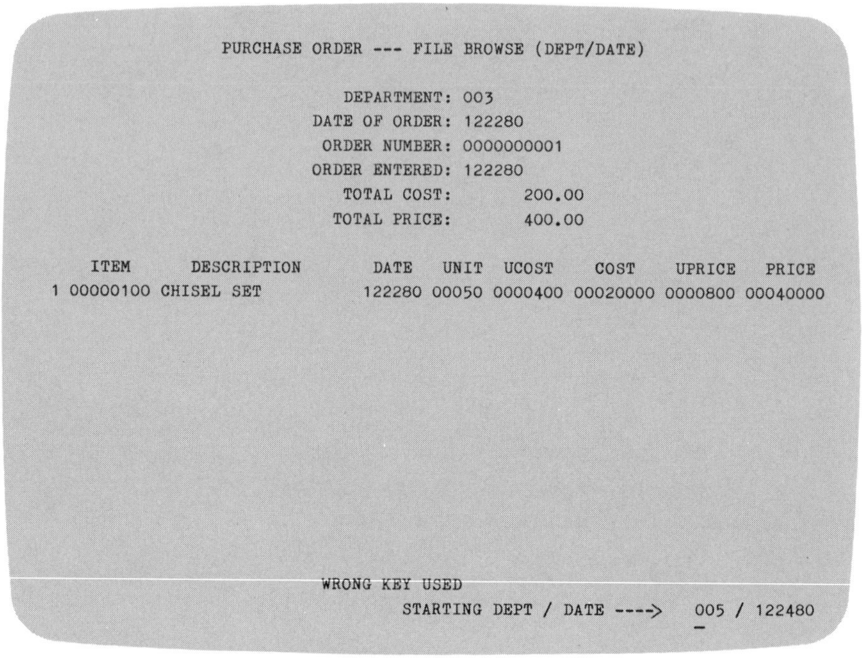

```
                    PURCHASE ORDER --- FILE BROWSE (DEPT/DATE)

                             DEPARTMENT: 003
                          DATE OF ORDER: 122280
                           ORDER NUMBER: 0000000001
                          ORDER ENTERED: 122280
                             TOTAL COST:         200.00
                            TOTAL PRICE:         400.00

     ITEM        DESCRIPTION          DATE   UNIT  UCOST     COST     UPRICE   PRICE
 1 00000100 CHISEL SET               122280 00050 0000400 00020000 0000800 00040000




                          WRONG KEY USED
                               STARTING DEPT / DATE ---->   005 / 122480
```

Fig. 23.17. If the operator keys in another browse starting point but then hits one of the PA keys instead of the ENTER key, the "WRONG KEY USED" message is displayed.

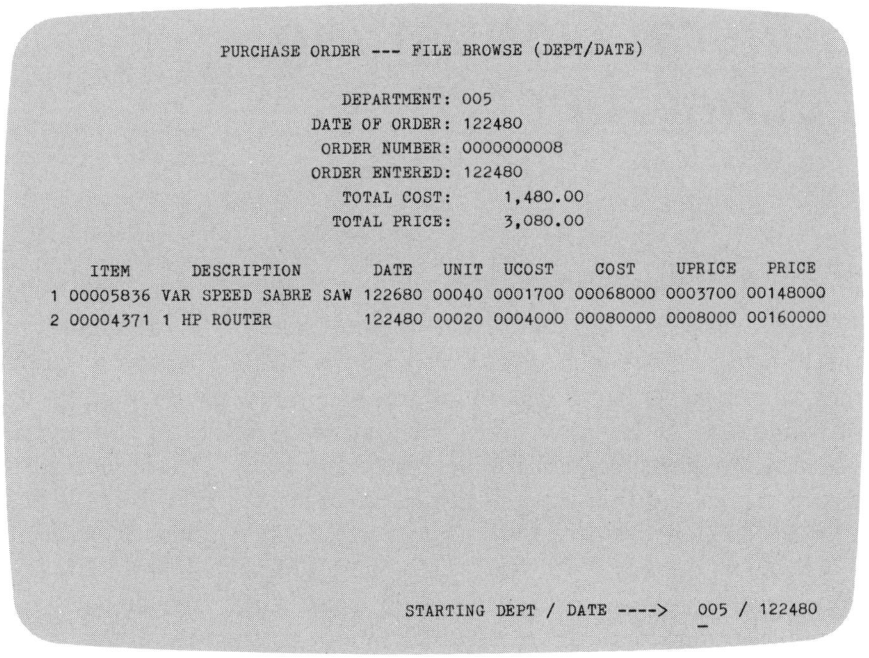

```
               PURCHASE ORDER --- FILE BROWSE (DEPT/DATE)

                          DEPARTMENT: 005
                       DATE OF ORDER: 122480
                        ORDER NUMBER: 0000000008
                       ORDER ENTERED: 122480
                          TOTAL COST:      1,480.00
                         TOTAL PRICE:      3,080.00

    ITEM        DESCRIPTION        DATE   UNIT  UCOST     COST     UPRICE    PRICE
1 00005836 VAR SPEED SABRE SAW 122680 00040 0001700 00068000 0003700 00148000
2 00004371 1 HP ROUTER         122480 00020 0004000 00080000 0008000 00160000




                                      STARTING DEPT / DATE ---->  005 / 122480
                                                                  -
```

Fig. 23.18. If the operator then hits the ENTER key, the session continues. The record selected in Fig. 23.17 is now displayed.

24

General Debugging Techniques

INTRODUCTION

CICS/VS programs may be tested in three ways. The first way is by the Execution Diagnostic Facility (EDF), which allows the programmer to, among other things, temporarily modify commands, results of commands, certain data areas, etc., interactively during testing. We will not, however, discuss the details of the EDF because such a discussion is beyond the scope of this book. Also, the EDF is really best learned through actual use.

The second method for testing CICS/VS programs is this: the programmer may simulate a terminal on a sequential device such as a card reader, magnetic tape, or disk. Then he prepares test data and tests the program as if it were a batch program. I do not recommend this method because the EDF method and the next method are superior; they allow the programmer to change test data during the test, making the test easier to conduct.

In the third method, the programmer can test the program interactively in the same manner that it would be used "live." He could then debug it using the terminal screen, and interpret a trace and a dump. This is the method that will be shown.

SCREEN DEBUGGING

Unlike batch programs, where the programmer has to prepare data in advance of the testing process, CICS/VS programs may be tested extemporaneously. The programmer should, however, have a plan to enable him to test as many functions as possible in a single sitting. He should also develop troubleshooting techniques. He can do both because a CICS/VS application program can be tested for as long as desired in a single sitting; after all, in case of an abend (*ab*normal *end*), the session can be restarted.

The first step in debugging is to make a visual inspection of how the terminal screen displays and accepts information. For instance, after each new map is displayed on the screen, the programmer may check:

Before Entering Data

1. Is the screen correct as far as display is concerned? Are all titles, field identifiers, etc., complete, correctly placed, and of the right intensity (bright, normal, dark)? If not, the map program has to be corrected.
2. Is there "garbage" showing? If so, maybe the previous SEND MAP command did not specify ERASE? Or maybe the map program itself has extra fields defined?
3. Is the cursor under the first field to be entered or modified? If not, maybe the IC operand was not specified or was misplaced in the map program.

While Entering Data

1. Are the shift (alphabetic or numeric) and intensity correct as you enter each unprotected field? If not, the attributes of the corresponding fields in the map program may have been incorrectly specified.
2. As you enter each unprotected field completely, does the cursor automatically go to the next unprotected field? If not, there may be something wrong with the use of SKIP or STOPPER fields in the map program.
3. On using the SKIP key continuously, does the cursor only fall under unprotected fields? If not, there is again something wrong with the use of SKIP or STOPPER fields.
4. After entering the last unprotected field on the screen, does the cursor wrap around to the first unprotected field? If not, there is no SKIP or STOPPER field after the last unprotected field.

5. Are there areas in the screen where the cursor goes to and it should not? If so, those fields may have been defined as unprotected erroneously.

On a terminal where a lot of data is to be entered for validation, the programmer should have a general plan of action. I suggest that the following sets of data mix be entered separately:

1. The minimum amount of data that will be accepted as complete by the program, with no errors entered.
2. All data that will be accepted by the program, with no errors entered.
3. Data entered with the number of errors equal to the maximum number of error message positions.
4. Data entered with the number of errors greater than the maximum number of error message positions.
5. No data entered.

After the programmer has entered the data mix, the ENTER key is then used to initiate the task. He may then check the following:

Data Without Errors (Data mix 1 and 2 above)

1. Does the program accept all data as correct? If so, the program probably will display a message like "DATA ACCEPTED – CONTINUE" on a fresh screen.
2. Is there some data that should be edited as correct but is treated as an error?
3. Is there a program check or a CICS/VS command error that aborts the session?

Data With Errors (Data mix 3 and 4)

1. Does the program really validate the errors as errors? If not, there is a logic error.

2. Is the cursor placed under the very first error detected? If not, there is probably something wrong with the use of the symbolic cursor positioning technique.

3. As you correct the data one by one (do not correct all of them at the same time; you want to see the effect of various combinations of error data), does the cursor remain under the very first error detected each time the data is validated? If not, we have the same problem as in 2.

4. For data mix 4, does the program easily deal with the extra errors, bypassing the editing of further errors as it should?

5. For data mix 4 again, when you correct all errors detected on the first pass, do the other errors appear on the second pass?

6. Is there a program check or a CICS/VS command error that aborts the session?

No Data Entered (Data Set 5)

1. Does the program catch this as an error? It should.

2. Is there a program check or a CICS/VS command error that aborts the session?

In addition, the operator may check the following:

PA Key Used After Data Entry

1. Do the messages "DATA BYPASSED – CONTINUE" or "WRONG KEY USED" appear when appropriate?

2. On the first message, is the screen that goes with the message a fresh screen so that the operator may enter a new set of data? If not, there is an error.

3. On the second message, does the screen remain the same? Also, when the operator uses the correct key (generally the ENTER key), does the program proceed from where it left off, accepting the data already entered?

After The Data Has Been Accepted

1. When the record is displayed (for instance, in a File Update application, the very same record just updated may be immediately recalled), does the display show that the input was indeed accepted? If not, something went wrong in writing out the record after data validation.

PROGRAM TRACE

Trace Tables

CICS/VS provides a facility to have trace entries generated as a debugging aid. A "regular" trace table in main storage is always maintained as part of the CICS/VS nucleus. All tasks generate entries on this table, which is automatically printed out only in cases involving most CICS/VS command exceptional conditions,* a transaction abend, or commands that request a dump (DUMP command for instance). Entries on this table are written in a wrap-around manner; that is, when the end of the table is reached, the next entry replaces the first entry of the table.

In addition, an auxiliary trace facility allows tasks to write the very same entries, time-stamped, into a trace table on a sequential device (generally a magnetic tape or disk), which may be printed out offline through the CICS/VS Trace Utility program. Unlike the regular trace table, this one will contain all entries written to it once CICS/VS is initialized. It is useful during a program test if the regular trace table is inadequate (in size) or if the programmer wants a trace independent of the result of the test. This may also be used for performance analysis to identify potential bottlenecks, because entries are time-stamped, and for other statistical analysis.

The auxiliary trace facility is activated only if the auxiliary trace program has been generated. Activation is done by the programmer through the master terminal using this CICS/VS service:

CSMT ATR, ON

---

*If a HANDLE CONDITION command was specified for the error or the ERROR condition was specified, the corresponding routine will be executed instead.

He should then get the message:

"AUXILIARY TRACE FUNCTION ACTIVATED"

The trace facility may also be deactivated by:

CSMT ATR, OFF

He should then get the message:

"AUXILIARY TRACE FUNCTION DEACTIVATED"

Trace Entries

There are two types of entries in trace tables. The system trace entries are totally CICS/VS controlled and include Execute Interface Program trace points (the only one really of importance to the application programmer) every time a CICS/VS command is executed. Two entries are made for most commands: first, when the command is issued; second, when the functions required in the command have been performed and control is about to be returned to the application program. In between these two entries, the flow of control, especially the control programs* that were executed, can be traced.

The user trace entry point is generated on the ENTER command and is used to provide a trace of the program in between CICS/VS commands. This command is generally used only during testing and should be removed when the program is released to production. The format of the command is:

```
enter traceid (data value)
      from    (data area)
```

The TRACEID operand is the trace identifier with value from 0 to 199 and appears in the first byte of the entry; the FROM operand is optional and places the value of the data area in bytes 8–15 of the entry.

---

*Many commands require several CICS/VS control programs.

Trace Header

All entries in the trace tables are 16 bytes long. The regular trace table contains a header that contains the following information:

Bytes	Contents
0–3	Address of the last-used entry.
4–7	Address of the beginning of the table.
8–11	Address of the end of the table.
12–15	Reserved.

A listing of the regular trace table is shown in Figure 24.1.

A points to the trace header; B is the address of the last entry used, which is 00146410; C is the address of the beginning of the table, which is 001457FO; D is the address of the end of the table, which is 00146460.

Execute Interface Trace Entry At Issuance

As we said before, of the system entries, the only ones of importance to the application programmer are the Execute Interface Program trace points. Most CICS/VS commands create two entries. The entry when the command is issued contains the following:

Bytes	Contents
0	X'E1' trace identifier.
1–3	Return point in the application program.
4	Not used.
5 (bits 0–3)	X'0', identifying the first entry for the command.
6–7	User task sequence number (packed decimal).
8–11	Address of the Working-Storage section (this is for ANS Cobol).
12, 13	Not used.
14, 15	Code identifying the CICS/VS command. This is identical to the EIBFN field codes of Fig. 24.7.

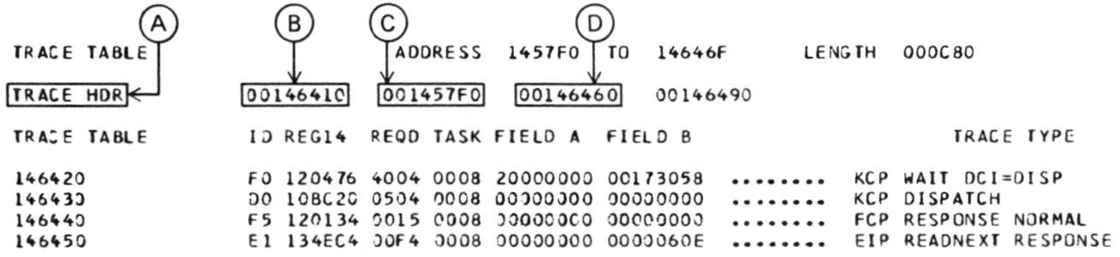
A
B
C
D
TRACE TABLE
ADDRESS 1457F0 TO 14646F LENGTH 000C80
TRACE HDR
00146410
001457F0
00146460
00146490
TRACE TABLE
ID REG14 REQD TASK FIELD A FIELD B
TRACE TYPE
146420 F0 120476 4004 0008 20000000 00173058 .... KCP WAIT DCI=DISP
146430 D0 10BC20 0504 0008 00000000 00000000 .... KCP DISPATCH
146440 F5 120134 0015 0008 000000C0 00000000 .... FCP RESPONSE NORMAL
146450 E1 134EC4 00F4 0008 00000000 0000060E .... EIP READNEXT RESPONSE

Fig. 24.1. The Regular Trace Table.

```
CUSTOMER INFORMATION CONTROL SYSTEM STORAGE DUMP   CODE=ERRS   TASK=ORAD      DATE=08/02/80   TIME=17 03 35   PAGE   3

TRACE TABLE        ID REG14  REQD TASK FIELD A  FIELD B                   TRACE TYPE

146460             E1 134EC4 0004 0008 0012FA2C 0000060E  ........  EIP READNEXT ENTRY


1457F0             F5 11E9C8 B003 0008 C4E2E7E3 C1C2E240  DSXTABS   FCP GETNEXT
145800             F0 120476 4004 0008 20000000 00173058  ........  KCP WAIT DCI=DISP
145810             D0 10BC20 0504 0008 00000000 00000000  ........  KCP DISPATCH
145820             F5 120134 0015 0008 00000000 00000000  ........  FCP RESPONSE NORMAL
145830             E1 134EC4 00F4 0008 00000000 0000060E  ........  EIP READNEXT RESPONSE
145840             E1 134EC4 0004 0008 0012FA2C 0000060E  ........  EIP READNEXT ENTRY
145850             F5 11E9C8 B003 0008 C4E2E7E3 C1C2E240  DSXTABS   FCP GETNEXT
145860             F0 120476 4004 0008 20000000 00173058  ........  KCP WAIT DCI=DISP
145870             D0 10BC20 0504 TC   00000000 00000000  ........  KCP DISPATCH
145880             F0 10DBB8 4004 TC   44000000 001007F8  .......8  KCP WAIT
145890             D0 10BC20 0504 0008 00000000 00000000  ........  KCP DISPATCH
1458A0             F5 120134 0015 0008 00000000 00000000  ........  FCP RESPONSE NORMAL
1458B0             E1 134EC4 00F4 0008 00000000 0000060E  ........  EIP READNEXT RESPONSE
1458C0             E1 134EC4 0004 0008 0012FA2C 0000060E  ........  EIP READNEXT ENTRY
1458D0             F5 11E9C8 B003 0008 C4E2E7E3 C1C2E240  DSXTABS   FCP GETNEXT
1458E0             F0 120476 4004 0008 20000000 00173058  ........  KCP WAIT DCI=DISP
1458F0             D0 10BC20 0504 0008 00000000 00000000  ........  KCP DISPATCH
145900             F5 120134 0015 0008 00000000 00000000  ........  FCP RESPONSE NORMAL
145910             E1 134EC4 00F4 0008 00000000 0000060E  ........  EIP READNEXT RESPONSE
145920             E1 134EC4 0004 0008 0012FA2C 0000060E  ........  EIP READNEXT ENTRY
145930             F5 11E9C8 B003 0008 C4E2E7E3 C1C2E240  DSXTABS   FCP GETNEXT
145940             F0 120476 4004 0008 20000000 00173058  ........  KCP WAIT DCI=DISP
145950             D0 10BC20 0504 0008 00000000 00000000  ........  KCP DISPATCH
145960             F5 120134 0015 0008 00000000 00000000  ........  FCP RESPONSE NORMAL
145970             E1 134EC4 00F4 0008 00000000 0000060E  ........  EIP READNEXT RESPONSE
145980             E1 134EC4 0004 0008 0012FA2C 0000060E  ........  EIP READNEXT ENTRY
145990             F5 11E9C8 B003 0008 C4E2E7E3 C1C2E240  DSXTABS   FCP GETNEXT
1459A0             F0 120476 4004 0008 20000000 00173058  ........  KCP WAIT DCI=DISP
1459B0             D0 10BC20 0504 0008 00000000 00000000  ........  KCP DISPATCH
1459C0             F5 120134 0015 0008 00000000 00000000  ........  FCP RESPONSE NORMAL
1459D0             E1 134EC4 00F4 0008 00000000 0000060E  ........  EIP READNEXT RESPONSE
1459E0             E1 134FDA 0004 0008 0012FA2C 00000A02  ........  EIP WRITEQ-TS ENTRY
1459F0             F1 12187A 8E04 0008 00130540 01100660  ... ....  SCP GETMAIN
145A00             C8 115222 0004 0008 00130740 8E130548  ... ....  SCP ACQUIRED TEMPSTRG STORAGE
145A10             F7 1218C6 4103 0008 D3F7F7F0 D6D9C1C4  L770ORAD  TSP PUTQ
145A20             F1 12231A F804 0008 00000038 01100660  ........  SCP GETMAIN-COND-INIT
145A30             C8 115222 0004 0008 0012C000 98000040  .......   SCP ACQUIRED TSTABLE STORAGE
145A40             F1 121AEA B704 0008 00120554 01100660  ........  SCP GETMAIN-CONDITIONAL
145A50             C8 115222 0004 0008 0012C040 97120560  ... ....  SCP ACQUIRED TSMAIN STORAGE
145A60             F7 121FCC 0015 0008 00000000 00000000  ........  TSP RESPONSE
145A70             F1 12183E 4004 0008 00130740 01100660  ... ....  SCP FREEMAIN
145A80             C9 11530C 0004 0008 00130740 8E130548  ... ....  SCP RELEASED TEMPSTRG STORAGE
145A90             E1 134FDA 00F4 0008 00000000 00000A02  ........  EIP WRITEQ-TS RESPONSE
145AA0             E1 135012 0004 0008 0012FA2C 00000C04  ........  EIP FREEMAIN ENTRY
145AB0             F1 11508A 4004 0008 0012FF90 01100660  ........  SCP FREEMAIN
145AC0             C9 11530C 0004 0008 0012FF90 8C120548  ........  SCP RELEASED USER STORAGE
145AD0             E1 135012 00F4 0008 00000000 00000C04  ........  EIP FREEMAIN RESPONSE
145AE0             E1 135060 0004 0008 0012FA2C 00000C02  ........  EIP GETMAIN ENTRY
```

Fig. 24.1. (Continued)

```
CUSTOMER INFORMATION CONTROL SYSTEM STORAGE DUMP   CODE=ERRS   TASK=ORAD        DATE=08/02/80   TIME=17 03 35   PAGE
                                                                (E)
145AF0          F1 115052 CC04 0008 000003BE 01100660  ........  SCP GETMAIN-INIT
145B00          C8 115222 0004 0008 00130800 8C0003C8  .......H  SCP ACQUIRED USER STORAGE
145B10          E1 135060 00F4 0008 00000000 00000C02  ........  EIP GETMAIN RESPONSE
145B20          E1 1350CE 0004 0008 0012FA2C 00001804  ........  EIP SEND-MAP ENTRY
145B30          FA 124F7E 0003 0008 000005E2 04000020  ...S....  BMS OUT MAP MAPSET SAVE ERASE
145B40          F2 1261AC 0804 0008 D6D9C1D7 E2F0F140  ORAPS01   PCP DELETE
145B50          F2 126200 0404 0008 D6D9C1C4 E2F0F140  ORADS01   PCP LOAD
145B60          F1 118572 8804 0008 00130096 01100660  ........  SCP GETMAIN
145B70          FD 00001C 0204 0008 E3C9D4C5 1702279F  TIME....  TIMING TRACE 17/02/27.9
145B80          C8 115222 0004 0008 00132800 88000800  ........  SCP ACQUIRED PGM STORAGE
145B90          F0 11862A 4004 0008 88000000 0011A746  ........  KCP WAIT DCI=CICS
145BA0          D0 10BC20 0904 0008 0000A746 EDC00000  ........  KCP SYSTEM RESUME
145BB0          D0 10BC20 0504 0008 00000000 00000000  ........  KCP DISPATCH
145BC0          F1 127F3A 9E04 0008 00130856 01100660  ........  SCP GETMAIN
145BD0          C8 115222 0004 0008 0012C800 9E130868  ..H.....  SCP ACQUIRED MAPCOPY STORAGE
145BE0          F1 124578 CC04 0008 000004E0 01100660  ........  SCP GETMAIN-INIT
145BF0          C8 115222 0004 0008 0012D070 8C0004E8  .......Y  SCP ACQUIRED USER STORAGE
145C00          F1 124846 8504 0008 001205D3 01100660  ...L....  SCP GETMAIN
145C10          C8 115222 0004 0008 00129170 851205E8  .......Y  SCP ACQUIRED TERMINAL STORAGE
145C20          F1 124A00 4004 0008 0012D070 01100660  ........  SCP FREEMAIN
145C30          C9 11530C 0004 0008 0012D070 8C0004E8  .......Y  SCP RELEASED USER STORAGE
145C40          F1 124A00 4004 0008 0012C800 01100660 (F) .H..... SCP FREEMAIN
145C50          C9 11530C 0004 0008 0012C800 9E130868  ..H.....  SCP RELEASED MAPCOPY STORAGE
145C60          FC 126CA8 0103 0008 00810000 00100660  ........  ZCP ZARQ APPL REQ ERASE WRITE
145C70          FA 125EE6 0005 0008 00000000 00000000  ........  BMS RESPONSE
145C80          E1 1350CE 00F4 0008 00000000 00001804  ........  EIP SEND-MAP RESPONSE
145C90          E1 13511C 0004 0008 0012FA2C 00000E08  ........  EIP RETURN ENTRY
145CA0          F1 11970C 9304 0008 00120019 01100660  ........  SCP GETMAIN
145CB0          C8 115222 0004 0008 0012C5A0 93120020  ..E.....  SCP ACQUIRED SHARED STORAGE
145CC0          F2 119760 1004 0008 D6D9C1C4 F0F1C140  ORAD01A   PCP RETURN
145CD0          F1 118A4A 4004 0008 0012F9E0 01100660  ..9.....  SCP FREEMAIN
145CE0          C9 11530C 0004 0008 0012F9E0 8C1303C8  ..9....H  SCP RELEASED USER STORAGE
145CF0          F0 118992 8004 0008 00000000 00000000  ........  KCP DETACH
145D00          D8 10AC20 0203 0008 02000000 001305B0  ........  SPP SYSTEM
145D10          F5 10D7F0 0003 0008 001305B0 00000000  ........  FCP DWE PROCESSOR
145D20          F1 120D70 4004 0008 001305B0 01100660  ........  SCP FREEMAIN
145D30          C9 11530C 0004 0008 001305B0 9D130038  ........  SCP RELEASED DWE STORAGE
145D40          F1 120D70 4004 0008 001305F0 01100660  ...0....  SCP FREEMAIN
145D50          C9 11530C 0004 0008 001305F0 8F1300C8  ...0...H  SCP RELEASED FILE STORAGE
145D60          F5 120134 0015 0008 00000000 00000000  ........  FCP RESPONSE NORMAL
145D70          D8 10D95C 0015 0008 00000000 00000000  ........  SPP RESPONSE
145D80          F0 10AC2A 0304 0008 0011A746 00000000  ........  KCP DEQALL
145D90          D0 10BC20 0504 0008 00000000 00000000  ........  KCP DISPATCH
145DA0          D0 10BC20 0704 0008 02C80400 00000000  .H......  KCP TERMINATE
145DB0          F1 10ADA0 4A04 KC   0012E800 00000000  ..Y.....  SCP FREEMAIN
145DC0          C9 11530C 0004 KC   00130800 8C0003C8  .......H  SCP RELEASED USER STORAGE
145DD0          C9 11530C 0004 KC   001306C0 8F130078  ........  SCP RELEASED FILE STORAGE
145DE0          C9 11530C 0004 KC   00130530 8C000078  ........  SCP RELEASED USER STORAGE
145DF0          C9 11530C 0004 KC   001304E0 8C000048  ........  SCP RELEASED USER STORAGE
145E00          C9 11530C 0004 KC   0012FF40 8C000048  ... ....  SCP RELEASED USER STORAGE
145E10          C9 11530C 0004 KC   0012FEF0 8C000048  ...0....  SCP RELEASED USER STORAGE
145E20          C9 11530C 0004 KC   0012FE70 8C000078  ........  SCP RELEASED USER STORAGE
145E30          C9 11530C 0004 KC   0012FE20 8C000048  ........  SCP RELEASED USER STORAGE
```

Fig. 24.1. (Continued)

```
CUSTOMER INFORMATION CONTROL SYSTEM STORAGE DUMP   CODE=ERRS   TASK=ORAD        DATE=08/02/80   TIME=17 03 35   PAGE    5

145E40          C9 11530C 0004 KC   0012FDB0 8C000068 ........ SCP RELEASED USER STORAGE
145E50          C9 11530C 0004 KC   0012F9C0 8C120018 ..9..... SCP RELEASED USER STORAGE
145E60          C9 11530C 0004 KC   0012F930 8C000088 ..9..... SCP RELEASED USER STORAGE
145E70          C9 11530C 0004 KC   0012F6A0 8C000288 ..6..... SCP RELEASED USER STORAGE
145E80          C9 11530C 0004 KC   0012F290 8C000408 ..2..... SCP RELEASED USER STORAGE
145E90          C9 11530C 0004 KC   0012E800 8A030598 ..Y..... SCP RELEASED TCA STORAGE
145EA0          D0 10BC20 0504 TC   00000000 00000000 ........ KCP DISPATCH
145EB0          F0 10DBB8 4004 TC   44000000 001007F8 .......8 KCP WAIT
145EC0          D0 10BC20 0904 JJ   0000CC20 88A00000 ........ KCP SYSTEM RESUME
145ED0          D0 10BC20 0904 JJ   0000CC20 C2B00000 ....B... KCP SYSTEM RESUME
145EE0          D0 10BC20 0904 JJ   0000CC20 3B700000 ........ KCP SYSTEM RESUME
145EF0          D0 10BC20 0504 TC   00000000 00000000 ........ KCP DISPATCH
145F00          F1 10EA54 4004 TC   00129170 80100660 ........ SCP FREEMAIN
145F10          C9 11530C 0004 TC   00129170 851205E8 .......Y SCP RELEASED TERMINAL STORAGE
145F20          F1 10EAF8 6004 TC   00000000 80100660 ........ SCP FREEMAIN ALL
145F30          C9 11530C 0004 TC   00129120 85000048 ........ SCP RELEASED TERMINAL STORAGE
145F40          F1 10E9F0 E404 TC   0000010F 80100660 ........ SCP GETMAIN-COND-INIT
145F50          C8 115222 0004 TC   00129000 84000118 ........ SCP ACQUIRED LINE STORAGE
145F60          F0 10DBB8 4004 TC   44000000 001007F8 .......8 KCP WAIT
145F70          D0 10BC20 0904 JJ   0000CC20 D1200000 ....J... KCP SYSTEM RESUME
145F80          D0 10BC20 0504 TC   00000000 00000000 ........ KCP DISPATCH
145F90          F0 10DBB8 4004 TC   44000000 001007F8 .......8 KCP WAIT
145FA0          D0 10BC20 0904 JJ   0000CC20 A6A00000 ........ KCP SYSTEM RESUME
145FB0          D0 10BC20 0504 TC   00000000 00000000 ........ KCP DISPATCH
145FC0          F0 10DBB8 4004 TC   44000000 001007F8 .......8 KCP WAIT
145FD0          D0 10BC20 0904 JJ   0000CC20 DE000000 ........ KCP SYSTEM RESUME
145FE0          D0 10BC20 0504 TC   00000000 00000000 ........ KCP DISPATCH
145FF0          F0 113464 1104 TC   01100660 D6D9C1C4 ....ORAD KCP ATTACH-CONDITIONAL
146000          F1 10A91E EA04 TC   000807B0 80100660 ........ SCP GETMAIN-COND-INIT
146010          C8 115222 0004 TC   0012D800 8A0307B8 ..Q..... SCP ACQUIRED TCA STORAGE
146020          D0 10BC20 0604 0009 D3F7F7F0 D6D9C1C4 L770ORAD KCP CREATE
146030          D0 10BC20 0504 TC   00000000 00000000 ........ KCP DISPATCH
146040          F0 10DBB8 4004 TC   44000000 001007F8 .......8 KCP WAIT
146050          D0 10BC20 0504 0009 00000000 00000000 ........ KCP DISPATCH
146060          F2 118804 0204 0009 D6D9C1C4 F0F1C140 ORAD01A  PCP XCTL
146070          F1 1190FC 8C04 0009 000003BC 01100660 ........ SCP GETMAIN
146080          C8 115222 0004 0009 0012DFC0 8C0003C8 .......H SCP ACQUIRED USER STORAGE
146090          F1 10C2A6 CC04 0009 00000128 01100660 ........ SCP GETMAIN-INIT
1460A0          C8 115222 0004 0009 0012E390 8C000138 ..T..... SCP ACQUIRED USER STORAGE
1460B0          E1 13399C 0004 0009 0012E00C 00000202 ........ EIP ADDRESS ENTRY
1460C0          E1 13399C 00F4 0009 00000000 00000202 ........ EIP ADDRESS RESPONSE
1460D0          E1 1339C2 0004 0009 0012E00C 00000206 ........ EIP HANDLE-AID ENTRY
1460E0          F1 10BC96 CC04 0009 00000059 01100660 ........ SCP GETMAIN-INIT
1460F0          C8 115222 0004 0009 0012E4D0 8C000068 ..U..... SCP ACQUIRED USER STORAGE
146100          F1 10BD98 CC04 0009 00000040 01100660 ... .... SCP GETMAIN-INIT
146110          C8 115222 0004 0009 0012E540 8C000048 ..V .... SCP ACQUIRED USER STORAGE
146120          E1 1339C2 00F4 0009 00000000 00000206 ........ EIP HANDLE-AID RESPONSE
146130          E1 133A1C 0004 0009 0012E00C 00000204 ........ EIP HANDLE-CONDITION ENTRY
146140          F1 10BC96 CC04 0009 00000070 01100660 ........ SCP GETMAIN-INIT
146150          C8 115222 0004 0009 0012E590 8C000078 ..V..... SCP ACQUIRED USER STORAGE
146160          F1 10BD98 CC04 0009 00000040 01100660 ... .... SCP GETMAIN-INIT
146170          C8 115222 0004 0009 0012E610 8C000048 ..W..... SCP ACQUIRED USER STORAGE
146180          E1 133A1C 00F4 0009 00000000 00000204 ........ EIP HANDLE-CONDITION RESPONSE
```

Fig. 24.1. (Continued)

```
CUSTOMER INFORMATION CONTROL SYSTEM STORAGE DUMP    CODE=ERRS    TASK=ORAD      DATE=08/02/80    TIME=17 03 35    PAGE    6
                                                                (G)
146190        E1 133ADC 0004 0009 0012E00C 00001A04  ........  EIP ENTER ENTRY
1461A0        6F 133ADC 0002 0009 0012E00C 00000000  ........  USER 111
1461B0        E1 133ADC 00F4 0009 00000000 00001A04  ........  EIP ENTER RESPONSE
1461C0        E1 133B3A 0004 0009 0012E00C 00001802  ........  EIP RECEIVE-MAP ENTRY
1461D0        FA 125080 0003 0009 00000505 00000020  ........  BMS MAP MAPSET MAP IN
1461E0        F1 12537E CC04 0009 00000274 01100660  ........  SCP GETMAIN-INIT
1461F0        C8 115222 0004 0009 0012E660 8C000288  ..W.....  SCP ACQUIRED USER STORAGE
146200        F1 15AD78 CC04 0009 00000074 01100660  ........  SCP GETMAIN-INIT
146210        C8 115222 0004 0009 0012E8F0 8C000088  ..YO....  SCP ACQUIRED USER STORAGE
146220        F2 126200 0404 0009 D6D9C1C4 E2F0F140  ORADS01   PCP LOAD
146230        F1 124AAC C504 0009 000003B1 01100660  ........  SCP GETMAIN-INIT
146240        C8 115222 0004 0009 00129120 850003C8  .......H  SCP ACQUIRED TERMINAL STORAGE
146250        F1 124E88 4004 0009 00129000 01100660  ........  SCP FREEMAIN
146260        C9 11530C 0004 0009 00129000 85000118  ........  SCP RELEASED TERMINAL STORAGE
146270        FA 125EE6 0005 0009 00000000 00000000  ........  BMS RESPONSE
146280        E1 133B3A 00F4 0009 00000000 00001802  ........  EIP RECEIVE-MAP RESPONSE
146290        E1 133BAA 0004 0009 0012E00C 00000A04  ........  EIP READQ-TS ENTRY
1462A0        F7 12192C 8903 0009 D3F7F7F0 D6D9C1C4  L770ORAD  TSP GETQ
1462B0        F1 121C38 AE04 0009 00120540 01100660  ... ....  SCP GETMAIN-CONDITIONAL
1462C0        C8 115222 0004 0009 0012E980 8E120548  ..Z.....  SCP ACQUIRED TEMPSTRG STORAGE
1462D0        F7 121FCC 0015 0009 00000000 00000000  ........  TSP RESPONSE
1462E0        E1 133BAA 00F4 0009 00000000 00000A04  ........  EIP READQ-TS RESPONSE
1462F0        E1 1347D8 0004 0009 0012E00C 00000C02  ........  EIP GETMAIN ENTRY
146300        F1 115052 8C04 0009 001201B1 01100660  ........  SCP GETMAIN
146310        C8 115222 0004 0009 0012EED0 8C1201C8  .......H  SCP ACQUIRED USER STORAGE
146320        E1 1347D8 00F4 0009 00000000 00000C02  ........  EIP GETMAIN RESPONSE
146330        E1 13486E 0004 0009 0012E00C 00001A04  ........  EIP ENTER ENTRY
146340        E1 12E610 02F4 0009 E0000000 00001A04  ........  EIP ENTER RESPONSE
146350        E1 1352F8 0004 0009 0012E00C 00001C02  ........  EIP DUMP ENTRY
146360        F4 1597FC FE04 0009 00000000 C5D9D9E2  ....ERRS  DCP TRANSACTION
146370        F0 155C58 4004 0009 80000000 00155E78  ........  KCP WAIT DCI=SINGLE
146380        FD 00001C 0204 0009 E3C9D4C5 1703355F  TIME....  TIMING TRACE 17/03/35.5
146390        D0 10BC20 0504 TC   00000000 00000000  ........  KCP DISPATCH
1463A0        F0 10DBB8 4004 TC   44000000 001007F8  .......8  KCP WAIT
1463B0        D0 10BC20 0904 0009 00005E78 6AA00000  ........  KCP SYSTEM RESUME
1463C0        D0 10BC20 0504 TC   00000000 00000000  ........  KCP DISPATCH
1463D0        F0 10DBB8 4004 TC   44000000 001007F8  .......8  KCP WAIT
1463E0        D0 10BC20 0504 0009 00000000 00000000  ........  KCP DISPATCH
1463F0        F0 155C58 4004 0009 80000000 00155E78  ........  KCP WAIT DCI=SINGLE
146400        D0 10BC20 0904 0009 00005E78 73D00000  ........  KCP SYSTEM RESUME
146410        D0 10BC20 0504 0009 00000000 00000000  ........  KCP DISPATCH
```

Fig. 24.1. (Continued)

An example of this is E on page 497. You will notice that on the right is a description of the entry. It is always the literal "EIP" (*E*xecute *I*nterface *P*rogram), followed by the command (in this case "SEND MAP"), followed by the literal "ENTRY," meaning that this is the issuance of the command.

Execute Interface Trace Entry At Completion

The trace entry upon completion of the command contains the following:

Bytes	Contents
0	X'E1' trace identifier.
1-3	Return point in the application program; if the response code in bytes 8-13 is nonzero and an appropriate HANDLE CONDITION command is active, these bytes will contain the address of the label specified in the HANDLE CONDITION command.
4	EIBGDI.
5 (bits 0-3)	X'F', identifying the second entry for the command.
5 (bits 4-7)	Not used.
6-7	User task sequence number (packed decimal).
8-13	Response code. Zero response code signifies that no exceptional condition occurred during execution of the command. If the response is nonzero, Figure 24.8 will identify the problem.
14, 15	Code identifying the CICS/VS command. Same as for Entry at Issuance.

An example of this is F on page 497, and you will notice that the description of the entry is now "RESPONSE," meaning the command has been completed. This entry will appear regardless whether there was a CICS/VS command exceptional condition or not. Bytes 8-13 will signify an exceptional condition if it is not zeroes, and the EIBRCODE field of the Execute Interface Block should then be investigated.

The specific control programs executed in a CICS/VS command are really only of academic importance to the programmer since they are provided automatically when required by the command. However,

	Description	Trace Identifier	Program
1.	BFP	X'FB'	Built-in Function
2.	BMP	X'FA', X'CD', X'CF'	Basic Mapping Support
3.	DCP	X'F4'	Dump Control
4.	DIP	X'D7'	Batch Data Interchange
5.	EIP	X'E1'	Execute Interface
6.	FCP	X'F5'	File Control
7.	ICP	X'F3'	Interval Control
8.	JCP	X'F9'	Journal Control
9.	KCP	X'F0', X'D0'	Task Control
10.	PCP	X'F2'	Program Control
11.	SCP	X'F1', X'C8', X'C9', X'CA'	Storage Control
12.	SPC	X'D8'	Sync Point
13.	TCP	X'FC'	Terminal Control
14.	TDP	X'F6'	Transient Data
15.	TSP	X'F7'	Temporary Storage
16.	USER	user specified	User Trace Entry

Fig. 24.2. Table of Trace Identifiers.

if the programmer is interested in knowing what they are, he may use the guide in Figure 24.2.

User Trace

The third trace entry of importance to the application programmer is the user trace entry and this is generated on the ENTER command. It contains the following information:

Bytes	Contents
0	Trace identifier, the hexadecimal equivalent of the data value specified in the TRACEID operand.
1-3	Return point in the application program.
4	Not used.
5 (bits 0-3)	Not used.
5 (bits 4-7)	X'2', identifying this entry as a user entry.

6–7	User task sequence number (packed decimal).
8–15	Value of the data area specified in the FROM operand.

An example of this is G on page 499. The description is the literal "USER" followed by the value specified in the TRACEID operand of the ENTER command. You will also notice that it is bracketed by the two Execute Interface entries.

TRANSACTION DUMP

While the trace tables provide the programmer with a trace of the programs as they execute, a transaction dump provides him with the contents of CICS/VS data blocks at the time the dump was initiated. This shows, among other things, the WORKING-STORAGE section, main storage corresponding to entries in the LINKAGE section, the Execute Interface Block, etc., all of which may be used in debugging.

The transaction dump is automatically generated on a program check; it is also the default in most CICS/VS command exceptional conditions not specified in a HANDLE CONDITION command, unless the ERROR condition is specified; it is an option in certain commands like DUMP or ABEND.

We will now show the procedure in debugging a program check. The program used is basically the File Add program but with certain statements removed to get the abend. The program and Data Division Map listing is shown in Figure 24.3.

The Procedure Division condensed listing is given in Figure 24.4.

The resulting transaction dump is shown in Figure 24.5.

The Transaction Work Area

The Transaction Work Area is part of the Task Control Area and always prints on page 1 of the transaction dump. It always starts at byte X'100' of the data block labeled "TASK CONTROL AREA (USER AREA)." This is A in Fig. 24.5 (page 536).

```
    1   IBM DOS VS COBOL                          REL 2.5 + PTF51   PP NO. 5746-CB1              18.38.45  07/27/80

 CBL  SUPMAP,STXIT,NOTRUNC,CSYNTAX,SXREF,OPT,VERB,CLIST,BUF=19069
 CBL  NOOPT,LIB
00001          IDENTIFICATION DIVISION.                                     00000030

00003          PROGRAM-ID. ORADC1A.                                         00000050


00005          ENVIRONMENT DIVISION.                                        00000070

00007          *************************************************************** 00000090
00008          *                                                             * 00000100
00009          *    1. THIS PROGRAM ADDS NEW ORDERS INTO THE PURCHASE ORDER  * 00000110
00010          *       MASTER FILE.                                          * 00000120
00011          *                                                             * 00000130
00012          *    2. AT LEAST ONE LINE ITEM MUST BE PRESENT FOR EACH ORDER. * 00000140
00013          *                                                             * 00000150
00014          *    3. A JOURNAL RECORD IS GENERATED FOR EACH NEW ORDER      * 00000160
00015          *       ENTERED.  THE JOURNAL DETAILS ARE                     * 00000170
00016          *             A) OPERATOR INITIAL.                            * 00000180
00017          *             B) DATE ENTERED.                                * 00000190
00018          *             C) ORDER NUMBER.                                * 00000200
00019          *             D) DOCUMENT NUMBER.                             * 00000210
00020          *             E) TOTAL COST OF ORDER.                         * 00000220
00021          *             F) TOTAL PRICE OF ORDER.                        * 00000230
00022          *                                                             * 00000240
00023          *************************************************************** 00000250
```

Fig. 24.3. Program Listing And Data Division Map.

```
2          ORAD01A        18.38.45        07/27/80

           DATA DIVISION.                                                  00000270

           WORKING-STORAGE SECTION.                                        00000290

           01  COMMUNICATION-AREA.                                         00000310
               05  COMMAREA-PROCESS-SW            PIC X.                   00000330

           01  AREA1.                                                      00000350

               05  VALIDATION-ERROR-MESSAGE.                               00000370
                 10  FILLER                       PIC X(5) VALUE 'LINE'.   00000380
                 10  VALIDATION-ERROR-LINE        PIC 9.                   00000390
                 10  FILLER                       PIC XXX  VALUE ' - '.    00000400
                 10  VALIDATION-ERROR-MSG         PIC X(19).               00000410

               05  JOB-NORMAL-END-MESSAGE  PIC X(23) VALUE                 00000430
                   'JOB NORMALLY TERMINATED'.                              00000440

               05  JOB-ABORTED-MESSAGE.                                    00000460
                 10  FILLER               PIC X(15) VALUE 'JOB ABORTED --'.00000470
                 10  MAJOR-ERROR-MSG      PIC X(16).                       00000480

               05  HEXADECIMAL-ZEROES     PIC 9999 COMP VALUE ZEROES.      00000500

               05  FILLER REDEFINES HEXADECIMAL-ZEROES.                    00000520
                 10  FILLER               PIC X.                           00000530
                 10  HEX-ZEROES           PIC X.                           00000540

               05  OLD-EIB-AREA.                                           00000560
                 10  FILLER               PIC X(7) VALUE 'OLD EIB'.        00000570
                 10  OLD-EIBFN            PIC XX.                          00000580
                 10  OLD-EIBRCODE         PIC X(6).                        00000590
```

Fig. 24.3. (Continued)

```
3           ORAD01A          18.38.45          07/27/80

00059          01  DFHEIVAR COPY DFHEIVAR.
00060 C        01  DFHEIVAR.                                                      04000000
00061 C            02    DFHEIV0  PICTURE X(26).                                  08000000
00062 C            02    DFHEIV1  PICTURE X(8).                                   12000000
00063 C            02    DFHEIV2  PICTURE X(8).                                   16000000
00064 C            02    DFHEIV3  PICTURE X(8).                                   20000000
00065 C            02    DFHEIV4  PICTURE X(6).                                   24000000
00066 C            02    DFHEIV5  PICTURE X(4).                                   28000000
00067 C            02    DFHEIV6  PICTURE X(4).                                   32000000
00068 C            02    DFHEIV7  PICTURE X(2).                                   36000000
00069 C            02    DFHEIV8  PICTURE X(2).                                   40000000
00070 C            02    DFHEIV9  PICTURE X(1).                                   45000000
00071 C            02    DFHEIV10 PICTURE S9(7) USAGE COMPUTATIONAL-3.            50000000
00072 C            02    DFHEIV11 PICTURE S9(4) USAGE COMPUTATIONAL.              55000000
00073 C            02    DFHEIV12 PICTURE S9(4) USAGE COMPUTATIONAL.              60000000
00074 C            02    DFHEIV13 PICTURE S9(4) USAGE COMPUTATIONAL.              65000000
00075 C            02    DFHEIV14 PICTURE S9(4) USAGE COMPUTATIONAL.              70000000
00076 C            02    DFHEIV15 PICTURE S9(4) USAGE COMPUTATIONAL.              75000000
00077 C            02    DFHEIV16 PICTURE S9(9) USAGE COMPUTATIONAL.              80000000
00078 C            02    DFHEIV17 PICTURE X(4).                                   81000000
00079 C            02    DFHEIV18 PICTURE X(4).                                   82000000
00080 C            02    DFHEIV19 PICTURE X(4).                                   83000000
00081 C            02    DFHEIV97 PICTURE S9(7) USAGE COMPUTATIONAL-3 VALUE ZERO.85000000
00082 C            02    DFHEIV98 PICTURE S9(4) USAGE COMPUTATIONAL VALUE ZERO.  90000000
00083 C            02    DFHEIV99 PICTURE X(1)  VALUE SPACE.                      95000000
00084          LINKAGE SECTION.                                                   00000610
00085          01  DFHEIBLK COPY DFHEIBLK.
00086 C        *     EIBLK EXEC INTERFACE BLOCK                                   02000000
00087 C         01   DFHEIBLK.                                                    04000000
00088 C        *          EIBTIME     TIME IN OHHMMSS FORMAT                      06000000
00089 C              02 EIBTIME     PICTURE S9(7) USAGE COMPUTATIONAL-3.          08000000
00090 C        *          EIBDATE     DATE IN OOYYDDD FORMAT                      10000000
00091 C              02 EIBDATE     PICTURE S9(7) USAGE COMPUTATIONAL-3.          13000000
00092 C        *          EIBTRNID    TRANSACTION IDENTIFIER                      16000000
00093 C              02 EIBTRNID    PICTURE X(4).                                 19000000
00094 C        *          EIBTASKN    TASK NUMBER                                 24000000
00095 C              02 EIBTASKN    PICTURE S9(7) USAGE COMPUTATIONAL-3.          29000000
00096 C        *          EIBTRMID    TERMINAL IDENTIFIER                         34000000
00097 C              02 EIBTRMID    PICTURE X(4).                                 37000000
00098 C        *          DFHEIGDI    RESERVED                                    40000000
00099 C              02 DFHEIGDI    PICTURE S9(4) USAGE COMPUTATIONAL.            43000000
00100 C        *          EIBCPOSN    CURSOR POSITION                             46000000
00101 C              02 EIBCPOSN    PICTURE S9(4) USAGE COMPUTATIONAL.            49000000
00102 C        *          EIBCALEN    COMMAREA LENGTH                             52000000
00103 C              02 EIBCALEN    PICTURE S9(4) USAGE COMPUTATIONAL.            55000000
00104 C        *          EIBAID      ATTENTION IDENTIFIER                        70000000
00105 C              02 EIBAID      PICTURE X(1).                                 73000000
00106 C        *          EIBFN       FUNCTION CODE                               76000000
00107 C              02 EIBFN       PICTURE X(2).                                 79000000
00108 C        *          EIBRCODE    RESPONSE CODE                               82000000
00109 C              02 EIBRCODE    PICTURE X(6).                                 85000000
00110 C        *          EIBDS       DATASET NAME                                88000000
00111 C              02 EIBDS       PICTURE X(8).                                 91000000
```

Fig. 24.3. (Continued)

```
     4        ORAD01A        18.38.45        07/27/80

00112 C       *        EIBREQID   REQUEST IDENTIFIER                       94000000
00113 C              02 EIBREQID  PICTURE X(8).                            97000000
00114          01  DFHCOMMAREA.                                            00000620

00116              05  PROCESS-SW              PIC X.                      00000640
00117                88  INITIAL-ENTRY-TIME        VALUE '0'.              00000650
00118                88  ORDER-VALIDATION-TIME     VALUE '1'.              00000660

00120              05  OPERATOR-INITIAL        PIC XXX.                    00000680


00122          01  LINKAGE-POINTERS.                                       00000700

00124              05  FILLER                  PIC S9(8) COMP.             00000720
00125              05  MAP1-POINTER            PIC S9(8) COMP.             00000730
00126              05  POM-POINTER             PIC S9(8) COMP.             00000740
00127              05  TWA-POINTER             PIC S9(8) COMP.             00000750
00128              05  TSA-POINTER             PIC S9(8) COMP.             00000760
00129              05  JOURNAL-POINTER         PIC S9(8) COMP.             00000770
00130              05  TABLE-POINTER           PIC S9(8) COMP.             00000780
```

Fig. 24.3. (Continued)

```
5         ORADO1A        18.38.45       07/27/80

00132     ****************************************************************** 00000800
00133     *                                                                * 00000810
00134     *              ORDER ENTRY MAP DESCRIPTION                       * 00000820
00135     *                                                                * 00000830
00136     ****************************************************************** 00000840


00138      01  MAP1-AREA.                                                    00000860

00140          05  FILLER                       PIC X(12).                   00000880
00141          05  MAP1-DUMMY-L                 PIC S9999 COMP.              00000890
00142          05  MAP1-DUMMY-A                 PIC X.                       00000900
00143          05  MAP1-DUMMY                   PIC X.                       00000910
00144          05  MAP1-ORDER-NUMBER-L          PIC S9999 COMP.              00000920
00145          05  MAP1-ORDER-NUMBER-A          PIC X.                       00000930
00146          05  MAP1-ORDER-NUMBER            PIC X(10).                   00000940
00147          05  MAP1-DOCUMENT-L              PIC S9999 COMP.              00000950
00148          05  MAP1-DOCUMENT-A              PIC X.                       00000960
00149          05  MAP1-DOCUMENT                PIC X(8).                    00000970
00150          05  MAP1-DEPARTMENT-L            PIC S9999 COMP.              00000980
00151          05  MAP1-DEPARTMENT-A            PIC X.                       00000990
00152          05  MAP1-DEPARTMENT              PIC XXX.                     00001000
00153          05  MAP1-ORDER-DATE-L            PIC S9999 COMP.              00001010
00154          05  MAP1-ORDER-DATE-A            PIC X.                       00001020
00155          05  MAP1-ORDER-DATE.                                          00001030
00156            10  MAP1-ORDER-DATE-MONTH      PIC XX.                      00001040
00157            10  MAP1-ORDER-DATE-DAY        PIC XX.                      00001050
00158            10  MAP1-ORDER-DATE-YEAR       PIC XX.                      00001060
00159          05  MAP1-LINE-ITEM           OCCURS 9                         00001070
00160                                       INDEXED BY MAP1-LINE-I.          00001080
00161            10  MAP1-ITEM-NUMBER-L         PIC S9999 COMP.              00001090
00162            10  MAP1-ITEM-NUMBER-A         PIC X.                       00001100
00163            10  MAP1-ITEM-NUMBER           PIC 9(8).                    00001110
00164            10  MAP1-ITEM-DESCRIPTION-L    PIC S9999 COMP.              00001120
00165            10  MAP1-ITEM-DESCRIPTION-A    PIC X.                       00001130
00166            10  MAP1-ITEM-DESCRIPTION      PIC X(19).                   00001140
00167            10  MAP1-UNIT-L                PIC S9999 COMP.              00001150
00168            10  MAP1-UNIT-A                PIC X.                       00001160
00169            10  MAP1-UNIT                  PIC 9(5).                    00001170
00170            10  MAP1-UNIT-COST-L           PIC S9999 COMP.              00001180
00171            10  MAP1-UNIT-COST-A           PIC X.                       00001190
00172            10  MAP1-UNIT-COST             PIC 9(5)V99.                 00001200
00173            10  MAP1-COST-L                PIC S9999 COMP.              00001210
00174            10  MAP1-COST-A                PIC X.                       00001220
00175            10  MAP1-COST                  PIC 9(6)V99.                 00001230
00176            10  MAP1-UNIT-PRICE-L          PIC S9999 COMP.              00001240
00177            10  MAP1-UNIT-PRICE-A          PIC X.                       00001250
00178            10  MAP1-UNIT-PRICE            PIC 9(5)V99.                 00001260
00179            10  MAP1-PRICE-L               PIC S9999 COMP.              00001270
00180            10  MAP1-PRICE-A               PIC X.                       00001280
00181            10  MAP1-PRICE                 PIC 9(6)V99.                 00001290
00182          05  MAP1-TOTAL-COST-L            PIC S9999 COMP.              00001300
```

Fig. 24.3. (Continued)

```
     6        ORAD01A          18.38.45        07/27/80

                05  MAP1-TOTAL-COST-A          PIC X.                    00001310
                05  MAP1-TOTAL-COST            PIC 9(7)V99.              00001320
                05  MAP1-TOTAL-PRICE-L         PIC S9999 COMP.           00001330
                05  MAP1-TOTAL-PRICE-A         PIC X.                    00001340
                05  MAP1-TOTAL-PRICE           PIC 9(7)V99.              00001350
                05  FILLER                 OCCURS 4                      00001360
                                           INDEXED BY ERROR-I.           00001370
                  10  MAP1-ERRORS-L            PIC S9999 COMP.           00001380
                  10  MAP1-ERRORS-A            PIC X.                    00001390
                  10  MAP1-ERRORS              PIC X(28).                00001400


     7        ORAD01A          18.38.45        07/27/80

              ************************************************************ 00000010
              *                                                          * 00000020
              *        PURCHASE ORDER MASTER -- FILE LAYOUT              * 00000030
              *                                                          * 00000040
              ************************************************************ 00000050

               01  ORDER-MASTER-RECORD.                                  00000070
                05  ORDER-NUMBER                   PIC X(10).            00000080
                05  ORDER-ALT-KEY.                                       00000090
                  10  ORDER-DEPARTMENT             PIC XXX.              00000100
                  10  ORDER-DATE.                                        00000110
                    15  ORDER-DATE-YEAR            PIC XX.               00000120
                    15  ORDER-DATE-MONTH           PIC XX.               00000130
                    15  ORDER-DATE-DAY             PIC XX.               00000140
                05  ORDER-DATE-ENTERED.                                  00000150
                  10  ORDER-DATE-ENTERED-MONTH     PIC XX.               00000160
                  10  ORDER-DATE-ENTERED-DAY       PIC XX.               00000170
                  10  ORDER-DATE-ENTERED-YEAR      PIC XX.               00000180
                05  ORDER-TOTAL-COST               PIC S9(7)V99  COMP-3. 00000190
                05  ORDER-TOTAL-PRICE              PIC S9(7)V99  COMP-3. 00000200
                05  ORDER-LINE-COUNT               PIC S9999     COMP.   00000210
                05  ORDER-ALL-LINES.                                     00000220
                  10  ORDER-LINE-ITEM          OCCURS 1 TO 9             00000230
                                               DEPENDING ON ORDER-LINE-COUNT 00000240
                                               INDEXED BY ORDER-LINE-I.  00000250
                    15  ORDER-ITEM-NUMBER          PIC X(8).             00000260
                    15  ORDER-ITEM-DESCRIPTION     PIC X(19).            00000270
                    15  ORDER-ITEM-DATE.                                 00000280
                      20  ORDER-ITEM-DATE-MONTH    PIC XX.               00000290
                      20  ORDER-ITEM-DATE-DAY      PIC XX.               00000300
                      20  ORDER-ITEM-DATE-YEAR     PIC XX.               00000310
                    15  ORDER-UNIT                 PIC S9(5)     COMP-3. 00000320
                    15  ORDER-UNIT-COST            PIC S9(5)V99  COMP-3. 00000330
                    15  ORDER-UNIT-PRICE           PIC S9(5)V99  COMP-3. 00000340
```

Fig. 24.3. (Continued)

```
    8          ORADO1A          18.38.45          07/27/80

00229          ***************************************************************** 00001440
00230          *                                                               * 00001450
00231          *          TRANSACTION WORK AREA                                * 00001460
00232          *                                                               * 00001470
00233          ***************************************************************** 00001480


00235           01  TWA-AREA.                                                    00001500


00237               05  TWA-LINE-ITEM-MAP.                                       00001520
00238                 10  TWA-ITEM-NUMBER-MAP-L          PIC S9999 COMP.         00001530
00239                 10  TWA-ITEM-NUMBER-MAP-A          PIC X.                  00001540
00240                 10  TWA-ITEM-NUMBER-MAP            PIC X(8).               00001550
00241                 10  TWA-ITEM-DESCRIPTION-MAP-L     PIC S9999 COMP.         00001560
00242                 10  TWA-ITEM-DESCRIPTION-MAP-A     PIC X.                  00001570
00243                 10  TWA-ITEM-DESCRIPTION-MAP.                              00001580
00244                   15  TWA-DESCRIPTION-FIRST-MAP    PIC X.                  00001590
00245                   15  FILLER                       PIC X(18).              00001600
00246                 10  TWA-UNIT-MAP-L                 PIC S9999 COMP.         00001610
00247                 10  TWA-UNIT-MAP-A                 PIC X.                  00001620
00248                 10  TWA-UNIT-MAP                   PIC 9(5).               00001630
00249                 10  TWA-UNIT-COST-MAP-L            PIC S9999 COMP.         00001640
00250                 10  TWA-UNIT-COST-MAP-A            PIC X.                  00001650
00251                 10  TWA-UNIT-COST-MAP              PIC 9(5)V99.            00001660
00252                 10  TWA-COST-MAP-L                 PIC S9999 COMP.         00001670
00253                 10  TWA-COST-MAP-A                 PIC X.                  00001680
00254                 10  TWA-COST-MAP                   PIC 9(6)V99.            00001690
00255                 10  TWA-UNIT-PRICE-MAP-L           PIC S9999 COMP.         00001700
00256                 10  TWA-UNIT-PRICE-MAP-A           PIC X.                  00001710
00257                 10  TWA-UNIT-PRICE-MAP             PIC 9(5)V99.            00001720
00258                 10  TWA-PRICE-MAP-L                PIC S9999 COMP.         00001730
00259                 10  TWA-PRICE-MAP-A                PIC X.                  00001740
00260                 10  TWA-PRICE-MAP                  PIC 9(6)V99.            00001750


00262               05  TWA-LINE-ITEM-ORDER.                                     00001770
00263                 10  TWA-ITEM-NUMBER-ORDER          PIC X(8).               00001780
00264                 10  TWA-ITEM-DESCRIPTION-ORDER     PIC X(19).              00001790
00265                 10  TWA-ITEM-DATE-ORDER            PIC X(6).               00001800
00266                 10  TWA-UNIT-ORDER                 PIC S9(5)     COMP-3.   00001810
00267                 10  TWA-UNIT-COST-ORDER            PIC S9(5)V99  COMP-3.   00001820
00268                 10  TWA-UNIT-PRICE-ORDER           PIC S9(5)V99  COMP-3.   00001830


00270               05  TWA-TOTAL-COST                   PIC S9(7)V99  COMP-3.   00001850


00272               05  TWA-TOTAL-PRICE                  PIC S9(7)V99  COMP-3.   00001870


00274               05  TWA-ORDER-RECORD-KEY             PIC X(10).              00001890
```

Fig. 24.3. (Continued)

```
      9         ORADO1A         18.38.45         07/27/80

00276             05  TSA-QUEUE-ID.                                             00001910
00277               10  TSA-TERM-ID                     PIC XXXX.               00001920
00278               10  TSA-TRANS-ID                    PIC XXXX.               00001930

00280             05  TWA-BINARY-FIELDS   COMP.                                 00001950
00281               10  TWA-LINE-DATA-CNT               PIC S9(8).              00001960
00282               10  TWA-JOURNAL-ID                  PIC S9(8).              00001970
00283               10  TWA-POM-LENGTH                  PIC S9(4).              00001980
00284               10  TSA-LENGTH                      PIC S9(4).              00001990
00285               10  TSA-QUEUE-NO                    PIC S9(4).              00002000
00286               10  TWA-JOURNAL-LENGTH              PIC S9(4).              00002010

00288             05  TWA-OPERATOR-MESSAGE              PIC X(31).              00002030

00290             05  TWA-CURRENT-DATE.                                         00002050
00291               10  TWA-CURRENT-DATE-MONTH          PIC XX.                 00002060
00292               10  FILLER                          PIC X.                  00002070
00293               10  TWA-CURRENT-DATE-DAY            PIC XX.                 00002080
00294               10  FILLER                          PIC X.                  00002090
00295               10  TWA-CURRENT-DATE-YEAR           PIC XX.                 00002100

00297             05  TWA-DEPT-TABLE-KEY.                                       00002120
00298               10  TWA-DEPT-TABLE-KEY-CODE         PIC X.                  00002130
00299               10  TWA-DEPT-TABLE-KEY-NUMBER       PIC 9(7)  COMP-3.       00002140
```

Fig. 24.3. (Continued)

```
        10          ORADO1A          18.38.45        07/27/80

00301        ****************************************************************** 00002160
00302        *                                                                * 00002170
00303        *              TEMPORARY STORAGE AREA                            * 00002180
00304        *                                                                * 00002190
00305        ****************************************************************** 00002200

00307         01  TSA-AREA.                                                       00002220

00309             05  TSA-POMAST-RECORD.                                          00002240
00310               10  TSA-ORDER-NUMBER              PIC X(10).                  00002250
00311               10  TSA-DEPARTMENT                PIC XXX.                    00002260
00312               10  TSA-ORDER-DATE.                                           00002270
00313                 15  TSA-ORDER-DATE-YEAR         PIC XX.                     00002280
00314                 15  TSA-ORDER-DATE-MONTH        PIC XX.                     00002290
00315                 15  TSA-ORDER-DATE-DAY          PIC XX.                     00002300
00316               10  TSA-ORDER-ENTERED.                                        00002310
00317                 15  TSA-ORDER-ENTERED-MONTH     PIC XX.                     00002320
00318                 15  TSA-ORDER-ENTERED-DAY       PIC XX.                     00002330
00319                 15  TSA-ORDER-ENTERED-YEAR      PIC XX.                     00002340
00320               10  TSA-TOTAL-COST                PIC S9(7)V99 COMP-3.        00002350
00321               10  TSA-TOTAL-PRICE               PIC S9(7)V99 COMP-3.        00002360
00322               10  TSA-LINE-COUNT                PIC S9999    COMP.          00002370
00323               10  TSA-LINE-ITEM             OCCURS 9                        00002380
00324                                             INDEXED BY TSA-LINE-I.          00002390
00325                 15  TSA-ITEM-NUMBER             PIC X(8).                   00002400
00326                 15  TSA-ITEM-DESCRIPTION        PIC X(19).                  00002410
00327                 15  TSA-ITEM-DATE               PIC X(6).                   00002420
00328                 15  TSA-UNIT                    PIC S9(5)    COMP-3.        00002430
00329                 15  TSA-UNIT-COST               PIC S9(5)V99 COMP-3.        00002440
00330                 15  TSA-UNIT-PRICE              PIC S9(5)V99 COMP-3.        00002450

00332             05  TSA-OPERATOR-INITIAL            PIC XXX.                    00002470

00334             05  TSA-DEPT-CNT                    PIC S9(8)    COMP.          00002490

00336             05  TSA-DEPTS                   OCCURS 300                      00002510
00337                                             DEPENDING ON TSA-DEPT-CNT       00002520
00338                                             ASCENDING KEY TSA-DEPT-NO       00002530
00339                                             INDEXED BY DEPT-I.              00002540
00340               10  TSA-DEPT-NO                   PIC XXX.                    00002550
```

Fig. 24.3. (Continued)

```
11   ORAD01A        18.38.45        07/27/80

00342  ****************************************************   00002570
00343  *                                                  *   00002580
00344  *                JOURNAL RECORD LAYOUT             *   00002590
00345  *                                                  *   00002600
00346  ****************************************************   00002610

00348  01  JOURNAL-RECORD.                                    00002630

00350      05  JOURNAL-OPERATOR-INITIAL    PIC XXX.           00002650
00351      05  JOURNAL-DATE-ENTERED        PIC X(6).          00002660
00352      05  JOURNAL-ORDER-NUMBER        PIC X(10).         00002670
00353      05  JOURNAL-DOCUMENT-NUMBER     PIC X(8).          00002680
00354      05  JOURNAL-TOTAL-COST          PIC S9(7)V99 COMP-3.  00002690
00355      05  JOURNAL-TOTAL-PRICE         PIC S9(7)V99 COMP-3.  00002700

12   ORAD01A        18.38.45        07/27/80

00357  ****************************************************   00002720
00358  *                                                  *   00002730
00359  *          DEPARTMENT TABLE --- RECORD LAYOUT      *   00002740
00360  *                                                  *   00002750
00361  ****************************************************   00002763

00363  01  DEPT-TABLE-RECORD.                                 00002780
00364      05  DEPT-TABLE-KEY.                                00002790
00365          10  DEPT-TABLE-KEY-CODE     PIC X.             00002800
00366              88  DEPT-RECORD              VALUE 'D'.    00002810
00367          10  DEPT-TABLE-KEY-NUMBER   PIC 9(7) COMP-3.   00002820
00368      05  DEPT-NO                     PIC XXX.           00002830
00369      05  FILLER                      PIC X(30).         00002840
00370      05  DEPT-DIVISION               PIC XX.            00002850
00371      05  FILLER                      PIC X(45).         00002860
```

Fig. 24.3. (Continued)

```
   13          ORADO1A          18.38.45          07/27/80

00373          PROCEDURE DIVISION USING DFHEIBLK DFHCOMMAREA.                     00002880
00374              CALL 'DFHEI1'.

00376          ****************************************************************** 00002900
00377          *                                                                * 00002910
00378          MAIN-LINE SECTION.                                                 00002920
00379          *                                                                * 00002930
00380          ****************************************************************** 00002940

00382          *   EXEC CICS
00383          *       ADDRESS TWA (TWA-POINTER)
00384          *   END-EXEC.
00385               MOVE '                   ' TO DFHEIVO CALL 'DFHEI1' USING     00002960
00386               DFHEIVO TWA-POINTER.
00387
00388          *   EXEC CICS
00389          *       HANDLE AID
00390          *           CLEAR (FINALIZATION)
00391          *             PA1 (BYPASS-INPUT)
00392          *             PA2 (BYPASS-INPUT)
00393          *             PA3 (BYPASS-INPUT)
00394          *   END-EXEC.
00395               MOVE '  0                ' TO DFHEIVO CALL 'DFHEI1' USING     00002990
00396               DFHEIVO GO TO FINALIZATION BYPASS-INPUT BYPASS-INPUT
00397               BYPASS-INPUT DEPENDING ON DFHEIGDI.
00398
00399
00400
00401
00402          *   EXEC CICS
00403          *       HANDLE CONDITION
00404          *           MAPFAIL (MAPFAIL-ERROR)
00405          *           ERROR   (MAJOR-ERROR)
00406          *   END-EXEC.
00407               MOVE '                   ' TO DFHEIVO CALL 'DFHEI1' USING     00003060
00408               DFHEIVO GO TO MAPFAIL-ERROR MAJOR-ERROR DEPENDING ON
00409               DFHEIGDI.
00410
00411
00412              IF EIBCALEN NOT EQUAL TO ZEROES                                00003110
00413                  IF ORDER-VALIDATION-TIME                                   00003120
00414                      GO TO ORDER-VALIDATION                                 00003130
00415                  ELSE IF INITIAL-ENTRY-TIME                                 00003140
00416                      GO TO INITIALIZATION                                   00003150
00417                  ELSE GO TO PROCESS-SWITCH-ERROR.                           00003160

00419              IF EIBCALEN EQUAL TO ZEROES                                    00003180
00420                  GO TO SIGN-ON-VIOLATION.                                   00003190
```

Fig. 24.3. (Continued)

```
14        ORADO1A        18.38.45        07/27/80

      ***************************************************************** 00003210
      *                                                               * 00003220
       ORDER-VALIDATION SECTION.                                        0C003230
      *                                                               * 00003240
      ***************************************************************** 00003250

      *     EXEC CICS
      *          RECEIVE MAP     ('ORADM01')
      *                  MAPSET ('ORADS01')
      *                  SET     (MAP1-POINTER)
      *     END-EXEC.
             MOVE 'ORADM01' TO DFHEIV1 MOVE 'ORADS01' TO DFHEIV2 MOVE '  00003270
      -      '           ' TO DFHEIV0 CALL 'DFHEI1' USING DFHEIV0
             DFHEIV1 MAP1-POINTER DFHEIV98 DFHEIV2.


            MOVE EIBTRMID    TO   TSA-TERM-ID.                          00003320
            MOVE EIBTRNID    TO   TSA-TRANS-ID.                         00003330

      *     EXEC CICS
      *          READQ TS
      *               QUEUE  (TSA-QUEUE-ID)
      *               SET    (TSA-POINTER)
      *               LENGTH (TSA-LENGTH)
      *               ITEM   (1)
      *     END-EXEC.
             MOVE 1 TO DFHEIV11 MOVE '  Y       ' TO DFHEIV0 CALL 'DFHEI1'00003350
             USING DFHEIV0 TSA-QUEUE-ID TSA-POINTER TSA-LENGTH DFHEIV99
             DFHEIV11.




            MOVE SPACES TO MAP1-ERRORS (1)                              00003420
                           MAP1-ERRORS (2)                              00003430
                           MAP1-ERRORS (3)                              0000344C
                           MAP1-ERRORS (4).                             00003450
            SET ERROR-I    TO  ZEROES.                                  00003460

       VALIDATE-FIXED-DATA.                                             00003480

            IF MAP1-ORDER-NUMBER NUMERIC                                00003500
                 MOVE MAP1-ORDER-NUMBER       TO   TSA-ORDER-NUMBER     00003510
            ELSE SET ERROR-I UP BY 1                                    00003520
                 MOVE 'INVALID ORDER NUMBER'  TO   MAP1-ERRORS (ERROR-I) 00003530
                 MOVE -1                      TO   MAP1-ORDER-NUMBER-L. 00003540

            IF MAP1-DOCUMENT NUMERIC                                    00003560
                 NEXT SENTENCE                                          00003570
            ELSE SET ERROR-I UP BY 1                                    00003580
                 MOVE 'INVALID DOCUMENT NUMBER' TO  MAP1-ERRORS (ERROR-I)00003590
```

Fig. 24.3. (Continued)

```
   15         ORAD01A          18.38.45        07/27/80

00473              IF ERROR-I EQUAL TO 1                                       00003600
00474                   MOVE -1                  TO  MAP1-DOCUMENT-L.          00003610

00476           SEARCH ALL TSA-DEPTS                                           00003630
00477              AT END                                                      00003640
00478                   GO TO DEPARTMENT-ERROR-RTN                             00003650
00479              WHEN MAP1-DEPARTMENT EQUAL    TO  TSA-DEPT-NO (DEPT-I)      00003660
00480                   MOVE MAP1-DEPARTMENT     TO  TSA-DEPARTMENT            00003670
00481                   GO TO EDIT-ORDER-DATE.                                 00003680


00483       DEPARTMENT-ERROR-RTN.                                              00003700

00485           SET ERROR-I UP BY 1.                                           00003720
00486           MOVE 'INVALID DEPARTMENT NUMBER' TO MAP1-ERRORS (ERROR-I).     00003730
00487           IF ERROR-I EQUAL TO 1                                          00003740
00488                MOVE -1                     TO MAP1-DEPARTMENT-L.         00003750


00490       EDIT-ORDER-DATE.                                                   00003770

00492           IF       MAP1-ORDER-DATE-MONTH (GREATER '00' AND LESS '13')    00003790
00493              AND MAP1-ORDER-DATE-DAY    (GREATER '00' AND LESS '32')     00003800
00494              AND MAP1-ORDER-DATE-YEAR   NUMERIC                          00003810
00495           THEN MOVE MAP1-ORDER-DATE-MONTH  TO  TSA-ORDER-DATE-MONTH      00003820
00496                MOVE MAP1-ORDER-DATE-DAY    TO  TSA-ORDER-DATE-DAY        00003830
00497                MOVE MAP1-ORDER-DATE-YEAR   TO  TSA-ORDER-DATE-YEAR       00003840
00498           ELSE SET ERROR-I UP BY 1                                       00003850
00499                MOVE 'INVALID ORDER-DATE'   TO  MAP1-ERRORS (ERROR-I)     00003860
00500                IF ERROR-I EQUAL TO 1                                     00003870
00501                     MOVE -1                TO  MAP1-ORDER-DATE-L.        00003880


00503       VALIDATE-FIXED-DATA-END.                                           00003900

00505           IF ERROR-I EQUAL TO 4                                          00003920
00506                GO TO DISPLAY-ERROR-SCREEN.                               00003930


00508       VALIDATE-VARIABLE-DATA.                                            00003950

00510           SET MAP1-LINE-I         TO  1.                                 00003970
00511           MOVE +99                TO  TWA-LINE-DATA-CNT.                 00003980
00512           MOVE MAP1-ORDER-DATE    TO  TWA-ITEM-DATE-ORDER.               00003990
00513           PERFORM VALIDATE-EACH-LINE THRU VALIDATE-EACH-LINE-EXIT        00004000
00514               UNTIL TWA-LINE-DATA-CNT EQUAL TO ZEROES                    00004010
00515                  OR ERROR-I           EQUAL TO 4                         00004020
00516                  OR MAP1-LINE-I       GREATER THAN 9.                    00004030
00517           GO TO VALIDATE-TOTALS.                                         00004040


00519       VALIDATE-EACH-LINE.                                                00004060
```

Fig. 24.3. (Continued)

```
16          ORADO1A          18.38.45          07/27/80

           MOVE ZEROES                  TO   TWA-LINE-DATA-CNT.
           SET VALIDATION-ERROR-LINE    TO   MAP1-LINE-I.
           MOVE MAP1-LINE-ITEM (MAP1-LINE-I) TO TWA-LINE-ITEM-MAP.

           IF TWA-ITEM-NUMBER-MAP-L NOT EQUAL TO ZEROES
           THEN IF TWA-ITEM-NUMBER-MAP NUMERIC
                     MOVE TWA-ITEM-NUMBER-MAP TO TWA-ITEM-NUMBER-ORDER
                     ADD 1 TO TWA-LINE-DATA-CNT
                ELSE MOVE 'INVALID ITEM NUMBER' TO VALIDATION-ERROR-MSG
                     SET ERROR-I UP BY 1
                     MOVE VALIDATION-ERROR-MESSAGE
                                         TO MAP1-ERRORS (ERROR-I)
                     IF ERROR-I EQUAL TO 1
                          MOVE -1 TO MAP1-ITEM-NUMBER-L (MAP1-LINE-I)
                     ELSE IF ERROR-I EQUAL TO 4
                               GO TO VALIDATE-EACH-LINE-EXIT.

           IF TWA-ITEM-DESCRIPTION-MAP-L EQUAL TO ZEROES
                MOVE SPACES TO TWA-ITEM-DESCRIPTION-ORDER
           ELSE IF TWA-DESCRIPTION-FIRST-MAP EQUAL TO SPACES
                     MOVE 'INVALID DESCRIPTION'
                                       TO VALIDATION-ERROR-MSG
                     SET ERROR-I UP BY 1
                     MOVE VALIDATION-ERROR-MESSAGE
                                       TO MAP1-ERRORS (ERROR-I)
                     IF ERROR-I EQUAL TO 1
                          MOVE -1
                               TO MAP1-ITEM-DESCRIPTION-L (MAP1-LINE-I)
                     ELSE IF ERROR-I EQUAL TO 4
                               GO TO VALIDATE-EACH-LINE-EXIT
                          ELSE NEXT SENTENCE
                ELSE MOVE TWA-ITEM-DESCRIPTION-MAP
                                       TO TWA-ITEM-DESCRIPTION-ORDER
                     ADD 2             TO TWA-LINE-DATA-CNT.

           IF TWA-UNIT-MAP-L NOT EQUAL TO ZEROES
           THEN IF TWA-UNIT-MAP NUMERIC
                     MOVE TWA-UNIT-MAP         TO  TWA-UNIT-ORDER
                     ADD 4 TO TWA-LINE-DATA-CNT
                ELSE MOVE ZEROES               TO  TWA-UNIT-ORDER
                     MOVE 'INVALID UNIT'       TO  VALIDATION-ERROR-MSG
                     SET ERROR-I UP BY 1
                     MOVE VALIDATION-ERROR-MESSAGE
                                               TO  MAP1-ERRORS (ERROR-I)
                     IF ERROR-I EQUAL TO 1
                          MOVE -1           TO  MAP1-UNIT-L (MAP1-LINE-I)
                     ELSE IF ERROR-I EQUAL TO 4
                               GO TO VALIDATE-EACH-LINE-EXIT.

           IF TWA-UNIT-COST-MAP-L NOT EQUAL TO ZEROES
           THEN IF TWA-UNIT-COST-MAP NUMERIC
                     MOVE TWA-UNIT-COST-MAP  TO  TWA-UNIT-COST-ORDER
                     ADD 8 TO TWA-LINE-DATA-CNT
```

Fig. 24.3. (Continued)

```
 17          ORAD01A          18.38.45          07/27/80

00574              ELSE MOVE ZEROES             TO  TWA-UNIT-COST-ORDER    00004610
00575                   MOVE 'INVALID UNIT COST'                           00004620
00576                                           TO  VALIDATION-ERROR-MSG   00004630
00577                   SET ERROR-I UP BY 1                                00004640
00578                   MOVE VALIDATION-ERROR-MESSAGE                      00004650
00579                                           TO  MAP1-ERRORS (ERROR-I)  00004660
00580                   IF ERROR-I EQUAL TO 1                              00004670
00581                        MOVE -1   TO   MAP1-UNIT-COST-L (MAP1-LINE-I) 00004680
00582                   ELSE IF ERROR-I EQUAL TO 4                         00004690
00583                             GO TO VALIDATE-EACH-LINE-EXIT.           00004700

00585          IF TWA-COST-MAP-L NOT EQUAL TO ZEROES                       00004720
00586          THEN IF      TWA-COST-MAP  NUMERIC                          00004730
00587                  AND TWA-COST-MAP =                                  00004740
00588                         TWA-UNIT-ORDER * TWA-UNIT-COST-ORDER         00004750
00589 <-(J)         THEN ADD TWA-COST-MAP  TO  TWA-TOTAL-COST              00004760
00590                   ADD 16           TO  TWA-LINE-DATA-CNT             00004770
00591              ELSE MOVE 'INVALID COST'  TO VALIDATION-ERROR-MSG       00004780
00592                   SET ERROR-I UP BY 1                                00004790
00593                   MOVE VALIDATION-ERROR-MESSAGE                      00004800
00594                                        TO MAP1-ERRORS (ERROR-I)      00004810
00595                   IF ERROR-I EQUAL TO 1                              00004820
00596                         MOVE -1 TO MAP1-COST-L (MAP1-LINE-I)         00004830
00597                   ELSE IF ERROR-I EQUAL TO 4                         00004840
00598                             GO TO VALIDATE-EACH-LINE-EXIT.           00004850

00600          IF TWA-UNIT-PRICE-MAP-L NOT EQUAL TO ZEROES                 00004870
00601          THEN IF TWA-UNIT-PRICE-MAP  NUMERIC                         00004880
00602                   MOVE TWA-UNIT-PRICE-MAP  TO  TWA-UNIT-PRICE-ORDER  00004890
00603                   ADD 32 TO TWA-LINE-DATA-CNT                        00004900
00604              ELSE MOVE ZEROES             TO  TWA-UNIT-PRICE-ORDER   00004910
00605                   MOVE 'INVALID UNIT PRICE'                          00004920
00606                                           TO  VALIDATION-ERROR-MSG   00004930
00607                   SET ERROR-I UP BY 1                                00004940
00608                   MOVE VALIDATION-ERROR-MESSAGE                      00004950
00609                                           TO  MAP1-ERRORS (ERROR-I)  00004960
00610                   IF ERROR-I EQUAL TO 1                              00004970
00611                        MOVE -1 TO MAP1-UNIT-PRICE-L (MAP1-LINE-I)    00004980
00612                   ELSE IF ERROR-I EQUAL TO 4                         00004990
00613                             GO TO VALIDATE-EACH-LINE-EXIT.           00005000

00615          IF TWA-PRICE-MAP-L NOT EQUAL TO ZEROES                      00005020
00616          THEN IF      TWA-PRICE-MAP  NUMERIC                         00005030
00617                  AND TWA-PRICE-MAP =                                 00005040
00618                           TWA-UNIT-ORDER * TWA-UNIT-PRICE-ORDER      00005050
00619              THEN ADD TWA-PRICE-MAP  TO  TWA-TOTAL-PRICE             00005060
00620                   ADD 64             TO  TWA-LINE-DATA-CNT           00005070
00621              ELSE MOVE 'INVALID PRICE'   TO VALIDATION-ERROR-MSG     00005080
00622                   SET ERROR-I UP BY 1                                00005090
00623                   MOVE VALIDATION-ERROR-MESSAGE                      00005100
00624                                         TO  MAP1-ERRORS (ERROR-I)    00005110
00625                   IF ERROR-I EQUAL TO 1                              00005120
00626                        MOVE -1 TO MAP1-PRICE-L (MAP1-LINE-I)         00005130
```

Fig. 24.3. (Continued)

```
18        ORAD01A          18.38.45          07/27/80

00627   00005140          ELSE IF ERROR-I EQUAL TO 4
00628   00005150                  GO TO VALIDATE-EACH-LINE-EXIT.

00630   00005170      IF TWA-LINE-DATA-CNT EQUAL TO (125 OR 127)
00631   00005180          IF ERROR-I EQUAL TO ZEROES
00632   00005190              SET TSA-LINE-I   TO MAP1-LINE-I
00633   00005200              MOVE TWA-LINE-ITEM-ORDER
00634   00005210                            TO TSA-LINE-ITEM (TSA-LINE-I)
00635   00005220          ELSE NEXT SENTENCE
00636   00005230      ELSE IF TWA-LINE-DATA-CNT EQUAL TO ZEROES
00637   00005240              NEXT SENTENCE
00638   00005250      ELSE SET ERROR-I UP BY 1
00639   00005260          MOVE 'INCOMPLETE DATA' TO VALIDATION-ERROR-MSG
00640   00005270          MOVE VALIDATION-ERROR-MESSAGE
00641   00005280                            TO MAP1-ERRORS (ERROR-I)
00642   00005290          IF ERROR-I EQUAL TO 1
00643   00005300              MOVE -1
00644   00005310                  TO MAP1-ITEM-NUMBER-L (MAP1-LINE-I)
00645   00005320          ELSE IF ERROR-I EQUAL TO 4
00646   00005330                  GO TO VALIDATE-EACH-LINE-EXIT.

00648   00005350      SET MAP1-LINE-I UP BY 1.
00649   00005360  VALIDATE-EACH-LINE-EXIT.   EXIT.

00651   00005380  VALIDATE-TOTALS.

00653   00005400      IF ERROR-I EQUAL TO 4
00654   00005410          GO TO DISPLAY-ERROR-SCREEN.

00656   00005430      IF    MAP1-LINE-I EQUAL TO 2
00657   00005440      AND TWA-LINE-DATA-CNT EQUAL TO ZEROES
00658   00005450  THEN SET ERROR-I UP BY 1
00659   00005460      MOVE 'NO LINE ITEM ENTERED' TO MAP1-ERRORS (ERROR-I)
00660   00005470      IF ERROR-I EQUAL TO 1
00661   00005480          MOVE -1 TO MAP1-ITEM-NUMBER-L (1)
00662   00005490      ELSE IF ERROR-I EQUAL TO 4
00663   00005500              GO TO VALIDATE-TOTALS-EXIT.

00665   00005520      IF    MAP1-TOTAL-COST NUMERIC
00666   00005530      AND MAP1-TOTAL-COST = TWA-TOTAL-COST
00667   00005540  THEN MOVE TWA-TOTAL-COST       TO TSA-TOTAL-COST
00668   00005550  ELSE SET ERROR-I UP BY 1
00669   00005560      MOVE 'INCORRECT TOTAL COST' TO   MAP1-ERRORS (ERROR-I)
00670   00005570      IF ERROR-I EQUAL TO 1
00671   00005580          MOVE -1            TO MAP1-TOTAL-COST-L
00672   00005590      ELSE IF ERROR-I EQUAL TO 4
00673   00005600              GO TO VALIDATE-TOTALS-EXIT.

00675   00005620      IF    MAP1-TOTAL-PRICE NUMERIC
00676   00005630      AND MAP1-TOTAL-PRICE = TWA-TOTAL-PRICE
00677   00005640  THEN MOVE TWA-TOTAL-PRICE      TO TSA-TOTAL-PRICE
00678   00005650  ELSE SET ERROR-I UP BY 1
```

Fig. 24.3. (Continued)

```
     19         ORAD01A         18.38.45        07/27/80

00679                  MOVE 'INCORRECT TOTAL PRICE'  TO  MAP1-ERRORS (ERROR-I)  00005660
00680                  IF ERROR-I EQUAL TO 1                                     00005670
00681                       MOVE -1                 TO  MAP1-TOTAL-PRICE-L       00005680
00682                  ELSE IF ERROR-I EQUAL TO 4                                00005690
00683                            GO TO VALIDATE-TOTALS-EXIT.                     00005700
00684           VALIDATE-TOTALS-EXIT.  EXIT.                                     00005710

00686           CHECK-IF-THERE-ARE-ERRORS.                                       00005730

00688               IF ERROR-I NOT EQUAL TO ZEROES                               00005750
00689                    GO TO DISPLAY-ERROR-SCREEN.                             00005760

00691           NO-ERRORS-RTN.                                                   00005780

00693               SET TSA-LINE-COUNT TO MAP1-LINE-I.                           00005800

00695               IF TSA-LINE-COUNT GREATER THAN 9                             00005820
00696                    IF TWA-LINE-DATA-CNT EQUAL TO ZEROES                    00005830
00697                         SUBTRACT 2 FROM TSA-LINE-COUNT                     00005840
00698                    ELSE SUBTRACT 1 FROM TSA-LINE-COUNT                     00005850
00699               ELSE SUBTRACT 2 FROM TSA-LINE-COUNT.                         00005860

00701         *     EXEC CICS
00702         *          GETMAIN
00703         *               SET     (POM-POINTER)
00704         *               LENGTH (433)
00705         *     END-EXEC.
00706                MOVE 433 TO DFHEIV11 MOVE '          ' TO DFHEIV0 CALL 'DFHEI00005880
00707         -     '1' USING DFHEIV0 POM-POINTER DFHEIV11.
00708
00709
00710
00711               MOVE TSA-LINE-COUNT      TO  ORDER-LINE-COUNT.               00005930
00712               MOVE TSA-POMAST-RECORD   TO  ORDER-MASTER-RECORD.            00005940
00713               COMPUTE TWA-POM-LENGTH = 37 + ORDER-LINE-COUNT * 44.         00005950
00714               MOVE TSA-ORDER-NUMBER    TO  TWA-ORDER-RECORD-KEY.           00005960

00716         *     EXEC CICS
00717         *          HANDLE CONDITION
00718         *               NOTOPEN (FILE-NOT-OPEN)
00719         *               DUPREC  (DUPLICATE-RECORD)
00720         *     END-EXEC.
00721               MOVE '                       ' TO DFHEIV0 CALL 'DFHEI1' USING   00005980
00722                DFHEIV0 GO TO FILE-NOT-OPEN DUPLICATE-RECORD DEPENDING ON
00723                DFHEIGDI.
00724
00725
00726         *     EXEC CICS
00727         *          WRITE DATASET ('ORTEST')
00728         *               LENGTH   (TWA-POM-LENGTH)
00729         *               FROM     (ORDER-MASTER-RECORD)
```

Fig. 24.3. (Continued)

```
20          ORADO1A          18.38.45          07/27/80

       *          RIDFLD  (TWA-ORDER-RECORD-KEY)
       *    END-EXEC.
             MOVE 'ORTEST' TO DFHEIV3 MOVE '  0        ' TO DFHEIVO CALL 'D000006030
       -    'FHEI1' USING DFHEIVO DFHEIV3 ORDER-MASTER-RECORD
             TWA-POM-LENGTH TWA-ORDER-RECORD-KEY.



       *    EXEC CICS
       *         FREEMAIN DATA (ORDER-MASTER-RECORD)
       *    END-EXEC.
             MOVE '          ' TO DFHEIVO CALL 'DFHEI1' USING DFHEIVO       00006090
             ORDER-MASTER-RECORD.

       *    EXEC CICS
       *         GETMAIN
       *              SET      (JOURNAL-POINTER)
       *              LENGTH (37)
       *    END-EXEC
             MOVE 37 TO DFHEIV11 MOVE '           ' TO DFHEIVO CALL 'DFHEI100006120
       -    '' USING DFHEIVO JOURNAL-POINTER DFHEIV11



            MOVE TSA-OPERATOR-INITIAL  TO  JOURNAL-OPERATOR-INITIAL.       00006170
            MOVE TSA-ORDER-ENTERED     TO  JOURNAL-DATE-ENTERED.           00006180
            MOVE TSA-ORDER-NUMBER      TO  JOURNAL-ORDER-NUMBER.           00006190
            MOVE TSA-TOTAL-COST        TO  JOURNAL-TOTAL-COST.             00006200
            MOVE TSA-TOTAL-PRICE       TO  JOURNAL-TOTAL-PRICE.            00006210
            MOVE MAP1-DOCUMENT         TO  JOURNAL-DOCUMENT-NUMBER.        00006220
            MOVE 37                    TO  TWA-JOURNAL-LENGTH.             00006230

       *    EXEC CICS
       *         JOURNAL JFILEID (02)
       *                 JTYPEID ('01')
       *                 FROM    (JOURNAL-RECORD)
       *                 LENGTH  (TWA-JOURNAL-LENGTH)
       *                 REQID   (TWA-JOURNAL-ID)
       *                 WAIT
       *    END-EXEC.
             MOVE 02 TO DFHEIV11 MOVE '01' TO DFHEIV7 MOVE '  8       ' TO00006250
             DFHEIVO CALL 'DFHEI1' USING DFHEIVO DFHEIV11 TWA-JOURNAL-ID
            DFHEIV7 JOURNAL-RECORD TWA-JOURNAL-LENGTH.






        DISPLAY-FRESH-SCREEN.                                              00006330

       *    EXEC CICS
       *         SEND MAP     ('ORADM01')
       *              MAPSET ('ORADS01')
```

Fig. 24.3. (Continued)

```
21          ORADO1A          18.38.45         07/27/80

00783       *              MAPONLY
00784       *              ERASE
00785       *    END-EXEC.
00786             MOVE 'ORADMO1' TO DFHEIV1 MOVE 'ORADSO1' TO DFHEIV2 MOVE '   00006350
00787       -     '            ' TO DFHEIVO CALL 'DFHEI1' USING DFHEIVO
00788             DFHEIV1 DFHEIV99 DFHEIV98 DFHEIV2.
00789
00790
00791
00792        RETURN-FOR-NEXT-ORDER.                                            00006410

00794            MOVE '1'  TO COMMAREA-PROCESS-SW.                             00006430

00796       *    EXEC CICS
00797       *         RETURN TRANSID  (EIBTRNID)
00798       *                COMMAREA (COMMUNICATION-AREA)
00799       *                LENGTH   (1)
00800       *    END-EXEC.
00801             MOVE 1 TO DFHEIV11 MOVE '          ' TO DFHEIVO CALL 'DFHEI1'00006450
00802             USING DFHEIVO EIBTRNID COMMUNICATION-AREA DFHEIV11.
00803
00804
00805
00806        DISPLAY-ERROR-SCREEN.                                             00006500

00808       *    EXEC CICS
00809       *         SEND MAP       ('ORADMO1')
00810       *              MAPSET    ('ORADSO1')
00811       *              FROM      (MAP1-AREA)
00812       *              DATAONLY
00813       *              CURSOR
00814       *    END-EXEC
00815             MOVE 'ORADMO1' TO DFHEIV1 MOVE 'ORADSO1' TO DFHEIV2 MOVE -1 00006520
00816            TO DFHEIV11 MOVE '  J          ' TO DFHEIVO CALL 'DFHEI1'
00817             USING DFHEIVO DFHEIV1 MAP1-AREA DFHEIV98 DFHEIV2 DFHEIV99
00818             DFHEIV99 DFHEIV99 DFHEIV11
00819
00820
00821
00822            GO TO RETURN-FOR-NEXT-ORDER.                                  00006590


00824        DUPLICATE-RECORD.                                                 00006610

00826            MOVE 'DUPLICATE -- NOT ACCEPTED' TO MAP1-ERRORS (1).          00006630
00827            MOVE -1       TO  MAP1-ORDER-NUMBER-L.                        00006640
00828            GO TO DISPLAY-ERROR-SCREEN.                                   00006650
```

Fig. 24.3. (Continued)

```
22          ORAD01A          18.38.45          07/27/80

            **************************************************************** 00006670
            *                                                              * 00006680
             BYPASS-INPUT SECTION.                                           00006690
            *                                                              * 00006700
            **************************************************************** 00006710

            *    EXEC CICS
            *         GETMAIN
            *              SET      (MAP1-POINTER)
            *              LENGTH   (958)
            *              INITIMG  (HEX-ZEROES)
            *    END-EXEC.
                  MOVE 958 TO DFHEIV11 MOVE '          ' TO DFHEIV0 CALL 'DFHEI00006730
            -    '1' USING DFHEIV0 MAP1-POINTER DFHEIV11 HEX-ZEROES.




                 MOVE 'ORDER BYPASSED - CONTINUE' TO MAP1-ERRORS (1).         00006790

            *    EXEC CICS
            *         SEND MAP    ('ORADM01')
            *              MAPSET ('ORADS01')
            *              FROM   (MAP1-AREA)
            *              ERASE
            *    END-EXEC.
                  MOVE 'ORADM01' TO DFHEIV1 MOVE 'ORADS01' TO DFHEIV2 MOVE '  00006810
            -    '        S    ' TO DFHEIV0 CALL 'DFHEI1' USING DFHEIV0
                  DFHEIV1 MAP1-AREA DFHEIV98 DFHEIV2.




                 MOVE '1' TO COMMAREA-PROCESS-SW.                              00006870

            *    EXEC CICS
            *         RETURN TRANSID  (EIBTRNID)
            *                COMMAREA (COMMUNICATION-AREA)
            *                LENGTH   (1)
            *    END-EXEC.
                  MOVE 1 TO DFHEIV11 MOVE '          ' TO DFHEIV0 CALL 'DFHEI1'00006890
                  USING DFHEIV0 EIBTRNID COMMUNICATION-AREA DFHEIV11.
```

Fig. 24.3. (Continued)

```
23          ORAD01A         18.38.45        07/27/80

       ******************************************************************* 00006950
       *                                                                 * 00006960
        INITIALIZATION SECTION.                                            00006970
       *                                                                 * 00006980
       ******************************************************************* 00006990

       *    EXEC CICS
       *         HANDLE CONDITION
       *              QIDERR (GET-STORAGE-FOR-TSA)
       *    END-EXEC.
             MOVE '                 ' TO DFHEIV0 CALL 'DFHEI1' USING      00007010
             DFHEIV0 GO TO GET-STORAGE-FOR-TSA DEPENDING ON DFHEIGDI.


            MOVE EIBTRMID    TO  TSA-TERM-ID.                               00007050
            MOVE 'ORAD'      TO  TSA-TRANS-ID.                              00007060

       *    EXEC CICS
       *         DELETEQ TS
       *              QUEUE (TSA-QUEUE-ID)
       *    END-EXEC.
             MOVE '         ' TO DFHEIV0 CALL 'DFHEI1' USING DFHEIV0      00007080
             TSA-QUEUE-ID.


        GET-STORAGE-FOR-TSA.                                               00007120

       *    EXEC CICS
       *         GETMAIN
       *              SET    (TSA-POINTER)
       *              LENGTH (1340)
       *    END-EXEC.
             MOVE 1340 TO DFHEIV11 MOVE '          ' TO DFHEIV0 CALL 'DFHE00007140
       -    'I1' USING DFHEIV0 TSA-POINTER DFHEIV11.



        LOAD-DEPARTMENT-TABLE.                                             00007190

            SET DEPT-I        TO  ZEROES.                                  00007210
            MOVE 'D'          TO  TWA-DEPT-TABLE-KEY-CODE.                 00007220
            MOVE  1           TO  TWA-DEPT-TABLE-KEY-NUMBER.               00007230

       *    EXEC CICS
       *         HANDLE CONDITION
       *              ENDFILE (READ-DEPT-TABLE-EXIT)
       *    END-EXEC.
             MOVE '                 ' TO DFHEIV0 CALL 'DFHEI1' USING      00007250
             DFHEIV0 GO TO READ-DEPT-TABLE-EXIT DEPENDING ON DFHEIGDI.


       *    EXEC CICS
```

Fig. 24.3. (Continued)

```
24          ORAD01A        18.38.45        07/27/80

       *        STARTBR DATASET ('DSXTABS')
       *                RIDFLD  (TWA-DEPT-TABLE-KEY)
       *                GTEQ
       *     END-EXEC.
              MOVE 'DSXTABS' TO DFHEIV3 MOVE '          ' TO DFHEIV0 CALL '00007290
       -     'DFHEI1' USING DFHEIV0 DFHEIV3 DFHEIV99 DFHEIV98
              TWA-DEPT-TABLE-KEY.


         READ-DEPT-TABLE.                                              00007340

       *     EXEC CICS
       *          READNEXT DATASET ('DSXTABS')
       *                   SET     (TABLE-POINTER)
       *                   RIDFLD  (TWA-DEPT-TABLE-KEY)
       *     END-EXEC.
              MOVE 'DSXTABS' TO DFHEIV3 MOVE '  M      ' TO DFHEIV0 CALL '00007360
       -     'DFHEI1' USING DFHEIV0 DFHEIV3 TABLE-POINTER DFHEIV98
              TWA-DEPT-TABLE-KEY DFHEIV98 DFHEIV98.


             IF DEPT-RECORD                                            00007410
             THEN IF DEPT-NO EQUAL '999'                               00007420
                       GO TO READ-DEPT-TABLE-EXIT                      00007430
                  ELSE IF DEPT-DIVISION LESS THAN '85'                 00007440
                            SET DEPT-I UP BY 1                         00007450
                            MOVE DEPT-NO TO TSA-DEPT-NO (DEPT-I).      00007460

             GO TO READ-DEPT-TABLE.                                    00007480
         READ-DEPT-TABLE-EXIT.  EXIT.                                  00007490


         CHECK-IF-TABLE-LOADED.                                        00007510

             IF DEPT-I EQUAL TO ZEROES                                 00007530
                  GO TO TABLE-NOT-LOADED-ERROR                         00007540
             ELSE SET TSA-DEPT-CNT TO DEPT-I.                          00007550


         INITIALIZE-TSA.                                               00007570

             MOVE CURRENT-DATE             TO  TWA-CURRENT-DATE.           00007590
             MOVE TWA-CURRENT-DATE-MONTH   TO  TSA-ORDER-ENTERED-MONTH.    00007600
             MOVE TWA-CURRENT-DATE-DAY     TO  TSA-ORDER-ENTERED-DAY.      00007610
             MOVE TWA-CURRENT-DATE-YEAR    TO  TSA-ORDER-ENTERED-YEAR.     00007620
             MOVE OPERATOR-INITIAL         TO  TSA-OPERATOR-INITIAL.       00007630
             MOVE 1340                     TO  TSA-LENGTH.                 00007640

       *     EXEC CICS
       *          WRITEQ TS
       *               QUEUE   (TSA-QUEUE-ID)
       *               FROM    (TSA-AREA)
       *               LENGTH  (TSA-LENGTH)
```

Fig. 24.3. (Continued)

```
25          ORAD01A        18.38.45        07/27/80

        *    END-EXEC.
              MOVE '            ' TO DFHEIVO CALL 'DFHEI1' USING DFHEIVO      00007660
              TSA-QUEUE-ID TSA-AREA TSA-LENGTH.




        *    EXEC CICS
        *         FREEMAIN DATA (TSA-AREA)
        *    END-EXEC.
              MOVE '            ' TO DFHEIVO CALL 'DFHEI1' USING DFHEIVO      00007720
              TSA-AREA.

        *    EXEC CICS
        *         GETMAIN
        *              SET      (MAP1-POINTER)
        *              LENGTH  (958)
        *              INITIMG (HEX-ZEROES)
        *    END-EXEC.
              MOVE 958 TO DFHEIV11 MOVE '          ' TO DFHEIVO CALL 'DFHEI00007750
        -    '1' USING DFHEIVO MAP1-POINTER DFHEIV11 HEX-ZEROES.




             MOVE 'ENTER FIRST ORDER' TO MAP1-ERRORS (1).                      00007810

        *    EXEC CICS
        *         SEND MAP    ('ORADM01')
        *              MAPSET ('ORADS01')
        *              FROM   (MAP1-AREA)
        *              ERASE
        *    END-EXEC.
              MOVE 'ORADM01' TO DFHEIV1 MOVE 'ORADS01' TO DFHEIV2 MOVE '   00007830
        -    '        S     ' TO DFHEIVO CALL 'DFHEI1' USING DFHEIVO
              DFHEIV1 MAP1-AREA DFHEIV98 DFHEIV2.




             MOVE '1' TO COMMAREA-PROCESS-SW.                                   00007890

        *    EXEC CICS
        *         RETURN TRANSID  ('ORAD')
        *                COMMAREA (COMMUNICATION-AREA)
        *                LENGTH   (1)
        *    END-EXEC.
              MOVE 'ORAD' TO DFHEIV5 MOVE 1 TO DFHEIV11 MOVE '          '  00007910
              TO DFHEIVO CALL 'DFHEI1' USING DFHEIVO DFHEIV5
              COMMUNICATION-AREA DFHEIV11.
```

Fig. 24.3. (Continued)

```
26        ORAD01A          18.38.45          07/27/80

      ****************************************************************** 00007970
      *                                                                * 00007980
       FINALIZATION SECTION.                                             00007990
      *                                                                * 00008000
      ****************************************************************** 00008010


       PREPARE-TERMINATION-MESSAGE.                                      00008030
           MOVE JOB-NORMAL-END-MESSAGE TO TWA-OPERATOR-MESSAGE.          00008040


       JOB-TERMINATED.                                                   00008060

      *    EXEC CICS
      *         SEND FROM   (TWA-OPERATOR-MESSAGE)
      *              LENGTH (31)
      *              ERASE
      *    END-EXEC.
            MOVE 31 TO DFHEIV11 MOVE '                 ' TO DFHEIV0 CALL '00008080
      -    'DFHEI1' USING DFHEIV0 DFHEIV99 DFHEIV98 TWA-OPERATOR-MESSAGE
            DFHEIV11.


      *    EXEC CICS
      *         HANDLE CONDITION
      *              QIDERR (END-OF-JOB)
      *    END-EXEC.
            MOVE '                    ' TO DFHEIV0 CALL 'DFHEI1' USING    00008130
            DFHEIV0 GO TO END-OF-JOB DEPENDING ON DFHEIGDI.


           MOVE EIBTRMID  TO  TSA-TERM-ID.                               00008170
           MOVE EIBTRNID  TO  TSA-TRANS-ID.                              00008180

      *    EXEC CICS
      *         DELETEQ TS
      *              QUEUE (TSA-QUEUE-ID)
      *    END-EXEC.
            MOVE '          ' TO DFHEIV0 CALL 'DFHEI1' USING DFHEIV0     00008200
            TSA-QUEUE-ID.



       END-OF-JOB.                                                       00008250

      *    EXEC CICS
      *         RETURN
      *    END-EXEC.
            MOVE '          ' TO DFHEIV0 CALL 'DFHEI1' USING DFHEIV0.    00008270


```

Fig. 24.3. (Continued)

```
27          ORADO1A         18.38.45        07/27/80

          ************************************************************ 00008310
          *                                                          * 00008320
           ABNORMAL-TERMINATION SECTION.                                00008330
          *                                                          * 00008340
          ************************************************************ 00008350

           FILE-NOT-OPEN.                                               00008370

          *    EXEC CICS
          *         XCTL PROGRAM ('TEL2OPEN')
          *    END-EXEC.
                MOVE 'TEL2OPEN' TO DFHEIV3 MOVE '          ' TO DFHEIVO CALL 00008390
               'DFHEI1' USING DFHEIVO DFHEIV3.

           MAPFAIL-ERROR.                                               00008420
               MOVE 'MAP FAILURE' TO MAJOR-ERROR-MSG.                   00008430
               GO TO PREPARE-ABORT-MESSAGE.                             00008440

           PROCESS-SWITCH-ERROR.                                        00008460
               MOVE 'PROCESS ERROR' TO MAJOR-ERROR-MSG.                 00008470
               GO TO PREPARE-ABORT-MESSAGE.                             00008480

           SIGN-ON-VIOLATION.                                           00008500
               MOVE 'SIGNON VIOLATION' TO MAJOR-ERROR-MSG.              00008510
               GO TO PREPARE-ABORT-MESSAGE.                             00008520

           TABLE-NOT-LOADED-ERROR.                                      00008540
               MOVE 'TABLE NOT LOADED' TO MAJOR-ERROR-MSG.              00008550
               GO TO PREPARE-ABORT-MESSAGE.                             00008560

           MAJOR-ERROR.                                                 00008580
               MOVE  EIBFN     TO  OLD-EIBFN.                           00008590
               MOVE  EIBRCODE  TO  OLD-EIBRCODE.                        00008600

          *    EXEC CICS
          *         DUMP DUMPCODE ('ERRS')
          *    END-EXEC.
                MOVE 'ERRS' TO DFHEIV5 MOVE '        ' TO DFHEIVO CALL 'DFH00008620
          -    'EI1' USING DFHEIVO DFHEIV5.

               MOVE 'MAJOR ERROR' TO MAJOR-ERROR-MSG.                   00008650
               GO TO PREPARE-ABORT-MESSAGE.                             00008660

           PREPARE-ABORT-MESSAGE.                                       00008680
               MOVE JOB-ABORTED-MESSAGE TO TWA-OPERATOR-MESSAGE.        00008690
               GO TO JOB-TERMINATED.                                    00008700
```

Fig. 24.3. (Continued)

28 ORADO1A 18.38.45 07/27/80

INTRNL NAME	LVL	SOURCE NAME	BASE	DISPL	INTRNL NAME	DEFINITION	USAGE	R	O	Q	M
DNM=3-000	01	COMMUNICATION-AREA	BL=1	000	DNM=3-000	DS 0CL1	GROUP				
DNM=3-031	02	COMMAREA-PROCESS-SW	BL=1	000	DNM=3-031	DS 1C	DISP				
DNM=3-060	01	AREA1	BL=1	008	DNM=3-060	DS 0CL99	GROUP				
DNM=3-078	02	VALIDATION-ERROR-MESSAGE	BL=1	008	DNM=3-078	DS 0CL28	GROUP				
DNM=3-115	03	FILLER	BL=1	008	DNM=3-115	DS 5C	DISP				
DNM=3-131	03	VALIDATION-ERROR-LINE	BL=1	00D	DNM=3-131	DS 1C	DISP-NM				
DNM=3-162	03	FILLER	BL=1	00E	DNM=3-162	DS 3C	DISP				
DNM=3-181	03	VALIDATION-ERROR-MSG	BL=1	011	DNM=3-181	DS 19C	DISP				
DNM=3-211	02	JOB-NORMAL-END-MESSAGE	BL=1	024	DNM=3-211	DS 23C	DISP				
DNM=3-243	02	JOB-ABORTED-MESSAGE	BL=1	03B	DNM=3-243	DS 0CL31	GROUP				
DNM=3-278	03	FILLER	BL=1	03B	DNM=3-278	DS 15C	DISP				
DNM=3-297	03	MAJOR-ERROR-MSG	BL=1	04A	DNM=3-297	DS 16C	DISP				
DNM=3-322	02	HEXADECIMAL-ZEROES	BL=1	05A	DNM=3-322	DS 1H	COMP				
DNM=3-350	02	FILLER	BL=1	05A	DNM=3-350	DS 0CL2	GROUP	R			
DNM=3-372	03	FILLER	BL=1	05A	DNM=3-372	DS 1C	DISP				
DNM=3-391	03	HEX-ZEROES	BL=1	05B	DNM=3-391	DS 1C	DISP				
DNM=3-411	02	OLD-EIB-AREA	BL=1	05C	DNM=3-411	DS 0CL15	GROUP				
DNM=3-436	03	FILLER	BL=1	05C	DNM=3-436	DS 7C	DISP				
DNM=3-455	03	OLD-EIBFN	BL=1	063	DNM=3-455	DS 2C	DISP				
DNM=3-474	03	OLD-EIBRCODE	BL=1	065	DNM=3-474	DS 6C	DISP				
DNM=4-000	01	DFHEIVAR	BL=1	070	DNM=4-000	DS 0CL106	GROUP				
DNM=4-021	02	DFHEIV0	BL=1	070	DNM=4-021	DS 26C	DISP				
DNM=4-041	02	DFHEIV1	BL=1	08A	DNM=4-041	DS 8C	DISP				
DNM=4-058	02	DFHEIV2	BL=1	092	DNM=4-058	DS 8C	DISP				
DNM=4-075	02	DFHEIV3	BL=1	09A	DNM=4-075	DS 8C	DISP				
DNM=4-092	02	DFHEIV4	BL=1	0A2	DNM=4-092	DS 6C	DISP				
DNM=4-109	02	DFHEIV5	BL=1	0A8	DNM=4-109	DS 4C	DISP				
DNM=4-126	02	DFHEIV6	BL=1	0AC	DNM=4-126	DS 4C	DISP				
DNM=4-143	02	DFHEIV7	BL=1	0B0	DNM=4-143	DS 2C	DISP				
DNM=4-160	02	DFHEIV8	BL=1	0B2	DNM=4-160	DS 2C	DISP				
DNM=4-177	02	DFHEIV9	BL=1	0B4	DNM=4-177	DS 1C	DISP				
DNM=4-194	02	DFHEIV10	BL=1	0B5	DNM=4-194	DS 4P	COMP-3				
DNM=4-212	02	DFHEIV11	BL=1	0B9	DNM=4-212	DS 1H	COMP				
DNM=4-230	02	DFHEIV12	BL=1	0BB	DNM=4-230	DS 1H	COMP				
DNM=4-248	02	DFHEIV13	BL=1	0BD	DNM=4-248	DS 1H	COMP				
DNM=4-269	02	DFHEIV14	BL=1	0BF	DNM=4-269	DS 1H	COMP				
DNM=4-287	02	DFHEIV15	BL=1	0C1	DNM=4-287	DS 1H	COMP				
DNM=4-305	02	DFHEIV16	BL=1	0C3	DNM=4-305	DS 1F	COMP				
DNM=4-323	02	DFHEIV17	BL=1	0C7	DNM=4-323	DS 4C	DISP				
DNM=4-341	02	DFHEIV18	BL=1	0CB	DNM=4-341	DS 4C	DISP				
DNM=4-359	02	DFHEIV19	BL=1	0CF	DNM=4-359	DS 4C	DISP				
DNM=4-377	02	DFHEIV97	BL=1	0D3	DNM=4-377	DS 4P	COMP-3				
DNM=4-395	02	DFHEIV98	BL=1	0D7	DNM=4-395	DS 1H	COMP				
DNM=4-413	02	DFHEIV99	BL=1	0D9	DNM=4-413	DS 1C	DISP				
DNM=4-431	01	DFHEIBLK	BLL=2	000	DNM=4-431	DS 0CL51	GROUP				
DNM=4-452	02	EIBTIME	BLL=2	000	DNM=4-452	DS 4P	COMP-3				
DNM=4-469	02	EIBDATE	BLL=2	004	DNM=4-469	DS 4P	COMP-3				
DNM=4-486	02	EIBTRNID	BLL=2	008	DNM=4-486	DS 4C	DISP				
DNM=5-000	02	EIBTASKN	BLL=2	00C	DNM=5-000	DS 4P	COMP-3				
DNM=5-021	02	EIBTRMID	BLL=2	010	DNM=5-021	DS 4C	DISP				

Fig. 24.3. (Continued)

29 ORAD01A 18.38.45 07/27/80

INTRNL NAME	LVL	SOURCE NAME	BASE	DISPL	INTRNL NAME	DEFINITION	USAGE	R	O	Q	M
DNM=5-039	02	DFHEIGDI	BLL=2	014	DNM=5-039	DS 1H	COMP				
DNM=5-057	02	EIBCPOSN	BLL=2	016	DNM=5-057	DS 1H	COMP				
DNM=5-075	02	EIBCALEN	BLL=2	018	DNM=5-075	DS 1H	COMP				
DNM=5-093	02	EIBAID	BLL=2	01A	DNM=5-093	DS 1C	DISP				
DNM=5-109	02	EIBFN	BLL=2	01B	DNM=5-109	DS 2C	DISP				
DNM=5-124	02	EIBRCODE	BLL=2	01D	DNM=5-124	DS 6C	DISP				
DNM=5-142	02	EIBDS	BLL=2	023	DNM=5-142	DS 8C	DISP				
DNM=5-157	02	EIBREQID	BLL=2	02B	DNM=5-157	DS 8C	DISP				
DNM=5-175	01	DFHCOMMAREA	BLL=3	000	DNM=5-175	DS 0CL4	GROUP				
DNM=5-202	02	PROCESS-SW	BLL=3	000	DNM=5-202	DS 1C	DISP				
DNM=5-225	88	INITIAL-ENTRY-TIME			DNM=5-225						
DNM=5-254	88	ORDER-VALIDATION-TIME			DNM=5-254						
DNM=5-286	02	OPERATOR-INITIAL	BLL=3	001	DNM=5-286	DS 3C	DISP				
DNM=5-312	01	LINKAGE-POINTERS	BLL=4	000	DNM=5-312	DS 0CL28	GROUP				
DNM=5-344	02	FILLER	BLL=4	000	DNM=5-344	DS 1F	COMP				
DNM=5-363	02	MAP1-POINTER	BLL=4	004	DNM=5-363	DS 1F	COMP				
DNM=5-385	02	POM-POINTER	BLL=4	008	DNM=5-385	DS 1F	COMP				
DNM=5-409	02	TWA-POINTER	BLL=4	00C	DNM=5-409	DS 1F	COMP				
DNM=5-430	02	TSA-POINTER	BLL=4	010	DNM=5-430	DS 1F	COMP				
DNM=5-451	02	JOURNAL-POINTER	BLL=4	014	DNM=5-451	DS 1F	COMP				
DNM=5-476	02	TABLE-POINTER	BLL=4	018	DNM=5-476	DS 1F	COMP				
DNM=6-000	01	MAP1-AREA	BLL=5	000	DNM=6-000	DS 0CL950	GROUP				
DNM=6-022	02	FILLER	BLL=5	000	DNM=6-022	DS 12C	DISP				
DNM=6-041	02	MAP1-DUMMY-L	BLL=5	00C	DNM=6-041	DS 1H	COMP				
DNM=6-063	02	MAP1-DUMMY-A	BLL=5	00E	DNM=6-063	DS 1C	DISP				
DNM=6-085	02	MAP1-DUMMY	BLL=5	00F	DNM=6-085	DS 1C	DISP				
DNM=6-105	02	MAP1-ORDER-NUMBER-L	BLL=5	010	DNM=6-105	DS 1H	COMP				
DNM=6-134	02	MAP1-ORDER-NUMBER-A	BLL=5	012	DNM=6-134	DS 1C	DISP				
DNM=6-163	02	MAP1-ORDER-NUMBER	BLL=5	013	DNM=6-163	DS 10C	DISP				
DNM=6-190	02	MAP1-DOCUMENT-L	BLL=5	01D	DNM=6-190	DS 1H	COMP				
DNM=6-218	02	MAP1-DOCUMENT-A	BLL=5	01F	DNM=6-218	DS 1C	DISP				
DNM=6-243	02	MAP1-DOCUMENT	BLL=5	020	DNM=6-243	DS 8C	DISP				
DNM=6-266	02	MAP1-DEPARTMENT-L	BLL=5	028	DNM=6-266	DS 1H	COMP				
DNM=6-296	02	MAP1-DEPARTMENT-A	BLL=5	02A	DNM=6-296	DS 1C	DISP				
DNM=6-323	02	MAP1-DEPARTMENT	BLL=5	02B	DNM=6-323	DS 3C	DISP				
DNM=6-348	02	MAP1-ORDER-DATE-L	BLL=5	02E	DNM=6-348	DS 1H	COMP				
DNM=6-375	02	MAP1-ORDER-DATE-A	BLL=5	030	DNM=6-375	DS 1C	DISP				
DNM=6-405	02	MAP1-ORDER-DATE	BLL=5	031	DNM=6-405	DS 0CL6	GROUP				
DNM=6-433	03	MAP1-ORDER-DATE-MONTH	BLL=5	031	DNM=6-433	DS 2C	DISP				
DNM=6-464	03	MAP1-ORDER-DATE-DAY	BLL=5	033	DNM=6-464	DS 2C	DISP				
DNM=7-000	03	MAP1-ORDER-DATE-YEAR	BLL=5	035	DNM=7-000	DS 2C	DISP				
DNM=7-030		MAP1-LINE-I			DNM=7-030		INDEX-NM				U
DNM=7-048	02	MAP1-LINE-ITEM	BLL=5	037	DNM=7-048	DS 0CL83	GROUP		O		
DNM=7-075	03	MAP1-ITEM-NUMBER-L	BLL=5	037	DNM=7-075	DS 1H	COMP				
DNM=7-106	03	MAP1-ITEM-NUMBER-A	BLL=5	039	DNM=7-106	DS 1C	DISP				
DNM=7-137	03	MAP1-ITEM-NUMBER	BLL=5	03A	DNM=7-137	DS 8C	DISP-NM				
DNM=7-166	03	MAP1-ITEM-DESCRIPTION-L	BLL=5	042	DNM=7-166	DS 1H	COMP				
DNM=7-202	03	MAP1-ITEM-DESCRIPTION-A	BLL=5	044	DNM=7-202	DS 1C	DISP				
DNM=7-238	03	MAP1-ITEM-DESCRIPTION	BLL=5	045	DNM=7-238	DS 19C	DISP				
DNM=7-272	03	MAP1-UNIT-L	BLL=5	058	DNM=7-272	DS 1H	COMP				

Fig. 24.3. (Continued)

30 ORADO1A 18.38.45 07/27/80

INTRNL NAME	LVL	SOURCE NAME	BASE	DISPL	INTRNL NAME	DEFINITION	USAGE	R	O	Q	M
DNM=7-296	03	MAP1-UNIT-A	BLL=5	05A	DNM=7-296	DS 1C	DISP				
DNM=7-320	03	MAP1-UNIT	BLL=5	05B	DNM=7-320	DS 5C	DISP-NM				
DNM=7-342	03	MAP1-UNIT-COST-L	BLL=5	060	DNM=7-342	DS 1H	COMP				
DNM=7-371	03	MAP1-UNIT-COST-A	BLL=5	062	DNM=7-371	DS 1C	DISP				
DNM=7-403	03	MAP1-UNIT-COST	BLL=5	063	DNM=7-403	DS 7C	DISP-NM				
DNM=7-430	03	MAP1-COST-L	BLL=5	06A	DNM=7-430	DS 1H	COMP				
DNM=7-454	03	MAP1-COST-A	BLL=5	06C	DNM=7-454	DS 1C	DISP				
DNM=7-478	03	MAP1-COST	BLL=5	06D	DNM=7-478	DS 8C	DISP-NM				
DNM=8-000	03	MAP1-UNIT-PRICE-L	BLL=5	075	DNM=8-000	DS 1H	COMP				
DNM=8-033	03	MAP1-UNIT-PRICE-A	BLL=5	077	DNM=8-033	DS 1C	DISP				
DNM=8-063	03	MAP1-UNIT-PRICE	BLL=5	078	DNM=8-063	DS 7C	DISP-NM				
DNM=8-091	03	MAP1-PRICE-L	BLL=5	07F	DNM=8-091	DS 1H	COMP				
DNM=8-116	03	MAP1-PRICE-A	BLL=5	081	DNM=8-116	DS 1C	DISP				
DNM=8-141	03	MAP1-PRICE	BLL=5	082	DNM=8-141	DS 8C	DISP-NM				
DNM=8-164	02	MAP1-TOTAL-COST-L	BLL=5	322	DNM=8-164	DS 1H	COMP				
DNM=8-194	02	MAP1-TOTAL-COST-A	BLL=5	324	DNM=8-194	DS 1C	DISP				
DNM=8-221	02	MAP1-TOTAL-COST	BLL=5	325	DNM=8-221	DS 9C	DISP-NM				
DNM=8-249	02	MAP1-TOTAL-PRICE-L	BLL=5	32E	DNM=8-249	DS 1H	COMP				
DNM=8-277	02	MAP1-TOTAL-PRICE-A	BLL=5	330	DNM=8-277	DS 1C	DISP				
DNM=8-305	02	MAP1-TOTAL-PRICE	BLL=5	331	DNM=8-305	DS 9C	DISP-NM				
DNM=8-331		ERROR-I			DNM=8-331		INDEX-NM				U
DNM=8-345	02	FILLER	BLL=5	33A	DNM=8-345	DS 0CL31	GROUP		O		
DNM=8-367	03	MAP1-ERRORS-L	BLL=5	33A	DNM=8-367	DS 1H	COMP				
DNM=8-393	03	MAP1-ERRORS-A	BLL=5	33C	DNM=8-393	DS 1C	DISP				
DNM=8-419	03	MAP1-ERRORS	BLL=5	33D	DNM=8-419	DS 28C	DISP				
DNM=8-446	01	ORDER-MASTER-RECORD	BLL=6	000	DNM=8-446	DS VLC=2	GROUP			Q	
DNM=8-478	02	ORDER-NUMBER	BLL=6	000	DNM=8-478	DS 10C	DISP				
DNM=9-000	02	ORDER-ALT-KEY	BLL=6	00A	DNM=9-000	DS 0CL9	GROUP				
DNM=9-026	03	ORDER-DEPARTMENT	BLL=6	00A	DNM=9-026	DS 3C	DISP				
DNM=9-052	03	ORDER-DATE	BLL=6	00D	DNM=9-052	DS 0CL6	GROUP				
DNM=9-078	04	ORDER-DATE-YEAR	BLL=6	00D	DNM=9-078	DS 2C	DISP				
DNM=9-103	04	ORDER-DATE-MONTH	BLL=6	00F	DNM=9-103	DS 2C	DISP				
DNM=9-132	04	ORDER-DATE-DAY	BLL=6	011	DNM=9-132	DS 2C	DISP				
DNM=9-159	02	ORDER-DATE-ENTERED	BLL=6	013	DNM=9-159	DS 0CL6	GROUP				
DNM=9-190	03	ORDER-DATE-ENTERED-MONTH	BLL=6	013	DNM=9-190	DS 2C	DISP				
DNM=9-224	03	ORDER-DATE-ENTERED-DAY	BLL=6	015	DNM=9-224	DS 2C	DISP				
DNM=9-259	03	ORDER-DATE-ENTERED-YEAR	BLL=6	017	DNM=9-259	DS 2C	DISP				
DNM=9-292	02	ORDER-TOTAL-COST	BLL=6	019	DNM=9-292	DS 5P	COMP-3				
DNM=9-318	02	ORDER-TOTAL-PRICE	BLL=6	01E	DNM=9-318	DS 5P	COMP-3				
DNM=9-348	02	ORDER-LINE-COUNT	BLL=6	023	DNM=9-348	DS 1H	COMP			Q	
DNM=9-374	02	ORDER-ALL-LINES	BLL=6	025	DNM=9-374	DS VLC=1	GROUP				
DNM=9-402		ORDER-LINE-I			DNM=9-402		INDEX-NM				U
DNM=9-421	03	ORDER-LINE-ITEM	BLL=6	025	DNM=9-421	DS 0CL44	GROUP		O		
DNM=9-452	04	ORDER-ITEM-NUMBER	BLL=6	025	DNM=9-452	DS 8C	DISP				
DNM=10-000	04	ORDER-ITEM-DESCRIPTION	BLL=6	02D	DNM=10-000	DS 19C	DISP				
DNM=10-035	04	ORDER-ITEM-DATE	BLL=6	040	DNM=10-035	DS 0CL6	GROUP				
DNM=10-069	05	ORDER-ITEM-DATE-MONTH	BLL=6	040	DNM=10-069	DS 2C	DISP				
DNM=10-106	05	ORDER-ITEM-DATE-DAY	BLL=6	042	DNM=10-106	DS 2C	DISP				
DNM=10-141	05	ORDER-ITEM-DATE-YEAR	BLL=6	044	DNM=10-141	DS 2C	DISP				
DNM=10-177	04	ORDER-UNIT	BLL=6	046	DNM=10-177	DS 3P	COMP-3				

Fig. 24.3. (Continued)

31 ORADO1A 18.38.45 07/27/80

INTRNL NAME	LVL	SOURCE NAME	BASE	DISPL	INTRNL NAME	DEFINITION	USAGE	R	O	Q	M
DNM=10-200	04	ORDER-UNIT-COST	BLL=6	049	DNM=10-200	DS 4P	COMP-3				
DNM=10-228	04	ORDER-UNIT-PRICE	BLL=6	04D	DNM=10-228	DS 4P	COMP-3				
DNM=10-260	01	TWA-AREA	BLL=7	000	DNM=10-260	DS OCL215	GROUP				
DNM=10-284	02	TWA-LINE-ITEM-MAP	BLL=7	000	DNM=10-284	DS OCL83	GROUP				
DNM=10-314	03	TWA-ITEM-NUMBER-MAP-L	BLL=7	000	DNM=10-314	DS 1H	COMP				
DNM=10-345	03	TWA-ITEM-NUMBER-MAP-A	BLL=7	002	DNM=10-345	DS 1C	DISP				
DNM=10-379	03	TWA-ITEM-NUMBER-MAP	BLL=7	003	DNM=10-379	DS 8C	DISP				
DNM=10-408	03	TWA-ITEM-DESCRIPTION-MAP-L	BLL=7	00B	DNM=10-408	DS 1H	COMP				
DNM=10-447	03	TWA-ITEM-DESCRIPTION-MAP-A	BLL=7	00D	DNM=10-447	DS 1C	DISP				
DNM=11-000	03	TWA-ITEM-DESCRIPTION-MAP	BLL=7	00E	DNM=11-000	DS OCL19	GROUP				
DNM=11-037	04	TWA-DESCRIPTION-FIRST-MAP	BLL=7	00E	DNM=11-037	DS 1C	DISP				
DNM=11-075	04	FILLER	BLL=7	00F	DNM=11-075	DS 18C	DISP				
DNM=11-094	03	TWA-UNIT-MAP-L	BLL=7	021	DNM=11-094	DS 1H	COMP				
DNM=11-118	03	TWA-UNIT-MAP-A	BLL=7	023	DNM=11-118	DS 1C	DISP				
DNM=11-142	03	TWA-UNIT-MAP	BLL=7	024	DNM=11-142	DS 5C	DISP-NM				
DNM=11-164	03	TWA-UNIT-COST-MAP-L	BLL=7	029	DNM=11-164	DS 1H	COMP				
DNM=11-196	03	TWA-UNIT-COST-MAP-A	BLL=7	02B	DNM=11-196	DS 1C	DISP				
DNM=11-228	03	TWA-UNIT-COST-MAP	BLL=7	02C	DNM=11-228	DS 7C	DISP-NM				
DNM=11-255	03	TWA-COST-MAP-L	BLL=7	033	DNM=11-255	DS 1H	COMP				
DNM=11-279	03	TWA-COST-MAP-A	BLL=7	035	DNM=11-279	DS 1C	DISP				
DNM=11-303	03	TWA-COST-MAP	BLL=7	036	DNM=11-303	DS 8C	DISP-NM				
DNM=11-325	03	TWA-UNIT-PRICE-MAP-L	BLL=7	03E	DNM=11-325	DS 1H	COMP				
DNM=11-358	03	TWA-UNIT-PRICE-MAP-A	BLL=7	040	DNM=11-358	DS 1C	DISP				
DNM=11-391	03	TWA-UNIT-PRICE-MAP	BLL=7	041	DNM=11-391	DS 7C	DISP-NM				
DNM=11-419	03	TWA-PRICE-MAP-L	BLL=7	048	DNM=11-419	DS 1H	COMP				
DNM=11-447	03	TWA-PRICE-MAP-A	BLL=7	04A	DNM=11-447	DS 1C	DISP				
DNM=11-472	03	TWA-PRICE-MAP	BLL=7	04B	DNM=11-472	DS 8C	DISP-NM				
DNM=12-000	02	TWA-LINE-ITEM-ORDER	BLL=7	053	DNM=12-000	DS OCL44	GROUP				
DNM=12-032	03	TWA-ITEM-NUMBER-ORDER	BLL=7	053	DNM=12-032	DS 8C	DISP				
DNM=12-063	03	TWA-ITEM-DESCRIPTION-ORDER	BLL=7	05B	DNM=12-063	DS 19C	DISP				
DNM=12-099	03	TWA-ITEM-DATE-ORDER	BLL=7	06E	DNM=12-099	DS 6C	DISP				
DNM=12-128	03	TWA-UNIT-ORDER	BLL=7	(K) 074	DNM=12-128	DS 3P	COMP-3				
DNM=12-155	03	TWA-UNIT-COST-ORDER	BLL=7	077	DNM=12-155	DS 4P	COMP-3				
DNM=12-184	03	TWA-UNIT-PRICE-ORDER	BLL=7	07B	DNM=12-184	DS 4P	COMP-3				
DNM=12-214	02	TWA-TOTAL-COST	BLL=7	07F	DNM=12-214	DS 5P	COMP-3				
DNM=12-241	02	TWA-TOTAL-PRICE	BLL=7	084	DNM=12-241	DS 5P	COMP-3				
DNM=12-269	02	TWA-ORDER-RECORD-KEY	BLL=7	089	DNM=12-269	DS 10C	DISP				
DNM=12-302	02	TSA-QUEUE-ID	BLL=7	093	DNM=12-302	DS OCL8	GROUP				
DNM=12-327	03	TSA-TERM-ID	BLL=7	093	DNM=12-327	DS 4C	DISP				
DNM=12-351	03	TSA-TRANS-ID	BLL=7	097	DNM=12-351	DS 4C	DISP				
DNM=12-373	02	TWA-BINARY-FIELDS	BLL=7	09B	DNM=12-373	DS OCL16	GROUP				
DNM=12-403	03	TWA-LINE-DATA-CNT	BLL=7	09B	DNM=12-403	DS 1F	COMP				
DNM=12-433	03	TWA-JOURNAL-ID	BLL=7	09F	DNM=12-433	DS 1F	COMP				
DNM=12-457	03	TWA-POM-LENGTH	BLL=7	0A3	DNM=12-457	DS 1H	COMP				
DNM=12-481	03	TSA-LENGTH	BLL=7	0A5	DNM=12-481	DS 1H	COMP				
DNM=13-000	03	TSA-QUEUE-NO	BLL=7	0A7	DNM=13-000	DS 1H	COMP				
DNM=13-022	03	TWA-JOURNAL-LENGTH	BLL=7	0A9	DNM=13-022	DS 1H	COMP				
DNM=13-053	02	TWA-OPERATOR-MESSAGE	BLL=7	0AB	DNM=13-053	DS 31C	DISP				
DNM=13-083	02	TWA-CURRENT-DATE	BLL=7	0CA	DNM=13-083	DS OCL8	GROUP				
DNM=13-115	03	TWA-CURRENT-DATE-MONTH	BLL=7	0CA	DNM=13-115	DS 2C	DISP				

Fig. 24.3. (Continued)

32 ORAD01A 18.38.45 . 07/27/80

INTRNL NAME	LVL	SOURCE NAME	BASE	DISPL	INTRNL NAME	DEFINITION	USAGE	R	O	Q	M
DNM=13-150	03	FILLER	BLL=7	0CC	DNM=13-150	DS 1C	DISP				
DNM=13-169	03	TWA-CURRENT-DATE-DAY	BLL=7	0CD	DNM=13-169	DS 2C	DISP				
DNM=13-202	03	FILLER	BLL=7	0CF	DNM=13-202	DS 1C	DISP				
DNM=13-221	03	TWA-CURRENT-DATE-YEAR	BLL=7	0D0	DNM=13-221	DS 2C	DISP				
DNM=13-252	02	TWA-DEPT-TABLE-KEY	BLL=7	0D2	DNM=13-252	DS 0CL5	GROUP				
DNM=13-286	03	TWA-DEPT-TABLE-KEY-CODE	BLL=7	0D2	DNM=13-286	DS 1C	DISP				
DNM=13-319	03	TWA-DEPT-TABLE-KEY-NUMBER	BLL=7	0D3	DNM=13-319	DS 4P	COMP-3				
DNM=13-357	01	TSA-AREA	BLL=8	000	DNM=13-357	DS VLC=3	GROUP			Q	
DNM=13-378	02	TSA-POMAST-RECORD	BLL=8	000	DNM=13-378	DS 0CL433	GROUP				
DNM=13-411	03	TSA-ORDER-NUMBER	BLL=8	000	DNM=13-411	DS 10C	DISP				
DNM=13-437	03	TSA-DEPARTMENT	BLL=8	00A	DNM=13-437	DS 3C	DISP				
DNM=13-461	03	TSA-ORDER-DATE	BLL=8	00D	DNM=13-461	DS 0CL6	GROUP				
DNM=14-000	04	TSA-ORDER-DATE-YEAR	BLL=8	00D	DNM=14-000	DS 2C	DISP				
DNM=14-032	04	TSA-ORDER-DATE-MONTH	BLL=8	00F	DNM=14-032	DS 2C	DISP				
DNM=14-065	04	TSA-ORDER-DATE-DAY	BLL=8	011	DNM=14-065	DS 2C	DISP				
DNM=14-093	03	TSA-ORDER-ENTERED	BLL=8	013	DNM=14-093	DS 0CL6	GROUP				
DNM=14-123	04	TSA-ORDER-ENTERED-MONTH	BLL=8	013	DNM=14-123	DS 2C	DISP				
DNM=14-156	04	TSA-ORDER-ENTERED-DAY	BLL=8	015	DNM=14-156	DS 2C	DISP				
DNM=14-187	04	TSA-ORDER-ENTERED-YEAR	BLL=8	017	DNM=14-187	DS 2C	DISP				
DNM=14-222	03	TSA-TOTAL-COST	BLL=8	019	DNM=14-222	DS 5P	COMP-3				
DNM=14-249	03	TSA-TOTAL-PRICE	BLL=8	01E	DNM=14-249	DS 5P	COMP-3				
DNM=14-274	03	TSA-LINE-COUNT	BLL=8	023	DNM=14-274	DS 1H	COMP				
DNM=14-301		TSA-LINE-I			DNM=14-301		INDEX-NM				U
DNM=14-318	03	TSA-LINE-ITEM	BLL=8	025	DNM=14-318	DS 0CL44	GROUP		O		
DNM=14-344	04	TSA-ITEM-NUMBER	BLL=8	025	DNM=14-344	DS 8C	DISP				
DNM=14-372	04	TSA-ITEM-DESCRIPTION	BLL=8	02D	DNM=14-372	DS 19C	DISP				
DNM=14-408	04	TSA-ITEM-DATE	BLL=8	040	DNM=14-408	DS 6C	DISP				
DNM=14-434	04	TSA-UNIT	BLL=8	046	DNM=14-434	DS 3P	COMP-3				
DNM=14-458	04	TSA-UNIT-COST	BLL=8	049	DNM=14-458	DS 4P	COMP-3				
DNM=15-000	04	TSA-UNIT-PRICE	BLL=8	04D	DNM=15-000	DS 4P	COMP-3				
DNM=15-030	02	TSA-OPERATOR-INITIAL	BLL=8	1B1	DNM=15-030	DS 3C	DISP				
DNM=15-063	02	TSA-DEPT-CNT	BLL=8	1B4	DNM=15-063	DS 1F	COMP			Q	
DNM=15-085		DEPT-I			DNM=15-085		INDEX-NM				U
DNM=15-101	02	TSA-DEPTS	BLL=8	1B8	DNM=15-101	DS 0CL3	GROUP		O		
DNM=15-123	03	TSA-DEPT-NO	BLL=8	1B8	DNM=15-123	DS 3C	DISP				
DNM=15-147	01	JOURNAL-RECORD	BLL=9	000	DNM=15-147	DS 0CL37	GROUP				
DNM=15-174	02	JOURNAL-OPERATOR-INITIAL	BLL=9	000	DNM=15-174	DS 3C	DISP				
DNM=15-208	02	JOURNAL-DATE-ENTERED	BLL=9	003	DNM=15-208	DS 6C	DISP				
DNM=15-238	02	JOURNAL-ORDER-NUMBER	BLL=9	009	DNM=15-238	DS 10C	DISP				
DNM=15-271	02	JOURNAL-DOCUMENT-NUMBER	BLL=9	013	DNM=15-271	DS 8C	DISP				
DNM=15-307	02	JOURNAL-TOTAL-COST	BLL=9	01B	DNM=15-307	DS 5P	COMP-3				
DNM=15-338	02	JOURNAL-TOTAL-PRICE	BLL=9	020	DNM=15-338	DS 5P	COMP-3				
DNM=15-370	01	DEPT-TABLE-RECORD	BLL=10	000	DNM=15-370	DS 0CL85	GROUP				
DNM=15-400	02	DEPT-TABLE-KEY	BLL=10	000	DNM=15-400	DS 0CL5	GROUP				
DNM=15-430	03	DEPT-TABLE-KEY-CODE	BLL=10	000	DNM=15-430	DS 1C	DISP				
DNM=15-465	88	DEPT-RECORD			DNM=15-465						
DNM=16-000	03	DEPT-TABLE-KEY-NUMBER	BLL=10	001	DNM=16-000	DS 4P	COMP-3				
DNM=16-031	02	DEPT-NO	BLL=10	005	DNM=16-031	DS 3C	DISP				
DNM=16-048	02	FILLER	BLL=10	008	DNM=16-048	DS 30C	DISP				
DNM=16-067	02	DEPT-DIVISION	BLL=10	026	DNM=16-067	DS 2C	DISP				

Fig. 24.3. (Continued)

```
37          ORADC1A          18.38.45          07/27/80

REG 6    BL =1

WORKING-STORAGE STARTS AT LOCATION 00100 FOR A LENGTH OF 000DC.
```

CONDENSED LISTING

373	ENTRY	000920	374	CALL	000938	385	MOVE	000940
385	CALL	000950	395	MOVE	000972	395	CALL	000982
396	GO	000998	407	MOVE	0009CC	407	CALL	0009DC
408	GO	0009F2	412	IF	000A22	413	IF	000A30
414	GO	000A3E	415	ELSE	000A44	415	IF	000A44
416	GO	000A52	417	ELSE	000A58	417	GO	000A58
419	IF	000A5E	420	GO	000A70	433	MOVE	000A76
433	MOVE	000A80	433	MOVE	000A8A	434	CALL	000A9A
438	MOVE	000AD4	439	MOVE	000AE2	448	MOVE	000AE8
448	MOVE	000AEE	448	CALL	000AFE	455	MOVE	000B44
459	SET	000B70	463	IF	000B78	464	MOVE	000B8C
465	ELSE	000B9A	465	SET	000BA0	466	MOVE	000BAC
467	MOVE	000BDC	469	IF	000BE6	471	ELSE	000C00
471	SET	000C00	472	MOVE	000C0C	473	IF	000C3C
474	MOVE	000C48	476	SEARCH ALL	000C52	478	GO	000C58
480	MOVE	000CAA	481	GO	000CB8	485	SET	000CC4
486	MOVE	000CD0	487	IF	000D00	488	MOVE	000D0C
492	IF	000D16	495	MOVE	000D5A	496	MOVE	000D68
497	MOVE	000D6E	498	ELSE	000D74	498	SET	000D7A
499	MOVE	000D86	500	IF	000DB6	501	MOVE	000DC2
505	IF	000DCC	506	GO	000DDA	510	SET	000DE0
511	MOVE	000DE6	512	MOVE	000DF0	513	PERFORM	000DFA
517	GO	000E46	521	MOVE	000E4C	522	SET	000E56
523	MOVE	000E74	525	IF	000E92	526	IF	000EA0
527	MOVE	000EB0	528	ADD	000EB6	529	ELSE	000EC2
529	MOVE	000EC8	530	SET	000ECE	531	MOVE	000EDA
533	IF	000EF4	534	MOVE	000F00	535	ELSE	000F12
535	IF	000F18	536	GO	000F26	538	IF	000F2C
539	MOVE	000F3E	540	ELSE	000F48	540	IF	000F4E
541	MOVE	000F5C	543	SET	000F62	544	MOVE	000F6E
546	IF	000F88	547	MOVE	000F94	549	ELSE	000FA6
549	IF	000FAC	550	GO	000FBA	551	ELSE	000FC0
552	ELSE	000FC6	552	MOVE	000FC6	554	ADD	000FD0
556	IF	000FDC	557	IF	000FEE	558	MOVE	000FFE
559	ADD	001012	560	ELSE	00101E	560	MOVE	001024
561	MOVE	00102E	562	SET	00103E	563	MOVE	00104A
565	IF	001064	566	MOVE	001070	567	ELSE	001082
567	IF	001088	568	GO	001096	570	IF	00109C
571	IF	0010AE	572	MOVE	0010BE	573	ADD	0010D2
574	ELSE	0010DE	574	MOVE	0010E4	575	MOVE	0010EE
577	SET	0010FE	578	MOVE	00110A	580	IF	001124
581	MOVE	001130	582	ELSE	001142	582	IF	001148
583	GO	001156	585	IF	00115C	586	IF	00116E
589	ADD	00119C ← (1)	590	ADD	0011A8	591	ELSE	0011B4
591	MOVE	0011BA	592	SET	0011CA	593	MOVE	0011D6
595	IF	0011F0	596	MOVE	0011FC	597	ELSE	00120E

Fig. 24.4. The Procedure Division Condensed Listing.

```
  38          ORAD01A          18.38.45          07/27/80

597   IF         001214     598   GO         001222     600   IF         001228
601   IF         00123A     602   MOVE       00124A     603   ADD        00125E
604   ELSE       00126A     604   MOVE       001270     605   MOVE       00127A
607   SET        001284     608   MOVE       001290     610   IF         0012AA
611   MOVE       0012B6     612   ELSE       0012C8     612   IF         0012CE
613   GO         0012DC     615   IF         0012E2     616   IF         0012F4
619   ADD        001322     620   ADD        00132E     621   ELSE       00133A
621   MOVE       001340     622   SET        001350     623   MOVE       00135C
625   IF         001376     626   MOVE       001382     627   ELSE       001394
627   IF         00139A     628   GO         0013A8     630   IF         0013AE
631   IF         0013CE     632   SET        0013DC     633   MOVE       0013F0
635   ELSE       00140E     636   ELSE       001414     636   IF         001414
638   ELSE       00142C     638   SET        00142C     639   MOVE       001438
640   MOVE       001448     642   IF         001462     643   MOVE       00146E
645   ELSE       001480     645   IF         001486     646   GO         001494
648   SET        00149A     649   EXIT       0014A6     653   IF         0014AC
654   GO         0014BA     656   IF         0014C0     658   SET        0014E0
659   MOVE       0014EC     660   IF         00151C     661   MOVE       001528
662   ELSE       001532     662   IF         001538     663   GO         001546
665   IF         00154C     667   MOVE       001576     668   ELSE       001584
668   SET        00158A     669   MOVE       001596     670   IF         0015C6
671   MOVE       0015D2     672   ELSE       0015DC     672   IF         0015E2
673   GO         0015F0     675   IF         0015F6     677   MOVE       001620
678   ELSE       00162E     678   SET        001634     679   MOVE       001640
680   IF         001670     681   MOVE       00167C     682   ELSE       001686
682   IF         00168C     683   GO         00169A     684   EXIT       0016A0
688   IF         0016A0     689   GO         0016AE     693   SET        0016B4
695   IF         0016CC     696   IF         0016DA     697   SUBTRACT   0016EC
698   ELSE       0016FC     698   SUBTRACT   001702     699   ELSE       001712
699   SUBTRACT   001718     706   MOVE       001728     706   MOVE       00172E
706   CALL       00173E     711   MOVE       001768     712   MOVE       00177C
713   COMPUTE    0017A0     714   MOVE       0017B8     721   MOVE       0017C2
721   CALL       0017D2     722   GO         0017E8     732   MOVE       001818
732   MOVE       001828     732   CALL       001838     741   MOVE       00187C
741   CALL       00188C     749   MOVE       0018B4     749   MOVE       0018BA
749   CALL       0018CA     754   MOVE       0018F4     755   MOVE       001902
756   MOVE       001908     757   MOVE       00190E     758   MOVE       001914
759   MOVE       00191A     760   MOVE       001924     770   MOVE       00192E
770   MOVE       001934     770   MOVE       00193A     771   CALL       00194A
786   MOVE       001990     786   MOVE       00199A     786   MOVE       0019A4
787   CALL       0019B4     794   MOVE       0019EA     801   MOVE       0019EE
801   MOVE       0019F4     801   CALL       001A04     815   MOVE       001A36
815   MOVE       001A40     815   MOVE       001A4A     816   MOVE       001A50
816   CALL       001A60     822   GO         001ABA     826   MOVE       001AC0
827   MOVE       001AD4     828   GO         001ADA     842   MOVE       001AE0
842   MOVE       001AE6     842   CALL       001AF6     848   MOVE       001B28
856   MOVE       001B3C     856   MOVE       001B46     856   MOVE       001B50
857   CALL       001B60     862   MOVE       001B96     869   MOVE       001B9A
869   MOVE       001BA0     869   CALL       001BB0     885   MOVE       001BE2
885   CALL       001BF2     886   GO         001C08     889   MOVE       001C36
890   MOVE       001C44     896   MOVE       001C4A     896   CALL       001C5A
907   MOVE       001C78     907   MOVE       001C7E     907   CALL       001C8E
914   SET        001CB8     915   MOVE       001CC0     916   MOVE       001CC8
```

Fig. 24.4. (Continued)

```
  39        ORAD01A        18.38.45        07/27/80

922    MOVE    001CCE        922    CALL    001CDE        923    GO      001CF4
931    MOVE    001D22        931    MOVE    001D2C        931    CALL    001D3C
943    MOVE    001D76        943    MOVE    001D80        943    CALL    001D90
948    IF      001DDE        949    IF      001DEC        950    GO      001DF8
951    ELSE    001DFE        951    IF      001DFE        952    SET     001E0E
953    MOVE    001E1A        955    GO      001E38        956    EXIT    001E3E
960    IF      001E3E        961    GO      001E4C        962    ELSE    001E52
962    SET     001E52        966    MOVE    001E70        967    MOVE    001E80
968    MOVE    001E8E        969    MOVE    001E94        970    MOVE    001E9A
971    MOVE    C01EA4        979    MOVE    001EAE        979    CALL    001EBE
988    MOVE    001EFA        988    CALL    001F0A        997    MOVE    001F32
997    MOVE    001F38        997    CALL    001F48        1003   MOVE    001F7A
1011   MOVE    001F8E        1011   MOVE    001F98        1011   MOVE    001FA2
1012   CALL    001FB2        1017   MOVE    001FE8        1024   MOVE    001FEC
1024   MOVE    001FF2        1024   MOVE    001FF8        1025   CALL    002008
1037   MOVE    002036        1046   MOVE    00204A        1046   MOVE    002050
1046   CALL    002060        1055   MOVE    00209A        1055   CALL    0020AA
1056   GO      0020C0        1059   MOVE    0020EE        1060   MOVE    0020FC
1066   MOVE    002102        1066   CALL    002112        1076   MOVE    002130
1076   CALL    002140        1091   MOVE    002156        1091   MOVE    00215C
1092   CALL    00216C        1095   MOVE    00218A        1096   GO      00219A
1099   MOVE    0021A0        1100   GO      0021B0        1103   MOVE    0021B6
1104   GO      0021BC        1107   MOVE    0021C2        1108   GO      0021C8
1111   MOVE    0021CE        1112   MOVE    0021D8        1117   MOVE    0021DE
1117   MOVE    0021E4        1117   CALL    0021F4        1120   MOVE    002212
1121   GO      002222        1124   MOVE    002228        1125   GO      002232

*STATISTICS*          SOURCE RECORDS =   1125   DATA ITEMS =     248    PROC DIV SZ =      411
*STATISTICS*          PARTITION SIZE = 200584   LINE COUNT =      56    BUFFER SIZE =    19069
*OPTIONS IN EFFECT*   PMAP RELOC ADR =   NONE   SPACING    =       1    FLOW        =     NONE
*OPTIONS IN EFFECT*     NOLISTX        APOST    SYM   NOCATALR        LIST        LINK        STXIT       LIB
*OPTIONS IN EFFECT*       CLIST        FLAGW    ZWB     SUPMAP      NOXREF        ERRS        SXREF       NOOPT
*OPTIONS IN EFFECT*     NOSTATE      NOTRUNC    SEQ   NOSYMDMP      NODECK        VERB      CSYNTAX       NOLVL
*OPTIONS IN EFFECT*                  NOCOUNT                     NOVERBSUM  NOVERBREF
*LISTER OPTIONS*           NONE
```

Fig. 24.4. (Continued)

```
CUSTOMER INFORMATION CONTROL SYSTEM STORAGE DUMP   CODE=ASRA (F)  TASK=ORAD (G)     DATE=07/27/80   TIME=18 43 53   PAGE    1

PSW       (H) 071D0007   CC13D9C8

REGS 14-4        5011812A  0013D9DA  00000000  0013D9DA        0013EE90  00000006  00129157

REGS 5-11        5013EB00  0012F00C  0012F2E3  0012F2E4        0013EAD0  0013C820  01100660
                 (A)
TASK CONTROL AREA (USER AREA)  ADDRESS  12E8B8  TO  12EFBF    LENGTH  000708

000000  0012E800 00107234 01100660 00108EF0  0012EBC0 0011A746 88400100 003100A0  *..Y........-...0..........  .......*  12E8B8
000020  4011862A 0015F1A0 00000000 0015F1B0  00118804 80118BA0 0013F808 00117F70  * .....1.......1.............8.....*  12E8D8
000040  0012E800 48000058 0011A728 0012EC18  00118888 01100660 5011812A 0012F980  *..Y....................-......9.*  12E8F8
000060  60121C38 00128800 AE120540 00000000  0000000A 00000540 00000000 0012D040  *-.........  ...........  ....... *  12E918
000080  FE00F988 D3F7F7F0 D6D9C1C4 C1E2D9C1  071D0007 C013D9C8 00000000 01F0F140  *..9.L770ORADASRA......RH.....01 *  12E938
0000A0  5011812A 0013D9DA 00000000 0013D9DA  0013EE90 00000006 00129157 5013EB00  *......R........R.................*  12E958
0000C0  0012F00C 0012F2E3 0012F2E4 0013EAD0  0013C820 01100660 0A040000 00010600  *..0...2T..2U......H....-.........*  12E978
0000E0  00000000 00000000 24F40000 00000000  00000000 00000000 00000000 00000000 (L)*...........4.....................*  12E998
000100  000400F0 F0F0F0F8 F5F7F300 0900C3C8  C1C9D540 E2C1E640 40404040 40404040  *...00008573...CHAIN SAW         *  12E9B8
000120  40000200 F0F0F0F2 F0000500 F0F0F1F0  F0F0F000 0600F0F0 F2F0F0F0 F0F00005  * ...00020...0010000...00200000..*  12E9D8
000140  00F0F0F2 F0F0F0F0 000600F0 F0F4F0F0  F0F0F0F0 F0F0F0F8 F5F7F3C3 C8C1C9D5  *.0020000...004000000000008573CHAIN*  12E9F8
000160  40E2C1E6 40404040 40404040 4040F1F0  F1F5F8F1 00020C00 10000C00 00000000  * SAW          101581............*  12EA18
000180  00000000 00000000 00000000 00000000  000000D3 F7F7F0D6 D9C1C400 00000F00  *...................L770ORAD.....*  12EA38
0001A0  00000000 00053C00 00000000 00000000  00000000 00000000 00000000 00000000  *................................*  12EA58
0001C0  00000000 00000000 00000000 00000000  00000000 00000000 00000000 00000000  *................................*  12EA78
0001E0  LINES TO 0002E0 SAME AS ABOVE                                                                                     12EA98
000300  D3C9C6D6 E2E3D6D9 42000088 00000000  FF12EC48 8012192C 001219D8 00000004  *LIFOSTOR.....................Q....*  12EBB8
000320  0012F360 0012F07C 0012EA4B 0012F328  0012EA5D 00000014 00000004 0010C700  *..3-..0........3....)..........G.*  12EBD8
000340  00121820 0012F0EC 0012F390 0012E8B8  001070F0 FE12EC48 F0000000 00000000  *......0...3...Y....0....0........*  12EBF8
000360  8B000028 00000000 00000000 0011A728  00000000 00000000 00000000 00000000  *................................*  12EC18
000380  00000000 00000000 8B000028 00000000  48000068 0012EBC0 00000000 4011862A  *..........................   ...*  12EC38
0003A0  0015F1A0 00000000 0015F1B0 00118804  80118BA0 0013F808 00117F70 0012E800  *..1.......1...........8.......Y.*  12EC58
0003C0  48000058 0011A728 0012EC18 00118888  01100660 00000000 00000000 FE12ECB0  *.....................-..........*  12EC78
0003E0  F700E3E2 00121A64 89040000 D3F7F7F0  D6D9C1C4 00000000 00000000 00000000  *7.TS.........L770ORAD............*  12EC98
000400  00000000 00000000 00000000 00000000  00000000 00000000 00000000 00000000  *................................*  12ECB8
000420  LINES TO 0006E0 SAME AS ABOVE                                                                                     12ECD8
000700  8A0307B8 0012F980                                                                      *......9.                        *  12EFB8

TASK CONTROL AREA (SYSTEM AREA)ADDRESS  12E800  TO  12E8B7    LENGTH  0000B8

000000  8A0307B8 0012F980 00000000 00000000  8000008C 00117120 00129880 00000000  *......9.........................*  12E800
000020  00109138 00000000 00000000 00000000  00000000 FF11A6E4 00000000 0012F0EC  *.......................U.......0.*  12E820
000040  0012EFC0 0012EC18 00000000 0012F660  00000000 00000000 00000000 00000000  *..............6-.................*  12E840
000060  00000000 00000000 00000000 C1E2D9C1  00000000 00000000 00000000 0012F390  *..............ASRA..............3.*  12E860
000080  FE12ECB0 00000000 FE12EBB0 FE12EFB8  00109A28 0012EBC0 00000000 00000000  *................................*  12E880
0000A0  00100660 00000000 00000000 00000000  D6D9C1C4 00000000                     *...-.............ORAD....       *  12E8A0
```

Fig. 24.5. The Transaction Dump.

```
CUSTOMER INFORMATION CONTROL SYSTEM STORAGE DUMP   CODE=ASRA   TASK=ORAD      DATE=07/27/80   TIME=18 43 53   PAGE    2

LIFO STACK ENTRY                ADDRESS  12EBC0  TO  12EC47      LENGTH  000088

000000   42000088 00000000 FF12EC48 B012192C   001219D8 00000004 0012F360 0012F07C   *...................Q......3-..0.*   12EBC0
000020   0012EA48 0012F328 0012EA5D 00000014   00000004 0010C700 00121820 0012F0EC   *.......3....)..........G.......0.*   12EBE0
000040   0012F390 0012E8B8 001070F0 FE12EC48   F0000000 00000000 8B000028 00000000   *..3...Y....0....0...............*   12EC00
000060   00000000 0011A728 00000000 00000000   00000000 00000000 00000000 00000000   *................................*   12EC20
000080   8B000028 00000000                                                           *........                        *   12EC40

       REGS  0 THRU 15          ADDRESS  155DCC  TO  155E0B      LENGTH  000040

000000   00000000 0013D9DA 0013EE90 00000006   00129157 5013EB00 0012F00C 0012F2E3   *......R...................0...2T*   155DCC
000020   0012F2E4 0013EAD0 0013C820 0013C820   0013CC98 0012F0EC 0012E9B8 0013D9DA   *..2U......H...H........0...Z...R.*   155DEC

COMMON SYSTEM AREA              ADDRESS  1070F0  TO  108EEF      LENGTH  001E00

000000   00000000 00000000 00000000 70155400   0013D9DA 00000000 0013D9DA 0013EE90   *.................R.......R.....*   1070F0
000020   00000006 00129157 5013EB00 0012F00C   0012F2E3 0012F2E4 0013EAD0 0013C820   *.............0...2T..2U......H.*   107110
000040   01100660 0012C0B8 0010023C 0012E8B8   1843539F 001298C0 17700000 00000000   *...-...........Y...............*   107130
000060   0066E567 00465000 00000000 000106EB   00002000 00100000 0018FFFF 0080209F   *..V.............................*   107150
000080   001096F8 F0FFFFFF 0000001E 0015EBD8   00000002 00000000 00128520 C434C614   *...80..........Q............D.F.*   107170
0000A0   00000000 00000000 00129840 00129840   00129880 001095A0 00109138 1000FF00   *..........  ...  ...............*   107190
0000C0   000C0001 00091E00 00108EF0 00000000   00000000 00000000 00100A10 00000000   *...........0....................*   1071B0
0000E0   4010A0C4 001150D0 00118804 0315D8F0   001553D8 00100310 0011F064 001231E4   * ..D...........Q0...Q......0....U*   1071D0
000100   001219D8 00000000 001464A0 8014F1DC   00000000 0010D054 0110D8D0 00146490   *...Q.........1..................*   1071F0
000120   00117090 001198F8 00100260 0011B250   00122A28 001284B0 00128800 00000000   *.......8...-....................*   107210
000140   00000000 00155E64 00100808 0011B090   001228B0 00000000 00000000 00000000   *...... .........................*   107230
000160   0014F1EA 00000000 00000000 871E80C5   01341C61 00000000 00000000 0014F4A0   *..1............E.../..........4.*   107250
000180   00000000 00000000 00000000 0015F4D4   00000000 00000000 00000000 FF1070A8   *...............4M...............*   107270
0001A0   07FE58F0 D19C07FF 0134B035 0134F685   00000000 000C0000 E6D6D9D2 C1D9C5C1   *...0J.........6.........WORKAREA*   107290
0001C0   0000000C 000C0000 003C003C 00008C00   00112C00 00080C00 0C000C00 0C000C00   *................................*   1072B0
0001E0   1C001C00 000C0000 0C000C00 0C00000C   00000C00 000C0000 0C00000C 00000C00   *................................*   1072D0
000200   00000000 00000000 00000000 00000000   00000000 00000000 00000000 00000000   *................................*   1072F0
000220   LINES TO 0006C0 SAME AS ABOVE                                                                                       107310
0006E0   00000000 00000000 00000000 00000000   00000000 00000000 00000000 00000000   *................................*   1077D0
000700   LINES TO 0016A0 SAME AS ABOVE                                                                                       1077F0
0016C0   00000000 00000000 00000000 00000000   00000000 00000000 00000000 00000000   *................................*   1087B0
0016E0   LINES TO 001DE0 SAME AS ABOVE                                                                                       1087D0

CSA OPTIONAL FEATURE LIST       ADDRESS  108EF0  TO  109077      LENGTH  000188

000000   00000000 00000000 00000000 00159BD0   0012532C 00000000 0015CC38 0015CC68   *................................*   108EF0
000020   0014F122 0014EE10 0014E7F4 00000000   00000000 0015C500 00000000 00000000   *..1.......X4...........E.........*   108F10
000040   00000000 00000000 00000000 00000000   00149C98 00000000 00000000 00000000   *................................*   108F30
000060   00000000 01F4D5D6 00000C00 000CFF00   00154D90 00000000 00000000 001070F0   *......4NO...........(............0*   108F50
000080   00109A28 00154B70 00153760 00150660   00000000 00000000 00000000 00000000   *..............-....-............*   108F70
0000A0   0010ADF0 00117F70 0010C260 0010BC60   0010E120 0011E770 00122FC0 00121820   *...0.......B-....-.......X.........*   108F90
0000C0   00115020 00119510 0015E4F0 0010A020   0015D720 0010D010 00124EC0 001486A0   *..............U0.......P.........+.....*   108FB0
0000E0   001597C0 00154DE0 0015A7D0 00000000   00000000 00000000 0014FCA0 00000000   *......(.........................*   108FD0
000100   00000000 00000000 00000000 00000000   00000000 0010DAF4 001141F0 00000000   *.........................4...0....*   108FF0
000120   00000000 001C000C 000C000C 000C001C   000C000C 000C000C 001C000C 000C000C   *................................*   109010
```

```
CUSTOMER INFORMATION CONTROL SYSTEM STORAGE DUMP   CODE=ASRA   TASK=ORAD      DATE=07/27/80   TIME=18 43 53   PAGE    3

CSA OPTIONAL FEATURE LIST      ADDRESS  108EF0  TO  109077      LENGTH  000188

000140    000C001C 000C000C 000C000C 001C000C    000C000C 000C001C 000C000C 000C000C   *................................*   109030
000160    001C000C 000C000C 000C001C 000C000C    000C000C 001C000C 000C000C 000C001C   *................................*   109050
000180    000C000C 000C000C                                                            *........                        *   109070

TRACE TABLE                    ADDRESS  1457F0  TO  14646F      LENGTH  000C80

TRACE HDR            00145920   001457F0   00146460   00146490

TRACE TABLE          ID REG14  REQD TASK FIELD A  FIELD B                 TRACE TYPE

145930               E1 132DFE 0004 0007 0012FA2C 0000060E  ........  EIP READNEXT ENTRY
145940               F5 11E9C8 B003 0007 C4E2E7E3 C1C2E240  DSXTABS   FCP GETNEXT
145950               F0 120476 4004 0007 20000000 00173058  ........  KCP WAIT DCI=DISP
145960               F5 120134 0015 0007 00000000 00000000  ........  FCP RESPONSE NORMAL
145970               E1 132DFE 00F4 0007 00000000 0000060E  ........  EIP READNEXT RESPONSE
145980               E1 132DFE 0004 0007 0012FA2C 0000060E  ........  EIP READNEXT ENTRY
145990               F5 11E9C8 B003 0007 C4E2E7E3 C1C2E240  DSXTABS   FCP GETNEXT
1459A0               F0 11B124 4004 0007 80000000 00173058  ........  KCP WAIT DCI=SINGLE
1459B0               F5 120134 0015 0007 00000000 00000000  ........  FCP RESPONSE NORMAL
1459C0               E1 132DFE 00F4 0007 00000000 0000060E  ........  EIP READNEXT RESPONSE
1459D0               E1 132DFE 0004 0007 0012FA2C 0000060E  ........  EIP READNEXT ENTRY
1459E0               F5 11E9C8 B003 0007 C4E2E7E3 C1C2E240  DSXTABS   FCP GETNEXT
1459F0               F0 120476 4004 0007 20000000 00173058  ........  KCP WAIT DCI=DISP
145A00               F5 120134 0015 0007 00000000 00000000  ........  FCP RESPONSE NORMAL
145A10               E1 132DFE 00F4 0007 00000000 0000060E  ........  EIP READNEXT RESPONSE
145A20               E1 132DFE 00C4 0007 0012FA2C 0000060E  ........  EIP READNEXT ENTRY
145A30               F5 11E9C8 B003 0007 C4E2E7E3 C1C2E240  DSXTABS   FCP GETNEXT
145A40               F0 120476 4004 0007 20000000 00173058  ........  KCP WAIT DCI=DISP
145A50               F5 120134 0015 0007 00000000 00000000  ........  FCP RESPONSE NORMAL
145A60               E1 132DFE 00F4 0007 00000000 0000060E  ........  EIP READNEXT RESPONSE
145A70               E1 132DFE 0004 0007 0012FA2C 0000060E  ........  EIP READNEXT ENTRY
145A80               F5 11E9C8 B003 0007 C4E2E7E3 C1C2E240  DSXTABS   FCP GETNEXT
145A90               F0 120476 4004 0007 20000000 00173058  ........  KCP WAIT DCI=DISP
145AA0               F0 10DBB8 4004 TC   44000000 001007F8  .......8  KCP WAIT
145AB0               F5 120134 0015 0007 00000000 00000000  ........  FCP RESPONSE NORMAL
145AC0               E1 132DFE 00F4 0007 00000000 0000060E  ........  EIP READNEXT RESPONSE
145AD0               E1 132DFE 0004 0007 0012FA2C 0000060E  ........  EIP READNEXT ENTRY
145AE0               F5 11E9C8 B003 0007 C4E2E7E3 C1C2E240  DSXTABS   FCP GETNEXT
145AF0               F0 120476 4004 0007 20000000 00173058  ........  KCP WAIT DCI=DISP
145B00               F5 120134 0015 0007 00000000 00000000  ........  FCP RESPONSE NORMAL
145B10               E1 132DFE 00F4 0007 00000000 0000060E  ........  EIP READNEXT RESPONSE
145B20               E1 132DFE 0004 0007 0012FA2C 0000060E  ........  EIP READNEXT ENTRY
145B30               F5 11E9C8 B003 0007 C4E2E7E3 C1C2E240  DSXTABS   FCP GETNEXT
145B40               F0 120476 4004 0007 20000000 00173058  ........  KCP WAIT DCI=DISP
145B50               F5 120134 0015 0007 00000000 00000000  ........  FCP RESPONSE NORMAL
145B60               E1 132DFE 00F4 0007 00000000 0000060E  ........  EIP READNEXT RESPONSE
145B70               E1 132DFE 0004 0007 0012FA2C 0000060E  ........  EIP READNEXT ENTRY
145B80               F5 11E9C8 B003 0007 C4E2E7E3 C1C2E240  DSXTABS   FCP GETNEXT
145B90               F0 120476 4004 0007 20000000 00173058  ........  KCP WAIT DCI=DISP
145BA0               F5 120134 0015 0007 00000000 00000000  ........  FCP RESPONSE NORMAL
```

Fig. 24.5. (Continued)

```
CUSTOMER INFORMATION CONTROL SYSTEM STORAGE DUMP   CODE=ASRA   TASK=ORAD      DATE=07/27/80   TIME=18 43 53   PAGE    4

TRACE TABLE         ID REG14  REQD TASK FIELD A  FIELD B                      TRACE TYPE

145BB0              E1 132DFE 00F4 0007 00000000 0000060E  ........  EIP READNEXT RESPONSE
145BC0              E1 132DFE 0004 0007 0012FA2C 0000060E  ........  EIP READNEXT ENTRY
145BD0              F5 11E9C8 B003 0007 C4E2E7E3 C1C2E240  DSXTABS   FCP GETNEXT
145BE0              F0 120476 4004 0007 20000000 00173058  ........  KCP WAIT DCI=DISP
145BF0              F5 120134 0015 0007 00000000 00000000  ........  FCP RESPONSE NORMAL
145C00              E1 132DFE 00F4 0007 00000000 0000060E  ........  EIP READNEXT RESPONSE
145C10              E1 132DFE 0004 0007 0012FA2C 0000060E  ........  EIP READNEXT ENTRY
145C20              F5 11E9C8 B003 0007 C4E2E7E3 C1C2E240  DSXTABS   FCP GETNEXT
145C30              F0 120476 4004 0007 20000000 00173058  ........  KCP WAIT DCI=DISP
145C40              F5 120134 0015 0007 00000000 00000000  ........  FCP RESPONSE NORMAL
145C50              E1 132DFE 00F4 0007 00000000 0000060E  ........  EIP READNEXT RESPONSE
145C60              FD 00001C 0204 0007 E3C9D4C5 1842534F  TIME....  TIMING TRACE 18/42/53.4
145C70              E1 132F14 0004 0007 0012FA2C 00000A02  ........  EIP WRITEQ-TS ENTRY
145C80              F1 12187A 8E04 0007 00120540 01100660  ... ....  SCP GETMAIN
145C90              C8 115222 0004 0007 0012C7B0 8E120548  ..G.....  SCP ACQUIRED TEMPSTRG STORAGE
145CA0              F7 1218C6 4103 0007 D3F7F7F0 D6D9C1C4  L770ORAD  TSP PUTQ
145CB0              F1 12231A F804 0007 00000038 01100660  ........  SCP GETMAIN-COND-INIT
145CC0              C8 115222 0004 0007 0012D000 98000040  .......   SCP ACQUIRED TSTABLE STORAGE
145CD0              F1 121AEA B704 0007 00120554 01100660  ........  SCP GETMAIN-CONDITIONAL
145CE0              C8 115222 0004 0007 0012D040 97120560  ... ....  SCP ACQUIRED TSMAIN STORAGE
145CF0              F7 121FCC 0015 0007 00000000 00000000  ........  TSP RESPONSE
145D00              F1 12183E 4004 0007 0012C7B0 01100660  ..G.....  SCP FREEMAIN
145D10              C9 11530C 0004 0007 0012C7B0 8E120548  ..G.....  SCP RELEASED TEMPSTRG STORAGE
145D20              E1 132F14 00F4 0007 00000000 00000A02  ........  EIP WRITEQ-TS RESPONSE
145D30              E1 132F4C 0004 0007 0012FA2C 00000C04  ........  EIP FREEMAIN ENTRY
145D40              F1 11508A 4004 0007 0012C000 01100660  ........  SCP FREEMAIN
145D50              C9 11530C 0004 0007 0012C000 8C120548  ........  SCP RELEASED USER STORAGE
145D60              E1 132F4C 00F4 0007 00000000 C0000C04  ........  EIP FREEMAIN RESPONSE
145D70              E1 132F9A 0004 0007 0012FA2C 00000C02  ........  EIP GETMAIN ENTRY
145D80              F1 115052 CC04 0007 000003BE 01100660  ........  SCP GETMAIN-INIT
145D90              C8 115222 0004 0007 0012C800 8C0003C8  ..H....H  SCP ACQUIRED USER STORAGE
145DA0              E1 132F9A 00F4 0007 00000000 00000C02  ........  EIP GETMAIN RESPONSE
145DB0              E1 133008 0004 0007 0012FA2C 00001804  ........  EIP SEND-MAP ENTRY
145DC0              FA 124F7E 0003 0007 000005E2 04000020  ...S....  BMS OUT MAP MAPSET SAVE ERASE
145DD0              F2 1261AC 0804 0007 D6D9C1D7 E2F0F140  ORAPS01   PCP DELETE
145DE0              F2 126200 0404 0007 D6D9C1C4 E2F0F140  ORADS01   PCP LOAD
145DF0              F1 118572 8804 0007 00120095 01100660  ........  SCP GETMAIN
145E00              C9 11530C 0004 0007 0013B800 88002800  ........  SCP RELEASED PGM STORAGE
145E10              C9 11530C 0004 0007 00136800 88002800  ........  SCP RELEASED PGM STORAGE
145E20              C9 11530C 0004 0007 0013A000 88001800  ........  SCP RELEASED PGM STORAGE
145E30              C9 11530C 0004 0007 00139000 88001000  ........  SCP RELEASED PGM STORAGE
145E40              C9 11530C 0004 0007 0013F800 88000800  ..8.....  SCP RELEASED PGM STORAGE
145E50              C9 11530C 0004 0007 0013E000 88001000  ........  SCP RELEASED PGM STORAGE
145E60              C9 11530C 0004 0007 00133800 88001000  ........  SCP RELEASED PGM STORAGE
145E70              C9 11530C 0004 0007 00135000 88001800  ........  SCP RELEASED PGM STORAGE
145E80              C9 11530C 0004 0007 00134800 88000800  ........  SCP RELEASED PGM STORAGE
145E90              C8 115222 0004 0007 00130800 88000800  ........  SCP ACQUIRED PGM STORAGE
145EA0              F0 11862A 4004 0007 88000000 0011A746  ........  KCP WAIT DCI=CICS
145EB0              F1 127F3A 9E04 0007 00130850 01100660  ........  SCP GETMAIN
145EC0              C8 115222 0004 0007 0012D800 9E130858  ..Q.....  SCP ACQUIRED MAPCOPY STORAGE
145ED0              F1 124578 CC04 0007 000004E0 01100660  ........  SCP GETMAIN-INIT
```

```
CUSTOMER INFORMATION CONTROL SYSTEM STORAGE DUMP   CODE=ASRA   TASK=ORAD        DATE=07/27/80   TIME=18 43 53   PAGE    5

TRACE TABLE         ID REG14  REQD TASK FIELD A  FIELD B                     TRACE TYPE

145EE0              C8 115222 0004 0007 0012E060 8C0004E8  .......Y  SCP ACQUIRED USER STORAGE
145EF0              F1 124846 8504 0007 001205D3 01100660  ...L....  SCP GETMAIN
145F00              C8 115222 0004 0007 00129170 851205E8  .......Y  SCP ACQUIRED TERMINAL STORAGE
145F10              F1 124A00 4004 0007 0012E060 01100660  ........  SCP FREEMAIN
145F20              C9 11530C 0004 0007 0012E060 8C0004E8  .......Y  SCP RELEASED USER STORAGE
145F30              F1 124A00 4004 0007 0012D800 01100660  ..Q.....  SCP FREEMAIN
145F40              C9 11530C 0004 0007 0012D800 9E130858  ..Q.....  SCP RELEASED MAPCOPY STORAGE
145F50              FC 126CA8 0103 0007 00810000 00100660  ........  ZCP ZARQ APPL REQ ERASE WRITE
145F60              FA 125EE6 0005 0007 00000000 00000000  ........  BMS RESPONSE
145F70              E1 133008 00F4 0007 00000000 00001804  ........  EIP SEND-MAP RESPONSE
145F80              E1 133056 0004 0007 0012FA2C 00000E08  ........  EIP RETURN ENTRY
145F90              F1 11970C 9304 0007 00120019 01100660  ........  SCP GETMAIN
145FA0              C8 115222 0004 0007 0012D5A0 93120020  ..N.....  SCP ACQUIRED SHARED STORAGE
145FB0              F2 119760 1004 0007 D6D9C1C4 F0F1C140  ORAD01A   PCP RETURN
145FC0              F1 118A4A 4004 0007 0012F9E0 01100660  ..9.....  SCP FREEMAIN
145FD0              C9 11530C 0004 0007 0012F9E0 8C1303C8  ..9....H  SCP RELEASED USER STORAGE
145FE0              F1 118B66 4004 0007 00131000 01100660  ........  SCP FREEMAIN
145FF0              C9 11530C 0004 0007 00131000 88002800  ........  SCP RELEASED PGM STORAGE
146000              F1 118B66 4004 0007 00130800 01100660  ........  SCP FREEMAIN
146010              C9 11530C 0004 0007 00130800 88000800  ........  SCP RELEASED PGM STORAGE
146020              F0 118992 8004 0007 00000000 00000000  ........  KCP DETACH
146030              D8 10AC20 0203 0007 02000000 0012C620  ......F.  SPP SYSTEM
146040              F5 10D7F0 0003 0007 0012C620 00000000  ..F.....  FCP DWE PROCESSOR
146050              F1 120D70 4004 0007 0012C620 01100660  ..F.....  SCP FREEMAIN
146060              C9 11530C 0004 0007 0012C620 9D120038  ..F.....  SCP RELEASED DWE STORAGE
146070              F1 120D70 4004 0007 0012C660 01100660  ..F.....  SCP FREEMAIN
146080              C9 11530C 0004 0007 0012C660 8F1200C8  ..F....H  SCP RELEASED FILE STORAGE
146090              F5 120134 0015 0007 00000000 00000000  ........  FCP RESPONSE NORMAL
1460A0              D8 10D95C 0015 0007 00000000 00000000  ........  SPP RESPONSE
1460B0              F0 10AC2A 0304 0007 0011A746 00000000  ........  KCP DEQALL
1460C0              F1 10ADA0 4A04 KC   0012E800 00000000  ..Y.....  SCP FREEMAIN
1460D0              C9 11530C 0004 KC   0012C800 8C0003C8  ..H....H  SCP RELEASED USER STORAGE
1460E0              C9 11530C 0004 KC   0012C730 8F120078  ..G.....  SCP RELEASED FILE STORAGE
1460F0              C9 11530C 0004 KC   0012C5A0 8C000078  ..E.....  SCP RELEASED USER STORAGE
146100              C9 11530C 0004 KC   0012C550 8C000048  ..E.....  SCP RELEASED USER STORAGE
146110              C9 11530C 0004 KC   0012FF40 8C000048  ... ....  SCP RELEASED USER STORAGE
146120              C9 11530C 0004 KC   0012FEF0 8C000048  ...0....  SCP RELEASED USER STORAGE
146130              C9 11530C 0004 KC   0012FE70 8C000078  ........  SCP RELEASED USER STORAGE
146140              C9 11530C 0004 KC   0012FE20 8C000048  ........  SCP RELEASED USER STORAGE
146150              C9 11530C 0004 KC   0012FDB0 8C000068  ........  SCP RELEASED USER STORAGE
146160              C9 11530C 0004 KC   0012F9C0 8C120018  ..9.....  SCP RELEASED USER STORAGE
146170              C9 11530C 0004 KC   0012F930 8C000088  ..9.....  SCP RELEASED USER STORAGE
146180              C9 11530C 0004 KC   0012F6A0 8C000288  ..6.....  SCP RELEASED USER STORAGE
146190              C9 11530C 0004 KC   0012F290 8C000408  ..2.....  SCP RELEASED USER STORAGE
1461A0              C9 11530C 0004 KC   0012E800 8A030598  ..Y.....  SCP RELEASED TCA STORAGE
1461B0              F0 10DBB8 4004 TC   44000000 001007F8  .......8  KCP WAIT
1461C0              F1 10EA54 4004 TC   00129170 80100660  ........  SCP FREEMAIN
1461D0              C9 11530C 0004 TC   00129170 851205E8  .......Y  SCP RELEASED TERMINAL STORAGE
1461E0              F1 10EAF8 6004 TC   00000000 80100660  ........  SCP FREEMAIN ALL
1461F0              C9 11530C 00C4 TC   00129120 85000048  ........  SCP RELEASED TERMINAL STORAGE
146200              F1 10E9F0 E404 TC   0000010F 80100660  ........  SCP GETMAIN-COND-INIT
```

Fig. 24.5. (Continued)

```
CUSTOMER INFORMATION CONTROL SYSTEM STORAGE DUMP   CODE=ASRA   TASK=ORAD        DATE=07/27/80   TIME=18 43 53   PAGE    6

TRACE TABLE       ID REG14  REQD TASK FIELD A  FIELD B                TRACE TYPE

146210            C8 115222 0004 TC   00129000 84000118 ........ SCP ACQUIRED LINE STORAGE
146220            F0 10DBB8 4004 TC   44000000 001007F8 .......8 KCP WAIT
146230            FD 00002C 0104 TC   0066CDE0 0066E548 ......V. ... REPEAT 00002 TIMES
146240            F0 113464 1104 TC   01100660 D6D9C1C4 ....ORAD KCP ATTACH-CONDITIONAL
146250            F1 10A91E EAC4 TC   00080780 80100660 ........ SCP GETMAIN-COND-INIT
146260            C8 115222 0004 TC   0012E800 8A0307B8 ..Y..... SCP ACQUIRED TCA STORAGE
146270            F0 10DBB8 4004 TC   44000000 001007F8 .......8 KCP WAIT
146280            F2 118804 0204 0008 D6D9C1C4 F0F1C140 ORAD01A  PCP XCTL
146290            F1 118572 8804 0008 000004F2 01100660 ...2.... SCP GETMAIN
1462A0            C8 115222 0004 0008 0013C800 88002800 ..H..... SCP ACQUIRED PGM STORAGE
1462B0            F0 11862A 4004 0008 88000000 0011A702 ........ KCP WAIT DCI=CICS
1462C0            F1 1190FC 8C04 0008 001303BC 01100660 ........ SCP GETMAIN
1462D0            C8 115222 0004 0008 0012EFC0 8C1303C8 .......H SCP ACQUIRED USER STORAGE
1462E0            F1 10C2A6 CC04 0008 00000128 01100660 ........ SCP GETMAIN-INIT
1462F0            C8 115222 0004 0008 0012F390 8C000138 ..3..... SCP ACQUIRED USER STORAGE
146300            E1 13D192 0004 0008 0012F00C 00000202 ..0..... EIP ADDRESS ENTRY
146310            E1 13D192 00F4 0008 00000000 00000202 ........ EIP ADDRESS RESPONSE
146320            E1 13D1B8 0004 0008 0012F00C 00000206 ..0..... EIP HANDLE-AID ENTRY
146330            F1 10BC96 CC04 0008 00000059 01100660 ........ SCP GETMAIN-INIT
146340            C8 115222 0004 0008 0012F4D0 8C000068 ..4..... SCP ACQUIRED USER STORAGE
146350            F1 10BD98 CC04 0008 00000040 01100660 ... .... SCP GETMAIN-INIT
146360            C8 115222 0004 0008 0012F540 8C000048 ..5 .... SCP ACQUIRED USER STORAGE
146370            E1 13D1B8 00F4 0008 00000000 00000206 ........ EIP HANDLE-AID RESPONSE
146380            E1 13D212 0004 0008 0012F00C 00000204 ..0..... EIP HANDLE-CONDITION ENTRY
146390            F1 10BC96 CC04 0008 00000070 01100660 ........ SCP GETMAIN-INIT
1463A0            C8 115222 0004 0008 0012F590 8C000078 ..5..... SCP ACQUIRED USER STORAGE
1463B0            F1 10BD98 CC04 0008 00000040 01100660 ... .... SCP GETMAIN-INIT
1463C0            C8 115222 0004 0008 0012F610 8C000048 ..6..... SCP ACQUIRED USER STORAGE
1463D0            E1 13D212 00F4 0008 00000000 00000204 ........ EIP HANDLE-CONDITION RESPONSE
1463E0            E1 13D2F4 0004 0008 0012F00C 00001802 ..0..... EIP RECEIVE-MAP ENTRY
1463F0            FA 125080 0003 0008 00000505 00000020 ........ BMS MAP MAPSET MAP IN
146400            F1 12537E CC04 0008 00000274 01100660 ........ SCP GETMAIN-INIT
146410            C8 115222 0004 0008 0012F660 8C000288 ..6..... SCP ACQUIRED USER STORAGE
146420            F1 15AD78 CC04 0008 00000074 01100660 ........ SCP GETMAIN-INIT
146430            C8 115222 0004 0008 0012F8F0 8C000088 ..80.... SCP ACQUIRED USER STORAGE
146440            F2 126200 0404 0008 D6D9C1C4 E2F0F140 ORADS01  PCP LOAD
146450            F1 118572 8804 0008 00120095 01100660 ........ SCP GETMAIN
146460            FD 00001C 0204 0008 E3C9D4C5 1843539F TIME.... TIMING TRACE 18/43/53.9


1457F0            C8 115222 0004 0008 0013F800 88000800 ..8..... SCP ACQUIRED PGM STORAGE
145800            F0 11862A 4004 0008 88000000 0011A746 ........ KCP WAIT DCI=CICS
145810            F0 10DBB8 4004 TC   44000000 001007F8 .......8 KCP WAIT
145820            F1 124AAC C504 0008 000003B1 01100660 ........ SCP GETMAIN-INIT
145830            C8 115222 0004 0008 00129120 850003C8 .......H SCP ACQUIRED TERMINAL STORAGE
145840            F1 124E88 4004 0008 00129000 01100660 ........ SCP FREEMAIN
145850            C9 11530C 0004 0008 00129000 85000118 ........ SCP RELEASED TERMINAL STORAGE
145860            FA 125EE6 0005 0008 00000000 00000000 ........ BMS RESPONSE
145870            E1 13D2F4 00F4 0008 00000000 00001802 ........ EIP RECEIVE-MAP RESPONSE
145880            E1 13D364 0004 0008 0012F00C 00000A04 ..0..... EIP READQ-TS ENTRY
145890            F7 12192C 8903 0008 D3F7F7F0 D6D9C1C4 L770ORAD TSP GETQ
```

Fig. 24.5. (Continued)

```
CUSTOMER INFORMATION CONTROL SYSTEM STORAGE DUMP    CODE=ASRA    TASK=ORAD        DATE=07/27/80    TIME=18 43 53    PAGE     7

1458A0              F1 121C38 AE04 0008 00120540 01100660  ... ....  SCP GETMAIN-CONDITIONAL
1458B0              C8 115222 0004 0008 0012F980 8E120548  ..9.....  SCP ACQUIRED TEMPSTRG STORAGE
1458C0              F7 121FCC 0015 0008 00000000 00000000  ........  TSP RESPONSE
1458D0              E1 13D364 00F4 0008 00000000 00000A04  ........  EIP READQ-TS RESPONSE
1458E0              F2 14F3C8 6004 0008 C1E2D9C1 00000000  ASRA....  PCP ABEND
1458F0              F4 11812A FE04 0008 00000000 C1E2D9C1  ....ASRA  DCP TRANSACTION
145900              F0 155C58 4004 0008 80000000 00155E78  ........  KCP WAIT DCI=SINGLE
145910              F0 10DBB8 4004 TC   44000000 001007F8  .......8  KCP WAIT
145920              F0 155C58 4004 0008 80000000 00155E78  ........  KCP WAIT DCI=SINGLE
                                         (B)
TRANSACTION STORAGE-TS          ADDRESS | 12F980   TO   12FECF       LENGTH  000550
                                        v
000000   8E120548 0012F8F0 05400000 F0F0F0F0   F0F0F0F5 F0F0F0F0 F3F8F1F1 F0F1F5F0   *......80. ..000000050000038110150*   12F980
000020   F7F2F7F8 F0000000 00000000 00000000   00000000 00000000 00000000 00000000   *72780............................*   12F9A0
000040   00000000 00000000 00000000 00000000   00000000 00000000 00000000 00000000   *................................*   12F9C0
000060   LINES TO 000180 SAME AS ABOVE                                                                                      12F9E0
0001A0   00000000 00000000 00000000 00000000   00000000 00000000 00000000 00D7C1D3   *.............................PAL*   12FB20
0001C0   000000BE F0F0F3F0 F0F4F0F0 F5F0F0F7   F0F0F8F0 F0F9F0F1 F0F0F1F2 F0F1F3F0   *....003004005007008009010012013O*   12FB40
0001E0   F1F4F0F1 F5F0F1F6 F0F1F7F0 F1F8F0F1   F9F0F2F0 F0F2F2F0 F2F3F0F2 F4F0F2F5   *1401501601701801902002202302402 5*   12FB60
000200   F0F2F6F0 F2F7F0F2 F8F0F2F9 F0F3F0F0   F3F2F0F3 F3F0F3F4 F0F3F5F0 F3F6F0F3   *0260270280290300320330340350360 3*   12FB80
000220   F7F0F3F8 F0F3F9F0 F4F0F0F4 F1F0F4F2   F0F4F3F0 F4F4F0F4 F5F0F4F6 F0F4F7F0   *7038039040041042043044045046047 0*   12FBA0
000240   F4F8F0F4 F9F0F5F0 F0F5F1F0 F5F2F0F5   F4F0F5F5 F0F5F6F0 F5F7F0F5 F8F0F5F9   *480490500510520540550560570580 59*   12FBC0
000260   F0F6F0F0 F6F1F0F6 F2F0F6F3 F0F6F4F0   F6F5F0F6 F7F0F6F8 F0F6F9F0 F7F0F0F7   *0600610620630640650670680690700 7*   12FBE0
000280   F1F0F7F2 F0F7F4F0 F7F5F0F7 F6F0F7F7   F0F7F8F0 F7F9F0F8 F0F0F8F1 F0F8F2F0   *1072074075076077078079080081082 0*   12FC00
0002A0   F8F4F0F8 F5F0F8F6 F0F8F7F0 F8F8F0F9   F0F0F9F1 F0F9F2F0 F9F3F0F9 F5F0F9F6   *8408508608708809009109209309509 6*   12FC20
0002C0   F0F9F7F0 F9F8F0F9 F9F1F0F1 F1F0F2F1   F0F3F1F0 F4F1F0F5 F1F0F6F1 F0F7F1F0   *0970980991011021031041051061071 0*   12FC40
0002E0   F8F1F0F9 F1F1F1F1 F1F3F1F1 F4F1F1F5   F1F1F6F1 F1F8F1F2 F1F1F2F2 F1F2F3F1   *8109111113114115116118121122123 1*   12FC60
000300   F2F4F1F2 F5F1F2F6 F1F2F7F1 F2F8F1F3   F0F1F3F1 F1F3F3F1 F3F4F1F3 F5F1F3F6   *2412512612712813013113313413513 6*   12FC80
000320   F1F3F7F1 F3F9F1F4 F0F1F4F2 F1F4F3F1   F4F4F1F4 F5F1F4F6 F1F4F7F1 F4F8F1F4   *1371391401421431441451461471481 4*   12FCA0
000340   F9F1F5F1 F1F5F2F1 F5F4F1F5 F5F1F5F6   F1F5F7F1 F5F9F1F6 F0F1F6F1 F1F6F3F1   *9151152154155156157159160161163 1*   12FCC0
000360   F6F4F1F6 F5F1F6F6 F1F6F7F1 F6F8F1F6   F9F1F7F0 F1F7F1F1 F7F2F1F7 F3F1F7F4   *6416516616716816917017117217317 4*   12FCE0
000380   F1F7F5F1 F7F6F1F7 F7F1F7F8 F1F7F9F1   F8F0F1F8 F1F1F8F2 F1F8F3F1 F8F4F1F8   *1751761771781791801811821831841 8*   12FD00
0003A0   F5F1F8F6 F1F8F7F1 F8F8F1F8 F9F1F9F0   F1F9F1F1 F9F2F1F9 F3F1F9F4 F1F9F5F1   *5186187188189190191192193194195 1*   12FD20
0003C0   F9F7F1F9 F8F1F9F9 F2F0F0F2 F0F3F2F0   F4F2F0F5 F2F0F6F2 F0F7F2F0 F8F2F0F9   *9719819920020320420520620720820 9*   12FD40
0003E0   F2F1F0F2 F1F5F2F1 F9F2F2F6 F2F2F9F2   F3F0F2F3 F4F2F4F1 F2F4F2F2 F4F70000   *21021521922622923023424124224 7..*   12FD60
000400   00000000 00000000 00000000 00000000   00000000 00000000 00000000 00000000   *................................*   12FD80
000420   LINES TO 000520 SAME AS ABOVE                                                                                      12FDA0
000540   00000000 00000000 8E120548 0012F8F0                                         *............80                  *   12FEC0

TRANSACTION STORAGE-USER        ADDRESS  12F8F0   TO   12F97F       LENGTH  000090

000000   8C000088 0012F660 D4D40000 00000001   00010001 00000000 00000000 00000000   *......6-MM......................*   12F8F0
000020   0013F808 00000000 00000000 00000000   00000000 00000000 D6D9C1C4 E2F0F140   *..8.....................ORADS01 *   12F910
000040   00000000 00000000 00000000 18500000   40000001 01015000 00000000 00000780   *............... ................*   12F930
000060   00000000 01100660 00404000 00000000   00000000 00000000 FFFFFFFF 00000000   *.......-.  .....................*   12F950
000080   00000000 00000000 8C000088 0012F660                                         *.............6-                 *   12F970
```

Fig. 24.5. (Continued)

```
CUSTOMER INFORMATION CONTROL SYSTEM STORAGE DUMP   CODE=ASRA   TASK=ORAD       DATE=07/27/80   TIME=18 43 53   PAGE    8

TRANSACTION STORAGE-USER        ADDRESS  12F660  TO  12F8EF      LENGTH  000290

000000   8C000288 0012F610 401256A6 0015A9C8   401258C0 001244CA 00000000 00000000   *......6. ......H ..............*   12F660
000020   00000000 00000000 00000000 00000000   00000000 00000000 00000000 00000000   *................................*   12F680
000040   00000000 00000000 00000505 C0000020   F0F1C140 00000000 D6D9C1C4 D4F0F140   *..............01A ....ORADM01 *   12F6A0
000060   D6D9C1C4 E2F0F140 0000C260 00000000   00000000 00000000 00000000 00000000   *ORADS01 ..B-...................*   12F6C0
000080   00000000 00000000 00000000 00000000   0012F8F0 0012F8F0 00000000 00000000   *..................80..80........*   12F6E0
0000A0   00000000 00000000 00000000 0010066C   00000000 00000000 00000000 00000000   *................................*   12F700
0000C0   00000000 00000000 00000000 00000000   1411A6E4 00000000 00000001 00000000   *................U...........*   12F720
0000E0   00000000 00000000 00000000 00000010   00000000 00000000 00000000 00000000   *................................*   12F740
000100   00000000 00000000 00000000 00000000   00000000 00000000 00000000 00000000   *................................*   12F760
000120   00000000 00000000 00000000 00000000   00000000 00000000 00000000 00000000   *................................*   12F780
000140   00000000 40126200 001252D8 000004B0   08129000 00000018 000000FF 0010066C   *.... ......Q...................*   12F7A0
000160   0013F814 90125884 48000058 0010C700   0012F660 0012F8F0 01100660 00000000   *..8...........G...6-..80...-....*   12F7C0
000180   00000000 00000000 00000000 00110000   00000000 00000000 00000000 00000000   *................................*   12F7E0
0001A0   00000000 00000000 00000000 00000000   00000000 00000000 00000000 00000000   *................................*   12F800
0001C0   LINES TO 000260 SAME AS ABOVE                                                                                   12F820
000280   00000000 00000000 8C000288 0012F610                                         *..............6.               *   12F8E0


TRANSACTION STORAGE-USER        ADDRESS  12F610  TO  12F65F      LENGTH  000050

000000   8C000048 0012F590 5013D212 0010C5A0   0012F00C 0012F360 5013D1CA 0013CCA8   *......5...K...E...0...3-..J.....*   12F610
000020   0012F420 5013EB00 0012F00C 0012F2E3   0012F2E4 0013EAD0 0013C820 0013C820   *..4.......0...2T..2U......H...H.*   12F630
000040   0013CC98 0012F0EC 8C000048 0012F590                                         *......0.......5.               *   12F650


TRANSACTION STORAGE-USER        ADDRESS  12F590  TO  12F60F      LENGTH  000080

000000   8C000078 0012F540 C012F5D7 00700302   00000000 00000000 00000000 00000000   *......5 ..5P.....................*   12F590
000020   00000000 00000000 00000000 00000000   00000100 00000000 00000000 00000000   *................................*   12F5B0
000040   00000000 00000000 00000000 00000001   12F61004 12F0EC02 12F61004 12F0EC00   *................6...0...6...0..*   12F5D0
000060   00000000 00000000 00000000 00000000   00000000 000000FF 8C000078 0012F540   *..............................5 *   12F5F0


TRANSACTION STORAGE-USER        ADDRESS  12F540  TO  12F58F      LENGTH  000050

000000   8C000048 0012F4D0 5013D1B8 0010C5A0   0012F00C 0012F360 0013EB40 00118BA0   *......4...J...E...0...3-... ....*   12F540
000020   0012F420 5013EB00 0012F00C 0012F2E3   0012F2E4 0013EAD0 0013C820 0013C820   *..4.......0...2T..2U......H...H.*   12F560
000040   0013CC98 0012F0EC 8C000048 0012F4D0                                         *......0.......4.               *   12F580


TRANSACTION STORAGE-USER        ADDRESS  12F4D0  TO  12F53F      LENGTH  000070

000000   8C000068 0012F390 0012F500 C0590500   00040201 03000000 00000000 00000000   *......3...5.....................*   12F4D0
000020   00000000 00000000 00000000 00000000   00000000 00000000 0112F540 0412F0EC   *..........................5 ..0.*   12F4F0
000040   0212F540 0412F0EC 0312F540 0412F0EC   0412F540 0412F0EC 00000000 00000000   *..5 ..0...5 ..0...5 ..0.........*   12F510
000060   FF000000 00000000 8C000068 0012F390                                         *..............3.               *   12F530
```

Fig. 24.5. (Continued)

```
CUSTOMER INFORMATION CONTROL SYSTEM STORAGE DUMP   CODE=ASRA   TASK=ORAD      DATE=07/27/80   TIME=18 43 53   PAGE    9

TRANSACTION STORAGE-USER        ADDRESS  12F390  TO  12F4CF      LENGTH  000140

000000   8C000138 0012EFC0 0012F488 00000000   00000000 00000000 00000000 00000000   *..........4.....................*   12F390
000020   00000000 00000000 00000000 00000000   00000000 00000000 00000000 00000000   *................................*   12F3B0
000040   0012F420 8012F424 0012F610 00000000   00129120 00000000 0012F980 00000000   *..4...4...6..............9......*   12F3D0
000060   00000000 00000000 00000000 00000000   00000000 0012F590 0012F4D0 00000000   *......................5...4.....*   12F3F0
000080   00000004 00000000 00010000 00000000   0012F488 8012D5B8 0012F0EC 0012F00C   *..................4...N...0...0.*   12F410
0000A0   00000000 00118DEC 0012F0EC 4010C43E   4013C822 00118DEC 0012F420 0013C8F0   *...........O. .D. .H......4...HO*   12F430
0000C0   0012EFD0 0013C868 00118E68 0012E800   0013C820 0010C260 0013D140 FF11A6E4   *.....H........Y...H...B-..J ...U*   12F450
0000E0   0012F390 0012E8B8 80000000 14000000   40C4C6C8 C5C9C240 0184353C 0080209F   *..3...Y......... DFHEIB ........*   12F470
000100   D6D9C1C4 0000008C D3F7F7F0 00000369   00017D0A 04000000 00000000 00000000   *ORAD....L770.......'............*   12F490
000120   00000000 00000000 00000000 00000000   00000000 00000000 8C000138 0012EFC0   *................................*   12F4B0


TRANSACTION STORAGE-USER        ADDRESS  12EFC0  TO  12F38F      LENGTH  0003D0
                                                                                                        (C)
000000   8C1303C8 0012E800 00000000 00000000   0013C920 5013EB18 0013EB40 00118BA0   *...H..Y............I........ ....*   12EFC0
000020   0013DCCC 5013EB00 0013C920 0013CBF7   0013CBF8 0013EAD0 0013C820 0013C820   *............I....7...8.......H...H.*   12EFE0
000040   0013CC98 0013CA00 C01190C6 00000000   00000000 D3C9D5C5 40F14060 40000000   *...........F........LINE 1 -....*   12F000
000060   00000000 00000000 00000000 00000000   D1D6C240 D5D6D9D4 C1D3D3E8 40E3C5D9   *................JOB NORMALLY TER*   12F020
000080   D4C9D5C1 E3C5C4D1 D6C240C1 C2D6D9E3   C5C44060 60400000 00000000 00000000   *MINATEDJOB ABORTED -- ..........*   12F040
0000A0   00000000 00000000 D6D3C440 C5C9C200   00000000 00000000 00000000 0A04E800   *.........OLD EIB..............Y.*   12F060
0000C0   04010089 00404040 40404040 40404040   40404040 4040D6D9 C1C4D4F0 F140D6D9   *.....                ORADM01 OR*   12F080
0000E0   C1C4E2F0 F1400000 00000000 00000000   00000000 00000000 00000000 00000000   *ADS01 ..........................*   12F0A0
000100   00000000 00000100 00000000 00000000   00000000 00000000 00000000 00000000   *................................*   12F0C0
000120   00000C00 00400000 00000000 00000000   0012F430 00000000 5013D364 0010C5A0   *..... ............4.......L...E.*   12F0E0
000140   0012F00C 0012F360 0013D264 00000001   0012F420 5013E800 0012F00C 0012F2E3   *..0...3-..K........4........0...2T*   12F100
000160   0012F2E4 0013EAD0 0013C820 0013C820   0013CC98 2010004B 00000000 00000000   *..2U.......H...H................*   12F120
000180   0010C3D4 00000000 00000000 FFF0F0F3   00000000 00000002 00000001 00000003   *..CM..........003...............*   12F140
0001A0   01000000 00000000 00000000 00000000   00000000 00000000 00000000 00000000   *................................*   12F160
0001C0   00000000 00000000 00000000 00000000   00000000 00000000 00000000 00000000   *................................*   12F180
0001E0   LINES TO 0002A0 SAME AS ABOVE                                                                                         12F1A0
0002C0   00000000 00000000 00000000 00000000   00000000 D6D9C1C4 F0F1C140 0013C820   *....................ORADO1A ..H.*   12F280
0002E0   00000000 00000000 00000000 00000000   00000000 00000000 00000000 00000000   *................................*   12F2A0
000300   00000000 00000000 00000000 00000000   00000000 00000000 00000000 00000000   *................................*   12F2C0
000320   0012F00C 00000000 0200000C 00000000   0200000F 00000000 0000001C 0012FB44   *..0.............................*   12F2E0
000340   000000BE 0013D478 01000003 00000000   0012F488 8012D5B8 0012F318 00129120   *......M............4...N...3......*   12F300
000360   00000000 0012E9B8 0012F98C 00000000   00000000 00000000 00000000 00000000   *......Z...9.....................*   12F320
000380   00000000 FFFFFFE1 00000000 00000000   00000000 00129157 0013DCCC 0013D62A   *..............................O.*   12F340
0003A0   0012F07C 0012EA48 0012F328 0012EA5D   0012F0E5 8012F0C5 00000000 00000000   *..0........3.....)..OV..OE.........*   12F360
0003C0   00000000 00000000 8C1303C8 0012E800                                         *............H..Y.               *   12F380


TERMINAL CONTROL TBL USER AREA ADDRESS  1007E8  TO  1007F7      LENGTH  000010

000000   00000000 00000000 00000000 00000000                                         *................                *   1007E8
```

Fig. 24.5. (Continued)

```
CUSTOMER INFORMATION CONTROL SYSTEM STORAGE DUMP    CODE=ASRA    TASK=ORAD         DATE=07/27/80    TIME=18 43 53    PAGE    10

TERMINAL CONTROL TABLE          ADDRESS  100660  TO  100723        LENGTH  0000C4

000000   D3F7F7F0 99F20404 00129120 00129120   0012E8B8 00000000 001007E8 10000000   *L770.2.............Y.........Y.....*   100660
000020   00000000 0C000000 00000100 00000900   03697D00 D6D9C1C4 E2F0F140 00000000   *..................'.ORADS01 ....*   100680
000040   00000000 00000000 07801850 00000000   00000000 00C40000 00000000 001005A8   *.....................D..........*   1006A0
000060   0010070E 00000000 0012D5A0 00000000   00000000 00000000 00840000 0000005C   *..........N....................**   1006C0
000080   00008C00 0C00005C 000C8100 00400000   40000000 00000000 00000000 00000000   *.......*..... .. ..............*   1006E0
0000A0   00000000 00000000 00000000 00001600   00000100 18500000 82000000 D4D40000   *...........................MM..*   100700
0000C0   00000000                                                                     *....                           *   100720

                                            (D)
TERMINAL STORAGE                ADDRESS  129120  TO  1294EF        LENGTH  0003D0

000000   850003C8 00100664 03AA0000 000100F1   000300F0 F0F0F0F0 F0F0F5F0 F0000400   *...H...........1...0000000500...*   129120
000020   F0F0F0F0 F2F3F5F6 000100F0 F0F30006   00F1F0F1 F5F8F100 0400F0F0 F0F0F8F5   *00002356...003...101581...000085*   129140
000040   F7F30009 00C3C8C1 C9D540E2 C1E64040   40404040 40404040 000200F0 F0F0F2F0   *73...CHAIN SAW           ...00020*   129160
000060   000500F0 F0F1F0F0 F0F00006 00F0F0F2   F0F0F0F0 F0000500 F0F0F2F0 F0F0F000   *...0010000...00200000...0020000.*   129180
000080   0600F0F0 F4F0F0F0 F0F00000 00000000   00000000 00000000 00000000 00000000   *..00400000......................*   1291A0
0000A0   00000000 00000000 00000000 00000000   00000000 00000000 00000000 00000000   *................................*   1291C0
0000C0   LINES TO 000300 SAME AS ABOVE                                                                                        1291E0
000320   00000006 00F0F0F0 F2F0F0F0 F0F00006   00F0F0F0 F4F0F0F0 F0F00000 00404040   *.....000200000...000400000...   *   129440
000340   40404040 40404040 40404040 40404040   40404040 40404040 40000000 40404040   *                           ...  *   129460
000360   40404040 40404040 40404040 40404040   40404040 40404040 00000040 40404040   *                          ...   *   129480
000380   40404040 40404040 40404040 40404040   40404040 40404000 00004040 40404040   *                         ...    *   1294A0
0003A0   40404040 40404040 40404040 40404040   40404040 40400000 00000000 00000000   *                      ..........*   1294C0
0003C0   00000000 00000000 850003C8 00100664                                         *...........H....                *   1294E0

                                                                          (E)
PROGRAM STORAGE                 ADDRESS  13C808  TO  13EF8F        LENGTH  002788

000000   C4C6C8C5 58F0F00C 07FF58F0 F00A07FF   001191B6 0010C760 05F00700 900EF00A   *DFHE.00....00..........G-.0....0.*   13C808
000020   47F0F082 00118DEC 0012F420 0013C8F0   0012EFD0 0013C868 00118E68 0012E800   *.00.......4...H0.......H.......Y.*   13C828
000040   0013C820 0010C260 0013D140 FF11A6E4   0012F390 0012E8B8 0012F430 4010C43E   *..H...B-..J ...U..3...Y...4. .D.*   13C848
000060   0013C920 5013EB18 0013EB40 00118BA0   0013DCCC 5013EB00 0013C920 0013CBF7   *..I........ ..............I....7*   13C868
000080   0013CBF8 0013EAD0 0013C820 0013C820   0013CC98 0013CA00 001190C6 58C0F0C6   *...8.......H...H............F..0F*   13C888
0000A0   58E0C000 58D0F0CA 9500E000 4770F0A2   9610D048 92FFE000 47F0F0AC 98CEF03A   *.......0........0..........00...0.*   13C8A8
0000C0   90ECD00C 185D989F F0BA9110 D0480719   07FF0700 0013EAD0 0013C820 0013C820   *.....)..0..................H...H.*   13C8C8
0000E0   0013CC98 0012F0EC 0013D140 0013EAB6   C3D6C2C6 F2F5F5F1 D6D9C1C4 F0F1C140   *......0...J ....COBF2551ORAD01A *   13C8E8
000100   0013CC24 F0F761F2 F761F8F0 F1F84BF3   F84BF4F5 00000000 00000000 00000000   *....07/27/8018.38.45............*   13C908
000120   D3C9D5C5 40004060 40000000 00000000   00000000 00000000 00000000 D1D6C240   *LINE . - ......................JOB *   13C928
000140   D5D6D9D4 C1D3D3E8 40E3C5D9 D4C9D5C1   E3C5C4D1 D6C240C1 C2D6D9E3 C5C44060   *NORMALLY TERMINATEDJOB ABORTED -*   13C948
000160   60400000 00000000 00000000 00000000   00000000 D6D3C440 C5C9C200 00000000   *- ..................OLD EIB.....*   13C968
000180   00000000 00000000 00000000 00000000   00000000 00000000 00000000 00000000   *................................*   13C988
0001A0   LINES TO 0001C0 SAME AS ABOVE                                                                                        13C9A8
0001E0   00000000 00000000 00000000 00000C00   00400000 00000000 00000000 00118DEC   *................ ...............*   13C9E8
000200   00000000 00000000 00000000 00000000   00000000 00000000 00000000 00000000   *................................*   13CA08
000220   00000000 00000000 00000000 00000000   00000000 00000000 00000000 00000000   *................................*   13CA28
000240   2010004B 00000000 00000000 001190C6   00000000 00000000 00000000 00000000   *...............F................*   13CA48
000260   00000000 00000000 00000000 00000000   00000000 00000000 00000000 00000000   *................................*   13CA68
000280   LINES TO 000380 SAME AS ABOVE                                                                                        13CA88
0003A0   D6D9C1C4 F0F1C140 0013C820 00000000   00000000 00000000 00000000 00000000   *ORAD01A ..H.....................*   13CBA8
0003C0   00000000 00000000 00000000 00000000   00000000 00000000 00000000 00000000   *................................*   13CBC8
0003E0   00000000 00000000 00000000 0013C920   00000000 00000000 00000000 00000000   *...............I................*   13CBE8
```

Fig. 24.5. (Continued)

```
CUSTOMER INFORMATION CONTROL SYSTEM STORAGE DUMP   CODE=ASRA   TASK=ORAD        DATE=07/27/80   TIME=18 43 53   PAGE   11

PROGRAM STORAGE                  ADDRESS  13C808  TO  13EF8F      LENGTH  002788

000400   00000000 00000000 00000000 00000000   00000000 00000000 00000000 00000000   *................................*   13CC08
000420   LINES TO 000440 SAME AS ABOVE                                                                                      13CC28
000460   00000000 00000000 0013DCCC 00000000   00000000 00000000 00000000 00000000   *................................*   13CC68
000480   00000000 00000000 00000000 00000000   0013EB40 0013C812 0013EE90 0013EB98   *................. ..H..........*   13CC88
0004A0   0013C820 0013D296 0013D4E4 0013D536   0013D5EC 0013D600 0013D66C 0013DCC6   *..H...K...MU..N...N...O...O....F*   13CCA8
0004C0   0013DCCC 0013DEC0 0013DED4 0013E20A   0013E256 0013E2E0 0013E300 0013E402   *...........M..S...S...S...T...U.*   13CCC8
0004E0   0013E498 0013E596 0013E65E 0013E856   0013E86A 0013E950 0013E976 0013E9AA   *..U...V...W ..Y...Y...Z...Z...Z.*   13CCE8
000500   0013E9C0 0013E9D6 0013E9E2 0013E9EE   0013EA48 0013EA58 0013EA88 0013EAA6   *..Z...ZO..ZS..Z.................*   13CD08
000520   0013EAAE 0013D27E 0013D264 0013D278   0013D3C0 0013D406 0013D420 0013D472   *.......K=..K...K...L...M...M...M.*   13CD28
000540   0013D4DE 0013D478 0013D47E 0013D59A   0013D62A 0013D65E 0013D74C 0013D6E8   *..M...M...M=..N...O...O ..P...OY*   13CD48
000560   0013D738 0013D76E 0013D7FC 0013D7E6   0013D7CC 0013D7E0 0013D88C 0013D844   *..P...P...P...PW..P...P...Q...Q.*   13CD68
000580   0013D8A8 0013D97C 0013D904 0013D968   0013DA48 0013D9DA 0013DA34 0013DB02   *..Q...R...R...R.........R.......*   13CD88
0005A0   0013DA90 0013DAEE 0013DBCE 0013DB60   0013DBBA 0013DBEE 0013DC34 0013DC2E   *..............-.................*   13CDA8
0005C0   0013DCBA 0013DC4C 0013DCA6 0013DCE0   0013DD6C 0013DD58 0013DDAA 0013DE16   *................................*   13CDC8
0005E0   0013DE02 0013DE54 0013DEAC 0013DF38   0013DF22 0013DF48 0013E658 0013E61E   *..........................W...W.*   13CDE8
000600   0013E672 0013DCCC 00000100 FFE1FFFF   00030000 00630000 00000001 00020004   *..W.............................*   13CE08
000620   00000C00 00080000 000C0010 00200040   007D007F 000901B1 002C0025 03BE053C   *.............. .'..............*   13CE28
000640   FFFD0000 001F0202 80000403 00000000   00000000 00000000 0206F000 04050406   *..........................O.....*   13CE48
000660   03000000 0C000000 00000204 C0000424   01000000 00000000 00000000 D6D9C1C4   *............................ORAD*   13CE68
000680   D4F0F1D6 D9C1C4E2 F0F11802 D0000401   00000005 09000000 200A04E8 00040100   *M01ORADS01..................Y....*   13CE88
0006A0   8900C9D5 E5C1D3C9 C440D6D9 C4C5D940   D5E4D4C2 C5D9C9D5 E5C1D3C9 C440C4D6   *..INVALID ORDER NUMBERINVALID DO*   13CEA8
0006C0   C3E4D4C5 D5E340D5 E4D4C2C5 D9C9D5E5   C1D3C9C4 40C4C5D7 C1D9E3D4 C5D5E340   *CUMENT NUMBERINVALID DEPARTMENT *   13CEC8
0006E0   D5E4D4C2 C5D9F0F0 F1F3F2C9 D5E5C1D3   C9C44006 D9C4C5D9 60C4C1E3 C5C9D5E5   *NUMBER00132INVALID ORDER-DATEINV*   13CEE8
000700   C1D3C9C4 40C9E3C5 D440D5E4 D4C2C5D9   C9D5E5C1 D3C9C440 C4C5E2C3 D9C9D7E3   *ALID ITEM NUMBERINVALID DESCRIPT*   13CF08
000720   C9D6D5C9 D5E5C1D3 C9C440E4 D5C9E340   C3D6E2E3 C9D5E5C1 D3C9C440 C3D6E2E3   *IONINVALID UNIT COSTINVALID COST*   13CF28
000740   C9D5E5C1 D3C9C440 E4D5C9E3 40D7D9C9   C3C5C9D5 E5C1D3C9 C440D7D9 C9C3C5C9   *INVALID UNIT PRICEINVALID PRICEI*   13CF48
000760   D5C3D6D4 D7D3C5E3 C540C4C1 E3C1D5D6   40D3C9D5 C540C9E3 C5D440C5 D5E3C5D9   *NCOMPLETE DATANO LINE ITEM ENTER*   13CF68
000780   C5C4C9D5 C3D6D9D9 C5C3E340 E3D6E3C1   D340C3D6 E2E3C9D5 C3D6D9D9 C5C3E340   *EDINCORRECT TOTAL COSTINCORRECT *   13CF88
0007A0   E3D6E3C1 D340D7D9 C9C3C5C0 02C00004   00008C00 0204C000 04130E00 00000000   *TOTAL PRICE.....................*   13CFA8
0007C0   00000000 0000D6D9 E3C5E2E3 0604F000   04280044 000C0480 00040000 4000D6F1   *......ORTEST..O............ .O1*   13CFC8
0007E0   1402F800 04000000 031804D0 00040000   00000562 04000020 0E08E000 0400001C   *..8.............................*   13CFE8
000800   001804D1 00040000 00001520 04000020   C4E4D7D3 C9C3C1E3 C5406060 40D5D6E3   *...J............DUPLICATE -- NOT*   13D008
000820   40C1C3C3 C5D7E3C5 C40C02E0 00040000   CC00D6D9 C4C5D940 C2E8D7C1 E2E2C5C4   * ACCEPTED.........ORDER BYPASSED*   13D028
000840   406040C3 D6D5E3C9 D5E4C518 04000004   00000000 05E20400 00200204 8000042C   * - CONTINUE..........S..........*   13D048
000860   00000000 00000000 00000000 0A068000   04000021 0C020480 00041400 00000000   *................................*   13D068
000880   00000000 000000C4 E2E7E3C1 C2E2060C   B0000400 20A00006 0ED40004 0100B000   *.......DSXTABS............M......*   13D088
0008A0   F9F9F9F8 F50A02E0 00040000 4100C5D5   E3C5D940 C6C9D9E2 E340D6D9 C4C5D904   *99985.........ENTER FIRST ORDER.*   13D0A8
0008C0   04300004 00000081 00004000 00000E08   00000400 001000E3 C5D3F2D6 D7C5D50E   *.......... ...........TEL2OPEN.*   13D0C8
0008E0   04800004 00000200 D4C1D740 C6C1C9D3   E4D9C5D7 D9D6C3C5 E2E240C5 D9D9D6D9   *.........MAP FAILUREPROCESS ERROR*   13D0E8
000900   E2C9C7D5 D6D540E5 C9D6D3C1 E3C9D6D5   E3C1C2D3 C540D5D6 E340D3D6 C1C4C5C4   *SIGNON VIOLATIONTABLE NOT LOADED*   13D108
000920   C5D9D9E2 1C028000 040000FE 00D4C1D1   D6D940C5 D9D9D6D9 5840D004 58404018   *ERRS.........MAJOR ERROR. ...  .*   13D128
000940   58104000 5010D224 58104004 5010D228   1B1158F0 C00405EF D2116070 C1B69240   *.. ...K... ...K....O....K.-.A.. *   13D148
000960   6082D206 60836082 41106070 5010D274   58E0D22C 4110E00C 5010D278 9680D278   *-.K.-.-...-...K...K........K...K.*   13D168
000980   4110D274 58F0C004 05EFD211 6070C1C8   92406082 D2066083 60824110 60705010   *..K..O.....K.-.AH. -.K.-.-...-...*   13D188
0009A0   D2749680 D2744110 D27458F0 C00405EF   58E0D224 4810E014 4130C010 4910C18E   *K...K...K..O.......K...........A.*   13D1A8
0009C0   05204720 20228B10 000147C0 20224811   20188910 00025811 300007F1 0013000E   *..............................1....*   13D1C8
0009E0   000E000E D2116070 C1DA9240 6082D206   60836082 41106070 5010D274 9680D274   *....K.-.A.. -.K.-.-...-...K...K.*   13D1E8
000A00   4110D274 58F0C004 05EF58E0 D2244810   E0144130 C0104910 C18C0520 4720201E   *..K..O.......K...........A.......*   13D208
000A20   8B100001 47C0201E 48112018 89100002   58113000 07F10017 00184830 E0184930   *..........................1.......*   13D228
000A40   C17858F0 C094078F 5820C098 58E0D228   95F1E000 07725810 C01407F1 5820C09C   *A..O...........K..1..........1....*   13D248
000A60   58E0D228 95F0E000 07725810 C04C07F1   5810C070 07F158E0 D2244830 E0184930   *..K..O..........1.....1..K.......*   13D268
```

Fig. 24.5. (Continued)

```
CUSTOMER INFORMATION CONTROL SYSTEM STORAGE DUMP   CODE=ASRA   TASK=ORAD      DATE=07/27/80   TIME=18 43 53   PAGE   12

PROGRAM STORAGE              ADDRESS 13C808  TO  13EF8F      LENGTH  002788

000A80  C17858F0 C014077F 5810C074 07F1D206   608AC1EC 92406091 D2066092 C1F39240   *A..0..........1K.-.A.. -.K.-.A3. *   13D288
000AA0  6099D20E 6070C1FA 9240607F D2096080   607F4110 60705010 D2744110 608A5010   *-.K.-.A.. -.K.-.-...-...K...-...*   13D2A8
000AC0  D27858E0 D22C4110 E0045010 D27C4110   60D75010 D2804110 60925010 D2849680   *K...K.........K...-P..K...-...K...*   13D2C8
000AE0  D2844110 D27458F0 C00405EF 58E0D238   58F0D224 D203E093 F010D203 E097F008   *K...K..0.......K..OK.K...0.K...0.*   13D2E8
000B00  D20160B9 C179D208 6070C209 92406079   D20F607A 60794110 60705010 D2744110   *K.-.A.K.-.B.. -.K.- -...-...K...*   13D308
000B20  E0935010 D27858E0 D22C4110 E0105010   D27C58E0 D2384110 E0A55010 D280411C   *....K...K........K...K.......K...*   13D328
000B40  60D95010 D2844110 60B95010 D2889680   D2884110 D27458F0 C00405EF 58E0D230   *-R..K...-...K...K...K..0.......K.*   13D348
000B60  9240E33D D21AE33E E33D9240 E35CD21A   E35DE35C 9240E37B D21AE37C E37B9240   *. T.K.T.T.. T*K.T)T*. T.K.T.T.. *   13D368
000B80  E39AD21A E39BE39A 4800C17C 5000D258   5820C008 58E0D230 DD09E013 20005810   *T.K.T.T...A...K........K..........*   13D388
000BA0  C0A00771 58E0D23C 58F0D230 D209E000   F0135810 C0A407F1 4100001F 5A00D258   *.......K..OK.K...0.......1.......K.*   13D3A8
000BC0  5000D258 58E0D230 4140E33D 5A40D258   5040D268 58E0D268 D213E000 C21258E0   *..K...K.. T.. K.. K...K.K...B...*   13D3C8
000BE0  D2689240 E01458E0 D26858F0 D268D206   E015F014 58E0D230 D201E010 C17E5820   *K.. ....K..OK.K...0...K.K...A=..*   13D3E8
000C00  C00858E0 D230DD07 E0202000 5810C0A8   07715810 C0AC07F1 4100001F 5A00D258   *....K.....................1.......K.*   13D408
000C20  5000D258 58E0D230 4140E33D 5A40D258   5040D268 58E0D268 D216E000 C22658E0   *..K...K.. T.. K.. K...K.K...B...*   13D428
000C40  D2689240 E01758E0 D26858F0 D268D203   E018F017 1B005900 D25858F0 C0AC077F   *K.. ....K..OK.K...0......K..0....*   13D448
000C60  58E0D230 D201E01D C17E5810 C0B007F1   5810C018 07F158E0 D23C4100 E1B85000   *..K.K...A=.....1.....1..K........*   13D468
000C80  D2105800 E1B45000 D214D203 D218C0B4   D201D21E C18058E0 D230D202 D208E02B   *K........K.K.K...K.K.A...K.K.K...*   13D488
000CA0  9201D21C 4100D208 4110D210 070058F0   C00C05EF 88030000 58101000 1B015000   *..K...K...K....0..................*   13D4A8
000CC0  D26458E0 D23C58F0 D230D202 E00AF02B   5810C01C 07F15810 C0B807F1 4100001F   *K...K..OK.K...0.......1......1....*   13D4C8
000CE0  5A00D258 5000D258 58E0D230 4140E33D   5A40D258 5040D268 58E0D268 D218E000   *..K...K...K.. T.. K.. K...K.K...*   13D4E8
000D00  C23D58E0 D2689240 E01958E0 D26858F0   D268D201 E01AF019 1B005900 D25858F0   *B...K.. ....K..OK.K...0......K..0*   13D508
000D20  C01C077F 58E0D230 D201E028 C17E5820   C0BC58E0 D230D501 E031C256 07D25820   *.......K.K...A=.......K.N...B..K..*   13D528
000D40  C0BCD501 E031C258 07B25820 C0BCD501   E033C256 07D25820 C0BCD501 E033C259   *..N...B........N...B..K.....N...B.*   13D548
000D60  07B25820 C008DD01 E0352000 5810C0BC   077158E0 D23C58F0 D230D201 E00FF031   *.......................K..OK.K...0.*   13D568
000D80  D201E011 F033D201 E00DF035 5810C020   07F14100 001F5A00 D2585000 D25858E0   *K...0.K...0.......1.......K...K...*   13D588
000DA0  D2304140 E33D5A40 D2585040 D26858E0   D268D211 E000C258 58E0D268 9240E012   *K.. T.. K.. K...K.K...B$..K.. ..*   13D5A8
000DC0  58E0D268 58F0D268 D208E013 F0121B00   5900D258 58F0C020 077F58E0 D230D201   *..K..OK.K...0......K..0.......K.K.*   13D5C8
000DE0  E02EC17E 4100005D 5900D258 58F0C024   077F5810 C04007F1 1B005000 D25458E0   *..A=...)..K..0......... .1....K...*   13D5E8
000E00  D238D203 E09BC182 58F0D230 D205E06E   F0315800 D2705000 D26C5800 C0C05000   *K.K...A..OK.K...0...K...K........*   13D608
000E20  D27058E0 D2385830 E09B4930 C17858F0   C0C4078F 4100005D 5900D258 58F0C0C4   *K...K.........A..0.D......)..K..0.D*   13D628
000E40  078F4100 02985900 D25458F0 C0C4074F   5810C028 07F15800 D26C5000 D2705810   *..........K..0.D.........1..K...K...*   13D648
000E60  C03007F1 58E0D238 D203E09B C1861B00   5810D254 41200053 1D024A10 C18A4E10   *...1..K.K...A......K...........A.+.*   13D668
000E80  D208F307 600DD208 96F0600D 58E0D230   4140E037 5A40D254 5040D268 58E0D238   *K.3.-.K..0-...K.. ... K.. K...K.*   13D688
000EA0  58F0D268 D252E000 F0004830 E0004930   C17858F0 C0C8078F 5820C008 DD07E003   *.0K.K...0.........A..0.H............*   13D6A8
000EC0  20005810 C0CC0771 D207E053 E0034830   C18A5A30 E09B5030 E09B5810 C0C807F1   *..........K.........A..............H.1*   13D6C8
000EE0  D2126011 C26D4100 001F5A00 D2585000   D25858E0 D2304140 E33D5A40 D2585040   *K.-.B.........K...K...K.. T.. K.. *   13D6E8
000F00  D26858E0 D268D21B E0006008 1B005900   D25858F0 C0D0077F 58E0D230 4140E037   *K...K.K...-.....K..0.......K.. ..*   13D708
000F20  5A40D254 D2014000 C17E5810 C0C807F1   4100005D 5900D258 58F0C0C8 077F5810   *. K.K. .A=...H.1...)..K..0.H.....*   13D728
000F40  C02C07F1 58E0D238 4830E00B 4930C178   58F0C0D4 077F9240 E05BD211 E05CE05B   *...1..K.........A..0.M... .$K..*.$*   13D748
000F60  5810C0D8 07F15820 C0DC58E0 D2389540   E00E0772 D2126011 C2804100 001F5A00   *...Q.1.......K.. ....K.-.B.........*   13D768
000F80  D2585000 D25858E0 D2304140 E33D5A40   D2585040 D26858E0 D268D21B E0006008   *K...K...K.. T.. K.. K...K.K...-.*   13D788
000FA0  1B005900 D25858F0 C0E0077F 58E0D230   4140E042 5A40D254 D2014000 C17E5810   *....K..0.......K.. ... K.K. .A=..*   13D7A8
000FC0  C0D807F1 4100005D 5900D258 58F0C0E4   077F5810 C02C07F1 5810C0D8 07F158E0   *.Q.1...)..K..0.U........1...Q.1..*   13D7C8
000FE0  D238D212 E05BE00E 4830C18C 5A30E09B   5030E09B 58E0D238 4830E021 4930C178   *K.K..$....A...............K.........A.*   13D7E8
001000  58F0C0E8 078F5820 C008DD04 E0242000   5810C0EC 0771F274 D1F8E024 F822E074   *.0.Y.........................2.J8..8...*   13D808
001020  D1FD94F0 E076960C E0764830 C18E5A30   E09B5030 E09B5810 C0E807F1 58E0D238   *J..0..........A...............Y.1..K.*   13D828
001040  D202E074 C190D20B 6011C293 9240601D   D205601E 601D4100 001F5A00 D2585000   *K...A.K.-.B.. -.K.-.-.........K...*   13D848
001060  D25858E0 D2304140 E33D5A40 D2585040   D26858E0 D268D21B E0006008 1B005900   *K...K.. T.. K.. K...K.K...-......*   13D868
001080  D25858F0 C0F0077F 58E0D230 4140E058   5A40D254 D2014000 C17E5810 C0E807F1   *K..0.0....K.. ... K.K. .A=...Y.1*   13D888
0010A0  4100005D 5900D258 58F0C0E8 077F5810   C02C07F1 58E0D238 4830E029 4930C178   *...)..K..0.Y.........1..K.........A.*   13D8A8
0010C0  58F0C0F4 078F5820 C008DD06 E02C2000   5810C0F8 0771F276 D1F8E02C F833E077   *.0.4.....................8..2.J8..8...*   13D8C8
```

Fig. 24.5. (Continued)

```
CUSTOMER INFORMATION CONTROL SYSTEM STORAGE DUMP   CODE=ASRA   TASK=ORAD        DATE=07/27/80   TIME=18 43 53   PAGE   13

PROGRAM STORAGE                  ADDRESS  13C808   TO   13EF8F      LENGTH  002788

0010E0   D1FC94F0 E07A960C E07A4830 C1945A30   E09B5030 E09B5810 C0F407F1 58E0D238   *J..0. ... ..A............4.1..K.*   13D8E8
001100   D203E077 C196D210 6011C293 92406022   D2006023 60224100 001F5A00 D2585000   *K...A.K.-.B.. -.K.-.-.......K...*   13D908
001120   D25858E0 D2304140 E33D5A40 D2585040   D26858E0 D268D21B E0006008 1B005900   *K...K.. T.. K.. K...K.K...-.....*   13D928
001140   D25858F0 C0FC077F 58E0D230 4140E060   5A40D254 D2014000 C17E5810 C0F407F1   *K..0......K.. .-. K.K. .A=...4.1*   13D948
001160   4100005D 5900D258 58F0C0F4 077F5810   C02C07F1 58E0D238 4830E033 4930C178   *...)..K..0.4.......1..K.......A.*   13D968
001180   58F0C100 078F5820 C008D007 E0362000   5810C104 0771F873 D1F8E077 FC62D1F9   *.0A..............A...8.J8....J9*   13D988
0011A0   E074F277 D200E036 F946D203 D1F958F0   C104077F F277D200 E036FA44 E07FD203   *..2.K...9.K.J9.0A...2.K.......K.*   13D9A8
0011C0   4830C19A 5A30E09B 5030E09B 5810C100   07F1D20B 6011C2A4 9240601D D205601E   *..A...........A..1K.-.B.. -.K.-.*   13D9C8
0011E0   601D4100 001F5A00 D2585000 D25858E0   D2304140 E33D5A40 D2585040 D26858E0   *-.......K...K...K.. T.. K.. K...*   13D9E8
001200   D268D21B E0006008 1B005900 D25858F0   C108077F 58E0D230 4140E06A 5A40D254   *K.K...-.....K..0A.....K.. ... K.*   13DA08
001220   D2014000 C17E5810 C10007F1 4100005D   5900D258 58F0C100 077F5810 C02C07F1   *K. .A=..A..1...)..K..0A........1*   13DA28
001240   58E0D238 4830E03E 4930C178 58F0C10C   078F5820 C008D006 E0412000 5810C110   *..K........A..0A...............A.*   13DA48
001260   0771F276 D200E041 F833E07B D20494F0   E07E960C E07E4830 C19C5A30 E09B5030   *..2.K...8...K..0.=...=..A.......*   13DA68
001280   E09B5810 C10C07F1 58E0D238 D203E07B   C196D211 6011C2B0 92406023 4100001F   *....A..1..K.K...A.K.-.B.. -.....*   13DA88
0012A0   5A00D258 5000D258 58E0D230 4140E33D   5A40D258 5040D268 58E0D268 D21BE000   *..K...K...K.. T.. K.. K...K.K...*   13DAA8
0012C0   60081B00 5900D258 58F0C114 077F58E0   D2304140 E0755A40 D254D201 4000C17E   *-.....K..0A.....K.. ... K.K. .A=*   13DAC8
0012E0   5810C10C 07F14100 005D5900 D25858F0   C10C077F 5810C02C 07F158E0 D2384830   *..A..1...)..K..0A.........1..K...*   13DAE8
001300   E0484930 C17858F0 C118078F 5820C008   DD07E04B 20005810 C11C0771 F873D200   *....A..0A..............A...8.K.*   13DB08
001320   E07BFC62 D201E074 F277D1F8 E04BF946   D1FBD201 58F0C11C 077FF277 D200E04B   *....K...2.J8..9.J.K..0A...2.K...*   13DB28
001340   FA44E084 D2034830 C19E5A30 E09B5030   E09B5810 C11807F1 D20C6011 C2C29240   *....K...A...........A..1K.-.BB. *   13DB48
001360   601ED204 601F601E 4100001F 5A00D258   5000D258 58E0D230 4140E33D 5A40D258   *-.K.-.-.......K...K...K.. T.. K.*   13DB68
001380   5040D268 58E0D268 D21BE000 60081B00   5900D258 58F0C120 077F58E0 D2304140   *. K...K.K...-.....K..0A.....K.. *   13DB88
0013A0   E07F5A40 D254D201 4000C17E 5810C118   07F14100 005D5900 D25858F0 C118077F   *... K.K. .A=..A..1...)..K..0A...*   13DBA8
0013C0   5810C02C 07F158E0 D2385830 E09B4930   C1A058F0 C124078F 5830E09B 4930C1A2   *.....1..K.......A..0A..........A.*   13DBC8
0013E0   58F0C128 077F4800 C17C5900 D25858F0   C12C077F 5810D254 4120002C 1C024120   *.0A.....A...K..0A.....K.........*   13DBE8
001400   00531D02 5010D260 58E0D23C 4140E025   5A40D260 5040D268 58E0D268 58F0D238   *......K-..K.. ... K-. K...K..0K.*   13DC08
001420   D22BE000 F0535810 C13007F1 58E0D238   5830E09B 4930C178 58F0C134 077F5810   *K...0...A..1..K.......A..0A......*   13DC28
001440   C13007F1 4100001F 5A00D258 5000D258   D20E6011 C2CF9240 6020D202 60216020   *A..1......K...K.K.-.B.. -.K.-.-.*   13DC48
001460   58E0D230 4140E33D 5A40D258 5040D268   58E0D268 D21BE000 60081B00 5900D258   *..K.. T.. K.. K...K.K...-.....K.*   13DC68
001480   58F0C138 077F58E0 D2304140 E0375A40   D254D201 4000C17E 5810C130 07F14100   *.0A......K.. ... K.K. .A=..A..1..*   13DC88
0014A0   005D5900 D25858F0 C130077F 5810C02C   07F14100 00535A00 D2545000 D2545810   *.)..K..0A.........1.......K...K..*   13DCA8
0014C0   D27007F1 41C0005D 5900D258 58F0C13C   077F5810 C04007F1 41000053 5900D254   *K..1...)..K..0A....... .1.......K.*   13DCC8
0014E0   58F0C140 077F58E0 D2385830 E09B4930   C17858F0 C140077F 4100001F 5A00D258   *.0A ....K.........A..0A .........K.*   13DCE8
001500   5000D258 58E0D230 4140E33D 5A40D258   5040D268 58E0D268 D213E000 C2DE58E0   *..K...K.. T.. K.. K...K.K...B...*   13DD08
001520   D2689240 E01458E0 D26858F0 D268D206   E015F014 1B005900 D25858F0 C144077F   *K.. ....K..0K.K....0.......K..0A...*   13DD28
001540   58E0D230 D201E037 C17E5810 C14007F1   4100005D 5900D258 58F0C140 077F5810   *..K.K...A=..A .1...)..K..0A .....*   13DD48
001560   C03407F1 5820C008 58E0D230 DD08E325   20005810 C1480771 F278D200 E32558E0   *...1........K...T.......A...2.K.T...*   13DD68
001580   D238F944 D203E07F 58F0C148 077F58E0   D23C58F0 D238F844 E019F07F 5810C14C   *K.9.K.....0A......K..0K.8...0...A.*   13DD88
0015A0   07F14100 001F5A00 D2585000 D25858E0   D2304140 E33D5A40 D2585040 D26858E0   *.1.......K...K...K.. T.. K.. K...*   13DDA8
0015C0   D268D213 E000C2F2 58E0D268 9240E014   58E0D268 58F0D268 D206E015 F0141B00   *K.K...B2..K.. ....K..0K.K...0...*   13DDC8
0015E0   5900D258 58F0C150 077F58E0 D2300201   E322C17E 5810C14C 07F14100 005D5900   *..K...0A......K.K.T.A=..A..1...)..*   13DDE8
001600   D25858F0 C14C077F 5810C034 07F15820   C00858E0 D230DD08 E3312000 5810C154   *K...0A.........1.......K...T......A.*   13DE08
001620   0771F278 D200E331 58E0D238 F944D203   E08458F0 C154077F 58E0D23C 58F0D238   *..2.K.T...K.9.K.....0A.....K..0K.*   13DE28
001640   F844E01E F0845810 C03407F1 4100001F   5A00D258 5000D258 58E0D230 4140E33D   *8...0.......1.......K...K...K.. T.*   13DE48
001660   5A40D258 5040D268 58E0D268 D214E000   C30658E0 D2689240 E01558E0 D26858F0   *. K.. K...K.K...C...K.. ....K..0*   13DE68
001680   D268D205 E016F015 1B005900 D25858F0   C158077F 58E0D230 D201E32E C17E5810   *K.K...0......K..0A......K.K.T.A=..*   13DE88
0016A0   C03407F1 4100005D 5900D258 58F0C034   077F5810 C03407F1 4800C17C 5900D258   *...1...)..K..0..........1..A...K.*   13DEA8
0016C0   58F0C038 078F5810 C04007F1 1B005810   D2544120 00531D02 4A10C18A 58E0D23C   *.0....... .1....K.........A...K.*   13DEC8
0016E0   4010E023 4830E023 4930C1A4 58F0C15C   07DF58E0 D2385830 E09B4930 C17858F0   * ..........A..0A*....K.........A...0*   13DEE8
001700   C160077F 58E0D23C 4830E023 4B30C18C   4030E023 5810C164 07F158E0 D23C4830   *A-.....K.........A. ......A..1..K...*   13DF08
001720   E0234B30 C18A4030 E0235810 C16407F1   58E0D23C 4830E023 4B30C18C 4030E023   *....A. ......A..1..K........A. ...*   13DF28
```

Fig. 24.5. (Continued)

```
CUSTOMER INFORMATION CONTROL SYSTEM STORAGE DUMP   CODE=ASRA   TASK=ORAD       DATE=07/27/80   TIME=18 43 53   PAGE   14

PROGRAM STORAGE                  ADDRESS  13C808   TO  13EF8F      LENGTH  002788

001740  D20160B9 C1A6D208 6070C31B 92406079   D20F607A 60794110 60705010 D27458E0   *K.-.A.K.-.C.. -.K.- -...-...K...*   13DF48
001760  D22C4110 E0085010 D2784110 60B95010   D27C9680 D27C4110 D27458F0 C00405EF   *K.......K...-...K...K...K..O....*   13DF68
001780  58E0D234 58F0D23C D201E023 F0235820   C08C0522 58E0D234 4100E000 4810D24E   *..K..OK.K...O..........K.......K+*  13DF88
0017A0  58E0D23C 4120E000 413001B1 BF38C19F   0E025820 C08C0522 58E0D234 4830E023   *..K...........A...........K.....*   13DFA8
0017C0  4C30C1A8 4A30C1AA 58E0D238 4030E0A3   58F0D23C D209E089 F000D211 6070C324   *..A...A...K. ....OK.K...O.K.-.C.*   13DFC8
0017E0  92406082 D2066C83 60824110 60705010   D2749680 D2744110 D27458F0 C00405EF   *. -.K.-.-...-...K...K...K..O....*   13DFE8
001800  58E0D224 4810E014 4130C010 4910C18C   05204720 201E8B10 000147C0 201E4811   *..K...........A.................*   13E008
001820  20188910 00025811 300007F1 0016000D   D205609A C3369240 60A0D200 60A160A0   *...........1....K.-.C.. -.K.-.-.*   13E028
001840  D2086070 C33C9240 6079D20F 607A6079   41106070 5010D274 4110609A 5010D278   *K.-.C.. -.K.- -...-...K...-...K.*   13E048
001860  58E0D234 4110E000 5010D27C 58E0D238   4110E0A3 5010D280 4110E089 5010D284   *..K........K...K.......K.......K.*  13E068
001880  9680D284 4110D274 58F0C004 05EF5820   C08C0522 D2086070 C3459240 6079D20F   *..K...K..O...........K.-.C.. -.K.*  13E088
0018A0  607A6079 41106070 5010D274 58E0D234   4110E000 5010D278 9680D278 4110D274   *- -...-...K...K........K...K...K.*  13E0A8
0018C0  58F0C004 05EF5820 C08C0522 D20160B9   C1AAD208 6070C31B 92406079 D20F607A   *.O...........K.-.A.K.-.C.. -.K.- *  13E0C8
0018E0  60794110 60705010 D27458E0 D22C4110   E0145010 D2784110 60B95010 D27C9680   *-...-...K...K........K...-...K...*  13E0E8
001900  D27C4110 D27458F0 C00405EF 58E0D240   58F0D23C D202E000 F1B1D205 E003F013   *K...K..O.......K .OK.K...1.K...O.*  13E108
001920  D209E009 F000F844 E01BF019 F844E020   F01E58F0 D230D207 E013F020 58E0D238   *K...O.8...O.8...O..OK.K...O...K.*   13E128
001940  D201E0A9 C1AAD201 60B9C18C D20160B0   C34ED208 607CC350 92406079 D20F607A   *K...A.K.-.A.K.-.C+K.-.C.. -.K.- *   13E148
001960  60794110 60705010 D2744110 60B95010   D2784110 E09F5010 D27C4110 60B05010   *-...-...K...-...K........K...-...*  13E168
001980  D28058E0 D2404110 E0005010 D28458E0   D2384110 E0A95010 D2889680 D2884110   *K...K .......K...K.........K...K...* 13E188
0019A0  D27458F0 C00405EF D206608A C1EC9240   6091D206 6092C1F3 92406099 D20E607C   *K..O.....K.-.A.. -.K.-.A3. -.K.-.*  13E1A8
0019C0  C3599240 607FD209 6080607F 41106070   5010D274 4110608A 5010D278 411060D9   *C.. -.K.-.-...-...K...-...K...-R*   13E1C8
0019E0  5010D27C 411060D7 5010D280 41106092   5010D284 9680D284 4110D274 58F0C004   *..K...-P..K...-...K...K...K..O..*   13E1E8
001A00  05EF92F1 6000D201 60B9C179 D2086070   C3689240 6079D20F 607A6079 41106070   *...1-.K.-.A.K.-.C.. -.K.- -...-.*   13E208
001A20  5010D274 58E0D224 4110E008 5010D278   41106000 5010D27C 411060B9 5010D280   *..K...K........K...-...K...-...K.*  13E228
001A40  9680D280 4110D274 58F0C004 05EFD206   608AC1EC 92406091 D2066092 C1F39240   *..K...K..O.....K.-.A.. -.K.-.A3. *  13E248
001A60  6099D201 60B9C17E D20E6070 C3719240   607FD209 6080607F 41106070 5010D274   *-.K.-.A=K.-.C.. -.K.-.-...-...K.*   13E268
001A80  4110608A 5010D278 58E0D230 4110E000   5010D27C 411060D7 5010D280 41106092   *..-...K...K.........K...-P..K...-.* 13E288
001AA0  5010D284 411060D9 5010D288 411060D9   5010D28C 411060D9 5010D290 411060B9   *..K...-R..K...-R..K...-R..K...-.*   13E2A8
001AC0  5010D294 9680D294 4110D274 58F0C004   05EF5810 C03C07F1 58E0D230 D218E33D   *..K...K...K..O...........1..K.K.T.* 13E2C8
001AE0  C3809240 E356D201 E357E356 D201E010   C17E5810 C04007F1 D20160B9 C1ACD208   *C.. T.K.T.T.K...A=... .1K.-.A.K.*   13E2E8
001B00  6070C399 92406079 D20F607A 60794110   60705010 D27458E0 D22C4110 E0045010   *-.C.. -.K.- -...-...K...K.......*   13E308
001B20  D2784110 60B95010 D27C4110 605B5010   D2809680 D2804110 D27458F0 C00405EF   *K...-...K...-$..K...K...K..O....*   13E328
001B40  58E0D230 D218E33D C3A29240 E356D201   E357E356 D206608A C1EC9240 6091D206   *..K.K.T.C.. T.K.T.T.K.-.A.. -.K.*   13E348
001B60  6092C1F3 92406099 D20E6070 C3B89240   607FD209 6080607F 41106070 5010D274   *-.A3. -.K.-.C.. -.K.-.-...-...K.*   13E368
001B80  4110608A 5010D278 4110E000 5010D27C   411060D7 5010D280 41106092 5010D284   *..-...K.........K...-P..K...-...K.* 13E388
001BA0  9680D284 4110D274 58F0C004 05EF92F1   6000D201 60B9C179 D2086070 C3689240   *..K...K..O.....1-.K.-.A.K.-.C.. *   13E3A8
001BC0  6079D20F 607A6079 41106070 5010D274   58E0D224 4110E008 5010D278 41106000   *-.K.- -...-...K...K.........K...-.* 13E3C8
001BE0  5010D27C 411060B9 5010D280 9680D280   4110D274 58F0C004 05EFD211 6070C3CA   *..K...-...K...K...K..O....K.-.C.*   13E3E8
001C00  92406082 D2066083 60824110 60705010   D2749680 D2744110 D27458F0 C00405EF   *. -.K.-.-...-...K...K...K..O....*   13E408
001C20  58E0D224 4810E014 4130C010 4910C18A   05204720 201C8B10 000147C0 201C4811   *..K............A.................*  13E428
001C40  20188910 00025811 300007F1 001058E0   D23858F0 D224D203 E093F010 D203E097   *.............1....K..OK.K...O.K...* 13E448
001C60  C1ECD208 6070C3DC 92406079 D20F607A   60794110 60705010 D2744110 E0935010   *A.K.-.C.. -.K.- -...-...K.......*   13E468
001C80  D2789680 D2784110 D27458F0 C00405EF   D20160B9 C1AED208 6070C31B 92406079   *K...K...K..O....K.-.A.K.-.C.. -.*   13E488
001CA0  D20F607A 60794110 60705010 D27458E0   D22C4110 E0105010 D2784110 60B95010   *K.- -...-...K...K........K...-...*  13E4A8
001CC0  D27C9680 D27C4110 D27458F0 C00405EF   4800C1B0 5000D264 58E0D238 92C4E0D2   *K...K...K..O.......A...K...K..D.K*  13E4C8
001CE0  D203E0D3 C1B2D211 6070C3E5 92406082   D2066083 60824110 60705010 D2749680   *K..LA.K.-.CV. -.K.-.-...-...K...*   13E4E8
001D00  D2744110 D27458F0 C00405EF 58E0D224   4810E014 4130C010 4910C18A 05204720   *K...K..O.......K.............A.....* 13E508
001D20  201C8B10 000147C0 201C4811 20188910   00025811 300007F1 0012D206 609AC3F7   *..........................1..K.-.C7* 13E528
001D40  924060A1 D2086070 C3FE9240 6079D20F   607A6079 41106070 5010D274 4110609A   *. -.K.-.C.. -.K.- -...-...K...-.*   13E548
001D60  5010D278 411060D9 5010D27C 411060D7   5010D280 58E0D238 4110E0D2 5010D284   *..K...-R..K...-P..K...K....K..K.*   13E568
001D80  9680D284 4110D274 58F0C004 05EFD206   609AC3F7 924060A1 D2086070 C4079240   *..K...K..O....K.-.C7. -.K.-.D.. *   13E588
```

Fig. 24.5. (Continued)

```
CUSTOMER INFORMATION CONTROL SYSTEM STORAGE DUMP   CODE=ASRA   TASK=ORAD       DATE=07/27/80   TIME=18 43 53   PAGE  15

PROGRAM STORAGE                 ADDRESS  13C808  TO  13EF8F      LENGTH  002788

001DA0   6079D20F 607A6079 41106070 5010D274   4110609A 5010D278 58E0D22C 4110E018   *-.K.- -...-...K...-...K...K......*   13E5A8
001DC0   5010D27C 41106CD7 5010D280 58E0D238   4110E0D2 5010D284 411060D7 5010D288   *..K...-P..K...K....K..K...-P..K.*   13E5C8
001DE0   411060D7 5010D28C 9680D28C 4110D274   58F0C004 05EF5820 C16858E0 D24495C4   *..-P..K...K...K..0......A...K..D*   13E5E8
001E00   E0000772 5820C16C D502F005 C4100772   5810C058 07F15820 C16858E0 D2440501   *......A.N...D........1..A...K.N.*   13E608
001E20   E026C413 07B24100 00035A00 D2645000   D26458E0 D23C4140 E1B85A40 D2645040   *..D.........K...K...K.. ... K.. *   13E628
001E40   D26858E0 D26858F0 D244D202 E000F005   5810C054 07F14800 C1B05900 D26458F0   *K...K..OK.K...0......1..A...K..0*   13E648
001E60   C170077F 5810C078 07F11B00 5810D264   41200003 1D024A10 C18A58E0 D23C5010   *A........1....K.........A...K...*   13E668
001E80   E1B45820 C0900522 58100014 0A2158E0   D238D207 E0CA1000 58E0D23C 58F0D238   *..............K.K.......K..OK.*   13E688
001EA0   D201E013 F0CAD201 E015F0CD D201E017   F0D058F0 D228D202 E1B1F001 58E0D238   *K...0.K...0.K...0..0K.K...0...K.*   13E6A8
001EC0   D201E0A5 C1AED208 6070C415 92406079   D20F607A 60794110 60705010 D2744110   *K...A.K.-.D.. -.K.- -...-...K...*   13E6C8
001EE0   E0935010 D27858E0 D23C4110 E0005010   D27C58E0 D2384110 E0A55010 D2809680   *....K...K.......K...K........K...*   13E6E8
001F00   D2804110 D27458F0 C00405EF 5820C090   0522D208 6070C345 92406079 D20F607A   *K...K..0..........K.-.C.. -.K.- *   13E708
001F20   60794110 60705010 D27458E0 D23C4110   E0005010 D2789680 D2784110 D27458F0   *-...-...K...K........K...K...K..0*   13E728
001F40   C00405EF 5820C090 0522D201 60B9C1AC   D2086070 C3999240 6079D20F 607A6079   *..........K.-.A.K.-.C.. -.K.- -.*   13E748
001F60   41106070 5010D274 58E0D22C 4110E004   5010D278 411060B9 5010D27C 4110605B   *..-...K...K.......K...-...K...-$*   13E768
001F80   5010D280 9680D280 4110D274 58F0C004   05EF58E0 D230D210 E33DC41E 9240E34E   *..K...K...K..0......K.K.T.D.. T+*   13E788
001FA0   D209E34F E34ED206 608AC1EC 92406091   D2066092 C1F39240 6099D20E 6070C3BB   *K.T.T+K.-.A.. -.K.-.A3. -.K.-.C.*   13E7A8
001FC0   9240607F D2096080 607F4110 60705010   D2744110 608A5010 D2784110 E0005010   *. -.K.-.-...-...K...-...K.......*   13E7C8
001FE0   D27C4110 60D75010 D2804110 60925010   D2849680 D2844110 D27458F0 C00405EF   *K...-P..K...-...K...K...K..0.....*   13E7E8
002000   92F16000 D20360A8 C1ECD201 60B9C179   D2086070 C3689240 6079D20F 607A6079   *.1-.K.-.A.K.-.A.K.-.C.. -.K.- -.*   13E808
002020   41106070 5010D274 411060A8 5010D278   41106000 5010D27C 411060B9 5010D280   *..-...K...-...K...-...K...-...K.*   13E828
002040   9680D280 4110D274 58F0C004 05EF58E0   D238D216 E0AB6024 9240E0C2 D206E0C3   *..K...K..0......K.K...-.. .BK..C*   13E848
002060   E0C2D201 60B9C1B4 D20E6070 C42F9240   607FD209 6080607F 41106070 5010D274   *.BK.-.A.K.-.D.. -.K.-.-...-...K.*   13E868
002080   411060D9 5010D278 411060D7 5010D27C   58E0D238 4110E0AB 5010D280 411060B9   *..-R..K...-P..K.........K...-.*   13E888
0020A0   5010D284 9680D284 4110D274 58F0C004   05EFD211 6070C3CA 92406082 D2066083   *..K...K...K..0....K.-.C.. -.K.-.*   13E8A8
0020C0   60824110 60705010 D2749680 D2744110   D27458F0 C00405EF 58E0D224 4810E014   *-...-...K...K...K..0.......K......*   13E8C8
0020E0   4130C010 4910C18A 05204720 201C8B10   000147C0 201C4811 20188910 00025811   *......A.........................*   13E8E8
002100   300007F1 001558E0 D23858F0 D224D203   E093F010 D203E097 F008D208 6070C3DC   *...1....K..OK.K...0.K...0.K.-.C.*   13E908
002120   92406079 D20F607A 60794110 60705010   D2744110 E0935010 D2789680 D2784110   *. -.K.- -...-...K.......K...K...*   13E928
002140   D27458F0 C00405EF D2086070 C43E9240   6079D20F 607A6079 41106070 5010D274   *K..0....K.-.D.. -.K.- -...-...K.*   13E948
002160   9680D274 4110D274 58F0C004 05EFD207   609AC447 D2086070 C44F9240 6079D20F   *..K...K..0....K.-.D.K.-.D.. -.K.*   13E968
002180   607A6079 41106070 5010D274 4110609A   5010D278 9680D278 4110D274 58F0C004   *- -...-...K...-...K...K...K..0..*   13E988
0021A0   05EFD20A 604AC458 924C6055 D2036056   60555810 C08007F1 D20C604A C4639240   *..K.-.D.. -.K.-.-.......1K.-.D.. *   13E9A8
0021C0   6057D201 60586057 5810C080 07F1D20F   604AC470 5810C080 07F1D20F 604AC480   *-.K.-.-......1K.-.D......1K.-.D.*   13E9C8
0021E0   5810C080 07F158E0 D224D201 6063E01B   D2056065 E01DD203 60A8C490 D2086070   *.....1..K.K.-...K.-...K.-.D.K.-.*   13E9E8
002200   C4949240 6079D20F 607A6079 41106070   5010D274 411060A8 5010D278 9680D278   *D.. -.K.- -...-...K...-...K...K.*   13EA08
002220   4110D274 58F0C004 05EFD20A 604AC49D   92406055 D2036056 60555810 C08007F1   *..K..0....K.-.D.. -.K.-.-.......1*   13EA28
002240   58E0D238 D21EE0AB 603B5810 C06007F1   1B004000 D24C4100 00254000 D24E58E0   *..K.K...-....-..1.. .K..... .K+..*   13EA48
002260   D2344810 E0234C10 C1A84A10 D24C4010   D24C4810 D24E4A10 D24C4010 D24E07F3   *K........A...K. .K...K+..K. .K+.3*   13EA68
002280   410001B8 4000D250 58E0D23C 5810E1B4   4C10C180 4A10D250 4010D250 07F35830   *.... .K...K.......A...K. .K..3..*   13EA88
0022A0   C0840533 05225830 C0880533 052250D0   50085050 D0045820 C0009500 20000779   *................................*   13EAA8
0022C0   92FF2000 9610D048 50E0D054 05F09120   D04847E0 F0165800 B048982D B05058E0   *.............0......0...........*   13EAC8
0022E0   D0540 7FE 9620D048 41600004 4110C010   4170C178 06700550 58401000 1E4B5040   *.........-........A...... ..... *   13EAE8
002300   10008716 50004180 D1F44170 D1F70510   58008000 1E0B5000 80008786 1000D203   *...........J4..J7..............K.*   13EB08
002320   D270C174 5860D1F4 58E0D1B0 906DE060   58E0D054 07FE0000 FFF5F7F4 F660C3C2   *K.A..-J4..J....-........5746-CB*   13EB28
002340   F140C3D6 D7E8D9C9 C7C8E340 C9C2D440   C3D6D9D7 4B40F1F9 F7F3F5F7 F4F660D3   *1 COPYRIGHT IBM CORP. 19735746-L*   13EB48
002360   D4F440C3 D6D7E8D9 C9C7C8E3 40C9C2D4   40C3D6D9 D74B40F1 F9F7F3C6 C540F2F4   *M4 COPYRIGHT IBM CORP. 1973FE 24*   13EB68
002380   F6F3F5F6 C6C540F2 F4F6F3F5 F7000000   47F0F018 C9D3C2C4 E2C3C8F0 F2F5F0F0   *6356FE 246357....00.ILBDSCH02500*   13EB88
0023A0   F1F261F2 F061F7F8 90ECF2B8 1BBB5841   000C8840 0018182E 58820000 89800008   *12/20/78..2........ ............*   13EBA8
0023C0   88800018 1AB84122 00044640 F028412D   00604132 000192FF 200018AB 1AA388A0   *........... 0....-.............*   13EBC8
0023E0   000289A0 000206B0 50BA0004 44B0F28A   5850F2C0 5841000C 88400018 504A0008   *..............2...2...... ......*   13EBE8
```

Fig. 24.5. (Continued)

```
CUSTOMER INFORMATION CONTROL SYSTEM STORAGE DUMP   CODE=ASRA   TASK=ORAD      DATE=07/27/80   TIME=18 43 53   PAGE   16

PROGRAM STORAGE             ADDRESS  13C808  TO  13EF8F      LENGTH  002788

002400   9200A010 188E47F0 F0DC4640 F2724132   00015880 F2C058BA 000444B0 F27E9201   *.......00.. 2.......2.......2=..*   13EC08
002420   A01058C1 00005871 00041897 06704841   000E504A 000C1C64 1A7C1889 88800001   *...A............................*   13EC28
002440   89800001 15891807 4770F0BE 1B041A0C   88000001 584A0008 44B0F28A 188E47F0   *..........0..............2....0*   13EC48
002460   F0D64188 00044858 00021A50 48980000   89900018 88900018 18690690 95888000   *00..............................*   13EC68
002480   4780F128 4720F110 95208000 4780F130   4720F214 95108000 4780F180 4740F19E   *..1...1......1...2.......1.. 1.*   13EC88
0024A0   95A08000 4780F1A6 4740F1FA 4490F290   97803000 47F0F21C 4490F290 47F0F21C   *.....1.. 1...2......02...2..02.*   13ECA8
0024C0   18B91AB5 9103B000 4740F15E 4490F2A2   18B94199 00018990 00041A9B 4490F29C   *......... 1 ..2..............2.*   13ECC8
0024E0   1AB341BB 000196FF B00047F0 F21C18B9   41990001 89900004 1A9B4490 F29696D0   *...........02..............2...*   13ECE8
002500   30001AB3 41BB0001 96FFB000 47F0F21C   18B91AB5 9130B000 4740F128 4710F19E   *.............02......... 1...1.*   13ED08
002520   4490F2A2 1A939730 900047F0 F21C4490   F2A247F0 F21C18B9 1AB59103 B0004740   *..2........02...2..02......... *   13ED28
002540   F1D418B9 41990001 89900004 1A9B4490   F29696F0 30001AB3 41BB0001 96FFB000   *1M............2..0.............*   13ED48
002560   47F0F21C 4490F2A2 18B94199 00018990   00041A9B 4490F29C 96203000 1AB341BB   *.02...2.................2......*   13ED68
002580   000196FF B00047F0 F21C18B9 1AB59130   B0004740 F19E4490 F2901A93 96F09000   *.......02......... 1...2....0..*   13ED88
0025A0   47F0F21C 4490F2A2 97803000 9101A010   4780F07A 4640F264 41320001 5890F2C0   *.02...2...........0 . 2.......2.*   13EDA8
0025C0   58BA0004 44B0F284 4780F2A8 584A000C   4720F24C 1B041870 47F0F250 1A0418C0   *......2...2.......2......02.....*   13EDC8
0025E0   15C74720 F26A1894 1A971B9C 1B881D84   47F0F0AA 1A3647F0 F0D258E1 000847F0   *.G..2............00....00K.....0*   13EDE8
002600   F2AC1A56 1A364188 000447F0 F0DCD200   80003000 D5009000 3000D200 30002000   *2...........00.K.....N.....K.....*   13EE08
002620   D2003000 5000F100 30005000 F1003000   3000D700 30005000 41E80004 58F0F2BC   *K.....1.....1.....P......Y...02.*   13EE28
002640   981CF2C4 07FE0000 4013D4BC 0013EB98   0012F2F4 0012F2FC 0013EE90 00000001   *..2D.... .M........24..2.........*   13EE48
002660   0012F420 5013EB00 0012F00C 0012F2E3   0012F2E4 0013EAD0 0013C820 0013C820   *..4........0...2T..2U......H...H.*   13EE68
002680   0013CC98 00000000 01010101 01010101   01010101 01010101 01010101 01010101   *................................*   13EE88
0026A0   01010101 01010101 01010101 01010101   01010101 01010101 01010101 01010101   *................................*   13EEA8
0026C0   LINES TO 002740 SAME AS ABOVE                                                                                        13EEC8
002760   01010101 01010101 01010101 01010101   01010101 01010101 00000000 00000000   *................................*   13EF68
002780   00000101 01010101                                                           *........                        *   13EF88

PROGRAM STORAGE             ADDRESS  13F808  TO  13FCA7      LENGTH  0004A0

000000   D6D9C1C4 E2F0F140 00404040 00000000   00000000 D6D9C1C4 D4F0F140 048F04B0   *ORADS01 .    ........ORADM01 ....*   13F808
000020   03B105C6 C0C200CC 001850FF FE000000   00000000 00000000 0001037D 0000F100   *...F.B....................'..1.*   13F828
000040   00001B02 F80018D7 E4D9C3C8 C1E2C540   D6D9C4C5 D9406060 6040C6C9 D3C540C1   *....8..PURCHASE ORDER --- FILE A*   13F848
000060   C4C40000 000D02F0 00BDD6D9 C4C5D940   D5E4D4C2 C5D97A00 00000A0D D800CB00   *DD.....0..ORDER NUMBER .....Q...*   13F868
000080   00000100 6000D600 00000802 F000DDC4   D6C340D5 D64B7A00 0000080D D800E600   *....-.0.......0..DOC NO. .....Q.W.*   13F888
0000A0   00000100 6000EF00 00000B02 F0010FC4   C5D7C1D9 E3D4C5D5 E37A0000 00030DD8   *....-........0..DEPARTMENT .....Q*   13F8A8
0000C0   011B0000 000100F0 011F0000 000E02F0   015CC4C1 E3C540D6 C640D6D9 C4C5D97A   *.......0........0.*DATE OF ORDER *   13F8C8
0000E0   00000006 0DD8016B 00000001 00F00172   00000004 02F002D6 C9E3C5D4 0000000B   *.....Q.,......0........0.OITEM....*   13F8E8
000100   02F002E0 C4C5E2C3 D9C9D7E3 C9D6D500   00000402 F002F9E4 D5C9E300 00000502   *.0..DESCRIPTION.....0.9UNIT.....*   13F908
000120   F002FFE4 C3D6E2E3 00000004 02F00308   C3D6E2E3 00000006 02F00310 E4D7D9C9   *0..UCOST.....0..COST.....0..UPRI*   13F928
000140   C3C50000 000502F0 0319D7D9 C9C3C500   00000102 F00322F1 00000008 0DD80324   *CE.....0..PRICE.....0..1.....Q..*   13F948
000160   00000013 01C8032D 00000001 00600341   00000005 0DD80348 00000007 0DD8034E   *.....H.......-.......Q.......Q.+*   13F968
000180   00000008 0DD80356 00000007 0DD8035F   00000008 0DD80367 00000001 00600370   *.....Q.......Q.......Q.......-..*   13F988
0001A0   00000001 02F00372 F2000000 080DD803   74000000 1301C803 7D000000 01006003   *.....0..2.....Q.......H.'......-.*   13F9A8
0001C0   91000000 050DD803 98000000 070DD803   9E000000 080DD803 A6000000 070DD803   *......Q.......Q.......Q.......Q.*   13F9C8
0001E0   AF000000 080DD803 B7000000 01006003   C0000000 0102F003 C2F30000 00080DD8   *......Q.......-.......0.B3.....Q*   13F9E8
000200   03C40000 001301C8 03CD0000 00010060   03E10000 00050DD8 03E80000 00070DD8   *.D.....H.......-.......Q.Y.....Q*   13FA08
000220   03EE0000 00080DD8 03F60000 00070DD8   03FF0000 00080DD8 04070000 00010060   *.......Q.6.....Q.......Q.......-*   13FA28
000240   04100000 000102F0 0412F400 0000080D   D8041400 00001301 C8041D00 00000100   *.......0..4.....Q.......H.......*   13FA48
000260   60043100 0000050D D8043800 0000070D   D8043E00 0000080D D8044600 0000070D   *-.......Q.......Q.......Q.......*   13FA68
000280   D8044F00 0000080D D8045700 00000100   60046000 00000102 F00462F5 00000008   *Q.......Q.......-.-......0..5....*   13FA88
0002A0   0DD80464 00000013 01C8046D 00000001   00600481 00000005 0DD80488 00000007   *.Q.......H.......-.......Q......*   13FAA8
```

Fig. 24.5. (Continued)

```
CUSTOMER INFORMATION CONTROL SYSTEM STORAGE DUMP   CODE=ASRA   TASK=ORAD      DATE=07/27/80   TIME=18 43 53   PAGE   17

PROGRAM STORAGE                 ADDRESS  13F808  TO  13FCA7      LENGTH  0004A0

0002CC   0DD8048E 00000008 0DD80496 00000007   0DD8049F 00000008 0DD804A7 00000001   *.Q.......Q.......Q.......Q......*   13FAC8
0002E0   00600480 00000001 02F004B2 F6000000   080DD804 B4000000 1301C804 BD000000   *.-.......0..6.....Q.......H.....*   13FAE8
000300   01006004 D1000000 050DD804 D8000000   070DD804 DE000000 080DD804 E6000000   *..-.J.....Q.Q.....Q.......Q.W...*   13FB08
000320   070DD804 EF000000 080DD804 F7000000   01006005 00000000 0102F005 02F70000   *..Q.......Q.7.....-.......0..7..*   13FB28
000340   00080DD8 05040000 001301C8 050D0000   00010060 05210000 00050DD8 05280000   *...Q.......H.......-.......Q....*   13FB48
000360   00070DD8 052E0000 00080DD8 05360000   00070DD8 053F0000 00080DD8 05470000   *...Q.......Q.......Q.......Q....*   13FB68
000380   00010060 05500000 000102F0 0552F800   0000080D D8055400 00001301 C8055D00   *...-.......0..8.....Q.......H.).*   13FB88
0003A0   00000100 60057100 0000050D D8057800   0000070D D8057E00 0000080D D8058600   *....-.......Q.......Q.=.....Q...*   13FBA8
0003C0   0000070D D8058F00 0000080D D8059700   00000100 6005A000 00000102 F005A2F9   *....Q.......Q.......-.......0..9*   13FBC8
0003E0   00000008 0DD805A4 00000013 01C805AD   00000001 006005C1 00000005 0DD805C8   *.....Q.......H.......-.A.....Q.H*   13FBE8
000400   00000007 0DD805CE 00000008 0DD805D6   00000007 0DD805DF 00000008 0DD805E7   *.....Q.......Q.O.....Q.......Q.X*   13FC08
000420   00000001 006005F0 0000000D 02F00666   E3D6E3C1 D3E24060 60606060 6E000000   *.....-.0.....0..TOTALS -----....*   13FC28
000440   090DD806 75000000 01006006 7F000000   090DD806 86000000 01006006 90000000   *..Q.......-.......Q.......-.....*   13FC48
000460   1C03F806 E0D6D9C4 C5D940C1 C3C3C5D7   E3C5C440 606040C3 D6D5E3C9 D5E4C540   *..8..ORDER ACCEPTED -- CONTINUE *   13FC68
000480   40000000 1C01F807 07000000 1C01F807   30000000 1C01F807 57FFFFFF FFFFFF00   * .....8.......8.......8.........*   13FC88

END OF CICS/VS STORAGE DUMP
```

Fig. 24.5. (Continued)

The Temporary Storage Area

Other main storage areas for the transaction are printed out after the regular trace table. Thus on page 542 are the blocks labeled "TRANSACTION STORAGE-XXX." You will notice a block labeled "TRANSACTION STORAGE-TS," which is the Temporary Storage Area. CICS/VS uses the first 12 bytes of this block, and thus the user area actually starts at B.

The Working-Storage Section

Other areas labeled "TRANSACTION STORAGE-USER" are those main storage areas secured for the task by CICS/VS or the application program. One of these is the task copy of the WORKING-STORAGE section that CICS/VS secures for a program written with the command level feature to make the program automatically quasi-reentrant. This is C on page 544 and it is easy to locate from the literals ("JOB NORMALLY TERMINATED," etc.) and is one of the last blocks labeled "TRANSACTION STORAGE-USER." This is different from the working storage that is part of the program and which is shown as the first part of "PROGRAM STORAGE" on page 545.

The Symbolic Description Map Area

The symbolic description map area is labeled "TERMINAL STORAGE." This is D on page 545 and the first 12 bytes corresponds to the 12-byte FILLER of the symbolic description map.

The Program Load Address

A literal defines the starting point of the program and its value is always constant for an installation regardless of whether this program is batch or on-line. It prints on the first line of the block labeled "PROGRAM STORAGE." In the case of a DOS/VSE system, this literal is "05F00700900EF00A47F0F082." This is E on page 545 and since the beginning of that line has the address 13C808 and E is offset from the beginning by 24 bytes (hexadecimal 18), the program address is thus 13C820 (13C808 + 18).

PROGRAM CHECK DEBUGGING

Of the several conditions that result in the abnormal termination of a task, only two are of importance to the application programmer. The first is a program check that happens on a logic error like the familiar data exception.* The second is an exceptional condition on a CICS/VS command.

CICS/VS automatically provides the programmer with a transaction dump that is used for debugging. For a program check, some additional information may also be read from the dump. Among these are:

1.	The abend code.**	"ASRA" identifies the problem as a program check. This is F on page 536 (Fig. 24.5).
2.	The transaction identifier	This is G.
3.	The PSW.	This is H.

The first step in debugging this type of problem is to find the instruction that caused the abend. This is done by taking the last 3 bytes of the PSW, which is the address of the next instruction which would have executed had the abend not occurred, and subtracting from it the address where the program was loaded, E on page 545. Thus:

```
   13D9C8
 - 13C820
     11A8
```

From Fig. 24.4, page 533, noting the PROCEDURE DIVISION condensed listing, 11A8 corresponds exactly to statement 590. The

*Certain CICS/VS exceptional conditions result in a transaction abend where CICS/VS treats the problem (as far as generating the dump) like a program check. For instance, if a map specified in a command is not in the CICS/VS program library, an abend with an abend code ABMO results.

**The meaning of abend codes are found in the CICS/VS Messages And Codes Manual (Form SC33-0081-1).

instruction that actually executed when the abend occurred is the one before it and the corresponding statement is thus 589. This is I.

From Fig. 24.3, page 517, we see that statement 589(J) is an ADD statement. The operand 'TWA-COST-MAP' is definitely numeric from statement 586; thus it is the operand 'TWA-TOTAL-COST' that is the problem. From the DATA DIVISION map, page 531, we see that this field (K) is offset from the start of the Transaction Work Area by 07F. This field is L on Fig. 24.5, page 536, and is hexadecimal zeroes.

In fact, this field was not zeroed out in this program. If you refer back to the original File Add program example, Fig. 19.4, statements 00513 and 00514 were removed.

THE CICS/VS COMMAND EXCEPTIONAL CONDITION

The system default for most CICS/VS command exceptional conditions is a transaction dump with the task being aborted. The programmer may then determine the problem by checking the values of the EIBFN and EIBRCODE fields of the Execute Interface Block. However, to simplify the debugging of this type of problem, I suggest the following techniques:

1. Instead of allowing the system to generate the transaction dump, in which case the programmer will have to look for the Execute Interface Block, put the values of EIBFN and EIBRCODE in the WORKING-STORAGE section so they can be easily traced.

2. These are the 'OLD-EIBFN' and 'OLD-EIBRCODE' fields. They are preceded by a tracer* with value 'OLD-EIB' for easier tracing.

---

*A tracer is a FILLER in working storage with a distinct value; it is placed in front of important fields. Its only function is to help locate such fields in a dump.

3. The fields 'OLD-EIBFN' and 'OLD-EIBRCODE' are set to the corresponding values in the Execute Interface Block on a major exceptional condition that terminates the session. These are done at the MAJOR-ERROR paragraph in the ABNORMAL-TERMINATION section. Major exceptional conditions are those covered by the ERROR exceptional condition for unusual conditions not covered by a specific HANDLE CONDITION command.

4. Since the default generation of the transaction dump is replaced by the user routine, the programmer must issue the DUMP command at the same ABNORMAL-TERMINATION section to generate the dump.

The format of the DUMP command is:

```
dump  dumpcode  (data value)
      task
```

The DUMPCODE operand specifies the literal (up to 4 bytes) that prints as the dump code in the listing to identify it. In the program examples, this literal is 'ERRS.' TASK is the default option and should be the one used to ensure that the dump is complete. Other options are not shown.

A transaction dump generated on a major CICS/VS exceptional condition, which will then cause the program to issue the DUMP command, is shown in Figure 24.6.

```
                                                          (A)
CUSTOMER INFORMATION CONTROL SYSTEM STORAGE DUMP    CODE=ERRS   TASK=ORAD       DATE=07/27/80   TIME=19 01 28   PAGE    1

REGS 14-4          401597FC  00000004  00000004  0012F360          0012F07C  8012F084  0012F420

REGS 5-11          5013EB02  00000038  00000002  0010C700          001597C0  0012F0EC  0012F390

TASK CONTROL AREA (USER AREA)  ADDRESS  12E8B8  TO  12EFBF      LENGTH  000708

000000   0012E800 00107234 01100660 00108EF0   0012EBC0 0017F040 80400100 00210000   *..Y........-...0.......0 . ......*   12E8B8
000020   7011B124 0011B0E6 806D9F4E 00183480   5011F096 00000001 00130400 406DABA4   *........W...+.......0.......... ...*   12E8D8
000040   00000000 0011BB18 4011B0E8 0011BAB0   44130170 001303C0 401597FC 401303C0   *........ ..Y........... ... ...*   12E8F8
000060   40120070 401210F4 C004C000 FE12EC48   5011F096 00120096 0012E81C 00000000   * ... ..4..........0........Y......*   12E918
000080   FE0000CA D6D9E3C5 E2E34040 C5D9D9E2   00000000 0000000F 00000000 0012EA41   *....ORTEST  ERRS.................*   12E938
0000A0   401597FC 00000004 00000004 0012F360   0012F07C 8012F084 0012F420 5013EB02   * .............3-...0...0...4......*   12E958
0000C0   00000038 00000002 0010C700 001597C0   0012F0EC 0012F390 1C020000 00010600   *...........G........0...3..........*   12E978
0000E0   00000000 00000000 24F40000 00000000   00000000 00000000 00000000 00000000   *.........4......................*   12E998
000100   00000000 00000000 00000000 00000000   00000000 00000000 00000000 00000000   *................................*   12E9B8
000120   00000000 00000000 00000000 00000000   00000000 00000000 00000000 00000000   *................................*   12E9D8
000140   00000000 00000000 00000000 00000000   000000F0 F0F0F0F8 F5F7F340 40404040   *...................00008573     *   12E9F8
000160   40404040 40404040 40404040 4040F0F1   F2F0F8F2 00020C00 10000C00 20000C00   *               012082...........*   12EA18
000180   0200000C 00040000 0CF0F0F0 F0F0F0F0   F2F1F5D3 F7F7F0D6 D9C1C400 00000000   *..........0000000215L770ORAD.....*   12EA38
0001A0   00000000 51053C00 00000000 00000000   00000000 00000000 00000000 00000000   *................................*   12EA58
0001C0   00000000 00000000 00000000 00000000   00000000 00000000 00000000 00000000   *................................*   12EA78
0001E0   LINES TO 0002E0 SAME AS ABOVE                                                                                    12EA98
000300   D3C9C6D6 E2E3D6D9 42000088 00000000   FF12EC48 5011EB20 8011EB82 9011EBDA   *LIFOSTOR........................*   12EBB8
000320   0012F360 0012F07C 0012F0A6 0012FF29   00000000 821303C0 0011EBE3 0010C700   *..3-..0...0..................T..G.*   12EBD8
000340   0011E770 0011BAB0 0012F390 0012E8B8   001070F0 FE12EC48 F0000000 00000000   *..X........3...Y....0.....0........*   12EBF8
000360   8B000028 00000000 00000000 0011A728   00000000 00000000 00000000 00000000   *................................*   12EC18
000380   00000000 00000000 8B000028 00000000   48000078 0012EBC0 00000000 7011B124   *................................*   12EC38
0003A0   0011B0E6 806D9F4E 00183480 5011F096   00000001 00130400 406DABA4 00000000   *...W...+.......0.......... ........*   12EC58
0003C0   0011BB18 4011B0E8 0011BAB0 44130170   001303C0 00000000 00000000 FE12ECC0   *.... ..Y..........................*   12EC78
0003E0   F500C6C3 0011F180 101303C0 D6D9E3C5   E2E34040 00010600 00000000 0000000F   *5.FC..1.....ORTEST  .............*   12EC98
000400   00000000 0012EA41 00000000 00000000   00000000 00000000 00000000 00000000   *................................*   12ECB8
000420   00000000 00000000 00000000 00000000   00000000 00000000 00000000 00000000   *................................*   12ECD8
000440   LINES TO 0006E0 SAME AS ABOVE                                                                                    12ECF8
000700   8A0307B8 001300F0                                                             *.......0                        *   12EFB8

TASK CONTROL AREA (SYSTEM AREA)ADDRESS  12E800  TO  12E8B7      LENGTH  000088

000000   8A0307B8 001300F0 00000000 00000000   8000008C 00117120 00129880 00000000   *........0.......................*   12E800
000020   00109138 00000000 00000000 00000000   00000000 FF11A6E4 00000000 0012F0EC   *........................U.......0.*   12E820
000040   0012EFC0 0012EC18 00000000 0012F660   00000000 00000000 00000000 00000000   *..............6-..................*   12E840
000060   00000000 00000000 00000000 00000000   00000000 00000000 00000000 0012F390   *..............................3.*   12E860
000080   FE12ECC0 00000000 FE12EBB0 FE12EFB8   00109A28 0012EBC0 00000000 00000000   *................................*   12E880
0000A0   00100660 00000000 00000000 00000000   D6D9C1C4 00000000                       *...-..............ORAD....      *   12E8A0

LIFO STACK ENTRY                  ADDRESS  12EBC0  TO  12EC47      LENGTH  000088

000000   42000088 00000000 FF12EC48 5011EB20   8011EB82 9011EBDA 0012F360 0012F07C   *..........................3-...0.*   12EBC0
000020   0012F0A6 0012FF29 00000000 821303C0   0011EBE3 0010C700 0011E770 0011BAB0   *..0...................T..G...X......*   12EBE0
000040   0012F390 0012E8B8 001070F0 FE12EC48   F0000000 00000000 8B000028 00000000   *..3...Y....0.....0..................*   12EC00
000060   00000000 0011A728 00000000 00000000   00000000 00000000 00000000 00000000   *................................*   12EC20
```

Fig. 24.6. The Transaction Dump, CICS/VS Exceptional Condition.

```
CUSTOMER INFORMATION CONTROL SYSTEM STORAGE DUMP   CODE=ERRS   TASK=ORAD        DATE=07/27/80   TIME=19 01 28   PAGE    2

LIFO STACK ENTRY                 ADDRESS  12EBC0  TO  12EC47        LENGTH  000088

000080    8B000028 00000000                                                              *........                        *   12EC40

COMMON SYSTEM AREA               ADDRESS  1070F0  TO  108EEF        LENGTH  001E00

000000    00000000 00000000 00000000 70155400    00000004 00000004 0012F360 0012F07C    *..........................3-..O.*   1070F0
000020    8012F084 0012F420 5013EB02 00000038    00000002 0010C700 001597C0 0012F0EC    *..O...4................G......O.*   107110
000040    0012F390 0012C0B8 0010023C 0012E8B8    1901289F 001298C0 17700000 00000000    *..3...........Y.................*   107130
000060    00688181 00465000 00008000 00010B10    00002000 00100000 0018FFFF 0080209F    *................................*   107150
000080    001096F8 F0FFFFFF 0000001E 0015EBD8    00000002 00000000 00128520 C434C614    *...80.........Q...........D.F.*   107170
0000A0    00000000 00000000 00129840 00129840    00129880 001095A0 00109138 1000FF00    *................................*   107190
0000C0    000C0001 00091E00 00108EF0 00000000    00000000 00000000 00100A10 00000000    *...........O....................*   1071B0
0000E0    4010A0C4 001150D0 00118804 0315D8F0    001553D8 00100310 0011F064 001231E4    *...D..........QO...Q......O....U*   1071D0
000100    001219D8 00000000 001464A0 0014F1DC    00000000 0010D054 0110DBD0 00146490    *...Q.........1..................*   1071F0
000120    00117090 001198F8 00100260 0011B250    00122A28 001284B0 00128800 00000000    *.......8...-....................*   107210
000140    00000000 00155E64 00100808 0011B090    001228B0 00000000 00000000 00000000    *................................*   107230
000160    0014F1EA 00000000 00000000 87227428    0138F72C 00000000 00000000 0014F4A0    *..1...............7..........4..*   107250
000180    00000000 00000000 00000000 0015F404    00000000 00000000 00000000 FF1070A8    *.................4M.............*   107270
0001A0    07FE58F0 D19C07FF 01398485 0139CA88    00000000 000C0000 E6D6D9D2 C1D9C5C1    *...OJ..................WORKAREA*   107290
0001C0    0000000C 000C0000 003C003C 00008C00    00118C00 00083C00 0C000C00 0C000C00    *................................*   1072B0
0001E0    0C001C00 000C0000 0C000C00 0C00000C    00000C00 000C0000 0C00000C 00000C00    *................................*   1072D0
000200    00000000 00000000 00000000 00000000    00000000 00000000 00000000 00000000    *................................*   1072F0
000220    LINES TO 000720 SAME AS ABOVE                                                                                        107310
000740    00000000 00000000 00000000 00000000    00000000 00000000 00000000 00000000    *................................*   107830
000760    LINES TO 001700 SAME AS ABOVE                                                                                        107850
001720    00000000 00000000 00000000 00000000    00000000 00000000 00000000 00000000    *................................*   108810
001740    LINES TO 001DE0 SAME AS ABOVE                                                                                        108830

CSA OPTIONAL FEATURE LIST        ADDRESS  108EF0  TO  109077        LENGTH  000188

000000    00000000 00000000 00000000 00159BD0    0012532C 00000000 0015CC38 0015CC68    *................................*   108EF0
000020    0014F122 0014EE10 0014E7F4 00000000    00000000 0015C500 00000000 00000000    *..1.......X4..........E.........*   108F10
000040    00000000 00000000 00000000 00000000    00149C98 00000000 00000000 00000000    *................................*   108F30
000060    00000000 01F4D5D6 00000C00 000CFF00    00154D90 00000000 00000000 001070F0    *......4NO...........(..........O*   108F50
000080    00109A28 00154B70 00153760 00150660    00000000 00000000 00000000 00000000    *...........-....-...............*   108F70
0000A0    0010ADF0 00117F70 0010C260 0010BC60    0010E120 0011E770 00122FC0 00121820    *...O.......B-....-.......X.......*   108F90
0000C0    00115020 00119510 0015E4F0 0010A020    0015D720 0010D010 00124EC0 001486A0    *...........UO......P.......+.....*   108FB0
0000E0    001597C0 00154DE0 0015A7D0 00000000    00000000 00000000 0014FCA0 00000000    *......(.........................*   108FD0
000100    00000000 00000000 00000000 00000000    00000000 0010DAF4 001141F0 00000000    *.......................4...O....*   108FF0
000120    00000000 001C000C 000C000C 000C001C    000C000C 000C000C 001C000C 000C000C    *................................*   109010
000140    000C001C 000C000C 000C000C 001C000C    000C000C 000C001C 000C000C 000C000C    *................................*   109030
000160    001C000C 000C000C 000C001C 000C000C    000C000C 001C000C 000C000C 000C001C    *................................*   109050
000180    000C000C 000C000C                                                              *........                        *   109070
```

Fig. 24.6. (Continued)

```
CUSTOMER INFORMATION CONTROL SYSTEM STORAGE DUMP   CODE=ERRS   TASK=ORAD        DATE=07/27/80   TIME=19 01 28   PAGE   3

TRACE TABLE                 ADDRESS  1457F0  TO  14646F      LENGTH  000C80

TRACE HDR         00145B40   001457F0   00146460   00146490

TRACE TABLE       ID REG14  REQD TASK FIELD A  FIELD B                   TRACE TYPE

145B50            F5 120134 0015 0007 00000000 00000000  ........  FCP RESPONSE NORMAL
145B60            E1 132E00 00F4 0007 00000000 0000060E  ........  EIP READNEXT RESPONSE
145B70            E1 132E00 0004 0007 0012FA2C 0000060E  ........  EIP READNEXT ENTRY
145B80            F5 11E9C8 B003 0007 C4E2E7E3 C1C2E240  DSXTABS   FCP GETNEXT
145B90            F0 120476 4004 0007 20000000 00173058  ........  KCP WAIT DCI=DISP
145BA0            F5 120134 0015 0007 00000000 00000000  ........  FCP RESPONSE NORMAL
145BB0            E1 132E00 00F4 0007 00000000 0000060E  ........  EIP READNEXT RESPONSE
145BC0            E1 132E00 0004 0007 0012FA2C 0000060E  ........  EIP READNEXT ENTRY
145BD0            F5 11E9C8 B003 0007 C4E2E7E3 C1C2E240  DSXTABS   FCP GETNEXT
145BE0            F0 120476 4004 0007 20000000 00173058  ........  KCP WAIT DCI=DISP
145BF0            F0 10DBB8 4004 TC   44000000 001007F8  .......8  KCP WAIT
145C00            F5 120134 0015 0007 00000000 00000000  ........  FCP RESPONSE NORMAL
145C10            E1 132E00 00F4 0007 00000000 0000060E  ........  EIP READNEXT RESPONSE
145C20            E1 132E00 0004 0007 0012FA2C 0000060E  ........  EIP READNEXT ENTRY
145C30            F5 11E9C8 B003 0007 C4E2E7E3 C1C2E240  DSXTABS   FCP GETNEXT
145C40            F0 120476 4004 0007 20000000 00173058  ........  KCP WAIT DCI=DISP
145C50            F5 120134 0015 0007 00000000 00000000  ........  FCP RESPONSE NORMAL
145C60            FD 00001C 0204 0007 E3C9D4C5 1900337F  TIME....  TIMING TRACE 19/00/33.7
145C70            E1 132E00 00F4 0007 00000000 0000060E  ........  EIP READNEXT RESPONSE
145C80            E1 132F16 0004 0007 0012FA2C 00000A02  ........  EIP WRITEQ-TS ENTRY
145C90            F1 12187A 8E04 0007 00120540 01100660  ... ....  SCP GETMAIN
145CA0            C8 115222 0004 0007 0012C7B0 8E120548  ..G.....  SCP ACQUIRED TEMPSTRG STORAGE
145CB0            F7 1218C6 4103 0007 D3F7F7F0 D6D9C1C4  L770ORAD  TSP PUTQ
145CC0            F1 12231A F804 0007 00000038 01100660  ........  SCP GETMAIN-COND-INIT
145CD0            C8 115222 0004 0007 0012D000 98000040  .......   SCP ACQUIRED TSTABLE STORAGE
145CE0            F1 121AEA B704 0007 00120554 01100660  ........  SCP GETMAIN-CONDITIONAL
145CF0            C8 115222 0004 0007 0012D040 97120560  ... ....  SCP ACQUIRED TSMAIN STORAGE
145D00            F7 121FCC 0015 0007 00000000 00000000  ........  TSP RESPONSE
145D10            F1 12183E 4004 0007 0012C7B0 01100660  ..G.....  SCP FREEMAIN
145D20            C9 11530C 0004 0007 0012C7B0 8E120548  ..G.....  SCP RELEASED TEMPSTRG STORAGE
145D30            E1 132F16 00F4 0007 00000000 00000A02  ........  EIP WRITEQ-TS RESPONSE
145D40            E1 132F4E 0004 0007 0012FA2C 00000C04  ........  EIP FREEMAIN ENTRY
145D50            F1 11508A 4004 0007 0012C000 01100660  ........  SCP FREEMAIN
145D60            C9 11530C 0004 0007 0012C000 8C120548  ........  SCP RELEASED USER STORAGE
145D70            E1 132F4E 00F4 0007 00000000 00000C04  ........  EIP FREEMAIN RESPONSE
145D80            E1 132F9C 0004 0007 0012FA2C 00000C02  ........  EIP GETMAIN ENTRY
145D90            F1 115052 CC04 0007 000003BE 01100660  ........  SCP GETMAIN-INIT
145DA0            C8 115222 0004 0007 0012C800 8C0003C8  ..H....H  SCP ACQUIRED USER STORAGE
145DB0            E1 132F9C 00F4 0007 00000000 00000C02  ........  EIP GETMAIN RESPONSE
145DC0            E1 13300A 0004 0007 0012FA2C 00001804  ........  EIP SEND-MAP ENTRY
145DD0            FA 124F7E 0003 0007 000005E2 04000020  ...S....  BMS OUT MAP MAPSET SAVE ERASE
145DE0            F2 1261AC 0804 0007 D6D9C1D7 E2F0F140  ORAPS01   PCP DELETE
145DF0            F2 126200 0404 0007 D6D9C1C4 E2F0F140  ORADS01   PCP LOAD
145E00            F1 118572 8804 0007 00120095 01100660  ........  SCP GETMAIN
145E10            C9 11530C 0004 0007 0013B800 88002800  ........  SCP RELEASED PGM STORAGE
145E20            C9 11530C 0004 0007 00136800 88002800  ........  SCP RELEASED PGM STORAGE
145E30            C9 11530C 0004 0007 0013A000 88001800  ........  SCP RELEASED PGM STORAGE
```

Fig. 24.6. (Continued)

CUSTOMER INFORMATION CONTROL SYSTEM STORAGE DUMP CODE=ERRS TASK=ORAD DATE=07/27/80 TIME=19 01 28 PAGE 4

TRACE TABLE	ID	REG14	REQD	TASK	FIELD A	FIELD B		TRACE TYPE
145E40	C9	11530C	0004	0007	00139000	88001000	....	SCP RELEASED PGM STORAGE
145E50	C9	11530C	0004	0007	0013F800	88000800	..8.....	SCP RELEASED PGM STORAGE
145E60	C9	11530C	0004	0007	0013E000	88001000	....	SCP RELEASED PGM STORAGE
145E70	C9	11530C	0004	0007	00133800	88001000	....	SCP RELEASED PGM STORAGE
145E80	C9	11530C	0004	0007	00135000	88001800	....	SCP RELEASED PGM STORAGE
145E90	C9	11530C	0004	0007	00134800	88000800	....	SCP RELEASED PGM STORAGE
145EA0	C8	115222	0004	0007	00130800	88000800	....	SCP ACQUIRED PGM STORAGE
145EB0	F0	11862A	4004	0007	88000000	0011A746	....	KCP WAIT DCI=CICS
145EC0	F1	127F3A	9E04	0007	00130850	01100660	....	SCP GETMAIN
145ED0	C8	115222	0004	0007	0012D800	9E130858	..Q.....	SCP ACQUIRED MAPCOPY STORAGE
145EE0	F1	124578	CC04	0007	000004E0	01100660	....	SCP GETMAIN-INIT
145EF0	C8	115222	0004	0007	0012E060	8C0004E8	.......Y	SCP ACQUIRED USER STORAGE
145F00	F1	124846	8504	0007	001205D3	01100660	...L....	SCP GETMAIN
145F10	C8	115222	0004	0007	00129170	851205E8	.......Y	SCP ACQUIRED TERMINAL STORAGE
145F20	F1	124A00	4004	0007	0012E060	01100660	....	SCP FREEMAIN
145F30	C9	11530C	0004	0007	0012E060	8C0004E8	.......Y	SCP RELEASED USER STORAGE
145F40	F1	124A00	4004	0007	0012D800	01100660	..Q.....	SCP FREEMAIN
145F50	C9	11530C	0004	0007	0012D800	9E130858	..Q.....	SCP RELEASED MAPCOPY STORAGE
145F60	FC	126CA8	0103	0007	00810000	00100660	....	ZCP ZARQ APPL REQ ERASE WRITE
145F70	FA	125EE6	0005	0007	00000000	00000000	....	BMS RESPONSE
145F80	E1	13300A	00F4	0007	00000000	00001804	....	EIP SEND-MAP RESPONSE
145F90	E1	133058	0004	0007	0012FA2C	00000E08	....	EIP RETURN ENTRY
145FA0	F1	11970C	9304	0007	00120019	01100660	....	SCP GETMAIN
145FB0	C8	115222	0004	0007	0012D5A0	93120020	..N.....	SCP ACQUIRED SHARED STORAGE
145FC0	F2	119760	1004	0007	D6D9C1C4	F0F1C140	ORAD01A	PCP RETURN
145FD0	F1	118A4A	4004	0007	0012F9E0	01100660	..9.....	SCP FREEMAIN
145FE0	C9	11530C	0004	0007	0012F9E0	8C1303C8	..9....H	SCP RELEASED USER STORAGE
145FF0	F1	118B66	4004	0007	00131000	01100660	....	SCP FREEMAIN
146000	C9	11530C	0004	0007	00131000	88002800	....	SCP RELEASED PGM STORAGE
146010	F1	118B66	4C04	0007	00130800	01100660	....	SCP FREEMAIN
146020	C9	11530C	0004	0007	C0130800	88000800	....	SCP RELEASED PGM STORAGE
146030	F0	118992	8004	0007	00000000	00000000	....	KCP DETACH
146040	D8	10AC20	0203	0007	02000000	0012C620	......F.	SPP SYSTEM
146050	F5	10D7F0	0003	0007	0012C620	00000000	..F.....	FCP DWE PROCESSOR
146060	F1	120D70	4004	0007	0012C620	01100660	..F.....	SCP FREEMAIN
146070	C9	11530C	0004	0007	0012C620	9D120038	..F.....	SCP RELEASED DWE STORAGE
146080	F1	120D70	4004	0007	0012C660	01100660	..F.....	SCP FREEMAIN
146090	C9	11530C	0004	0007	0012C660	8F1200C8	..F....H	SCP RELEASED FILE STORAGE
1460A0	F5	120134	0015	0007	00000000	00000000	....	FCP RESPONSE NORMAL
1460B0	D8	10D95C	0015	0007	00000000	00000000	....	SPP RESPONSE
1460C0	F0	10AC2A	0304	0007	0011A746	00000000	....	KCP DEQALL
1460D0	F1	10ADA0	4A04	KC	C012E800	00000000	..Y.....	SCP FREEMAIN
1460E0	C9	11530C	0004	KC	0012C800	8C0003C8	..H....H	SCP RELEASED USER STORAGE
1460F0	C9	11530C	0004	KC	0012C730	8F120078	..G.....	SCP RELEASED FILE STORAGE
146100	C9	11530C	0004	KC	0012C5A0	8C000078	..E.....	SCP RELEASED USER STORAGE
146110	C9	11530C	0004	KC	0012C550	8C000048	..E.....	SCP RELEASED USER STORAGE
146120	C9	11530C	0004	KC	0012FF40	8C000048	... .	SCP RELEASED USER STORAGE
146130	C9	11530C	0004	KC	0012FEF0	8C000048	...0....	SCP RELEASED USER STORAGE
146140	C9	11530C	0004	KC	0012FE70	8C000078	....	SCP RELEASED USER STORAGE
146150	C9	11530C	0004	KC	0012FE20	8C000048	....	SCP RELEASED USER STORAGE
146160	C9	11530C	0004	KC	0012FDB0	8C000068	....	SCP RELEASED USER STORAGE

Fig. 24.6. (Continued)

```
CUSTOMER INFORMATION CONTROL SYSTEM STORAGE DUMP   CODE=ERRS   TASK=ORAD      DATE=07/27/80   TIME=19 01 28   PAGE   5

TRACE TABLE        ID REG14  REQD TASK FIELD A  FIELD B                  TRACE TYPE

14617C             C9 11530C 0004 KC   0012F9C0 8C120018 ..9.....  SCP RELEASED USER STORAGE
146180             C9 11530C 0004 KC   0012F930 8C000088 ..9.....  SCP RELEASED USER STORAGE
146190             C9 11530C 00C4 KC   0012F6A0 8C000288 ..6.....  SCP RELEASED USER STORAGE
1461A0             C9 11530C 0004 KC   0012F290 8C000408 ..2.....  SCP RELEASED USER STORAGE
1461B0             C9 11530C 00C4 KC   0012E800 8A030598 ..Y.....  SCP RELEASED TCA STORAGE
1461C0             F0 10DBB8 4004 TC   44000000 001007F8 .......8  KCP WAIT
1461D0             F1 10EA54 4004 TC   00129170 80100660 ........  SCP FREEMAIN
1461E0             C9 11530C 0004 TC   00129170 851205E8 .......Y  SCP RELEASED TERMINAL STORAGE
1461F0             F1 10EAF8 6004 TC   00000000 80100660 ........  SCP FREEMAIN ALL
146200             C9 11530C 0004 TC   00129120 85000048 ........  SCP RELEASED TERMINAL STORAGE
146210             F1 10E9F0 E404 TC   0000010F 80100660 ........  SCP GETMAIN-COND-INIT
146220             C8 115222 0004 TC   00129000 84000118 ........  SCP ACQUIRED LINE STORAGE
146230             F0 10DBB8 4004 TC   44000000 001007F8 .......8  KCP WAIT
146240             FD 00001C 0104 TC   00686C18 00686C18 ........  ... REPEAT 00001 TIMES
146250             F0 113464 1104 TC   01100660 D6D9C1C4 ....ORAD  KCP ATTACH-CONDITIONAL
146260             F1 10A91E EA04 TC   000807B0 80100660 ........  SCP GETMAIN-COND-INIT
146270             C8 115222 0004 TC   0012E800 8A0307B8 ..Y.....  SCP ACQUIRED TCA STORAGE
146280             F0 10DBB8 4004 TC   44000000 001007F8 .......8  KCP WAIT
146290             F2 118804 0204 0008 D6D9C1C4 F0F1C140 ORAD01A   PCP XCTL
1462A0             F1 118572 8804 0008 000004F2 01100660 ...2....  SCP GETMAIN
1462B0             C8 115222 0004 0008 0013C800 88002800 ..H.....  SCP ACQUIRED PGM STORAGE
1462C0             F0 11862A 4004 0008 88000000 0011A702 ........  KCP WAIT DCI=CICS
1462D0             F1 1190FC 8C04 0008 0013038C 01100660 ........  SCP GETMAIN
1462E0             C8 115222 0004 0008 0012EFC0 8C1303C8 .......H  SCP ACQUIRED USER STORAGE
1462F0             F1 10C2A6 CC04 0008 00000128 01100660 ........  SCP GETMAIN-INIT
146300             C8 115222 0004 0008 0012F390 8C000138 ..3.....  SCP ACQUIRED USER STORAGE
146310             E1 13D18C 0004 0008 0012F00C 00000202 ..0.....  EIP ADDRESS ENTRY
146320             E1 13D18C 00F4 0008 00000000 00000202 ........  EIP ADDRESS RESPONSE
146330             E1 13D1B2 0004 0008 0012F00C 00000206 ..0.....  EIP HANDLE-AID ENTRY
146340             F1 10BC96 CC04 0008 00000059 01100660 ........  SCP GETMAIN-INIT
146350             C8 115222 0004 0008 0012F4D0 8C000068 ..4.....  SCP ACQUIRED USER STORAGE
146360             F1 10BD98 CC04 0008 00000040 01100660 ... ....  SCP GETMAIN-INIT
146370             C8 115222 0004 0008 0012F540 8C000048 ..5 ....  SCP ACQUIRED USER STORAGE
146380             E1 13D1B2 00F4 0008 00000000 00000206 ........  EIP HANDLE-AID RESPONSE
146390             E1 13D20C 0004 0008 0012F00C 00000204 ..0.....  EIP HANDLE-CONDITION ENTRY
1463A0             F1 10BC96 CC04 0008 00000070 01100660 ........  SCP GETMAIN-INIT
1463B0             C8 115222 0004 0008 0012F590 8C000078 ..5.....  SCP ACQUIRED USER STORAGE
1463C0             F1 10BD98 CC04 0008 00000040 01100660 ... ....  SCP GETMAIN-INIT
1463D0             C8 115222 0004 0008 0012F610 8C000048 ..6.....  SCP ACQUIRED USER STORAGE
1463E0             E1 13D20C 00F4 0008 00000000 00000204 ........  EIP HANDLE-CONDITION RESPONSE
1463F0             E1 13D2EE 0004 0008 0012F00C 00001802 ..0.....  EIP RECEIVE-MAP ENTRY
146400             FA 125080 0003 0008 00000505 00000020 ........  BMS MAP MAPSET MAP IN
146410             F1 12537E CC04 0008 00000274 01100660 ........  SCP GETMAIN-INIT
146420             C8 115222 0004 0008 0012F660 8C000288 ..6.....  SCP ACQUIRED USER STORAGE
146430             F1 15AD78 CC04 0008 00000074 01100660 ........  SCP GETMAIN-INIT
146440             C8 115222 0004 0008 0012F8F0 8C000088 ..80....  SCP ACQUIRED USER STORAGE
146450             F2 126200 0404 0008 D6D9C1C4 E2F0F140 ORADS01   PCP LOAD
146460             F1 118572 8804 0008 00120095 01100660 ........  SCP GETMAIN
```

Fig. 24.6. (Continued)

```
CUSTOMER INFORMATION CONTROL SYSTEM STORAGE DUMP    CODE=ERRS    TASK=ORAD        DATE=07/27/80    TIME=19 01 28    PAGE    6

1457F0          F0 00001C 0204 0008 E3C9D4C5 1901286F  TIME....  TIMING TRACE 19/01/28.6
145800          C8 115222 0004 0008 0013F800 88000800  ..8.....  SCP ACQUIRED PGM STORAGE
145810          F0 11862A 4004 0008 88000000 0011A746  ........  KCP WAIT DCI=CICS
145820          F0 10DBB8 4004 TC   44000000 001007F8  .......8  KCP WAIT
145830          F1 124AAC C504 0008 000003B1 01100660  ........  SCP GETMAIN-INIT
145840          C8 115222 0004 0008 00129120 850003C8  .......H  SCP ACQUIRED TERMINAL STORAGE
145850          F1 124E88 4004 0008 00129000 01100660  ........  SCP FREEMAIN
145860          C9 11530C 0004 0008 00129000 85000118  ........  SCP RELEASED TERMINAL STORAGE
145870          FA 125EE6 0005 0008 00000000 00000000  ........  BMS RESPONSE
145880          E1 13D2EE 00F4 0008 00000000 00001802  ........  EIP RECEIVE-MAP RESPONSE
145890          E1 13D35E 0004 0008 0012F00C 00000A04  ..0.....  EIP READQ-TS ENTRY
1458A0          F7 12192C 8903 0008 D3F7F7F0 D6D9C1C4  L770ORAD  TSP GETQ
1458B0          F1 121C38 AE04 0008 00120540 01100660  ... ....  SCP GETMAIN-CONDITIONAL
1458C0          C8 115222 0004 0008 0012F980 8E120548  ..9.....  SCP ACQUIRED TEMPSTRG STORAGE
1458D0          F7 121FCC 0015 0008 00000000 00000000  ........  TSP RESPONSE
1458E0          E1 13D35E 00F4 0008 00000000 00000A04  ........  EIP READQ-TS RESPONSE
1458F0          E1 13DF8C 0004 0008 0012F00C 00000C02  ..0.....  EIP GETMAIN ENTRY
145900          F1 115052 8C04 0008 001201B1 01100660  ........  SCP GETMAIN
145910          C8 115222 0004 0008 0012FED0 8C1201C8  .......H  SCP ACQUIRED USER STORAGE
145920          E1 13DF8C 00F4 0008 00000000 00000C02  ........  EIP GETMAIN RESPONSE
145930          E1 13E00C 0004 0008 0012F00C 00000204  ..0.....  EIP HANDLE-CONDITION ENTRY
145940          F1 10BD98 CC04 0008 00000040 01100660  ... ....  SCP GETMAIN-INIT
145950          C8 115222 0004 0008 001300A0 8C000048  ........  SCP ACQUIRED USER STORAGE
145960          E1 13E00C 00F4 0008 00000000 00000204  ........  EIP HANDLE-CONDITION RESPONSE
145970          E1 13E098 0004 0008 0012F00C 00000604  ..0.....  [EIP WRITE ENTRY] <-- (C)
145980          F1 11E830 CC04 0008 00000068 01100660  ........  SCP GETMAIN-INIT
145990          C8 115222 0004 0008 001300F0 8C000078  ...0....  SCP ACQUIRED USER STORAGE
1459A0          F5 11E9C8 2803 0008 D6D9E3C5 E2E34040  ORTEST (E) FCP GETAREA
1459B0          F1 120BD8 CF04 0008 000001F1 01100660  ...1....  SCP GETMAIN-INIT
1459C0          C8 115222 0004 0008 00130170 8F000208  ........  SCP ACQUIRED FILE STORAGE
1459D0          F5 120134 0015 0008 00000000 00000000  ........  FCP RESPONSE NORMAL
1459E0          F5 11E9C8 4403 0008 D6D9E3C5 E2E34040  [ORTEST]  FCP PUT-NEW
1459F0          F1 120E62 9D04 0008 00130030 01100660  ........  SCP GETMAIN
145A00          C8 115222 0004 0008 00130380 9D130038  ........  SCP ACQUIRED DWE STORAGE
145A10          F1 120BC8 8F04 0008 00130094 01100660  ........  SCP GETMAIN
145A20          C8 115222 0004 0008 001303C0 8F1300A8  ........  SCP ACQUIRED FILE STORAGE
145A30          F0 11B124 4004 0008 83000000 0017F040  ......0   KCP WAIT DCI=SINGLE
145A40          FD 00001C 0104 0008 00688180 00688180  ........  ... REPEAT 00001 TIMES
145A50          F1 120D70 4004 0008 00130170 01100660  ........  SCP FREEMAIN
145A60          C9 11530C 0004 0008 00130170 8F000208  ........  SCP RELEASED FILE STORAGE
145A70          F5 120134 8215 0008 00000000 00000000  ........  FCP RESPONSE
145A80          F5 11EB20 1003 0008 101303C0 00000000  ........  FCP RELEASE
145A90          F1 120D70 4004 0008 00130380 01100660  ........  SCP FREEMAIN
145AA0          C9 11530C 0004 0008 00130380 9D130038  ........  SCP RELEASED DWE STORAGE
145AB0          F1 120D70 4004 0008 001303C0 01100660  ........  SCP FREEMAIN
145AC0          C9 11530C 0004 0008 001303C0 8F1300A8  .....(B)  SCP RELEASED FILE STORAGE
145AD0          F5 120134 0015 0008 00000000 00000000  ........  FCP RESPONSE NORMAL
145AE0          E1 12F610 02F4 0008 82000000 00000604  ........  [EIP WRITE RESPONSE] <-- (D)
145AF0          E1 13EA34 0004 0008 0012F00C 00001C02  ..0.....  EIP DUMP ENTRY
145B00          F4 1597FC FE04 0008 00000000 C5D9D9E2  ....[ERRS] DCP TRANSACTION
145B10          F0 155C58 4004 0008 80000000 00155E78  ........  KCP WAIT DCI=SINGLE
145B20          F0 10DBB8 4004 TC   44000000 001007F8  .......8  KCP WAIT
145B30          F0 155C58 4004 0008 80000000 00155E78  ........  KCP WAIT DCI=SINGLE
```

Fig. 24.6. (Continued)

```
CUSTOMER INFORMATION CONTROL SYSTEM STORAGE DUMP   CODE=ERRS    TASK=ORAD        DATE=07/27/80   TIME=19 01 28    PAGE    7

145B40            F0 10DBB8 4004 TC    44000000 001007F8  .......8 KCP WAIT

TRANSACTION STORAGE-USER        ADDRESS  1300F0  TO  13016F       LENGTH  000080

000000   8C000078 001300A0 D6D9E3C5 E2E34040   00000000 0811BAB0 00000000 00000000   *.........ORTEST ................*   1300F0
000020   00000000 00000000 00000000 00000000   00000000 00000000 00000000 00000000   *................................*   130110
000040   00000000 00000000 00000000 00000000   00000000 00000000 00000000 00000000   *................................*   130130
000060   00000000 00000000 00000000 FF000000   00000000 00000000 8C000078 001300A0   *................................*   130150

TRANSACTION STORAGE-USER        ADDRESS  1300A0  TO  1300EF       LENGTH  000050

000000   8C000048 0012FED0 5013E00C 0010C5A0   00000025 0012F360 6013EAB0 00000051   *.............E........3--.......*   1300A0
000020   001291AA 5013EB02 0012F00C 0012F2E3   0012F2E4 0013EAD2 0013C820 0013C820   *..........0...2T..2U...K..H...H.*   1300C0
000040   0013CC98 0012F0EC 8C000048 0012FED0                                         *......0.........                *   1300E0

TRANSACTION STORAGE-USER        ADDRESS  12FED0  TO  13009F       LENGTH  0001D0

000000   8C1201C8 0012F980 F0F0F0F0 F0F0F0F2   F1F5F0F0 F5F8F2F0 F1F2F0F0 F7F2F7F8   *...H..9.0000000215005820120072 78*   12FED0
000020   F0000200 000C0004 00000C00 01F0F0F0   F0F8F5F7 F3C3C8C1 C9D540E2 C1E64040   *0............00008573CHAIN SAW  *   12FEF0
000040   40404040 40404040 F0F1F2F0 F8F20002   0C001000 0C002000 0C000000 00000000   *        012082..................*   12FF10
000060   00000000 00000000 00000000 00000000   00000000 00000000 00000000 00000000   *................................*   12FF30
000080   LINES TO 000100 SAME AS ABOVE                                                                                       12FF50
000120   00000000 00000000 00000130 00000000   00000800 00000000 00000000 00000000   *................................*   12FFF0
000140   00000000 00000000 00000000 00000000   00000000 00000000 00000000 00000000   *................................*   130010
000160   LINES TO 0001A0 SAME AS ABOVE                                                                                       130030
0001C0   00000000 00000000 8C1201C8 0012F980                                         *...........H..9.                *   130090

TRANSACTION STORAGE-TS          ADDRESS  12F980  TO  12FECF       LENGTH  000550

000000   8E120548 0012F8F0 05400000 F0F0F0F0   F0F0F0F2 F1F5F0F0 F5F8F2F0 F1F2F0F0   *......80. ..0000000215005820120 0*   12F980
000020   F7F2F7F8 F0000200 000C0004 00000C00   01F0F0F0 F0F8F5F7 F3C3C8C1 C9D540E2   *72780............00008573CHAIN S*   12F9A0
000040   C1E64040 40404040 40404040 F0F1F2F0   F8F20002 0C001000 0C002000 0C000000   *AW              012082..............*   12F9C0
000060   00000000 00000000 00000000 00000000   00000000 00000000 00000000 00000000   *................................*   12F9E0
000080   LINES TO 000180 SAME AS ABOVE                                                                                       12FA00
0001A0   00000000 00000000 00000000 00000000   00000000 00000000 00000000 0007C1D3   *.............................PAL*   12FB20
0001C0   000000BE F0F0F3F0 F0F4F0F0 F5F0F0F7   F0F0F8F0 F0F9F0F1 F0F0F1F2 F0F1F3F0   *....003004005007008009010012013 0*   12FB40
0001E0   F1F4F0F1 F5F0F1F6 F0F1F7F0 F1F8F0F1   F9F0F2F0 F0F2F2F0 F2F3F0F2 F4F0F2F5   *14015016017018019020022023024025*   12FB60
000200   F0F2F6F0 F2F7F0F2 F8F0F2F9 F0F3F0F0   F3F2F0F3 F3F0F3F4 F0F3F5F0 F3F6F0F3   *02602702802903003203303403503603*   12FB80
000220   F7F0F3F8 F0F3F9F0 F4F0F0F4 F1F0F4F2   F0F4F3F0 F4F4F0F4 F5F0F4F6 F0F4F7F0   *70380390040041042043044045046047 0*   12FBA0
000240   F4F8F0F4 F9F0F5F0 F0F5F1F0 F5F2F0F5   F4F0F5F5 F0F5F6F0 F5F7F0F5 F8F0F5F9   *48049050051052054055056057058059*   12FBC0
000260   F0F6F0F0 F6F1F0F6 F2F0F6F3 F0F6F4F0   F6F5F0F6 F7F0F6F8 F0F6F9F0 F7F0F0F7   *06006106206306406506706806907007*   12FBE0
000280   F1F0F7F2 F0F7F4F0 F7F5F0F7 F6F0F7F7   F0F7F8F0 F7F9F0F8 F0F0F8F1 F0F8F2F0   *10720740750760770780790800810820*   12FC00
0002A0   F8F4F0F8 F5F0F8F6 F0F8F7F0 F8F8F0F9   F0F0F9F1 F0F9F2F0 F9F3F0F9 F5F0F9F6   *84085086087088090091092093095096*   12FC20
0002C0   F0F9F7F0 F9F8F0F9 F9F1F0F1 F1F0F2F1   F0F3F1F0 F4F1F0F5 F1F0F6F1 F0F7F1F0   *09709809910110210310410510610710*   12FC40
0002E0   F8F1F0F9 F1F1F1F1 F1F3F1F1 F4F1F1F5   F1F1F6F1 F1F8F1F2 F1F1F2F2 F1F2F3F1   *81091111131141151161181211221231*   12FC60
000300   F2F4F1F2 F5F1F2F6 F1F2F7F1 F2F8F1F3   F0F1F3F1 F1F3F3F1 F3F4F1F3 F5F1F3F6   *24125126127128130131133134135136*   12FC80
000320   F1F3F7F1 F3F9F1F4 F0F1F4F2 F1F4F3F1   F4F4F1F4 F5F1F4F6 F1F4F7F1 F4F8F1F4   *13713914014214314414514614714814*   12FCA0
000340   F9F1F5F1 F1F5F2F1 F5F4F1F5 F5F1F5F6   F1F5F7F1 F5F9F1F6 F0F1F6F1 F1F6F3F1   *91511521541551561571591601611631*   12FCC0
000360   F6F4F1F6 F5F1F6F6 F1F6F7F1 F6F8F1F6   F9F1F7F0 F1F7F1F1 F7F2F1F7 F3F1F7F4   *64165166167168169170171172173174*   12FCE0
```

Fig. 24.6. (Continued)

```
CUSTOMER INFORMATION CONTROL SYSTEM STORAGE DUMP   CODE=ERRS   TASK=ORAD       DATE=07/27/80   TIME=19 01 28   PAGE   8

TRANSACTION STORAGE-TS          ADDRESS  12F980  TO  12FECF       LENGTH  000550

000380   F1F7F5F1 F7F6F1F7 F7F1F7F8 F1F7F9F1   F8F0F1F8 F1F1F8F2 F1F8F3F1 F8F4F1F8   *17517617717817918018118218318418*   12FD00
0003A0   F5F1F8F6 F1F8F7F1 F8F8F1F8 F9F1F9F0   F1F9F1F1 F9F2F1F9 F3F1F9F4 F1F9F5F1   *51861871881891901911921931941951*   12FD20
0003C0   F9F7F1F9 F8F1F9F9 F2F0F0F2 F0F3F2F0   F4F2F0F5 F2F0F6F2 F0F7F2F0 F8F2F0F9   *97198199200203204205206207208209*   12FD40
0003E0   F2F1F0F2 F1F5F2F1 F9F2F2F6 F2F2F9F2   F3F0F2F3 F4F2F4F1 F2F4F2F2 F4F70000   *210215219226229230234241242247..*   12FD60
000400   00000000 00000000 00000000 00000000   00000000 00000000 00000000 00000000   *................................*   12FD80
000420   LINES TO 000520 SAME AS ABOVE                                                                                       12FDA0
000540   00000000 00000000 8E120548 0012F8F0                                         *..............80                *   12FEC0

TRANSACTION STORAGE-USER        ADDRESS  12F8F0  TO  12F97F       LENGTH  000090

000000   8C000088 0012F660 D4D40000 00000001   00010001 00000000 00000000 00000000   *......6-MM......................*   12F8F0
000020   0013F808 00000000 00000000 00000000   00000000 00000000 D6D9C1C4 E2F0F140   *..8.....................ORADS01 *   12F910
000040   00000000 00000000 00000000 18500000   40000001 01015000 00000000 00000780   *............... ................*   12F930
000060   00000000 01100660 00404000 00000000   00000000 00000000 FFFFFFFF 00000000   *......-.  ......................*   12F950
000080   00000000 00000000 8C000088 0012F660                                         *..............6-                *   12F970

TRANSACTION STORAGE-USER        ADDRESS  12F660  TO  12F8EF       LENGTH  000290

000000   8C000288 0012F610 401256A6 0015A9C8   401258C0 001244CA 00000000 00000000   *......6. ......H ...............*   12F660
000020   00000000 00000000 00000000 00000000   00000000 00000000 00000000 00000000   *................................*   12F680
000040   00000000 00000000 00000505 00000020   F0F1C140 00000000 D6D9C1C4 D4F0F140   *................01A ....ORADM01 *   12F6A0
000060   D6D9C1C4 E2F0F140 0000C260 00000000   00000000 00000000 00000000 00000000   *ORADS01 ..B-....................*   12F6C0
000080   00000000 00000000 00000000 00000000   0012F8F0 0012F8F0 00000000 00000000   *................80..80..........*   12F6E0
0000A0   00000000 00000000 00000000 0010066C   00000000 00000000 00000000 00000000   *................................*   12F700
0000C0   00000000 00000000 00000000 00000000   1411A6E4 00000000 00000001 00000000   *.....................U..........*   12F720
0000E0   00000000 00000000 00000000 00000010   00000000 00000000 00000000 00000000   *................................*   12F740
000100   00000000 00000000 00000000 00000000   00000000 00000000 00000000 00000000   *................................*   12F760
000120   00000000 00000000 00000000 00000000   00000000 00000000 00000000 00000000   *................................*   12F780
000140   00000000 40126200 001252D8 000004B0   08129000 00000018 000000FF 0010066C   *.... ......Q....................*   12F7A0
000160   0013F814 90125884 48000058 0010C700   0012F660 0012F8F0 01100660 00000000   *..8...........G...6-..80...-....*   12F7C0
000180   00000000 00000000 00000000 00110000   00000000 00000000 00000000 00000000   *................................*   12F7E0
0001A0   00000000 00000000 00000000 00000000   00000000 00000000 00000000 00000000   *................................*   12F800
0001C0   LINES TO 000260 SAME AS ABOVE                                                                                       12F820
000280   00000000 00000000 8C000288 0012F610                                         *..............6.                *   12F8E0

TRANSACTION STORAGE-USER        ADDRESS  12F610  TO  12F65F       LENGTH  000050

000000   8C000048 0012F590 5013D20C 0010C5A0   0012F00C 0012F360 5013D1C4 0013CCA8   *......5...K...E...0...3-..JD....*   12F610
000020   0012F420 5013EB02 0012F00C 0012F2E3   0012F2E4 0013EAD2 0013C820 0013C820   *..4.......0...2T..2U...K..H...H.*   12F630
000040   0013CC98 0012F0EC 8C000048 0012F590                                         *......0.......5.                *   12F650

TRANSACTION STORAGE-USER        ADDRESS  12F590  TO  12F60F       LENGTH  000080

000000   8C000078 0012F540 0012F5D7 00700402   00000000 00000000 00000000 00000000   *......5 ..5P....................*   12F590
000020   00030000 00000000 00000000 00000000   00000100 00000000 00000000 00000000   *................................*   12F5B0
000040   00000000 00000000 00000000 00000001   12F61004 12F0EC02 12F61004 12F0EC01   *................6...0...6...0..*   12F5D0
000060   1300A004 12F0EC00 00000000 00000000   00000000 000000FF 8C000078 0012F540   *.....0.......................5 *   12F5F0
```

Fig. 24.6. (Continued)

```
CUSTOMER INFORMATION CONTROL SYSTEM STORAGE DUMP   CODE=ERRS   TASK=ORAD        DATE=07/27/80   TIME=19 01 28   PAGE    9

TRANSACTION STORAGE-USER        ADDRESS  12F540   TO  12F58F       LENGTH  000050

000000   8C000048 0012F4D0 5013D1B2 0010C5A0    0012F00C 0012F360 0013EB40 00118BA0   *......4...J...E...0...3-... ....*   12F540
000020   0012F420 5013EB02 0012F00C 0012F2E3    0012F2E4 0013EAD2 0013C820 0013C820   *..4........0...2T..2U...K..H...H.*  12F560
000040   0013CC98 0012F0EC 8C000048 0012F4D0                                          *......0........4.               *   12F580

TRANSACTION STORAGE-USER        ADDRESS  12F4D0   TO  12F53F       LENGTH  000070

000000   8C000068 0012F390 0012F500 00590500    00040201 03000000 00000000 00000000   *......3...5.....................*   12F4D0
000020   00000000 00000000 00000000 00000000    00000000 00000000 0112F540 0412F0EC   *.......................5 ..0.*      12F4F0
000040   0212F540 0412F0EC 0312F540 0412F0EC    0412F540 0412F0EC 00000000 00000000   *..5 ..0...5 ..0...5 ..0.........*   12F510
000060   FF000000 00000000 8C000068 0012F390                                          *..............3.               *    12F530

TRANSACTION STORAGE-USER        ADDRESS  12F390   TO  12F4CF       LENGTH  000140

000000   8C000138 0012EFC0 0012F488 00000000    00000000 00000000 00000000 00000000   *..........4.....................*   12F390
000020   00000000 00000000 00000000 00000000    00000000 00000000 00000000 00000000   *................................*   12F3B0
000040   0012F420 8012F424 001300A0 A011ECAA    00129120 00000000 0012F980 00000000   *..4...4...................9.....*   12F3D0
000060   00000000 00000000 001300F8 001300F8    00000000 0012F590 0012F4D0 00000000   *............8...8.......5...4.....*  12F3F0
000080   01000004 00000000 00010000 00000000    0012F488 8012D5B8 0012F0EC 0012F00C   *.................4...N...0...0.*   12F410
0000A0   00000000 00118DEC 0012F0EC 4010C43E    4013C822 00118DEC 0012F420 0013C8F0   *..........0. .D. .H.......4...HO*   12F430
0000C0   0012EFD0 0013C868 00118E68 0012E800    0013C820 0010C260 0013D13A FF11A6E4   *......H.......Y...H...B-..J....U*   12F450
0000E0   0012F390 0012E8B8 80000000 010E0000    40C4C6C8 C5C9C240 0190128C 0080209F   *..3...Y.........  DFHEIB ........*  12F470
000100   D6D9C1C4 0000008C D3F7F7F0 0000068D    00017D1C 02000000 000000D6 D9E3C5E2   *ORAD....L770.......'........ORTES*  12F490
000120   E3404000 00000000 00000000 00000000    00000000 00000000 8C000138 0012EFC0   *T  .............................*   12F4B0

TRANSACTION STORAGE-USER        ADDRESS  12EFC0   TO  12F38F       LENGTH  0003D0
                                                        (F)          (G)
000000   8C1303C8 0012E800 00000000 00000000    0013C920 5013EB1A 0013EB40 00118BA0   *...H..Y............I......... ....*  12EFC0
000020   0013C820 5013EB02 0013C920 0013CBF7    0013CBF8 0013EAD2 0013C820 0013C820   *..H.......I....7...8...K..H...H.*   12EFE0
000040   0013CC98 0013CA00 001190C6 00000000    00000000 D3C9D5C5 40F24060 40000000   *............F........LINE 2 - ...*  12F000
000060   00000000 00000000 00000000 00000000    D1D6C240 D5D6D9D4 C1D3D3E8 40E3C5D9   *...................JOB NORMALLY TER*  12F020
000080   D4C9D5C1 E3C5C4D1 D6C240C1 C2D6D9E3    C5C44060 60400000 00000000 00000000   *MINATEDJOB ABORTED -- ..........*   12F040
0000A0   00000000 00000000 D6D3C440 C5C9C206    04820000 00000000 00000000 1C028000   *.........OLD EIB.................*  12F060
0000C0   040000FE 00404040 40404040 40404040    40404040 4040D6D9 C1C4D4F0 F140D6D9   *.....                ORADM01 OR*    12F080
0000E0   C1C4E2F0 F140D6D9 E3C5E2E3 40400000    00000000 C5D9D9E2 00000000 00000000   *ADS01 ORTEST  ......ERRS........*   12F0A0
000100   00000000 0001B100 00000000 00000000    00000000 00000000 00000000 00000000   *................................*   12F0C0
000120   00000C00 00400000 00000000 00000000    0012F430 00000000 5013EA34 0010C5A0   *..... ............4...........E.*   12F0E0
000140   0012F00C 0012F360 4013D21E 0013CCA8    0012F420 5013EB02 0012F00C 0012F2E3   *..0...3-  .K.......4.......0...2T*  12F100
000160   0012F2E4 0013EAD2 0013C820 0013C820    0013CC98 2010004B 00000000 00000000   *..2U...K...H...H.................*  12F120
000180   0010C3D4 00000000 00000000 FFF0F0F5    00000000 00000002 00000001 00000003   *..CM..........005...............*   12F140
0001A0   01000000 00000000 00000000 00000000    00000000 00000000 00000000 00000000   *................................*   12F160
0001C0   00000000 00000000 00000000 00000000    00000000 00000000 00000000 00000000   *................................*   12F180
0001E0   LINES TO 0002A0 SAME AS ABOVE                                                                                        12F1A0
0002C0   00000000 00000000 00000000 00000000    00000000 D6D9C1C4 F0F1C140 0013C820   *.....................ORAD01A ..H.*  12F280
0002E0   00000000 00000000 00000000 00000000    00000000 00000000 00000000 00000000   *................................*   12F2A0
000300   00000000 00000000 00000000 00000000    00000000 00000000 00000000 00000000   *................................*   12F2C0
000320   0012F00C 00000000 0400000F 00000000    0400000F 00000000 0000002C 0012FB44   *..0.............................*   12F2E0
000340   000000BE 0013D472 01000003 00000000    0012F488 8012D5B8 0012F318 00129120   *.......M............4...N...3.......*  12F300
000360   0012FED8 0012E9B8 0012F98C 00000000    00000000 00000000 002C0051 00000000   *...Q..Z...9.....................*   12F320
```

Fig. 24.6. (Continued)

```
CUSTOMER INFORMATION CONTROL SYSTEM STORAGE DUMP   CODE=ERRS   TASK=ORAD       DATE=07/27/80   TIME=19 01 28   PAGE   10

TRANSACTION STORAGE-USER         ADDRESS  12EFC0  TO  12F38F       LENGTH  0003D0

000380   000000A6 FFFFFFE1 00000000 00000000   00000006 001291AA 0013DCD0 0013DCD0   *................................*   12F340
0003A0   0012F07C 8012F0B4 0012FED8 0012EA5B   8012EA41 8012F0C5 00000000 00000000   *..0...0....Q...$......0E........*   12F360
0003C0   00000000 00000000 8C1303C8 0012E800                                         *...........H..Y.                *   12F380

TERMINAL CONTROL TBL USER AREA ADDRESS  1007E8  TO  1007F7       LENGTH  000010

000000   00000000 00000000 00000000 00000000                                         *................                *   1007E8

TERMINAL CONTROL TABLE           ADDRESS  100660  TO  100723       LENGTH  0000C4

000000   D3F7F7F0 99F20404 00129120 00129120   0012E8B8 00000000 001007E8 10000000   *L770.2..........Y........Y.....*   100660
000020   00000000 0C000000 00000100 00000900   068D7D00 D6D9C1C4 E2F0F140 00000000   *.................'.ORADS01 ....*   100680
000040   00000000 00000000 07801850 00000000   00000000 00C40000 00000000 001005A8   *....................D.........*   1006A0
000060   0010070E 00000000 0012D5A0 00000000   00000000 00000000 00840000 0000005C   *..........N.....................**   1006C0
000080   00008C00 0C00005C 000C8100 00400000   40000000 00000000 00000000 00000000   *.......*..... .. ..............*   1006E0
0000A0   00000000 00000000 00000000 00001600   00000100 18500000 82000000 D4D40000   *...........................MM..*   100700
0000C0   00000000                                                                    *....                            *   100720

TERMINAL STORAGE                 ADDRESS  129120  TO  1294EF       LENGTH  0003D0

000000   850003C8 00100664 03AA0000 000100F1   000300F0 F0F0F0F0 F0F0F2F1 F5000400   *...H...........1...0000000215...*   129120
000020   F0F0F0F0 F5F3F2F8 000100F0 F0F50006   00F0F1F2 F0F8F200 0400F0F0 F0F0F8F5   *00005328...005...012082...000085*   129140
000040   F7F30009 00C3C8C1 C9D540E2 C1E64040   40404040 40404040 000200F0 F0F0F2F0   *73...CHAIN SAW             ...00020*   129160
000060   000500F0 F0F1F0F0 F0F00006 00F0F0F2   F0F0F0F0 F0000500 F0F0F2F0 F0F0F000   *...0010000...00200000...0020000.*   129180
000080   0600F0F0 F4F0F0F0 F0F00000 00000000   00000000 00000000 00000000 00000000   *..00400000......................*   1291A0
0000A0   00000000 00000000 00000000 00000000   00000000 00000000 00000000 00000000   *................................*   1291C0
0000C0   LINES TO 000300 SAME AS ABOVE                                                                                         1291E0
000320   00000006 00F0F0F0 F2F0F0F0 F0F00006   00F0F0F0 F4F0F0F0 F0F00000 00404040   *.....000200000...000400000...   *   129440
000340   40404040 40404040 40404040 40404040   40404040 40404040 40000000 40404040   *                          ...   *   129460
000360   40404040 40404040 40404040 40404040   40404040 40404040 00000040 40404040   *                         ...    *   129480
000380   40404040 40404040 40404040 40404040   40404040 40404000 00004040 40404040   *                        ...     *   1294A0
0003A0   40404040 40404040 40404040 40404040   40404040 40400000 00000000 00000000   *                      ..........*   1294C0
0003C0   00000000 00000000 850003C8 00100664                                         *...........H....                *   1294E0

PROGRAM STORAGE                  ADDRESS  13C808  TO  13EF8F       LENGTH  002788

000000   C4C6C8C5 58F0F00C 07FF58F0 F00A07FF   001191B6 0010C760 05F00700 900EF00A   *DFHE.00....00.........G-.0....0.*   13C808
000020   47F0F082 00118DEC 0012F420 0013C8F0   0012EFD0 0013C868 00118E68 0012E800   *.00.......4...HO.......H.......Y.*   13C828
000040   0013C820 0010C260 0013D13A FF11A6E4   0012F390 0012E8B8 0012F430 4010C43E   *..H...B-..J....U..3...Y...4. .D.*   13C848
000060   0013C920 5013EB1A 0013EB40 00118BA0   0013C820 5013EB02 0013C920 0013CBF7   *..I........ ......H.......I....7*   13C868
000080   0013CBF8 0013EAD2 0013C820 0013C820   0013CC98 0013CA00 001190C6 58C0F0C6   *...8...K..H...H............F..0F*   13C888
0000A0   58E0C000 58D0F0CA 9500E000 4770F0A2   9610D048 92FFE000 47F0F0AC 98CEF03A   *......0.......0.........00...0.*   13C8A8
0000C0   90ECD00C 185D989F F0BA9110 D0480719   07FF0700 0013EAD2 0013C820 0013C820   *.....)..0...............K..H...H.*   13C8C8
0000E0   0013CC98 0012F0EC 0013D13A 0013EAB8   C3D6C2C6 F2F5F5F1 D6D9C1C4 F0F1C140   *......0...J.....COBF2551ORAD01A *   13C8E8
000100   C013CC24 F0F761F2 F761F8F0 F1F848F5   F64BF3F5 00000000 00000000 00000000   *....07/27/8018.56.35.............*   13C908
000120   D3C9D5C5 40004060 40000000 00000000   00000000 00000000 00000000 D1D6C240   *LINE . - ..................JOB *   13C928
000140   D5D6D9D4 C1D3D3E8 40E3C5D9 D4C9D5C1   E3C5C4D1 D6C240C1 C2D6D9E3 C5C44060   *NORMALLY TERMINATEDJOB ABORTED -*   13C948
```

Fig. 24.6. (Continued)

```
CUSTOMER INFORMATION CONTROL SYSTEM STORAGE DUMP   CODE=ERRS   TASK=ORAD        DATE=07/27/80   TIME=19 01 28   PAGE   11

PROGRAM STORAGE                  ADDRESS  13C808  TO  13EF8F      LENGTH  002788

000160   60400000 00000000 00000000 00000000   00000000 D6D3C440 C5C9C200 00000000   *- .................OLD EIB.....*   13C968
000180   00000000 00000000 00000000 00000000   00000000 00000000 00000000 00000000   *...............................*   13C988
0001A0   LINES TO 0001C0 SAME AS ABOVE                                                                                         13C9A8
0001E0   00000000 00000000 00000000 00000C00   00400000 00000000 00000000 00118DEC   *............... .............*     13C9E8
000200   00000000 00000000 00000000 00000000   00000000 00000000 00000000 00000000   *...............................*   13CA08
000220   00000000 00000000 00000000 00000000   00000000 00000000 00000000 00000000   *...............................*   13CA28
000240   20100048 00000000 00000000 001190C6   00000000 00000000 00000000 00000000   *..............F................*   13CA48
000260   00000000 00000000 00000000 00000000   00000000 00000000 00000000 00000000   *...............................*   13CA68
000280   LINES TO 000380 SAME AS ABOVE                                                                                         13CA88
0003A0   D6D9C1C4 F0F1C140 0013C820 00000000   00000000 00000000 00000000 00000000   *ORAD01A ..H....................*   13CBA8
0003C0   00000000 00000000 00000000 00000000   00000000 00000000 00000000 00000000   *...............................*   13CBC8
0003E0   00000000 00000000 00000000 0013C920   00000000 00000000 00000000 00000000   *..............I................*   13CBE8
000400   00000000 00000000 00000000 00000000   00000000 00000000 00000000 00000000   *...............................*   13CC08
000420   LINES TO 000440 SAME AS ABOVE                                                                                         13CC28
000460   00000000 00000000 0013DCD0 00000000   00000000 00000000 00000000 00000000   *...............................*   13CC68
000480   00000000 00000000 00000000 00000000   0013E840 0013C812 0013EE90 0013EB98   *.................. ..H.........*   13CC88
0004A0   0013C820 0013D290 0013D4DC 0013D52E   0013D5E4 0013D5F8 0013D670 0013DCCA   *..H...K...M...N...NU..N8..O.....*  13CCA8
0004C0   0013DCD0 0013DEC4 0013DED8 0013E20C   0013E258 0013E302 0013E404 0013E49A   *.......D...Q..S...S...T...U...U.*  13CCC8
0004E0   0013E598 0013E660 0013E858 0013E86C   0013E952 0013E978 0013E9AC 0013E9C2   *..V...W-..Y...Y...Z...Z...Z...ZB*  13CCE8
000500   0013E9D8 0013E9E4 0013E9F0 0013EA4A   0013EA5A 0013EA8A 0013EAA8 0013EAB0   *..ZQ..ZU..ZO...................*   13CD08
000520   0013D278 0013D25E 0013D272 0013D3BA   0013D400 0013D41A 0013D46C 0013D4D6   *..K...K ..K...L...M...M...M...MO*  13CD28
000540   0013D472 0013D478 0013D592 0013D62E   0013D662 0013D750 0013D6EC 0013D73C   *..M...M...N...O...O...P...O...P.*  13CD48
000560   0013D772 0013D800 0013D7EA 0013D7D0   0013D7E4 0013D8C0 0013D848 0013D8AC   *..P...Q...P...P...PU..Q...Q...Q.*  13CD68
000580   0013D980 0013D908 0013D96C 0013DA4C   0013D9DE 0013DA38 0013DB06 0013DA94   *..R...R...R.......R............*   13CD88
0005A0   0013DAF2 0013DBD2 0013DB64 0013DBBE   0013DBF2 0013DC38 0013DC32 0013DCBE   *...2...K...........2...........*   13CDA8
0005C0   0013DC50 0013DCAA 0013DCE4 0013DD70   0013DD5C 0013DDAE 0013DE1A 0013DE06   *...........U.......*...........*   13CDC8
0005E0   0013DE58 0013DEB0 0013DF3C 0013DF26   0013DF4C 0013E65A 0013E620 0013E674   *.......................W...W...W.*  13CDE8
000600   0013DCD0 0013C820 00000100 FFE1FFFF   00030000 00630000 00000C00 00010002   *......H........................*   13CE08
000620   00040008 00100020 0040007D 007F0009   01B1002C 002503BE 053CFFFD 0000001F   *......... .'...................*   13CE28
000640   02028000 04030000 00000000 00000000   00000206 F0000405 04060300 00000000   *...................0...........*   13CE48
000660   00000000 0204C000 04240100 00000000   00000000 0000D6D9 C1C4D4F0 F1D6D9C1   *....................ORADM01ORA*    13CE68
000680   C4E2F0F1 1802D000 04010000 00050900   0000200A 04E80004 01008900 C9D5E5C1   *DS01.................Y.......INVA*  13CE88
0006A0   D3C9C440 D6D9C4C5 D940D5E4 D4C2C5D9   C9D5E5C1 D3C9C440 C4D6C3E4 D4C5D5E3   *LID ORDER NUMBERINVALID DOCUMENT*  13CEA8
0006C0   40D5E4D4 C2C5D9C9 D5E5C1D3 C9C440C4   C5D7C1D9 E3D4C5D5 E340D5E4 D4C2C5D9   * NUMBERINVALID DEPARTMENT NUMBER*  13CEC8
0006E0   F0F0F1F3 F2C9D5E5 C1D3C9C4 40D6D9C4   C5D960C4 C1E3C5C9 D5E5C1D3 C9C440C9   *00132INVALID ORDER-DATEINVALID I*  13CEE8
000700   E3C5D440 D5E4D4C2 C5D9C9D5 E5C1D3C9   C440C4C5 E2C3D9C9 D7E3C9D6 D5C9D5E5   *TEM NUMBERINVALID DESCRIPTIONINV*  13CF08
000720   C1D3C9C4 40E4D5C9 E340C3D6 E2E3C9D5   E5C1D3C9 C440C3D6 E2E3C9D5 E5C1D3C9   *ALID UNIT COSTINVALID COSTINVALI*  13CF28
000740   C440E4D5 C9E340D7 D9C9C3C5 C9D5E5C1   D3C9C440 D7D9C9C3 C5C9D5C3 D6D4D7D3   *D UNIT PRICEINVALID PRICEINCOMPL*  13CF48
000760   C5E3C540 C4C1E3C1 D5D640D3 C9D5C540   C9E3C5D4 40C5D5E3 C5D9C5C4 C9D5C3D6   *ETE DATANO LINE ITEM ENTEREDINCO*  13CF68
000780   D9D9C5C3 E340E3D6 E3C1D340 C3D6E2E3   C9D5C3D6 D9D9C5C3 E340E3D6 E3C1D340   *RRECT TOTAL COSTINCORRECT TOTAL *  13CF88
0007A0   D7D9C9C3 C50C02C0 00040000 8C000204   80000413 00000000 00000000 00000000   *PRICE..........................*   13CFA8
0007C0   D6D9E3C5 E2E30604 F0000428 0044000C   04800004 00004000 D6F11402 F8000400   *ORTEST..0............ .O1..8...*   13CFC8
0007E0   00000318 04D00004 00000000 05620400   00200E08 E0000400 00100018 04D10004   *..........................J..*     13CFE8
000800   00000000 15200400 0020C4E4 D7D3C9C3   C1E3C540 606040D5 D6E340C1 C3C3C5D7   *..........DUPLICATE -- NOT ACCEP*  13D008
000820   E3C5C40C 02E00004 0000CC00 D6D9C4C5   D940C2E8 D7C1E2E2 C5C44060 40C3D6D5   *TED.........ORDER BYPASSED - CON*  13D028
000840   E3C9D5E4 C51804D0 00040000 000005E2   04000020 02048000 042C0000 00000000   *TINUE..........S...............*   13D048
000860   00000000 00000A06 80000400 00210002   04800004 14000000 00000000 00000000   *...............................*   13D068
000880   00C4E2E7 E3C1C2E2 060C8000 040020A0   00060ED4 00040100 B000F9F9 F9F8F50A   *.DSXTABS............M.......99985.*  13D088
0008A0   02E00004 00004100 C5D5E3C5 D940C6C9   D9E2E340 D6D9C4C5 D9040430 00040000   *.........ENTER FIRST ORDER.......*  13D0A8
0008C0   00810000 40000000 0E080000 04000010   00E3C5D3 F2D6D7C5 D50E0480 00040000   *.... .............TEL2OPEN.......*  13D0C8
0008E0   0200D4C1 D740C6C1 C9D3E4D9 C5D7D9D6   C3C5E2E2 40C5D9D9 D6D9E2C9 C7D5D6D5   *..MAP FAILUREPROCESS ERRORSIGNON*  13D0E8
```

Fig. 24.6. (Continued)

```
CUSTOMER INFORMATION CONTROL SYSTEM STORAGE DUMP   CODE=ERRS   TASK=ORAD      DATE=07/27/80   TIME=19 01 28   PAGE  12

PROGRAM STORAGE                ADDRESS  13C808  TO  13EF8F     LENGTH  002788

000900  40E5C906 D3C1E3C9 D6D5E3C1 C2D3C540   D5D6E340 D3D6C1C4 C5C4C5D9 D9E21C02   * VIOLATIONTABLE NOT LOADEDERRS..*   13D108
000920  80000400 00FE00D4 C1D1D6D9 40C5D9D9   D6D95840 D0045840 40185810 40005010   *.......MAJOR ERROR. ...  ... ...*   13D128
000940  D2245810 40045010 D2281811 58F0C004   05EFD211 6070C180 92406082 D2066083   *K... ...K.....0....K.-.A.. -.K.-.*  13D148
000960  60824110 60705010 D27458E0 D22C4110   E00C5010 D2789680 D2784110 D27458F0   *-...-...K...K.......K...K...K..0*   13D168
000980  C00405EF D2116070 C1C29240 6082D206   60836082 41106070 5010D274 9680D274   *....K.-.AB. -.K.-.-...-...K...K.*   13D188
0009A0  4110D274 58F0C004 05EF58E0 D2244810   E0144130 C0104910 C1900520 47202022   *..K..0......K...........A.......*   13D1A8
0009C0  88100001 47C02022 48112018 89100002   58113000 07F10012 000D000D 000D0211   *.......................1.......K.*  13D1C8
0009E0  6070C1D4 92406082 D2066083 60824110   60705010 D2749680 D2744110 D27458F0   *-.AM. -.K.-.-...-...K...K...K..0*   13D1E8
000A00  C00405EF 58E0D224 4810E014 4130C010   4910C18E 05204720 201E8B10 000147C0   *......K............A............*   13D208
000A20  201E4811 20188910 00025811 300007F1   0016001A 4830E018 4930C178 58F0C090   *..............1..........A..0...*   13D228
000A40  078F5820 C09458E0 D22895F1 E0000772   5810C014 07F15820 C09858E0 D22895F0   *........K..1.........1.......K..0*  13D248
000A60  E0000772 5810C048 07F15810 C06C07F1   58E0D224 4830E018 4930C178 58F0C014   *.........1.....1..K........A..0..*  13D268
000A80  077F5810 C07007F1 D206608A C1E69240   6091D206 6092C1ED 92406099 D20E6070   *.......1K.-.AW. -.K.-.A.. -.K.-.*   13D288
000AA0  C1F49240 607FD209 6080607F 41106070   5010D274 4110608A 5010D278 58E0D22C   *A4. -.K.-.-...-...K...-...K...K.*   13D2A8
000AC0  4110E004 5010D27C 411060D7 5010D280   41106092 5010D284 9680D284 4110D274   *......K...-P..K...-...K...K...K.*   13D2C8
000AE0  58F0C004 05EF58E0 D23858F0 D2240203   E093F010 D203E097 F008D201 60B9C179   *.0.......K..0K.K...0.K...0.K.-.A.*  13D2E8
000B00  D2086070 C2039240 6079D20F 607A6079   41106070 5010D274 4110E093 5010D278   *K.-.B.. -.K.- -...-...K.......K.*   13D308
000B20  58E0D22C 4110E010 5010D27C 58E0D238   4110E0A5 5010D280 411060D9 5010D284   *..K........K...K.......K...-R..K.*  13D328
000B40  411060B9 5010D288 9680D288 4110D274   58F0C004 05EF58E0 D2309240 E33DD21A   *..-...K...K...K..0.......K.. T.K.*  13D348
000B60  E33EE33D 9240E35C D21AE35D E35C9240   E37BD21A E37CE37B 9240E39A D21AE39B   *T.T.. T*K.T)T*. T.K.T.T.. T.K.T.*   13D368
000B80  E39A4800 C17C5000 D2585820 C00858E0   D230DD09 E0132000 5810C09C 077158E0   *T...A...K.......K...............*   13D388
000BA0  D23C58F0 D230D209 E000F013 5810C0A0   07F14100 001F5A00 D2585000 D25858E0   *K..0K.K...0.......1.......K...K...*  13D3A8
000BC0  D2304140 E33D5A40 D2585040 D26858E0   D268D213 E000C20C 58E0D268 9240E014   *K.. T.. K.. K...K.K...B...K.. ..*   13D3C8
000BE0  58E0D268 58F0D268 D206E015 F01458E0   D230D201 E010C17E 5820C008 58E0D230   *..K..0K.K...0...K.K...A=......K.*   13D3E8
000C00  DD07E020 20005810 C0A40771 5810C0A8   07F14100 001F5A00 D2585000 D25858E0   *.................1.......K...K...*  13D408
000C20  D2304140 E33D5A40 D2585040 D26858E0   D268D216 E000C220 58E0D268 9240E017   *K.. T.. K.. K...K.K...B...K.. ..*   13D428
000C40  58E0D268 58F0D268 D203E018 F01718B00  5900D258 58F0C0A8 077F58E0 D230D201   *..K..0K.K....0......K..0.......K.K.*  13D448
000C60  E01DC17E 5810C0AC 07F15810 C01807F1   58E0D23C 4100E1B8 5000D210 5800E1B4   *..A=.....1.....1..K.......K.....*   13D468
000C80  5000D214 D203D218 C0B0D201 D21EC180   58E0D230 D202D208 E02B9201 D21C4100   *..K.K.K...K.K.A...K.K.K.....K...*   13D488
000CA0  D2084110 D21058F0 C00C05EF 88030000   58101000 1B015000 D26458E0 D23C58F0   *K...K..0...............K...K..0*   13D4A8
000CC0  D230D202 E00AF02B 5810C01C 07F15810   C0B407F1 4100001F 5A00D258 5000D258   *K.K...0......1.....1......K...K.*   13D4C8
000CE0  58E0D230 4140E33D 5A40D258 5040D268   58E0D268 D218E000 C23758E0 D2689240   *..K.. T.. K.. K...K.K...B...K.. *   13D4E8
000D00  E01958E0 D26858F0 D268D201 E01AF019   1B005900 D25858F0 C01C077F 58E0D230   *.....K...0K.K...0.....K...0......K.*  13D508
000D20  D201E028 C17E5820 C0B858E0 D230D501   E031C250 07D25820 C0B8D501 E031C252   *K...A=.......K.N...B..K.....N....B.*  13D528
000D40  07B25820 C0B8D501 E033C250 07D25820   C0B8D501 E033C253 07B25820 C008DD01   *......N...B..K.....N...B.........*  13D548
000D60  E0352000 5810C0B8 077158E0 D23C58F0   D230D201 E00FF031 D201E011 F033D201   *............K..0K.K...0.K...0.K.*   13D568
000D80  E00DF035 5810C020 07F14100 001F5A00   D2585000 D25858E0 D2304140 E33D5A40   *..0.......1.......K...K...K.. T.. *  13D588
000DA0  D2585040 D26858E0 D268D211 E000C255   58E0D268 9240E012 58E0D268 58F0D268   *K.. K...K.K...B...K.. ....K..0K.*   13D5A8
000DC0  D208E013 F0121B00 5900D258 58F0C020   077F58E0 D230D201 E02EC17E 4100005D   *K...0......K..0......K.K...A=...)*  13D5C8
000DE0  5900D258 58F0C024 077F5810 C04007F1   18005000 D25458E0 D238D203 E09BC182   *..K..0....... .1....K...K.K....A.*  13D5E8
000E00  58F0D230 D205E06E F031D204 E07FC186   D204E084 C1865800 D2705000 D26C5800   *.0K.K...0.K...A.K...A...K...K...*   13D608
000E20  C0BC5000 D27058E0 D2385830 E09B4930   C17858F0 C0C0078F 4100005D 5900D258   *....K...K.......A..0........)..K.*  13D628
000E40  58F0C0C0 078F4100 02985900 D25458F0   C0C0074F 5810C028 07F15800 D26C5000   *.0...........K..0..........1..K...*  13D648
000E60  D2705810 C03007F1 58E0D238 D203E09B   C1861B00 5810D254 41200053 1D024A10   *K.......1..K.K...A.....K..........*  13D668
000E80  C18C4E10 D208F307 600DD208 96F0600D   58E0D230 4140E037 5A40D254 5040D268   *A.+.K.3.-.K..0-...K.. ... K.. K.*   13D688
000EA0  58E0D238 58F0D268 D252E000 F0004830   E0004930 C17858F0 C0C4078F 5820C008   *..K..0K.K...0........A..0.D.....*   13D6A8
000EC0  DD07E003 20005810 C0C80771 D207E053   E0034830 C18C5A30 E09B5030 E09B5810   *..........H..K.......A...........*  13D6C8
000EE0  C0C407F1 D2126011 C2674100 001F5A00   D2585000 D25858E0 D2304140 E33D5A40   *.D.1K.-.B.......K...K...K.. T.. *   13D6E8
000F00  D2585040 D26858E0 D268D21B E0006008   1B005900 D25858F0 C0CC077F 58E0D230   *K.. K...K.K...-......K..0.......K.*  13D708
000F20  4140E037 5A40D254 D2014000 C17E5810   C0C407F1 4100005D 5900D258 58F0C0C4   *. ... K.K. .A=...D.1...)..K..0.D*   13D728
000F40  077F5810 C02C07F1 58E0D238 4830E00B   4930C178 58F0C0D0 077F9240 E05BD211   *........1..K........A..0..... .$K.*  13D748
```

Fig. 24.6. (Continued)

```
CUSTOMER INFORMATION CONTROL SYSTEM STORAGE DUMP    CODE=ERRS    TASK=ORAD         DATE=07/27/80    TIME=19 01 28    PAGE   13

PROGRAM STORAGE                ADDRESS  13C808   TO   13EF8F       LENGTH  002788

000F60   E05CE05B 5810C0D4 07F15820 C0D858E0   D2389540 E00E0772 D2126011 C27A4100   *.*.$...M.1...Q..K.. ....K.-.B ..*   13D768
000F80   001F5A00 D2585000 D25858E0 D2304140   E33D5A40 D2585040 D26858E0 D268D21B   *....K...K...K.. T.. K.. K...K.K.*   13D788
000FA0   E0006008 1B005900 D25858F0 C0DC077F   58E0D230 4140E042 5A40D254 D2014000   *..-.....K..O.......K.. ... K.K. .*   13D7A8
000FC0   C17E5810 C0D407F1 4100005D 5900D258   58F0C0E0 077F5810 C02C07F1 5810C0D4   *A=...M.1...)..K..O..........1...M*   13D7C8
000FE0   07F158E0 D238D212 E05BE00E 4830C18E   5A30E09B 5030E09B 58E0D238 4830E021   *.1..K.K..$....A............K.....*   13D7E8
001000   4930C178 58F0C0E4 078F5820 C008DD04   E0242000 5810C0E8 0771F274 D1F8E024   *..A..O.U.................Y..2.J8..*   13D808
001020   F822E074 D1FD94F0 E076960C E0764830   C1905A30 E09B5030 E09B5810 C0E407F1   *8...J..O.........A..............U.1*   13D828
001040   58E0D238 D202E074 C188D20B 6011C28D   9240601D D205601E 601D4100 001F5A00   *..K.K...A.K.-.B.. -.K.-.-.......*   13D848
001060   D2585000 D25858E0 D2304140 E33D5A40   D2585040 D26858E0 D268D21B E0006008   *K...K...K.. T.. K.. K...K.K...-.*   13D868
001080   1B005900 D25858F0 C0EC077F 58E0D230   4140E058 5A40D254 D2014000 C17E5810   *....K..O.......K.. ... K.K. .A=..*   13D888
0010A0   C0E407F1 4100005D 5900D258 58F0C0E4   077F5810 C02C07F1 58E0D238 4830E029   *.U.1...)..K..O.U........1..K.....*   13D8A8
0010C0   4930C178 58F0C0F0 078F5820 C008DD06   E02C2000 5810C0F4 0771F276 D1F8E02C   *..A..O.O.................4..2.J8..*   13D8C8
0010E0   F833E077 D1FC94F0 E07A960C E07A4830   C1925A30 E09B5030 E09B5810 C0F007F1   *8...J..O. ... ..A..............O.1*   13D8E8
001100   58E0D238 D203E077 C187D210 6011C28D   92406022 D2006023 60224100 001F5A00   *..K.K...A.K.-.B.. -.K.-.-.......*   13D908
001120   D2585000 D25858E0 D2304140 E33D5A40   D2585040 D26858E0 D268D21B E0006008   *K...K...K.. T.. K.. K...K.K...-.*   13D928
001140   1B005900 D25858F0 C0F8077F 58E0D230   4140E060 5A40D254 D2014000 C17E5810   *....K..O.8....K.. .-. K.K. .A=..*   13D948
001160   C0F007F1 4100005D 5900D258 58F0C0F0   077F5810 C02C07F1 58E0D238 4830E033   *.O.1...)..K..O.O........1..K.....*   13D968
001180   4930C178 58F0C0FC 078F5820 C008DD07   E0362000 5810C100 0771F873 D1F8E077   *..A..O..................A...8.J8..*   13D988
0011A0   FC62D1F9 E074F277 D200E036 F946D203   D1F958F0 C100077F F277D200 E036FA44   *..J9..2.K...9.K.J9.OA...2.K.....*   13D9A8
0011C0   E07FD203 4830C194 5A30E09B 5030E09B   5810C0FC 07F1D20B 6011C29E 9240601D   *..K...A................1K.-.B.. -.*   13D9C8
0011E0   D205601E 601D4100 001F5A00 D2585000   D25858E0 D2304140 E33D5A40 D2585040   *K.-.-........K...K...K.. T.. K.. *   13D9E8
001200   D26858E0 D268D21B E0006008 1B005900   D25858F0 C104077F 58E0D230 4140E06A   *K...K.K...-.......K..OA......K.. ..*   13DA08
001220   5A40D254 D2014000 C17E5810 C0FC07F1   4100005D 5900D258 58F0C0FC 077F5810   *. K.K. .A=......1...)..K..O.......*   13DA28
001240   C02C07F1 58E0D238 4830E03E 4930C178   58F0C108 078F5820 C008DD06 E0412000   *...1..K........A..OA..............*   13DA48
001260   5810C10C 0771F276 D200E041 F833E07B   D20494F0 E07E960C E07E4830 C1965A30   *..A...2.K...8...K..O.=....=..A...*   13DA68
001280   E09B5030 E09B5810 C10807F1 58E0D238   D203E07B C187D211 6011C2AA 92406023   *.........A..1..K.K...A.K.-.B.. -.*   13DA88
0012A0   4100001F 5A00D258 5000D258 58E0D230   4140E33D 5A40D258 5040D268 58E0D268   *.......K...K...K.. T.. K.. K...K.*   13DAA8
0012C0   D21BE000 60081B00 5900D258 58F0C110   077F58E0 D2304140 E0755A40 D254D201   *K...-......K..OA......K.. ... K.K.*   13DAC8
0012E0   4000C17E 5810C108 07F14100 005D5900   D25858F0 C108077F 5810C02C 07F158E0   * .A=..A..1...)..K..OA..........1..*   13DAE8
001300   D2384830 E0484930 C17858F0 C114078F   5820C008 DD07E04B 20005810 C1180771   *K.........A..OA..................A...*   13DB08
001320   F873D200 E07BFC62 D201E074 F277D1F8   E04BF946 D1FBD201 58F0C118 077FF277   *8.K......K...2.J8..9.J.K..OA...2.*   13DB28
001340   D200E04B FA44E084 D2034830 C1985A30   E09B5030 E09B5810 C11407F1 D20C6011   *K.........K...A..............A..1K.-.*   13DB48
001360   C2BC9240 601ED204 601F601E 4100001F   5A00D258 5000D258 58E0D230 4140E33D   *B.. -.K.-.-.........K...K...K.. T.*   13DB68
001380   5A40D258 5040D268 58E0D268 D21BE000   60081B00 5900D258 58F0C11C 077F58E0   *. K.. K...K.K...-......K..OA......*   13DB88
0013A0   D2304140 E07F5A40 D254D201 4000C17E   5810C114 07F14100 005D5900 D25858F0   *K.. ... K.K. .A=..A..1...)..K..O*   13DBA8
0013C0   C114077F 5810C02C 07F158E0 D2385830   E09B4930 C19A58F0 C120078F 5830E09B   *A.........1..K.........A..OA.........*   13DBC8
0013E0   4930C19C 58F0C124 077F4800 C17C5900   D25858F0 C128077F 5810D254 4120002C   *..A..OA......A...K..OA......K.......*   13DBE8
001400   1C024120 00531D02 5010D260 58E0D23C   4140E025 5A40D260 5040D268 58E0D268   *............K-..K.. ... K-. K...K.*   13DC08
001420   58F0D238 D22BE000 F0535810 C12C07F1   58E0D238 5830E09B 4930C178 58F0C130   *.OK.K...O...A..1..K.........A..OA.*   13DC28
001440   077F5810 C12C07F1 4100001F 5A00D258   5000D258 D20E6011 C2C99240 60200202   *.....A..1.......K...K.K.-.BI. -.K.*   13DC48
001460   60216020 58E0D230 4140E33D 5A40D258   5040D268 58E0D268 D21BE000 60081B00   *-.-...K.. T.. K.. K...K.K...-...*   13DC68
001480   5900D258 58F0C134 077F58E0 D2304140   E0375A40 D254D201 4000C17E 5810C12C   *..K..OA......K.. ... K.K. .A=..A.*   13DC88
0014A0   07F14100 005D5900 D25858F0 C12C077F   5810C02C 07F14100 00535A00 D2545000   *.1...)..K..OA..........1.......K....*   13DCA8
0014C0   D2545810 D27007F1 4100005D 5900D258   58F0C138 077F5810 C04007F1 41000053   *K...K..1...)..K..OA....... .1.....*   13DCC8
0014E0   5900D254 58F0C13C 077F58E0 D2385830   E09B4930 C17858F0 C13C077F 4100001F   *..K..OA......K.........A..OA.........*   13DCE8
001500   5A00D258 5000D258 58E0D230 4140E33D   5A40D258 5040D268 58E0D268 D213E000   *..K...K...K.. T.. K.. K...K.K....*   13DD08
001520   C2D858E0 D2689240 E01458E0 D26858F0   D268D206 E015F014 1B005900 D25858F0   *BQ..K.. ....K..OK.K...O......K..O*   13DD28
001540   C140077F 58E0D23C D201E037 C17E5810   C13C07F1 4100005D 5900D258 58F0C13C   *A ....K.K...A=..A..1...)..K..OA.*   13DD48
001560   077F5810 C03407F1 5820C008 58E0D230   DD08E325 20005810 C1440771 F278D200   *........1.......K...T.....A...2.K.*   13DD68
001580   E32558E0 D238F944 D203E07F 58F0C144   077F58E0 D23C58F0 D238F844 E019F07F   *T...K.9.K.....OA......K..OK.8...O.*   13DD88
0015A0   5810C148 07F14100 001F5A00 D2585000   D25858E0 D2304140 E33D5A40 D2585040   *..A..1.......K...K...K.. T.. K.. *   13DDA8
```

Fig. 24.6. (Continued)

```
CUSTOMER INFORMATION CONTROL SYSTEM STORAGE DUMP   CODE=ERRS   TASK=ORAD        DATE=07/27/80   TIME=19 01 28   PAGE   14

PROGRAM STORAGE              ADDRESS  13C808   TO  13EF8F       LENGTH  002788

0015C0   D26858E0 D268D213 E000C2EC 58E0D268   9240E014 58E0D268 58F0D268 D206E015   *K...K.K...B...K.. ....K..OK.K...*   13DDC8
0015E0   F0141800 5900D258 58F0C14C 077F58E0   D230D201 E322C17E 5810C148 07F14100   *0.....K..OA.....K.K.T.A=..A..1..*   13DDE8
001600   005D5900 D25858FC C148077F 5810C034   07F15820 C00858E0 D230DD08 E3312000   *.)..K..OA.........1.......K...T...*   13DE08
001620   5810C150 0771F278 D200E331 58E0D238   F944D203 E08458F0 C150077F 58E0D23C   *..A...2.K.T...K.9.K.....OA......K.*   13DE28
001640   58F0D238 F844E01E F0845810 C03407F1   4100001F 5A00D258 5000D258 58E0D230   *.OK.8...0.......1.......K...K...K.*   13DE48
001660   4140E33D 5A40D258 5040D268 58E0D268   D214E000 C30058E0 D2689240 E01558E0   *. T.. K.. K...K.K...C...K.. ....*   13DE68
001680   D25858F0 D268D205 E016F015 18005900   D25858F0 C154077F 58E0D230 D201E32E   *K..OK.K...0......K..OA......K.K.T.*   13DE88
0016A0   C17E5810 C03407F1 4100005D 5900D258   58F0C034 077F5810 C03407F1 4800C17C   *A=......1...)..K..0...........1..A.*   13DEA8
0016C0   5900D258 58F0C038 078F5810 C04007F1   18005810 D2544120 00531D02 4A10C18C   *..K..0........ .1....K...........A.*   13DEC8
0016E0   58E0D23C 4010E023 4830E023 4930C19E   58F0C158 07DF58E0 D2385830 E09B4930   *..K. ..........A..OA......K........*   13DEE8
001700   C17858F0 C15C077F 58E0D23C 4830E023   4830C18E 4030E023 5810C160 07F158E0   *A..OA*.....K.........A. ......A-.1..*   13DF08
001720   D23C4830 E0234830 C18C4030 E0235810   C16007F1 58E0D23C 4830E023 4830C18E   *K.........A. ......A-.1..K.........A.*   13DF28
001740   4030E023 D20160B9 C1A0D208 6070C315   92406079 D20F607A 60794110 60705010   * ...K.-.A.K.-.C.. -.K.- -...-...*   13DF48
001760   D27458E0 D22C4110 E0085010 D2784110   60B95010 D27C9680 D27C4110 D27458F0   *K...K........K...-...K...K...K..0*   13DF68
001780   C00405EF 58E0D234 58F0D23C D201E023   F0235820 C0880522 58E0D234 4100E000   *.......K..OK.K...0...........K......*   13DF88
0017A0   4810D24E 58E0D23C 4120E000 413001B1   BF38C199 0E025820 C0880522 58E0D234   *..K+..K.............A..............K.*   13DFA8
0017C0   4830E023 4C30C1A2 4A30C1A4 58E0D238   4030E0A3 58F0D23C D209E089 F000D211   *........A....A...K. ....OK.K...0.K.*   13DFC8
0017E0   6070C31E 92406082 D2066083 60824110   60705010 D2749680 D2744110 D27458F0   *-.C.. -.K.-.-...-...K...K...K..0*   13DFE8
001800   C00405EF 58E0D224 4810E014 4130C010   4910C18C 05204720 201C8B10 000147C0   *.......K.............A...............*   13E008
001820   201C4811 20188910 00025811 300007F1   0015D205 609AC330 924060A0 D20060A1   *.................1..K.-.C.. -.K.-.*   13E028
001840   60A0D208 6070C336 92406079 D20F607A   60794110 60705010 D2744110 609A5010   *-.K.-.C.. -.K.- -...-...K...-...*   13E048
001860   D27858E0 D2344110 E0005010 D27C58E0   D2384110 E0A35010 D2804110 E0895010   *K...K.........K...K.........K........*   13E068
001880   D2849680 D2844110 D27458F0 C00405EF   5820C088 0522D208 6070C33F 92406079   *K...K...K..0..............K.-.C.. -.*   13E088
0018A0   D20F607A 60794110 60705010 D27458E0   D2344110 E0005010 D2789680 D2784110   *K.- -...-...K...K.........K...K...*   13E0A8
0018C0   D27458F0 C00405EF 5820C088 0522D201   60B9C1A4 D2086070 C3159240 6079D20F   *K..0..............K.-.A.K.-.C.. -.K.*   13E0C8
0018E0   607A6079 41106070 5010D274 58E0D22C   4110E014 5010D278 411060B9 5010D27C   *- -...-...K...K.........K...-...K.*   13E0E8
001900   9680D27C 4110D274 58F0C004 05EF58E0   D24058F0 D23CD202 E000F1B1 D205E003   *..K...K..0........K .OK.K...1.K...*   13E108
001920   F013D209 E009F000 F844E01B F019F844   E020F01E 58F0D230 D207E013 F02058E0   *0.K...0.8...0.8...0..OK.K...0...*   13E128
001940   D238D201 E0A9C1A4 D20160B9 C18ED201   60B0C348 D2086070 C34A9240 6079D20F   *K.K...A.K.-.A.K.-.C.K.-.C.. -.K.*   13E148
001960   607A6079 41106070 5010D274 411060B9   5010D278 4110E09F 5010D27C 411060B0   *- -...-...K...-...K.........K...-.*   13E168
001980   5010D280 58E0D240 4110E000 5010D284   58E0D238 4110E0A9 5010D288 9680D288   *..K...K .......K...K.........K...K.*   13E188
0019A0   4110D274 58F0C004 05EFD206 608AC1E6   92406091 D2066092 C1ED9240 6099D20E   *..K..0.....K.-.AW. -.K.-.A.. -.K.*   13E1A8
0019C0   6070C353 9240607F D2096080 607F4110   60705010 D2744110 608A5010 D2784110   *-.C.. -.K.-.-...-...K...-...K...*   13E1C8
0019E0   60D95010 D27C4110 60D75010 D2804110   60925010 D2849680 D2844110 D27458F0   *-R..K...-P..K...-...K...K...K..0*   13E1E8
001A00   C00405EF 92F16000 D20160B9 C179D208   6070C362 92406079 D20F607A 60794110   *......1-.K.-.A.K.-.C.. -.K.- -...*   13E208
001A20   60705010 D27458E0 D2244110 E0085010   D2784110 60005010 D27C4110 60B95010   *-...K...K.........K...-...K...-...*   13E228
001A40   D2809680 D2804110 D27458F0 C00405EF   D206608A C1E69240 6091D206 6092C1ED   *K...K...K..0.....K.-.AW. -.K.-.A.*   13E248
001A60   92406099 D20160B9 C17ED20E 6070C36B   9240607F D2096080 607F4110 60705010   *. -.K.-.A=K.-.C,. -.K.-.-...-...*   13E268
001A80   D2744110 608A5010 D27858E0 D2304110   E0005010 D27C4110 60D75010 D2804110   *K...-...K...K.........K...-P..K...*   13E288
001AA0   60925010 D2844110 60D95010 D2884110   60D95010 D28C4110 60D95010 D2904110   *-...K...-R..K...-R..K...-R..K...*   13E2A8
001AC0   60B95010 D2949680 D2944110 D27458F0   C00405EF 5810C03C 07F158E0 D230D218   *-...K...K...K..0...........1..K.K.*   13E2C8
001AE0   E33DC37A 9240E356 D201E357 E356D201   E010C17E 5810C040 07F1D201 60B9C1A6   *T.C . T.K.T.T.K...A=... .1K.-.A.*   13E2E8
001B00   D2086070 C3939240 6079D20F 607A6079   41106070 5010D274 58E0D22C 4110E004   *K.-.C.. -.K.- -...-...K...K......*   13E308
001B20   5010D278 411060B9 5010D27C 4110605B   5010D280 9680D280 4110D274 58F0C004   *..K...-...K...-$..K...K...K..0..*   13E328
001B40   05EF58E0 D230D218 E33DC39C 9240E356   D201E357 E356D206 608AC1E6 92406091   *.....K.K.T.C.. T.K.T.T.K.-.AW. -.*   13E348
001B60   D2066092 C1ED9240 6099D20E 6070C3B5   9240607F D2096080 607F4110 60705010   *K.-.A.. -.K.-.C.. -.K.-.-...-...*   13E368
001B80   D2744110 608A5010 D2784110 E0005010   D27C4110 60D75010 D2804110 60925010   *K...-...K.........K...-P..K...-...*   13E388
001BA0   D2849680 D2844110 D27458F0 C00405EF   92F16000 D20160B9 C179D208 6070C362   *K...K...K..0......1-.K.-.A.K.-.C.*   13E3A8
001BC0   92406079 D20F607A 60794110 60705010   D27458E0 D2244110 E0085010 D2784110   *. -.K.- -...-...K...K.........K...*   13E3C8
001BE0   60005010 D27C4110 60B95010 D2809680   D2804110 D27458F0 C00405EF D2116070   *-...K...-...K...K...K..0.....K.-.*   13E3E8
001C00   C3C49240 6082D206 60836082 41106070   5010D274 9680D274 4110D274 58F0C004   *CD. -.K.-.-...-...K...K...K..0..*   13E408
```

Fig. 24.6. (Continued)

```
CUSTOMER INFORMATION CONTROL SYSTEM STORAGE DUMP   CODE=ERRS   TASK=ORAD        DATE=07/27/80   TIME=19 01 28   PAGE   15

PROGRAM STORAGE                ADDRESS  13C808  TO  13EF8F      LENGTH  002788

001C20   05EF58E0 D2244810 E0144130 C0104910   C18C0520 4720201C 8B100001 47C0201C   *....K............A...............*   13E428
001C40   48112018 89100002 58113000 07F1000F   58E0D238 58F0D224 D203E093 F010D203   *............1....K..OK.K...O.K.*   13E448
001C60   E097C1E6 D2086070 C3D69240 6079D20F   607A6079 41106070 5010D274 4110E093   *..AWK.-.CO. -.K.- -...-...K.....*   13E468
001C80   5010D278 9680D278 4110D274 58F0C004   05EFD201 60B9C1A8 D2086070 C3159240   *..K...K...K..O....K.-.A.K.-.C.. *   13E488
001CA0   6079D20F 607A6079 41106070 5010D274   58E0D22C 4110E010 5010D278 411060B9   *-.K.- -...-...K...K.......K...-.*   13E4A8
001CC0   5010D27C 9680D27C 4110D274 58F0C004   05EF4800 C1AA5000 D26458E0 D23892C4   *..K...K...K..O.......A...K...K..D*   13E4C8
001CE0   E0D2D203 E0D3C1AC D2116070 C3DF9240   6082D206 60836082 41106070 5010D274   *.KK..LA.K.-.C.. -.K.-.-...-...K.*   13E4E8
001D00   9680D274 4110D274 58F0C004 05EF58E0   D2244810 E0144130 C0104910 C18C0520   *..K...K..O......K...........A...*   13E508
001D20   4720201C 8B100001 47C0201C 48112018   89100002 58113000 07F10011 D20660 9A   *.........................1..K.-.*   13E528
001D40   C3F19240 60A1D208 6070C3F8 92406079   D20F607A 60794110 60705010 D2744110   *C1. -.K.-.C8. -.K.- -...-...K...*   13E548
001D60   609A5010 D2784110 60D95010 D27C4110   60D75010 D28058E0 D2384110 E0D25010   *-...K...-R..K...-P..K...K...K...*   13E568
001D80   D2849680 D2844110 D27458F0 C00405EF   D206609A C3F19240 60A1D208 6070C401   *K...K...K..O....K.-.C1. -.K.-.D.*   13E588
001DA0   92406079 D20F607A 60794110 60705010   D2744110 609A5010 D27858E0 D22C4110   *. -.K.- -...-...K...-...K...K...*   13E5A8
001DC0   E0185010 D27C4110 60D75010 D28058E0   D2384110 E0D25010 D2844110 60D75010   *....K...-P..K...K...K..K...-P..*   13E5C8
001DE0   D2884110 60D75010 D28C9680 D28C4110   D27458F0 C00405EF 5820C164 58E0D244   *K...-P..K...K...K..O.......A...K.*   13E5E8
001E00   95C4E000 07725820 C168D502 E005C40A   07725810 C05407F1 5820C164 58E0D244   *.D.......A.N...D........1..A...K.*   13E608
001E20   D501E026 C40D07B2 41000003 5A00D264   5000D264 58E0D23C 4140E1B8 5A40D264   *N...D..........K...K...K.. ... K.*   13E628
001E40   5040D268 58E0D268 58F0D244 D202E000   F0055810 C05007F1 4800C1AA 5900D264   *. K...K...OK.K...O.......1..A...K.*   13E648
001E60   58F0C16C 077F5810 C07407F1 1B005810   D2644120 00031D02 4A10C18C 58E0D23C   *.0A........1....K..........A...K.*   13E668
001E80   5010E1B4 5820C08C 05225810 00140A21   58E0D238 D207E0CA 100058E0 D23C58F0   *.................K.K.........K..O*   13E688
001EA0   D238D201 E013F0CA D201E015 F0CDD201   E017F0D0 58F0D228 D202E1B1 F00158E0   *K.K...O.K...O.K...O..OK.K...O...*   13E6A8
001EC0   D238D201 E0A5C1A8 D2086070 C40F9240   6079D20F 607A6079 41106070 5010D274   *K.K...A.K.-.D.. -.K.- -...-...K.*   13E6C8
001EE0   4110E093 5010D278 58E0D23C 4110E000   5010D27C 58E0D238 4110E0A5 5010D280   *.......K...K........K...K.......K.*   13E6E8
001F00   9680D280 4110D274 58F0C004 05EF5820   C08C0522 D2086070 C33F9240 6079D20F   *..K...K..O..........K.-.C.. -.K.*   13E708
001F20   607A6079 41106070 5010D274 58E0D23C   4110E000 5010D278 9680D278 4110D274   *- -...-...K...K..........K...K...K.*   13E728
001F40   58F0C004 05EF5820 C08C0522 D20160B9   C1A6D208 6070C393 92406079 D20F607A   *.O..........K.-.A.K.-.C.. -.K.- *   13E748
001F60   60794110 60705010 D27458E0 D22C4110   E0045010 D2784110 60B95010 D27C4110   *-...-...K...K..........K...-...K...*   13E768
001F80   605B5010 D2809680 D2804110 D27458F0   C00405EF 58E0D230 D210E33D C4189240   *-$..K...K...K..O.......K.K.T.D.. *   13E788
001FA0   E34ED209 E34FE34E D206608A C1E69240   6091D206 6092C1ED 92406099 D20E6070   *T+K.T.T+K.-.AW. -.K.-.A.. -.K.-.*   13E7A8
001FC0   C3B59240 607FD209 6080607F 41106070   5010D274 4110608A 5010D278 4110E000   *C.. -.K.-.-...-...K...-...K......*   13E7C8
001FE0   5010D27C 411060D7 5010D280 41106092   5010D284 9680D284 4110D274 58F0C004   *..K...-P..K...-...K...K...K..O..*   13E7E8
002000   05EF92F1 6000D203 60A8C1E6 D20160B9   C179D208 6070C362 92406079 D20F607A   *...1-.K.-.AWK.-.A.K.-.C.. -.K.- *   13E808
002020   60794110 60705010 D2744110 60A85010   D2784110 60005010 D27C4110 60B95010   *-...-...K...-...K...-...K...-...*   13E828
002040   D2809680 D2804110 D27458F0 C00405EF   58E0D238 D216E0AB 60249240 E0C2D206   *K...K...K..O.......K.K...-.. .BK.*   13E848
002060   E0C3E0C2 D20160B9 C1AED20E 6070C429   9240607F D2096080 607F4110 60705010   *.C.BK.-.A.K.-.D.. -.K.-.-...-...*   13E868
002080   D2744110 60D95010 D2784110 60D75010   D27C58E0 D2384110 E0AB5010 D2804110   *K...-R..K...-P..K...K.......K...*   13E888
0020A0   60B95010 D2849680 D2844110 D27458F0   C00405EF D2116070 C3C49240 6082D206   *-...K...K...K..O....K.-.CD. -.K.*   13E8A8
0020C0   60836082 41106070 5010D274 9680D274   4110D274 58F0C004 05EF58E0 D2244810   *-.-...-...K...K...K..O.......K...*   13E8C8
0020E0   E0144130 C0104910 C18C0520 4720201C   8B100001 47C0201C 48112018 89100002   *.........A......................*   13E8E8
002100   58113000 07F10014 58E0D238 58F0D224   D203E093 F010D203 E097F008 D2086070   *.....1....K..OK.K...O.K...O.K.-.*   13E908
002120   C3D69240 6079D20F 607A6079 41106070   5010D274 4110E093 5010D278 9680D278   *CO. -.K.- -...-...K........K...K.*   13E928
002140   4110D274 58F0C004 05EFD208 6070C438   92406079 D20F607A 60794110 60705010   *..K..O....K.-.D.. -.K.- -...-...*   13E948
002160   D2749680 D2744110 D27458F0 C00405EF   D207609A C441D208 6070C449 92406079   *K...K...K..O....K.-.D.K.-.D.. -.*   13E968
002180   D20F607A 60794110 60705010 D2744110   609A5010 D2789680 D2784110 D27458F0   *K.- -...-...K...-...K...K...K..O*   13E988
0021A0   C00405EF D20A604A C4529240 6055D203   60566055 5810C07C 07F1D20C 604AC45D   *....K.-.D.. -.K.-.-......1K.-.D)*   13E9A8
0021C0   92406057 D2016058 60575810 C07C07F1   D20F604A C46A5810 C07C07F1 D20F604A   *. -.K.-.-......1K.-.D......1K.-.*   13E9C8
0021E0   C47A5810 C07C07F1 58E0D224 D2016063   E01BD205 6065E01D D20360A8 C48AD208   *D .....1..K.K.-...K.-...K.-.D.K.*   13E9E8
002200   6070C48E 92406079 D20F607A 60794110   60705010 D2744110 60A85010 D2789680   *-.D.. -.K.- -...-...K...-...K...*   13EA08
002220   D2784110 D27458F0 C00405EF D20A604A   C4979240 6055D203 60566055 5810C07C   *K...K..O....K.-.D.. -.K.-.-......*   13EA28
002240   07F158E0 D238D21E E0AB603B 5810C05C   07F11B00 4000D24C 41000025 4000D24E   *.1..K.K...-....*.1.. .K..... .K+*   13EA48
002260   58E0D234 4810E023 4C10C1A2 4A10D24C   4010D24C 4810D24E 4A10D24C 4010D24E   *..K.......A...K. .K...K+..K. .K+*   13EA68
```

Fig. 24.6. (Continued)

```
CUSTOMER INFORMATION CONTROL SYSTEM STORAGE DUMP   CODE=ERRS   TASK=ORAD        DATE=07/27/80   TIME=19 01 28   PAGE   16

PROGRAM STORAGE                ADDRESS  13C808  TO  13EF8F      LENGTH  002788

002280   07F34100 01B84000 D25058E0 D23C5810   E1B44C10 C1804A10 D2504010 D25007F3   *.3.... .K...K........A...K. .K..3*   13EA88
0022A0   5830C080 05330522 5830C084 05330522   50D05008 5050D004 5820C000 95002000   *.................................*   13EAA8
0022C0   077992FF 2000961C D04850E0 D05405F0   9120D048 47E0F016 5800B048 982DB050   *...............0.......0.........*   13EAC8
0022E0   58E0D054 07FE9620 D0484160 00044110   C0104170 C1780670 05505840 10001E4B   *...........-.........A...... ....*   13EAE8
002300   50401000 87165000 4180D1F4 4170D1F7   05105800 80001E0B 50008000 87861000   *. ........J4..J7.................*   13EB08
002320   D2030270 C1705860 D1F458E0 D1B0906D   E06058E0 D05407FE FFF5F7F4 F660C3C2   *K.K.A..-J4..J....-.......5746-CB*   13EB28
002340   F140C3D6 D7E8D9C9 C7C8E340 C9C2D440   C3D6D9D7 4B40F1F9 F7F3F5F7 F4F660D3   *1 COPYRIGHT IBM CORP. 19735746-L*   13EB48
002360   D4F440C3 D6D7E8D9 C9C7C8E3 40C9C2D4   40C3D6D9 D74B40F1 F9F7F3C6 C540F2F4   *M4 COPYRIGHT IBM CORP. 1973FE 24*   13EB68
002380   F6F3F5F6 C6C540F2 F4F6F3F5 F7660001   47F0F018 C9D3C2C4 E2C3C8F0 F2F5F0F0   *6356FE 246357....00.ILBDSCH02500*   13EB88
0023A0   F1F261F2 F061F7F8 90ECF2B8 1BBB5841   000C8840 0018182E 58820000 89800008   *12/20/78..2........ ............*   13EBA8
0023C0   88800018 1AB84122 00044640 F028412D   00604132 000192FF 200018AB 1AA388A0   *........... 0....-.............*   13EBC8
0023E0   000289A0 000206B0 50BA0004 44B0F28A   5850F2C0 5841000C 88400018 504A0008   *.............2...2...... ......*   13EBE8
002400   9200A010 188E47F0 F0DC4640 F2724132   00015880 F2C058BA 000444B0 F27E9201   *.......00.. 2.......2.......2=..*   13EC08
002420   A01058C1 00005871 00041897 06704841   000E504A 000C1C64 1A7C1889 88800001   *...A.............................*   13EC28
002440   89800001 15891807 4770F0BE 1B041A0C   88000001 584A0008 44B0F28A 188E47F0   *..........0...............2....0*   13EC48
002460   F0D64188 00044858 00021A50 48980000   89900018 88900018 18690690 95888000   *00...............................*   13EC68
002480   4780F128 4720F110 95208000 4780F130   4720F214 95108000 4780F180 4740F19E   *..1...1........1...2........1.. 1.*   13EC88
0024A0   95A08000 4780F1A6 4740F1FA 4490F290   97803000 47F0F21C 4490F290 47F0F21C   *.......1.. 1...2.......02...2..02.*   13ECA8
0024C0   18B91AB5 9103B000 4740F15E 4490F2A2   18B94199 00018990 00041A9B 4490F29C   *......... 1 ..2...............2.*   13ECC8
0024E0   1AB341BB 000196FF B00047F0 F21C18B9   41990001 89900004 1A9B4490 F29696D0   *...........02...............2...*   13ED08
002500   30001AB3 41BB0001 96FFB000 47F0F21C   18B91AB5 9130B000 4740F128 4710F19E   *.............02.......... 1...1.*   13ED28
002520   4490F2A2 1A939730 900047F0 F21C4490   F2A247F0 F21C18B9 1AB59103 B0004740   *..2.........02...2..02......... *   13ED48
002540   F1D418B9 41990001 89900004 1A9B4490   F29696F0 30001AB3 41BB0001 96FFB000   *1M..............2..0............*   13ED68
002560   47F0F21C 4490F2A2 18B94199 00018990   00041A9B 4490F29C 96203000 1AB341BB   *.02...2.................2........*   13ED88
002580   000196FF B00047F0 F21C18B9 1AB59130   B0004740 F19E4490 F2901A93 96F09000   *........02........... 1...2....0..*   13EDA8
0025A0   47F0F21C 4490F2A2 97803000 9101A010   4780F07A 4640F264 41320001 5890F2C0   *.02...2............0 . 2........2.*   13EDC8
0025C0   58BA0004 44B0F284 4780F2A8 584A000C   4720F24C 1B041870 47F0F250 1A0418C0   *........2...2.......2.......02......*   13EDE8
0025E0   15C74720 F26A1894 1A971B9C 1B881D84   47F0F0AA 1A3647F0 F0D258E1 000847F0   *.G..2............00.....00K......0*   13EE08
002600   F2AC1A56 1A364188 000447F0 F0DCD200   80003000 D5009000 3000D200 30002000   *2..........00.K......N.....K......*   13EE28
002620   D2003000 5000F100 30005000 F1003000   3000D700 30005000 41E80004 58F0F28C   *K.....1.....1......P.......Y...02.*   13EE48
002640   981CF2C4 07FE0000 4013D4B4 0013EB98   0012F2F4 0012F2FC 0013EE90 00000001   *..2D.... .M.......24..2..........*   13EE68
002660   0012F420 5013EB02 0012F00C 0012F2E3   0012F2E4 0013EAD2 0013C820 0013C820   *..4.......0...2T..2U...K..H...H.*   13EE88
002680   0013CC98 00000000 01010101 01010101   01010101 01010101 01010101 01010101   *.................................*   13EEA8
0026A0   01010101 01010101 01010101 01010101   01010101 01010101 01010101 01010101   *.................................*   13EEC8
0026C0   LINES TO 002740 SAME AS ABOVE                                                                                       13EF68
002760   01010101 01010101 01010101 01010101   01010101 01010101 00000000 00000000   *.................................*   13EF88
002780   00000101 01010101                                                            *........                         *

PROGRAM STORAGE                ADDRESS  13F808  TO  13FCA7      LENGTH  0004A0

000000   D6D9C1C4 E2F0F140 00404040 00000000   00000000 D6D9C1C4 D4F0F140 048F0480   *ORADS01 .   ........ORADM01 ....*   13F808
000020   03B105C6 C0C200CC 001850FF FE000000   00000000 00000000 0001037D 0000F100   *...F.B......................'..1.*   13F828
000040   00001B02 F80018D7 E4D9C3C8 C1E2C540   D6D9C4C5 D9406060 6040C6C9 D3C540C1   *....8..PURCHASE ORDER --- FILE A*   13F848
000060   C4C40000 000D02F0 00BDD6D9 C4C5D940   D5E4D4C2 C5D97A00 00000A0D D800CB00   *DD.....0..ORDER NUMBER .....Q...*   13F868
000080   00000100 6000D600 00000802 F000DDC4   D6C340D5 D64B7A00 0000080D D800E600   *....-.O......0..DOC NO. .....Q.W.*   13F888
0000A0   00000100 6000EF00 00000B02 F0010FC4   C5D7C1D9 E3D4C5D5 E37A0000 00030DD8   *....-.......0...DEPARTMENT .....Q*   13F8A8
0000C0   011B0000 000100F0 011F0000 000E02F0   015CC4C1 E3C540D6 C640D6D9 C4C5D97A   *.........0........0.*DATE OF ORDER *   13F8C8
0000E0   00000006 0DD8016B 00000001 00F00172   00000004 02F002D6 C9E3C5D4 00000008   *.....Q.,......0........0.OITEM....*   13F8E8
000100   02F002E0 C4C5E2C3 D9C9D7E3 C9D6D500   00000402 F002F9E4 D5C9E300 00000502   *.0..DESCRIPTION.....0.9UNIT.....*   13F908
000120   F002FFE4 C3D6E2E3 00000004 02F00308   C3D6E2E3 00000006 02F00310 E4D7D9C9   *0..UCOST.....0..COST.....0..UPRI*   13F928
```

Fig. 24.6. (Continued)

```
CUSTOMER INFORMATION CONTROL SYSTEM STORAGE DUMP   CODE=ERRS   TASK=ORAD      DATE=07/27/80   TIME=19 01 28   PAGE   17

PROGRAM STORAGE               ADDRESS  13F808  TO  13FCA7      LENGTH  0004A0

000140   C3C50000 000502F0 03190709 C9C3C500   00000102 F00322F1 00000008 0DD80324   *CE......0..PRICE......0..1......Q..*   13F948
000160   00000013 01C8032D 00000001 00600341   00000005 0DD80348 00000007 0DD8034E   *.....H........-........Q........Q.+*   13F968
000180   00000008 0DD80356 00000007 0DD8035F   00000008 0DD80367 00000001 00600370   *.....Q........Q.......Q........-..*   13F988
0001A0   00000001 02F00372 F2000000 080DD803   74000000 1301C803 7D000000 01006003   *......0..2......Q.........H.'......-.*   13F9A8
0001C0   91000000 0500D803 98000000 070DD803   9E000000 080DD803 A6000000 070DD803   *.......Q.........Q.........Q.........Q.*   13F9C8
0001E0   AF000000 080DD803 B7000000 01006003   C0000000 0102F003 C2F30000 00080DD8   *.......Q........-.........0.B3......Q*   13F9E8
000200   03C40000 001301C8 03CD0000 00010060   03E10000 00050DD8 03E80000 00070DD8   *.D......H........-........Q.Y......Q*   13FA08
000220   03EE0000 00080DD8 03F60000 00070DD8   03FF0000 00080DD8 04070000 00010060   *........Q.6......Q.........Q........-*   13FA28
000240   04100000 000102F0 0412F400 0000080D   D8041400 00001301 C8041D00 00000100   *.........0..4......Q.........H.........*   13FA48
000260   60043100 0000050D D8043800 0000070D   D8043E00 0000080D D8044600 0000070D   *-........Q.........Q.........Q.........*   13FA68
000280   D8044F00 0000080D D8045700 00000100   60046000 00000102 F00462F5 00000008   *Q........Q........-.-.......0..5.....*   13FA88
0002A0   0DD80464 00000013 01C8046D 00000001   00600481 00000005 0DD80488 00000007   *.Q.........H.........-.........Q........*   13FAA8
0002C0   0DD8048E 00000008 0DD80496 00000007   0DD8049F 00000008 0DD804A7 00000001   *.Q.........Q.........Q.........Q........*   13FAC8
0002E0   00600480 00000001 02F00482 F6000000   080DD804 B4000000 1301C804 BD000000   *.-.........0..6......Q.........H.......*   13FAE8
000300   01006004 D1000000 050DD804 D8000000   070DD804 DE000000 080DD804 E6000000   *..-.J.......Q.Q.......Q.........Q.W....*   13FB08
000320   070DD804 EF000000 080DD804 F7000000   01006005 00000000 0102F005 02F70000   *..Q.........Q.7......-.........0..7..*   13FB28
000340   00080DD8 05040000 001301C8 050D0000   00010060 05210000 00050DD8 05280000   *...Q.........H.........-.........Q.....*   13FB48
000360   00070DD8 052E0000 00080DD8 05360000   00070DD8 053F0000 00080DD8 05470000   *...Q.........Q.........Q.........Q.....*   13FB68
000380   00010060 05500000 000102F0 0552F800   0000080D D8055400 00001301 C8055D00   *...-.........0..8......Q.........H.).*   13FB88
0003A0   00000100 60057100 0000050D D8057800   0000070D D8057E00 0000080D D8058600   *....-.........Q.........Q.=.......Q....*   13FBA8
0003C0   0000070D D8058F00 0000080D D8059700   00000100 6005A000 00000102 F005A2F9   *.....Q.........Q.........-.........0..9*   13FBC8
0003E0   00000008 0DD805A4 00000013 01C805AD   00000001 006005C1 00000005 0DD805C8   *......Q.........H.........-.A.......Q.H*   13FBE8
000400   00000007 0DD805CE 00000008 0DD805D6   00000007 0DD805DF 00000008 0DD805E7   *......Q.........Q.O.......Q.........Q.X*   13FC08
000420   00000001 006005F0 0000000D 02F00666   E3D6E3C1 D3E24060 60606060 6E000000   *......-.0.......0..TOTALS ------.....*   13FC28
000440   090DD806 75000000 01006006 7F000000   090DD806 86000000 01006006 90000000   *..Q.........-.........Q.........-......*   13FC48
000460   1C03F806 E0D6D9C4 C5D940C1 C3C3C5D7   E3C5C440 606040C3 D6D5E3C9 D5E4C540   *..8..ORDER ACCEPTED -- CONTINUE *   13FC68
000480   40000000 1C01F807 07000000 1C01F807   30000000 1C01F807 57FFFFFF FFFFFF00   * .....8.........8.........8...........*   13FC88

END OF CICS/VS STORAGE DUMP
```

Fig. 24.6. (Continued)

A on page 557 is the literal 'ERRS,' which is the dump code. The command that caused the abend itself can be seen easily from the trace table. The same dump code 'ERRS' prints in the last entries of the trace table. This is B on page 562. The CICS/VS command that precedes this is the one that caused the problem, and it is the WRITE command. In between the Execute Interface Trace Entry at Issuance ("EIP WRITE ENTRY"), C, and the Execute Interface Trace Entry at Completion ("EIP WRITE RESPONSE"), D, the file is identified as "ORTEST," E. Therefore, the problem occurred on a write command to the ORTEST file.

To get a more accurate picture of the problem, the WORKING-STORAGE section will be investigated. From the 'TRANSACTION STORAGE-USER' data block at the bottom of page 563, we can see that:

1. EIBFN = X'0604' F
2. EIBRCODE = X'820000000000' G

The table of EIBFN codes are shown in Figure 24.7.

We can see that X'0604' is indeed the WRITE command (H).
The table of EIBRCODE values is shown in Figure 24.8.

You can see from I that if the first byte of EIBRCODE is X'82', and the first byte of EIBFN is X'06', the exceptional condition is DUPREC. This means that the CICS/VS error occurred because there was an attempt to write a new record and the key was a duplicate of the key of an existing record.

Code	Command
02 02	ADDRESS
02 04	HANDLE CONDITION
02 06	HANDLE AID
02 08	ASSIGN
04 02	RECEIVE
04 04	SEND
04 06	CONVERSE
04 08	ISSUE EODS
04 0A	ISSUE COPY
04 0C	WAIT TERMINAL
04 0E	ISSUE LOAD
04 10	WAIT SIGNAL
04 12	ISSUE RESET
04 14	ISSUE DISCONNECT
04 16	ISSUE ENDOUTPUT
04 18	ISSUE ERASEAUP
04 1A	ISSUE ENDFILE
04 1C	ISSUE PRINT
04 02	READ
06 04	WRITE ← (H)
06 06	REWRITE
06 08	DELETE
06 0A	UNLOCK
06 0C	STARTBR
06 0E	READNEXT
06 10	READPREV
06 12	ENDBR
06 14	RESETBR
08 02	WRITEQ TD
08 04	READQ TD
08 06	DELETEQ TD
0A 02	WRITEQ TS
0A 04	READQ TS
0A 06	DELETEQ TS
0C 02	GETMAIN
0C 04	FREEMAIN
0E 02	LINK
0E 04	XCTL
0E 06	LOAD
0E 08	RETURN
0E 0A	RELEASE
0E 0C	ABEND
0E 0E	HANDLE ABEND
10 02	ASKTIME
10 04	DELAY
10 06	POST
10 08	START
10 0A	RETRIEVE
10 0C	CANCEL

Fig. 24.7. Table of EIBFN Codes.

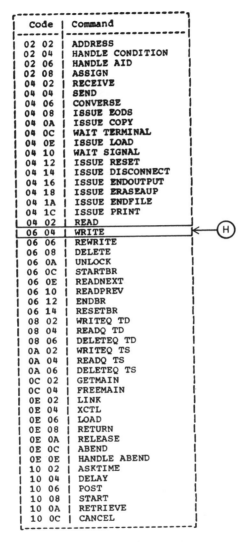

Code	Command
12 02	WAIT EVENT
12 04	ENQ
12 06	DEQ
12 08	SUSPEND
14 02	JOURNAL
14 04	WAIT JOURNAL
16 02	SYNCPOINT
18 02	RECEIVE MAP
18 04	SEND MAP
18 06	SEND TEXT
18 08	SEND PAGE
18 0A	PURGE MESSAGE
18 0C	ROUTE
1A 02	TRACE ON/OFF
1A 04	ENTER
1C 02	DUMP
1E 02	ISSUE ADD
1E 04	ISSUE ERASE
1E 06	ISSUE REPLACE
1E 08	ISSUE ABORT
1E 0A	ISSUE QUERY
1E 0C	ISSUE END
1E 0E	ISSUE RECEIVE
1E 10	ISSUE NOTE
1E 12	ISSUE WAIT
20 02	BIF DEEDIT

Fig. 24.7. (Continued)

EIBFN	EIBRCODE		
Byte 0	Byte	Bit(s)	Meaning
02	0	E0	INVREQ
04	0	04	EOF
04	0	10	EODS
04	0	C1	EOF
04	0	C2	ENDINPT
04	0	E1	LENGERR
04	0	E3	WRBRK
04	0	E4	RDATT
04	0	E5	SIGNAL
04	0	E6	TERMIDERR
04	0	E7	NOPASSBKRD
04	0	E8	NOPASSBKWR
04	1	20	EOC
04	1	40	INBFMH
04	3	F6	NOSTART
04	3	F7	NONVAL
06	0	01	DSIDERR
06	0	02	ILLOGIC[1]
06	0	04	SEGIDERR
06	0	08	INVREQ
06	0	0C	NOTOPEN
06	0	0F	ENDFILE
06	0	80	IOERR[1]
06	0	81	NOTFND
06	0	82	DUPREC ← (1)
06	0	83	NOSPACE
06	0	84	DUPKEY
06	0	D0	SYSIDERR
06	0	D1	ISCINVREQ
06	0	E1	LENGERR
08	0	01	QZERO
08	0	02	QIDERR
08	0	04	IOERR
08	0	08	NOTOPEN
08	0	10	NOSPACE
08	0	C0	QBUSY
08	0	D0	SYSIDERR
08	0	D1	ISCINVREQ
08	0	E1	LENGERR
0A	0	01	ITEMERR
0A	0	02	QIDERR
0A	0	04	IOERR
0A	0	08	NOSPACE

[1] When this condition occurs during File Control operations, further information is provided in field EIBRCODE, as follows:
bytes 1-4 = DAM response (OS/VS only)
bytes 1 and 2 = ISAM response
byte 1 = VSAM return code;
byte 2 = VSAM error code

Fig. 24.8. Table of EIBRCODE Codes.

EIBFN	EIBRCODE		
Byte 0	Byte	Bit(s)	Meaning
0A	0	20	INVREQ
0A	0	D0	SYSIDERR
0A	0	D1	ISCINVREQ
0A	0	E1	LENGERR
0C	0	E2	NOSTG
0E	0	01	PGMIDERR
0E	0	E0	INVREQ
10	0	01	ENDDATA
10	0	04	IOERR
10	0	11	TRANSIDERR
10	0	12	TERMIDERR
10	0	14	INVTSREQ
10	0	20	EXPIRED
10	0	81	NOTFND
10	0	D0	SYSIDERR
10	0	D1	ISCINVREQ
10	0	E1	LENGERR
10	0	E9	ENVDEFERR
10	0	FF	INVREQ
12	0	32	ENQBUSY
14	0	01	JIDERR
14	0	02	INVREQ
14	0	05	NOTOPEN
14	0	06	LENGERR
14	0	07	IOERR
14	0	09	NOJBUFSP
18	0	01	INVREQ
18	0	02	RETPAGE
18	0	04	MAPFAIL
18	0	08	INVMPSZ[a]
18	0	20	INVERRTERM
18	0	40	RTESOME
18	0	80	RTEFAIL
18	0	E3	WRBRK
18	0	E4	RDATT
18	1	10	INVLDC
18	1	80	TSIOERR
18	2	01	OVERFLOW
1E	2	04	EODS
1E	2	08	EOC
1E	2	10	IGREQID
1E	0	04	DSSTAT
1E	0	08	FUNCERR
1E	0	0C	SELNERR
1E	0	10	UNEXPIN
1E	0	E1	LENGERR
1E	1	11	EODS
1E	2	20	EOC

[a] When this condition occurs during BMS operations, byte 3 of field EIBRCODE contains the terminal code. (See Figure 3.3-1)

Fig. 24.8. (Continued)

Index